War, Violence and the Modern Condition

European Cultures
Studies in Literature and the Arts

Edited by
Walter Pape
Köln

Volume 8

Walter de Gruyter · Berlin · New York
1997

War, Violence
and the Modern Condition

Edited by
Bernd Hüppauf

Walter de Gruyter · Berlin · New York
1997

♾ Printed on acid-free paper
which falls within the guidelines of the ANSI to ensure
permanence and durability.

Library of Congress Cataloging-in-Publication Data

War, violence, and the modern condition / edited by Bernd Hüppauf.
(European cultures : v. 8)
Includes bibliographical references (p.) and index.
ISBN 3-11-014702-5 (alk. paper)
1. War and civilization. 2. World War, 1915-1918 – Social aspects
– Europe, German-speaking. 3. World War, 1914-1918 – Literature
and the war. 4. War in literature. 5. German literature – 20th century
– History and criticism. 6. Austrian literature – 20th century –
History and criticism. I. Hüppauf, Bernd-Rüdiger II. Series
CB481.W36   1996
940,3´1 – dc21   96-48552
                                                                       CIP

Die Deutsche Bibliothek — Cataloging-in-Publication Data

War, violence and the modern condition / ed. by Bernd
Hüppauf. – Berlin ; New York : de Gruyter, 1997
(European cultures ; Vol. 8)
ISBN 3-11-014702-5
NE: Hüppauf, Bernd [Hrsg.]; GT

Printed in Germany
Typesetting: Greiner & Reichel, Köln
Printing: Arthur Collignon GmbH, Berlin
Binding: Lüderitz & Bauer GmbH, Berlin
Cover design: Rudolf Hübler, Berlin
Cover illustration: Otto Dix, Leuchtkugeln, 1917.
Stiftung Sammlung Walther Groz in der Städtischen Galerie Albstadt

Contents

BERND HÜPPAUF
New York University

Introduction
Modernity and Violence:
Observations Concerning a Contradictory Relationship

I.

The twentieth century opened with the first modern war which killed almost ten million, experienced another world war, the Holocaust and other genocides, the explosion of nuclear bombs and the ensuing fear of holocide, forty years of a dubious peace for which it coined the term 'cold war', and after this period of warfare without military battles finally came to an end, it is marred by an unprecedented omnipresence of violence in wars, civil wars and civil societies. There can be little doubt that this century was characterized by an extraordinary presence of violence. However, surprisingly little theorization has been devoted to violence. Throughout the history of philosophy and political and social theory, the concept of violence has rarely attracted attention commensurate with its importance and has often been discussed only implicitly under concepts such as 'war', 'state', 'city', 'power' or 'civilization'. In the history of the European literature from Homer onwards, violence has been addressed prominently, its abstract and even fleeting character leading, however, to representations through concrete images, constellations of characters and scenes. It was only during the twentieth century, and in particular with the rise of abstraction, that codes and specific aesthetic techniques have emerged which can be interpreted as representations of violence. Apart from few precursors such as Kleist, Georg Büchner or the late Beethoven, it was not before the turn of this century that literature, arts and music changed perception and aesthetic representation by redefining violence as their integral element. A new awareness of a hitherto unknown 'violence of representation' emerged.[1] Ex-

---

This volume would not have gone to print without the help of Mr. Kyung Tae Ahn.

1   Cf. Armstrong and Tennenhouse, ed.: *The Violence of Representation*.

perimental psychology and theories of perception developed in the school of Empirico-criticism were instrumental in developing techniques of experimentation, categories and approaches for observing and theorizing the violent nature of perception and the artistic process. Radical changes in the structure of modern literature, the arts and music can be attributed to a changing attitude towards violence which was no longer understood in terms of individual acts of deviant behavior but as a constitutive element of the very process of constructing and relating to reality under conditions of modern Western civilization. The experience of the First World War was paradigmatic for this change in the mentality of the West. Strong and continued attempts notwithstanding, the experience of this war could no longer be integrated in traditional patterns of creating meaning through ideals of heroism and identification with the nation. Instead, it generated a new consciousness and lasting memory of the destructiveness of modern technology and civilization which can be observed at the center of the contradictory relationship to violence characteristic of the century. It was this turning point in the definition of Western civilization in terms of philosophical and anthropological conditions rather than the end of heroism or questions in relation to the nation state or morality and war guilt which made this war paradigmatic for, and for some witnesses indeed identical with, the experience of a crisis of Western civilization.

The contrast between an under-theorization in relation to violence and the significance of violence for the construction of social reality is particularly noteworthy in a century in which war and various forms of open and concealed violence have affected so many millions of lives and shaped collective memory as never before and in which, it can be argued, an unprecedented outburst of violence, namely the First World War, led to the creation of a global collective memory. It is even more surprising to note the continuation of the common faith, originating during the eighteenth century, in modern civil society's incompatibility with violence. It is one of the disturbing experiences of this century that the line dividing war and peace has been blurred beyond recognition and civil society does not lead to the eradication of but continues to co-exist with violence. Yet, despite the ever more threatening presence of violence in the worlds of both physical and emotional experiences and their representations, there is evidence that Western civilization continues to perceive itself in terms of one of its foundation myths which tells a story concerning the intertwining of a process of rationalization and the abolition of violence, of progressing civility and peace. The vision that Western civilization continues to project of itself as one concerned with creating conditions for the emergence of a world free from war and violence is at variance with its own collective memory and continued political and cultural practices. It is the obsequious maintenance of this self image, it can be argued, which has become one of the major obstacles for the development of more effective and rational approaches towards the persistent problem of war and violence under conditions of the modern world. It is an injudicious image of self that can be interpreted as the precondition for the many ill-conceived attempts to fight violence with violence and create peace through increased armament. The USA, at present arguably the most violent and militaristic among the industrialized western societies and obsessed with ever more graphic representations of violence and brutality,[2] is at the same time guided by the belief that its domestic and international policies are making a major contribution to the creation of a future free from wars and violence. Its collective consciousness is in the firm grip of the image of modern western civilization en route to its ultimate destination and therefore considers violence a legitimate means to protect itself from its adversaries. More guns, more military actions, more police and more prisons are therefore not perceived as contradictions but rather as contributions to achieving the propagated objective of a world of peace and justice.

Representations, in words and images, of violence in the families, at the work place, in the cities or between religious or ethnic groups as well as the violence between states in other parts of the world from Bosnia to Argentina provide striking examples of resistance against an insight into the violent nature of modernity. Dominant practices of representing violence and destruction are characterized by *techniques of relegation*. It is the other both spatially and temporally where illegiti mate violence and senseless destruction can be observed. It is this technique of relegation which makes it possible to perceive one's own world as a sphere where violence and destruction are exceptions to the rule of the otherwise peaceful and rational reality. Banishing violence to a contained sphere separated from one's own is a prerequisite for maintaining the cherished image of modernity engaged in redeeming the pledge of its own origin.

In this respect, the Holocaust is the most challenging of the deranging experiences of the century. Until recently, there was little dissent from the dominant approach to the extermination of six million Jews which is couched in a language of historical and social-psychological atavism. The murderous program is regarded as a disastrous deviation from the standards of modernity, a

---

2   In his recent book "On Killing", Dave Grossman argues that a continuous presence of images of violence threatens to blur the line between entertainment and the conditioning of army soldiers. He refers to a "stage of desensitization at which the infliction of pain and suffering has become a source of entertainment ... We are learning to kill, and we are learning to like it." Dave Grossman: *On Killing. The Psychological Cost of Killing in War*, p. 311.

return to humanity's dark past, often summed up in terms such as barbarism or primitivism. This pattern based on the polar opposites of civilization and barbarism was persuasive enough to remain without serious alternative for a long time, penetrating deeply into the semantics of academic as well as public discourse. An increasing dissatisfaction with this approach has for some years now led to challenging its basic assumption and creating a growing body of research demonstrating the extent to which the mass murder was intertwined with and dependent upon the conditions of a modern society, its bureaucracy, industrial-military complex, transportation system, division of labor, the sciences, work attitudes, abstraction, and many other aspects of the modern society.[3] The smooth organization of the Holocaust was based upon the infrastructure of an advanced urban society. The individual perpetrators (and often their victims) operated efficiently even under the most extreme conditions, never questioning their role. This division of labor and responsibility is characteristic of the operations of modern production and presupposes mental structures of the kind Max Weber identified at the center of the process of rationalization. Indeed, the icon of modernization and industrialization during the nineteenth and early twentieth centuries, the smoking chimney, has been identified as the symbol of Auschwitz.[4] The concept of production is common to both. The production of goods and the production of corpses were registered by meticulous book-keepers. It was in particular Zygmund Bauman's work which made this changing approach popular.

In Bauman's view, Auschwitz was the logical outcome of a civilization that is not the opposite of but a modern version of barbarism. He argues that the Holocaust has "uncovered another face of the same modern society whose other, more familiar, face we so admire. And that the two faces are perfectly comfortably attached to the same body." He refers to "Holocaust-style phenomena" as the "legitimate outcomes of ... the civilizing tendency, and its constant potential."[5] In Bauman's account, the process of civilization has created a sphere of civility only by concealing the simultaneously growing destructiveness and violence underneath its surface. Through increased concen-

---

3   Among other aspects, the implication of the ideology of racial purity in Darwinism, biological theory and the international politics of eugenics has recently attracted considerable attention. Weingart, Kroll, Bayertz: *Rasse, Blut und Gene*; Friedlander: *The Origins of Nazi Genocide: From Euthanasia to the Final Solution*.

4   Feingold: "How unique is the Holocaust?," pp. 399f. Raul Hilberg writes: "The machinery of destruction ... was structurally no different from organized German society as a whole." *The Destruction of the European Jewry*, vol III, p. 994.

5   Bauman: *Modernity and the Holocaust*, p. 7 ff.

tration and intensification of power vested in the state, modern man is increasingly subjected to anonymous techniques of coercion and threatened with violence. The separation of agents of power and violence from ethical discourse, characteristic of the process of rationalization of modern societies, he argues, inevitably leads to a-morality and subsequently to outbursts of cruelty on a scale larger than it was possible in previous and less organized and modernized societies. Under modern conditions, he argues, civilization is continuously creating a mentality and social fabric designed for the perfection of structures ready to be applied towards any goal including massive violence and mass murder. Bauman's position is the reversed image of the optimism displayed in the theories of civilization which, since the eighteenth century Enlightenment invented the pattern of progressing civility, credited Western civilization with the emancipation of mankind and the creation of a world of peace. It appears that the simplicity of the thesis which maintains the basic structure of the argument replacing the optimistic by a pessimistic result has made Bauman's books popular. Skepticism in relation to the process of civilization expressed in terms of political theory by Max Weber or philosophy in Martin Heidegger's investigation into the condition of technology[6] is of a different and more complex structure. In the tradition of Nietzsche, Sigmund Freud and Weber's philosophical writings, Horkheimer and Adorno's seminal study "Dialectics of Enlightenment" (1946) provided the first attempt to deal with the experience of fascism and industrialized mass murder by examining their relationship to modernity and its process of rationalization. It presupposes ambivalence and, instead of reversing the judgment as to the valence of the teleological paradigm, makes an attempt to define the problem in different terms. The presupposed simultaneity of Odysseus and modern man, theses concerning the continued productivity of mythology, the ambiguity of reason, expressed in their term 'instrumental reason', or the violence vested in conceptual language contribute to defining a paradigm for the investigation into the modern condition in which the Holocaust and modernity are inextricably linked without, however, resorting to a language of inevitability or necessity.

Such insight into the conditions and structure of the Holocaust forms only a thin layer of knowledge which has failed to have a deeper effect on the image which modern civilization constructs of itself. The authors' reluctance for many years to authorize a new edition of their book was indicative of their own ambivalence in relation to their interpretation of modernity. In Germa-

---

6   Heidegger: "The Question concerning Technology," p. 283–317.

ny, the organized and highly efficient destruction of the European Jewry tends to be treated as *unique* and is thereby, interpreted as an aberration from the path of civilization, involuntarily excluded from the history of modernity and relegated to a sphere of atavism. Public opinion of the USA tends to perceive the Holocaust as a specific national and German problem.[7] Neither mounting evidence nor compelling theoretical considerations have made a significant contribution to changing the common image that perceives this outbreak of murderous destructiveness as one contained in terms of time and space but not related to the construction of the modern condition. As a result, the Holocaust can be remembered in isolation from the construction of self.[8]

The relationship between fascism and modernity is crucial to the understanding of modernity. In an essay on violence, Adorno once argued that every relapse (Rückfall) to open and physical violence in the present period is atavistic and deserves the term barbarism.[9] It is precisely this model of modernity – which places our own society at one end and barbarism at the other and sees them as separated by a 'process of civilization' – that needs examination.[10] As long as the concept of Western history as one of progressing civilization is maintained, open and brutal violence will never be perceived as part of our own world. In this construction of self, violence tends to become part of another world, a world beyond the northern border of Greece, where the barbarians lived, a world beyond the border of our own civilization, where all the others live. Violence becomes an intruder from this outer sphere and is present in our world by default, as an exception, a deplorable relic, a foreign

---

7   Fischer analyses such "fallacious or misleading theories of political causation and psychological motivation," which are based on the assumption that the Holocaust is "rooted deeply in German history and in the German character" and he demonstrates that this perspective results in necessary twistings and turnings of German history. Fischer: *Nazi Germany: A New History*.

8   Goldhagen: *Hitler's Willing Executioners. Ordinary Germans* appeared after his essay had been completed, and there is no space for more detailed comments. Its extraordinary success, it seems to me, is not only due to marketing strategies but corresponds to a strong demand on the part of the majority of readers that had been frustrated by previous Holocaust studies. Goldhagen's book reduces complexity by applying on oversimplifying pattern based on the category of 'national character', and relegates violence to a clearly defined other: the Germans before our present time. It thus produces relief for many whose image of self had been troubled by recent trends of Holocaust studies. It is regrettable that the more insightful aspects of this book are lost in its streamlined reception.

9   Adorno: *Erziehung zur Mündigkeit*, p. 130.

10 Elias: *Der Prozeß der Zivilisation. Soziogenetische und psychogenetische Untersuchungen*. Vols. 1 and 2.

body in an otherwise civilized system. The disbelief that such brutalities are 'still' possible in our world is a hidden part of the semantics and visual codes with which violence in Yugoslavia, Nigeria, Georgia and the far side of our town is commonly referred to. The atrocities of the twentieth century give rise to reactions of disbelief, Walter Benjamin wrote, "but this is not a philosophical" response, he added. "It is not the beginning of new insight, safe the one that the concept of history that gives rise to it, has become untenable."[11] Individuals and societies have a tendency to see violence associated not with themselves but with others, distanced by space and time, in pre-modern, primitive or developing societies, societies of the East or the South, people in the poor and uneducated quarters of our cities. But is there a difference between a sniper in a Sarajevo street and the frustrated worker in Detroit who pulls a gun, or between looting an aid-convoy in Mogadishu and drug dealing in affluent quarters of Berlin or New York?

Just how deeply the image of the peaceful society in the tradition of the eighteenth century moral imperative is anchored in the public image which the USA prefers to create of itself was demonstrated at the occasion of a planned exhibition commemorating the dropping the atomic bombs on Hiroshima and Nagasaki.[12] Protests from veterans' organizations, senators and a wave of public opposition made the Smithsonian Institute in Washington withdraw its original plan and change the concept of the exhibition in such a way that it did not harm the cherished self image of a nation that had fought a just war with justified means. This debate ensured once again that the problem of the bomb is kept within the framework of a debate concerned with military strategy and political decision making. Among the popular issues was the numbers game calculating how many thousands of lives had been saved by dropping the bombs and shortening the war.[13] However, the problem of the atomic bomb, Karl Jaspers wrote in his "Reflections on the Atomic Bomb

11 Benjamin: *Über den Begriff der Geschichte*. Gesammelte Schriften vol. 1, 2 p. 697.
12 In a substantial essay entitled "War over the Bomb," p. 26–34, Ian Buruma reviews major contributions to the heated debate concerning the bombing of Hiroshima and Nagasaki including the domestic scene in the USA. Among the noteworthy contributions to the debate are: Nobile, ed.: *Judgment at the Smithsonian's 50th Anniversary Exhibit of the Enola Gay*; Alperowitz et al.: *The Decision to use the Atomic Bomb and the Architecture of an American Myth*; Lifton and Mitchell: *Hiroshima and America: Fifty Years of Denial*; Allen and Polmar: *Code-Name Downfall: The Secret Plan to Invade Japan - and why Truman Dropped the Bomb*.
13 In the present debate the argument of the small number of casualties has been given prominen ce, whereas in 1945 it played no significant role in the decision making process. The figure of 500 000 American casualties as the likely result of an invasion of Japan was inflated at the time and has not gained credibility since.

and the Future of Humanity" (1958),[14] cannot be understood as one among other questions. The importance of questions concerning military opportunity and political decision making notwithstanding, Hiroshima poses the problem of an absolute standard for human behavior.

In an interview with the New York Times at the occasion of the fiftieth anniversary of August 6, 1945, the director of the Hiroshima Memorial, Akihiro Takahashi again raised Jasper's question, irritating the American interviewer who continued to ask his 'American questions' concerned with political and strategic issues. For Takahashi, however, the incommensurability of the political and military rationale on the one side and the philosophical problem of the bomb on the other was self evident to the extent that he did not bother to address this issue explicitly. As a result, communication was almost impossible. The interviewer asked questions about a specific event in the history of the USA, whereas Takahashi referred to a crime against humanity, not because of the number of casualties. In the twentieth century, 300 000 victims is a figure that pales in comparison with many other events. The decisive issue is a different one and concerned with the question as to whether human behavior is at all restrained by inhibitions or recklessly prepared to turn into reality the ultimate consequence of modern technology of destruction and risking the end of humanity. The nuclear threat has radicalized the question concerned with the relationship between war and morality. The distinction between conventional and nuclear war is significant in as far as the possibility of nuclear war forces us to acknowledge that "anything short of a radical change in our thinking has the remotest prospect of success"[15] in dealing with the issue of war and violence. Thinking Hiroshima has the potential of subverting conventional illusions inherent in attitudes towards war and violence. However, as long as Hiroshima is being remembered in terms of military and political history, its image will continue to provide the means for remaining blind in relation to its most challenging dimension. "Any line can be crossed, whether in the use of weaponry or in their production when the capability is possessed. What makes the difference is the attitudes toward war itself. The risk of nuclear war is the function of more than the mere possession of nuclear weapons; it is a function of attitudes concerning ideology, national interest, self-defense, conflict resolution, and, perhaps most importantly, toward the use of violence and the taking of human life."[16] Hiroshima has led to a change

---

14   Jaspers: *Die Atombombe und die Zukunft des Menschen.*
15   Holmes: *On War and Morality*, p. 10.
16   Ibid., p. 9.

in the conditions of modern existence in as far as the absolute termination of live has become a real and is no longer a mere hypothetical possibility. The taboo of pre-modern societies has no equivalent under the conditions of modernity. The sectarian motto of the Persian *Assassins* "Everything is permissible and nothing prohibited!" has become universally acceptable and is kept in check only by pragmatic considerations and superior military power. However, the ways in which the issue is being framed in public debate provides the means for shielding the collective consciousness from realizing this threat. One of the lessons of Hiroshima is that human behavior, under the extreme conditions of war, is not governed or restricted by ethical imperatives.[17] However, in order to become effective for changing *attitudes*, this lesson needs to be included in the forms of collective remembrance. Only once the images remembered and the story publicly told will associate Hiroshima with the transgression of the threshold which separates relative prohibition, such as killing in warfare, from absolute taboo will Hiroshima make a contribution to changing a collective mentality deeply implicated in violence. To date, Hiroshima has contributed to maintaining the self deceptive conviction that it is possible to maintain a system driven by a mentality of violence but eliminate its consequences, namely individual acts of violence and wars.[18]

A comparison of Hiroshima and Auschwitz would be absurd in most respects. What has made several critical observers link the two heterogeneous events is their significance for the concept of modern history. We find Auschwitz beyond comprehension because it is impossible to conceive of it as a part of a *human* history. Industrialized mass murder cannot be reconciled with the concept of history produced by man believed to be made in the image of God. The novel forms of death require a new language and imagery and cannot be constructed in terms of traditional military or political history without losing their specific significance for the history of humanity. Traditional discourse, Jaspers argued, remains blind in relation to the problem posed by the nuclear threat and therefore more often than not will turn into aggression.[19]

---

17 In 1945, neither the nuclear physicists nor the politicians involved were plagued by moral scruples. Cf. Barton Bernstein's *Afterword* to Nobile, ed.: *Judgment at the Smithsonian's 50th Anniversary Exhibit of the Enola Gay*. Summing up the position of US politicians, Bernstein writes that the use of the A-Bomb "did not create ethical or political problems for them … " (235) In: "Understanding the Atomic Bomb and the Japanese Surrender: Missed Opportunities, Little-Known Near Disasters, and Modern Memory."

18 Argued from a combined psychoanalytical and moral position, cf: Lifton and Markusen: *The Genocidal Mentality*.

19 Jaspers: *Die Atombombe und die Zukunft des Menschen*, p. 20.

Focusing on the rationality in the motivation, planning and execution of the bombing bars the gaze from perceiving the threat inherent in the memory of Hiroshima for imaging the future. Only in as far as an approach concerned with national responsibility and its complement, that is national victimization, can be overcome, will the reflection upon the bomb be liberated from ritual. Auschwitz and Hiroshima are linked in this one respect namely that both signify a historical experience that gives rise to the problem of nihilism. Despite fundamental differences separating the two events, both demonstrate that under extreme conditions no ethical imperative will create an inhibition from making use of all means available, even of those leading to unlimited destruction. The memory of human beings who evaporated in a fraction of a second leaving behind nothing but shadows on walls has changed the image of history in a way not dissimilar to the memory of the reduction of men, women and children to moving objects of destruction in the extermination camps. Both Hiroshima and Auschwitz have led to the experience of man as the animal with no biologically inherited inhibition whose culturally learned inhibitions are unlearned under extreme conditions. The violence unfolding in the memory of these two events has produced an irreparable fissure in the image of the human face. However, public rituals, ceremonies and narratives all contribute to creating modes of memorializing which veil the fissure to the extent that it is absorbed in meaning and becomes invisible.

A perception in which violence tends to be excluded from our own civilized world as a deplorable digression from its 'true' constitution is not only one of self-deception but has the paradoxical effect of making violence acceptable. It could be time not so much for the revision of moral positions in relation to violence and attempts to return to conventional values but for a change in the very perception of violence. The response which the experience with modern macro-violence requires is a change in perspective and a novel concern with perception rather than morality. An inquiry into the grammar of seeing rather than the standards of evaluation is needed.[20] The understanding of the ways in which reality, including the enemy, is constructed rather than a critique of ideologies and systems of belief will more appropriately respond to the challenge posed by the insights into the violent nature of the modern condition.

As long as events such as Auschwitz or Hiroshima are being perceived in terms of national history, ideologies and moral justification, the dimension of

---

20   Among the stimulating more recent attempts in this regard are the essays by Virilio: *War and Cinema*.

structural violence and its relationship to technological society will remain invisible. It seems too harmful to the cherished self-image to accept a perspective from which violence appears to be inextricably intertwined with modernity. It is much safer to continue defining violence as individual acts in terms of civil law and remain fixated on issues of ideology. It seems doubtful, however, whether the specific violence of the modern world can adequately be comprehended as long as an essentialist position is being maintained and identifiable nations, groups, or individuals are being defined as the respective agents of violence whereas anonymous structures and macro-scale conditions determining individual and group behavior are excluded from the construction of violence. This reduction of complexity makes it possible to relegate violence to the sphere of the other and, as a result, perceive violence in one's own sphere as either regrettable exceptions and relapses to atavistic acts or as justified by a greater good.

The strategy of relegation can be observed at the center of the contradictory relationship of modernity to violence. It is the result of a specific way of constructing rather than morally evaluating self and the other. The strong resistance against deconstructing the grand narrative concerning the peaceful nature of the process of civilization adheres to the fundamental belief that violence is a legitimate element of modern society in as far and only in as far as it contributes to the aim of the final eradication of violence. Violence that cannot be justified in theses terms needs to be excluded from the sphere of modernity defined as civility and peaceful civilization and consequently eludes the gaze. While it continues to determine the conditions of existence, it is made disappear through techniques of relegation. Foucault analyses the violence vested in asylums and institutions of discipline which confine, against their will, those who have broken rules, are insane, deranged, mentally or physically distorted or otherwise do not correspond to the image of perfectible man. These institutions, created in order to protect the public from having to face bodies that physically represent disorder and rupture, make disappear from public sight the bodies of those stigmatized and legally incapacitated. Such eye sores must not mar the cultivated image that the civil society projects of itself. Locking them away guarantees that violence of nature and society is removed from public sight and memory sanitized. What might disturb harmony is hidden from the public eye through institutionalized violence. Most of these institutions are now closed and their system of coercion has been abandoned. But modern public ceremonies, celebrations and narrations have a function not dissimilar to these institutions of discipline and order. They make disappear the mutilated face of modernity without having to use open violence. They are designed and the public are educated in such a way as to guarantee mutual consent in the confinment of memory and the incapacitation of the visualizing faculty.

II.

In the genesis of violence and the relationship to it, two turning points can be determined. As a result of the process of centralizing power and monopolizing it under the authority of the state,[21] violence was subjected to a process of *de-naturalization*. It was declared a predicament of a past governed by prejudice, irrationalism and arbitrary power relations and considered an illegitimate product of modernity. The Encyclopedists in France, English and Scottish philosophers and historians such as Edward Gibbon, James Dunbar, Adam Ferguson or Adam Smith and German philosophers of the Enlightenment movement like Wolff, Kant and his student Ehrhard produced a body of literature devoted to the idea of the beginning of a new period in world history distinguished by civility and progressive exclusion of violence and cruelty from civilization. In their view, modern European society was guided by the ideal of self determination, absence of coercion and employing force "only for the obtaining of justice, and for the preservation of national rights."[22] With growing skepticism in relation to these ideals of reason and progress and a teleological concept of history, another turning point emerged. Now the position of violence in the modern world of technology was radically reevaluated. Only the first of the two turning points in the relationship to violence has been incorporated into the Western vision of civilization and has shaped its collective memory. The disillusioning critique of the modernist concept of civil society has remained marginal ever since its emergence in the late nineteenth century. It has had only a superficial impact beyond the philosophical and intellectual margins of collective consciousness. It was Friedrich Nietzsche who used the most provocative metaphors, often taken from the language of war, in his attempt to unmask modernity and enlighten the Enlightenment about its intrinsic violence. His theory of the violent nature of representation itself prepared the foundation for the coming century's skepticism in relation to the optimism of the Enlightenment heritage and, in particular, Horkheimer's and Adorno's inquiry into the dialectics of the process of Enlightenment or Foucault's theory of power relations.

---

21   Elias: *Über den Prozess der Zivilisation. Soziogenetische und psychogenetische Untersuchungen.* Vols. 1 and 2.

22   Ferguson: *An Essay on the History of Civil Society* (1767).

The denaturalization of violence was an intrinsic and constitutive element of the emerging definition of modern Western civilization in contradistinction to all previous cultures. Civilization, defined as both a process and the desired outcome of this process, targeted violence, defined as pre-modern barbarism, savagery, nature and incivility, as its adversary. Edward Gibbon's history of the decline and fall of Rome provided a widely recognized model of civilization and its fragility in confronting barbarian violence.[23] It was read as a warning against the possibility of regress in history and the reassurance that modern Europe was better equipped on its path toward civilization and would therefore not fall victim to renewed threats of uncivilized barbarians. As a result of their alleged irrational principles of constitution, violence was constructed as an accepted part of an organic or God-given order of 'primitive' or 'natural' societies. It was open, endemic, always associated with identifiable agents and normality. It has been demonstrated that in pre-modern revolts an adequate concept of collective social practice was absent.[24] These revolts were directed against specific acts of violence and domination, but lacked an appropriate understanding of violence as an element of the construction of social reality, and therefore were not driven by visions of a just and peaceful society. Beginning in the seventeenth century, violence was no longer considered a natural element of life but increasingly defined as an undesirable heritage of times gone by or an equally undesirable by-product of the present. Called before the court of reason, violence had to produce a legitimation of its existence and, as it was unable to do so, the objective of a society free from violence began to emerge. Consequently, ethical discourse, from the eighteenth century on, demanded the complete eradication of violence in a society under the rule of reason.[25]

Evolutionary social theories of the nineteenth century resonate with trust in the power of reason to create a non-violent society, now defined as an unfailing implication of the process of rationalization. In Herbert Spencer's concept of social evolution or Fustel de Coulange's history of the city as a spatial realization of reason, violence is associated with the irrational religious beginnings of human civilization and is increasingly mastered by the forces of civilization progressing towards the age of reason and a modern, rationally designed space of urban life. Another example of this faith in progress was Alfred Nobel's dream of the inevitability of a society free from wars and vio-

---

23   Gibbon: *The History of the Decline and Fall of the Roman Empire* (1776–1788).

24   Fourquin: *Les soulèvements populaires au Moyen Age.*

25   Kant: Mutmasslicher Anfang der Menschengeschichte – *Werke* vol. 6, p. 99–101. See also: *Der Streit der Facultäten*, ibid., p. 365f.

lence as a result of innovations in military technology leading to such power of destruction that waging war would become self-destructive and therefore irrational to the degree that it was impossible. In these constructions of modern civilization, violence is destined to lose its right of residence in a world increasingly governed by reason. The emergence of a society free from wars and violence was considered inevitable and during the decades preceding the outbreak of war in 1914, there was no shortage of political theories arguing that, as a result of international trade, economic integration and mutual dependence, war had become impossible. The logic of the process of modernization had, according to this view, finally taken care of this atavistic relic of a despised past.

Paradoxically, the denaturalization of violence and its construction as a product of social and cultural conditions also marks the birth of a new concept of *legitimate* violence. The end of its natural history led to the emancipation of violence from ritual mythical and religious structures. Violence was turned into a means and within the spheres of politics, social institutions and the military was freed from conventional restrictions as long as it could be justified by moral reasoning. It could now be defined as violence against oppression that is, against unjustified violence and was therefore justified even before the court of reason. In November 1793, in his address 'Sur la situation politique de la Republique', Robespierre coined the term 'violence progressive' initiating a modern discourse on 'just violence' of revolutions, strikes, wars and terrorism. Definitions of violence in the service of equality and liberation from oppression provided the origin of the modern contradictory relationship to violence. Marx's, Sorel's or Fanon's theories of liberation are prominent examples of this ethical justification of violence in the name of peace and justice.

Once modernity freed violence from traditional, ritual or metaphysical restrictions, it was not only justified through moral theory but could also become part of an instrumental and extra-moral means-end relationship. Under these conditions, violence is no longer a partial element embedded in social-cultural constructions which define its time, space and dimensions nor is it restricted by morality. Instead, it becomes a constitutive element of modern societies developing its own momentum within their various sub-systems. An early example of this tendency is provided by Carl von Clausewitz's reflections on the nature of modern warfare, written during the years following the anti-Napoleonic 'Wars of Liberation'. This analysis from the perspective of an enlightened rationalist discovers a tendency of modern war towards the *absolute*. Modern warfare, he argues, is not regulated by ritual conventions or restricted by moral considerations. Its limitations, which he calls 'inertia' and 'friction', are intrinsic to war itself. He defines them as qualities generated by and inherent in its system.[26] As soon as technology overcomes these limitations, the path from 'absolute' war, which for Clausewitz was a 'tendency', to total war will be clear. It is this tendency of violence, 'liberated' from rules and restrictions of pre-modern societies, to determine its own rules and turn into a force aiming toward totality and omnipresence that is significant of modernity. Hannah Arendt was among the first to reflect on such disturbing changes in the nature of violence. While modernity defined itself in opposition to pre-modern times by banishing violence from its self-image and branding it as an outlaw, its political and cultural practices were being built on an emerging omnipresence of open as well as disguised and diffused forms of violence.

In an attempt to capture this tendency, Johan Galtung invented the term *structural violence*.[27] Because this is a very loosely defined concept, its analytical value has been doubted. Nonetheless, it is an emotionally suggestive term that also draws attention to a distinction between violence that originates in social actors, both individuals and groups, and a novel form of violence which is inherent in anonymous structures. In doing so, it has the potential to draw analytical attention to a central aspect of violence in modern societies which can be interpreted in terms of *spaces of violence*. The structure of the technological battlefield, of which the First World War was the first example and which historical research only recently began to explore in greater detail, seems to provide us with a number of clues for the understanding of structural violence in terms of spaces of violence.[28] This space is characterized by an apparently unlimited and ubiquitous threat, despite the absence of visible actors. Associated with this is the experience of helplessness in the face of anonymous forces. In the wake of the First World War, the view became popular that violence under the conditions of modern technology has led to the re-emergence of a public space not dissimilar to that of a "natural state" of society, associated by Hobbes[29] and his school of thought with the regime of unrestricted violence. Structural similarities between primitivism and moder-

---

26   von Clausewitz: *On War*, p. 75–89.

27   Galtung: *Strukturelle Gewalt*.

28   Lewin: "Kriegslandschaft"; cf. Hüppauf: "Walter Benjamin's Imaginary Landscape," p. 33–54.

29   Hobbes interpreted "the condition of Man" in primitive societies as "a condition of Warre of every one against every one; in which case every one is governed by his own Reason; and there is nothing he can make use of, that may not be a help unto him , in preserving his life against his enimyes ... " Hobbes: *Leviathan, or the Matter, Forme, and Power of a Common-Wealth Ecclesiastical and Civil*, 1,14.

nity were observed – and propagated – not only in the arts but also in the ways in which modern societies constructed their public spheres and collective practices. In the grip of an uncontrollable technology, modern Europe seemed to experience conditions similar to that of cultures which, in the absence of developed means of controlling their social and natural environment, lived under the spell of animistic beliefs. Abstract space of modernity can be interpreted in terms of a return of violence that pervaded pre-modern space. Under pre-modern conditions it was endemic, originating in physical or meta-physical agents, while, under the conditions of modernity, it has been transformed into an abstract and anonymous constituent increasing its threatening might. One of the major manifestations of anonymous violence in this new space can be called macro-criminality.

Linked to the denaturalization of violence was its psychological redefinition in terms of *ambivalence*. The combination of pleasure and horror seems particular to modern forms of a subconscious desire of imagining and experiencing violence both as actor and victim. The poetics of many of the most remarkable and at the same time disorientating works of modernism is indebted to images of an inescapable violence. A confrontation of banalities and blind routine of the every-day with extraordinary and radical fantasies of violence can be seen as a matrix of modernist imagination. Desires of destruction, mutilation, dismembering and disfiguration are indicative of production techniques of modernist theater, film, photography, art, music and literature. The human body became the most important site of such artistic practices after the end of the First World War.[30] The inescapability of violence is reiterated in Freud's theory of culture and, based upon Gestalt psychology, the beliefs of the ethological school of Konrad Lorenz, Eibl Eibesfeld and others. Freud's concept of the *uncanny* has provided a conceptual context within which the exclusion of death "from sight," leading to a heightened sense of death as "uncomfortable, uneasy, gloomy, dismal," is connected with transformations of violence in images and imaginations.[31] The culture industry successfully transforms this desire into a large and profitable market.

As far as literary reflections on this issue are concerned, authors associated with the concept of modernism such as Kafka, Musil, Benn, the early Döblin and, with expressions of satisfaction if not of triumph, Ernst Jünger, share this view. Some of the most intriguing and disturbing pieces of modern-

---

30 See now Tatar: *Lustmord. Sexual Murder in Weimar Germany.*
31 Freud: *The Uncanny.* Freud: *The Standard edition of the Complete Psychological Works,* vol. 17, pp. 219–52.

ist literature are the product of this image of inescapable violence. The confrontation between the banalities of everyday life and extraordinary and radical forms of the desire for destruction and violence are at the core of modern literary imagination. Many of Kafka's parables, say, or Musil's figure Moosbrugger, murderer of a prostitute who mutilates his victim and to whom the narrator feels more closely related than to his own ego represented in a photograph from his early childhood, should prevent the common but inappropriate reference to these authors as representatives of 'classical modernity'. It has to be realized that this literature is not, as the term might suggest, one of timeless beauty and classical harmony but to the contrary; it gives shape to a specific modern form of violence that is ambivalent and, in as much as it is constitutive for the aesthetic process, also inescapable.

Much reflection has been devoted to the relationship of destruction and production which, under the modern condition, have become indistinguishable. Destruction is no longer a relic of a barbarian past, a deplorable by-product or an unforeseen implication of the process of production that will be eliminated with time. In fact, destruction has in the twentieth century become another form of production. In his many scattered remarks and essays, Walter Benjamin was among the first to suggest that the modern mentality has reversed the relationship replacing the central category of capitalist society, productivity, with its opposite, the 'destructive character'. In this interpretation, the quest for innovation and incessant change, quintessential quality of the modern, inevitably leads to destruction and the production of the destructive mentality. Examples are numerous and, again, the structure of the battlefield after 1916 is well suited to serve as an illustration. The ingenuity and innovative power of the most advanced industrial societies in Europe turned war into an extension of the industrial complex. War was no longer experienced as the exception, a time that suspended the rules of the world of capitalism and, for a short period of time, introduced into the world of bourgeois order conditions for the creation of heroes. Instead, this war turned battlefields into gigantic systems of production which, devoted to the destruction of lives, landscapes and material and symbolic goods, followed the rules of capitalist order more thoroughly than in times of peace. Contemporary photographs convey this inversion of the traditional concept of production. With the gestures of pride and success normally displayed by owners of factories or merchants looking at the visible symbols of their entrepreneurial success, German officers pose on huge piles of rubble.[32] Standing on the

---

32 Many of these photographs were taken as attempts to demonstrate the recklessness of the enemy whose artillery had destroyed its own villages.

ruins of blown-up houses, castles, forts and whole villages, these officers demonstrate to the viewer the astounding success of the latest technological innovation: 42 cm guns, shells so heavy that they needed cranes to be lifted into the barrels, long-distance bombardments which depended on sophisticated ballistic calculations and precision work of designers and engineers at Krupp, Skoda or Schneider-Creuzot, and aerial photography and new techniques of cartography that required new skills of reading abstract representations of geographical space. The gaze of these proud soldiers is consistently directed to the lens of the camera expecting the consent of the viewer. It is an expectation of mutual agreement that directs the desired fusion of the perpetrator's gaze with that of the distanced viewer. This is significant of the fact that this destruction was not one confined to the battle field but transcended the time of war. Henri Barbusse was the first to coin a term that captures this inversion: he called modern soldiers 'les ouvriers de la destruction'. Arnold Zweig and Ernst Jünger used their own terms respectively: 'Arbeiter der Zerstörung' and 'Proletarier der Zerstörung'. This is a further example of the inversion of labor, in which the production of goods is transformed into the production of destruction. With it, the character of representation changed and images were not only representations of acts of destruction but became themselves intrinsic to the process of destruction.

Theories of perception[33] and modern aesthetics from the late nineteenth century have stressed the paramount importance of *fragmentation* as a constitutive element in the process of both production and reception. Perception under the conditions of modern cities, through window frames of fast-moving vehicles, discontinuities in the flow of time and the breaking-up of the homogeneity of space, new images of the body represented in states of dismemberment, or the dislocation of subjectivity have been analyzed as contributions to the emergence of a world which is no longer experienced as cohesive. Modern reality is no longer perceived as an object of the senses but the product of a complex process of construction. The violence inherent in this process is of a constitutive nature and beyond the level of moral value judgments. It may well be that the apparent failure of pacifism and peace movements results from confusing these levels. If the modern period is characterized by violence inherent in the structure of producing and perceiving reality, then the moral approach adopted by all peace movements locates the problem on an inappropriate level. War defined as "a problem of our own

---

33 Of the first and most highly influential studies concerned with the dismemberment of the self in terms of a psychology of the senses was Mach: *Die Analyse der Empfindungen.*

making" in such a way that an understanding of "the moral problem of war" will contribute to resolve this problem through acts of willed "determination" and "courage"[34] presupposes a continued rational control over collective practices which have disengaged themselves from systems of morality and reason. In as much as theories of modernity based upon fragmentation as one of its fundamental characteristics are an appropriate reflection of the modern condition, violence would have to be seen in *anthropological* terms as an element of modernity's very structure rather than of individual and political decision making, which is subject to moral evaluation. In contrast to conventional theory which is predicated upon a subject of destruction who "*chooses* to do these things"[35] and which disqualifies a language of anonymity and contingency as mere rationalization, the shift to theories of perception and construction requires a different focus including a suspension of moral assessment.

I can only briefly point at the ambivalence of this argument. The gradual dismemberment of philosophical systems based on concepts of a homogenous world centered around the commanding subjectivity and engaged in a continuous process of rationalization has been perceived as a threat to civilization. But it has also been hailed as the liberation from the intrinsic violence of order and the fetters of integrated systems. The shattering of inherited systems and the ensuing loss of orientation, Döblin wrote in the twenties, does not at all lead to feelings of loss or despair but to those of a newly gained freedom and self-determination. In a scene that is as disturbing as it is funny,[36] Robert Musil makes an officer of the Austrian army discover that life cannot exist without structures of cohesion and systems of order which require force, but that order pursued to its essence consequently equals death. Life therefore requires the destruction of systems which impose order onto it.[37] Michel Foucault's archeological approach to the systems of signification is the extension of this anti-programmatic program. Musil's fascination with the mode of the subjunctive interpreted as a category of grammar and of ontology, is a precursor of Foucault's commanding attempt to demonstrate history's contingency by demonstrating that comprehensible grounds and reasons for the emergence of events can be found without, however, subscribing to notions of necessity or teleology. It is the destruction of conventional systems of order and progress designed in the name of the grandiose foundation

34   Holmes: *On War and Morality*, p. 14.
35   Ibid, p. 3.
36   Musil: *Der Mann ohne Eigenschaften,* p. 127–28.
37   Ibid., p. 19.

myths of modernity, of freedom, equality and eternal peace, which lead Foucault to the celebration of new experiences of freedom and self determination. Only once the self-deceiving narrative of Western civilization's commitment to the eradication of violence is being debunked will, according to this view,[38] the liberation from the powerful coercion of these systems clear the path for the creation of local regions of and spontaneous approaches to self determination and non-violence.

The critique of this position as one of dark pessimism and cynical nihilism is widespread. An implication of the ongoing disintegration of the grand narratives, namely the erosion of conventional systems of ethics, has been interpreted as an exercise in the preparation of inhumanity and fascism through perversions of attitudes and inhuman distortions of mental dispositions. Frequently associated with a postmodern position, a skeptical assessment of the relationship between modernity and violence tends to be identified with an antimoral position that plays with and even advocates violence.[39] However, an association of a critique of the position of the Enlightenment in relation to violence with an antimoral position is misguided. It confuses wishful thinking with analysis. The responses to the civil war in Bosnia can be interpreted as a case in point.

The world was to an unusual extent united in opinion and, as far as it was in a position to articulate its position, condemned the continuation of the senseless killing and destruction while politicians and, it can be assumed, the large majority of their voters, were equally determined to do nothing. Statements of outrage and moral declarations provided a verbal smokescreen behind which inertia could be maintained with great comfort. No economic or strategic interests of those who had the power to intervene were affected. Nearly three years of cruel civil war and 300 000 casualties failed to persuade those who morally condemned the war to turn their words into action. Pragmatic considerations were so strong and the power of morality so weak that all nations involved did not even bother when the credibility of the United Nations was shattered. Once its term 'safe haven' had been turned from a grandiose promise into a grotesque joke, the credibility of the UN which rests upon moral grounds was destroyed beyond repair. The only power remaining was that of armed forces, of NATO and American military supremacy. In the name of the 'greater good' the international community was prepared even to

---

38 Michel Foucault: *Discipline and Punish. The Birth of the Prison.*

39 Critical and often polemical responses to Enzensberger's recent essays on civil war have fallen victim to this common misunderstanding. Cf. A. Glucksmann: "Ein neuer Vogel Strauss," *Der Spiegel*, No. 37, 1993, p. 247–49.

live with war criminals and mass murderers elevated to positions of presidents, ministers and senior statesmen. In his account of the events, David Owen goes so far as to suggest that the Vance-Owen plan failed to receive support from the US government because it had the wrong originators, namely European and not American diplomats.[40] He claims that the USA were prepared to run the risk of renewed war and then watch three years of bloodshed for no other reason but its interest in demonstrating its superior role as a world super-power. It is remarkable that for years it was possible to keep moral arguments separated from political and diplomatic action and both co-existed as if they belonged to two separate worlds.

Acceptance that morally grounded positions vis a vis war and violence have lost their credibility and persuasive power must not be confused with accepting war and violence. While Nietzsche's philosophical speculations about the violent nature of Western civilization have at times been confused with war mongering and Sigmund Freud's anthropological speculation about patricide as the origin of human culture dismissed or ridiculed, more recent studies that closely associate the construction of cultural order and violence are supported by an abundance of anthropological, historical and mythological evidence. It has been argued with considerable persuasion that violence exists at the very origin of human society, and is transformed into cultural practices. René Girard's association of the holy and bloody sacrifice[41] is an example of the conversion of earlier speculation into disciplined academic theory. Also, while the theses of Konrad Lorenz and his school[42] have remained controversial because of their oversimplifying analogy between human and animal behavior, the basic pessimism concerning the human evolutionary heritage is currently experiencing strong support through research in experimental psychology and neuro-physiology. By now it appears beyond reasonable doubt that no human society has ever been free from violence and war. Anthropologists and historians seem to have abandoned their search for a peaceful hu-

---

40   David Owen: *Balkan Odyssey.*
41   René Girard: *La Violence et Le Sacre.*
42   Konrad Lorenz is still the best known exponent of a school of ethologists who explain human aggressive behavior on the basis of a theory of 'instinct' and therefore as an element of natural history. Initially developed in contradiction to Sigmund Freud's theory of aggression as a culturally conditioned impulse of destruction directed towards others and the self, Lorenz maintains that aggressive behavior among animals, and for much of human history, served a purposeful function and is therefore not evil but has, under the conditions of modern society, been distorted and lost its legitimate place in society. His 'solution' to the problem of the inevitability of aggression is 'sublimation', not unlike Freud's view. K. Lorenz: *Das sogenannte Böse. Zur Naturgeschichte der Aggression.*

man society. Acceptance that the world has never been free from war and violence must not be confused, however, with a position in support of violence. Acceptance that modernity is inextricably intertwined with structures of violence and attitudes of destructiveness must not be confused with fatalism and a resigned acceptance of violence and destructiveness.

Any serious attempt to come to terms with modern forms of violence is conditional upon developing perceptions and attitudes that are not built upon the exclusion of the devastating experiences of this century. In his popular theory of aggression, Erich Fromm argues that there are two forms of aggression which need to be kept apart, a productive and a destructive one. It seems to me that this distinction has remained popular not only because it introduces a simple and binary moral opposition, but also because it suggests to neglect this century's experiences with violence since the First World War. Theoretical insights to which Nietzsche and Fromm's own mentor, Sigmund Freud, made substantial contributions in relation to ambivalence and modernity's implication in a destructive system are sacrificed in favor of simplicity and exclusion. The two aspects of aggression, modern experience suggests, are inseparably intertwined and, more than this, under the modern condition destruction appears to have liberated itself from specific acts and is no longer in need of specific objects. Instead, it has become a pervasive force which can be called *destructiveness*, a term that refers to a general attitude towards life which manifests in individual acts of destruction. The subjective condition called destructiveness can be interpreted as the mental equivalent of the social concept of 'structural violence'. The continued co-existence of a flattering self image that civil society maintains of itself and conflicting practices requires a considerable degree of reduction of complexity, a process to which the printed and electronic media make invaluable contributions day and night.

In this context two general issues need clarification. What is the social-cultural locus of these two complementary concepts and in what way can they be seen as characteristic of the modern period? When Walter Benjamin introduced the terms barbarism and new barbarians into discourse on modernity, he made use of a favorite theoretical tool of his time, namely the construction of ideal types. His 'destructive character' is a representation of the major characteristics of a society based upon a destructive mentality; it is not a portrait of an individual person nor does it refer to a statistical mean value. This then opens the question as to the relationship between individual violence and the violent structure of modern society. It seems obvious that the violent structure of modern societies cannot be understood as the sum total of individual acts of violence. Individual acts of violence can be seen as manifestations of a violent structure generated in the space of modern technological society. With the emergence of a post-industrial society these spaces are again subjected to fundamental changes which create new forces of violence and destruction. Contemporary wars and civil wars have perforated the dividing line between war and crime contributing to the emergence of a violent space of "criminal anarchy."[43] The ways in which individual responsibility is being affected by structural violence remains an open question which, to my knowledge, has never been seriously debated by theoreticians of the law. The maintenance of civil society as well as all reasonable expectations of justice require individual accountability. Yet, the alarming inclination towards macrocriminality and the growing number of jails and those sent to prison should provide sufficient reason to face this issue in a serious fashion. The unforgettable ending of Kafka's *Der Prozeß* in which the victim is killed like a dog makes the two perpetrators insignificant in relation to the violent and anonymous power structure of which they are but contingent agents. Kafka's cool account of this structural violence and the complementary mentality of destructiveness are paradigmatic of the approach taken by many authors of modernism.

III.

One of the underlying assumptions of this collection of essays is that a very specific and intricate relationship between violence and the modern condition exists. It is further assumed that the First World War was experienced as a paradigm of this constitutive relationship, and the unprecedented wave of literature in its wake consequently associated this experience with a crisis of Western civilization. There is good reason to believe that the project of modernity, to quote Jürgen Habermas, entered its terminal phase during the First World War or, to be more precise, in the wake of this war, in the process of gradually understanding the events of 1916 and the following years of the war.

(1) The violence of the First World War spelt the end of the belief that violence can be controlled and ultimately eradicated by reason. It unleashed a destruction out of proportion to any reasonable aim that developed independence and a momentum of its own. It came to an end not as a result of a conscious decision imposed on it from outside but only because of intrinsic necessity. Like the period of modernity, this war accepted no scale outside its system and defined its standards with no reference to a transcendent authority. (2) This war created a new space which became paradigmatic for the expe-

---

43   Kaplan: *The Coming Anarchy*. Atlantic Monthly 273, February 1994, p. 44–76.

rience of space in the twentieth century. Its morphology requires continuous destruction and is signified by movement without changing places. The violence generated in this space of destruction has no point of termination and is continuous by its own nature. This type of violence did not end with the end of the war. It returns as a constitutive element of the city[44] and of life in modern industrialized society and is reflected in the art and literature of the present. (3) The structure of technological destruction for ever changed the relationship between violence and morality, liberating violence from the confinement of ethics. This war gave rise to the most forceful movement of pacifism in history and at the same time spelt the end of moral pacifism. One of the powerful moral maxims of the century: 'Never again!', 'Nie wieder Krieg!' mobilized masses and turned out to be one of the greatest illusions of the century. I make this point without the slightest feeling of satisfaction. However, intellectual rigor requires us to call a dream a dream, even if that dream describes a desirable world.

The relevance of considerations of the nature of violence and war is beyond doubt. Wars and civil wars, new forms of undeclared war in the cities, from Los Angeles to Calcutta, and a hidden and often not so hidden daily violence of normal life: the violence in families, schools, factories and offices, and of public and private languages leave no doubt that contemporary modern reality and violence are inseparable. In a recent collection of essays Hans Magnus Enzensberger argued that we now live in an age of global civil war.[45] According to his diagnosis, traditional conflicts between nation states are being replaced by new forms of conflict which, he argues, are the result of changing definitions of ethnic, ethical, religious and economic interests, the global distribution of wealth and the trend towards the decentralization of state powers. These conflicts produce a ubiquity of violence which is reinforced by the omnipresence of its images. It has become common for families to continue their dinner while graphic images of violence, death and mutilations appear on their television screens. Recent research has shown that mental disturbances of children after watching horror movies in which the dismemberment of human bodies is shown in graphic detail seem to have become part of the experience of every day or night.

Until recently, a specific pattern of argument was commonly used for providing justification for apparent contradictions between academic discourse on violence and its subject matter. It was argued that by advancing our understanding of war and violence, research contributes to bring about a society

---

44   Hüppauf: *Die Stadt als imaginierter Kriegsschauplatz*, p. 317–335.
45   Enzensberger: *Civil War.*

free from wars and violence. When viewed in the light of this century's experiences, the optimistic conceptual framework for this work appears ill-founded and dated.[46] An admission of ignorance in relation to violence seems more pertinent than the maintenance of a cherished ideal. The ideal of a society in eternal peace, which Kant in his small book *Zum Ewigen Frieden,* published in 1795, so persuasively developed and which was based upon a broad consensus of eighteenth-century authors to whom this phrase was like an icon, has lost much of its persuasiveness. It appears to be one of the victims of the end of an era of grand narratives. Once this ideal is debunked, academic discourse on violence acquires a certain aspect of perversity and at the same time of urgency. The loss of faith in the inevitability of growing civilization provides the debate with a new openness and indeterminacy, and an increasing skepticism in relation to the current knowledge about violence makes attempts to understand it even more urgent.

The common fuzziness and contradictory use of the terms "war," "violence" and "modernity" are significant of the larger problem. Conceptual problems in distinguishing between war and peace are exaggerated in the attempt to distinguish between violence and its opposite that can be denoted only through negativity, non-violence. Its relationship to concepts such as power, aggression, coercion, domination, destruction varies from discipline to discipline, language to language and with time. Translations of this terminological field in other European languages create insoluble problems. Medieval and early modern as well as non-European art and literature remind us that standards vary significantly and acts which were once considered acceptable or entertaining become, with changing contexts and perceptions, unacceptable cruelties. Public floggings and executions or the new awareness of domestic violence and child abuse are but few extreme examples of radically changing standards of evaluation. Under close scrutiny, distinctions between actors and victims often begin to blur and, to add a final point, answers to the question as to the origin of violence vary from narrow legal definitions in terms of identifiable subjects breaking articles of the positive law to philo-

---

46   The sixties and early seventies, a number of institutes devoted to research on war and peace were founded world wide. The optimistic mood of these years created great expectations and in Germany the term 'Friedensforschung' was coined in an attempt to create a new interdisciplinary field of study. After a decade of research, conferences and publications, few projects and even fewer institutes had survived an atmosphere of growing disillusionment and dwindling financial support. Well endowed institutes (for example in Starnburg or Kronberg) were discontinued. The Institute at Stockholm continued to publish highly valuable data about international developments of the military complex but the time for publications on 'theories of peace' is clearly over.

sophical responses which, in the tradition of Nietzsche, Foucault or Derrida, will associate language with violence in as far as it is the means of domination over reality.

The following collection of essays makes an attempt to contribute to the clarification of some of the issues raised. A history of interpretations of the First World War has not yet been written. It could be revealing in many respects. Diaries, letters and literature from the years after 1915 and the period immediately following the war bear witness to the disturbing effects which the killing and devastation at the front and the hunger and privation at the home front had on men, women and children. However, nothing else could be expected. The interpretation of the war as the first modern war of technology which led to a fundamental crisis of European civilization emerged only many years after the end of the war and is associated with a wave of literature emerging during the late twenties. To date, no other war has given rise to such a huge number of works of prose, poetry, drama and essays as well as of the visual arts. Later in the century, concern with the Second World War overshadowed that of its predecessor. Soon after that war ended, a view was developed merging the two wars into one period of a new Thirty Year War of the twentieth century, incorporating the violent inter-war years into an epoch of war without battles or peace without peace. During the two decades after 1918, the ways of remembering World War I differed significantly between societies which were able to cushion their memories by celebrating a victory and those of the vanquished. At the end of the century, a difference in referring to this war as either the "Great War" or "World War I" can still be felt. After 1945, even greater discrepancies emerged creating memories of the war that greatly differed from nation to nation. For many years the First World War disappeared from public memory in Germany and Austria, until the publication of Fritz Fischer's controversial book re-opened an emotionally charged debate about guilt and the politics of the war. In contrast, memories of the invasion had remained very much alive in Belgium and in eastern France, and the issue of war guilt was of a lesser importance there as it had been settled previously. In some English speaking countries, Armistice Day is celebrated to date keeping alive ambivalent feelings in relation to the military and political history of the war.

A turning point in the history of the war came in the seventies when books by Paul Fussell and Eric Leed, soon followed by others, made this war the subject of a reconstituted cultural history.[47] Historians now discovered a

---

47 Fussell: *The Great War and Modern Memory*; Eric J. Leed: *No Man's Land. Combat and Identity in the First World War*

dimension of this war which literary authors, philosophers and cultural critics such as Walter Benjamin, Martin Heidegger, Ernst Jünger, Alain (Emile Auguste Chartier), or Marc Bloch had begun to investigate during the inter-war years. The war was discovered as an *experience*. Local histories of the war, histories of the every-day life at the front and the home front were written. New questions concerning the impact of the war on collective memory, changing patterns of perception and imagery, public manifestations of changing mentalities and collective psychology, artistic practices or the role of technology began and continue to be developed. A broad consensus emerged, ascribing to this war a central position for the history of the modern condition and collective experience in the twentieth century. This view has never been uncontested. The volume opens with an essay that challenges this approach. *J.M. Winter* argues that conventional ways of responding to the war enabled the bereaved to live with their losses and finally come to terms with their experience. The essay refers to an opposition between 'modernist' and 'traditional' forms of imaging war and argues that the modernist view has been overstretched and needs to be reevaluated. This essay is juxtaposed with a decidedly modernist attempt to read the landscape of devastation produced by this war in terms of a spatial history of the early twentieth century. *Cornelia Vismann* observes an extension of the front line to a zone of combat, danger, annihilation and nihilism, linking this geographical and military space to philosophical and juridical conceptions of modern reality. *Frank Trommler*'s essay addresses the ambiguous issue of turning the war experience into a factor for social integration. Healing wounds through political, social, or psychological therapy can be interpreted either as another way of instrumentalizing victims or, alternatively, the appropriate way of addressing the consequences of nationalist violence. Therapy, as much as reckless destruction, seems to be part of a specific modern concept of war. *Wolfgang Michalka* follows the traces of specific structures of the war economy in the designing of economic concepts for the early twentieth century. He refers to an ideal of an economy modeled in analogy to a machine or to the rationalized battle field, shedding light on military aspects of modern economic systems.

The following chapters are concerned with clarifying individual aspects of the relationship between modernity and violence in wars and in civil society. *Jeffrey Verhey* demonstrates that propaganda, which was systematically used during for the first time in history World War I, is ill-understood as a habit of lying. His underlying assumption that language in modern media is never a representation of a given reality but makes a substantial contribution to the construction of reality, necessarily blurs the dividing line between war propaganda and the genre of news information. An interpretation of the term

"Blitzkrieg" serves *Karlheinz Barck's* discussion of fascism's tendency to substitute cognition with will and transforming will into violent action. His examples of overlap between political, cultural and military discourse based on
the common use of the metaphor Blitzkrieg are striking. Based on literary reflections on the destruction of Dresden, *Andy Spencer* demonstrates to what
extent the relationship between modernity and destruction is an unresolved
issue. Spencers's juxtaposition of two approaches, a biographical one and a
generalizing one that removes the events from any historical concreteness, reveals the undesirable implication of constructing a universal story of violence
that may make death and destruction acceptable as a given part of life. In her
contribution, *Andrea Slane* discusses twenty years of associating fascism and
sexual license by both juxtaposing and fusing sexuality and brutality, emotional perversion and violence. She pursues the intriguing questions how it was
possible that the movement of philistine brown shirts, congregating in Munich beer halls and led by a celibate, could be turned into images of sexual
subversion, freedom from state control and radical experimentation. The essay presents fascinating elements of a pictorial and linguistic history of responses to Nazism, empirical and fantastic.

Wolfgang Eckart opens a dark chapter in the relationship between modernity and violence, namely the deep involvement of the sciences and medicine in
modern warfare. The medical profession and, in particular, neurology, psychology and also psychoanalysis made a considerable contribution to the war
effort and, in turn, enjoyed a period of innovation, growth, and increased
respectability by using the battlefield as their laboratory and sphere for experimentation. After the end of the war, this involvement continued, as the medical profession was then involved in designing large programs of rehabilitation and reintegration of war cripples into the production process. The
opposites of war and love, in *Lisabeth During's* reading of texts of modern literature, no longer exclude one another but enter into unusual relationships
and states of mutual exchanges. *Crystal Mazur Ockenfuss* approaches Gottfried
Benn, radical innovator of poetic language through aggressive violations of
conventional aesthetic codes and, for a short time supporter of the NS revolt,
through a reading of the body as a metaphor. *Phillip D'Alton* is concerned
with a specific aspect of the construction of the female. Women's continued
exclusion from central areas of the military may well give rise to ambivalent
responses. Why should women wish to be included in the 'privilege' to kill
which has been a male domain for most of human history? D'Alton's argument is a different one. He raises the issue of the cultural construction of images of masculinity and femininity in relation to violence that serves specific
political purposes in discourse on power.

Richard Cork provides the reader with an authoritative survey of German artistic representations of the war experience and is puzzled by the artists' determination to continue to produce even under the most adverse conditions. Literary reflections on war and violence are being pursued in a group of essays ranging from interpreting a novel on the Thirty Years War by Alfred Döblin, to Heiner Müller's and Thomas Bernhard's fascination with destruction and violence in our own contemporary world. *Robert Cohen* writes about Arnold Zweig's changing and at the same time surprisingly consistent attitude toward war. *Harro Müller* compares Döblin's early and experimental novel about Wallenstein and his much more conventional, late three volumes on the First World War and its aftermath. *Tim Mehigan* pursues traces of continuity in dealing with violence in the works of two Austrian authors, Robert Musil and Thomas Bernhard; and *Justus Fetscher's* essay reconstructs representations of the French Revolution in German literature and theater after World War I. Finally, *Wolf Kittler* analyses Heiner Müller's texts and theater about the war mentality and the destruction of bourgeois society.

Violence and Modernity

J. M. WINTER
Pembroke College, Cambridge

The Great War and the Persistence of Tradition: Languages of Grief, Bereavement, and Mourning

Abstract: Those who argue that the First World War was a landmark in the history of Modernism ignore a salient feature of the war: it's legacy of universal bereavement. The strength of what may be termed 'traditional' forms in cultural life, in art, poetry and ritual, lay in their power to mediate bereavement. The cutting edge of 'modern memory', its multi-faceted sense of dislocation, paradox and the ironic, could express anger and despair, and did so in enduring ways; it was melancholic but by and large it could not heal. Traditional modes of seeing the war, while at times less challenging intellectually, aesthetically or philosophically, provided a way of remembering which enabled the bereaved to live with their losses, and perhaps to leave them behind.

The history of the Great War is a subject of perennial fascination. In some ways the end of the twentieth century appears disturbingly close to its beginnings. We have witnessed recently the collapse of elements of the European state system and the ideological and geo-political divide which grew out of the 1914–18 conflict. The end of the 'Cold War' has brought us back not to 1939 or 1945, but in a sense back to 1914. Ethnic and nationalist divisions that seemed past history are painfully present today, resurrected by unscrupulous leaders as if nothing had occurred between 1914 and 1994.

In other ways the chequered recent history of European integration makes even clearer the need to recall the bloody history of European disintegration. If we want to understand and ultimately to put behind us the cataclysmic record of European history in this century, we must revisit the war that set in motion these enduring centrifugal and centripetal forces, propelling us away from and towards a unified Europe.

In some respects, this historical terrain is very familiar. Whole libraries exist on the military, economic and diplomatic history of the period. Less attention has been paid, though, to the process whereby Europeans tried to find ways to comprehend and then to transcend the catastrophes of the war. The

many sites of memory and sites of mourning, both public and private, created in the wake of the conflict have only recently been treated to study in a
comparative framework.

Remembrance is part of the landscape. Anyone who walks through northern France or Flanders will find traces of the terrible, almost unimaginable,
human losses of the war, and of efforts to commemorate the fallen. War memorials dot the countryside, in cities, towns, and villages, in market squares,
churchyards, schools and obscure corners of hillsides and fields. Scattered
throughout the region are larger sites of memory, the cemeteries of Verdun,
the Marne, Passchendaele and the Somme.

Contemporaries knew these names and the terrible events that happened
there all too well. The history of bereavement was universal history during
and immediately after the Great War in France, Britain, and Germany. In the
military service of these three countries alone, more than four million men
died, or roughly one in six of those who served. This figure represents nearly
half the total death toll in the bloodiest war in history to date.[1] Among the
major combatants, it is not an exaggeration to suggest that every family was in
mourning: most for a relative – a father, a son, a brother, a husband – others
for a friend, a colleague, a lover, a companion.

Transcendence was a privilege, not a commonplace experience. To remember the anxiety of 1500 days of war necessarily entailed how to forget; in
the interwar years those who couldn't obliterate the nightmares were locked
in mental asylums throughout Europe. Most people were luckier. They knew
both remembering and forgetting, and by living through both, they had at
least the chance to transcend the terrible losses of war.

In the years following the war, in the face of the army of the dead, the effort to commemorate went beyond the conventional shibboleths of patriotism. Yes, these millions died for their country, but to say so was merely to
begin, not to conclude, the search for the 'meaning' of the unprecedented
slaughter of the Great War. Even to pose that question was bound to be appallingly difficult; full of ambivalence and confusion, charged with tentative-
ness and more than a fragment of futility. But that search went on in all the
major combatant countries from the first months of the war.

---

1   For full casualty figures, see J. M. Winter: *The Great War and the British People*, ch. 3.

I. The 'Traditional' and the 'Modern'

Current historical interpretations of the cultural history of the Great War focus on two basic components of that process of understanding. The first is
encapsulated in the term "modern memory".[2] It describes the creation of a
new language of truth-telling about war in poetry, prose and the visual arts.
'Modernism,'[3] thus defined, was a cultural phenomenon, the work of the elite
whose legacy has touched millions. It had sources in the pre-war period, but
flowered during and after the 1914–18 conflict. As Samuel Hynes has argued,
the war turned back the clock on cultural experimentation at home. But at the
same time, soldier/writers brought the 'aesthetics of direct experience' to
bear on imagining the war in a way far removed from the 'lies' or 'Big Words'
of the older generation which sent them to fight and die in France and Flanders. Their vision paralleled that of the non-combatant modernists – Eliot,
Pound, Joyce – whose break with literary tradition seemed so valid after the
upheaval of the war.[4]

The second way of understanding the war entails what many modernists
rejected: patriotic certainties, "high diction"[5] incorporating euphemisms
about battle, 'glory,' and the 'hallowed dead,' in sum, the sentimentality and
lies of wartime propaganda. Some modernists, notably the Italian futurists,
struck nationalist poses during the war; most were more ambivalent about the
war. But the power of patriotic appeals derived from the fact that they were
distilled from a set of what may be called 'traditional values' – classical, romantic, or religious images and ideas widely disseminated in both elite and
popular culture before and during the war. It is this set of values and the languages in which they were expressed which I call the 'traditional' approach to
imagining war.[6]

Of course, both the 'modernist' and the 'traditional' forms of imagining
the war were evident long before the Armistice. Furthermore, the distinction
was at times more rhetorical than real. Modernists didn't obliterate traditions;

---

2 Fussell: *The Great War and Modern Memory*.
3 The best formulation of this position is by Samuel Hynes in his remarkable book *A War Imagined: The Great War and English Culture*. It subtly develops and goes beyond the earlier,
   seminal work of Fussell. For the latest (though certainly not the last) study in this tradition,
   see Christopher Coker: *War and the Twentieth Century*.
4 Hynes: *A War Imagined*.
5 See Fussell: *The Great War and Modern Memory*, and Bogacz: "'A Tyranny of words': language,
   poetry, and antimodernism in England in the First World War."
6 For a similar argument, see Rosa Bracco: *Merchants of Hope: Middlebrow Writers of the First
   World War*.

they stretched, explored and reconfigured them in ways that alarmed conventional artists, writers, and the public at large. Frequently that shock to the cautious was part of the program of modernist art and literature,[7] but it is important to bear in mind the continuing affinities between avant-garde artists and mainstream styles and modes of thought.[8]

Perhaps it is time for us to go beyond the cultural history of the Great War as a phase in the onward ascent of modernism. This now fashionable and widely-accepted interpretation will not stand scrutiny primarily for two reasons. First, the rupture of 1914–18 was much less complete than previous scholars have suggested. The overlap of languages and approaches between the old and the new, the 'traditional' and the 'modern,' the conservative and the iconoclastic, was apparent both during and after the war. The ongoing dialogue and exchange among artists and their public, between those who self-consciously returned to nineteenth-century forms and themes and those who sought to supersede them, makes the history of modernism much more complicated than a simple, linear divide between 'old' and 'new' might suggest.

Secondly, though, the identification of the 'modern' positively with abstraction, symbolic representation, and an architectural exploration of the logical foundations of art, and negatively through its opposition to figurative, representational, 'illusionist,' naturalistic, romantic or descriptive styles in painting and sculpture,[9] is so much a part of cultural history, that it is almost impious to question it, but question it we must. What is at issue is both whether such a distinction is accurate and whether it contributes to an understanding of the cultural consequences of the Great War. On both counts, I dissent from the 'modernist' school.

Equally sacrosanct is the view that there was a 'modernist' moment in literary history, beginning in the 1860s, maturing before 1914, but coming of

---

7   See the stimulating remarks in Modris Eksteins' *Rites of Spring: The Modern in Cultural History*, and in Clement Greenberg: "Beginnings of modernism." Chefdor *et al.*, eds., *Modernism: Challenges and perspectives*, pp. 17–24.

8   In the visual arts, the best statement of this position is Ken Silver's *Esprit de Corps: The Parisian Avant-garde in the period of the Great War*. A similarly sensitive approach is adopted in Robert Wohl: "The generation of 1914 and Modernism." Chefdor et al., eds.: *Modernism*, pp. 66–78.

9   The literature on this subject is mountainous. One could do worse than start with Clement Greenberg's seminal remarks in his "Modernist painting," in Geoffrey Battock, ed., *The New Art: A Critical Anthology*, pp. 100–110; see also the essays in his *Art and Culture*. For an earlier and even more trenchant exposition of the modernist revolution, see Wilenski: *The Modern Movement in Art* (1927).

age after the Great War.[10] "Modernism," one literary scholar tells us, "is part of the historical process by which the arts have dissociated themselves from nineteenth-century assumptions, which had come in the course of time to seem like dead conventions." In this process, the war of 1914–18 had both a crystallizing and hastening effect.[11] A second literary historian has added, "The Great War created one world by freeing us from that old one …"[12] A third view is that the war "uncovered" the "decay" of Edwardian values,[13] and helped provoke a rejection of what had come before, "two gross of broken statues," "a few thousand battered books," the cultural artefacts of what Pound called "an old bitch gone in the teeth," "a botched civilization".[14]

The iconoclastic element in 'modernism,' "a rage against prevalent traditions"[15] is taken frequently as its chief defining feature. Artist and audience are separated at times by an almost unbridgeable gulf. Gone is the comfort of conventional art and literature, for example, the safe, sentimental narrative of Dickens's prose or the warm embrace of the yellows and greens in Monet's water lilies. In its place are the harsher disciplines and forms of Joyce and Picasso, and the paradoxical, esoteric, fractured images of a host of their contemporaries.[16] They offered, in the words of T. S. Eliot, "something stricter" than conventional art, as a means "of controlling, of ordering, of giving a shape and a significance to the immense panorama of futility and anarchy which is contemporary history." Eliot wrote this essay in 1923, a year after the publication of James Joyce's *Ulysses*. In that work, Stephen Dedalus "com-

---

10 Fokkema: *Literary History, Modernism and Postmodernism* (1984); René Wellek: "The Term and Concept of Symbolism in Literary History"; Stark: "'The Murder of Modernism': Some Observations on Research into Expressionism and the Post-modernism Debate." Sheppard, ed.: *Expressionism in Focus*, pp. 27–46; Paul de Man: *Blindness and Insight: Essays in the rhetoric of contemporary criticism*, chs. 8–9.

11 Faulkner: *Modernism*, pp. 1, 14.

12 Schneidau: *Waking Giants: The Presence of the Past in Modernism*, p. 20.

13 Brian A. Rowley: "Anticipations of modernism in the age of romanticism." Janet Garton, ed.: *Facets of European Modernism*, p. 17.

14 Ezra Pound: "Hugh Selwyn Mauberley." *Selected Poems*, pp. 171–87

15 Eysteinsson: *The Concept of Modernism*, p. 8.

16 Once again, the literature in this field is vast. Two key essays on the notion are Harry Levin: "What was modernism?", and Raymond Williams: "When was modernism?" For some other recent explorations, see: Calinescu: *Five Faces of Modernity: Modernism, Avant-garde, Decadence, Kitsch, Postmodernism*; Karl: *Modern and Modernism: The Sovereignty of the Artist, 1885–1925*; Huyssens, *After the Great Divide: Modernism, Mass Culture, Postmodernism* (1986); Levenson: *A Geneology of Modernism: A Study of English Literary Doctrine, 1908–1922* (1984); Clark: *Sentimental Modernism: Women Writers and the Revolution of the Word* (1991).

plains that history is a nightmare from which he is trying to awake."[17] In the same spirit, two critics writing in the 1970s argued that "Modernism is our art; it is the one art that responds to the scenario of our chaos" defined in many ways, but marked indelibly by "the destruction of civilization and reason in the First World War".[18] Once again, I would like to offer a dissenting point of view on these widely-held convictions about the location of the 1914–18 war within European cultural history.

That some aspects of twentieth-century art and literature are revolution-ary goes without saying. And it seems equally inoffensive to identify modern-ism as both an 'aesthetic project' – an exploration of the foundations of art – and as a 'cultural force' – its capacity to comment critically and powerfully on contemporary events.[19] What is more difficult to accept is that 'modernism' – more a temperament than a set of fixed beliefs – left behind as neatly and sur-gically as some scholars suggest the host of images and conventions derived from eighteenth and nineteenth-century religious, romantic or classical tradi-tions.[20] Furthermore, those outside the 'modernist' canon, – Kipling, Luty-ens, Käthe Kollwitz – were hardly as banal and barren of innovation as this argument has it. Lutyens's Cenotaph was described by one champion of mod-ernism as "derivative popular modern architectural sculpture. Not being an original work it has no intrinsic value".[21]

It is the very teleology of this position – the search for precursors or expo-nents of what later critics have admired or rejected – which makes the 'mo-dernist' hypothesis about the cultural history of the early twentieth century just as misleading as other tendentious interpretations of recent or not so re-cent history. To array the past in such a way is to invite distortion by losing a sense of its messiness, its non-linearity, its vigorous and stubbornly visible in-compatibilities.

The history of the Great War and its aftermath is full of them, requiring scholars to go beyond the so-called modernist/traditionalist divide to a more sophisticated appreciation of the ways Europeans imagined the war and its terrible consequences. I would like to suggest one way do so: by concentrat-

---

17 Eliot: "Ulysses, order and myth." *Selected Prose*, p. 177; as cited in Eysteinnson: *The Concept of Modernism*, p. 9.
18 Bradbury and McFarlane: "The Name and Nature of Modernism." Bradbury and McFar-lane, eds.: *Modernism 1890–1930* (1976), pp. 27, 29.
19 Eysteinnson: *The Concept of Modernism*, p. 16.
20 In its extreme form, the argument states that "today modernism negates the notion of tra-dition itself." See Adorno: *Aesthetic Theory*, p. 31. For a neat demolition of this position, see Shils: *Tradition* (1981), pp. 160ff.
21 Wilsenski: *The Modern Movement in Art*, p. 165n.

ing on aspects of one particular theme in the cultural history of the war: the
theme of mourning and its private and public expression.

II. Tradition and the Mediation of Bereavement

The Great War brought the search for an appropriate language of loss to the
center of cultural and political life.[22] In this search, older motifs took on new
meanings and new forms. Some derived them from classical strophes. Others
explicitly elaborated religious motifs, or explored romantic forms. This vigorous mining of eighteenth and nineteenth-century images and metaphors to
accommodate expressions of mourning is one central reason why it is unacceptable to see the Great War as the moment when 'modern memory' replaced something else, something timeworn and discredited, which (following contemporaries) I have called 'tradition'.

It is my fundamental argument that the enduring appeal of many traditional motifs – defined as an eclectic set of classical, romantic, or religious images and ideas – is directly related to the universality of bereavement in the
Europe of the Great War and its aftermath. The strength of what may be
termed 'traditional' forms in social and cultural life, in art, poetry, and ritual,
lay in their power to mediate bereavement. The cutting edge of 'modern
memory,' its multi-faceted sense of dislocation, paradox and the ironic, could
express anger and despair, and did so in enduring ways; it was melancholic,
but it could not heal.[23] Traditional modes of seeing the war, while at times less
challenging intellectually or philosophically, provided a way of remembering
which enabled the bereaved to live with their losses, and perhaps to leave
them behind.

III. Facets of the Cultural History of Mourning
Catastrophe and Consolation

There is no alternative to starting with the palpable shock of the catastrophe
of the war. We could begin with a scene from the 1919 film of Abel Gance
J'accuse, in which the dead arise and return home to see if their sacrifice has

---

22 David Cannadine: "War and death, grief and mourning in modern Britain." Whaley, ed.:
    Mirrors of Mortality: Studies in the Social History of Death, pp. 187–219.
23 For a discussion of melancholy and mourning in the context of postmodernism, see Mar-
    tin Jay: *Force Fields: Between intellectual history and cultural critique*, pp. 84–97.

been in vain. This terrifying metaphor had an all too material reality to it. The question of finding the dead, gathering their remains in cemeteries or bringing them home, was posed in all combatant countries and answered in very different ways. There is much evidence available to enable us to follow those in mourning from the shock of discovery and through the painful effort to understand what had happened and to accept their loss.

Almost all towns and villages in the major European combatant countries were, in another sense, communities of the bereaved. Primary mourners – those directly related to the men who died in the war – numbered in the tens of millions. The construction, dedication, and repeated pilgrimages to war memorials in the interwar years provided a ritual expression of their bereavement, and that of their local communities. The grief of widows, orphans, parents, friends was 'seen' at the annual commemorative ceremonies, and to a degree we will never know, their loss was shared by their neighbors and friends. Community here had a very local character, some of the rich variety of which has been disclosed in great works of literature, such as Jean Giono's *Le grand troupeau* (1931) and more recently in Jean Rouault's novel *Champs d'honneur* (1991).

Through these works, and in many other sources, we find considerable evidence of the power of traditional modes of commemoration within communities, from small groups of men and women in family circles, to séances, to those gathered in more conventional forms of religious worship, to universities, ex-servicemen's associations, widows' organizations, to communities unveiling war memorials, and finally, to the 'imagined community' of the nation itself.[24] How to accept the shock of the war; how to remember the 'Lost Generation' were questions with disturbing communal and political repercussions, which in some sense still echo to this day. Witness the debate over what should be the appropriate German national war memorial for the *Neue Wache* in Berlin.[25]

The history of mourning discloses much about social solidarity in the wake of the war. Yes, in some ways, the Great War brought brutality into the

---

24 For the *locus classicus*, see Benedict Anderson: *Imagined Communities: Reflections on the origin and spread of nationalism*; for some doubts on the usefulness of national boundaries in the study of social history see J. M. Winter's introduction to Robert and Winter: *Paris, London, Berlin: Capital Cities at War 1914–1919* (Cambridge University Press, 1995).

25 Reinhart Koselleck: "Bilderverbot. Welches Totengedenken?" *Frankfurter Allgemeine Zeitung*, 8 April 1993. See also the profound comments in Koselleck's "Kriegerdenkmale als Identitätsstiftungen der Überlebenden," and "Der Einfluss der beiden Weltkriege auf das soziale Bewusstsein," in Wette, ed.: *Der Krieg des kleinen Mannes: Eine Militärgeschichte von unten*, pp. 324–43.

center of social life. But brutalization was not the only or even the dominant response in many quarters. Compassion was there too, and deserves to be recognized as an essential component in the process of recovery from the war.[26]

IV. Cultural Codes and Languages of Mourning

There is much in the history of cultural forms which enable us to explore the power of traditional motifs in the search for a language of mourning during and after the Great War. Cinematic visions of war drew on an older tradition of popular religious art. Here film emerged as a language of aesthetic redemption, and present what was, for the time, a very modern, cinematic way of 'seeing' the dead. Here the most 'modern' techniques are used to present ancient motifs and images about sacrifice, death and resurrection.

Gance's film is a remarkable mixture of two visions of war: the first is full of conventional romanticism; the second supersedes it by imagining the Apocalypse. I find in this film two facets of the romantic temperament confronting the problem of mourning the dead of the Great War. Very similar responses may be observed in the self-conscious naiveté of the French graphic art tradition of *l'imagerie d'Epinal* and similar modes of expression drawing on popular piety and religion; and in a different register, in the apocalyptic visions of artists who reflected on the war and who, in very different ways, resurrected the dead.

The search for appropriate languages of mourning went on in other ways, but among the most salient, and most relevant for the 'modernist' argument, are war literature, in fiction, plays and poetry. Here too 'seeing' the war meant more a return to older patterns and themes, than the creation of new ones. Among the most powerful was the reformulation of the sacred, as an exploration of apocalyptic themes in prose, or as a poetic language of communication about and with the dead.

V. Aspects of Cultural History: the Great War in the Twentieth Century

My argument is that the best way to show the need to go beyond the 'modernist-traditionalist' divide is to focus on one central theme: the form and content of mourning for the dead of the Great War. I make no claim to present a

---

26   For the 'brutalizing' effects of the war, see George Mosse: *Fallen Soldiers: Reshaping the Memory of the World Wars.*

tour d'horizon of the effect of the Great War on systems of representation of gender, social groups or nations.[27]

I have reformulated the question to what extent was the Great War a moment of discontinuity in cultural history, by reference to the history of bereavement. My emphasis is on the enduring character of what I have termed 'traditional' languages of mourning. But I recognize as equally true that the 1914–18 war was, if not the end of one phase of European cultural history, at least the beginning of the end. In contrast to the post-1918 period, the rupture of language and imagery which followed the Second World War was profound and enduring.

1. Continuities and discontinuities: 1939 and 1914

It is evident that by no means all 'traditional' languages survived the 1914–18 war and its aftermath intact. Slowly but surely, expressions of patriotism, or inhumanely idealized images of combat, suffering and death as 'glory,' began to fade away. It is true too that because of the 1914–18 conflict and popular understanding of its costs and uncertain outcome, the outbreak of war in 1939 was not greeted with patriotic bravado. Partly this was a result of the newsreels of the 1930s, and the knowledge, drawn from the Spanish Civil War, they spread about air raids and civilian casualties. But as Samuel Hynes has shown, by the 1930s the "Big Words" – duty, honor, country – had a hollow ring for many people who had never read the war poets. The Dean of Durham, Henley Henson, noted that clerical patriotism had to be muted in 1939; the patriotic lexicon of 1914 could no longer be used in the same way as before. Romantic notions about war did indeed take a battering during the 1914–18 war, and some wartime and postwar literature helped to discredit them further.

Nevertheless, in 1939 war could still be justified. What had changed in Western European culture is that the days of its glorification were over.[28] Whatever was true in Nazi Germany, Fascist Italy and (after June 1941) the Soviet Union, the rest of European society greeted war as the abomination that it was.

The men and women who went to war in 1939 knew more about the cruelties of modern warfare than did the generation of 1914. They enlisted or supported the men in uniform without much patriotic fanfare, in part be-

---

27 For a beginning, see Becker, et al., eds.: *Guerres et cultures: Vers une histoire comparée de la grande guerre.*

28 See the thoughtful remarks of Antoine Prost: "Les représentations de la guerre dans la culture française de l'entre deux guerres".

cause they felt they had no other choice. But when the time came to mourn fallen soldiers, many of the survivors did so in the somber languages and forms which derived from the memory of the Great War. After 1945 the names of the fallen were added to communal war memorials, and in Britain it is the poetry of the 1914–18 war which is still intoned to recall the 'lost generation' of both world conflicts.

2. 1945 and after

There is a sense in which the dead of the two world wars formed one community of the fallen. But in time both the political character of the Second World War and some of its horrific consequences made it impossible for many survivors to return to the languages of mourning which grew out of the 1914–18 war when they tried to express their sense of loss after 1945.

The sources of this rupture are not hard to find. Many of the commemorative forms created after 1918 were intended to warn; when the warning was not heard, when the Nazis forced war upon reluctant Western European democracies in 1939, that message of hope, of using the witness of those who had suffered during the war to prevent its recurrence, was bound to fade away.[29]

Warfare too had changed. In the 1939–45 conflict, more than half of the approximately 50 million people who died directly as a result of hostilities were civilians. And the ways millions of innocent people perished were new. The nuclear bombardment of Hiroshima and Nagasaki was new. So was the extermination of the Jews of Europe, an act with affinities to earlier mass atrocities, but which transcended them in method, character, and scale. Both of these catastrophes raised the possibility that the limits of language had been reached; perhaps there was no way adequately to express the hideousness and scale of the cruelties of the 1939–45 war.[30]

Those doubts were present both during and after the First World War, but a host of writers, sculptors, poets, and others stilled them – at least for a time – to create some enduring works of art and monuments to those who died in war. After Hiroshima and Auschwitz, the earlier commemorative effort simply could not be duplicated. As Julia Kristeva has observed, the Second

---

29   I am grateful to Elisabeth Domansky for discussions on this point.

30   For an introduction to the vast literature on Holocaust commemoration, see Young: *The Texture of memory. Holocaust memorials and meaning*; Domansky: "Die gespaltene Erinnerung."

World War undermined the very symbols through which meaning – any meaning – could be attached to the "cataclysm" of war.[31]

Before 1939, the reverse was the case. An examination of commemorative forms and practices during and after the Great War discloses striking convergences in the search for meaning in all combatant countries. For this reason, we would do well to consider the implications of a well-known sketch by Paul Klee, entitled *Angelus Novus*. The drawing grew out of a caricature of Kaiser Wilhelm II as the 'iron eater'. But Klee's search for the meaning of history did not end with this national stereotype. Instead, he transformed the image into the angel of history, a transcendental figure whose gaze embraces us all.[32]

In his ninth 'Thesis on the Philosophy of History,' Walter Benjamin meditated on the drawing and its implications. Benjamin recalls:

> A Klee painting named 'Angelus Novus' shows an angel looking as though he is about to move away from something he is fixedly contemplating. His eyes are staring, his mouth is open, his wings are spread. This is how one pictures the angel of history. His face is turned towards the past. Where we perceive a chain of events, he sees one single catastrophe which keeps piling wreckage upon wreckage and hurls it in front of his feet. The angel would like to stay, awaken the dead, and make whole what has been smashed. But a storm is blowing from Paradise; it has got caught in his wings with such violence that the angel can no longer close them. This storm irresistibly propels him into the future to which his back is turned, while the pile of debris before him grows skyward. This storm is what we call progress.[33]

No image does more to capture the subtle and contradictory elements embedded in European cultural history in the period of the Great War. Benjamin's "angel of history" did indeed float into the future with his gaze fixed firmly on the past. His back was turned on us, those who have come after; the onward march towards 'modernism' did not concern him. Instead his eyes were directed towards the 'wreckage' strewn at his feet, the 'pile of debris' left by the 'storm' we call the Great War.[34]

---

31 See Julia Kristeva: *Black Sun: Depression and melancholy*, p. 223.

32 Stéphane Mosès: *L'ange de l'histoire: Rosenzwieg, Benjamin, Scholem.*

33 Benjamin: *Illuminations*, pp. 259–60. On Benjamin's use of this image, see Susan Buck-Morss: *The Dialectics of Seeing: Walter Benjamin and the Arcades Project*; Stéphane Mosès: *L'Ange de l'histoire*; and Werckmeister: *The Making of Paul Klee's Career, 1914–1920*, pp. 241–2.

34 See Adorno's comments on the painting: "During the First World War or shortly after, Klee drew cartoons of Kaiser Wilhelm as an inhuman iron eater. Later, in 1920, these became – the development can be shown quite clearly – the *Angelus Novus*, the machine angel, who, though he no longer bears any emblem of caricature or commitment, flies far beyond both. The machine angel's enigmatic eyes face the onlooker to try to decide whether he is announcing the culmination of disaster of salvation hidden with it. But, as Walter Benja-

It is my central contention that the backward gaze of so many writers, artists, politicians, soldiers, and everyday families in this period reflected the universality of grief and mourning in Europe from 1914. A complex traditional vocabulary of mourning, derived from classical, romantic or religious forms, flourished, largely because it helped mediate bereavement. The 'sites of memory,' like Benjamin's "Angelus Novus," faced the past, not the future.

The Second World War helped put an end to the rich set of traditional languages of commemoration and mourning which flourished after the First World War. Before 1939, before the Death Camps, and the thermonuclear cloud, most men and women were still able to reach back into their 'traditional' cultural heritage to express amazement and anger, bewilderment and compassion, in the face of war and the losses it brought in its wake. If this essay has drawn attention to their achievement, so human and so sad, then in part it will have realized its aim.

---

min, who owned the drawing, said, he is the angel who does not give but takes." From Adorno: "Commitment," in Arato and Gebhardt, eds: *The Essential Frankfurt School Reader*, p. 318. Werckmeister locates the drawing in the context of Klee's ruminations on aircraft and on the 'flying man' as the new angel. This interpretation sees Klee's drawing as a twentieth-century variant of Leonardo's and Swedenborg's sense of manned flight as angelic. See Werckmeister, *Klee's career*, p. 241. In this reading of the drawing, once again we find the most modern forms transformed into carriers of ancient images of transformation and redemption.

CORNELIA VISMANN

Europa Universität Viadrina, Frankfurt (Oder)

Starting From Scratch:
Concepts of Order in No Man's Land

> "Vor allem wissen, an welchem Punkt der Landkarte wir aus der
> blutverschmierten, undeutlichen, verdammten Erdkruste
> herausgekrochen sind."
>
> *Heiner Müller / Bertolt Brech: Fatzer, p. 17.*

Abstract: "No-man's-land" is the metaphorical territory wrought by a highly effective encounter between the military and legal discourse during World War I. The concept of order during this period was markedly spatial. Changes in the perception of space inevitably altered the perception of order. The destruction of landscape, extreme deterritorialization, and complete dissociation of habitual systems of order contained in the notion of no-man's-land required new definitions of order in the realm of military strategy. Order becomes concrete and dynamic, immediately responsive to war's marks in the soil and to the changing demarcations of space. German jurisprudence during the period following World War I is characterized by the same desire for new concepts of order. Carl Schmitt's idea of concrete order ("konkretes Ordnungsdenken") belongs here, as does the prefascistic notion of dynamical law, which is both chtonic and spatial. In the name of jus terrendi, Schmitt's "Nomos der Erde," a new order emerges, an order which not only reflects the war experiences of no-man's-land but also posits war itself as a concept of order. No-man's-land becomes the subtext of law as a state of war, transferring the violence of an occupation, as restored in the idea of a terra nullius, into the spheres of law.

I.

The primordial scene of the *nomos* opens with a drawing of a line in the soil. This very act initiates a specific concept of law, which derives order from the notion of space. The plough draws lines – furrows in the field – to mark the space of one's own. As such, as ownership, the demarcating plough touches the juridical sphere. The space of what is owned marks either a private or a public sphere of control,[1] either a possession of land or a state-territory. Cultivation defines the order of ownership in space. In the language of Roman Law: *Urbare est aratro definire*. This initial scene of the law can still be found in the Anglo-American common law: The common law divisions base themselves upon a civilian definition of dimensions, the underlying principle of which can be found initially in the Digest, where 'the term urbs is to mark out by a plough.'[2] The primordial act as described here brings together land and law, cultivation and order, space and *nomos*. Moreover – although barely perceptible – it already contains the split between two competing orders of law depending on two different notions of space: the homogenous space of geography on one side and the specific space of the soil on the other.

Both order, the universal measurement of land and the specific order of the soil, start by drawing a line. Lines can either be the arbitrary, orthogonal and exactly measured lines drawn by the *agrimensores*,[3] which surround and demarcate a certain territory,[4] or it can be the line as traces of the land use, evidence of pro ductivity, which fill out the territory with signs of ownership.[5] The order of the soil claims to have a primordial writing in the scripture of furrows.[6] Such writing performs the about-face of an ox, alternating from left to right and right to left. Thus it produces a certain order of space, due to the economy of cultivating the land. Jacques Derrida points out in his comment of Jean-Jacques Rousseau, that the writing by an ox – Bustrophedon-writing it

---

Thanks to Jane B. Malmo for her kind help with the translation, thanks also to Peter Berz for his critical comments.

1   Fustel de Coulange: *Histoire*, p. 4, who confirms the correspondence of *potestas* and *proprietas* (here also to the primordial scene). Further on the topic of *ager privatus* and *ager publicus* in Roman law Theodor Mommsen in his reply to Max Weber's *History of Roman Agriculture*. A general overview on Roman rural Law by Ruddy: *Res nullius and Occupation*.

2   Goodrich: *Eating the Law*, p. 260 with reference to Hachamovitch: *The Ideal Object*, p. 92 (note 27): where the passage of the Digest (50.239.6) is cited at length: "and Varus says that *urbus* is the name of the curved part of a plough which is customarily used in the foundation of an *urbs*."

3   About the agrimensores see note 1 and Dilke: *The Roman Land Surveyors*.

4   Prescott: *Boundaries*, p. 68.

5   The two competing orders can be discovered in the property claims made for land. Here paper titles compete with "practical senses of property which arose from land use, and which lay in local memory," see Pottage: *Measure of Land*, pp. 364–367; all together a brilliant study about the relation of paper and land in the legal system of land property.

6   A so-called "Kehr-Pflug" (turn-back-plough) draws this kind of lines; Leser: *Entstehung und Verbreitung des Pfluges*, for the possible different 'scriptures' of a plough, pp. 7–12; (I am grateful to Ulrich Raulff for this reference); also Raulff: *Ein Historiker*, pp. 120–124.

is called – is not yet in force as a universal order. Before any kind of universal or homogeneous order "ordnet sich der gesamte Raum um ihre Behausung und die Einschreibung des 'eigenen' Körpers in ihn."[7] This space is then as heterogeneous as the bodies inscribed in it. Different parts of the body set up different spaces. The economical imperative, which agriculture as well as law seem to be subjected to, produces a particularly different writing depending on whether it is the eye or the hand that dictates the drawing of lines. The order of body and soil refers to a law before any positive law, before any uniform writing or orthography, and before any homogenized space. The phantasm of such a primordial writing initiates what one would call, though a bit spectacular, the terror of the terrain that the texts of the law unfold. What is meant by the terror of the terrain should become clearer in what follows.

The imprints that bodies leave in the soil mark the unique, the authentic, according to the discourse that considers agriculture as a physical and even spatial inscription of the owned in the soil.[8] "Raumordnender Urakt des *Nomos*," (ordering of space according to the primordial act of the *nomos*) as Carl Schmitt, who emphasizes 'space' and not 'script,' dubs it. Therefore the spatial, the chtonic, the telluric law, the *jus terrendi*, has its founding scene in the cultivation of the soil. It defends this ground against a law that starts not from scratch but from an already homogenized land. This is the land of geometry, in which the line is the graph of a map, with a universalized scale, with a unified economy – bodiless, abstract and arbitrary in its ordering units. Such land is associated in legal thought with Hermann Kelsens's legal positivism,[9] with empty normatism and spaceless norms. Withdrawn from the originary ground, it is referred to as mere paper. For Schmitt this 'geographical principle is not convincing as a basis for legal thought.[10] Only common law, he stresses, has restored some of the essential spatial boundedness of law,[11] which he tries to regain for the notion of law. At war here is abstract normativism versus concrete order, arbitrary rules versus self-legitimizing lawfulness, universal law versus spatial *nomos*, empty statehood versus 'Großraum.'[12] Briefly: the ground becomes a battleground for a *jus terrendi* versus a *jus scriptum*.

Between the two World Wars, the power of a spatial order, even the power of space ordering, possesses a certain attraction not only for those whose dai-

---

7   Derrida: *Grammatologie*, p. 494: "the whole space is configured around its lodging and the inscription of the specific body in it."
8   Ibid., p. 461.
9   Schmitt: "Der neue Raumbegriff in der Völkerrechtswissenschaft," p. 440.
10 Schmitt: *Völkerrechtliche Großraumordnung*, p. 33.
11 Schmitt: *Der Nomos der Erde*, p. 66.
12 Schmitt: "Der neue Raumbegriff in der Völkerrechtswissenschaft," p. 442.

ly business is occupations – the military. Also for legal discourse, a project that seeks concrete order in the land fills the gap, rather fulfills the desire for the concrete, for the just, which abstractions of land by law leave behind. From a German perspective, World War I consists of those abstractions of the land ranging from the devastation in the terrain of war to the topos of 'Heimatlosigkeit,' homelessness, after a lost war.

The project of gaining ground again for a concrete law is not as organic and fruitful as the agriculture jargon suggests. Incisions in the ground are overall inscriptions of property and identity. As pointed out in the beginning: spatial law starts by drawing a line. In this country one would probably say by 'staking a claim.'[13] The term 'claim' might indicate the juridical violence contained in the primordial act. The writing of agriculture bears the traits of a reclamation – a claim for land, 'Landnahme.' But because the scene takes place in the ground, this concept has no problem grounding – in the sense of legitimizing – the primordial violence. The rhetoric of economy, which is at work as soon as drawing a line is associated with the writing of agriculture, justifies violence, the violence of a claim as functional, necessary, inevitable, and existential. A specific autopoiesis, the founding of law by cultivating the land, provides the legitimizing discourse with arguments.

This figure of justifying the primordial act of violence in law explains to some extent the attraction exerted by a notion of law stemming from the soil. Whereas the pure *jus scriptum* is set out by a superior authority, the *jus terrendi* bears out its own order within. It is 'ontonom,' as Schmitt designates this legitimizing figure of factual necessity.[14] The cultivation of a piece of land with a plough is an act, that is – in terms of its purpose – necessary. It is an economic imperative and not a juridical command that shapes order here. Because the power to establish an order by claiming land contains its own legitimation, it does not need the authority of a law. It justifies the incisions in the soil by virtue of the *nomos* inherent in this same soil. The economical cultivation of the land submits to a self-justifying order which is thus natural and almost organic. By contrast with these attributes of a chtonic law, it follows that all other forms of order, which do not stem from the soil, are uneconomical, not necessary and therefore arbitrary and frail.

The body plays an important role for the legitimation of a *jus terrendi*. The body that marks the soil attests to the human power executed in the land. And that is what actually functions as legitimation: the evidence of the body in the

---

13   Bolz: *Peri Trans Beyond*, p. 14.
14   Schmitt: *Der Nomos der Erde*, p.16.

soil. Occupations of land are executed by bodies, the bodies of soldiers. In Schmitt's agricultural terms, an occupation consists in cultivating the soil, which is accomplished in three steps: "Dem Nehmen [...] folgt das Teilen und Weiden."[15] To translate this apparent etymological interpretation – *nemein* as the root for *nomos* and for grazing – into the language of international law: occupation of land is followed by erecting boundaries and by colonizing.

For the major occupations in the colonizing era of the 16th century, legitimation was bound to the same three steps. And the actions took place on the same unmarked land, in the terra nullius as this terrain is called in international legal discourse. This is the uncultivated land that belongs to no one, sometimes the land that no one inhabits. In the 16th century, the mere act of discovering a piece of land or accidental acts of taking possession did not suffice as a legal foundation for proprietorship. Addressing the Spanish ambassador, Queen Elizabeth declares in 1580:

> She would not persuade herself that the Indies are the rightful property of Spain [...] only on the ground that the Spaniards have touched here and there, have erected shelters, have given names to a river or a promontory, acts which cannot confer property. So that [...] this imaginary proprietorship ought not to hinder other princes from carrying on commerce in these regions and from establishing colonies where Spaniards are not residing without the least violation of law of the nations.[16]

To turn an imaginary proprietorship into one legally acknowledged, an act of efficiency had to follow; the signs of executive state power had to be evident. Legal discourse specified that such signs meant the defining of boundaries and the erection of a visible and durable order. Or, again in Schmitt's agricultural terms: 'dividing and grazing come after the act of taking.' What was the economy of ploughing appears in the colonial discourse as effectiveness of occupation.

Occupation consists, according to international lawyers mostly of the beginning of the 20th century, in a bodily act such as cultivation. In this sense Queen Elizabeth is quoted by these jurists to emphasize that ephemeral acts such as naming the land, cannot found proprietorship. It is an effective execution of property and not some kind of juridical act that mediates a *jus in occupationem*. With the legal doctrine of effective occupation, factual acts replace

---

15 Schmitt: *Theorie des Partisanen*, p. 83: "The taking [of a piece of land] is followed by dividing and grazing."

16 Heydte: *Discovery, Symbolic Annexation*, p. 459; about the doctrine of effective occupation in general see Grewe: *Völkerrechtsgeschichte*, p. 467.

papal authorizations. The soil takes the place of an authorizing instance of the sort Queen Elizabeth explicitly rejected. The legal requirement of effectiveness in land claiming, land taking, rather its economy comes from the aim itself: the occupation that provides its own legitimation.

Schmitt's order producing *nomos* operates on a similar legitimation basis. A 'superior allocation agency or instance' ("oberste Zuteilungsinstanz")[17] is made superfluous when the authorizing instance becomes the effectiveness of the occupation itself. Both concepts, the one of effective occupation and Schmitt's nomos, begin with unmarked land. The land that has no visible order imprinted in the soil is the land that authorizes, merely by the absence of any order, the imprinting of such an order, which is to say, the occupation of the land. Furthermore, the object of occupation is simultaneously the agency of its legitimation. According to this concept the order emerges directly from the soil. That is the logic of the doctrine of effective occupation in the 16th century as it is translated into the nomos of the earth of the 20th century. Effective occupation is spatial order.

II.

On the other side operates the logic of geometry in occupational acts. The interaction between the accuracy of maps and the mobility of warfare can be traced back to the 17th century. And even before, in the 16th century, military maps were in use at least for tactical reasons.[18] Wars in and over territories were fought on a cartographic basis. Not only in terms of strategy and tactics did *maps* – ordnance survey – meet the needs of warfare and alter them. Due to the anticipatory and almost substitory tendency of maps they also change the theater of war itself: with the introduction of *maps* warfare became a battle over borders and names, and maps became part of treaties between countries. But far from replacing the 'real' wars by map-wars, the claim for the right borders in maps seemed to evoke new and other wars.

Thus it is not astonishing that World War I begins with an occupation on paper – an imaginary proprietorship in Elizabethan terms. In 1909 countries began occupying the world by surveying the very countries with whom they would be at war just five years later.[19] The prelude for that war was an interna-

---

17   Schmitt: *Der Nomos der Erde*, p. 68.
18   Skelton: *The Military Surveyor's Contribution*.
19   Engelmann: *Die internationale Weltkarte*, p. 33.

tional project of a world map,[20] a kind of *cartographical* war over correct boundaries, national interests, and spheres of influence in the world. Whether it was because Great Britain, which the Germans accused of exploiting the map as a means to prepare for war,[21] or whether it was because of Germany, which gave up paper occupation on the legal principle: "Nur auf dem Papier kann man nicht rechtswirksam occupieren,"[22] in 1914 a World War started, that put an end to the worldmap project. And yet the surveying of the world was so advanced at that time that the material provided a sufficient base for ordnance survey maps for national military.[23] In Schmitt's monograph "Nomos der Erde," this fact emerges as follows:

> [...] als das geschichtliche und wissenschaftliche Bewußtsein der Menschen die ganze Erde bis in die kartographischen und statistischen Einzelheiten hinein in jedem Sinne des Wortes aufgenommen hatte, steigerte sich die praktisch politische Notwendigkeit einer nicht nur geometrisch flächenhaften Teilung, sondern einer inhaltlich erfüllten Raumordnung unserer Erde.[24]

Here he assembles all the motifs of a chtonic way of thinking: the detesting of the plane, the unifying measurement, the homogenization of space, its reduction of two dimensions and the expulsion of a primordial writing by cartographic ideograms – as if the seizing of the world within a unifying scale on paper, in legal contracts or through other empty norms could be blamed for the assumed degeneration of the *nomos*. Against the flattening of the world in the format of maps, Schmitt set up the spatial order, which began to take shape after the First World War.

And Germany? Germany quits the international *map* project in 1914 and draws its lines in the soil of Europe: frontlines of barbed wire, firing batteries and trenches, spatial lines of its claims for land. That is where the idea of *Großraum* deve lops, more spatial than the territory of a state represented in maps and more legitimate than the boundaries fixed in international con-

---

20   About the project, see the special issue No. 1 of the Bibliographica Cartograhica compiled by Emil Meyen.

21   Penck: *Die Weltkarte 1: 1,000,000*, p. 82: Albrecht Penck, the Austro-German initiator of the world-map-project, writes that he had discovered shortly before World War I, that the map was intended to be used as the British map for operations in the world war.

22   Dahm: *Völkerrecht*, p. 585: "Only on paper one can not occupy a country effectively."

23   Eckert: *Die Kartographie im Kriege*, p. 282.

24   Schmitt: *Der Nomos der Erde*, p. 54: "when the historical and scientific conscience of men had seized the whole earth up to every cartographic and statistical detail in every sense, the practical political necessity was enhanced for a not only geometrical and plane division but a substantially accomplished spatial order of our world."

tracts. In wartime, territory is treated like an unmarked piece of land, a *terra nullius* that has not yet been occupied. It is exactly this treatment of the terrain as unmarked that makes it possible to turn it into the primordial scene for *nomos*.

Necessity – this rhetoric of agricultural efficiency – had further, direct resonances in a discourse of military tactics. In this discourse the binary order built upon the dividing function of a geometrical line would fail to meet the goal of effective occupation in its most literal sense which is the exploitation of the depth of space. Therefore a shift occurred on the tactical level in 1916 whose significance cannot be overestimated. It has spread into all kinds of discourses from there on: cognitive as well as psychological, cultural and legal. It is the shift from the perception of a 'line' to a formation called the '*zone*.' The zone reaches for the depth of the space and structures the terrain of war spatially – according to military *necessities*. "Tiefengliederung der Befestigungsanlagen und Führung des Kampfes im Großen nicht um Linien, sondern in Kampfzonen" – that is what the German High Command enacts under Erich Ludendorff.[25] His decree contains two kinds of zones. The first is concerned with fortifications and the second with the conduct of the battle. The zone as a spatial unit of combat is shaped by the so-called 'Sperrfeuer,' which is followed by a 'Feuer-Walze,' an artillery barrage that de-cultivates, de-ploughs the zone for combat in order to prepare the ground for the infinity to come.[26] It calls for an accurate cooperation – "auf die Minute genau" – between the artillery and the infantry.[27]

The zone can either be between or behind the frontlines.

> Zwischen den einzelnen Linien, zwischen und hinter den Grabensystemen ist jede Verteidigung auszunutzen und vorzubereiten. Hierzu dienen Stützpunkte – größere, oft geschlossene Anlagen unter Ausnutzung von Dörfern, Waldstücken usw. und Anklammerungspunkte – kleine Gräben, Trichter, Hausruinen, Waldstücke, Hecken und ähnliches – [...]. Die Tiefe einer in dieser Weise vorbereiteten Zone soll bis zu mehreren Kilometern betragen; ihre Begrenzung muß schwer erkennbar sein.[28]

---

25 "Depth structure of the fortifications and conduct of war in general not around lines but in zones of combat," Ludendorff: *Urkunden der Obersten Heeresleitung*, ("Allgemeines über den Stellungsbau") p. 594.

26 Ibid., ("Der Angriff im Stellungskriege"), pp. 648, 652, 674.

27 Ibid., p. 645.

28 Ibid., p. 598: "Between the particular lines, between and behind the trench systems every possibility has to be utilized and prepared. Every strong point serves that purpose, larger, mostly closed layouts under utilization of villages, pieces of forests etc., and clamp points – small trenches, craters, ruins of houses, pieces of forests, bushes and such things – [...].

The structuring '*zone*' is formed under the eyes and by the moves of infantry-men. The virtual line, which runs from one point to the next, produces the zone. Thus the zone is unique, it differs for each fighting unit and changes with the moves this particular unit makes. This is what is so remarkable about the zone: it is an arrangement of perception in the moment of death threat, a construction of highly semiotized elements of landscape. For soldiers in the zone it becomes an order of survival. Its shape depends on the position and the situation of the battle. It is a virtual yet effective order. In the particular moment of action, and only in this moment, the landscape is coded according to tactical values, not aesthetic ones. Forests turn into strong points, bushes into clamp points.

When the line no longer applies, when every structuring element in the landscape has been rolled flat, military-trained eyes will perceive a zonal order, where untrained eyes see nothing. That there is nothing to see, precisely that the habitual structures of perception and models of order do not fit, finds expression in what eventually became the emblem of World War I: the *no man's land*. This composition of words was hardly known before the First World War and never became an official military term. It refers to the zone in respect to what the zone negates: that is, aesthetical perception and habitual order and, after all, 'men.' The military requirement reads: "Adapt to the terrain," which, apart from the recreation of a maternal order and the penetration of body and soil, means 'disappear!' It means to disappear by transforming into a stone, furrow, tree. Therefore the battlefield is "abandoned by men,"[29] or "menschenleer," as Ernst Jünger likes to say. And, although this land is suffused with bodies – not to talk about corpses –, the landscape looks abandoned, because someone who assimilates to the elements of a landscape becomes a no man. For identity is based on the order of a dividing line. Without the line, this order breaks down. In the zone identity is negated. And no man's land precisely designates this condition. Dismemberment, destruction, disappearance: such annihilating effects of the zone are well expressed by the term *"no man's land,"* as yet another fact confirms: the *zone* of combat is gradually transformed until it becomes impassable. Weapons turn it into a terrain, where no one could dwell. Ein "schmale[r] Streifen Erdstrich, der aber dennoch immer unüberwindbarer wird."[30] This is how Ernst Jünger defines the no man's land. The terrain becomes untrespassable, because it is devastated

---

    The depth of a thus prepared zone should expand up to several kilometers, its boundaries
    should hardly be visible."

29   Leed: *No Man's Land*, p. 14.

30   Jünger: *Kriegerische Mathematik*, p. 270: "A small strip in the earth, but nevertheless more and
    more intransgressable."

by constant combat. An amorphous mush of terrain emerges, through which it is impossible to move.

Bernd Hüppauf writes most clearly about this deterritorializing process, about the decomposition of an orderly landscape.

> Bilderserien, über längere Zeiträume hinweg aufgenommen, zeigen Waldregionen, die langsam sich lichten, bis lediglich Baumstümpfe übrig bleiben, die durch fortgesetztes Bombardement auch verschwinden und schließlich nur noch eine unkonturierte Fläche aus Schwarz und dunklen Grautönen, zerwühltes Erdreich, Schlamm, durchsetzt mit Resten der Kampfhandlungen übrig lassen.[31]

Only the strategic gaze trained in the zone still finds among the craters and furrows clamp points structuring the terrain. In contrast, an untrained gaze only discovers vast, deserted territory. The absence of structure and negation of a visible order lead directly into the indeterminacy of the no man's land.

In his memoirs on World War I Charles Carrington writes about the state of indeterminacy. "In fifty years I have never been able to rid myself of the obsession of No Man's Land and the unknown world beyond it."[32] Whenever no man's land is mentioned in war memories it refers to the collapse of any known order and of clearly defined boundaries. The break-down takes place in the borderland between the fronts. This border-experience in the zone which is at the same time the experience of the break-down of all borders is "… the very image of the marginal, the liminal, the 'betwixt and between' – *No Man's Land*," as Eric Leed puts it in his book of the same title about combat and identity in World War I.[33] And simultaneously this transitional *zone* becomes something like an ultimate border because of its impassability. The boundary that effaces all boundaries. The line that negates all lines, that is a zone.

III.

But no man's land not only refers to the absence of habitual order. It also produces a new order under the name '*zone*,' which is structured by clamp points and strong points. Fusing the cultural discourse of no man's land with the mi-

---

31 Hüppauf: *Räume der Destruktion und Konstruktion von Raum*, p. 117: "A series of pictures taken over a longer period of time show regions of forests, which slowly begin to clear until only stumps of trees remain. Even those disappear under continuous bombardment, and finally all that stays are a plane of black and dark tones of gray, rooted up ground without any contours, and mud interspersed with remainders of combat-actions."

32 Fussell: *The Great War*. p. 79; also Leed: *No Man's Land,* p. 14.

33 Ibid., p. 21.

litary discourse of the zone leads to a spatial notion of order. Here the nihilism of *no man's land* coincides with the spatiality of the zone. Such a discourse is characterized by a mixture of no man and land, nihilism and zone, nothingness and space. Ernst Jünger's "mobil-gemachte Landschaft" (mobilized landscape), as Walter Benjamin has dubbed it, Martin Heidegger's "Zone des vollendeten Nihilismus" (zone of complete nihilism) and Carl Schmitt's state of emergency all belong here. Norbert Bolz combined these three discourses on the line in an admirable paper called "Peri Trans Beyond": Jünger's essay "Über die Linie," dedicated to Heidegger, and Heidegger's reply to it, as well as Schmitt's "Nomos der Erde."

Those who claim to think about the line in terms of 'over,' 'above' and 'beyond' the line, find themselves in the zone, thinking in zones – because there is no other side of the line, because there is no line. In this respect all three discourses by Jünger, Heidegger, and Schmitt are very similar. For them an order, which begins somewhere behind the line, where the zone ends, is of no importance. It does not even exist. The terrain of indeterminacy, of nihilism, of chaos cannot be limited by simply drawing a line; in order to find an orderly world behind the line, for no man's land is the terminus a quo for their notion of order. The line has to be produced anew in the zone, where friend and foe are no longer separated by a visible boundary. Soldiers in World War I experienced this indeterminacy when reporting that during an attack they could not tell whether they were already on hostile ground or not.

For purposes of orientation the zonal discourse seeks a deeper order beneath the surface. Thus Jünger writes about the chaotic-anarchic landscape of war: "Nur die Oberfläche ist anarchisch – da muß die Mobilisierung hindurch" in order to make the underlying structure evident.[34] This recalls the order of furrows that the plough makes visible by throwing up soil. In his reply to Jünger,[35] Heidegger latches onto the idea of a deeper order beneath the surface of chaos and calls for an attempt to gain a new order of being. "In der Zone der Linie nähert sich der Nihilismus seiner Vollendung."[36] Appointed briefly as a 'Luftschiffer' at the meteorological station of the western front in 1918,[37] he must know. At that time, decisions about poison gas attacks were

---

34 Jünger: *Der Arbeiter*, p. 167: "Only the surface is anarchical – there mobilization must pass through."

35 Heidegger: *Zur Seinsfrage*, p. 41.

36 "In the zone of the line nihilism approaches its own completeness," ibid., p. 393.

37 About *Frontwetterwarte 414*, see Ott: *Martin Heidegger*, p. 104, also Heidegger/Blochmann: *Briefwechsel*. p. 135, (notes to letters no. 2 und 3); Farias: *Heidegger*, p. 95.

being made on the basis of meteorological prognosis, within the framework of weather-zones.

Less lethal but no less annihilating are the ordering effects of the zone. The zone not only negates identity but also stands for the negation of all kinds of orders linked with identity. Such negations make room for a completely new order which emerges with the expansion of the zone. It therefore fits well that Heidegger talks about the 'zone of the line.' The military zone is the unpassable and ultimate border, a transcendental line. Those three thinkers of the zone stay there, because – speaking in tactical terms – the zone cannot be overcome by drawing a line. As during the war, when the zonal border disseminates beyond the surveyable, the end of the zone is unpredictable, i. e. the point where the zero-line begins, from whence on a new order can develop remains indeterminable. "Mit der Vollendung des Nihilismus beginnt erst die Endphase des Nihilismus. Deren Zone is vermutlich […] ungewöhnlich breit. Deshalb ist die Null-Linie, wo die Vollendung zum Ende wird, am Ende noch gar nicht sichtbar."[38]

In Carl Schmitt's theory of an "Ausnahmezustand" – the *state of exception, the state of emergency* – the zone of nihilism finds its legal equivalent. The state of emergency is topographically defined as the place where the enforcement of positive law is suspended. By choosing the word 'suspension' instead of 'negation,' Schmitt takes into account the temporal and provisional aspect of this state that annihilates the positive law only to invoke what he calls the *concrete* order, which is hidden or repressed by the legal system. Suspension is more than just the absence of order. It makes room for a new, spatial order.

In Schmitt's essay about the state of siege, given as an inaugural speech in 1916, this type of order is already indicated. As a war volunteer, assigned to the homefront at Munich in the infantry-regiment (Infanterie-Leibregiment), Schmitt defines in this essay an internal and an external, a fictitious and a factual state of siege as a return to the primordial state of a lawless (rechtsfrei) space ("Rückkehr zum Urzustand").[39] Although Schmitt explicitly rejected this interpretation, his discussion in effect supplied the later so-called "dictatorship of the German High Command" with legal arguments for their claim to authority even in non-military matters.[40] The situation of 1916 was indeed formed by the High Command's struggle for power in Germany. At that time,

---

38 Heidegger: *Zur Seinsfrage,* p. 393: "With the completion of nihilism does the final phase of nihilism first begin. Their zone is presumably […] unusually wide. Therefore the zero-line is not yet visible at the end where the completion approaches the end."

39 Schmitt: *Diktatur und Belagerungszustand,* p.159.

40 Ibid., p. 161, note 52.

the *state of siege* declared for a more efficient mobilization was still in force, and a legal debate was abrew over the interpretation of the relation between the act of the state of siege and article 68 of the German constitution.[41] Article 68 authorized the German Emperor to declare a state of siege but referred to the legal situation of 1851. Enacted under the influence of the Revolution of 1848, at a time without a German Emperor, the act of 1851 decreed that the executive power was to pass over directly to the military commander-in-chief. The legal debate consequently focused on the question of how to interpret article 68. Who had the power to declare the state of siege and who holds the command under the altered conditions of 1916: the German Emperor or the military commander himself? This controversy was resolved de facto when the first Generalquartermeister (military commander) Erich Ludendorff "took over" on August 29, 1916 and thus suspended the Emperor's command.

Schmitt's essay, published in February 1916, does not focus on the question of who is the responsible body during the state of siege; instead he emphasizes that the state of siege is not susceptible to legal interpretation, precisely because it rests on a return to the natural state. In contrast, a dictatorship takes place *within* a constitution and thus is a thoroughly juridical matter. Thus the state of siege excludes any further legal debates. Schmitt's trick to immunize – at least indirectly – the German High Command against legal measures appears to be the definition of the state of siege as a lawless primordial natural state, so to speak a *terra nullius* of law.

According to Schmitt the definition of the legal institution of a 'state of siege' as lawlessness can be found in the positive law of the Anglo-Saxon *Martial Law*. He cites a directive that the American government handed down during the civil war in 1863:

> Martial Law in a hostile county consists in the suspension by the occupying Military Authority of the Criminal and Civil Law and the domestic Administration and Government in the occupied place or territory, and the substitution of Military rule and force by the same, as well as in the dictation of the general laws, as far as Military necessity requires this suspension, substitution or dictation.[42]

Military necessity, not arbitrary definition, defines the area in which the Martial Law is enforced. This area resembles the zone of military discourse which

41   Kitchen: *The Silent Dictatorship*, especially Chapter 2; Boldt: *Rechtsstaat und Ausnahmezustand*, pp. 196–222.
42   Schmitt: *Diktatur und Belagerungszustand*, p. 144.

derives from tactical expediency, and it follows the rhetoric of necessity without being confined by constructed borders.[43] Schmitt writes about the amazing and also effective intersection between the military and the law: "Der Zweck ist [...] beim Belagerungszustand rein faktisch bestimmt: ein Aufruhr soll niedergeschlagen, ein bestimmter militärischer Erfolg soll gesichert werden" and "[...] der Raum [der Suspension des Rechts ist] nur noch durch den bloß tatsächlichen Zweck [...] abgegrenzt."[44] Legal authority is replaced with factual necessity, the same figure of ipso-facto legitimation discussed previously.

With his inaugural speech Schmitt qualified as a government-official (Beamter) in the deputy general command (Stellvertretendes Generalkommando) of the first Bavarian army corps, for which he wrote reports from 1917 on about the law in the state of war.[45] By gradually removing the state of siege from its position as an exception, it became the regular model for the concept of *concrete* order as it is unfolded in Schmitt's "Nomos der Erde." Thirty-four years after the 'state of siege' had been written, its mature version was submitted in this monograph. It argues that the state in general consists of zones, temporal enforcements of particular orders according to particular situations. What, compared to the inaugural speech, is added in the 1940 version is the emphasis on the *spatiality* of order, which emerges as soon as the positive law is suspended. The return to a primordial state as it appeared in 1916 can then be localized: where else could that happen but in the no man's land of Hobbes' natural state, as Schmitt puts it in "Nomos der Erde?"[46]

Space and necessity instead of law and definition are the coordinates of this order. It is the order of the zone. The zonal order casts light on the notion of 'Reich' and 'Großbaum' in opposition to the state. Crucial is the expansion of the notion of terrain. Whereas the state territory is enclosed by a line, the extent of a terrain stems from the zonal order. *Zone* and *line* are both border-notions. The line is either a purely legal notion, such as the papal de-

---

43   The notion of military necessity substituting for legal proof goes along with the war crimes doctrine that "what constitutes devastation *beyond military necessity* requires detailed proof of operational and tactical nature." (*Law Report of War Criminals* 6 (1948), p. 52. In return military tactics produce proof of their own necessity.

44   Schmitt: *Diktatur und Belagerungszustand*, pp. 159, 158: "The goal of a state of siege is defined purely by facts: a riot must be put down, a certain military success should be secured. [...] The space [of a suspension of the law] ist delineated only by a shere factual purpose."

45   Villinger: *Verortung des Politischen*, p. l0.

46   Schmitt: *Der Nomos der Erde*, p. 64.

marcation line, or the effect of precise geography. A zonal order, however, comes from filling in, not from exclusion. To come back to the plough: the movements of a plough define the shape of the piece of land almost as if hatching it by furrows. Ploughing draws no exact boundaries. The turn about of the plough, like Bustrophedon writing, produces an area, a zone of a border. In Germanic law this zone is legally acknowledged as the "Pflugwenderecht," the right to turn the plough on the neighbor's ground.[47]

Thus the boundary replaces the frontier, a zonal border,[48] as soon as geography and the invention of the state as territory coincide. Schmitt alludes to medieval times, which were on the verge of inventing geometry, cartography, and the state – notions that for him are linked to the decline of a spatial sense ("Raum-sinn").[49] Thus the 'empty notion of the state' has to be replaced by a 'territorial concrete order of space' ("territorial konkrete Großraumordnung"). The borderline that usually defines the state then becomes a 'zone of defense' ("Zone der Selbstverteidigung") as every 'real empire' claims to have.[50] And indeed, in fifteenth century terminology one will find zones, in German also called 'Mark,' and mega-landscapes with 'overlapping borders' ("grenzübergreifende Großlandschaften"), that take into account a variety of formations, shiftings and overlappings of different powers.[51] In the zone, change and expansion can be expressed by emphasizing the *elasticity* of a spatially organized order. Therefore, Schmitt prefers expressions like "Grenzzone" or "Mark"[52] as opposed to the linear boundary. 'Elastic and yet effective' ("Elastisch und doch wirksam"),[53] he characterizes them. And as in military discourse, it is movement that creates the zone as the outline of an empire's terrain.[54] The investment of the body, of labor, of physical self-defense and control defines the space of an empire. This kind of empire is congruent with its actual power-expansions, that is all kinds of labors, which convey effective occupation: movement, cultivation, war. This kind of empire is strong but not built to last. It can break down just as a body can die, where-

---

47 W. Ogris: "Anwenderecht [Pflugwenderecht]." *Handwörterbuch zur Deutschen Rechtsgeschichte* vol. 1, p. 191.
48 Prescott: *Boundaries*, p. 57.
49 Schmitt: *Der Nomos der Erde*, pp. 54, 188.
50 Ibid., p. 256, also Schmitt: "Raum und Großraum im Völkerrecht," p. 153: Here he differentiates line and zone parallel to state and empire.
51 Moraw: *Von offener Verfassung*, pp. 22, 43.
52 Schmitt: "Der neue Raumbegriff in der Völkerrechtswissenschaft," p. 442.
53 Schmitt: "Raum und Großraum im Völkerrecht," p. 176.
54 Schmitt: "Der neue Raumbegriff in der Völkerrechtswissenschaft," p. 442.

as the state has gained eternity not least of all through an abstract inventory of its territory on maps.[55]

The primordial act of the *nomos* can thus be deciphered as the 'natural state' of World War I as, in fact, it has been by national socialist legal theorists. Schmitt provided the national socialist legal discourse with catchwords like 'Zone,' 'Großraum,' or 'raumschaffender Urakt' which were then reduced to the sheer struggle for space. Schmitt's territorial 'agonal character' of the no-mos, an order where 'factual necessity happens' ("das faktisch Notwendige geschieht")[56] was then translated into war and a short circuit between factual necessity and the authority of the law was made in the legal theory of the Sec-ond World War. The order of law becomes the 1:1 order of war.

Three attributes for a kind of war-law can be derived from this equation: combat as legal order is concrete, dynamic and bodily. Such attributes are of-ten involved whenever greater justice and more modernizing impulses are proposed for the law. Influential jurists of the twenties in Germany, among them Rudolph Smend, emphasized that the law should obtain concreteness through war, others referred to soil (Boden) (Karl Larenz) or to Erich Kaufmann's often discussed "Regula sic stantibus," in which the result of war is seen as the final proof of the just law.

The dynamical notion of the law, for which national-socialist legal theory is known, reflects the dynamics of combat and echoes Schmitt's elasticity of order. This point is explicitly made in the writings of the assistant judge and later jurists for the Gestapo, Werner Best.[57] In an essay collection "Krieg und Krieger" edited by Ernst Jünger in 1930, Best argues that the state's role is one of affirming, by legal means the power relations set up by military action. He defines the law as a 'function of combat' ("Funktion eines Kampfes"),

---

55 Because it is a certain investment of productivity that defines the zone, it becomes 'the own' uno actu with occupying it. In this sense the zone is where home is. There everybody is put into a Partisan situation, that is someone who defends his own ground. Maybe that the resentment against maps derive from the connotation of zone-home. 'At home' maps are not needed. The Partisan-myth is that of a deeply rooted local knowledge of the piece of land he defends.

56 Schmitt: *Der Nomos der Erde*, p. 67.

57 Müller: *Furchtbare Juristen*, pp. 30, 47, 249: In 1931 Best wrote the 'Boxheimer Dokumente,' the plans for a coup d'etat of the National Socialists. Since1933 he worked for the Gestapo; during the war he became the Reich's deputy (Reichsbevollmächtigter) in Denmark and later the organizer of the SS-troops in Poland. After the war, an investigation into the case of Best never took place – officially because of too little evidence. When in 1969 a trial against him began, he obtained a certificate for "Verhandlungsunfähigkeit." For further in-formation on Best see now also Herbert: *Best: Biographische Studien* (1996).

and 'interval in the rhythm of life' ("Intervall im Takte des Lebens"), the 'fixation of a certain state of combat' ("Festsetzung eines bestimmten Kampfzustandes").[58]

For supporting his notion that order is bodily, Schmitt refers to Otto von Gierke's studies on the law of corporations from the turn of the century. Gierke's concept of law is – according to Schmitt – devoted to the 'penetration of body and territory in opposition to the planeness' of the law. ("Durchdringung von Körper und Gebiet [...] gegen die Flächenhaftigkeit").[59] How will this concept sound to someone trained to "adapt to the terrain" as cited previously? And finally does the penetration of body and territory find its most literal realization in the dead bodies that give the landscape of war a new shape? Or as Ernst von Salomon defines the bodily borders of state-territory in his war-enthusiasm: 'the boundaries are drawn with bodies.'[60]

IV.

For Schmitt, who derives his concept of order from spatial notions, no man's land serves as the primordial scene for the *nomos*. At the same time it explains the decline of the legal order, which bears the name of abstract normativism. As noted, the topographical notion of order contains two competing orders, the spatial order and the plane, the physical and the cartographical, the concrete and the abstract. In the image of a contourless plane Schmitt discovers the loss of a spatial sense and the rise of normativism. Thus no man's land serves not only as the blank space on which the primordial act of *nomos* can be performed, it also explains why the legal order became spaceless, bodiless, and rigid.

This explanation has to be sought in the major shift of space, of spatial experience in World War I, when every point of orientation vanished and a "hoch formalisierte und technisierte Frontlandschaft" gained ground, to quote Bernd Hüppauf once again.

> Die Uniformität dieses Riesenraumes wurde in der Abwesenheit einer zugrundeliegen den Struktur durch Gleichförmigkeit und Simultaneität hergestellt, so daß diese Einheit zugleich die Atomisierung in unverbundene Segmente bedeutete.[61]

---

58 Best: *Der Krieg und das Recht*, p. 156.
59 Schmitt: "Raum und Großraum im Völkerrecht," p. 150.
60 von Salomon: *Der verlorene Haufe*, p. 124.
61 Hüppauf: *Räume der Destruktion und Konstruktion von Raum*, p. 122: "highly formalized and technical frontlandscape. The uniformity of that gigantic space was produced, in the absence of an underlying structure by monotony and simultaneity, so that this unity, meant at the same time an atomization into unconnected segments."

Homogeneity and interchangeability are the consequences. Without an underlying structure territory begins to resemble the sea.

For Schmitt the end of concrete space is the starting point for the expansion of a universal order, which he characterizes through abstraction, formalism, and interchangeability. If the terrain resembles the sea, the British sea power is in charge again. "Die britische Meeresherrschaft" mit ihren "konstruierten, raumaufhebenden, generalisierenden Normen, die den universalistischen […] Kern britischer Weltherrschaft ausmachen," represents according to Schmitt the adversary to a concrete and spatial order.[62] In Schmitt's view it is the British power since 1815 that has brought a certain "Raumscheu" to international law.[63] The "uferlose Meeresbezogenheit des englischen Völkerrechtsdenkens" (borderless sea-centeredness of British international legal thinking)[64] gradually transferred to the airspace, although air supremacy is not comparable to sea- or land- based power.

Schmitt takes the General of the British Air Force James Spaight as a representative of the British idea of a 'universal world law,'[65] because this law receives its order from the aerial perspective.[66] From up there, sea and terrain are likewise structured as a flat plane. Points in the flat plane are located by a universally matching coordinate system – the scale on maps, the screen of a trigonometer installed on machine guns and in airplanes. Air-space seems to engender constructed images of space rather than space-experience. Constructed space-images are after all based on aerial photographs, which are connected to maps. A target can then be determined exactly by the intersection of a horizontal and a vertical line on a two-dimensional representation.

Because of its target precision, Air Force General Spaight praised the air bombardment in the thirties. Since air bombardments are more precise than other weapons they make it possible "to minimize slaughter."[67] However in the fifties, Schmitt warns against the "spacelessness of a global war"[68] as suggested by the air-bombardment Spaight had in mind. Reterritorialization is

---

62 Schmitt: "Raum und Großraum im Völkerrecht," p. 169: "its artificially constructed, space-annihilating, generalizing norms, which make up the universalistic core of British world power."

63 Ibid., p. 145.

64 Ibid., p. 159.

65 Schmitt: *Völkerrechtliche Großraumordnung*, p. 84.

66 The aerial photography that was mainly developed during the first war, led only in England, not in Germany, to the institutionalization of a ministry for aerial war photography. For aerial photography in war see Bernhard Siegert: *Luftwaffe Fotografie*.

67 Spaight: *Air Power*, pp. 4, 23.

68 Schmitt: *Der Nomos der Erde*, p. 219.

therefore Schmitt's project. His spatial order is opposed to Spaight's aerial one.

Combat in the name of space and for space is finally a combat against air warfare. From the air came, after 1945, the order of the victorious powers. 'Air' destroys the notion of space in Schmitt's telluric perspective. Air is linked to a loss of space, rise of the rule of cartography and the state, defeat in war, the Anglo-American victorious powers, and finally, universal law. Even a minor event like the continuation of the international map project after World War I in London, with the cooperation of the International Aeronautical Conference but in Germany's absence[69] seems to affirm in retrospect this division of the world into space-powers and air-powers.

What follows on the German side, as a project of regaining ground of re-territorializing no man's land, is a combat for space, a war declared as an occupation. No-men are nomads – homeless soldiers – their destiny is taking, dividing, and grazing. From their perspective World War II is not a self-contradictory colonization of what already belongs to the territory of Europe – a 'geographical lapsus' as Heiner Müller once coined it.[70] From their perspective, the occupation takes place in no man's land, ready to be colonized anew. And where no man's land did not exist, their mission was to produce one, precisely to produce desert-*zones*.[71] Their mission was to erase all lines in order to start from scratch. It is the *terra nullius* (for them still the Europe of 1918) that authorized their mission to effective occupation. Thus before colonization comes the production of a no man's land. And after all, what else were German machines called 'Schienenwolf' (track-wolf) doing in Russia in 1943 by extricating rails, those lines that cultivate a country, other than producing a *no man's land*?

---

69   Penck: *Die Weltkarte 1: 1,000,000*, p. 82: However the conference had already agreed on London as the next conference-city at the conference in Paris before the First World War. Another characteristic detail is the intention on the German side to restore at least the German geographical names for the lost territories. But the maps by the German Landesaufnahme (No. 4 und 5 for the world map project) were not accepted.

70   Müller referred to European Genocide: *Material*, p. 53.

71   Bartov: *The Eastern Front*, p. 104: As in 1941/2 at the Eastern Front when the no man's land appears as the zone again: The 18th tank division "issued further instructions regarding the new defensive line it was erecting. A so-called desert-zone, nine miles deep, was to be created, from which all men and their possessions were to be evacuated [...] later yet another desert-zone was declared in which all houses were burned, all wells poisoned with dead cattle, all men taken to the rear and all children instructed to wander off to the area northwest of the desert-zone in the midst of a bitter winter."

FRANK TROMMLER
University of Pennsylvania

The Therapeutic Response:
Continuities from World War I to National Socialism

Abstract: This essay is concerned with the other side of violence created by modern warfare, namely the social contextualization of death and physical mutilations. The basic hypothesis is that a social reading of a wide range of therapeutic responses to violence helps avoiding the danger of either aestheticizing it as something incommensurable and therefore specifically modern or its petrification as an example of modern civilization's failure.

I.

Some years ago when political scientists ruled the academic discourse on violence, there was little interest in the correlation of violence with modernity. In the preface to their standard text of 1974, *The Ideologies of Violence*, Kenneth Grundy and Michael Weinstein emphasized in their definition the normalcy of violence as part of the political conflict, not the "aberrations or exotic outbursts."[1] In their Parsonian view, the authors included the use of violence for revolutionary purposes, but leveled its impact in the context of other forces of historical transformation. Averse to conceding any period or group a unique claim on violence, political scientists focused on the importance of the defining agent. In the words of Grundy and Weinstein:

> There is no single correct definition of violence. The term tends to be defined by political actors and sometimes differently by the same political actors, depending on the purposes they wish to achieve, the context in which the term is used, and their relationship to established political authority. Each group of political actors finds the source of violence in a different common experience in everyday life.[2]

---

1 Grundy and Weinstein: *The Ideologies of Violence*, p. VI.
2 Ibid., p. 8.

Or in a useful summary: "The actor who succeeds in defining the context of meaning gains an advantage over his adversaries."[3]

As cultural and literary historians develop a new interest in violence, the correlation with the phenomenon of modernity has become a crucial topic, leading invariably to a reflection of the changes that the industrialized slaughter of World War I brought to the experience and the definition of violence. It has become commonplace to include the forms of mechanized violence that dominated the battles of Verdun and at the Somme in definitions of modernity. Cultural historians, eager to relate the innovations in the areas of aesthetic perception and creation to the great landmarks of history, have returned to the once bold and provocative proclamations of early twentieth-century avant-gardes that war is at the roots of the ruptures without which traditions would rule forever, forestalling the growth of a genuinely modern art.[4] This view helps refocus on the traumatizing experience of millions of soldiers as a cultural, social, and even biological shock which has shaped twentieth-century life, exceeding the normative systematization of violence in handbooks of political science.[5] Yet it also tends to entangle the definition of the historical transformations caused by violence with the aesthetic vocabulary of shock and rupture that isolates, in order to illuminate its representative potential, the individual experience from its concrete social and psychological context. The rediscovery of technology as part of modernism has made the universalistic claims of the avant-gardes regarding the effects of violence an attractive, yet dubious reference. Here Grundy's and Weinstein's comment that the definition of violence strongly depends on the orientation of the actor seems fitting. As modernity itself has not found a single comprehensive definition, the correlation with violence remains tentative.

Taking a different perspective on this correlation, this article attempts to broaden the definition of violence through a consideration of its social and psychological effects or, more to the point, of the concrete response to World War I violence. Thanks to Eric Leed's *No Man's Land*, Robert Weldon Whalen's *Bitter Wounds: German Victims of the Great War, 1914–1939*, Bernd Ulrich's research project "Nerven und Krieg," and other studies, we are in a better position to understand that the impact of war violence after 1914 was not just a matter of shock, death, and destruction but also the focus of a construction which guaranteed some form of physical, mental, and – both for the wounded and the widowed – economic survival. The organization of medical and eco-

---

3   Ibid., p. 7.
4   See Klaus Kiefer: "Erster Weltkrieg und Avantgarde – Ein Projekt."
5   Gurr, ed.: *Handbook of Political Conflict*, esp. pp. 331–60.

nomic assistance took many different forms. Private and state institutions re-formed the outdated pre-war system for the collection and distribution of funds for the war-disabled and casualties' next of kin. In its cruel application of military psychiatry, the treatment of soldiers with war neurosis was similar in the armies of the warring nations. The organizations for the provision of medical care, pensions, and vocational rehabilitation paralleled each other at least in the effort of reintegrating the victims of war into society. In an un-spoken consensus across the frontlines, those involved in building a welfare system for these victims defined the overwhelming violence of this war in con-junction with the equally overwhelming need for a response. The victims tend-ed to define the violence more and more through the response itself – which often seemed to equal the pain and humiliation on the battlefield. To call the response therapeutic does not necessarily mean that it broke the cycle of pain.

It is my thesis that the immense aggregation of violence in World War I need be contextualized with the formidable therapeutic response in order to avoid its mythification in two opposing ways: its aestheticization as something incommensurable and therefore modern on the one hand and its petrification as a monument for the failure of modern civilization on the other. The con-struction of the response in its manifold layers was not only a strong catalyst for individual and collective success and failure until long after the war, but al-so became the litmus-test for the credibility of the Weimar Republic as a state which owed its existence to Germany's defeat in the war. Overshadowed by the outrage over the Treaty of Versailles, this whole phenomenon has been shortchanged by contemporaries and historians alike.

If one insists on the correlation between modernity and violence, one can-not overlook the fact that this response, with its unprecedented formation of a welfare bureaucracy, represents no less an aspect of modernity than the shock of the encounter with mechanized death. Measuring the shock without the alienation which the war victims experienced vis-à-vis the bureaucracy hardly leads to a full understanding of the phenomenon. The soldier who had gone through hell could not count on the reality of the experienced violence and pain until the bureaucracy gave official recognition of his encounter, ne-cessary for a pension or other life-saving support.

II.

An obvious point of departure for tracing the various forms of response to violence in World War I is the treatment of war neurosis which increasingly involved substantial segments of the medical and psychiatric establishment.

Psychological disorders in soldiers exposed to the horrors of modern warfare had long been recognized. After the Russo-Japanese War in 1904/05 Russian officials diagnosed soldiers as suffering from "organic disorders."[6] Differentiating between psychosis and neurosis, officials in World War I applied the term "neurotic disorder" to this phenomenon. Initially called "shell shock," on the mistaken assumption that it was caused by injury to the brain from the air blast of high explosives, it came to be recognized as war neurosis, for which Sigmund Freud delineated important arguments.[7] Since the Vietnam War the term "posttraumatic stress disorder" (PTSD) has dominated the issue.[8] With its unwieldy and costly aftereffects of violence, the Vietnam War has generated new attention to this phenomenon which remained underreported mainly due to the assumed lack of political qualities.

In World War I, psychiatrists and military officers learned to understand the direct connection between the mechanized nature of war and the breakdown of increasing numbers of combatants, especially after 1915. Under the impact of long-term artillery and the newly introduced machine-gun, combat was immobilized. "The cause of neurosis lay in the dominance of material over the possibilities of human movement," Eric Leed concluded. "In a real sense the neuroses of war were the direct product of the increasingly alienated relationship of the combatants to the modes of destruction."[9] Aware of the ambiguity of the term 'neurosis,' military and medical personnel functionalized it since it described a category of behavior – of removing oneself from the sphere of military obedience to the more lenient sphere of medical obedience – for which a response could be articulated. There were many forms of grueling treatment for shell shock. At first they were dominated by the clearly hostile attitude of military officers who insisted on the power of the moral, the "will-power," over the mechanical, blaming the soldiers of cowardice and insisting that discipline, chastisement, and punishment represented the best therapy. During the course of the war, especially after 1916, this reaction lost some of its force in all armies. The change seems to have been particularly problematic in Great Britain where the reassertion of the character and the will, the core of all educational efforts, disavowed 'mental' therapies even if medically justified. The number of soldiers who were convicted by courts-

---

6   Verkamp: *The Moral Treatment of Returning Warriors*, pp. 72–85.
7   Freud: "Thoughts for the Times on War and Death." Freud: *The Standard Edition of the Complete Psychological Works* vol. 14, pp. 273–302. – See also his "Introduction to Psychoanalysis and the War Neuroses" (1919) ibid., and Fornari: *The Psychoanalysis of War*, pp. 80–4.
8   See Sonnenberg, Blank, Ralbott, eds.: *The Trauma of War*.
9   Leed: *No Man's Land*, p. 164.

martial for cowardice and executed – 346 of 3000 soldiers – was especially high in the British army.[10] Yet the adjustment to the conscript armies of 1916–18, which were the rule in other countries, furthered a more "analytical" response even there.

While in "disciplinary" treatment the therapy serves "to dramatize and clarify the moral issues involved in the conflict between public duty and the private intentions of the patient,"[11] the "analytic" approach attempts to reach to the level of subconscious conflicts which often rage between a strong sense of duty and an equally strong instinct for survival, from which the soldier's mind, independent from his will, takes refuge in neurotic symptoms. This treatment, although designed to return the soldier to the battlefield, is not meant as punishment, – but, of course, was often experienced as such.

In 1917, Generaloberarzt Robert Gaupp asserted: "The neurotic patients represent by far the largest contingent of all patients in our army."[12] As immense as the dimensions of this phenomenon were, it remained underreported in every army. And in every army, the medical, psychiatric, and religious authorities became deeply compromised in their therapeutic collaboration with the military command, so that the soldier had to choose whether he preferred the tortures of the front to those in the psychiatric hospitals. Siegfried Sassoon, famous for his anti-war poetry, made every effort to return to the front from his confinement in the hospital. Many others chose to undergo de-individualization within medical and social welfare, many were thrown into it, even long after the war was over. Certainly, most of them cherished the hope to have a shot – to use the appropriate expression – at a disability pension; in bureaucratic German, they entertained "Rentenbegehrungsvorstellungen" (pension neurosis).

This leads to the next step in the pursuit of the various forms of response: to the development of a partly public, partly private system of medical care and economic support for the victims and their kin. Wounded veterans, war widows, woman workers and heads of large families who had suffered losses during the war firmly believed that they had a right to qualitatively better welfare services than those which were provided by the traditional poor-relief system. Mass distress and the gradual polarization of social relations made the institution of a coherent social welfare policy a priority of the state. The death of male heads of family and the participation of most war widows in the labor

---

10   Bogacz: "War Neurosis and Cultural Change in England, 1914–22," p. 228.
11   Leed: *No Man's Land*, p. 170.
12   Robert Gaupp: *Die Nervenkranken des Krieges, ihre Beurteilung und Behandlung.* Stuttgart 1917, p. 4, quoted in Ulrich: "Nerven und Krieg," p. 178.

market helped focus the multitude of individual cases around the larger, politically sensitive issue of the disintegration of the family and the existing social
structure. In Germany, the term *Volksgemeinschaft* was increasingly favored
over the reference to *Kaiser* and *Reich*. The efforts of transforming the frag-
mented public and private welfare services for war widows into a comprehensive program increased the importance of professional counseling and the
role of social workers as 'social physicians.'

The essentially political nature of the process of restructuring the welfare
system remained hidden behind legal battles about recognizing the specifics
of suffering as well as 'scientific' debates concerning the rationalization and
professionalization of social work. As Michael Geyer has shown in his comparative study of Germany, France, and England, creating the legal foundations for the recognition of the special needs of war victims and veterans presented a big hurdle in each country.[13] Even if the privilege of having suffered
unbearable pain for the glory of the nation eventually found expression in
various welfare laws, the process of recognizing violence and injury hardly
lifted the victims out of the perception of having become objects of bureaucratic decisions. Geyer maintains that while the British legislative process was
geared less towards the official privileging of war victims than the French, the
German initiatives were characterized by the high number of rehabilitative
and social therapeutic measures, embracing the individual with more bureaucratic *Betreuung* (care) than elsewhere. He lists the specifics of the German efforts for social re-integration under the heading of "Arbeitstherapie" (work
therapy)[14] which indeed has deep roots in the German conceptualization of
social integration in *Volk* and *Volksgemeinschaft*. While more interventionist
and goal-oriented, and to some extent more explicitly therapeutic than others,
the German organizational efforts, due to their expert-oriented bureaucrati-
zation, had a hard time to be considered by the public as the best possible national response. The centrifugal politics of the Weimar Republic did not spare
this area. Of course, the effects of the defeat in the war and the feeling of humiliation through the Treaty of Versailles made a policy of national reconcili-
ation with the war victims a particularly thorny issue.

And yet, if one looks at modernity as practiced rationalization of social
advancement and integration, one can find it here, in the construction of this
organizational response which has been considered another step toward the
modern welfare state – the therapeutic state. Its rationality lay in the existence

---

13   Geyer: "Ein Vorbote des Wohlfahrtsstaates."
14   Ibid., p. 248: "Die deutsche Militärversorgung war die einzige, die einen sozialtherapeu-
     tischen Anspruch erhob."

of the value-neutral, scientifically justified, and professionalized system of welfare services. And as in so many other bureaucratic creations which accommodate Max Weber's verdict of *Entzauberung* (disenchantment), it also produced what has been called quintessentially modern: alienation.[15]

Although modernity and antimodernity were not employed as discursive terms in the public debate in Germany, the dynamics of contrasting an alienating bureaucracy that frustrated the individual with a wholesome response to suffering and death signaled a similar thinking mode. George Mosse has made a convincing case that the "cult of the fallen soldier"[16] has to be located in this dynamics which juxtaposed the excesses of the age of the masses – from mass production to mass entertainment – with the dignified peace of the war dead. From the moment that war cemeteries and monuments to the fallen soldiers were planned as manifestations of national mourning, they ostensibly carried an antimodernist message: "From these places of worship [the dead] descended to plead against mass society and for the restoration of those genuine, pre-industrial virtues which were exemplified by the very design and construction of their cemeteries."[17] The design had to emphasize the fact that the cemeteries were part of the landscape, conveying the impression of eternity by eschewing any modern stylistic features as merely transitory.

Many veterans expressed satisfaction with this kind of dignified response, especially on the local level, though not without frustration and cynicism concerning the lack of unity in its political support. While the Weimar Republic was able to activate public awareness of the moral and national symbolism of these memorials, the government was unable to rally the population behind a national monument, symbol, or ritual which would reconcile the living with the dead. Parties and veterans' organizations constantly bickered about a national war memorial. Not until 1931 the government adopted the Neue Wache at Berlin as such. There were continuous disputes about a Memorial Day (*Volkstrauertag*) which never materialized until the end of the Republic. The Republic's inability to provide symbolic identification as part of the process of participating in democratic politics came to diminish also the therapeutic effect of its commemorative endeavors.

Measuring the political capital accumulated in the two crucial domains of official response to the victims of the war – in the social bureaucracy and the realm of public symbolism – the results are disappointing for the first German democracy. The comments turn increasingly critical in the last years of

15   See Crew: "Wohlfahrtsbrot ist bitteres Brot."
16   Mosse: "National Cemeteries and National Revival."
17   Ibid., p. 15.

the Republic when economic depression and political radicalization worsened the disillusionment and a wave of war literature, triggered by the success of Erich Maria Remarque's novel, *All Quiet on the Western Front*, and other documentary novels, captured the imagination of a broad audience. Typically, Remarque himself boasted after the initial surprise about the phenomenal success of his book that his autobiographically based report functioned as a kind of therapy for thousands, even millions of former soldiers. The young man of his generation, he explained in an interview, who had escaped the war finally learned that the experience of violence and death was still with him. "It continued to effect him in a gloomy way, it remained a blurred nightmare, a condition of restlessness, of skepticism, of harshness or staggering aimlessness."[18] Writing *All Quiet on the Western Front* had turned out to be therapeutic for Remarque's efforts to overcome these ruminations. He felt reassured by the letters of many readers: "They all perceived the book not as pessimistic but as liberating; those matters under which they had suffered as long as they had remained unconscious had lost their power over them, because they had been clearly addressed."[19]

While the political impact of this kind of literature has been widely discussed by scholars, the political impact of the work of the welfare bureaucracies for the war victims still needs attention. Robert Weldon Whalen concluded that it was not just the lack of money that led to the perception of failure:

> Organized benevolence failed partly because it was torpedoed by Germany's governing elites in the early 1930s. Deep cuts in welfare radicalized millions of people, including the war victims, and this provided a priceless opportunity for reckless demagogues like the National Socialists. But German organized benevolence failed even when it was funded. It failed because it was technocratic, bureaucratic, and propelled by a pseudo-social science. This rationalized charity spoke in a language so jargon-filled, it functioned in a matter so ponderous, it was so abstract, that it created for its wards a mysterious, capricious, and inhuman world.[20]

III.

When the National Socialists came to power in 1933, they lost little time in instituting an official day of mourning for the fallen soldiers of World War I. The first such day, called *Heldengedenktag* (heroes memorial day) instead of

---

18   Eggebrecht: "Gespräch mit Remarque," p. 1.
19   Ibid., p. 2. – See also Müller, *Der Krieg und die Schriftsteller*, pp. 42–44.
20   Whalen: *Bitter Wounds*, p. 192.

Volkstrauertag, was celebrated in 1934. They not only inaugurated a cult of mourning, a *Totenkult,* but also initiated public events in which the individual got the feeling of being able to participate, not just being a bystander. The new regime took advantage of the sense of frustration that had developed despite the Republic's far-reaching efforts in meeting the needs of the war victims. Already in the 1920s, the National Socialists had made it known that they heeded the importance of social assistance. They were aware that going to the welfare bureaucracy often was, for millions of Germans, the only direct contact with the state and national politics. In the 1930s, they established, in addition and partly in competition with the extended governmental, regional, and social bureaucracies, the network of *Nationalsozialistische Volkswohlfahrt* (NSV). It is one of the typical cases where the dual administration created competition, control, and a lot of mix-up, yet there is no doubt that the social welfare organization NSV with its subdivisions *Winterhilfswerk* and the *Hilfswerk Mutter und Kind* contributed substantially to the feeling of the German people that they were taken care of – though sometimes in the double meaning of the word.[21] In this connection, *Volksgemeinschaft* was not just a propaganda term; it often summarized a genuine feeling of integration based on authentic care, *Fürsorge.*

It is hardly surprising that scholars preferred to focus on the violence- and power-oriented political manifestations since the early 1920s. Connecting the experience of death and violence in World War I with, in George Mosse's word, "the brutalization of German politics,"[22] has become a standard procedure in the analysis of the continuities between war and National Socialism. Indeed, long before Ernst Jünger wrote about the emergence of the *Gestalt* of the worker-soldier as a sober professional user of violence, military authorities promoted an attitude toward death and destruction that was supposed to be *sachlich,* matter-of-fact. Jünger's continually revised and polished myth-making of the violent war experience certainly broadened the frame of reference for National Socialists who insisted that only the full dedication to the rationale of war would help Germany recover its standing as a world power.

There can be little doubt as to which response National Socialists endorsed vis-à-vis war neurosis and the accompanying symptoms: of course, the "therapy of will" (*Willens-Therapie*). Ironically, or rather characteristically, this therapy, in all its brutality, was embraced by Hitler who had gone through his own case of war neurosis after hours of artillery fire in which he tempo-

---

21   Zolling: *Zwischen Integration und Segregation.*
22   Mosse: *Fallen Soldiers,* pp. 159–81.

rarily went blind, as thousands did. Having been exposed to the extremely brutal proceedings at the hospital at Pasewalk in 1918, Hitler concluded that the aims of his physician, the notorious Edmund Forster, to create an absolutely inured, hardened soldier type through tough treatment should be feasible for a whole nation. His conviction that the Germans lost the war because they lost their nerves, above all at the home front, contributed to his devastating gamble in risking another world war for which the Germans would be better equipped both in material and in psychological terms.

And yet, the overall picture shows that the National Socialists were much too shrewd to overlook the manipulative power of the therapeutic response, particularly since it allowed to build on the shortcomings of the Weimar Republic. There might have been indeed a thorough reflection on the traumatizing effect of the encounter with violence, an encounter that carried into the "brutalization of politics" the important insight: that violence is not fully defined without the response to it. It meant, in political terms, that the manipulation of the response was at least as meaningful as the exerted violence. There is enough evidence that Hitler and the Nazis did not just concentrate on the usefulness of violence as a means of acquiring political power. They also focused on the longing of people for being protected permanently from such forms of violence. As World War I had opened this can or worms, violence – i. e. violence exerted by militant men in uniforms with loaded guns – became a permanent feature of post-Versailles reality, while society built a network of *Angst* and social welfare. After 1930, the Nazis stirred the spread of violence with hundreds of militant confrontations. They created the violence in Germany from which Hitler promised to save the Germans. After 1933, the Nazis fine-tuned their tactics which combined the intimidation of the populace through their monopoly on violence with the expansion of a therapeutic policy through the creation of a 'caring' *Volksgemeinschaft*.

This assessment is corroborated by the acceptance, even support of psychotherapy on the part of Nazi authorities. As Geoffrey Cocks stated in his path-breaking study of the *Deutsches Institut für Psychologische Forschung und Psychotherapie*, the so-called *Göring-Institut*, in Berlin, the Third Reich provided "more opportuni ty than oppression for the existing profession of psychotherapy:" "Between 1933 and 1945 the discipline of psychotherapy made major strides toward an established professional and institutional status within the German medical profession and German society as a whole."[23] Cocks is less sanguine about the attitude toward psychoanalysis which labored under

---

23   Cocks: *Psychotherapy in the Third Reich*, p. 249. – See also Ulfried Geuter: *Die Professionalisierung der deutschen Psychologie im Nationalsozialismus*.

the disadvantage of being branded as a Jewish science. Concerning the race question in a wider sense, National Socialists did not automatically regard mental illness as evidence of a racial-biological defect. Pure Aryans simply could not be fundamentally defective, and therefore therapy would readily restore them to full health. Because homosexuality was found within the ranks of the SS, it came to be regarded as a curable 'disorder' rather than hopeless racial degeneracy, and officers were marched along to the Göring-Institut to be straightened out. Göring, its director, was, of course, not Hermann, the politician, but Matthias, his cousin, a neuropsychiatrist and Adlerian psychotherapist.

While the discussion about the fortunes of psychotherapy in Nazi Germany calls long-accepted notions into question, the political implications of the shrewd manipulation of the therapeutic response to violence still deserve more attention. Their study helps answer some of the more vexing questions concerning the violent character of the Nazi regime and its acceptance on the part of the German population. Were the Germans so enthralled with violence and terror? Didn't they experience enough of it during war, revolution, and the putsch years during inflation, and later in the street fights during the depression? Or were they so intimidated by the Gestapo apparatus that they accepted everything? It is telling that Timothy Mason, the foremost British historian of the German working class under National Socialism, later found himself ready to modify his views of Nazi politics and concede that the constant emphasis on caring, *Fürsorge*, and social welfare indeed ingratiated the regime to some extent even with the working class. His and other scholars' hesitation to include these features in the analysis is understandable. And for those who like to draw conclusions from visual evidence, the instruments of violence and terror are usually more photogenic than these features.[24]

The unqualified association of National Socialism with violence and terror obviously fails to take account of the emphasis on social welfare as part of a therapeutic concept of *Volksgemeinschaft*. Certainly, the reality of violence and terror to which the regime subjugated its adversaries and victims cannot be disputed. But there is good reason to presuppose a more sophisticated concept of violence on the part of the Nazis that emerged with the war experience and its aftermath in the early years of the Weimar Republic. Only a differentiated approach to this double-strategy can help clarify the discrepancies between intimidation and affirmation under National Socialism. It also will

---

24 Mason: "Die Bändigung der Arbeiterklasse im nationalsozialistischen Deutschland," pp. 23, 34.

help understanding the strong support for Hitler and his movement on the part of women. Furthermore, it might help explain the shortcomings of the Marxist reduction of National Socialism to a Fascism which, in turn, might throw light on the inadequacies of the concept of Antifascism which communist leaders in the former German Democratic Republic used as a justification for their own monopoly of violence.

Finally, a reflection of this strategy may even contribute to a better understanding of the reasons why writers such as Gottfried Benn and Ernst Jünger who had hoped for the consequential installation of a regime of steely fascism, turned away in disappointment. This new state was too "völkisch" for them, too soft, too opportunistic, lacking in form and character. As we know from Auschwitz: when National Socialists developed the facilities for unmitigated violence, they covered it up.

WOLFGANG MICHALKA
Militärgeschichtliches Forschungsamt, Potsdam

From War Economy to "New Economy": World War I and the Conservative Debate About the 'Other' Modernity in Germany[1]

Abstract: This essay is concerned with the emergence, during the First World War, and the later developments of the concept of an economic structure that combined elements of a free market economy with those of central control; required by a war economy. The debate about this *cooperative economy* (Gemeinwirtschaft) is significant both of attempts to design a different approach to modernity and a tendency towards a militarization of civil society after the end of the first modern war.

I.

Great Britain's economic blockade during the first few days of the war in 1914 severed the Central Powers from the world market. There were raw materials which were either missing or growing short in supply and they had to be replaced, seized and allocated according to the criteria of war. The establishment of the *Kriegsrohstoffabteilung* (1914, War Raw Materials Department) and the *Kriegsamtes* (1916, War Department), as well as the establishment of the *Demobilmachungsamtes* (Department of Demobilization) and the *Sozialisierungskommissionen* (Socializing Commissions) following the war led to an intensive discussion of the structure of the economy for the post-war period. Models for state-controlled or partially state-controlled, "mixed economic" (gemischtwirtschaftler) institutions had already begun to emerge prior to 1914 and were made concrete through the experiences of the War Economy. Concepts such as *Gemeinwirtschaft* (Corporative Economy), *Staatssozialismus* (state socialism) *organisierter Kapitalismus* (organized capitalism), "corporate collecti-

---

1 Revised edition of Michalka, Wolfgang: "Kriegsrohstoffbewirtschaftung, Walther Rathenau und die 'kommende Wirtschaft.'" Michalka, ed.: *Der Erste Weltkrieg*, pp. 485–505.

vism," were an outgrowth of these institutions and offered an alternative to *Wirtschaftsliberalismus* (economic liberalism).[2]

The individualistic, market economy structure of the economy sank more and more into the vortex of the regulating, planning and governing State. The development of regulating principles was advanced markedly due to the economic and social crises, which were brought about partly by the capitalist Industrial System and partly by political and military conflicts. Industry showed a diminishing ability to gain control over these crises in government intervention. World War I, with its economic and social effects, and the years of political insecurity, economic reces sion and social unrest following the break-up of the Wilhelminian Empire serve as the zenith of this state of national crisis. During this time, the social and economic structure of the Reich was subjugated by cutting interventions of the State, due to the war and blockade. These interventions were aimed against privileged interest groups within the economy, as well as being aimed toward the public planning and control of production and distribution. These interventions also contributed to the change and ultimate weakening of established industrial structures. Alternatives, of varying scope, for a new ordering of society and the economy grew simultaneously out of economic and social crises of the military conflict and the meager situation and democratic emancipation movement of the working class.

A model for a *Gemeinwirtschaft*, which was oriented on the common good was conceptualized; the attempt was made to put it into practice in its beginning stages. However, only after the collapse did the champions of the concept of a Common Economy have the opportunity to organize individual branches of industry in accord with their vision.[3] This collapse represents a caesura with regard to the economic and social aspects of the politics of organization, despite all subsuming developmental processes. This is similar to the goal of a socialist economic and societal structure,[4] which was only theoretically possible in a social democracy during the war and which was first able to achieve practical meaning under the changed political power dynamics after the overthrow.[5]

---

2   For the state of the discussion, compare: Winkler, ed.: *Organisierter Kapitalismus*; Kocka: "Organisierter Kapitalismus im Kaiserreich"; Mommsen, ed.: *Die Organisierung des Friedens: Demobilmachung 1918–1920*; Puhle: "Historische Konzepte des Industriekapitalismus. 'Organisierter Kapitalismus' und 'Korporativismus'".

3   Biechele: *Der Kampf um die Gemeinwirtschaftskonzeption im Jahre 1919.*

4   Kügeigen: *Kriegswirtschaft und Sozialismus.*

5   Compare Zunkel: *Industrie und Staatssozialismus. Der Kampf um die Wirtschaftsordnung in Deutschland*, p. 9ff. Likewise, Haupts: *Deutsche Friedenspolitik 1918–1919. Eine Alternative zur Machtpolitik im Ersten Weltkrieg?*, p. 93.

What follows is a sketch of the reactions to the economic war and the measures for the War Economy, which arise from the former. In addition, I shall provide an overview of the contemporary discussions of politicians, industrialists and scientists with regard to the process of change in the triangular relationship between State, Economy and Society. This process of change is especially the product of the interdependence of the economic war and the War Economy. Conservative, nationalist opinions shall be given special attention in the description and evaluation of the clash of opinions and interests of the post-war economy. The concentration on the ideas of Walther Rathenau in this debate suggests itself not only because he prompted and even ran the War Raw Materials Department (Kriegsrohstoffabteilung) in its beginning, but also because he, as a well-read writer on the contemporary discussions on the "new economy," offered prominent accents to the discussion, though not without strong criticism.

II.

The strong dependency of the German Empire on the world market allowed for only a short war. The economic blockade of the Central Powers, which began with Britain's declaration of War on August 4, 1914, expanded the war from one, which had been prepared primarily as a military war, to an economic war. The blockade had not been entirely unexpected, but the various commercial interests, especially those of the United States,[6] had been expected to hinder the complete isolation of Germany from the world market. This hope soon proved to be an illusion. The blockade gave the British Empire, in conjunction with the United States, control over the world market and it provided them the opportunity to take over the German export markets. In doing so, they simultaneously drove the German Empire from the world market as an economic competitor. The loss of access to foreign markets must necessarily drive any country as dependent on foreign trade for its raw materials, as Germany was, to a crisis and ensuing physical jeopardy. In this way, the British sea blockade became the "Constitution" of the looming Economic World War (Weltwirtschaftskrieg).[7]

---

6 Compare here Fiebig-von Haase: "Die deutsch-amerikanischen Wirtschaftsbeziehungen, 1890–1914, im Zeichen von Protektionismus und internationaler Integration," pp. 329–57. Likewise, Fiebig-von Haase: "Der Anfang vom Ende des Krieges: Deutschland, die USA und die Hintergründe des amerikanischen Kriegseintritts am 6. April 1917." Michalka, ed.: *Der Erste Weltkrieg*, pp. 125–58.

7 Hardach: *Der Erste Weltkrieg 1914-1918*, esp. pp. 62–84.

The supply of raw materials serves as an example of both the lack of goal conscious of the economy in preparation for the war and also demonstrates the necessity of a centrally organized and led War Economy in Germany.[8] In view of the fact that far more than forty percent of its industrial raw materials had to be imported to Germany during the last years of peace, the rationing of raw materials as a result of the British economic blockade shifts to the center of the discussion of the German War Economy.[9]

The first initiatives aimed at improving the raw materials situation came from the private economy quite at the beginning of the war. In response to Wichard von Moellendorff, a leading force at AEG, Walther Rathenau was able to convince the Prussian Minister of War, von Falkenhayn, of the necessity of a centralized War Raw Materials Department (KRA) on August 9th, 1914. The KRA was promptly established[10] under the Ministry of War a few days later under Rathenau's supervision and was directed by him until March, 1915. On the legal basis of the Enabling Act (Ermächtigungsgesetz) of the Bundesrat and in accordance with the proclamation of a State of Siege, the KRA was the first institution established for the centralized War Economy and was responsible for all rationing of raw materials in Germany.[11]

Perhaps the most well-known accomplishment of the KRA is the development of replacement materials, especially the synthetic production of nitrogen by the chemical industry. This accomplishment is representative of the close interlinking of state and private industry which can take place.

The rationing of raw materials was an important component of the German weapons industry, but it is by no means synonymous with it.[12] Neither the state-run War Raw Materials Department, nor the private raw materials associations were directly involved in the decision and leadership levels of the politics of armament. The long-term armaments programs and contracts were agreed upon during negotiations between the State and industrialists. The Prussian Ministry of State was primarily responsible for the State's role in

---

8   Burchard: *Friedenswirtschaft und Kriegsvorsorge. Deutschlands wirtschaftliche Rüstungsbestrebungen vor 1914*; Michalka, Wolfgang: "Kriegswirtschaft und Wirtschaftskrieg." *Deutschland und der Erste Weltkrieg*, pp. 169–92.

9   Wiedenfeld: *Die Organisation der Kriegsrohstoff-Bewirtschaftung im Weltkrieg*.

10 Burchardt: "Walther Rathenau und die Anfänge der deutschen Rohstoffbewirtschaftung im ersten Weltkrieg," pp. 169–96; Williamson: "Walther Rathenau and the KRA. August 1914 – March 1915," pp. 118–36; Hecker: *Walther Rathenau und sein Verhältnis zu Militär und Krieg*, pp. 201–67.

11 Koeth: "Rohstoffbewirtschaftung," pp. 224–35; Delbrück: *Die wirtschaftliche Mobilmachung in Deutschland 1914*.

12 Compare esp. to: Feldman: *Armee, Industrie und Arbeiterschaft in Deutschland 1914 bis 1918*.

these negotiations, although the highest levels of the military command and the regional commander had their competing contacts to the armament industry. The "War Committee for German Industry"[13] was the primary representative of Industry in these negotiations. This committee consisted of both the "Bund der Industriellen" and the "Centralverband deutscher Industrieller," which had united immediately after the outbreak of war.

Along with industry, agriculture also found itself greatly impaired and was forced to undergo changes to its traditional structure. The German Empire had been dependent on imports for feeding its population before the war, despite high domestic production levels. Now the German Empire had to make due with what it itself could produce and what could be imported from neutral or allied (later occupied) countries. There were shortages not only in manure and plow animals, but also in workers to meet the increased demand. For these reasons, as early as the end of 1914 the population was being instructed to use recycling measures, such as the use of kitchen waste. By the beginning of 1915, bread and flour were being rationed and the supply of foodstuffs was drastically impaired. In the so-called "Turnip Winter" 1916/17, the food situation reached its catastrophic low. The caloric consumption per person sank markedly due to poor harvests and difficulties in distribution. Consequently, the rates of sickness and death rose enormously.[14]

The short supply of foodstuffs led to increased prices and profiteering. Despite the governments efforts to control and equilibrate the problem by setting maximum prices, they were unable to control the problem until the end of the war. The black market trade and smuggling flowered and led to increased discontent and resignation.[15]

In the summer of 1916, there was a new shift in the highest levels of command (OHL, Oberste Heeresleitung). Generalfieldmarshall Hindenburg and his trusted counselor, First General Quartermaster Ludendorff, comprised the third OHL and were given nearly dictatorial powers. Together they wanted to improve the worsening state of the war and economic situation through drastic measures. The so-called "Hindenburg Program" of August 31, 1916

---

13 Gutsche: "Die Entstehung des Kriegsausschusses der deutschen Industrie und seine Rolle zu Beginn des Ersten Weltkriegs," and generally, Ullmann: *Interessenverbände in Deutschland,* pp. 77–84.

14 Burchardt: "Die Auswirkungen der Kriegswirtschaft auf die Zivilbevölkerung im Ersten und Zweiten Weltkrieg"; Baudis: "Vom 'Schweinemord zum Kohlrübenwinter'"; Roerkohl: *Hungerblockade und Heimatfront. Stahl und Steckrüben.*

15 Wette: "Reichstag und 'Kriegsgewinnerei' (1916–1918)"; Burchardt: "Zwischen Kriegsgewinnen und Kriegskosten. Krupp im Ersten Weltkrieg."

called for a two to three hundred percent increase in production. A reorganization of the war-time administrative body[16] was to be simultaneously undertaken with the goal of making it more efficient and to provide a better overview. The War Raw Materials Department (KRA), the War Replacement and War Employment Department, which was responsible for enlisting and making available labor resources, and the Office of Weapons and Munitions Acquisition (WUMBA, Waffen- und Ammunitionsbeschaffungsamt) were placed under the jurisdiction of a newly created War Department (Kriegsamt), under the direction of General Wilhelm Groener. A long overdue and centralizing concentration of the war-time economic administrative structure was thereby formally achieved, though there remained questions of authority between the new War Department (Kriegsamt) and the Ministry of War (Kriegsministerium) and the OHL (Oberste Heeresleitung).[17]

In addition to the concentration of the bureaucratic infrastructure, the third OHL tried to reach a complete and thorough mobilization and militarization of the economy and society. Under the "Gesetz über den vaterländischen Hilfsdienst" (Fatherland Service Duty Law) of December 5, 1916, a general requirement for employment for the entire population was established. The draft for men was extended to the ages of fifteen to sixty, with draftees being called either to military service or work in the armament industry.[18]

Finally by the end of 1916, the "Ständiger Ausschuß für die Zusammenlegung von Betrieben" (Permanent Commission for the Merging of Plants) was established and given the task of shutting down production plants not essential to the war and those small operations which had lesser capacity. The intent was to gain labor, raw materials, and production equipment for the larger operations in the armament industry. This move had a likewise drastic effect on the economic structure of the German Empire during the war.

It was not long under the "Hindenburg Program" before the German war economy demonstrated that it was overtaxed. As the first casualty, the transportation infrastructure fell apart, which had especially negative effects with regard to the supply of coal during the "Winter of Hunger" of 1916/17. The deciding bottleneck was the overtaxed labor resources. The expectation that the Fatherland Service Duty Law would provide a marked increase in the number of workers available to the armament industry soon proved to be an illusion as well.

---

16   Dieckmann: *Die Behördenorganisation in der deutschen Kriegswirtschaft 1914–1918.*

17   Goebel: *Deutsche Rohstoffwirtschaft im Weltkrieg einschließlich des Hindenburgprogramms.*

18   Feldmann: *Industrie und Arbeiterschaft,* pp. 169–206.

III.

The War Economy led to an intensive discussion about the structure of the economy in Germany.[19] Out of the breadth of models of organization for state socialism, which were developed during the war and which were representative of different agendas, two related models are especially notable. They are Wichard von Moellendorff's "Gemeinwirschaft"[20] and Walther Rathenau's "Neue Wirtschaft." Both models gathered their experience through the rationing of raw materials and both models assert the role of the system for state control and industrial self-determinance which they both responded to and developed during the war and which, they believed, must form the foundation of the future economy.[21]

Walther Rathenau was, along with Wichard von Moellendorff, initiator and head of the KRA until the beginning of 1915. During this time he developed a state-controlled economic model, under which strong market-economy (privatwirtschaftlich) retention of expansive parts of the economy were a distinguishing feature. He reflected on this model in several publications:

> Die neue Wirtschaft wird keine Staatswirtschaft sein, sondern eine der bürgerlichen Entschlußkraft anheimgestellte Privatwirtschaft, die freilich zum organischen Zusammenschluß, zur Überwindung innerer Reibung und zur Vervielfältigung ihrer Leistung und Tragkraft staatlicher Mitwirkung bedarf.[22]

---

19 A contemporary overview of the state socialist and war socialist literature is offered in: Köppe: "Schriften über den Kriegssozialismus." Compare esp. Zunkel: *Industrie und Staatssozialismus*; compare also Feldman: "War Economy and Controlled Economy: The Discrediting of 'Socialism' in Germany during the First World War," and Krüger: "Kriegssozialismus. Die Auseinandersetzung der Naionalökonomen mit der Kriegswirtschaft 1914–1918," pp. 506–29.

20 Moellendorff: *Deutsche Gemeinwirtschaft* and Moellendorff: *Konservativer Sozialismus*. Compare Brown: *German Theories of the Corporate Sate. With Special Reference to the Period 1870–1890*, pp. 164–218; Braun: *Konservatismus und Gemeinwirtschaft. Eine Studie über Wichard v. Moellendorff*; Barclay: "A Prussian Socialism? Wichard von Moellendorff and the dilemmas of Economic Planning in Germany. 1918–1919"; Schmid: *Wichard v. Moellendorff. Ein Beitrag zur wirtschaftlichen Selbstverwaltung.*

21 Kruse: "Kriegswirtschaft und Gesellschaftsvision. Walther Rathenau und die Organisierung des Kapitalismus."

22 Rathenau: "Die neue Wirtschaft." *Gesammelte Schriften*, Vol. 5, pp. 179–261: "The 'Neue Wirtschaft' will not be a state-controlled economy, but rather an economy of the private sector, governed by the decision-making of the people. It will admittedly require the cooperation of the State to be able to grow to an organic inclusion, to the conquering of inner tensions and to the multiplication of its productivity and influence." p. 250.

The coexistence of self-determination and being directed, of capitalist private ventures and centrally guided state socialism was possible to this extent due to the already existing degree of concentration and cartelization in the economy,[23] which established the necessary organizational foundation. State and Business were so efficiently linked; just as Rathenau would have liked to have had in the peace-time electric industry. They were not linked by simple state-run centralization, but by the founding of Kriegswirtschaftsgesellschaften (War-economy Associations). These Kriegswirtschaftsgesellschaften were agencies responsible for the acquisition and distribution of individual raw materials and were, in effect, similar to public stock companies. In addition, these entities were regulated by the state. These associations were organized upon existing syndicates, cartels and associations; "they were actually state-controlled and protected cartels."[24]

This mixed economic form of organization had had practical success and was to serve as the structural basis for "Neue Wirtschaft" (New Economy) and "Gemeinwirtschaft" (cooperative economy) after the war, according to Walther Rathenau's conception. This was because the growing length of a war of destruction and positioning demonstrated the impossibility of a victory for the German Empire and portended an economic war to be measure in decades with increasing clarity, as far as Rathenau was concerned. He often expounded the opinion: If there were any worthwhile goal for the war, it would be more efficient and fairer production. Business was no longer a private matter, but rather a matter for the community, Rathenau suggested.[25]

The KRA is generally held[26] to be the most effective state organization for control of the economy during the war in Germany and Rathenau's work had a lasting impression on him. Through practical tests he was able to observe the effects of the State's involvement into a free market economy and observe, to his surprise, the nearly frictionless functioning of these measures. At the moment of confiscation, "the Peace Economy ended"; a "decided step

23   Müller: *Die Kriegsrohstoffbewirtschaftung 1914–1918 im Dienste des deutschen Monopolkapitals*; Stolper: *Deutsche Wirtschaft seit 1870*, pp. 76–78; Baudis and Nussbaum: *Wirtschaft und Staat in Deutschland vom Ende des 19. Jahrhunderts bis 1918/19*, pp. 261–70.

24   Schulin: "Krieg und Modernisierung. Rathenau als philosophierender Industrieorganisator im Ersten Weltkrieg," p. 60.

25   Rathenau: "Probleme der Friedenswirtschaft." (Lecture, held on Dec. 18, 1916), *Gesammelte Schriften* vol. 5, pp. 59–93, here p. 71; Rathenau: "Die neue Wirtschaft" (1917). Ibid., pp. 179–261, here p. 181. Compare to *Walther Rathenau. Industiralist, Banker, Intellectual, Politician. Notes and Diaries 1907–1922*, p. 20.

26   Kocka: "Kriegssozialismus? Unternehmer und Staat 1914–1918," p. 160.

towards State Socialism had been taken."[27] The "Kriegsrohstoffgesellschaften" had an especially strong impression on Rathenau. He saw them as "a median form between stock company (Aktiengesellschaft), which embodied the free market, capitalist form, and a bureaucratic organism."[28] He was sure that this form of self-governing would also retain its importance into the future. For Rathenau, the War Economy demonstrated state socialist qualities, which were paired with individual initiatives from industry, evidenced in the form of the Kriegsgesellschaften (War-time Associations). These War-time Associations were born of the "image of self-determination and yet not of the image of unbridled freedom," according to Rathenau.[29]

In his highly regarded writings, "Von kommenden Dingen" (1917, Of Things to Come), "Vom Aktienwesen" (1917, On the Stock Company), and "Die neue Wirtschaft" (1918, The New Economy), Rathenau developed a self-contained economic program. Under this program, he repeated time and time again, business "was not a private concern, but the concern of the community, not an end in itself, but a means towards the absolute, not to be a privilege, but a responsibility."[30] He was convinced that the war had accelerated this progression. He believed to be able to observe a symbol of this change in the growing disdain for sheer wealth, in the advancing de-personalization of ownership through stock companies and war time associations and the development from oligarchy to democracy. Admittedly, Rathenau's perspective was very idealized. In Rathenau's opinion, neither the capitalist nor communist economic structure would be able to meet the task of being a transition economy in the coming years of peace. Only a New Economy would be able to do this. On the one hand, the Neue Wirtschaft would preserve the circumstances for property as in the commercial structural model. However, the high frictional costs of the, to his way of thinking, useless consumption, unbridled competition, economic special interests, and the "eternal" feud with labor. All these ills were to be alleviated through "conscientious organization," "consensual responsibility," and through the dissolution of "proletarian bonds."

Rathenau's goal was the *optimal rationalizing* of the industrial system of pro-

---

27 Rathenau: "Deutschlands Rohstoffversorgung." (Lecture, held Dec. 20, 1915) *Gesammelte Schriften* vol. 5, pp. 23–58, here: pp. 38 and 40.

28 Ibid., p. 41; compare also Lederer: *Deutschlands Wiederaufbau und weltwirtschaftliche Neueingliederung durch Sozialisierung*, pp. 15ff.

29 Rathenau: "Deutschlands Rohstoffversorgung." (Lecture, held Dec. 20, 1915) *Gesammelte Schriften* vol. 5, pp. 23–58, here: p. 41.

30 Rathenau: "Von kommenden Dingen." *Gesammelte Schriften* vol. 3, p. 102.

duction. Rathenau envisioned individual branches of industry as the upholders
of this idea. These branches were to form occupational guilds, which would retain the rights of sole distribution, of the export and import of domestic and
foreign products, of the planing and implementation of the division of labor,
and represent their interests in discussions with the State and other guilds. According to Rathenau's vision, workers were also to be involved in the management, while the state would control the administration, the fixing of prices, social services and privilege. Profits were to be subject to appropriate taxation
and should benefit the state, the workers, the owners, and the reduction in
price of the product. In addition, Rathenau recommended a policy of national
autarky to defend against the buy out of German assets and labor for the benefit of foreign capitalist and, in general, to keep the German economy free
from foreign capital. A state-controlled foreign trade policy would be responsible for re-establishing active balance of payments and trade balance as well as
renewing the mint par of exchange (Währungsparität). Imports should be restricted to necessary raw materials and goods, while exports of capital and raw
materials should be controlled while the export of labor intensive goods
should be forced at the expense of domestic demand. Domestically, the preference of internal sources of raw materials, the reduction in superfluous consumption and luxury, the abolishment of "idleness" and waste of labor should
be fostered to resurrect the national economy by its own power.

For Rathenau, the individualistic structure of society and the economy
that had heretofore existed seemed now to have given way inevitably to a *gemeinwirtschaftlich* and *staatssozialistisch* (state socialist) direction due to the new
economic structure developed during the war. This change was provisional,
but perhaps also permanent. These "Erkenntnisse" (insights, recognition) of
Rathenau are prophetic and are above all to be found in his writings dealing
with economic problems, but they were first articulated in a letter to Hermann Stehr on August 14th, 1914. This letter, which was intended to serve as
a document of ground-laying experience for his third work, "Things to
Come," is of special importance.[31] In it, Rathenau outlines the difficulties and
the necessity of establishing this New Economy:

> It is clear to me that the methods by which I must proceed to reach this goal reach
> deep into the organizational structure of the capitalist economic model and must,
> therefore, meet with strong opposition from industrialist and the Reichstag (par-

---

31 According to Schulin: "Zu Rathenaus Hauptwerken." Rathenau: *Hauptwerke und Gespräche*,
     pp. 499–595, here p. 557.

liament) alike. When I listen inside myself, I am of the opinion that I must make myself an instrument of this transformation. In doing this, I myself take part in toppling the gods that the world worshipped until August 1914, a world to which I belong and which has made me what I am: an individualist ...

We stand before an unforeseeable period of restructuring, both intellectual and material, a period which, I shudder to say it, will seem to many as the decline of Europe. But only where the old has toppled, can the new emerge and the fortunes of men and peoples have never been born out of beginnings, but always out of upheaval.[32]

Rathenau held another of the effects of the organization of the War Economy for indispensable.[33] The KRA would form "the core of an economic General Staff" during peace time, in preparation for a future war.[34] Additionally, Rathenau was of the opinion that a new "concept of raw materials" had been developed during the War Economy. The importance of these materials for the German economy was, according to Rathenau, perceived in a higher degree and would eventually rise to the "concept of the protection of raw materials."

Rathenau judged the importation of raw materials, which the German economy had always been dependent on, to be bad, especially with regard to the balance of payments, since each purchase abroad must lead to a disadvantage for Germany. The War Economy had prompted a strong desire for autarky, which would lead to a new "Mercantilism" and which would grow in importance for the time after a peace treaty.[35]

The future economic fortune of Germany was of deep concern to Rathenau throughout the entire war and afterwards. In a speech on "The Problems of a Peace Economy," held on December 18, 1916 in the "Deutsche Gesellschaft," he demonstrated the great difficulties for the German economy after the war. Each year of war, he maintained, set Germany back about four years. After the peace treaty, the loans and debts must be repaid to the creditors, which would bring about a great redistribution of wealth and, in turn, social problems along with it. The economy would also have to deal with the anticipated worsening relationship to foreign powers all by itself and would have to

---

32 Merides-Stehr, ed.: *Hermann Stehr – Walther Rathenau. Zwiesprache über den Zeiten,* pp. 25ff.

33 Ibid., pp. 25, 41, 53. Compare also Feldman: "Die Demobilmachung und die Sozialordnung der Zwischenkriegszeit in Europa," pp. 156ff. Likewise, Schieder: "Rathenau und die Probleme der deutschen Außenpolitik," pp. 250ff.

34 Rathenau: "Deutschlands Rohstoffversorgung." (Lecture, held Dec. 20, 1915) *Gesammelte Schriften* vol. 5, pp. 23–58, here: pp. 55ff.

35 Ibid., p. 54.

depend on the experience gathered during the War Economy: we have established organisms in the form of our war-time associations, which know these problems as they know their daily bread.[36]

Rathenau believed that the entire economy would have to divide itself into the material economy, the labor economy, and the capital economy and that the protection of raw materials would receive stronger attention, due to the "new thinking that the necessity of war has taught us." Nothing could be wasted and each new source must be tapped so that Germany not fall into dependency on foreign powers. Therefore, Rathenau spoke of a "Neo-mercantilism," which would embody "the correct positioning of the trade balance." The importation of goods and services from other countries must be kept in hand with great caution. "The politics of our sources of power and of the distribution of that power will form one of the basic questions of our economy."[37] This economic policy was to find support through the limitation of the production and importation of luxury items.

Rathenau expected a maximum exertion of strengths from another economic complex, the "labor economy." This complex would be strengthened by means of the rationalizing and advancing concentration of corporations.

Along with an increase in production, he required a simplification of wholesale and retail trade as an additional factor. The standardization of the product line, of warehouses, and of stock would free up the power of "youthful manhood," which had formerly waited uselessly and senselessly behind the store-counter.[38]

Rathenau demanded intervention on behalf of the interests of the country by the capital economy (Kapitalwirtschaft). No German capital should be allowed to flow into foreign countries. As to the question of whether or not guilds (Gesellschaften) and entrepreneurs could remain "continually private economic elements," Rathenau did not yet wish to give any answer.[39]

The measures of the War Economy were not to be equated[40] with the

---

36 Ibid., "wir haben in unseren Kriegsgesellschaften die Organismen geschaffen, die damit vertraut sind, wie mit ihrem täglichen Brot." pp. 70ff.; compare also Rathenau: "Die Neue Wirtschaft," pp. 182ff., where these thoughts are offered in a similar form and carried further.

37 Ibid., p. 75.

38 Ibid., pp. 78ff.

39 Ibid., p. 85.

40 Rathenau understands his concepts as alternatives to Socialism, strictly speaking. Thus he writes in "Von kommenden Dingen." *Gesammelte Schriften* vol. 3, p. 16: "This book strikes at the heart of dogmatic Socialism."Compare with Toch: *Vergesellschaftung in Österreich,* p. 57.

goals of Socialism, but the organization of the former was seen as forming part of the transition to a socialist economy.[41]

In July of 1917, Rathenau wrote "Die Neue Wirtschaft"[42] (The New Economy), in which he developed concrete steps for the transformation of the economic situation in Germany. This work was a direct continuation of the ideas in Rathenau's "Probleme der Friedenswirtschaft" (The Problems with a Peace Economy).

Rathenau recommended a combining of similar operations in industry, manual labor, and commerce into trade guilds. These trade guilds would "appear in form as stock companies and in their commerce as syndicates." The state would transfer to the trade guilds decisions regarding the induction of new entrepreneurs and would give the right for the liquidation or closure of non economical working operations.

The trade guilds especially show clear features of the KRA (War Raw Materials Department), which similarly managed individual branches, closed small operations and whose members participated with differing levels of capital.[43] However, these new guilds did not have the goal of the raw materials associations, namely to limit trade, but rather the opposite goal, to strengthen and extend trade.[44] Rathenau had no doubt received the deciding stimuli for his plans in the KRA: "Unsere Kriegswirtschaft [...] bietet [...] gerade den Beweis, daß die scheinbar unveränderlichsten Systeme [...] auf viele Weisen abgewandelt werden können."[45] Rathenau retained firmly, however, the principal of private industry. He placed his hope to a great extent on the coming "Gemeinschaftswillen" (desire for community) and on "civility and responsibility." For this reason, the "New Economy" would not be a state-run economy, "but rather a discretionary private economy comprised of the people's decisions, which admittedly requires the state's cooperation."[46]

Rathenau believed, similarly to Moellendorff, that the recognition is dawning, that all economic life is founded on the base of the State, that the

---

41 Compare Kranold: *Sozialisierung: Warum, Was, Wie, Wann?* p. 15; Stephinger: *Grundsätze der Sozialisierung*, pp. 90ff.

42 Rathenau: "Die neue Wirtschaft." *Gesammelte Schriften* vol. 5, pp. 232ff.

43 Compare Goebel: *Deutsche Rohstoffwirtschaft*, p. 52.; Müller: *Die Kriegsrohstoffbewirtschaftung*, pp. 130, 135; Mai: *Das Ende des Kaiserreichs. Politik und Kriegführung im Ersten Weltkrieg*, p. 92.

44 Rathenau: "Die neue Wirtschaft." *Gesammelte Schriften* vol. 5, pp. 179–261, here: pp. 232ff.

45 Ibid., p. 249: "Our War Economy provides exactly the evidence that seemingly unchangeable systems can be transformed in many ways."

46 Ibid.,: "die Erkenntnis [dämmert], daß alles Wirschaftsleben auf dem Urgrund des Staates ruht, daß Staatspolitik der Geschäftlichkeit vorangeht, daß jeder, was er besitzt und kann, allen schuldet." p. 250.

politics of state take precedence over business and that each one owes what
he has and can do to the whole. He saw that the time had to come to make a
general summary of all his fundamental perspectives and war economy experience, which he did in his "System des wirtschaftlichen Ausgleichs und der
sozialen Freiheit" (System of Economic Equilibration and Social Freedom).
He formulated the main theoretical lines of reason in this work as follows:

> 1) State allocation of the available factors of production between consumption
> and investment in accordance with a fixed, planned rate of economic growth.
> 2) A fairer, more egalitarian division of national income and property,
> 3) Prohibition of every type of monopolizing relationship, which function as, in
> modern capitalism, the foremost source of unfair accumulation of wealth,
> 4) Drastic limitations on the right of inheritance, in connection with a wide-scale
> vocational training program in order to diminish social difference and accomplish
> greater social mobility in the long term.

The realization of these ground principals should be produced through the
own economic functioning of the state and comprehensive control of wages,
profit, interest rates and foreign trade. Rathenau saw a powerful instrument
for influencing prices and interest rates in the interest of common social goals
and for the protection of the middle class from the competition of monopolizing groups.[47] This instrument was the public economic sector, state-run
operations and investment. "The social ethic" which is everywhere in Rathenau's works arose from his critical view of the industrialist-capitalist development in Wilhelminian Germany and which saw the "things to come" prophe-
sied in the maelstrom of his time. In his social consciousness, he was kindred
to his katheder-socialist contemporaries, even though he often felt their criticism for his radically far-reaching plans and recommendations.[48]

IV.

In contrast to Rathenau, who ultimately never called the capitalist economic
model into question, Wichard von Moellendorff systematically purported the
concept of a Gemeinwirtschaft (cooperative economy). He was convinced
that it was possible to "produce in times of peace from the perspective of a

---

47   Rathenau: "Von kommenden Dingen." *Gesammelte Schriften* vol. 3, pp. 96, 139, 97, 158, 159.
     Compare Barkai: *Das Wirtschaftssystem des Nationalsozialismus: Ideologie. Theorie. Politik
     1933–35*, p. 88.
48   Ibid., p. 89.
49   Braun: *Konservatismus und Gemeinwirtschaft*, p. 63. Compare also Barclay: *A Prussian Socialism?*

war economy."[49] After the war, he wanted to realize his *gemeinwirtschaftlich* and *staatssozialistisch* (state socialist) vision as an economic structural model, which he posited as a "third way" between Socialism and Capitalism. As Under-Secretary in the Empire's Department of the Economy (Reichswirtschaftsamt) from the end of 1918 until July 1919, he saw concrete possibilities for the systematic implementation of a politics of socialization, but these possibilities always faltered in the face of opposition from entrepreneurs. This was because most industrialists saw the return to a market economy after the war as being beyond question. In the last years of the war and the first years of the post-war period, they were pursuing the abolition of the offices and controls developed during the war in an effort to regain the economic freedom they had had. For example, as early as December of 1914, Alfred Hugenberg, the Head of the Directorship at Krupp, sought support among other industrialists for an opposition party in the fear that the war might represent "the irreversible end of the era of economic individualism."[50] After 1918, the industrialists argued with the Empire's Department of the Economy over the supervision of the so-called Transition Economy.[51] It is no wonder, therefore, that Rathenau's and Moellendorff's plans for the coming economy were soundly rejected by politicians and industrialist of a conservative order, especially because an "insider" opposed those who were working for the establishment of the *status quo ante*.[52]

The model of a "cooperative economy" was taken up by national economists with not unchecked rejection. Johannes Plenge, for instance, who coined the term "The ideas of 1914," contrasted the German revolution of 1914 with the French Revolution. According to Plenge, where the latter was the product of the collapse of state or a change of system, the former was marked primarily by organization and new development, by state socialism and Volksgemeinschaft (the unity of the people). He said: "Here a new spirit is born: the spirit of the strongest combination of all state and economic powers to an new whole, in which all the parts live equally; the New German State! The Ideas of 1914!" For Plenge, the German war economy was nothing

---

50 Hugenberg an Beukenberg. Dec. 8, 1914. Mannesmann-Archiv. P 2/2501; qouted in: Epkenhens: *Die wilhelminische Flottenrüstung 1908-1914*, p. 390.

51 Schieck: *Der Kampf um die deutsche Wirtschaftspolitik nach dem Novemberumsturz 1918*.

52 Compare here Strandmann: *Unternehmenspolitik und Unternehmungsführung*, pp. 139–48. There is a complete reaction to Rathenau by Mannesmann, cf. Max Steinthal's review of Rathenau's "Die neue Wirtschaft," quoted ibid., pp. 167–84. The latter is said to "do away with the free market through the introduction of the "compulsion market "in one fell swoop. It kills progress, in that it stuffs the initiative into a state uniform." p. 167.

other than the realization of Socialism, the blueprint for a new society: "Under the necessity of the war, the idea of Socialism thrust its way into German economic life, its organization grew together into a new spirit and thus was born from the self-assertion of our nation for humanity the Idea of 1914, the Idea of German Organization, and the Volksgenossenschaft (People's League) of National Socialism."

In opposition to the ideas of 1789, the "Spirit of 1914" had a decidedly anti-liberal point and a new type of Anti-Capitalism showed itself in the concept of the "Volksgenossenschaft (People's League) of National Socialism." This new concept opposed certain forms of capitalism in "the national interest," yet strove for a greater efficiency in the economy. National Socialism was conceived of as a form of "state socialism," which had turned away from the "idea of boundless freedom" and had trained its sights on the "Idea of a healthy combination of all powers," just as Plenge demanded.[53] Seemingly an economy oriented on the common good had been achieved, just as an entire school of political idealists, corporatists and state socialists had demanded during the past century. "Even among bureaucrats in Berlin, who had accepted the myth of Prussian bureaucracy in the classrooms of Wagner and Schmoller, were convinced that the end of capitalism was upon them and that they were experiencing the birth of a new epoch, in which the economy would serve the 'whole' again under the leadership of the state."[54]

Fichte's Deutschtumsmetaphysik (The Metaphysics of Germanity) and its connection to Rathenau's and Moellendorff's philosophies of life and corporatism were being particularly emphasized in the conception of the cooperative economy. It is therefore notable that Moellendorff sought out, among others, Friedrich II., Fichte, and Lagarde as the progenitors of his German "Gemeinwirtschaft,"[55] which he saw as a genuine German economic structure, in contrast to the English economic liberalism. In addition, both Moellendorff and Rathenau sought to integrate their ideas for economic structuring into the rationalizing teachings of the American, Frederick W. Taylor.[56] Taylor was of the opinion that the rationalization of the workers' activities would allow an increase in production, which would satisfy the requirements of both the employees and employers. These ideas gained entry into Germa-

---

53 Reinhard Rürup: "Die Ideologisierung des Krieges: Die 'Ideen von 1914.'" Böhme and Kalkenberg, eds.: *Deutschland und der Erste Weltkrieg,* pp. 121–41. Also for the prior.

54 Krüger: *Nationalökonomen im wilhelminischen Deutschland,* p. 121; compare Glum: *Zwischen Wissenschaft, Wirtschaft und Politik,* pp. 156ff.

55 Moellendorff: "Von Einst zu Einst."

56 Compare Moellendorff: *Konservativer Sozialismus,* pp. 31ff. Compare as well Braun: *Konservativismus und Gemeinwirtschaft,* pp. 42ff., 143ff., 155ff.; Schmid: *Wichard v. Moellendorff,* pp. 24ff.

ny and Europe before the World War; they found a home in the ideology of "Industrialism."[57] These ideas are reflected not only in the organizations mythology of Rathenau and Moellendorff, but also in those of national economists like Plenge and Jaffe, as well as Friedrich Naumann and others, however different their political visions might be. Especially by Rathenau and Moellendorff one cannot shake the impression that they intended the transmission of taylorian ideals to society, which should "function" in the machine-like manner of the rationalized large factory. "These theories gained their particularly German character, inasmuch as they tied into the conservative / anti-capitalist concepts and emphasized their opposition to western Liberalism."[58]

It is, therefore, hardly surprising that the best-known protagonists of "the Third Way" between the antagonism of the capitalist "*Verkehrswirtschaft*" (economy of commerce) and the "*Eisenbartrezepten*"[59] (strong men's prescriptions) of a socialist planned economy focused their new visions of economic structuring on the War Economy, whose structure they participated measurably in constructing. Walther Rathenau and Wichard von Moellendorff, the managers of German big business, embody for all intents and purposes the vision of "*Industriebeamten*" (industrial bureaucrats), which the National economists Plenge, Schulze-Gävernitz and even Rathenau himself had formulated. For the time being, all of hope of these things seemed to be coming true under the War Economy, which, with its *Durchstaatlichung* (state-ification) and/or planned production was viewed as the exodus from the opposition of Capitalism and the danger of social revolution.[60] This heterogeneous concept of a new economic and societal system, which grew out of the border situation of the national military and societal battles for existence, found a further echo in the public sector. This concept held fast to the instrument of a planned economy (Wirtschaftsführung), which it had itself created.[61]

Rathenau's writings met with limited approval in the SPD and USPD.[62]

---

57 Best compare Maier: "Zwischen Taylorismus und Technokratie."
58 Krüger: *Nationalökonomen*, p. 125.
59 Rathenau: "Von kommenden Dingen." *Gesammelte Schriften* vol. 3, p. 125.
60 Rathenau produced this in his election handbill, "Die Wirtschaft der Zukunft" on Nov. 29, 1918 in the following formulation: "We shall establish an economy that is not marxist, but which offers all parts of the population greater fairness, peace and joy at work than any other. [...] The goal of true and healthy Socialism is not the *Verstaatlichung*, but rather the *Durchstaatlichung*; it is the order, the forethought and the regulation of the formerly unbridled and mercurial production." Rathenau: *Nachgelassene Schriften* vol. 1, p. 87.
61 Compare Gutsche, Klein, Petzold: *Der Erste Weltkrieg*, p. 256, similarly Zunkel: *Industrie und Staatssozialismus*, pp. 30ff.
62 Strandmann: "Rathenau zwischen Politik und Wirtschaft," pp. 102ff. Compare that to Bendixen: *Das Staatsdenken Walther Rathenaus*, pp. 302ff.

This is astounding, since the idea of "organized capitalism" was introduced by Rudolf Hilferding in 1915 into the discussion of the politics of economic structure. This idea was little more than a modified version of the Marxist doctrine of "state-monopolized capitalism"[63] and was entirely in harmony with Rathenau and Moellendorff's concept of *Gemeinwirtschaft*. In addition, the Social Democrats and the Unions both witnessed major structural changes in the economy and society[64] during the war, especially "the dissolution of a competitive economy, initiated by individual entrepreneurs and which was shielded in a great degree from state intervention. This system was replaced by a highly concentrated and internally bureaucratic and guild-style economic structure, whose ability to function was guaranteed by state intervention of various qualities."[65] Hilferding defined the "transition from the capitalism of free competition to organized capitalism" as the development of increasing concentration of "Finance Capital," similar to cartels and the developments of trusts. This was the product of the war and post-war period, which is denoted by the term "Organized Capitalism."

Other Social Democrats such as Rudolf Wissel, Minister of the Economy in 1919, who was influenced by his Secretary of State, v. Moellendorff,[66] and Max Cohen, who intervened on behalf of a cooperative Upper House, and also Georg Bernhard, Publisher of the liberal "Vossische Zeitung," who was closely aligned with the Democratic Party and who supported the "Imperial Council on Economics" (Reichswirtschaftsrat) were all active in the debate surrounding the politics of economic structure. Their participation in the restructuring of the economy was evidenced in their taking elements of the various ideologies of different councils and binding them into an *organism* made up of state and community. What they envisioned was a pyramid of the organs of state planning, which would be comprised of representatives of business, labor and the state. With the authority to fix prices, to allot raw materials and market shares and the power to delineate the policy lines of the politics of the economy, these new institutions were to embody the partnership of the classes for the common good. Even when champions of this idea, such as Wissell, were reckoned among the Social Democrats, they did not by any means take action for the rule of the proletariat, but rather they demanded the greatest possible production for "the whole." The institutional models for

---

63 Könke: *Organisierter Kapitalismus. Sozialdemokratie und Staat.*

64 Compare this with the numerous evidence in Kruse: *Krieg und nationale Integration,* pp. 116–24.

65 According to the definition of Winkler, ed.: *Organisierter Kapitalismus,* p. 8.

66 Ehlert: *Die wirtschaftliche Zentralbehörde des Deutschen Reiches 1914 bis 1919,* pp. 225–387.

a planned economy were, more than anything else, borrowed from the war economy, including the armaments industry, which was of mixed state and private ownership.[67] Rathenau saw this step as a middle stage towards the development from capitalism to state socialism.

It is, however, noteworthy that Rathenau's concept of the KRA and the model for the organization of the "New Economy" that arose from it, met largely with strong criticism among his German contemporaries, but with strong attention and even agreement abroad. As early as October 11th, 1915, the Times ("A Businessman and a War") prized Rathenau's rationing of raw materials as "one of the best ideas of modern times" and honored his deeds as being decisive in the war on the order of commanders Falkenhayn, Hindenburg and Mackensen. Lloyd George, leader of the British Office of Munitions, took the KRA to be the effective weapon against the sea blockade that it was. As such, this weapon was the paradigm for an effective planned economy.[68] Rathenau's futuristic blueprints met with a strong audience in Sweden, where his writings appeared in large numbers. However, it was in the nascent Soviet Union that the German war economy was especially honored as the most developed combination of high capitalist technology and methodical organization. Even Bucharin and Lenin, as well has his economic advisor Larin and Miljutin referred explicitly to Rathenau's concept of *Gemeinwirtschaft*, whose modern structure was to be implemented under the dictatorship of the proletariat in the socialist revolution.[69]

Later the National Socialist usurped the idea from the Jew Rathenau, whom they spurned. As Albert Speer, who had just been named Imperial Minister for Armament and War-time Production in 1942, transformed the foundering *NS-Kommandowirtschaft* (NS Command Economy) into a managed war economy, which was still based on the principal of industrial self-determination, he was inspired by the KRA of Walther Rathenau. His war-socialist and shared economic ideas seemed to the National Socialists an opportune means by which to perhaps be able to win the war from an economic standpoint, since they had long lost it from a military standpoint.

---

67 Compare Maier: *Zwischen Taylorismus und Technokratie*, p. 198.
68 Compare Wendt: "Vom Interventionsstaat zum Industrieparlamanet. Ordnungspolitische Vorstellungen in England nach dem Ersten Weltkrieg"; Milward: *The Economic Effects of the Two World Wars on Britain*.
69 Kruse: *Kriegswirtschaft und Gesellschaftsvision*, p. 160.

Codes of War and Violence

Jeffrey Verhey
University of Siegen

Some Lessons of the War:
The Discourse on Propaganda and Public Opinion
in Germany in the 1920s

Abstract: In World War I, the first "mass" war, German leaders attempted to sustain internal morale through a vast propaganda campaign. "Propaganda," German leaders asserted, was one of the most effective weapons of modern warfare. This conceptualization of the role of propaganda had profound implications for the postwar understanding of the nature of civil society. A scientific discourse on propaganda and public opinion grew up, whose assumptions – the manipulable masses, the absence of rules of decent rhetoric, and the like – had profoundly anti-democratic implications. This discourse played an important role in the demise of Weimar democracy, for the scientific discourse was also a popular discourse, underlying the "stab-in-the-back" legend, and the conservative conceptualizations of how to create the *Volksgemeimschaft*.

I.

On 11 July 1914 there was the following advertisement in the *Kölnische Zeitung*: "A large Berlin printing firm seeks an ambitious person to assist in propaganda […]." One year later, this advertisement could not have appeared. By the middle of 1915 "propaganda" no longer denoted advertising, it denoted advertising for a political purpose.[1] In the course of this shift in definition,

---

1   In the years before the war there was even a trade journal entitled *Propaganda*. Originally, of course, propaganda denoted the Catholic church's efforts to win believers to the faith. In the course of the nineteenth century, the word became applied more broadly. See Wolfgang Schieder and Christof Dipper: "Propaganda." Brunner, Conze, Koselleck, eds.: *Geschichtliche Grundbegriffe* vol. 5, pp. 69–112.

"propaganda" also developed negative connotations absent before.[2] "Propaganda" became synonymous with demagogy (*Verhetzung*: indeed, in 1915 "*Verhetzung*" was the more popular label for this rhetorical category), with lying, as in the lies of foreign newspapers concerning Germany's military successes,[3] and, especially, the lies of foreign governments and newspapers concerning the German "atrocities" in Belgium.[4] Moreover, "propaganda" was foreign. In his wartime analysis of the "cultural war" Ernst Troeltsch argued that, in contrast to the Allies, Germany had no propaganda; Germans remained committed to the truth.[5]

This shift in definition was not the last the word would undergo during the war. By 1918 "propaganda" most often signified those rhetorical and advertising efforts organized for the nation by the state. As "propaganda" continued to suggest manipulation, lying and deceit, it remained foreign. Accordingly, when in 1917 General Erich Ludendorff established a propaganda organization within the German army he labelled his efforts at persuasion not "propaganda" but enlightenment (*Aufklärung*) or teaching (*Unterricht*). Soldiers and citizens participated in "patriotic instruction" (*vaterländischer Unterricht*); they were instructed by "enlightenment officers" (*Aufklärungsoffiziere*). (Actually, Ludendorff himself was not much concerned with "propaganda's" negative connotations. From 1916 onward he repeatedly asked the civilian government to establish a "propaganda" ministry, and had to be persuaded to find a different label for his own persuasion organization.[6])

---

2   For example, Paul Eltzbacher's remarks in "Die politische Propaganda der Franzosen," *Norddeutsche Allgemeine Zeitung*, 28 February 1914 (#109), are neutral concerning the moral value of propaganda.

3   Anton: *Am Pranger. Der Lügenfeldzug unserer Feinde.*

4   Avenarius: *Das Bild als Verleumder. Bemerkungen zur Technik der Völkerverhetzung*; and Becker: *Ein Beitrag zur Aufklärung der feindlichen Greuelberichte.* Of course, there were atrocities. See Wieland: *Belgien 1914. Die Frage des belgischen "Franktireurkrieges"*; and Horne and Kramer: "German 'Atrocities' and Franco-German Opinion, 1914: The Evidence of German Soldier's Diaries." But, especially after 1914, almost all Allied atrocity stories were invented. See Read: *Atrocity Propaganda, 1914-1919.*

5   Troeltsch: *Der Kulturkrieg. Rede am 1. Juli 1915*, pp. 5–6. Similarly, Troeltsch: "Das Wesen des Weltkrieges," p. 10; Dr. Frosch: "Die Dämonen der Lüge." *Die Welt am Montag*, 26 April 1915, Beilage; Leopold Ziegler: "Haß," *Die Schaubühne* 1 (1915), p. 5; and many, many others.

6   For Ludendorff's efforts to get the civilian government to create a "Propaganda Ministry," see his memoirs, Ludendorff: *Ludendorff's Own Story. August 1914 – November 1918*, pp. 352–353; and the letters reprinted in Ludendorff, ed.: *Urkunden der Obersten Heeresleitung über ihre Tätigkeit 1916–1918*; and in Deist, ed.: *Militär und Innenpolitik im Weltkrieg 1914–1918.* On the "patriotic instruction," see Mai: "'Aufklärung der Bevölkerung' und 'vaterländischer Unterricht' in Württemberg 1914–1918"; and the documents in Deist.

This shift in the definition of "propaganda" reflected a shift in the conceptualization of the role of rhetoric in war. Whereas Bismarck had claimed
that "one does not shoot at the enemy with public opinion but with gunpow-
der and lead,"[7] in World War I all governments employed "propaganda" as a
tool of war, as a "weapon." Moreover, although rhetoric in wartime is as old
as war itself, there was something modern about the nature of the violence
the propagandistic language was supposed to accomplish. If in the nineteenth
century wartime rhetoric had aimed largely to deceive the enemy or to improve the army's morale, in World War I rhetoric centered on sustaining the
morale of the civilian population and weakening the morale of the enemy
population. This shift in emphasis grew out of an awareness that this war was
different than the wars of the past. Not armies but the collective power of the
nations as a whole were at war. Victory in this war, generals and politicians
came to believe, would not be achieved on the battlefield alone. Victory was a
function of "nerves," and would come to the nation whose "nerves" broke
last.[8] Propaganda was the means, the "weapon" employed to strengthen one's
own morale and to weaken the enemy. A victory over Russia would come
quicker, so the German General Staff, through a revolution in Russia, and
thus the German army conducted a vast propaganda campaign on the Russian front.[9] A victory over England in 1918, so Erich Ludendorff warned in
two letters to the German civilian leadership in early 1918, could only be
achieved through a two-pronged attack – on the ground and at the English
mind.[10]

This shift in the understanding of the role of rhetoric in war had profound
implications for the normative understanding of the nature of modern collective violence. If war is understood, according to the famous Clausewitzian
formula, as the use of violence "to compel the enemy to do our will,"[11] then
in World War I the weapons of war were not only physical but psychological,
and the understanding of the nature of violence had to be expanded to in-

---

7   Quoted in Stern-Rubath: *Die Propaganda als politisches Instrument*, p. 68.
8   Ulrich: "Nerven und Krieg. Skizzierung einer Beziehung."
9   Zeman: *Germany and the Revolution in Russia, 1915–1918*, as well as the documents in Golder,
    ed.: *Documents of Russian History 1914–1917*, pp. 385 ff.
10 The two letters with "Suggestions for a German political offensive in 1918" ("Zwei Vor-
    schläge zu einer deutschen politischen Offensive im Jahre 1918"), both of which were writ-
    ten by the Major von Haeften and passed on by Ludendorff to the Chancellor can be found
    in Ludendorff (ed.), *Urkunden der Obersten Heeresleitung über ihre Tätigkeit 1916–1918*, pp. 473
    ff.
11 Clausewitz: *On War*, p. 75.

clude this psychological component. What were to be the boundaries of the moral, the limits of psychological violence, the limits of manipulation?

This shift in the understanding of the role of rhetoric in war, this "democratization" of warfare had profound implications as well for the normative conceptualization of "public opinion." Conservatives, for example, found that the wartime experiences delegitimated one of the central tenets of the conservative ideology, the belief that because the German bureaucratic state (*Obrigkeitsstaat*) was above "public opinion," because governmental elites were "unpolitical," German politics was more immune to the whims of an irrational public opinion than were democratic states.[12] Although well before 1914 conservative elites had begun a "pseudo- democratization" of their conservative political practice,[13] only in World War I was this aristocratic conceptualization of the proper relationship between public opinion and the government proven without question to be anachronistic. In this war, when the state's military success depended upon the courage, ability, and will of the common man, the opinions of the people acquired a special significance. The experiences of the war encouraged the further "democratization" of conservative thought, a reconstruction of the concept of leadership which recognized the significance of mass opinion.

Although the war seemed to validate the democratic idea, democratically minded Liberals and Social Democrats also found themselves forced to reevaluate many of their assumptions and beliefs as a result of the war experiences. The very success of World War I propaganda – and almost all contemporaries saw propaganda as an effective tool of war – raised a number of difficult questions. Whereas the autocracies of the past had demanded only passive obedience – Thomas Hobbes, for example, thought it pointless to probe into people's consciences, law and order required only passive obedience – all warring states in World War I, including the democratic states, demanded from their citizens a complete personal identification with the war effort. If democracy was to be defined as the rule of the people over themselves, as the identity between the will of the government and the will of the people, how was this identity to come about and to be represented? If a people could be falsely led, was it not the duty of society's elites to direct public opinion, thus prohibiting the people's seduction by dangerous men?

---

12   The classic account is Delbrück: *Regierung und Volkswille.*
13   The classic account of this process of "pseudo-democratization" is Rosenberg: "The Pseudo- Democratisation of the Junker Class." See also Eley: *Reshaping the German Right*; Chickering: *We Men Who Feel Most German. A Cultural Study of the Pan-German League 1886–1914*; and Blackbourn: "The Politics of Demagogy."

What was to be the role and nature of a civil society separate and immune from rhetorical manipulation?

II.

There were many attempts to answer questions like these, answers often couched as "lessons of the war," in the years following the war. Bibliographies on "propaganda" and "public opinion" listed hundreds of works spanning many disciplines:[14] works by advertising men,[15] dissertations in media studies (*Publizistik*) and in law,[16] historical and pseudo-historical studies,[17] works in the new military science that would come to be called "psychological warfare,"[18] and, especially, works in the burgeoning field of mass psychology.[19]

Very quickly a "discourse" grew up within the field of propaganda and public opinion studies, "characterized by the delimitation of a field of object, the definition of a legitimate perspective for the agent of knowledge, and the fixing of norms for the elaboration of concepts and theories."[20] The works within this dis course shared not only an object of study – the laws of rhetorical manipulation in the modern mass public sphere, they also shared a methodology, mass psychology, and a purpose, the good of the German nation. Within this discourse the definition of "propaganda" shifted. Whereas during the war "propaganda" suggested an immoral form of manipulative rhetoric, within this postwar discourse "propaganda" was viewed in morally neutral terms, as a collection of techniques of manipulation. Thus, although propaganda continued to suggest lying, continued to suggest manipulative persua-

---

14   See, for example, Scherke and Vitzthum: *Bibliographie der geistigen Kriegführung.*

15   Exemplary are Schmidt: *Das politische Werbewesen im Kriege*; Schmidt: *Das politische Werbewesen in der Umsturzzeit*; and Schultze-Pfaelzer: *Propaganda, Agitation, Reklame.*

16   Huber: *Die französische Propaganda im Weltkrieg gegen Deutschland 1914 bis 1918*; Prosch: *Die Propaganda. Ihre Anwendung in der Politik und ihre Bedeutung für Deutschlands Wiederaufstieg*; Holzapfel: "Politische Propaganda."

17   Exemplary are Thimme: *Weltkrieg ohne Waffen*; and Knesebeck: *Die Wahrheit über den Propagandafeldzug und Deutschlands Zusammenbruch.*

18   The leader of this division in 1932 was Max Simoneit. See his *Wehrpsychologie.* One of the officers who participated in the "psychological warfare" division of the German General Staff was Kurt Hesse. See his *Der Feldherr Psychologos.*

19   There are good critical accounts of these works in Berking: *Masse und Geist. Studien zur Soziologie in der Weimarer Republik*; Möding: "Die domestizierte Masse. Gedanken zu den Affinitäten von 'Massen'- und Volks-'Begriff;" and Sodhi: "Zur Problematik der Massenpsychologie."

20   Foucault: "History of Systems of Thought," p. 199.

sive efforts, those who wrote within this discourse argued that propaganda was legitimate if employed for a good cause.

Accordingly, most authors concentrated on "propaganda" and treated public opinion as a function of propaganda. Only a few works in the 1920s dealt with "public opinion" per se, and only one, Ferdinand Tönnies' *Kritik der öffentlichen Meinung* (1922), attempted an abstract, sociological definition of this modern phenomenon.[21] Although written by the most important sociologist of his day, Tönnies book was a flop. It was rarely criticized; it was largely ignored. Not only was it written in an abstract, sociological German, not only was it full of internal contradictions, more importantly, it was out of step both with the neutral, amoral definitions of propaganda and public opinion and with the methodology of the growing discourse on propaganda and public opinion. Still, as Tönnies book is representative of the common wisdom concerning propaganda and public opinion during the war – as distilled, for example, in the changes in the definition of "propaganda" – and of an important strain of postwar academic thought on public opinion and propaganda, it is worth setting out here the central arguments of Tönnies's book before turning to the popular discourse on propaganda and public opinion.[22]

In this massive, 583 page work Tönnies attempted, first, an ideal-typical definition of "public opinion." In *Gemeinschaft und Gesellschaft* Tönnies had defined "public opinion" within the framework of "social will:" "The forms of will themselves are defined as follows: (a) that of the *Gemeinschaft*; from the point of view of the individual faith; from the point of view of the whole, religion; (b) that of the *Gesellschaft*: individually considered, theory; generally considered, public opinion."[23] The war convinced him, however, that this framework was insufficient.[24] In *Zur Kritik der öffentlichen Meinung* Tönnies now distinguished between a "Public Opinion" (capitalized) of the community of scholars (*Gelehrtenrepublik*), that is, a "knowledgeable, educated, informed public,"[25] and many popular "public opinions" (*Volksstimmungen*).[26] The two

---

21	Tönnies: *Zur Kritik der öffentlichen Meinung.* I have discussed this work in more depth in "Tönnies Begriff der 'öffentlichen Meinung.'"

22	The contemporary reception of this work is briefly described in Gollin and Gollin: "Toennies on Public Opinion," The book was such a flop that it is rarely discussed in treatments of Tönnies' work. Thus, for example, there is no discussion of this book in Mitzman: *Sociology and Estrangement. Three Sociologists of Imperial Germany*; Bellebaum: "Ferdinand Tönnies;" or even in Bickel's recent monograph, *Ferdinand Tönnies. Soziologie als skeptische Aufklärung zwischen Historismus und Rationalismus.*

23	Tönnies: *Community and Society*, p. 218.

24	Tönnies discussed the history of his interest in "public opinion" in his introduction to *Zur Kritik der öffentlichen Meinung*, pp. v ff.

forms of public opinion differed as their subjects differed. "Public Opinion" was by definition rational; it avoided appeals to base instincts, remained scientific, *sachlich*.[27] "Public opinions" in contrast, were by definition common, "vulgar," characterized by sensationalism, emotionalism, an uninformed moralistic tone.[28] In this framework, "propaganda" was defined as the organized expression of mass public opinions. Indeed, in some sense this book can be understood as an effort, in Tönnies own words, to give "a scientific foundation to those wisdoms of our common language usage," to provide a scientific foundation to the common definition of propaganda during the war.[29] The special tragedy of World War I, the increase in violence compared to the wars of the nineteenth century, was to be explained at least in part by the increase in the importance of popular public opinion, of propaganda during the war, by the decline of "Public Opinion."

This conceptualization of the nature of the modern public sphere was, of course, scarcely original. Indeed as Fritz Ringer, Rüdiger vom Bruch, Walter Struve and others have noted, the distinction between a "rational" elite and an "irrational," popular "public opinion," accompanied by a warning of the danger to culture caused by an increasingly important "mass society," was the accepted academic wisdom concerning "public opinion" before and during the war.[30] Yet Tönnies retained these elitist definitions in his 1922 book, in

---

25 Ibid., p. 77.

26 Ibid., p. 154.

27 Ibid., p. 279.

28 See his discussion of "Vulgar Forms of Public Opinion (*Vulgäre Erscheinungen der Öffentlichung Meinung*)," in Ibid., pp. 178 ff. See also the arguments he made in his *Der englische Staat und der deutsche Staat*, pp. 33 ff.; and in *Warlike England as seen by Herself*, p. 16, where he writes of the dangers of "feminine intelligences."

29 This is Tönnies description of his motivation for writing *Community and Society* but it pertains here, too. Tönnies: "Gemeinschaft und Gesellschaft. Vorrede zu der Dritten Auflage," p. 59.

30 Ringer: *The Decline of the German Mandarins*; vom Bruch: *Weltpolitik als Kulturmission*; vom Bruch: *Wissenschaft, Politik und öffentliche Meinung. Gelehrtenpolitik im Wilhelminischen Deutschland (1890–1914)*; and Struve: *Elites Against Democracy*. There are good discussions of liberal intellectuals' fear of the "masses" during the Weimar Republic in Döring: *Der Weimarer Kreis*; Mayer: *Linksbürgerliches Denken. Untersuchungen zur Kunsttheorie, Gesellschaftsauffassung und Kulturpolitik in der Weimarer Rrepublik (1919–1924)*; and Schürgers: *Politische Philosophie in der Weimarer Republik*. This was an especially popular argument during the war. Tönnies himself charged in a wartime piece that the German constitution was to be preferred to the English constitution because in Germany the whims of public opinion had less of an impact on the government; that is, a mixed constitution was to be preferred to a democracy. Tönnies: *Der englische Staat und der deutsche Staat*, p. 32. Probably the most famous wartime

spite of the fact that after 1918 Tönnies interpreted the wartime experiences
as evidence that the *Obrigkeitsstaat* was anachronistic, and in spite of the fact
that this definition was clearly inadequate for understanding and explaining
the World War I experiences which had inspired him to write this book in the
first place. For example, neutral "Public Opinion" during World War I largely
blamed Germany with having begun the First World War. Arguing from a patriotic perspective, Tönnies charged that as English propaganda had deceived
these intellectuals, as they had failed to act "scientifically," they were not true
"intellectuals."[31] But this only raised the issue of power: who gets to define
what is "true," and what is a true "intellectual?"

The intellectuals in the enemy nations presented Tönnies with a similar
problem. Tönnies was forced to admit that during World War I education had
not vaccinated effectively against hatred, base emotions, and brutality, that intellectuals had acted just as emotionally and as inadequately as the masses.
Tönnies described this phenomena along lines that Julien Benda would later
term "the treason of the intellectuals."[32] Yet it was unrealistic to expect intellectuals to remain "above the battle," in Romain Rolland's famous phrase.
During the war Tönnies himself had written one-sided "propaganda" pieces,
and in the postwar internal political struggles he, too, sometimes employed an
irrational, *ad hominem* form of argumentation.[33] On the basis of his own experiences, how could Tönnies argue that the defining characteristic of "Public
Opinion" was that it was rational, *sachlich*, unemotional, in comparison to
mass public opinion, which was emotional and irrational?

Thus, although Tönnies saw correctly that there was a modern danger associated with the triumph of the irrational over the rational, his description of
the nature of that danger was peculiarly anachronistic. It was also profoundly
fatalistic. For while Tönnies decried the effects of an irrational public opinion
and made "propaganda" responsible for the peculiar violence of this war, and
while he acknowledged that mass public opinion was increasing in importance as a part of the process of modernization, he offered no way out of this
dilemma. The works in the growing discourse on propaganda and public
opinion, in contrast, generally viewed the rise of mass society as an opportu-

---

work in this vein was: Harnack, Hintze, Meinecke, Sering, and Troeltsch: *Die Deutsche Freiheit.*

31   Tönnies: Zur Kritik der öffentlichen Meinung, pp. 544 ff. Tönnies argued similarly in *Fortschritt und soziale Entwicklung. Geschichtsphilosophische Ansichten*, p. 103.

32   Benda: *The Treason of the Intellectuals.* Tönnies: *Zur Kritik der öffentlichen Meinung*, pp. 544 ff.

33   Lembcke: "Die Auseinandersetzung Tönnies mit Grelling und Kautsky," pp. 495 ff.

nity, if one learned to channel the masses' powerful creative energies. What were the characteristics of this discourse on the techniques of manipulation?

First, almost all works within the discourse assumed that public opinion was, as one Pan-German, Hans Freiherr von Liebig, wrote during the war, "always a matter of direction," that there was no such thing as a free collective will, that the masses were inherently stupid, were always led.[34] Thus, whereas Tönnies distinguished between two realms of public opinion and refused to draw any necessary lines of influence between these realms, the authors in this discourse charged that there was only one public opinion, and that elites always and everywhere manipulated public opinion.[35] This, of course, had profound implications for the concept of the elite. If the political elite were previously understood to be those who best understood the rational demands of national interest, the authors in this discourse defined the political elite as those with charisma, those capable of achieving and sustaining popularity, a mass following.

Second, the authors within this discourse assumed that public opinion could best be understood by applying the laws of "mass psychology," that the masses were always and everywhere manipulable in the same way. The success of propaganda was defined as a function of the degree to which the propagandists understood and applied these laws. Edgar Stern-Rubath, for example, who wrote one of the two most influential works within the discourse (the other was by Johann Plenge), charged that the success of British World War I propaganda came because the British had had no moral scruples in applying these rules:

> working on the basis of these assumptions [mass psychology], almost all the English propaganda work during the war was directed toward the psyche of the masses, that is, the propagandists were willing to do without the applause of the intellectuals. Indeed, the propagandists were willing to have their work criticized by independent and intelligent minds such as Bernard Shaw or Jerome, not to mention those in the enemy camp, rather than hold back, if they could win the masses.[36]

This implied that it was less the set of ideas than the method that made a good propagandist.

Third, "public opinion" mattered a great deal; indeed, it was the most important factor in modern politics. Conceptualizing the nature of victory in World War I as a battle of wills, the authors within this discourse argued that

---

34   Liebig: *Die Politik von Bethmann-Hollwegs,* p. 92.
35   For Tönnies' position, see *Zur Kritik der öffentlichen Meinung,* p. 154.
36   Stern-Rubath: *Die Propaganda als politisches Instrument,* pp. 78–79.

government propaganda had played the essential role in organizing and directing these wills. Edgar Stern-Rubath, for example, began his important book by charging that Germany did not lose the war militarily, but lost it to "propaganda:"

> the conviction that Germany's defeat did not result from the military superiority of its opponents is a common one [...]. It must then logically follow that we succumbed to other weapons than military ones. This is correct. Then in truth we were defeated by the enemy propaganda, the battle of words and of ideas.[37]

Enemy propaganda had broken the German will to fight. In contrast, in the section of his book on the German World War I propaganda experience, Tönnies made an impassioned plea against the claim that more and better propaganda would have sustained morale and won the war. The Allies material and manpower superiority, he charged, not the loss of will, caused the German defeat.[38]

If public opinion mattered a great deal, and if there was no such thing as an independent "public opinion," then there was not only nothing inherently immoral about propaganda; propaganda was a necessary tool of modern politics.[39] Thus, it was only logical for the authors in this discourse to reject the negative connotations which had grown up around "propaganda" during wartime, to take an essentially neutral, amoral approach. Whereas Tönnies was appalled with the inherent characteristics of a "propagandistic" style of rhetoric, with this emotional, irrational political discourse, with the "Machiavellian" manipulation techniques employed by the propagandist, those writing within the discourse on propaganda and public opinion charged that political rhetoric should not be judged as rational or irrational, as moral or immoral on the basis of the style of argumentation itself. Rather, rhetoric was to be judged solely on the value of the goal that it served.

The practical political lessons from this discourse were clear. "Propaganda" was an essential part of modern politics.[40] It was also the only way out of the difficult position of the 1920s, and the quicker the German politicians got over their old-fashioned moralistic qualms about using this "weapon," the better. For "propaganda," charged Johann Plenge, was the means to "organize" public opinion, the means to unite the people and thus to increase the power of the nation: "our system of thought concerning society aims to teach

---

37   Ibid., p. 3.
38   Tönnies: *Zur Kritik der öffentlichen Meinung,* pp. 550 ff.
39   Ibid., pp. 7, 21.
40   Ibid., p. 3; Plenge: *Deutsche Propaganda,* p. 12.

the practical art of bringing human wills together, making them act as a unit. The practical side of our teachings is inconceivable without propaganda."[41] And indeed, given this view of the masses, it was not cynical hypocrisy for the National Socialists to claim that propaganda was an essential component of a government of and for the people, for Goebbels to claim in a speech on 16 March 1933 that the establishment of a Propaganda ministry four days earlier was a "revolutionary action showing that the government does not intend to leave the public on their own. This government is in the truest sense of the word a government of the people [*Volksregierung*]."[42]

This discourse on propaganda and public opinion had a profound impact. Although it never became the accepted academic wisdom (except in the field of "mass psychology"), it did have powerful and intelligent proponents in many academic disciplines such as the sociologists Othmar Spann and Hans Freyer, and the jurist Carl Schmitt.[43] More importantly, almost all the non-academic articles written in popular magazines and newspapers – and outside the Social Democratic public realm – followed, at least broadly, the tenets of this discourse.[44] Most important of all, this discourse had a central position in the ideology of the so-called conservative revolutionaries,[45] and of the National Socialists.[46] Thus, for example, the section on propaganda in *Mein Kampf*, the most important part of the book, the only part that was widely reprinted, was little more than a compendium of the wisdom of the popular discourse on propaganda and public opinion.[47]

III.

In October 1918, newspapers informed the German people that the war was going very badly. After four years during which the German people had been told that the war was going well, that they were certain to win if they would

---

41   Ibid., p. 13.

42   Goebbels: "Rede vor der Presse, 16.3.33," p. 135.

43   Their most important works in this regard are: Spann: *Der Wahre Staat;* Freyer: *Revolution von Rechts;* and Schmitt: *The Crisis of Parliamentary Democracy.* See also Bolz: *Auszug aus der entzauberten Welt.*

44   See, for example, the collection of newspaper articles on "propaganda" collected by the "Deutsche Arbeitsfront," in BA (Bundesarchiv) Potsdam, 62 DAF, #17395.

45   Klemperer: *Germany's New Conservatism;* Sontheimer: *Antidemokratisches Denken in der Weimarer Republik;* and Faye: *Totalitäre Sprachen.*

46   See most recently Michels: *Ideologie und Propaganda;* Paul: *Aufstand der Bilder. Die NS-Propaganda vor 1933;* as well as the excellent discussion in Stern: *Hitler. The Führer and the People.*

47   This is noted by McClelland: *The Crowd and the Mob,* p. 283.

only "hold out," this news came as a shock. Morale collapsed, and so, too, did support for the existing system. Many citizens expressed outrage at having been duped, and felt that any system which had lied to them in such a manner had lost its legitimacy. On 9 November the German people therefore deposed the monarchy. This, at least, was the interpretation of the revolution proposed on 10 November by Theodor Wolff, the editor of the *Berliner Tageblatt*, and a number of other prominent democratic liberals. According to Wolff, the disgust felt with "propaganda," the feeling that one had not been treated as an intelligent citizen, capable of making informed and responsible decisions, but as an *Untertan*, was the primary motivation behind the 1918 revolution. Moreover, Wolff charged, the motivation was justified. The war experience had shown that "propaganda" alone could sustain neither morale nor win for the government the support of the population.[48] Democracy was to be preferred because democracy, in the words of Hugo Preuß, was the form of government "in which the will of the state is the organized will of the people."[49] In other words, many German liberals and democrats in 1918 sought legitimation for the new Republic in the argument that democracy was needed for "reasons of state" (*Staatsräson*). Democracy, they charged, would best provide a strong modern state, because strength in a modern state came from national unity.[50]

Radical or "revolutionary" conservative elites, that is, those who were willing to break with the monarchical idea, such as the Pan Germans, responded with arguments culled from the popular discourse on propaganda and public opinion. They agreed with the Republicans that the war had shown, first, that modern state power was a function of the unity of the people, and, second, that the old system, the *Obrigkeitsstaat*, was inherently unable to create and sustain this unity. They charged that a "Republican" democracy, however, would also not produce national unity, that a "Republican" democracy would only sustain the internal division of Germany. National unity was not to be obtained through a process of compromise and consensus accomplished through discussion. National unity, they claimed, could only be produced through effective leadership, by someone who was able to unite the nation behind him, and through national myths.[51]

---

48   Theodor Wolff, Untitled, *Berliner Tageblatt*, No. 534, 10. November 1918, (Morgen).

49   Preuß: *Obrigkeitsstaat und großdeutscher Gedanke*, p. 19. Similarly, H: Preuß, *Das deutsche Volk und der Weltkrieg*, pp. 159 ff.

50   National unity as the most important factor of national strength was a central aspect in the thought of the so-called "rational republicans," (*Vernunftrepublikanern*). See Schmidt: *Deutscher Historismus und der Übergang zur parlamentarischen Demokratie*.

51   The classic version of this response is Schmitt's *The Crisis of Parliamentary Democracy*.

Thus, the discourse on propaganda and public opinion allowed the leading military figures to state with conviction – already in 1918, and especially in the first few years after the war – that they had never lied. They did not claim to have portrayed reality objectively. Rather, "reality," they charged, was a very slippery thing. In his memoirs, Erich Ludendorff, for example, while admitting that the enemy had vastly outnumbered and outgunned Germany, that the enemy had had more soldiers, more material and more food, charged that this material inferiority had been compensated by a greater German "will to victory." Defeat came not because the enemy's material superiority had finally grown to the point where it produced victory, but because the German will to victory had subsided to the point where it produced defeat. In other words, according to Ludendorff, Germany had lost the war not because of the enemy's military but because of their psychological superiority. The enemy had had the better nerves, the stronger will; the German nerves and will had broken in the revolution of 1918. A weak civilian leadership was responsible for this loss of will, so Ludendorff and others, for it left the German masses without direction. But the masses, being inherently docile and tractable, ab-hor a vacuum. Without direction, they easily succumbed to defeatist and ene-my propaganda. Thus, while agreeing that morale had been deeply affected by propaganda, the military leaders charged that it was not the military but the civilian leadership and the defeatist and enemy propaganda which had weakened morale.[52]

Of course, it was only a small step to take to seek definite political gains from this interpretation of the revolution by identifying one's own political enemies, the Social Democratic Party (SPD) and democratic newspapers, as those who had taken advantage of this leadership vacuum in order to "stab the army in the back."[53] This step was taken immediately. Already in the 1918 elections for the National Assembly the Conservative German National

---

52 Ludendorff: *Ludendorff's Own Story*. Similar remarks can be found in the postwar writings of many leading military figures such as Wrisberg: *Der Weg zur Revolution 1914–1918*; Bauer: *Konnten wir den Krieg vermeiden, gewinnen, abbrechen?*; and the "Gutachten des Sachverständigen General der Infanterie a. D. [Hans] von Kuhl: "Entstehung, Durchführung und Zusammenbruch der Offensive von 1918," Philipp, ed.: *Ursachen des Zusammenbruchs* vol. 3, pp. 1–238.

53 On the "stab-in-the-back legend," see especially Gärtringen: "'Dolchstoß'-Diskussion und 'Dolchstoßlegende' im Wandel von vier Jahrzehnten;" but also Fries-Thiessenhusen: "Politische Kommentare deutscher Historiker 1918/19 zu Niederlage und Staatsumsturz;" Petzold: *Die Dolchstosslegende*; Thimme: *Flucht in den Mythos*, pp. 68 ff.; and Kaehler: "Neuere Geschichtslegenden und ihre Überwindung." More generally, see Heinemann: *Die verdrängte Niederlage*.

People's Party (DNVP) asked the German people not to vote for the so-called "November criminals," – the left-liberals and especially the Social Democrats – who, they claimed, had taken the weapons out of the hands of the German people.[54] In the latter half of the Weimar Republic the National Socialists were the most vocal and most able proponents of this legend. Adolf Hitler, for example, began his first speech as Chancellor on 1 February 1933 with the words:

> fourteen years have passed since those unfortunate days when the German people, blinded by various internal and external promises, forgot the highest values of our past, our empire, and our freedom, and accordingly lost everything. Since this day of treason God has taken away his grace from our people. Disunity and hatred have entered. The promised equality and fraternity have not appeared. But we have lost our freedom. Because of the loss of the unity of the will of our people we have lost our political position in the world.[55]

In the 1920s, democrats responded to these charges largely by attempting to point out how ridiculous the legend was as history. It was not the morale at home, they charged, which had worsened the morale at the front; the morale of the soldiers had collapsed on its own – because of the soldiers' experience of Prussian militarism or because of the soldier's recognition of the ever growing material superiority of the enemy.[56] They pointed out, too, that morale at home was damaged not by the Social Democrats or by the liberal press, but by the poor social and economic conditions and by the actions of the right, especially when the right set forth vast war aims, suggesting to many Germans that they wished to extend the war.

The democrat's response to the conservative legend was often characterized by that tone of disbelief rational people feel when faced with profound irrationality. Hans Delbrück, for example, wrote in a pamphlet on Ludendorff:

> one simply pulls out one's hair when one reads such thoughts. Every sentence is either an absurdity or it is historically false. How were the German people to be whipped up to ever greater accomplishments? According to Ludendorff through propaganda. What a conception of the nature of the press, of the possibility of the

---

54 Gärtringen: "'Dolchstoß'-Diskussion und 'Dolchstoßlegende' im Wandel von vier Jahrzehnten," pp. 134–135.

55 "Aufruf der Reichsregierung von Adolf Hitler im Rundfunk verkündet." *Völkischer Beobachter* (München), 3 February 1933, p. 1. Paul: *Aufstand der Bilder. Die NS- Propaganda vor 1933*, has an excellent account of the importance of the "stab-in-the-back" legend in the National Socialist propaganda of the late 1920s and early 1930s.

56 Lehmann-Russbüldt: *Warum erfolgte der Zusammenbruch an der Westfront?*; Gothein: *Warum verloren wir den Krieg?*; and Koester: *Fort mit der Dolchstosslegende!*

government to influence the people, of the nature of the people, who see their freedom in the fact that each one of them of their own free will has chosen to serve the fatherland. Certainly, the government can influence the press and thus the people. Yet there are limits to this influence, and the experience of the last few years has shown us that such attempts to influence can often cause more harm than good.[57]

The democrats were undoubtedly correct – historical research since 1945 has effectively debunked the stab-in-the-back legend[58] – but the problem was that the debate was not historical but conceptual – between differing views as to the nature of the "masses," the "people," and differing views as to the nature of "history." If one believed, as did Hans Delbrück, Ferdinand Tönnies, and Theodor Wolff, that the people fight best when they fight of their own free will for things they had chosen of their own free will, then clearly, as one liberal wrote: "[…] one can no longer look down upon the 'masses,' as without the sacrifices of the masses we could not have fought this last war, no matter how great our generals. […] One can not direct the will of these masses through the whip toward a goal."[59]

Democracy was a necessity, as was a free public realm, characterized by the absence of what they called negatively "propaganda," characterized by tolerance and respect. If one believed, however, that the people, the "masses," were stupid and malleable and were impressed most by strength,[60] if one believed, as did Colonel Bauer, Ludendorff's political advisor, that the "united will of the people does not exist," that individual leaders always "seek the base instincts of the masses in order to become their leaders and bring forward a rule by the mob which does away with all that is noble and good,"[61] that to leave the masses to themselves meant to deliver them to unscrupulous demagogues,[62] then clearly the 1918 revolution could only have been inspired by foreign, enemy elements.

---

57 Delbrück: *Ludendorff, Tirpitz, Falkenhayn*, p. 17, quoted in Tönnies: *Zur Kritik der öffentlichen Meinung*, pp. 547–548.

58 Deist: "Der militärische Zusammenbruch des Kaiserreichs. Zur Realität der 'Dolchstoßlegende.'"

59 Dr. K. E. M: "Politische Wochenschau," *Münchener Neueste Nachrichten*, 21 Oktober 1917, #533, p. 1.

60 Ludendorff: *Kriegführung und Politik*, p. 125.

61 "Auszug aus der Aufzeichnung Bauer," 23 April 1918, in Deist, ed.: *Militär und Innenpolitik*, p. 1214.

62 "Entwurf einer Stellungnahme der Obersten Heeresleitung zur Denkschrift des preußischen Ministers des Innern über die innenpolitische Lage," written by Bauer, 21 February 1918, in Deist, ed.: *Militär und Innenpolitik*, p. 1200.

The stab-in-the-back legend was not only conceived of as history, was not only a central part of conservative belief, it was, more importantly, a central part of the right's strategy for winning popularity during the 1920s. In other words, the stab-in-the-back legend was used not only as a mythic narrative which defined German political culture, "the values, expectations and implicit rules" that conservatives believed should "express and shape collective intentions and actions,"[63] it was also the most important narrative through which conservative hegemony should make itself popular, in spite of the fact that history – at least as we would write it today – was largely on the side of the democrats, and in spite of the fact that in this conservative discourse on propaganda and the public the people were conceptualized as marionettes who were easily controlled and manipulated by propaganda.[64] The "stab-in-the-back" legend was, by all accounts, a very popular and effective narrative. It seems inconceivable that a free people should choose to be chained. But was that how they conceptualized it themselves? What are the explanations for the popularity of the stab-in-the-back legend, the popularity of the conservative discourse on propaganda and public opinion?

The answers to these questions are, of course, largely psychological, and thus to some degree speculative. The legend offered a number of psychological supports. German elites, for example, gladly saw the causes of the military defeat not in their own foolish foreign policy, in their own hubris, in their own military decisions, or in the nature of their bureaucratic government, but in the actions of foreign or traitorous elements. In his remarks in front of the parliamentary committee investigating the causes of the German defeat, Vize-Admiral a. D. von Trotha characteristically claimed that, as he was responsible for the morale on his ship, the revolutionary mood had to have been brought in from the outside.[65]

The people, too, wished to hide from unpleasant truths about themselves. As Ernst Deutelmoser, who had been a very important figure in the German propaganda organization during the war, noted after the war, "it takes two for someone to go down the wrong path: one who points in the wrong direction, and one who allows himself to be guided."[66] Many Germans who believed the lies had wanted to be lied to; indeed, those Germans who cast doubt upon the

---

63   This is L. Hunt's definition of "political culture" in her *Politics, Culture, and Class in the French Revolution*, p. 10.

64   See Vondung: "Propaganda oder Sinndeutung?," p. 13.

65   Reichstag, Untersuchungsausschuß über die Weltkriegsverantwortlichkeit, 4. Untersuchungsausschuß, session of February 9, 1926, Philipp, ed.: *Die Ursachen des Deutschen Zusammenbruchs im Jahre 1918* vol. 4, p. 221.

66   Deutelmoser: "Die amtliche Einwirkung auf die deutsche Öffentlichkeit im Kriege," p. 22.

veracity of the propaganda were in danger of being castigated as traitors.[67] This desire to believe that one had not acted foolishly during the war was all too human, reminding one of the truth of one of Nietzsche's famous dictum: "'This is what I have done,' says my memory. 'You could not have done that,' says my pride, and insists. Finally, my memory gives in." And it was a feeling that extended far beyond those who voted for parties on the middle or the right.

Yet self-deception is less important a motivation than is often assumed. More importantly, the conservative discourse on propaganda and public opinion met a widespread desire for faith. This desire sprang less from the recognition that one's fate was in the hands of forces greater than oneself than from the hope that with faith one could accomplish more than one could with a rational, pragmatic approach to one's problems. Thus, paradoxically, conservative elites claimed that by giving up aspects of one's freedom – one's critical intellect – one could regain a certain amount of control over one's destiny. Not with one's intellect could one construct one's future, only with one's will could one again become the subject and not the object of history. Clearly, the National Socialists profited from this desire; their emphasis on the power of belief was an important part of their appeal.[68]

The proposition that will accomplishes wonders (*Glaube versetzt Berge*), at the heart of all wartime propaganda, is, of course, a part of the soldier's ethos. In World War I all generals in all armies emphasized that the will to victory was an essential part of military strategy. If one accepted the truth of these assumptions there was a certain validity in the military leader's claims that the wartime news releases had not been false, for they were at the service of the will to victory, and if the will to victory had been sustained this would have made these releases true. As Gerhard Ritter once noted, "soldiers live with the idea that mere will power can overcome all obstacles; but such a primitive notion will not hold in the sphere of politics, and especially not in diplomacy with its many subtleties."[69] The tragedy of World War I was that this aspect of the soldier's ethos became a part of the "home front's" ethos as well.[70]

---

67 See, for example, Dr. Karl Heldmann's description of his experiences during the war, when he had tried to point out the government's lies, in his *Kriegserlebnissse eines deutschen Geschichtspofessors in der Heimat.*

68 There are interesting remarks on the religiosity of the National Socialist movement and the importance of this as a part of their appeal in Stern: *Hitler. The Führer and the People*; and Rhodes: *The Hitler Movement: A Modern Millenarian Revolution.*

69 Ritter: *The Sword and the Scepter* vol. 2, p. 104.

70 Tönnies' remarks on "Belief as a Duty" in *Zur Kritik der Öffentlichen Meinung*, pp. 15 ff., are interesting here: "Thus one experiences during the war that any expression of doubt con-

For the practical lessons drawn from this proposition produced terrible results. "Fanatic" and "total," terms which before the war had possessed negative connotations, became positive values.[71] Violence was a central element in showing, in demonstrating one's intensity, one's fanaticism, one's will. A person just as a nation could only be "fully mobilized," to employ Ernst Jünger's famous phrase, if they were willing to live dangerously.[72] To be truly committed to one's ideals meant to follow them without consideration for anything else. War became a metaphor for life itself. And many hoped that a greater will would bring success in a future war, as Michael Balfour has noted: "[...] by exaggerating the extent to which the German failure in 1918 had been due to a failure of will rather than to material inferiority, they encouraged the belief that greater will-power, derived from a more fervent conviction, would by itself be enough to produce a different result."[73]

IV.

Since the 1960s it has become one of the truisms of propaganda studies that the ideas of a certain propaganda campaign only work within a receptive cultural terrain. This necessary correction to the manipulation thesis put forward in the popular discourse on propaganda and public opinion after World War I has led to too much emphasis on studying the content or the rhetoric of the myths being propagated in order to understand their popularity.[74] For the popularity of a discourse which privileges propaganda often lies less in the ideas, that is, in the myths themselves, than in the ability of the myth-makers to evoke the positive aspects of an act of faith. As Eric Hoffer has noted:

> A rising mass movement attracts and holds a following not by its doctrine and promises but by the refuge it offers from the anxieties, barrenness and meaninglessness of an individual existence. It cures the poignantly frustrated not by conferring on them an absolute truth or by remedying the difficulties and abuses which made their lives miserable, but by freeing them from their ineffectual selves

---

cerning the justice of one's own cause [...] is perceived as a sign of heresy, and as such a sort of treason that for those stating such beliefs publicly produces a heavy punishment."

71   Bork: *Mißbrauch der Sprache.*

72   Jünger: *Die totale Mobilmachung.*

73   Balfour: *Propaganda in War, 1939-1945,* p. 10.

74   There are trenchant criticisms of the "manipulation thesis" employed by German historians in the 1950s in Haug: *Der hilflose Antifaschismus.* More generally, see Bessel: "The Rise of the NSDAP and the Myth of Nazi Propaganda;" and Welch: *The Third Reich. Politics and Propaganda.*

– and it does this by enfolding and absorbing them into a closely knit and exultant corporate whole.[75]

In the 1920s, the German proponents of the discourse on propaganda and public opinion, including, of course, the radical conservative politicians, were able to couch the essential political choice not as one between different forms of taxation, school budgets, the color of the flag, or of unemployment insurance, not even as one between different forms of the constitution, but as to different forms of *Weltanschauung*, between a "materialistic" and an "idealistic" *Weltanschauung*. The materialist, Houston Stewart Chamberlain, for example, charged (and by materialist he meant not only the Marxist but also the utilitarian, capitalist vision of society) believes that man is a "machine," that he is acted upon by the outer world, that his "consciousness is simply a mirror, and that there is no freedom."[76] The idealist believes that man creates his own world through the set of ideas and concepts with which he or she chooses to view the world. In other words, so Chamberlain, the idealist believes that man can master his fate; the materialist believes he or she can not.

In stark contrast to the "materialist" vision of the nature of society during the 1920s, a time perceived by many Germans as a time of crisis, radical conservatives offered the comforts of myth. Only through the power of faith, they charged, could the German people accomplish the *Volksgemeinschaft* they so desired. According to the *Völkischer Beobachter* on 30 January 1939 only a community of belief could provide the foundation for a true modern community: "This is the effect of the power of faith, a power one has to submit to – that millions of people become one, that every individual receives the conviction that he and his life will grow up as and be a part of the *Volksgemeinschaft*."[77] Faith not only provided the foundation for community; it also gave people the belief that they were creating their own reality, that they were masters of their fate. "A myth," said Mussolini in October 1922 in a speech often quoted by National Socialists, "is a belief, a passion. The myth does not have to be real. It creates reality."[78]

---

75 Hoffer: *The True Believer*, p. 39. My understanding of the popularity of modern mythic movements has also benifited from my reading of Kolwakowski: *The Presence of Myth*; Frank: *Der Kommende Gott. Vorlesungen über die Neue Mythologie*; Frank: *Gott im Exil. Vorlesungen über die Neue Mythologie*; and Hüppauf: "Mythisches Denken und Krisen der deutschen Literatur und Gesellschaft."

76 Chamberlain: "Deutsche Weltanschauung," p. 10.

77 Quoted in Bork: *Mißbrauch der Sprache* p. 80.

78 Quoted in Peterson: "Mussolini: Wirklichkeit und Mythos eines Diktators," p. 246.

The myth of the "stab-in-the-back" is an especially good example of the powerful charms of the appeal to faith in a time of crisis, for not only was it historically ludicrous, it was also in some sense insulting. Those who believed in it must have had an especially strong reason for doing so, and the reason lay less in the realm of ideas than in the fact that the myth offered them the possibility of total commitment. If I may paraphrase Ernst Jünger, who said that it does not matter why we are fighting, only that we fight, the appeal of the discourse on propaganda can be summarized as something like this: it does not matter what we believe, only that we believe fully.

It would be foolish – and it was foolish for many democrats in the 1920s – to underestimate the appeal of faith, to underestimate the hope that by giving up a part of one's personality, by subsuming oneself in a greater whole, one receives something in return – such as community in this lonely world, or even just the hope in the possibility of hope – the hope that in a time of crisis through will alone one could escape one's fate. As William James has noted, there is an ancient phrase that fear is the mother of myth. Especially in a time of crisis democrats neglect the popularity of a mythic discourse – not so much the myths themselves – at their own peril.

KARLHEINZ BARCK

Zentrum für Literaturforschung, Berlin

Blitzkrieg:
"God Stinnes" or the Depoliticization of the Sublime

Abstract: This paper pursues some traces of the astounding career of the term Blitzkrieg from its invention by fascist military strategists and its subsequent ideologically charged use in European fascist cultural discourse to its aggressive role in later critical and socialist literature and, finally, its currency in present every-day language and re-occurrence in military phraseology. After its dissociation from the sublime, the current and common use of Blitzkrieg has been emptied of its political and ideological content and its initial significance replaced with an empty notion of destruction by sheer technology.

Blitzkrieg, one of those international notions of German origin such as *Kitsch* or *Kindergarten,* originated in military or strategic language and was soon incorporated in socio-political or socio-psychological discourse[1]. Let me briefly characterize them.

In October 1941, shortly after the beginning of the Nazi onslaught against the Soviet Union in accordance with the "Aufmarschanweisung Barbarossa," one could read the following, written in August of that year in a book published in London by Faber and Faber:

> It is too early to see more than the widest outline of what is happening in the largest Blitzkrieg of the lot, that on the Russian front. All we can tell is that there are some signs that the German forces have been slowed down, and a number of signs to show that they are meeting with an opposition not only powerful in numbers and materials, but more effective in its tactics than has been met by the Nazi Army in almost all its previous campaigns. We cannot tell whether this opposition will

---

Thanks to Fiona Greenwood for reviewing the English version of my text.

1   On war-propaganda see Blau: *Geistige Kriegführung*; Blau: *Propaganda als Waffe*; Hadamovsky: *Propaganda und nationale Macht*; Hesse: *Der Feldherr Psychologos*; Lasswell, Casey and Smith: Propaganda and Promotional Activities.

succeed; but we can say already that the Russians seem to have attempted on a very large scale the creation of a web of defense that separates the armored spear-head of the Blitzkrieg from the infantry divisions following it [...]. The Blitzkrieg has decided the fate of too many nations. The principles that I have emphasized here are to my kind the essence of the Blitzkrieg: concentration for a [rolling thrust], the linking of various arms in combat teams, large scale counter-attack as one main element in the only sort of defense possible, and a web of tank-proof islands of resistance as the other main element.[2]

This was written by Tom Wintringham in his introduction to the first and best description of Blitzkrieg doctrine we have, Ferdinand Otto Miksche's "Blitzkrieg." The contemporaneous book by Fritz Sternberg, friend of Brecht and member of the SAP (Socialist Workers' Party),[3] first published in German in 1939 in Paris by the Münzenberg-Editions' Sebastian Brant and in that same year by Faber and Faber in London, is distinguished by its more political and economic orientation. Miksche and Wintringham both participated in the Spanish Civil War, which was the first "Nazi laboratory" for the Blitzkrieg. Miksche was a Czechoslovak major on the General Staff of the Spanish Republican Army, while Wintringham was commander of the British battalion. Miksche's book is the only serious study of the epoch, written by an expert and an eyewitness, for whom the principles of Blitzkrieg "were well known by 1939, at the end of the Spanish War. The road that the evolution of war was taking could not fail to be seen by an attentive observer who studied it in Spain."[4]

---

2   Tom Wintringham, introduction to Mischke: *Blitzkrieg*. – On Blitzkrieg see also: Arazi: "Horchdienst und Blitzkrieg"; Buchfink: *Der Krieg von Gestern und Morgen*; Deighton: *Blitzkrieg*; Förster: *Totaler Kreig und Blitzkrieg*; Hadamovsky: *Blitzmarsch nach Warschau*; Harrison: *Living through the Blitz*; Justrow: *Der technische Krieg im Spiegelbild der Kriegserfahrungen und der Weltpresse*; Kittler: "Media Wars: Trenches, Lightening, Stars"; Messenger: *The Art of Blitzkrieg*; Moisy: *Luftkrig – Zukunftskrieg*; Negt and Kluge: "Einige 'Beobachtungen zum Entstehungsprozeß' des Blitzkrieges." A recent study by a German military historian, Uwe Bitzel, has analyzed in detail the complementary economic factors as another driving force of Blitzkrieg strategy. This book, entitled "Die Entstehung der Blitzkrieg-Konzeption in der deutschen Wehrmacht" ("Emergence of the Blitzkrieg Conception in the German Wehrmacht," 1991) describes the direct and indirect interests of competing German monopoly groups and their international relations in Blitzkrieg. It is well known that many of the big US companies such as DuPont, Esso, Ford, General Electric, General Motors, IBM and ITT participated from the very beginning in the Nazi rearmament and continued even during the war. Cf. Trepp: *Bankgeschäfte mit dem Feind*; see also Helms: "Adlerorden aus der Hand des Führers"; Thomas: *Geschichte der deutschen Wehr- und Rüstungswirtschaft (1918–1943/45)*.

3   Cf. also Sternberg: *Der Dichter und die Ratio: Erinnerungen an Bertolt Brecht.*

4   Tom Wintringham, introduction to Mischke: *Blitzkrieg*, p. 7.

What is well known by military historians to-day as the basic concept of Blitzkrieg has been analyzed by Miksche as a sort of combination of two factors which may be characterized as dromological (or speed-making) and territorial (or space-making) factors:

> The first ones are surprise, speed and material superiority; the second ones are motorization, as method of transport, mechanization as method of breakthrough (Durchbruch), air action as method of support, protection and communication – that gives the warfare of to-day a character entirely different from that of the last World War.[5]

Speed and communication, their articulation or linking by means of new hard- and software technologies, can be seen as the differentia specifica that distinguish Blitzkrieg from the war machine of World War I. The new era which Blitzkrieg opened in the history of war is characterized by the use and performance of "communication weapons" and "transmission media." By what Heinz Guderian, commander of the tank troops and one of the first theorists of Blitzkrieg, called the "concert of weapons," made possible by new communication technologies like FM radio facilitating the control of command.[6]

The other critical reflection mentioned has another horizon and another dimension. After the beginning of World War II several entries in the "Arbeitsjournal" of Brecht refer to the speed of "German Blitzkrieg" as an astonishing new quality of the war machine. Signifying this new quality as the substitution of the traditional "battlefield" by what Brecht called a "Schlachtwürfel," a "battle cube" or "battle dice", Brecht demonstrated a certain amount of knowledge of Blitzkrieg strategy and tactics, which he may have owed to his friend Fritz Sternberg.

But what is even more striking in Brecht's brief notes which may be considered in relation to the later "Kriegsfibel" (the "War Primer" composed together with Ruth Berlau), is his question about the specific type of energy which the Nazis brought into being and put on wheels ("Krupp steel on

---

5   Ibid., p. 9. On speed see Charnay: "Vitesse et stratégie"; Fuller: *Pegasus*; Fuller: *The Conduct of War 1789-1961*;

6   The original reads: "Konzert der Waffen," Guderian: *Achtung Panzer*, p. 6. See also Guderian: *Panzer – Marsch!* and Eimannsberger: *Der Kampfwagenkrieg*. On miltary strategy and tactics see also Böhmel: "Das Geheimnis des Sieges"; Groos: *Seekriegslehren im Lichte des Weltkriegs*; Hierl: *Grundlagen einer deutschen Wehrpolitik*; Liddell-Hart: *Infanterie von morgen*; Liddell-Hart: *The British Way in Warfare*; Metzsch: *Krieg als Saat*; Metzsch: *Zeitgemäße Gedanken um Clausewitz*; Paret, ed.: *Makers of Modern Strategy. From Machiavelli to the Nuclear Age*; Visconti-Prasca: *Der Entscheidungskrieg*; Wallach: *Das Dogma der Vernichtungsschlacht*.

wheels") with their Blitzkrieg tactics. This question which Brecht rated for himself as important for the better understanding of the destructive mobilizing drive of the Nazi war machine, is seen as a consequence of deeper structures underlying the relation between civil society and violence. He thought that many "brave antifascists" had failed to understand those relations and therefore remained bound to what later on has been called a "helpless and hopeless antifascism" ("hilfloser Antifaschismus").[7]

Let me quote just some of his reflections about the new quality of "German Blitzkrieg" from his "Arbeitsjournal" in order to illustrate this idea:

30.6.40 […] Der langsame Krieg bringt den schnellen hervor (wie der stehende den beweglichen). Aber wie dieses Tempo alles verändert! Dabei handelt es sich nicht nur um einen Blitzkrieg bei den Deutschen, sondern auch um eine Blitzaufrüstung. und welche Kraft zieht dieses Regime aus Bruch aller Konventionen. Mit den modernsten Waffen der Luft mischen sich die Dampfer mit Touristen, Karl May ergänzt Clausewitz.

9.4.41 Die Welt hält wieder den Atem an. Die deutsche Armee rollt nach Saloniki in genau dem Tempo, das die Autos eben hergeben. Man hatte sich einen monatelangen Kampf vorgestellt, es waren Tage. Man erwartete dort die englische Wavellarmee zu sehen, es war nichts. Es ist, als ob nur diese Armee sich bewegen könnte. Sie allein schafft und beherrscht den Schlachtwürfel, der das Schlachtfeld abgelöst hat. Die veralteten Armeen konkurrieren da wie der Spinnrocken gegen die Jenny. Tapferkeit verliert gegen Fahrkunst, Unermüdlichkeit gegen Pünktlichkeit, Ausdauer gegen Fleiß. Die Strategie ist zur Chirurgie geworden. Ein feindliches Land wird „geöffnet", nachdem es betäubt worden ist, dann wird tamponiert, desinfiziert, genäht usw. Alles mit der Ruhe.

29.6.42 Die „hohe Moral" der deutschen Truppen macht vielen braven Antifaschisten enormes Kopfzerbrechen. Sie haben in den parlamentarischen Regierungsformen nie die Elemente der Gewalt entdeckt: die Parlamente repräsentieren den Consensus des Volkes. Jetzt ist der parlamentarische Apparat zertrümmert, und hervortritt die „nackte" (aller Verhüllung entkleidete) Gewalt. Sie erkennen diese Nudität nicht wieder … Für die unteren Volksschichten scheint die Versklavung durch die Nazis nur eine relative zu sein, d. h. das *Mehr* übt keinen wirklichen Einfluß auf das Verhalten dieser Schichten aus, wenigstens so lang nicht, als nicht gerade dieses *Mehr* das gesamte System der Sklaverei anfällig macht.[8]

---

7   "Amerika 21.7.41–31.12.41." *Werke* vol. 27: *Journale 2*, p. 109: 29. 6. 1942; cf. Haug: *Der hilflose Antifaschismus.*

8   Brecht: "Journale 1938–1941." *Werke* vol. 26: *Journale 1*, pp. 396, 30. 6. 1940: "The slow war brings about the fast one (as the inactive precipitates the active). But now this speed changes everything! whereas with the Germans it is not only a question of blitzkrieg, but also of blitz-armament. And oh what power this regime wrests from the breaking of all conventions! the most modern weapons of the sky mingle with tourist cruisers, Karl May com-

Now, the point I want to stress, taking Brecht's reflections in a certain sense as symptomatic in considering Blitzkrieg as the violent eruption of a specific group mentality and configuration among people fallen into deep crisis and despair after World War I, is what has been stressed by Karl Korsch in his war time correspondence with his friend Bertolt Brecht as "Blitzkrieg als geballte linke Energie" ("Blitzkrieg as concentrated left energy").

It was Heiner Müller who remembered this idea as a figura of the dramatic and dilemma-ridden history of German (and other) socialist movement(s). So he wrote in his preface entitled "News from Moscow" to Curzio Malaparte's war reports: "In the GDR it would have been a text of 'Aufklärung' about an aspect ignored by the ideological consensus of the workers' and peasants' state, an aspect which Karl Korsch was the first to articulate in a letter to Brecht with his thesis on Blitzkrieg as concentrated left energy."[9]

It was in the same sense, for example, that Karl Korsch in a letter (12. 3. 1942) recommends to Brecht Sidney Rogerson's book, "Propaganda in the next war," and discussed critically at some length Heinz Langerhans' "Implications of the Allied Counterblitz," where Langerhans took for granted a "world-wide equality of globally accepted Blitzkrieg tactics."[10] What is remarkable are certain affinities between this judgment of the two friends and those made by Curzio Malaparte in his war reports from the Russian front, written between June 1941 and November 1942 for the Italian "Corriere della Sera." Those reports were considered as a provocation by the Nazi propaganda officials because of Malaparte's early opinion that World War II on the

---

plements Clausewitz," p. 471: 9. 4. 1941: Again considering the driving force of the Blitzkrieg war machine: "It is as though only this army could move. It alone creates and controls the '3-D battle-zone', that has replaced the battlefield. Conventional armies will compete this way like the bobbin with the 'Spinning Jenny'. Courage is lost to the maneuverability of a vehicle, alertness is lost to punctuality, endurance to industriousness. The strategy has become surgery. An offensive country is 'opened' after it has been anesthetized, then blotted, disinfected, sutured, and so on, all in excellent time." Ibid., vol. 27: *Journale 2*, p. 109: 29. 6. 1942: "The 'high morale' of the German troops created a major headache for many well-meaning anti-fascists. they had never before encountered the elements of violence in parliamentary forms of government: the parliaments supposedly represented the consensus of the people. now the parliamentary apparatus has been torn to shreds and the naked violence (stripped of all its veils) has become visible. this nudity is no longer recognizable … For the lower social strata, enslavement by the Nazis appeared only a relative one, that is to say the intensification (of violence) did not exercise any real influence upon the behavior of these strata, at least so long as this intensification did not itself threaten the whole system of slavery."

9   Müller preface to Malaparte: *Die Wolga entspringt in Europa.*
10 Brecht-Korsch-Korrespondenz: *Brecht-Archiv-Berlin, Sign. Z* 34/42. 50–51.

Eastern front had to be seen as a war of two "worker armies," and that the morality of the Red Army was by no means inferior to that of the Wehrmacht soldiers.

As we remember, in 1932 Curzio Malaparte wrote his book *Der Staats-streich* (*The Coup d'Etat*), a comparative study of armed putchism in Europe after World War I. From the perspective of Blitzkrieg (and of Malaparte's own war reports) , these studies may illuminate an important difference and also a connection between a "total state" (or totalitarism) and "total war" as described in the famous, widely-read book by General Erich Ludendorff in 1935, Blitzkrieg being the extreme and ultimate form of "total war." Brecht and Korsch discussed the impacts of Blitzkrieg strategy while they were under the impression that the German Wehrmacht was successful in its offensive against Poland, France and the Soviet Union. They saw it as the coming into being of a new form of "strategischer Überfall," of strategic raid, qualified as such in one of the first appearances of the notion in an article published in spring 1938 by Oberstleutnant a. D. Braun in the "Militär-Wochen-blatt": "The importance of the strategic raid – called also Blitzkrieg – is nothing less than a gigantic Stoßtruppunternehmen. Everything depends on velocity and surprise."[11]After Stalingrad however, the draconic measures taken by the Nazis in order to totalize the war ("Totalisierung des Krieges" as Goebbels called it on 18 February 1943) were propagated as being the better way to shorten the war. "Totaler Krieg – kürzester Krieg!" the audience could read on the huge banner around the wall of the Sportpalast. In reality this change in the war strategy was a sort of mad drive precipitated by the prospect of the military defeat and the turning point in World War II. Thus Goebbels' statement at this moment: "Wir wissen heute ganz genau, daß der Blitz-krieg des Polen- und Westfeldzuges für den Osten nur noch eine bedingte Gültigkeit hat," was followed by the order: "Der totale Krieg ist also das Gebot der Stunde!"[12]

The Nazi war-machine took over all activities of state and civil institutions in a way described by Gilles Deleuze and Félix Guattari in "Mille Plateaux":

---

11 Militär-Wochenblatt, No. 18, 1938, p. 1135.

12 "Today we know very well that the blitzkrieg employed in the Poland and West front cam-paigns will be one of limited utility for the East" and "The total war is therefore the com-mand of the hour." Goebbels: *Reden*, vol. 2 p. 184s. On Total War see Daudet: *La guerre to-tale*; *Denkschrift des OKW* v. 4. 4. 1938 "Kriegführung als Problem der Organisation"; Forsthoff: *Der totale Staat*; Heider: "Der totale Krieg – seine Vorbereitung durch Reichs-wehr und Wehrmacht"; Jünger: *Die totale Mobilmachung*; Ludendorff: *Der totale Krieg*; Masson: *Une guerre totale 1939-1945*; Possony: *L'economia della Guerra Totale*; Virilio: *Der reine Krieg*.

Car le totalitarisme est affaire d 'Etat: il concerne essentiellement le rapport de l'E-
tat comme agencement localisé avec la machine abstraite de surcodage, qu'il effec-
tue [...]. Le totalitarisme est conservateur par excellence. Tandis que, dans le fascisme, il s'agit bien d'une machine de guerre. Et quand le fascisme se construit un
Etat totalitaire, ce n'est plus au sens où une armée d'Etat prend le pouvoir, mais au
contraire au sens ou une machine de guerre s'empare de l'Etat.[13]

This was exactly the theory of Ludendorff's book in which he responded to
the experience of World War I, criticizing Clausewitz and calling for a total
militarization of society at all levels. Or, as Malaparte wrote in his *Der Staats-
streich*, pointing out the same difference: "The police defend the state as if it
were a city; but the army attacks the state as if it were a fortress."[14]

I want to comment now briefly on two examples which may illustrate the
idea from the Korsch-Brecht-Correspondence, referring to "Blitzkrieg as
concentrated left energy." These examples may illustrate a collective mentality formed under the pressure of a configuration which had been sickening
Europe between World War I and World War II. Two examples which may
help us to consider from new perspectives what has been called recently "a bizarre compatibility of elitism and populism in fascism" and which made, as
Alice Yeager Kaplan puts it, that "the appeal of fascism had to do with its
presentation as a total state – one that could reconcile the nationalism of the
right and the syndicalist revolt of the left."[15] This perspective may help us as
well, I think, not to fall back in the traps of "helpless antifascism," facing in a
critical way the different right-wing movements of our own time.

The first example refers to the Fiume-Adventure of Gabriele d'Annunzio,
who occupied the Adriatic city of Fiume for 14 months after the famous
march from Ronchi on 11 September 1919.

The "Poet as Commander" himself, making use of the prophetic semantics of his name, saw in the Fiume-action an announcement of Mussolini's
later march to Rome in 1922. In this sense Fiume could be considered as a

---

13   Deuleuze/Guattari: *Capitalisme et Schizophrenia*, vol. 2: *Mille plateaux*, p. 281. – "Totalitaria-
     nism is a State affair: it essentially concerns the relation between the State as a localized as-
     semblage and the abstract machine of overcoding it effactuates. [...] Totalitarianism is
     quintessentially conservative. Fascism, on the other hand, involves a war machine. When
     fascism builds itself a totalitarian State, it is not in the sense of a State army taking power,
     but of a war machine taking over the State," Deleuze/Guattari: *A Thousand Plateaus: Capital-
     ism and Schizophrenia*, p. 230.
14   Malaparte: *Der Staatsstreich*, p. 125. See also Schmitt: *Die Wendung zum diskriminierenden Kriegs-
     begriff* (1938); Schmitt *Völkerrechtliche Großraumordnung mit Interventionsverbot für raumfremde
     Mächte* (1941).
15   Yeager Kaplan: *Reproductions of Banality*, p. 32.

double figure (in the sense of Erich Auerbach's concept) , connecting two
events: that of Garibaldi's march in 1862 and that of Mussolini's in 1922. As
Emilio Gentile recently pointed out in an essay on "Fascism as Political Religion" (1990), the Fiume adventure revealed a clear connection with the national movement of the Risorgimento which has been obscured by the Mussolini
movement and was later on forgotten by post-war historians for a long time.[16]
But Fiume, according to Gentile's convincing study and a recent analysis by
Hans Ulrich Gumbrecht[17] on the nationalist prophecy of this event, cannot
be seen as a mere "symbol of fascism" any more than the figure of d'Annunzio can be seen as merely one who invented much of the rhetoric and the gesture of Italian fascism. One dare not forget either the driving force of the
Garibaldian tradition which provided the elements of the large popular support for d'Annunzio's adventure, nor the force of the other one coming from
the syndicalism of Georges Sorel and which is present in the Constitution of
Fiume, known as the Carta del Carnaro.

In d'Annunzio's speeches on the eve of Fiume which constitute the collection of "La Penultima Ventura," we can see the difference between him
and Mussolini: d'Annunzio a more authentic representation of national and
social desires for emancipation while Mussolini emerges as a violent and repressive "disciplining of exuberant energies" (as the Fascist newspaper La Pa-
tria del Popolo, once wrote in November 1922)[18].

At the same time this becomes clear when we consider the notion of the
sublime, which works as a sort of leitmotiv in the speeches of d'Annunzio.
The creation "di un sublime eroe novissimo"[19] to overcome the decadent
values of western culture is carried out in the tradition of Georges Sorel. It
was he who thought that the liberal bourgeoisie had lost every sense and possibility of "sublime ethics," the moment when it adopted the Marseillaise (as
Sorel wrote metaphorically) as a mere "party hymn," a new sublime (and a
sublime politics) being possible only in relation with the emancipatory struggle of the proletariate. And this was, for Sorel, a general strike and "action di-
recte": "Pourquoi les actes de violence peuvent-ils, dans certains pays, se
grouper autour du tableau de la grève générale et produire ainsi une idéologie

---

16   Gentile: "Fascism as Political Religion." See also Hartrecht: "The Ideologies and Semiotics
     of Fascism: Analyzing Pound's Cantos"; Glucksmann: *Le discours de la guerre*; Link: "Über
     die strategische Funktion normalistischer Medien im exterministischen Krieg."

17   Gumbrecht: *I Redentori della Vittoria. Über Fiumes Ort in der Genealogie des Faschismus.* Type-
     script, 1993.

18   D'Annunzio: *La penultima ventura*, p. 135.

19   Ibid.: "of a new sublime hero."

socialiste, riche en sublime, et ne semblent-ils pas le pouvoir dans d'autres?"[20] The other example refers to the subtitle of my paper and is connected direct-ly with d'Annunzio's Fiume Action. It marks also a clear distinction between prefascist discourse and rhetoric in Italy and Germany.

In 1922 the 32 year old Eugen Ortner published a sharply polemical essay with the title *Gott Stinnes: Ein Pamphlet gegen den vollkommenen Menschen* (*God Stinnes: A Pamphlet against Perfect Man*). Today nearly forgotten, Ortner was in the twenties, mainly in southern Germany, an author of some renown, writing plays and novels in the line of Gerhart Hauptmann and Frank Wedekind. The interest and the significance of his God-Stinnes-essay lies in the fact that amidst a large mass of disillusioned post-war-writings pertaining to the per-ceived negative consequences of the Versailles treaty, against the Dolchstoß legend, amidst, therefore, all sorts of utopic visions offered to people in de-spair, Ortner proceeded to integrate those aimless energies in accordance with the principles of a totally collectivistic society, whose dignified and sub-lime symbol is Hugo Stinnes. Stinnes represents as an idolized figure the modern energies of industry and of the masses, incorporating thus the busi-nessman and the leader of the masses at the same time:

> Denn bei Stinnes und bei Lenin ist alles aufgebaut auf Massen, ist alles kollektivi-stisch, gibt es keine persönliche Kultur mehr. Auch das ist gewiß richtig, daß bei Stinnes wie bei Lenin letztlich das ganze System auf Gehorsam aufgebaut ist, oh-ne den es nie und nirgends organisierte Massen gibt.
>
> Es kann wohl auch von den schärfsten Individualisten nicht mehr bestritten werden, daß wir einer Epoche des Massenmenschen entgegengehen.[21]

Whereas at the same time in Spain an Ortega y Gasset in his essay on "Inver-tebrated Spain" (1923) wrote his diagnosis of the mass-era in a critical way, Ortner's prophecy is purely apologetic, but realistic however in pointing at the authoritarian tendencies in the post-war society of Germany (and of Europe in general). Ten years later the analysis made by a group from the Frankfurt Institute for Social Research among German workers and low-level employ-

---

20 "Why is it that in certain countries acts of violence grouiping themselves round the idea of a general strike, produce a Socialist ideology capable of inspiring sublimity, and why in oth-ers do they seem not to have that power?" Sorel: *Réflexions sur la violence*, p. 329.

21 Ortner: *Gott Stinnes: Ein Pamphlet gegen den vollkommenen Menschen*, pp. 19 and 23: "Because in Stinnes and in Lenin, everything is founded upon masses, everything is collective, and the-re is no longer any such thing as personal culture. And it is also certainly true in Stinnes as well as in Lenin that in the end the entire system is based upon obedience, without which there can and never will be organized masses. [...] It can certainly no longer be denied, even by the most extreme individualist, that we are approaching an era of the mass human being."

ees, carried out using sociological methods, revealed the dangers of a wide-spread authoritarian mentality. In the aftermath of the treaty between the German entrepreneurs and the Federation of Labor signed in November 1918, known as the "Stinnes-Legien-Treaty," Ortner's text can be read as an apologia for this treaty. More significant, however, is the rhetorical dispositif concentrating social energies in only one point: the integrated power of the machines and the masses. It is this same point which then constitutes, trans-ferred into pure destructive power, the Blitzkrieg war machine. The sublime becoming pure sublime in its fascist form: that is to say, eliminating all ele-ments such as fear, horror and critical self-consciousness which have consti-tuted since Kant the notion of the modern sublime, substituting for them pu-re monumentalism, heroism, populism and "Führer-Kult."

In a way Ortner described it as the substitution of the "totality man" by the "combinatory man," the symbolic figure of the former being d'Annunzio. Thus sounds his "good bye to d'Annunzio":

> Aus dem Erlebniskomplex eines Hugo Stinnes in den eines Gabriele d'Annunzio führt kein Weg. Nirgends erkennen wir klarer, als an diesen beiden Typen eine Welt, die Abschied nimmt und eine Welt, die kommt. Ein Mensch, der auch nur ei-nigermaßen d'Annunzio ähnlich ist, wird in fünzig Jahren in Europa nicht mehr möglich sein. Nicht, daß ich ihn irgendwie vergliche mit all den eitlen Köpfen, die ich aufgezählt habe. Von ihm scheiden wir mit der heiteren Wehmut, die der letzte Totalitätsmensch einer sterbenden, großen Kultur von uns beanspruchen darf. Stinnes vernichtet d'Annunzio, Stinnes vernichtet die Künstler.[22]

The annihilation of the artist by "God Stinnes" can be read as an image of the dissolution of the sublime: d'Annunzio's still political sublime is deconstruct-ed by "God Stinnes" as the new energetic artist, be it as politician in the figure of the fascist Führer, or in that of the commander of the Blitzkrieg war ma-chine (as for example the commander of the tank troops Heinz Guderian who considered himself an artist).

As we know, a modern concept of the sublime can be seen historically as emerging from the experience of war and of revolution. In different ways Ed-mund Burke wrote on behalf of the sublime and against the French Revolu-

---

22   Ortner: *Gott Stinnes*, p. 48: "There is no path joining Hugo Stinnes's world of experience to that of Gabriele D'Annunzio. No clearer illustration can be found of two worlds, one in decline and the other on the rise, than in these two types. In fifty years, a person who even slightly resembles D'Annunzio will no longer be possible in Europe. Not that I am com-paring him in any way with all of those vain individuals who I have listed here. We take leave of him with the kind of cheerful melancholy to which the last totalitarian member of a great, dying culture is entitled. Stinnes destroys D'Annunzio, Stinnes destroys the artists."

tion. Francisco Goya represented another figure of the sublime in his "Collosus," in the "Caprichos" and in the "Desastres de la guerra," shaping a critical sublime which in Picassos "Guernica," facing the first experience of Blitzkrieg attacks by the Nazi "Legion Condor" in 1937, opened a new era of the political sublime as art-form. The configurations of a specific fascist sublime, which according to Walter Benjamin can be considered an epicenter of the aestheticization of politics, contributed to the generalized suspicion of the sublime as conduit of ideological mystification and the operator of reification. However, the sublime it seems is more than ever with us.

> The very condition of late capitalism is to render thought (but not the writing of critical essays) impossible. Commodities circulate in a dizzying vortex of speed, simulacra hollow out a vast abyss in the place of the real; Elvis is everywhere. F. Jameson calls this a 'hysterical sublime'; Baudrillard stays cool [...]. A reminder from Kant can be this way: the sublime presents an object that exceeds cognition, and the subject experiences a mixture of pleasure and pain, pain at the incapacity of the faculties to come to terms with this object and pleasure at the capacity of the faculties to recognize their own incapacity.[23]

The apparently seamless forms of commodification that now characterize global capital, the boundless configuration of a New World Order, would present us with a dynamic sublime: the excessively large and all-present. Money in capitalism thus becomes, in Terry Eagleton's words, "an infinitely spawning signifier which has severed all relation to the real, a fantastical idealism which blots out specific value as surely as those more conventional figures of sublimity – the raging ocean, the mountain crags – engulf all particular identities in their unbound expanse."[24]

And the movement of the commodity is "an unstoppable metonymic chain in which one object refers itself to another and that to another, to infinity."[25] At the same time, the electronic technology that permits the accelerated solubility of one commodity into another, that speeds up circulation by eliminating the weight of the material in the commodity, making it more and more virtual, introduces the mathematical sublime, the unthinkably small mechanical and logical components of artificial intelligence.

These are, basically, the arguments whose roots lie in the critical theory of the Frankfurt School, which was, alongside (but in a different way) with the Toronto School of Communication, among the first to recognize the critical

---

23   Readings: "Sublime Politics: The End of the Party Line," pp. 409, 411.
24   Eagleton: *The Ideology of the Aesthetic*, p. 213.
25   Ibid., p. 212.

problems posed once information itself becomes matter for work and com-modification, once a 'culture industry' causes or allows representation to in-habit the base as well as the superstructure, confounding the distinction be-tween production and reproduction.

We may remember Adorno's assertion that "the Absolute became abso-lute horror," considering that German culture, the insistence on the autono-my of the spirit and the absolute idea of idealism, participated in a motion that culminated in Auschwitz. This is, according to Joshua Halberstam, the inhuman and cruel consequence of every idealism led to its extreme. "Kant does not entail Auschwitz. That charge would be an outrageous calumny. But Kant leads to Auschwitz. He leads to other places as well – some heroic and ennobling. But any moral theory which begins by disregarding human senti-ment, caring and sympathy, might well end in crematoria. In the legend, God takes hold of compassion and creates a world. In the twentieth-century the Nazis renounce compassion and almost destroy that world."[26]

So what about the sublime (and a politics of the sublime) in this perspec-tive? We have to distinguish a Fascist sublime in the sense of the German Na-zis who originally considered themselves to be the movement of national "Erhebung," making use of the original German term for the sublime, of the "Erhabene," and another notion of the sublime. Since "all efforts to render politics aesthetic culminate in one thing: war" (Walter Benjamin)[27], and since Kant himself had noted war as an example of the dynamic sublime in the *Kri-tik der Urteilskraft* (*Critique of Judgment*, 1790)[28], it is tempting to assume that the invocation of the sublime belongs entirely on the side of Fascism in this di-chotomy. The sublime introduces terror and death into aesthetics, Fascism seeks to return them to society having accepted terror and death as primarily aesthetic rather than political criteria. Fascism's aestheticization of politics would be the extraction of all political meaning in favor of aesthetic criteria.

Thus the depoliticization of the sublime, for which "Blitzkrieg" and its justifying discourse offers a symptomatic collective symbol (or figure), con-sists in the application of indeterminate judgments (judgments of taste) to the political as if they were determinate: we have an idea of the beautiful, and we will make society that way. The idea of beauty, for example, will find its fulfill-ment in the social order: in the ordered hierarchy alongside a return to feudal elements, to "Blut and Boden." This "backward" understanding goes hand in

---

26   Halberstam: "From Kant to Auschwitz," p. 54.
27   Benjamin: "The Work of Art in the Age of Mechanical Reproduction." Benjamin: *Illumina-tions*, p. 241. See also Hartung: "Walter Benjamins Anti-Kriegsschriften."
28   Kant: *Kritik der Urteilskraft*. Kant: *Werke* vol. 5, § 28, p. 351 (A 106).

hand with an appeal to the dynamic sublime on the grounds of technical modernization, an attempt to make society present the idea of pure energy rather than simple order. Blitzkrieg for example, as we can see by a statement made by Hitler in 1935, speaking at the Nuremburg Party Rally to foreign delegates of the League of German Girls (BDM) , which can be considered one of the first recorded allusions to the term Blitzkrieg: "I shouldn't negotiate for months beforehand and make lengthy preparations, but – as I have always done throughout my life – I should suddenly, like a flash of lightening in the night, hurl myself upon the enemy."[29]

Fascist politics of the sublime in this sense attempt to present the unpresentable, to materialize the idea of energy. The effect of such realization is to make politics entirely a matter of representation and hence of cognition, a domination which is essentially totalitarian. Fascist totalitarianism proceeds from the claim that the idea can be an object of cognition, that the law can be fully represented, so that determinate judgments can be made in reference to it. The effect of this, the essence of such "gleichgeschaltete" society (emerging in the post World War I era as a movement to "total war," "total state," "total enemy," as described and justified for example by Carl Schmitt in his 1938 text *Die Wendung zum diskriminierenden Kriegsbegriff*), is to preclude any possibility of dispute: the terror of Fascism consists in saying that we are just because we know what justice is. (Remember Göring: "Wer bei mir Jude ist, bestimme ich!," claiming against those who tried to criticize him because of his retaining a jewish director of the Lufthansa[30]). Fascism's politics of the sublime, integrating and sublimating people's fear of existence, consists in a replacement of cognition by will. Blitzkrieg is the ruthless transformation of will into violence.

In conclusion I would say that Blitzkrieg, after its success at the beginning of World War II and its failure after Stalingrad and beyond its application in further wars, has become a myth representing dangerous tendencies and sentiments of despair in the collective mind. We need not look too far in order to observe that Blitzkrieg as a concept has become something like a collective symbol. Its use may be dazzling, creating blindness, or illuminating, creating pain, which may be signs of a critical sublime.

A few examples of the current actual and metaphorical use of Blitzkrieg in that sense may suffice. During a program on German TV concerning problems of new radical movements in Germany, the reporter interviewed young members of different so-called right-wing movements. Among them a young

---

29 Quoted in Messenger: *The Art of Blitzkrieg*, p. 80.
30 Cf. Irving: *Die Tragödie der deutschen Luftwaffe*, p. 72: Feldmarschall Milch only reported Goebbel's remark; Milch himself was said to have had jews among his ancestors.

girl of about 20, Uschi, named as her hobbies: combative sports, skinheads, Germany, music – and as her nickname "Blitzkrieg." The reporter, visibly astonished, couldn't do much with this and passed by.[31]

At a big manifestation in the summer of 1994 on Berlin Alexanderplatz Käthe Reichel, famous actrice in the Brecht tradition, referred to the disaster of German unification in the cultural area in Blitzkrieg-terms:

> Alle Eroberer, ob sie nun mit Waffen, blendenden Glasperlen, Geld oder Waren in die Länder kamen, haben immer zuerst die Kultur des eroberten Landes erschlagen. Und wenn es jetzt eines beweises in Deutschland braucht, daß hier seit November ein Krieg stattgefunden hat, ein deutscher Blitzkrieg, dann ist das der Umgang der Sieger und ihrer bezahlten Vollstrecker mit der Kultur dieses Landes.[32]

In October 1990 the *London Guardian* published in its weekend edition an article by Günter Grass under the headline: "The Business Blitzkrieg." Grass explained to his English readers his well-known critical position on the German unification process and its universal significance. He mentioned that the media after the monetary union in July 1990 used the term "Blitzkrieg" in a hugely euphoric manner:

> The way in which the D-Mark has been held up as an article of faith is frightening, as if thoughtlessness could be compensated for by money […]. In both parliaments the initial State Treaty was thoughtlessly rushed through [the German term 'durchpeitschen' forms part of the Blitzkrieg semantics]. And it was frightening to read reports of success according to which the strategy of the Blitzkrieg is now showing its strength in peacetime by means of a politico-financial pincer movement.
>
> Who should not feel ever more anxious, when German recidivism is demonstrated on a daily basis, when carefully learned democratic virtues lose their market value overnight, when there is even to be unification of the State Security Services, when – once again – the largest opposition party ducks the issue because it has to worry about the slightest reproach of 'lack of patriotism'?[33]

In another context, but in the same way, Heiner Müller explained his conviction that Japan and Germany are the real winners of World War II by the ap-

---

31 Panorama, ARD, 15. 7. 1993.
32 Cf. *Neues Deutschland*, September 3, 1994, p. 1: "All conquerors, regardless of whether they came with weapons, dazzling glass beads, money, or goods, always began by destroying the culture of the conquered land. And if any proof is now necessary in Germany that since November a war has been taking place, a German blitzkrieg, then let it be the interaction of the victors and their paid enforcers with the culture of this land."
33 Grass: "The Business Blitzkrieg." *The Guardian* (London), Oct. 20–21, weekend edition, p. 6.

plication of Blitzkrieg strategies to market economy. Blitzkrieg being a result of the modern industrialization of war, "the continuation of economy by other (military) means, leading through total realization (Verwertung) of labor power in the concentration camps, to annihilation of production in extermination. Auschwitz as an industrial product."[34] Blitzkrieg, may we conclude, is seen as a sort of coupling (or crisis reducing) figure between pre-war and post-war economic struggles.

That media not only played an important role in the Blitzkrieg war machine, but have created a particular space of perception, has been related by Marshall McLuhan in his Playboy interview of 1969, describing, we could say, the shift from "ivory tower" to "control tower" as a possible orientation for our work as critical "headworkers":

> The first and most vital step of all [...] is simply to understand media and its revolutionary effects on all psychic and social values and institutions. Understanding is half the battle. The central purpose of all my work is to convey this message, that by understanding media they extend man, we gain a measure of control over them. And this is a vital task, because the immediate interface between audile-tactile and visual perception is taking place everywhere around us. No civilian can escape this environmental blitzkrieg, for there is, quite literally, no place to hide. But if we diagnose what is happening to us we can reduce the ferocity of the winds of change and bring the best elements of the old visual culture, during its transitional period, into peaceful coexistence with the new retribalized society.[35]

Whatever this McLuhan-Utopia of a new tribalism may be, his warning may be accepted, it seems to me, as a message we must become aware of when facing violence, and in view of our experience with this new electronic media Blitzkrieg of the Gulf War, that has been characterized as an "exterminate Blitzkrieg," opening up a new era in the modern history of warfare and of civil society, becoming more and more threatened by tendencies toward a "total state."

---

34 Müller: Preface to Malaparte: *Die Wolga entspringt in Europa.*

35 McLuhan: "A Candid Conversation with the High Priest of Popcult and Metaphysics of Media." *Playboy*, March 1969, p. 74.

ANDY SPENCER

The Fiftieth Anniversary of the Allied Air Raids on Dresden: A Half Century of Literature and History Writing

Abstract: The present essay isolates two distinct approaches to writing on the bombing of Dresden of February 13/14, 1945. These two approaches, is argued, have failed to meaningfully come to terms with historical processes which led to Dresden, and continue to lead to cities such as Sarajevo. The two approaches, a concentration on biography and a mythologizing of the events of February, 1945, have left the way for the imperfectly understood history of Dresden to be employed as revitalizing symbol by revisionist historian Ernst Nolte.

Rolf Hochuth's 1967 drama *Soldaten* is discussed as an example of the equation of biography with history. The primacy of such an understanding is illustrated with reference to the controversy surrounding the unveiling of a statue of Air Marshall Harris in London in 1992. One novel from the GDR and two from the BRD are discussed as examples for the mythologizing of the raids. The essay includes a brief discussion of the role played by Dresden in the Historikerstreit and concludes with Martin Walser's use of Dresden as symbol for a "lost" history in his 1991 novel *Die Verteidigung der Kindheit*.

Since April, 1993 Susan Sontag has been traveling to Sarajevo to teach and work on theatrical projects. In August of that year she spoke with journalist Alfonso Armada of *El Pais* about the significance of the city towards the end of this century. "I believe," she told him,

> that the twentieth century began here and that the twenty first will also begin here. This has been a short century. The First World War began in this city. [...] I suppose the twenty first century really began in 1989 with the suicide of the Soviet Union, but you could also say – in a more ironic way – that it began with Sarajevo because now we have a total picture of what the twentieth century was.[1]

---

1   Sontag: "Waiting for something that does not arrive." *The Guardian Weekly*, vol. 149/6, August 8, 1993, p. 24.

Sarajevo has indeed come to possess great symbolic value for the history of Europe in this century. A century which began with the War-to-end-all-Wars, triggered, however spuriously, by events in that city, is drawing to a close with yet another conflict, this time being fought in and around the Bosnian capital.

The twentieth century, Sontag makes clear, has been characterized by a continuing succession of wars, and for this reason it might seem somewhat arbitrary to single out for investigation one (albeit momentous) wartime atrocity, namely the combined British/American bombing of Dresden of February 13/14, 1945. 1995 does of course mark the 50th anniversary of the raids but the choice of Dresden was motivated not solely by the appropriateness of commemoration but by the fact that aerial bombardment has come to characterize the conduct of modern warfare: from the first experiments during the latter half of the First World War, to Guernica, to Hamburg, Dresden, Hiroshima, and Nagasaki, to Vietnam, to Panama, to Sarajevo. If we are to understand and act upon the nature of the relationship between war, violence and the modern condition, then clearly we would do well to look at the historical processes which have resulted in this uniquely modern method of destruction. While it is of course true that the raids have already received the attentions of historians and writers, it is my contention that the works produced, far from illuminating the relationship, have actually mitigated against a considered coming to terms with historical processes and consistently denied or camouflaged the uniquely modern character of aerial bombardment. It is a grim irony of the destruction of Dresden that while the writers to be discussed below were proving to be little more than distractions, the twentieth anniversary of the raids was being marked (to the day) by the launch of Operation Rolling Thunder, the sustained US air war against North Vietnam. The fiftieth anniversary, as we are all aware, is bearing witness to two further slaughters, in Bosnia and in Chechnya.

A survey of the available literature on Dresden reveals two distinct and widely-employed approaches to writing history. The first is the focusing on the question of immediate responsibility for the bombing, on, as it were, who pushed the button. Historians of Dresden have consistently opted to concentrate on biography, thereby personalizing and ahistoricizing the raids.

The second approach, to be discussed later, is the banishment of Dresden to a period which somehow stands outside the continuum of twentieth century history. In mythologizing the raids, the second group of writers has separated them from the context of the condition of modernity, and isolated them from the historical processes which led to them.

In searching for individuals responsible for the Dresden raids, the biographer-historians agree that it is clearly unsatisfactory to single out the crews of the planes which flew over Germany since they merely executed orders handed down to them on the day of operation. They represent the penultimate human link in a process which is completed by the victims on the ground. Both the crews of the planes and eye-witnesses on the ground tell us about only one facet of an historical process, and that is its end. Brecht provides an apt simile in his notes for *Mutter Courage*:

> Die Zuschauer bei Katastrophen erwarten ja zu Unrecht, daß die Betroffenen daraus lernen werden. Solang die Masse das Objekt der Politik ist, kann sie, was mit ihr geschieht, nicht als einen Versuch, sondern nur als ein Schicksal ansehen; sie lernt so wenig aus der Katastrophe wie das Versuchskarnickel über Biologie lernt.[2]

The need to look elsewhere has led the biographer-historian to attempt histories from above; histories which identify the historical subjects (the great men), parcel out guilt and tie up the loose ends of an already closed chapter. They have traced back the military chain of command in the belief that it is entirely possible to find the spot where the history of the Dresden raids started. Thus it should not be surprising that Air Marshall Sir Arthur "Bomber" Harris, and his superior, British wartime Prime Minister Winston Churchill, loom large in histories of Dresden, histories which actually reduce the bombing to an aspect of the biography of whoever of the two is cast in the role of perpetrator.

GDR historians, such as Max Seydewitz (*Zerstörung und Wiederaufbau von Dresden*, ("Destruction and Rebuilding of Dresden," 1955) were content to adhere to this model because it enabled them to ask if there was really any difference between the actions of the capitalist Churchill and the fascist Hitler. Seydewitz was certainly not alone in posing the question. In a speech to commemorate the tenth anniversary of the raids, then Minister-President Otto Grotewohl made the comparisons clear. The raids, "wurden von den anglo-amerikanischen Imperialisten aus dem gleichen imperialistischen Macht- und Eroberungswahn begangen, aus dem die deutschen Faschisten den Zweiten Weltkrieg inszenierten."[3]

Poet Max Zimmering identified the raids as fundamentally capitalist in nature:

> War Dresdens Sterben letztes Strafgericht?
> War es gerechten Zornes letzter Fluch?

---

2 Brecht: "Anmerkung zu 'Mutter Courage und Ihre Kinder'." *Werke* vol. 24: *Schriften 4. Texte zu Stücken*, p. 264: "The observers of catastrophes unjustly expect the victims to learn something. For as long as the masses remain the object of politics, they will regard what happens to them not as an experiment, but as fate; they learn as much from a catastrophe as the guinea pig learns of biology."
3 Grotewohl: *Der Morgen*, vol. 11/38, February 15, 1955.

> War da kein Stempel auf dem Leichentuch?
> Kein Dollar-Zeichen? Sagt, wer sah es nicht?[4]

Such an argumentation opened the way for a linking of the destructive nature of capitalism/fascism with the western-oriented Federal Republic. Once this enemy image had been created it was a relatively simple matter to contrast it with the life-affirming, regenerative power of socialism by drawing attention to the rebuilding of the city. Zimmering again,

> Der Zwingerbau mit seinen Todesschwären,
> er, den Barbaren aus den "freien" Staaten
> mit ihren Bombenstiefeln niedertraten,
> begann dem Licht sein Antlitz zuzukehren.[5]

During the first half of the 1950's it was this symbolic value of Dresden's reconstruction which was trumpeted in the GDR and the fact that no histories of the raids appeared in the ten years following Seydewitz's work[6] can be attributed chiefly to the snail's pace of reconstruction after the much-heralded re-opening of the Zwinger in 1955 – the paeans of praise to the reborn city simply ceased to ring true.

In the Federal Republic the raids were treated only slightly more subtly. The first book-length historical study to appear, Axel Rodenberger's *Der Tod von Dresden* ("The Death of Dresden") of 1951, was claimed by its author to be entirely free of tendentiousness. Writing in 1977, however, Götz Bergander dismissed Rodenberger's claim of objectivity and described the text more accurately as a narrative touching on actual events.[7]

Rodenberger also claimed that his history was not a charge against this person or that.[8] In the light of such a claim it is instructive to follow the course of the book's reprintings, to which the author each time added new prefaces and afterwords. By the eighth edition of 1963, all pretensions of re-

---

4   Zimmering: "Frage und Antwort." *Im herben Morgenwind*, p. 277: "Was Dresden's dying a final judgement? / Was it righteous anger's last curse? / Wasn't there a stamp on the winding sheet? / A dollar sign? Say, who didn't see it?"

5   Zimmering: "Melodie an der Elbe." Ibid, p. 299: "The Zwinger building with its sores of death, / that, which the barbarians of the "free" nations / had trampled with their boots made of bombs, / began to turn its face to the light."

6   Former Dresden Mayor Walter Weidauer's *Inferno Dresden* of 1965 (reprinted 1987) is the only major post-Seydewitz history.

7   Bergander: *Dresden im Luftkrieg*, p. 129: "eine auf wahren Vorkommnisen beruhende Erzählung."

8   Rodenberger: *Der Tod von Dresden*, p. 11: "keine Anklage ... gegen diesen oder jenen."

sisting the urge to aportion blame had vanished. Rodenberger added an afterword which answered a still open, but legitimate question: Who gave the order for the destruction of Dresden?[9]

In Rodenberger's view the raids were motivated purely and simply by hatred for all things German on the part of the British military command, particularly Harris. This hatred was present also at Yalta and the author concluded his new afterword, which of course followed a narrative detailing German suffering, with the following disingenuous comparison:

> Durch diesen Vertrag wurden aber Millionen Deutscher entrechtet und Millionen gezwungen, ihre Heimat zu verlassen. Die Erklärung der Kollektivschuld aller Deutschen ergab das scheinbare Recht der Vertreibung, das genausowenig eine Berechtigung hatte, als wenn man den noch in der Ostzone verbliebenen Deutschen eines Tages die Kollektivschuld für Ulbrichts Regime auferlegen wollte.[10]

Rodenberger sowed seeds which David Irving, among others, harvested. Irving is an English historian and Nazi sympathizer, now lacking in any credibility, who nevertheless continues to cut a high public profile. It was he who in 1977 proposed that Hitler had known nothing of the Holocaust, and who as recently as July 7, 1992, told the English *Guardian* newspaper that the Holocaust was "a legend built on baloney." Such sentiments are not to be found in *The Destruction of Dresden* (1963), but this book can indeed be viewed as one of the first steps in what has become a full-scale revisionist argument. It paved the way most effectively by foregrounding German suffering and contrasting it with the ruthlessness of the Allies. Yet even in this Irving exaggerated his case, for three years after the book's appearance the author was forced to concede in a letter to *The Times* (July 7, 1966) that the casualty figures in Dresden were "very much lower than those I quoted." Irving's recounting of events sparked great controversy because of the author's insistence on Churchill's culpability. He was roundly condemned by the British establishment for sullying the name of the wartime leader, but should perhaps be better rebuked for having determined for years to come the parameters for debate on Dresden.

---

9 Ibid., p. 14: "das eine offen gebliebene, aber auch berechtigte Frage beantwortet: 'Wer gab den Befehl zur Vernichtung Dresden?'"

10 Ibid, pp. 197–98: "By this treaty millions of Germans were dispossessed and millions forced to leave their homeland. The declaration of the collective guilt of all Germans provided seeming justification for the expulsions, a justification as baseless as would be the attempt in the future to saddle those Germans who have remained in the Eastern zone with collective guilt for Ulbricht's regime."

In both Britain and Germany the centrality of biography, and specifically Churchill was again enforced with the appearance in 1967 of Rolf Hochhuth's *Soldaten*. Hochhuth relied on, and worked with Irving in researching his morality drama, although it should be noted here that the playwright soon distanced himself from the historian once the latter's revisionist intentions became clearer.

Hochhuth's stated aim in writing *Soldaten* was to dramatize the need for aerial bombardment to be covered by the provisions of the Geneva Convention. The playwright had written an open letter to Federal Republic President Lübke in 1964, as the twentieth anniversary of the Dresden raids approached and also the centenary of the original signing of the Geneva Convention, appealing to him to agitate for the change. When the letter failed to achieve results he turned to the stage.

Soldaten is often called the "Churchill Play" and for good reason. Rarely is the Prime Minister off stage. Hochhuth's relationship to Churchill was ambivalent: he viewed the British PM as a glorious war-time leader who was the most decisive influence in the defeat of Nazi Germany, but who also, in a phrase reminiscent of Grotewohl's comments cited above, sunk to Hitler's level ("sich auf Hitlers Niveau herabbegab").[11] Here is the stuff of tragedy. Hochhuth's Schillerian drama personifies the tragic decisions which must be made during wartime in the historical characters of Churchill, Polish Prime Minister in exile Sikorski, and others, in an attempt to show that unless there is legal proscription acts of atrocity will be carried out during times of war also by a power with right on its side. The play suffers, however, owing to the inconsistency of its structure, that of a play-within-a-play. In the Prologue we see the preparations for a performance of "The Little London Theater of the World" ("Das Londoner Kleine Welttheater"), which is being staged in the ruins of Coventry Cathedral to commemorate the two anniversaries which Hochhuth had himself marked with his letter to Lübke. The author/director of this play, Dorland, who twenty years previously had flown in the raid on Dresden and had been forced to bail out over the city, is introduced as a latter-day Everyman. Everyman has become a soldier. But as soon as "Das Londoner Kleine Welttheater" begins the Everyman theme disappears and we are confronted with Churchill, the man pushing the globe with his forehead ("der Mann, der mit der Stirn den Erdball bewegt"),[12] an almost mythological figure

---

11   Hochhuth: "Vom Soldaten zum Berufsverbrecher." *Krieg und Klassenkrieg*, pp. 106–29, here p. 115.

12   Hochhuth: *Soldaten*, p. 77.

in Hochhuth's hands. The play-within-the- play is fundamentally inconsistent with the Prologue.

The situations surrounding two decisions of Churchill's made during the summer of 1943 are the subject matter of the play- within-the-play: the fire-bombing of Hamburg (although it is Dresden which is "shown" on stage through Hochhuth's use of a photograph of the carnage in that city as back projection), and the imputed murder of the Polish Prime Minister. Decisions made during times of war, Hochhuth would like to show, can be possessed of a tragic dimension. The "murder" of Sikorski, for example, was deemed necessary by Churchill in order that good relations with Stalin be maintained and the fight against Nazi Germany continued. Yet no such dimension is given to the bombing raids and one is left with the distinct impression that Churchill is the single responsible individual, a man who mercilessly bombed civilians over the protests of religious leaders and others who had appealed for an end to the slaughter. The pairing of the two decisions appears forced and the parallels between them are never clear. The play is further weakened by the fact that the imputed murder of Sikorski has never been proven and its inclusion struck many at the time as little more than an attack on the person of Churchill. The outcry which resulted from Hochhuth's imputation (based on information from Irving, who subsequently published his own study of the Sikorski incident) focused attention squarely on the biography of Churchill, not the history of Dresden.

In the United States Dresden entered the public consciousness by way of Kurt Vonnegut's 1969 novel *Slaughterhouse Five*. This work, along with Joseph Heller's *Catch 22*, was seized upon by those opposed to the Vietnam War as an expression of the "absurdist tenor of the modern revulsion."[13] In the European context, however, Vonnegut's maxim from the first chapter of the novel, "there is nothing intelligent to say about a massacre,"[14] translated into almost complete silence on the subject of the raids.

With the exception of Bergander's *Dresden im Luftkrieg*, and Alexander McKee's *Dresden 1945: The Devil's Tinderbox* (1982), the '70s and '80s saw little interest in the bombing. Predictably it was not until the surfacing of another biographical controversy that the raids came back into view. In perhaps the most incendiary chapter of Anglo-German relations since the war, a statue of Air Marshall Harris was erected in London in May, 1992 in callous disregard for German feelings. The statue was intended to honor the dead of Bomber

---

13   Amis: "Kurt Vonnegut: After the Slaughterhouse." *The Moronic Inferno*, pp. 132–37, here p. 135.

14   Vonnegut: *Slaughterhouse Five*, p.19.

Command, but in its decision to place Harris on a pedestal and not, for example, an unknown airman or, better yet, a grieving victim, it certainly seemed as if the sponsoring veterans' group of Bomber Command Association, fully sanctioned by the British establishment, had decided that it was time to respond in kind for any doubts which still lingered about the morality of the actions of Britain's wartime leaders.

The statue (cost $ 180,000) was unveiled during a "private" ceremony which was nevertheless attended by the entire Royal Air Force hierarchy, the Queen Mother in her capacity as patron of the Bomber Command Association, and former Prime Minister Mrs. Thatcher. Described by the *Guardian* newspaper (June 1, 1992) as "an uncompromisingly bullish likeness of Harris, chin and chest jutting, legs thrust apart," the nine feet high statue also bore an inscription, "honoring him and Bomber Command's 55,000 dead but leaving out references to civilian victims of bombings which peace groups and a group of German mayors had requested." Bomber Command Association rode roughshod over all complaints, exhibiting its own insensitivity most strikingly in the comments of Association Secretary Douglas Radcliffe who parried criticism by asking, "You don't think (the Germans would) be doing this if the Berlin Wall hadn't come down, do you?" (*Guardian*, May 18, 1992)

The signals sent to the rest of the world by this whole appallingly orchestrated affair were clear. First, as Humphrey Fisher pointed out in *The Observer* (May 24, 1992), that Britain felt no contrition; second, as noted by John Harris in a letter to the *Guardian Weekly* (June 28, 1992), that Britain wished to perpetuate "the myths that war can be waged with honor and that national pride is an unmitigated virtue"; third, that British history would continue to be written through identification with the perpetrators alone.[15]

In 1993 the pendulum swung away from Harris and back to Churchill again. English historian John Charmley's biography of the PM argues that he was wrong to go to war with Nazi Germany because he thereby brought about Britain's future dependence on the economic power of the United States. Charmley cites David Irving but is careful to distance himself from the disgraced historian by way of a defensive footnote: "It is perhaps necessary to say that Mr. Irving is cited only when his sources have been checked out and

---

15   As a side note, the controversy over monuments shows no sign of letting up. A mere five months after the Harris affair German aerospace organizations were forced to cancel a planned ceremony commemorating the 50th anniversary of the launch of the first V-2 rocket. The ceremony was to have been attended by a junior minister in Chancellor Kohl's government, but despite the city of Peenemünde's argument that it needed the tourism, international protests forced the organizers to back down.

seem reliable. [...] The current author admires Mr. Irving's assiduity, energy and courage, even if he differs from him in his conclusions."[16]

In reviewing the biography in the *Guardian Weekly* (September 12, 1993), John Lukacs mused as to the exact nature of the difference between the two historians, citing examples from Charmley's text of similarities with Irving: Churchill's father was "bank-rolled by his Jewish friends," Winston by "wealthy Jews" and an "ardent Zionist." Charmley asks if Churchill was not the "'hired help' (Irving) for a Jewish lobby, which, regarding Jewish interests as superior to those of the British Empire, was determined to embroil that Empire in a war on their behalf?" Lukacs rightly calls the study "denigration by a pamphleteer."

Despite the low regard in which Charmley's book is held there are no signs that biography will not continue as the dominant model for the writers of popular history. The writing of history has been devalued to an ever-continuing series of claims and counter-claims which grab newspaper headlines but ultimately lead us nowhere.

The second approach in writing about Dresden, the consignment of it to a period somehow existing outside of history, has had an equally debilitating effect on our understanding of the place of the air raid in the world of the twentieth century. The determination in the GDR that the history of Nazi Germany was a legacy with which the FRG alone had to struggle, combined with the headlong rush into the new socialist society, left Dresden consigned to pre-history. Wilhelm Rudolph, a Dresden graphic artist who produced a remarkable series of sketches and woodcuts of the destroyed city which were subsequently criticized for being behind the time and its progressive tendencies,[17] noted in a 1981 interview that this charge forward meant: "Es war einem ganzen Volke nicht gestattet, um seine Toten zu trauern, nach einem opferreichen Kriege."[18]

The open sore that was the memory of Dresden was not aided by crudely ideologized literary treatments of the theme such as Max Zimmering's 1954 novel *Phosphor und Flieder. Vom Untergang und Wiederaufstehung der Stadt Dresden* ("Phosphorus and Lilac. The Destruction and Resurrection of the city of Dresden"). The novel actually has very little to do with "Untergang" since the raids are over within the first thirty pages of a work which stretches to over five hundred. The subject matter of Zimmering's text is the rebuilding of the city which, as mentioned above, served as symbol for the regenerative powers

---

16   Charmley: *Churchill: The End of Glory*, p. 675.

17   E. L.: "Ruinenromantik. Ruinendämonie," p. 18.

18   Drescher: "Der Alte Wilhelm Rudolph," p. 970: "An entire people had not been allowed to mourn for its dead after a war which had claimed so many victims."

of socialism. One could easily be led to believe that history began in 1945 with the arrival of the Soviet troops in Dresden and the end of the war, and that violence and destruction are solely Western phenomena.

Wolfgang Paul wrote similarly schematized and ideologically charged novels in the West, but with the opposite intent: he concentrated his attention on the Soviet occupation of the city after 1945 and declared, in the novel *Dresden 1953*, that Dresden had been destroyed twice: "Einmal in der Nacht, in der sie Bomben zerstörten, und noch einmal unter den fremden Truppen, die sich in der Stadt auf Jahrzehnte einrichteten."[19] For both Zimmering and Paul the raids pre-date the real story of Dresden.

More instructive than these works, however, are two novels which appeared in the Federal Republic in 1949: Bruno Werner's *Die Galeere* ("The Slave Galley") and Erhart Kästner's *Das Zeltbuch von Tumilat* ("The Tent Book of Tumilat"). They deserve attention because they illustrate well an ahistoricization of Dresden which actually began immediately after the raids with the appearance in the Nazi Press of Gerhart Hauptmann's unsolicited eulogy for his beloved city. Nowhere in this piece does Hauptmann actually describe the raids but instead he begins the mythologizing of them, incorporating references to both the Bible – "Sodom und Gomorra-Höllen der englischen und amerikanischen Flugzeuge" – and Classical mythology.[20] From the text it is not even evident that the destruction occurred during wartime. The Western Allies are condemned for their Godless act but no mention is made of context. Thomas Mann, keeping a diary in his Californian exile, succinctly laid bare the false premise of Hauptmann's piece: "Hauptmann [...] vergoß Tränen [...] über Dresden. Über sonst nichts."[21]

Both Werner and Kästner, who incidentally served for two years as Gerhart Hauptmann's personal secretary, assign two important roles to the destruction of Dresden. First, it is offered as evidence of the suffering of non-Nazi Germany. Even though Kästner was in uniform, both writers claim for themselves the moral highground of the innocent bystander, unable to act alone against the all-powerful forces of evil. The destruction of the city (for Kästner) and of the city and its inhabitants (for Werner) represent the pin-

---

19 Paul: *Dresden 1953*, p. 36: "Once in the night, in which it was destroyed by bombs, and once again under the foreign troops who had established themselves in the city for decades to come."

20 Hauptmann: "Dresden." *Sämtliche Werke* vol. 11, pp. 1205–06, here p.1205: "Sodom and Gomorrah hells of the English and American airplanes."

21 Mann: *Tagebücher 1944–1. 4. 1946*, p. 206: "Hauptmann shed tears for Dresden. For nothing else."

nacle of retribution for Nazi crimes and proof that penance had been paid. From this is developed the second role, which sees Dresden representing the closing of a period of history, an anomalous period which can now be consigned to the margins. This is particularly evident in Kästner's autobiographical novel. From the distance of a British-administered prisoner of war camp in immediate post-war Tumilat, Egypt, Kästner and a fellow prisoner collect as much information as they can about the destroyed cultural treasures of Europe, with particular emphasis on Dresden, and "einen Katalog dessen zu machen, was nicht mehr da war – einen Unkatalog also."[22]

Kästner sets about recreating for himself the pre-war Europe of his memory, refusing to see the war itself as anything other than an intrusion into history of an other-worldly force. The destruction of Dresden, he writes, was something special which Satan had saved for last ("Den Untergang dieser Stadt schien sich der Satan als etwas Besonderes bis zum Schlusse aufgehoben zu haben").[23] And what of Kästner's own complicity in the destruction? His only crime was that of belonging to an age in which such destruction occurred. In fact he goes so far as to say that he himself had escaped that time by way of his literary endeavors.[24] After the interlude of the destructive forces ("die zerstörenden Mächte") is over, Kästner chooses to rejoin the world and history is allowed to start up again, picking up on the tradition which was interrupted. It is not clear, however, if the interruption began in 1933 or 1939.

Werner's novel also posits the existence of mythical forces deciding the course of events. The angels Metos and Seragul are sent to earth to unleash terrible suffering and test the faith of protagonist Georg Forster and other slaves like him on the galley that is Nazi Germany. Dresden in the novel represents the apotheosis of suffering for these slaves, the final act of a tragedy whose outcome they were in no position to influence. Again, penance is shown to have been paid and a chapter of history is closed as the little man ends the novel heading into a hopeful sunset. The book's popular success attested to the resonance of Werner's wish-history. The writer himself went on to become the Federal Republic's cultural attaché in Washington DC between 1954 and 1961, after which he assumed the post of President of the German PEN Center.

---

22   Kästner: *Zeltbuch von Tumilat*, p. 103: "make a catalogue of that, which was no longer there – a non-catalogue, as it were."

23   Ibid., p. 106.

24   Kästner: *Ölberge, Weinberge: Ein Griechenlandbuch*, p. 36: "So war ich aus der Zeit ausgestiegen. Muß man schon in der Zeit sein, ist es gut wenn man hier und da aussteigen kann."

Overseas critics of the novel were not so sure of its virtues. Robert Pick, writing in the *Saturday Review of Literature* (June 9, 1951), succinctly summed up protagonist Forster as "smaller than the sum total of his sufferings."

Clearly, neither Kästner nor Werner offer any kind of understanding of the raids and indeed push them further away from view. Which is essentially where they stayed for the overwhelming majority of West Germans. Yet precisely because the raids remained under-researched, they retained from these early post-war years the symbolic values of marking the end of something and of settling accounts. This symbolic value was never far from just below the surface in discussions of Dresden and was tapped again, despite the passing of the years, by contributors to the Historikerstreit of the 1980's, wherein Dresden was occasionally pressed into service as relativizing symbol by those who would argue against the uniqueness of the Holocaust. While an in-depth look into the employment of Dresden in the Historikerstreit lies beyond the scope of this essay, I think it pertinent to the topic at hand to note that it was the Dresden raids as symbol of specifically Allied atrocity which was exploited by the revisionist historians. The aim of such an approach to history, as stated by Ernst Nolte, Michael Stürmer, and others during the time of the Historikerstreit, has been to create a German history which de-emphasizes the importance of the Holocaust. In its crudest form, the revisionist argument balances one crime-against-humanity against another, thereby negating them both. In defending the 1986 visit of then President Reagan to the military cemetery in Bittburg, Nolte argued that although that visit had prompted an emotional debate on German history, the fear of being accused of settling old scores, indeed the fear of making comparisons at all, had resulted in one very simple question remaining unasked: "[…] was es bedeutet haben würde, wenn der damalige Bundeskanzler sich 1953 geweigert hätte, den Soldatenfriedhof von Arlington zu besuchen, und zwar mit der Begründung, dort seien auch Männer begraben, die an den Terrorangriffen gegen die deutsche Zivilbevölkerung teilgenommem hätten."[25] In a response, Jürgen Habermas rejected such a comparison and wondered at the naiveté ("Unbefangenheit") of an internationally renowned German historian such as Nolte balancing Auschwitz against Dresden.[26]

---

25 Nolte: "Vergangenheit, die nicht vergehen will." *Historikerstreit*, pp. 29–47, here p. 42: "what it would have meant if in 1953 the chancellor of the Federal Republic had refused to visit the national cemetery in Arlington, arguing that men were buried there who had participated in terror attacks on the German civilian population."

26 Habermas: "Vom öffentlichen Gebrauch der Historie." *Historikerstreit*, pp. 243–55, here p. 245- 46.

In recent years the author Martin Walser has proved as controversial as Nolte. In 1988 Walser had claimed for himself a blameless childhood: he had been a six to eighteen year old who had not noticed Auschwitz.[27] Yet this innocent childhood had been wrongfully stripped from him, and in his 1991 novel *Die Verteidigung der Kindheit* ("In Defense of a Childhood") it is stripped from his protagonist, Dresden-born Alfred Dorn. Dresden is depicted not as the end of a period of history (à la Werner) but as the beginning of a period of unjust German punishment which continued with the division of Germany. In the same 1988 essay cited above Walser labeled the division a punishment ("Straf-Aktion")[28] which had served its purpose. Germany should be allowed to unify on the basis of a history which stretches back not just to 1871 but a thousand years. The bombings and division had destroyed the continuum of German history. The necessity of resurrecting that continuum is personified in the novel in the character of Alfred Dorn, a six to eighteen year old during the Nazi period, who becomes obsessed in his later life with recovering his lost childhood, all physical traces of which had been destroyed in the firestorm at Dresden. The mementos he most dearly misses are photographs and home movies from before 1945: "One should not complain about two dozen photo albums and three films, when between 100 and 200,000 people are killed. But he nevertheless wanted to have the pictures back."[29]

Dorn castigates himself for not having taken the time to search for his "history" after the bombing and realizes that his own ambitions to leave Dresden and study law had caused him to neglect the search, just as the economic ambitions of the FRG had caused it to switch attention from its past to the future. The effects of this switch of attention are dramatized in the person of Dorn to suggest fatal consequences: he dies, clutching in his hand a biography of Kaspar Hauser. German history is shown as victim and one wonders what becomes of the true victims of Nazism. The answer is that there is no place for them in Walser's symbolic tale.

The combined result of the various roles into which Dresden has been massaged into playing is a woefully inadequate understanding of a defining characteristic of modern warfare. Whether the raids are assigned to the margins of biography, placed within the confines of an imaginary history, or employed as relativizing symbol, they are each time separated from the context of modernity. For as long as this particular context remains unexplored it is to

---

27 Walser: "Über Deutschland reden. Ein Bericht." *Über Deutschland reden*, pp. 76–100, here p. 76: "Ein sechs- bis Achtzehnjähriger, der Auschwitz nicht bemerkt hatte."

28 Ibid, p. 83.

29 Walser: *Die Verteidigung der Kindheit*, p. 197.

be feared that aerial bombardment and the slaughter of civilians will continue to be viewed as arbitrary, unforeseeable, and thus inescapable.

Andrea Slane
Old Dominion University

Sexy Nazis and Daddy's Girls:
Fascism and Sexuality in Film and Video since the 1970s

Abstract: Since its arrival on the political scene of the 1920's in Germany, national socialism has been written, imaged and theorized in relation to "abnormal" sexuality by its critics across the globe. This article examines the last twenty-five years of the ongoing association, by considering the prominent trope of the incestuous father/daughter dyad. In charting the recent history of uses of these images, "Sexy Nazis and Daddy's Girls" reveals shifts in the rhetorical manipulation of gender, sexuality, and feminism for divergent political agendas in the United States, and thus exposes the changing functions of fascism for contemporary political and social debates.

SS Kommandant Amon Goeth, the central Nazi character of Steven Spielberg's multiple-academy award winning *Schindler's List* (1993) has a penchant for random acts of violence and sexual debauchery. Goeth's actions, presented in stark relief against the miserable existence of the film's Jewish victims, are generalized to the underlying moral laxity of the Nazis overall. Spielberg's camera stays tight on Goeth's hands as he nearly caresses then strikes his Jewish maid, cutting to match movement on the seductive advances of an opulently-clad nightclub singer as she approaches Oskar Schindler. Spielberg welds together sexual and political excess, making *Schindler's List* the most recent example of a long history of deeply contradictory images of Nazis that developed both out of the 20th century's liberal humanist preoccupation with sexual explanations for human behavior, and a mostly conservative tendency toward reading acts of immorality willy-nilly across different moral registers (social, political, and religious).[1]

---

1   This article is a summary of several chapters of my dissertation, *The Erotics of Violence: Sexy Nazis and the Transformation of Psycho-Sexual Explanation and Political Rhetoric in Film, Video and Fiction, 1930-1994*.

In 1972, raunchy transvestite folk dancers in lederhosen spanked themselves in *Cabaret*'s Kit Kat Klub as Nazi brownshirts brutally beat the nightclub owner. In 1993, Schindler wins his first round of Nazi friends by throwing a raucous drunken party with loose women and dancing girls in bowling derbies, tuxedo jackets and hotpants, as countless Jews are herded and harassed. These two film blockbusters, *Schindler's List* and Bob Fosse's *Cabaret*, represent two comparable moments twenty years apart on the more than seventy year history of the association of German fascism with sexual license. The crosscutting of sexual play and political brutality are structurally similar in these two films, their anti-fascist critique resting on these direct juxtapositions to underscore their moral conclusions. Yet it would be a mistake to assume that the politics of images of sexualized Nazis has not changed over the course of these twenty years. There are significant differences in the climates of the production and reception of these films and others, which can help flesh out some of the transformations in the relationship between sexual and political morality in the second half of this century.

German fascism is a highly examined phenomenon in the nexus of sexual, political and ethical knowledge, providing both an historical and an imaginary locus for problematizing sexuality and violence. The long history of intellectual fascination with the sexuality of German fascism stems partly from the fact that Germany was the most active seat of developments in sexual theories in the late 19th and early 20th century.[2] Nazi writings and policy grew out of another version of the fascination, namely panic around the degradation of German "blood" through miscegenation and venereal disease (blamed on Jews), both of which are strikingly prominent specters in Hitler's *Mein Kampf*. Outrage against the policies of the Nazis outside of Germany very often shared this belief in a world wracked with sex-based moral decay, but focused on Nazism's own violations of traditional family and religious values.[3] From the outset, the variety of political aims achieved from understanding German fascism through sexuality informed one another, creating a large field of sex-

2 The early merger of psychology (especially psychoanalysis) and political theory around German fascism includes work by Wilhelm Reich (*The Mass Psychology of Fascism*), Erich Fromm and the Frankfurt School (*Studies on Authoritarianism*), and rather indirectly by Sigmund Freud in *Civilization and its Discontents*. These political theories grew out of the prominence of Germany in the development of Sexology through figures like Magnus Hirschfeld, Karl Westphal and Richard von Krafft-Ebing.

3 See for instance Ramona M. Rose's study *The Position and Treatment of Women in Nazi Germany: As viewed from the perspective of the English Language press 1933-1945*. For a conservative report on Nazi family policy that tacitly approves of some of their concerns to garner women for reproduction see *Nazi Germany: its women and family life* by Clifford Kirkpatrick.

ual knowledge, beliefs, and lore around the "sexy" Nazi. As such, German fascism serves as a rich example of the pliability of political rhetoric around sexuality more generally, in which liberal and conservative rhetoricians pirate concepts from each other.

The development of psychology and psychiatry in the nineteenth century was contemporaneous to the cultural production of the novel; the development of sexology should likewise be seen as occurring in a cultural context invested in the production of texts revolving around sex. The genesis of the Sexy Nazi has everything to do with the twentieth century ascendancy of sexuality as a primary locus of human behavior from which to establish motives and through which to express them. Political morality (i. e. the protection of human rights) and sexual morality (i. e. what is not permissible) could not be kept distinct in this climate. Film theories, reviews and popular journalism around films invariably reveal broader cultural beliefs about morality, not unlike the judicial system, where moral decisions are handed down through verdicts, or the legislature, where policy decisions about the use of public funds for sexually related services are spoken through moral arguments. Using selected examples of films and videos in which the "sexy Nazi" appears, in what follows I will examine the critical apparatus around these texts as they provide a portrait of the moral uses to which this figure has been put, and thus illustrate how film and video functions within a history of rhetoric on sexuality.

The long-standing practice of spreading sexual propaganda against enemies of war is one place where one might expect to have seen the sexualized Nazi. Indeed, Magnus Hirschfeld et al's 1930 study *The Sexual History of the World War* used evidence garnered from leaflets, letters, newspaper articles and other sources that depicted the various players in World War One as "perverts" to expose this moral aspect of warfare. As they write in the chapter on "Propaganda and Sex Lies,"

> [...] French artists and journalists all made it appear as though they seriously believed that all Germans, without exception, were homosexual. The Germans revenged themselves by asserting that all the other aberrations of psychopathia sexualis were French specialties.[4]

But in the case of the Nazis in the next World War, this sexualization became more intense after they were defeated, as they would subsequently come to be associated with "perversion" in general. Since war time climates inflame such tendencies to incite hatred against enemies, what is significant is that this enemy (to some measure severed from the German people, to some measure

---

4   Magnus Hirschfeld et al.: *The Sexual History of the World War,* p. 282.

not) came to serve so many uses in the *post*-war sexual/political arena. German fascism is thus a unique figure in the dual histories of sexuality and politics; it is a premiere example for sexual theories of political behavior, and more directly, it became a rich terrain for noting rhetorical uses of sexuality for political ends.

The role of the film industry in these histories is pernicious. By the end of the war, the politically motivated emigration of many members of the European film industry had insured a high output of anti-fascist films in the United States. When these films featured women, they quite regularly fixed on the story of a young girl compelled into state-enforced promiscuity in keeping with the most common conservative sex-based critique of fascism that it destroyed the family.[5] At war's end, the overtly propagandistic function of these films of course ended, but production of films featuring Nazis and their sexual impropriety by no means did. Instead Nazis took on a longer list of potential perversions in the image bank of post-war cinema.[6] The film industry's simultaneously growing love affair with psychology would permanently meld these Nazis and psycho-sexology, producing an ever growing catalogue of Nazi characters whose actions were narratively explained via conscientious deployment of psycho-sexual information.

In this paradigm, psycho-sexual information ostensibly either explains how ordinary (read morally justifiable) desires can become entangled with out-of-the-ordinary violence, or else exposes the cruelty potentially present in all human relationships. But what it masks is how sexuality operates epistemologically, that is, precisely as an explanation or knowledge system, that obscures as well as illuminates other ways of understanding the same information.[7] Sex-based behavioral theories can become decoy "solutions" to

---

5 See Jan-Christopher Horak's *Anti-Nazi-Filme der deutschsprachigen Emigration von Hollywood 1939-1945*. Horak does not discuss the function of sexuality in these films per se, but his short analyses of films like *Women in Bondage* and *Hitler's Children* can be read with a view to extracting the anti-fascist critique of Nazi morality.

6 For example Roberto Rossellini's *Rome: Open City* (1945) and Alfred Hitchcock's *Notorious* (1946), produced under very different circumstances, elaborate imaginatively on sexual themes. Rossellini makes his two key Nazis homosexual and sadistic; Hitchcock uses tangled Nazi Oedipal relations as the thrilling backdrop for the manipulative relationship between the film's hero and heroine. The use of sexual peril in film narrative of course dates back practically to its inception: its political use is certainly evident in films such as D. W. Griffith's *Birth of a Nation* (1915), to invoke a familiar example.

7 Psychology often provides the answer to vexing turns of plot, motives for unlikely criminals, resolutions for post-climactic denouements (i. e. Hitchcock's *Spellbound* (1945)). Michel Foucault writes in *The History of Sexuality* (1976) that while Western society has come to believe in the "truth" offered up by the sexual version of any story, sexuality ceases to re-

insoluble problems. In the case of Nazism, the primary theory involves the interchangeability of sex and violence, which for women involves a slippage between pleasure and abuse. The emphasis on female masochism appears as the most fundamental problem for women's sexual subjectivity.[8]

The most common figures in the list of diagnosed Sexy Nazi players are the Daddy and the Daddy's Girl. Oskar Schindler is one such Daddy; Helena Hirsch, the maid, one such girl. The staging of the above scene from *Schindler's List* is parallel to a very similar earlier scene which features our soon-to-be-transformed hero Schindler similarly interacting with Hirsch. Again located in the dark and expressively lit basement, Schindler instills sexual fear in the quivering young girl. In what is supposed to be read as a gesture of magnanimity, he offers her chocolate and kisses her on the forehead despite her obvious physical protest, saying "it's not that kind of kiss." With the megalomaniacal statement "I am Schindler," Spielberg's character is awash in a sea of sexual ambiguity, in which Schindler's creepy paternalism is deployed as a sign of his later potential for dubious heroism, while at the same time linking him to the kind of materialism and pleasure-oriented license the film attaches to Nazi brutality more generally.

This paternal sexuality is part of an ongoing prominence of the figure of incest in films and videos featuring Nazis, insuring that the image is anything but *simply* benevolent. Sally Bowles cries when she's stood up by her father in *Cabaret*; Lucia of Liliana Cavani's *The Night Porter* (1974) dons a little girl's dress to pair her partner Max's SS uniform; Gabrielle, the skinhead's moll in Geoffrey Wright's *Romper Stomper* (1992), sicks her boyfriend's neo-Nazi gang on her sexually abusive father. These figures comment on whether women can be entrusted with authority, what role they play in their own victimization, and whether their participation in political movements is intellectually or sexually driven, generally with the intent of denigrating their choices in the latter. Depictions of women entangled with Nazism illustrate some of the varied functions psycho-sexual explanation continues to play in the realm of political behavior, most prominently in the tangled uses of the figure of incest as at the root of women's relationship to authority *and* as the seat of future social pathology.

---

veal "truths" but rather manufactures them. This phenomenon is easily visible with the popularization of psychoanalysis (and psychology more generally) as a plot structuring device in film.

8   For men, the slippage between pleasure and abuse is most often imaged as a product of repressed (or overt) homosexuality, or of personal insecurity which makes men sadists (the grown up version of "boys will be boys").

I. Daddy's Girls Come of Age: Sexy Nazis and Feminism

What *Cabaret*, *Night Porter*, *Romper Stomper* and *Schindler's List* share is an ongoing belief that psycho-sexual dynamics lie at the core of political behavior: fascism is usually the outgrowth of some kind of sexual and/or familial dysfunction, or else metaphorical for a dysfunction so widespread it no longer reads as such. What distinguishes the images that emerge from these films is a surprisingly diverse set of erotic logics that lend political meaning to these images in the form of both moral judgment and either intentional or inadvertent titillation.[9]

Films of the 1970s marked a fundamental change in the focus on sexualized Nazis. Earlier films imagined sexualized Nazism as a given political leaning which had to be explained (so it could be cured). In the 1970s, Nazis were cast as metaphors for sexual proclivities themselves, or else Nazism was seen as a possible consequence of sexual debauchery. In the Sixties Nazism had become a widely used metaphor for abuses of state-sanctioned authority, with accusations of fascism not at all uncommon in radical rhetoric, including that of radical feminists.[10] The sexual politics of the period, in a complicated and often indirect fashion, deployed sexual freedoms against a repressive establishment; free love sat across political picket lines from "fascist" government practices. But in the early 70s, pornographic literature, films, and low budget exploitation movies with historically illogical titles like *Girls of the SS* moved the Nazi metaphors into another realm entirely. What had been a tacit content in many Nazi images before then now became overt; sex did not just fly in the face of repressive authority but rather repressive authority was in itself found to be sexy. This latter rendition provoked voluminous critical outpourings decrying these figurations of the sexualized Nazi on the basis of either sexism, historical disrespect for fascism's victims, or a generalized moral depravity.

In 1972, *Cabaret* was retrieved from such criticism by means of a claim of critical distance, insisting that the film *illustrated* the damning connection between Nazis and marginal sexual practices. Others would find the film to be politically conservative precisely for that reason, hypocritical in that it was trying to speak from a moral high ground which continued to cash in on images of illicit sexuality. The range can be seen in the characterization of

---

9   The history of cinema includes the ongoing debates about film and morality, where the titillating potential of film was recognized practically at the same moment that film came into public viewing. See for instance Annette Kuhn: *Cinema, Censorship and Sexuality, 1909–1925*.

10   See for instance Kate Millet's *Sexual Politics*, or Naomi Weisstein's "'Kinder, Küche, Kirche' as Scientific Law: Psychology Constructs the Female."

Cabaret as carrying "a general theme of sick sexual ambiguity [...] as a kind of working motif" to the admonition that the film "implies a simple causal relationship between decadence and totalitarianism."[11] *The Night Porter*, which came out two years later, entered an escala ted version of this debate, being well received in Europe and miserably received in the United States, mostly on the grounds that the film was itself fascist for showing fascism to be erotic.

The Academy award success of *Cabaret* seems to indicate that the final verdict on that film was that it was morally acceptable; the mostly thoroughgoing trashing *The Night Porter* received by comparison indicates that it was not. The major difference between *Cabaret* and *Night Porter* in fact is that *Cabaret* ultimately passes moral judgment on the improper combination of sex and violence in what ends up being a commentary on German national character (i. e. an explanation for fascism) while Cavani's film more likely takes the reverse trajectory, claiming that morality is not in fact an issue in the realm of desire. Brian and Max merely touch hands in *Cabaret* and a Hitler youth starts belting some version of the Horst Wes sel Song; Lucia and her Max have intense sex in *Night Porter* and they share a blue-tinted theatrical flashback to a stylized concentration camp. *Cabaret* makes gestures toward delimiting a boundary between violent excesses and perversions which would be linked with fascism (i. e. homosexuality, transvestism and sadism), and more "acceptable" forms of experimental sexuality (like heterosexual promiscuity or extramarital sex, to which even the "nice Jewish girl" succumbs). *Cabaret* thus tries to maintain the politics of some kind of sexual license as radical, while both encouraging the notion that fascism is sexy, *and* implying that because its sexiness is perverse it is morally condemnable. *Night Porter* instead turns unacceptable sexuality into something carried out in the service of love, with fascism as part of its internal vocabulary.[12] These two films together mark an important historical turning point in the understanding of fascism as a metaphor for sexual relations in general.

---

11   Roger Greenspun's review "Liza Minelli Stirs a Lively Cabaret," and Stephen Farber's review "Cabaret May Shock Kansas ..." respectively.

12   *Schindler's List*, characteristic now of a more conservative bent in the 90s, equates all forms of sexual liberalism with amorally achieved power: there is no legitimate sexuality in Spielberg's film; except perhaps the paternal sexuality Schindler exhibits in the scene discussed above. The libertarianism of the gleeful raunchiness of *Cabaret* is thus not to be entirely relegated to the conservativism of the film's moral judgments, but rather should be used to point out the precise line that the American film industry would then define as the limit point of acceptable political alliances around sexualized Nazis, and how different that is today.

The costuming and visual style of *Cabaret* are garish and strikingly characteristic of the 70s rather than 30s, from the excessive use of robin's egg-blue
eyeshadow and false eyelashes to the uniform of the 70s prostitute: halter tops
and hotpants (think of Jody Foster in *Taxi Driver* (Scorcese, 1976)). What is
supposed to make this characteristic of Berlin, 1931, is the gender ambiguity of
the cabaret dancers; while they are all "women" (with the occasional exception
of Joel Gray's emcee) they could be genitally male or female. What is "sinister"
about the sexuality portrayed in the nightclub is not just that it is raunchy, but
that it involves deviance that is consistently played out as grotesquely female,
homosexual, sadistic and, *consequently*, fascist. Of course, the film also has a lot
of fun with that, so the anti-fascist critique it offers is extremely troubled.

Susan Sontag addressed the phenomenon of eroticized Nazis in her 1974
article "Fascinating Fascism." She blames both the "predilections of the fascist leaders themselves for sexual metaphors" and the coincidence of theatrical sensibilities in fascism and sado-masochism, then the most prominent
subculture of the sexual "underground."[13] She did not yet go so far in that essay to ask why sado-masochism, or theatricality, would be so apt to appeal to
the sexual sensibilities of the 70s. Linda Mizejewski, writing in the 90s, offers
that *Cabaret* is characteristic of the 70s because it reflects a sensibility about
politics as spectacle common to the era:

> [*Cabaret's*] continual play with spectatorship and performance as a continuum of
> politics reworks a constellation of anxieties that had been latent in the ongoing
> historical confrontations of that era: the "guilt" of passivity (spectatorship) as a
> motivation for activism, the conflation of spectator/spectacle, the radical posi-
> tionings that quickly cast figures of authority on the side of the 'fascist pigs.'[14]

But, as Mizejewski also acknowledges, another echo of the phenomenon of
political spectacle would be the swelling influence of camp sensibilities. Borrowed from the irony of gay subculture, reinscription of what were meant to
be morally damaging associations of German fascism with homosexuality
quickly expanded into other areas of sexual marginality (sado-masochism,
transvestitism, fetishism, etc.) which, by the acts they entail, are spectacular
and performative – and lend themselves easily to camp irony.[15]

---

13   Susan Sontag: "Fascinating Fascism," p. 102.
14   Linda Mizejewski: *Divine Decadence: Fascism, Female Spectacle, and the Makings of Sally Bowles*,
     p. 208.
15   Of course, the film and Broadway scripts also make Brian bisexual, at least partly hetero-
     sexualizing Christopher Isherwood's secretly gay and largely asexual character in *Goodbye to
     Berlin*. The film's appropriation of gay camp sensibilities does not extend to its depiction of
     gay characters.

Against this spectacular and performative play of marginal sexualities however, *Cabaret* posits the psycho-sexual diagnoses of a Sally driven by unresolved Oedipal attachments. The neglect she suffers from her "fabulously important" diplomat father provides an opening for Brian to step in as her (albeit inadequate) Daddy. Although all sexual relations in the film entail performances of some sort, what remains unperformative is the original reference to the negligent father. What appears as the first sexual attachment is unalterable, all the rest are merely substitutes. Sally's moral flightiness with regard to power (represented mainly as men with money) has to do with her inability to distinguish between the different forms of authority she is subject to – she expects all of them to "take care of her" in one way or another, to provide her with what she wants, even when they repeatedly fail to do so. *Cabaret* thus sets up distinct boundaries between what it determines to be theatrical displays of sexual perversity akin to Nazi brutality, and the repetitive casting of one man after another as authoritative Daddy to Sally's little girl, a pattern which contributes to her indifference to the rise of Nazism all around her.

Complicating this belief in the fundamental unresolved Oedipus at the root of female sexual subjectivity, however, is the only other prominent female character in the film, Natalia, the daughter of a wealthy Jewish family. She is also extremely constrained by the strict expectations of her family's class status and religious doctrine, and a Daddy's girl, although the film does not associate this total deference to authority on the part of a female character with authoritarianism. The reasons for this may be obvious (i. e. the situation of the Jews as a persecuted religious minority) but my point here is that the film is completely uncritical of women's troubled relationship to authority in the construction of their sexuality, while using grotesque femininity (i. e. the performing transvestites) to stand for the kind of excess underlying authoritarianism.

By contrast, *The Night Porter* entirely collapses these boundaries of pleasure and abuse which might explain why the film outraged so many critics when it first appeared in the United States. Many critics were simply irate about *The Night Porter*, usually from the perspective that it was itself fascist and belittled the gravity of the Holocaust because it presented a masochist's view of the female victim's psyche. Henry Giroux for instance, wrote of the film that it was "a thinly-disguised fascist propaganda film that glorifies sadism, brutality and exaggerated machismo [...]. Its barbarism rests not only in its audacity to extol fascist principles, but also in its attempt to legitimize the death of millions of innocent victims at the hands of the Nazi machine."[16]

---

16   Henry Giroux: "The Challenge of Neo-fascist Culture," p. 31.

Giroux's reading of the film that follows is startlingly inaccurate, obviously guided by an anger-blindness which he shares with many other critics. What is interesting in this is that the exaggerations the film's critics committed often tended to provide additional prurient content, heightening the connection between sex and violence that so appalled them. Paul Zimmerman wrote in *Newsweek*, that *The Night Porter* was "just obscene sentimentality disguised as sophisticated cynicism [...]. We are supposed to like [Max], even as we watch him jam broken glass into Rampling's mouth (it's OK, she loves it)."[17] The last sentence in Zimmerman's series of criticisms is highly symptomatic, in that Dirk Bogard's character Max never "jams" glass into Lucia's mouth, nor do we see him "abusing the nude Charlotte Rampling, cutting her arm, forcing objects up her vagina, and teaching her the pleasures of fellatio," as critic Lester Keyser would have us believe.[18] Marking the film as somehow porno-graphic ("romantic pornography" (Canby), "porno-gothic" (Kael), "political pornography" (Sarris)[19]) is very often the foundation for a sarcastic denigra-tion of the film. The critics brought out these sometimes vaguely implied sex-ual acts to their most extreme and literal manifestation, betraying a tremen-dous anxiety around the generalizability of the psychological connection of sex and violence that the film suggests.

The sins of *The Night Porter* rack up on two counts: the acknowledgment of a relationship between female sexual subjectivity and authoritarianism (de-nied though illustrated in *Cabaret*) and the critics' reading of a parallel gener-alization to the sexual psychology of all victims (especially Jews). In actuality, Cavani explicitly evades the race question, never once speaking the word "Jew" in the film and explaining Lucia's presence in the camp through her be-ing the daughter of a socialist. Any racial motivation for violence is sub-merged in fleeting glances at Stars of David, which serve as a visual counter-point to the more prominent display of the swastika. In an act of directorial evasion, *The Night Porter* moves away from the touchy territory of racial vio-lence and firmly onto the terrain of gender-based violence.[20] This move then sparks the mobilization of the popularly-held belief in the fundamental mas-

---

17   Paul D. Zimmerman: "Trampling on Rampling," p. 95.
18   Lester J Keyser: "Three Faces of Evil: Fascism in Recent Movies," p. 29.
19   See Vincent Canby's "'Porter' is Romantic Pornography," p. 284; Pauline Kael's "Stuck in the Fun," pp. 151–52; and Andrew Sarris's "The Nasty Nazis: History or Mythology," pp. 77–8.
20   A great many reviewers, including the one's I've mentioned, missed the evasion of the ra-cial issue and listed among their complaints the wrongs committed against the erroneously labelled "little Jewish girl" who comes to love her torturer.

ochism of the female sexual psyche, brought out in overt and performative manifestations. But unlike *Cabaret* which reserves the authority- dependence of its female characters for uncriticized moments of truth, *The Night Porter* eliminates any point of origin making both the "original" interactions in the flashback concentration camp and the "recreated" scenarios in the present equally theatrical.

Feminist film theory's rescue of *The Night Porter* from condemnations calling it fascist largely fixed on the value of highlighting the masochistic construction of the female sexual psyche, but denied its performativity. Feminist film scholars claimed that what was abhorrent about the sexualization of the concentration camp in the film was serving as a valuable metaphor for women in general who experienced their oppression sexually. Because these theorists heavily favored psychoanalytic reading strategies, the relationship between the main characters always deferred to the father and daughter roles.

In these writings therefore, like in *Cabaret*, it is state authority which is cast as spectacular, against the ground of family relations. Beverly Houston and Marsha Kinder wrote the first feminist academic article on the film, basing their reclamation strategy on insisting that the film is primarily about sex and secondarily about Nazis:[21]

> It's as if Cavani begins with the desire to create a powerful sado/masochistic story and then draws from the past the most extreme setting possible – the Nazi concentration camp – in order to enhance its imaginative power. This is quite different from setting out to make a film about the historical reality of Nazi brutality and then reducing it to a romantic love story, which would be grotesquely immoral and obscene. The film has been attacked on just these grounds by many critics who have mistaken its mode and intentions.[22]

---

21 See also Teresa de Lauretis' article "Cavani's *Night Porter*: A Woman's Film?" where she writes, "it is not Lucia's experience (her victimization, initiation, and subsequent unbreakable bondage to her oppressor-father-lover) that serves as a metaphor for the infamy perpetrated by the Nazis on humanity, but Nazism and the atrocities committed in the camps that are the allegorical framework chosen by Cavani to investigate the dialectics of the male-female relationship in our contemporary, post-Nazi, society." (pp. 35–6) What makes this a "woman's film" she wrote then was "[t]he way in which Lucia is victimized, the truth she discovers in herself and lives out, the imagery of her bondage to the Father [...] a true metaphor, however magnified, of the female condition." (p. 37) The importance of this twist in reading sexual imagery is not to be underestimated; I only suggest they need to be read in the context of a series of turns which the political reading of sexual images has taken.

22 Beverly Houston and Marsha Kinder: "*The Night Porter* as Daydream," pp. 366–67.

Critics of the film are cast as disavowing the fundamental truth of the perverse nature of the father-daughter dyad, but Houston and Kinder's argument relies on the subsequent disavowal of the eroticism of the setting into which it is placed. It still seems impossible to come to terms with the sexiness of Nazis themselves. Another version of the "mistake" then might lie in not considering the possibility that both familial authority *and* state authority are simultaneously erotic, fantastic, and capable of wreaking material and psychical consequences.[23] Houston and Kinder's claim that the film's use of the historical context of German fascism is imaginary and only of secondary importance is novel and marks an important shift in how these images are used, but the recasting of an Oedipal ground to explain the appeal ignores the significance of the fact that it is Nazism more often than any other scenario which provides the stage.[24]

In 1974, partly in direct response to the release of *The Night Porter*, Michel Foucault was among those who asked how a thoroughly unsexy bunch of fascists could end up as the ultimate symbol of sexual experimentation. He speculates that "[n]obody loves power anymore," at least in the form of fetishizing leaders, and so the erotic relationship between political leaders and subjects had been lost. The Nazi fad in the 70s would then be a symptom of "the beginnings of a re-eroticization of power, taken to a pathetic, ridiculous extreme by the porn-shops with Nazi insignia that you can find in the United States."[25] Political power was being experienced, at least theoretically, as more diffuse and impersonal under a then-new rubric of "politics as spectacle," making the

---

23 Kinder and Houston expressly delineate the psycho-sexual appeal of the film as follows: "Despite its apparently exotic nature, the basic emotional situation is universally accessible partly because the acting out of the father/child harkens back to everyone's childhood, where the master/slave relationship is first infused with love. Who among the audience has not wanted to ease back into utter dependence, to be totally cared for by another? Thus, as Lucia stands quietly, arms upraised, waiting for Max to slip on her Sunday dress, she evokes identification even among those who must reject other aspects of the sado/masochism." (p. 369).

24 Two prominent versions of the debates within feminism around the separation of fantasy and material conditions concerned the problems of pornography and feminist sado-masochism. These debates have left the enduring legacies of rhetoric around victimization and censorship. The debate about feminist sado-masochism prominently invoked Nazism as either invariably having to do with historical Nazis (the anti-S/M side) or having nothing to do with historical Nazis (the pro-S/M side). See for example, Pat Califia: "Feminism and Sadomasochism," or Susan Leigh Star: "Swastikas: The Street and the University."

25 Michel Foucault: "Film and Popular Memory," an interview conducted by the editors of *Cahiers du Cinema*, p. 98.

re-eroticization of power not about individual leaders but rather about the general category of authority figures, encapsulated in an office or a uniform.

The persistent use of the Nazi trope then could lie in the significance that like *Cabaret*, *Night Porter* foregrounds theatricality, with *Night Porter* going one step further. Cavani's concentration camp scenes do not pretend to be historical recreations, but rather are more like stylized photoplays, or silent opera. The register of the real is in the film's present, 1957, where managers, therapists, service workers, and nosy neighbors act as agents of the remnants of the Nazis former political power, a sinister audience to the dramas of Max and Lucia's romance. The flashback cabaret-like scene, for instance, functions as theater in a number of ways. Lucia literally performs a sultry song and dance number, and Max's retelling of the story becomes part of the evidence which brings on the scrutiny of Max's Nazi colleagues; Max's watching Lucia in the cabaret will soon be echoed by the Nazis menacing scrutiny over both of them. Their sexual relationship depends on theater both privately and publicly, making control and evasion, watching and performing, the tug-of-war which constitutes the erotics of the film.

In fact, every scene featuring the sexual exchanges of the protagonists is framed by another scene involving the restrictions imposed on them by Max's former Nazi friends. The Oedipal story is enacted with the same theatricality as the concentration camp roles, unlike the Oedipal plotline in *Cabaret* (Sally's negligent Daddy) which is depicted as a moment of psychological truth. In Cavani's story, authority is primarily exercised by surveillance, so the theatricality of the central character's private moments (both psychological and sexual) are performed in acknowledgment of a state of always being watched. This performativity undermines the efficacy of a belief in the originary value of a father-daughter dyad as it is but one way of conceiving of watchful control. By way of understanding the specific appeal of the Nazi scenario then, the most important logic operating in the film is that external disapproval structures the couple's sexual excitement. This is underscored by the final sequences, when Max dresses in his well preserved SS uniform, and Lucia does not wear her nifty cabaret outfit but rather the little girl's dress which has appeared recursively throughout. The mixing of two versions of role inequity does not necessarily privilege the Daddy and his Little Girl game across the board, but rather implies that for Lucia's character, the Little Girl is the most comparable to Max's SS persona as a public icon. As they finally leave the apartment they've been holed up in for two weeks, the cabaret song is reprised on the soundtrack. When they go out into public in these representative costumes from their erotic repertoire, they are exhibitionists coming under the direct gaze of their pursuers who are only then inclined to gun them down. The implication is that the erotic logic of authoritarianism necessitates a strict disavowal of its own perversions. The public nature of their execution is linked to their "going public" with their sexual proclivities, making this very crucially a drama about individual freedom and state control.

Common to both then-current feminist film theory and Foucault's commentary is the figure of overarching surveillance. *The Night Porter* engages the system of gendered gazes which fix the female image in the service of a heterosexual male psyche as feminist film scholars were elaborating concurrently with the release of this film, and it also operates in a manner more in line with Foucault's also concurrent theory of a logic of official surveillance.[26] *The Night Porter* eroticizes public scrutiny of private relationships by drawing on the Nazi trope with its history of public/private boundary violations. It is this particular trajectory which carries its continued use through the Eighties and into the Nineties.

II. Erotic Surveillance and Anti-Censorship Politics: The Sexy Nazi as Bad Girl

The intrusion of state authority into private/sexual matters thematizes many of the political controversies in the United States in the Eighties. Mostly this was due to the resurgence of a strong and politically powerful Christian Fundamentalist Right which called for intense restrictions in sexual freedoms, the elimination of public funding to artwork deemed "obscene," the banning of record albums on the basis of offensive lyrics, and legislation restricting pornography. The anti-abortion movement, the perception of escalating crime rates, and the looming specter of AIDS also helped foster the spread of rhetoric claiming that the United States had become a place sorely lacking in moral fortitude.[27] This "Moral Majority" cast its solutions under the umbrella-term "family values," issuing protests that taxpayers' money should not be spent on supporting "immoral" activities. In this way government institutions could be faulted for becoming too permissive, requiring a healthy dose

---

26 Laura Mulvey's seminal article "Visual Pleasure and the Narrative Cinema" and Michel Foucault's *Discipline and Punish* were both published in 1975.

27 Pope John Paul II was chosen as 1994 Man of the Year by *Time* magazine with the justification that "[i]n a year when so many people lamented the decline in moral values or made excuses for bad behavior, Pope John Paul II forcefully set forth his vision of the good life and urged the world to follow it." This statement implies that the other side of recognizing moral decline is to "make excuses" via sociological or psychological explanation. The obviously greater value placed on moral judgment is indicative of the current state of this belief.

of conservatism to correct these wrongs. To counter the mounting restrictions, media projects explicitly challenging censors dominated the music and art scenes. This gave rise to a tendency already discernable in the visual and narrative strategies of *The Night Porter*, involving the further eroticization of surveillance: "anti-censorship" politics became melded with "anti-censorship" eroticism, making censorship itself sexy.

Oppositional sex politics judged that what is most *politically* sexy in such a climate is that which ensures the response of censoring authorities.[28] But as this erotic fever caught on, new sometimes imaginary specters of censorship were erected perhaps most prominently, within feminism itself. Over the course of the Eighties, a monolithically perceived feminism became associated with sexual conservatism and an over-controlling liberal establishment. The growing perceived-validity of this belief involved the inadvertent collusion of feminists who opposed other feminist campaigns to censor representations of women (i. e. anti-pornography feminism) with the narrow focusing the Right used to deny diversity within feminism in the interests of discrediting it.[29]

Key to this sexy controversiality, however, is a reliance on a belief in the efficacy of these censoring authorities. Both the conservative forces within the state funding institutions and the "Politically Correct" establishment (which a certain kind of feminism was thought to exemplify) had to be underwritten as powerful censors if such a politics was to continue to be persuasive. Madonna's 1990 music video for *Justify My Love* functioned as an "anti-censorship" statement on multiple registers, concluding with the line "poor is the man whose pleasures depend on the permission of others."

The controversy around *Justify My Love* basically concerned MTV's wavering on whether or not the clip was too risqué for their often underage viewers.

---

28   Sylvere Lotringer makes a related case in his book *Overexposed* which examines a new technique for treating prisoners convicted of sexual crimes with more rather than less access to prurient material. The logic behind this is that the perverse activity which landed the perpetrator in jail would become "boring" instead of arousing. Arguments against mental conditioning notwithstanding, the logic behind the practice Lotringer examines is that some form of censorship is necessary for something to become arousing.

29   Most of this came out of the "anti-pornography" movement which advocated extreme restrictions on sexually explicit material and hence came to be allied with conservative religious forces. Catherine MacKinnon and Andrea Dworkin are the two most prominent figures here. That this particular strand of feminism be singled out is a very complicated move on the part of anti-feminists: feminists get to be associated with authoritarianism (i. e. "political correctness") and thus are figured as the powerful force against which the poor, victimized reactionaries need to defend themselves. This is rhetorical acrobatics at its best.

The tape features a catalogue of sexual alternatives, including threesomes, voyeurism, the much-discussed lesbian kiss, and some glimpses of bondage and domination. The most interesting among these for my argument is an image lifted directly out of *The Night Porter* of a bare-chested Charlotte Rampling look-alike in suspenders and something like an SS officer's cap. The latter was not necessarily read as such, partly because by this time the image exclusively represented a shorthand for sado-masochism with the guarantee that most of Madonna's viewers would never think of historical Nazis at all. In the "pro-sex" feminist criticism around Madonna which also considered its counter-part to be a repressive "cultural feminism," the reference to Nazism is buried under notations of Madonna's pirating "European Art Films." Sexy feminists then, like their predecessors writing about *The Night Porter*, insisted on claim-ing that Madonna's references to Nazism were severed from the historical ref-erence to German fascism.[30] In this way, Madonna's anti-censorship gestures play out the continued legacy of an erotics of state surveillance, trying to take the "Nazi" out of the Sexy Nazi.

Meanwhile the Right was gearing up to put the "Nazi" back into sex − "perverse" sex that is. Riding somewhat alongside the above rhetoric of a lib-eral establishment perceived to be suppressing the rights of others came the anti-abortion movement harping on the "murder" of "unborn children" of a magnitude warranting the label "an American Holocaust." Rush Limbaugh's more recent labeling of feminist pro-choice activists as "Feminazis" further marks the Right's re-appropriation of the use of Nazism as an epithet, as does the claim in the voter's pamphlet issued by the Oregon Citizen's Alliance in support of their 1994 anti-gay ballot measure that "Nazism was largely the outgrowth of Germany's gay rights movement."[31] The connection between sexuality and Nazism is therefore persistent on this end of the political spec-trum as well.

Again the huge split in uses of the Sexy Nazi comes to bear in the present. Sexualized Nazi images are associated with anti-repressive art practices while

---

30 See for instance many of the articles in *The Madonna Connection: Representational Politics, Sub-cultural Identities, and Cultural Theory*, ed. Cathy Schwichtenberg.

31 Limbaugh writes, "A feminazi is a woman to whom the most important thing in life is see-ing to it that as many abortions as possible are performed" (*The Way Things Ought to Be*, p. 194). A discussion of the Oregon Citizens Alliance statements and those of their member-ship director Scott Lively as he attempted to clarify the invocation of Nazism occurred on the Internet where one subscriber, Lynda King, wrote, "In the past, the OCA has been compared with the Nazis in its campaigning methods and goals, so this time around, they are turning the tables by claiming that not they, but the gays are the ones who should be compared to Nazis." (October 20, 1994).

simultaneously being redeployed against what the Christian Right claim to be sexually immoral feminists and gays and lesbians. Nazis are in both cases thoroughly sexualized in terms of libertarian pleasures on the one hand, and in terms of the Right's own veritable obsession with sexual matters on the other.[32] "Family values" are set against what the Christian Right sees as a morally bankrupt government, echoing of the original response of conservatives to fascism in wartime. For them the Nazi is not "sexy" but continues to most definitely have to do with sex. Left/liberal anti-censorship politics in the Eighties thus continued to try to take the "nazi" out of the "sexy Nazi," while Right/reactionary forces tried to underline the "nazi" in what they deemed to be unacceptable sexual practices. In both cases, the figure of the Nazi is thoroughly saturated in sexualization.

III. Daddy's Little Girl Files a Lawsuit: Child Abuse and the Sexy Nazi

The resurgence of a conservative trend in the US of the Eighties ought to be analyzed not only in terms of the effect of the dissemination of diluted psychoanalytic beliefs and the way these can dove-tail around the perception of a concretely repressive cultural environment, but also in terms of the tremendous anxiety occurring concurrently around incest, personal victimization, addiction, and child sexual abuse. This history reveals a sexual dynamic, again with both psychical and material registers, in which the primary locus of erotic energy is state intervention into "private" sexual realms. Among the effects of these changing psycho-sexual climates is the shift in the psychical meaning of childhood from the seat of desire to the seat of dysfunction (i. e. "healing the inner child"). The incest paradigm still operates as an originary moment, but not of object choice or desire so much as a motivation for later violence.

The wildfire spread of the recovery movement in the 80s and the use of childhood sexuality in the courts to defend all kinds of behaviors has radically altered this particular paradigm in Sexy Nazi history in more recent texts. This is evident in Beth B. and Ida Applebroog's 1989 art video *Belladonna*, in which the collision of these two uses of the Daddy/Little Girl dyad symptomatically undermines the stated political intentions of the artists. *Belladonna* brings together three versions of sexuality and violence which produce an unsettling blend of psycho-sexual confession, Nazi brutality as a form of pater-

---

32 Most prominent agendas of the Christian Right in the United States include virulent opposition to all Gay Rights measures, opposition to sex education except for the teaching of abstinence, and claims that the welfare state encourages promiscuity.

nalism, and modern-day child abuse. To do so, the tape intermingles Freud's 1919 case history "A Child is Being Beaten" on masochism, the testimony from the posthumous trial of Dr. Josef Mengele (1985), and testimony from the trial of Joel Steinberg and Hedda Nussbaum for the abuse/murder of their young daughter (1988). What links *Belladonna* to the trajectory I've traced out from *The Night Porter* is its primary strategy of leveling private and public tribunals. Through the exclusive use of talking heads, each character speaks fragments of each kind of testimony, thereby making court and couch equivalent, and signaling a breakdown of the difference between public and private disclosure.

Beth B. has said that "Repression causes so much violence in our society and particularly violence towards women [...]. To me, exorcism is the best approach to life – to deal with problems you need to confront them, not bury them."[33] In light of the entirely overdetermined association of Nazism with psychoanalysis, *Belladonna* in fact does more toward illuminating the effects of saturation brought on by extensive testimonial, rather than alleviate any kind of "repression" by means of such testimonial. What the tape reveals is the erotic potency of the judicial system, where the telling of stories through testimony has an eroticizing effect. Joseph Di Mattia, who conducted the interview from which the above quote is taken, likens *Belladonna* to "a segment from 'Nightline' from an alternative uni verse where the guests can only speak the subtext of their most intimate thoughts," a subtext made primary, in which "childhood fears, sexual guilt and anxiety about physical punishment" are no longer subtextual. This seems a fitting strategy, perhaps *not* because it runs counter to current trends but rather because it *duplicates* them. *Belladonna* stages a battle between not entirely coinciding tendencies: child hood sexuality as an explanation for adult behavior and childhood sexual abuse as the most voyeuristically riveting crime, two versions of contemporary sensationalism. Because of the addition of Nazism into the brew, reported with the same intimacy and emphasis on voyeuristic witnessing, all three types of testimony end up drifting toward the psychoanalytic, eroticism winning out over repulsion as the net effect.

In *Belladonna's* news format of talking heads, confession and testimony, therapy and justice collide to produce an effect governed by an erotics of "telling all." Witnessing and voyeurism are interchangeable, and the audience as jury stands in as an agent of generalized pleasurable surveillance not unlike that available to habitual viewers of talk shows or Court TV. The artists at-

---

33 Joseph Di Mattia: "No More Happy Endings," p. 9.

tempt to encourage the viewer to look at these stories "objectively," to encourage "judicial impartiality," since the identities of the speakers of the testi-
monies are not revealed until the last moment of the tape. As Beth B said,

> Maybe by not knowing who is speaking or where the source material comes from,
> the viewer can hear and understand what's being said more than they would if the
> identity of the speakers was known. When the media portrays a person like Joel
> Steinberg or Mengele, the information is filtered for you. You have certain expec-
> tations about the way you see that person and you make certain judgments. In a
> sense, the media makes up your mind for you.[34]

But the generalizable meaning of both the Freudian and Nazi texts insures that
the information is always already "filtered," already conflated. In this sense, the
Steinberg story gets lost under Freud's recantation long ago which erased the reality of child abuse and replaced it with a fantasy, while Nazi violence, stylized
and theatrical, cannot escape the recognizability of Nazi eroticism. The issue of
"Jewishness" is completely submerged and obscured in the text where again, as
in *Night Porter*, the word "Jew" is never uttered. The racial constitution of the
concentration camp inmates and the Jewishness of the Steinbergs is elided, only
to escape in the traces of the assorted accents of the speakers, or what the viewer
might assume about their ethnic physical characteristics. In an effort to general-
ize and decontextualize the various stories to produce "objectivity," the Nazi
trope is not "retrieved" from its eroticization, but quite the opposite: the presence of the Nazi insures that between two versions of childhood sexual experience – guilty pleasure and abuse – the former will dominate and absorb the latter.

The cumulative effect of the Freudian and Nazi narratives is to obscure
the actual victims (those killed by the Nazis and the daughter of the Steinberg
couple) into the general diagnosis of a male sexual subject with a guilty conscience. Ironically, the persistence with which violence against women and
against children is figured insures its sexualization precisely because it functions not on its own but in relation to the therapy of the perpetrator. The various ways in which the death of a female inmate is recounted highlights its
"perversion," in keeping with the theatricality common to the uses of the
Sexy Nazi since the 70s, with a ring of witnesses and a guard who sometimes
"whistles an aria from Madame Butterfly." Finally, this one repeatedly invoked
victim comes to stand in for the body of the Steinberg child, whose death is
never explicitly mentioned, and who thus remains the true subtext of the tape.

Belladonna stands at a point where psychoanalysis has run a ragged course
and has come to work as an erotic language rather than as a functional tool

---

34   Ibid., pp. 8–9.

for analysis. Child abuse stories carry a more publicly-oriented erotic charge than ever before in the current therapeutic climate that encourages public confrontation and legal action as remedies to enduring psychological trauma. The arena within which the Sexy Nazi circulates has changed with the increasing prominence of sexual testimony in courtrooms and other confessional formats (i. e. talk shows) that this therapeutic climate entails.[35] What *Belladonna* illustrates is not that there is a secret psychical desire at work beneath these acts of public disclosure, but rather that the disclosure itself, the point where private acts and public censure meet, is the new locus for an erotic cast on state authority.

IV. Daddy's Girl Gets a Boyfriend: the Sexy Skinhead

The verdict on the Sexy Nazi figure is that it has come to stand primarily for a sexual scenario and has nearly ceased to have resonance as an actual historical figure (except, of course, to the people who were actually there). But the legacy of German fascist doctrine does carry on in the figure of the neo-Nazi skinhead, a figure that does not emerge clean of the association of fascism with sexuality even as he has radically altered the terms.[36] Neo-nazi skinheads are vehemently anti-gay, anti-race mixing, and anti-Semitic, but they are not sexually repressive within the confines of same-race heterosexuality. In fact, they have come to represent a kind of raw sexual energy, fueled as much by their potential for violence as their disregard for "conventional" morality which, in the twisted rhetoric swapping of the Right from the Left, can include supposed "PC" conventionality of the tolerance of homosexuality and mixed-race sexual relations. This swapping rests on the rhetorical trick whereby the "liberal establishment" and the "liberal media" (typically thought to be controlled by Jews) are cast as the forces which dictate convention. As rebels against this "establishment," skinheads have captured the erotic imagination of the Nineties.

---

35 Prominent cases in 1993 and 1994 include the Menendez brothers' televised trial in which they claimed to have killed their parents because of past sexual abuse, and a series of cases in which adults have brought charges against their parents after having "recovered" memories of sexual abuse as children. The validity of recovered memories is currently hotly contested.

36 Not all skinheads are White supremacist or even anti-gay, although the mainstream representations of them are mainly of these factions. Skinheads more generally represent a youth subculture with a range of political goals, although their style is arguably contingent on the eroticism lent to all of them by their association with fascism.

Geoffrey Wright's 1992 film *Romper Stomper* follows the logic of the above texts in that psychology is once again favored over any other method of understanding social phenomena. The shape of this new Sexy Nazi's psyche, however, has changed. Instead of looking at Nazis as a by-product of sexual perversion, or linking the deep rooted sexual perversion-in-all-of-us to an attraction to Nazism, the depiction of skinheads is more in keeping with trends of the last decade, in which every form of behavior can be explained by deference to past victimization. Wright has said that he "wanted to do a story that revealed the pathetic personal vulnerability of young neo-Nazis and remind them that whatever they think, they are primarily motivated by a profound sense of inadequacy."[37] The skinheads in Wright's film see themselves as underdog heroes pitted against the whole world which is out to get them. This is a dressed up way of saying they see themselves as victims. This line of logic is what allows for a very disturbing equivalence that the film draws between this mentality and that of the central female character Gabrielle, lashing out against her own powerlessness at the hands of the men around her, most acutely those of her father who has coerced her into a long-standing incestuous relationship.

Looking at the four major fight scenes in the film as a recursive figure illuminates how this parallel is visually woven. Together with the unaccountability of the skinheads to authorities other than their own, the incest paradigm makes another appearance, this time around the erotic power of rage. The first fight scene occurs in the opening sequence, where three young Vietnamese immigrants fall prey to the gang of skinheads who will be the focus of the film. The skinheads are introduced from the Asian woman's perspective in slow motion, as she sits on a skateboard and pans by them at a low angle. This low-angle panning shot will be repeated at the beginning of each fight thereafter, allowing the skinheads the image of threat and power that they desire. After this first true point of view, the shot is appropriated by the skinheads, reflecting how they would like to be seen, in a visual example of the kind of appropriative rhetoric this essay has traced.

The Asian woman who provides the introduction does not appear again in the film, although she is mentioned in the following sequence when her brother tries to rally support for a vigilante retaliation against the skins among other young Asian men. They refuse to become involved, insuring that the primary motor of the next fight does not have to do with the traditional romantic story of men protecting women, but is rather exclusively about men of one race competing for territory with men of another. Women remain inci-

---

37   Academy Entertainment: "Romper Stomper" (Press material for U.S. release), p. 2.

dental to this logic. The introduction of Gabrielle in the next scene, then, is not immediately lucid in its connection to the skinhead story. She is tangled in a breakup with a tantrum-throwing boyfriend, waiting for her sexually snaky father to arrive with a hired thug to clear up the situation. Her imperviousness to the violence we hear off-screen as the thug beats the loudly protesting Ex prepares us for her later thrill at proximity to the skinheads' rumbles. Her constant need to ward off the advances of her father will come up every time he appears, leading finally to her own violent outburst. Her retaliation against her father appears as just retribution because of the way incest has come to function as a legitimate motive for later retaliatory violence in judicial proceedings. The incest figure, so prominent throughout the psychological profiles of women connected to fascism, will henceforth serve as psychological motivation for many of her actions. And it will serve as a metaphor for ultimate injustice, which could just as easily be claimed by the skinhead men against their perceived displacement by the Asian immigrants.

Sexuality does not function similarly for the men and the women in this film. Gabrielle will never be fought over ideologically (i. e. as a white woman who is part of the cause) but rather will be fought over on a romantic, individual level, causing the fatal split between Hando and his second-in-command Davey. Sex therefore does not function as part of the neo-Nazi doctrine of the male characters, but rather only as part of the narrative motor behind the violent female psyche. Sex for the skinhead men functions not psychologically but rather narratively, as an augmentation to their erotic cast as "decadent," having sex in front of each other, pouring alcohol over copulating couples and the like. The image of the Sexy Neo-Nazi is no longer the sleek and stylized performative decadence of *Cabaret* or *Night Porter* or even the product of the overindulgence of men with too much money and power as in *Schindler's List*. The decadence pictured is closer to that associated with the Stormtroopers of the early Nazi movement, of vulgar "underdog" men and their slutty women, carousing, drinking and having sex with wild abandon, running against bourgeois norms in this as well as in their lack of adherence to legal means of achieving their version of "justice."

But Gabrielle's victim-based sexual psychology will come to rhyme with the retaliatory social logic of the skinhead men, bringing together the decadent image and the persuasive explanation for rage to a sexually potent effect. The second fight opens again with the low-angle panning shot across the faces of the skinhead men in repose, menacing in this moment of calm before the battle. The fight begins with similar odds as the last one, the skinheads outnumbering their foes who have no chance of fighting back. But this time the community of young Vietnamese men is mobilized and comes streaming in from all directions. The situation worsens and the skinheads, now them-

selves vastly outnumbered, retreat, fighting, to their warehouse squat. They
barricade themselves inside in what is ultimately a metaphor for the skinhead
position; against a formidable threat trying to take over their turf, they can appear justified in their battle. The stage is now set for the rest of the film,
which will not feature any more racially motivated fights, and instead centers
on how the skinheads are themselves persecuted by the police.

Wright says, "it isn't the story of skinhead kids vs. Vietnamese kids, but
skinhead kids against the whole world around them […]. The objective of the
neo-Nazis in *Romper Stomper* is not the thrill of real power, but the power of
real thrill."[38] Wright claims that underneath the thrilling adrenaline rush of
fighting and vandalism, are the "scared, small people who need reassurance
and some kind of love."[39] This is where the story of Gabrielle and her growing involvement with Davey is supposed to intercede as an alternative to the
skinhead's credo of violence. But as the film so deeply imbricates Gabrielle in
a logic of "justifiable retaliation" that is just as thrilling as any in which the
skinhead men engage, the "love" she offers is completely tainted. In the next
fight, Gabrielle directs the skinheads to do a "hit" on her father's mansion,
ostensibly in order to steal goods to trade for money and arms. Gabrielle's
one-on-one confrontation with her father is peppered with the self-righteous
violence that she has "learned" watching and participating in the skinheads'
activities against the immigrants. Here, the legitimacy garnered by feminists in
bringing the reality of child sexual abuse to light is transformed into a parallel
to skinhead "vengeance" against the people who they deem have disempow-
ered them. Although largely incompatible in their needs and desires, abused
women and skinhead men are here made out to be similarly positioned with
respect to legitimized authority: they both wage a battle against forces that are
institutionally supported, and the means of redress depicted is violent retribution. The violence is cathartic, and even if it doesn't solve any problems, as is
ultimately the case in the film, it is, fundamentally, satisfying.

The final sequence, touted by Wright above as the instance where "love"
wins over the destructiveness of the skinheads, ultimately does not offer any
kind of alternative to violence at all. It reads instead as a classic "demise of a
buddydom" movie, in which a manipulative little bitch with no loyalties and
nothing but the desire to lash out against those she feels have wronged her,
succeeds in destroying the friendship of what used to be two really good pals.
Davey kills Hando because Hando wanted to kill Gabrielle, a logical urge

---

38   Ibid., p. 6.
39   Ibid., p. 8.

since she turned the gang over to the police. In fact, Gabrielle's finking is part of a series of actions she commits in which she invokes exactly those authorities to whom she is otherwise seen to be in opposition: her father (who rescues her from her tantrum-throwing boyfriend), the skinheads (who help her wreak havoc on her father), and the police (who essentially carry out her revenge for having been unceremoniously discarded by Hando). None of her acts are motivated by moral conscience, and so it is just as narratively supported to think that Davey is blinded by Gabrielle who doesn't really deserve his loyalty, and that it is tragic that he kills Hando, who, despite being a Nazi, was after all a loyal friend. What her patterned behavior does reveal, however, is the tight fit between familial, heterosexual, and state authority.

Like *The Night Porter*, *Romper Stomper* sat in the center of a critical controversy, this time in its country of origin, Australia. The controversy had mainly to do with the young, strong, charismatic appeal of the skinhead subculture. In the United States, the critics repeatedly fixed on the problem of the film's "excessive violence," a strange accusation in light of what passes for acceptable in other graphically violent genres like action or horror. Also criticized was its perspective from within the gang, and especially the "sexy rebel with the wrong cause"[40] persona of Russell Crowe's Hando. There is hardly any mention of the bearing Gabrielle's story has on that appeal, which I have been arguing is less of an alternative as Wright suggests, than a parallel line.

David Sterritt's review of the film is highly symptomatic when he writes,

> The appalling violence of the main characters, inflicted first on Asian immigrants and later on the heroine's dysfunctional father, goes far beyond the once notorious excesses of "A Clockwork Orange," which clearly influenced some aspects of the movie; the sex is rough as well.[41]

First, the erasure of the father's abuse in the blameless term "dysfunctional" colludes with the film's parallel between these two "threats" (that of immigrant encroachment and that of child abuse). Second, the separation of the discussion of "appalling violence" via semi-colon from "the sex is rough as well" further erases the function of incest in this story. Third, the very common comparison with "A Clockwork Orange" is used in such a way as to make a totally random judgment that the violence in *Romper Stomper* exceeds that of Kubrick's film. This latter point again totally negates the fact that *Clockwork Orange* prominently features rape as its most central expression of

---

40   Stephen Holden: "Of Skinheads High on Hate and Violence," p. 17.
41   David Sterritt: "Romper Stomper," *Christian Science Monitor*, June 11, 1993, p. 12.

violence, whereas there are no rapes in *Romper Stomper* except those that took place before the start of the film, perpetrated by Gabrielle's father.

Aside from what are probably Sterritt's personal blindnesses, this review does reveal a tendency around writing on skinheads that elevates their potential for violence as a (sexual) thrill of its own. This is another way to read the rhetorical impact of the semi-colon. The appeal of the skinheads, however, also lies in what this review overlooks: the psychological justifiability of counter-authoritarian behavior, perfectly capsulized in the rape or incest survivor with whom the skinheads in some manner identify. This does not mean that skinheads are depicted as any more sensitive to women, but rather that the new image of the fascist outlaw finds the incest survivor's experience rhetorically useful.[42]

Skinheads consistently are represented in the media as building an identity around the idea that "everybody hates us."[43] Like much of the rest of the Right, a lot of the rhetoric they have used to describe themselves and the appeal for their members stems from idealized and compensatory notions of family and community, a strange mixture of a counter-culture image based on pervasive "persecution" by the status quo and highly traditional "family values."[44] Kathy Dobie describes one skingirl's image of a lost America as "daddy-worship – erotic and childlike; and very wishful. It's a fantasy about strong men, men who are competent and secure enough to protect their families, about sweet, deep job satisfaction."[45] These two tendencies, the erotic thrill of

---

42 The neo-Nazi or White Supremacist woman is often scripted as having gained her political convictions by way of the rage she carries from having been sexually victimized. This is the case not only with *Romper Stomper*, which claims to be critical of the skinheads, but with White Supremacist novels like *Hunter* by Andrew Macdonald and *Serpent's Walk* by Randolph D. Calverhall.

43 As stated by "Eva" in "Young, White and Surrounded," Jennifer Allen: *Rolling Stone*, June 30, 1994. She relates how when she first joined the Fourth Reich skinheads of Los Angeles, they all "shared a racial moment" from their recent past "like being threatened on a public bus or having your brother's bike get stolen or even hearing your mom getting mugged in the driveway." (pp. 60–1) The gay skinzines like "The GSM" (Gay Skinhead Movement) are similarly into their own victimization, except with the added thrill of homophobia among their brethren. When not hooked into race politics, these whiny accounts tend to be about how "everybody" is against them because of the way they dress.

44 See for instance "Long Day's Journey into White" by Kathy Dobie in *The Village Voice*, April 28, 1992. This is very different from the portrayal of neo-Nazi youth in Germany, who are always written about as part of a disturbing nationalist resurgence (i. e. "Germany's Troubles" by Tamara Jones in *The Los Angeles Times Magazine*, March 7, 1993).

45 Kathy Dobie: "Long Day's Journey into White," p. 25. Another film which illustrates this configuration in Martin Campbell's 1994 film *No Escape*. The film takes place on an island prison colony in the future, run by an extremely violent, aggressive and authoritarian gang

a "fight and fuck" subculture and the uniquely American cast to the story as somehow nostalgic of lost family values, clash but, in an act of rhetorical acrobatics, they also can be non-contradictory.

V. Conclusion

Operation Grow Hair, a program developed to give the Fourth Reich skin-heads of Los Angeles a "dose of reality" after being rounded up by the FBI in the summer of 1993 included the requirement that they see *Schindler's List*.[46] After all that I have so far delineated about the history of the Sexy Nazi and what it has to say about the political climate in which the relationship between sexuality and politics are being discussed, the movie poster for *Schindler's List* suddenly becomes too dense to read: a father clasping a child's hand. In the enormous amount of journalism generated around Spielberg's film, there is very little mention of the role of sexuality in the film, revealing a vastly differ-ent focus than those around *Cabaret* and *The Night Porter* twenty years ago. Over the course of those years, the nature of the discussion around Sexy Na-zis has changed to fit a current arena of discussion which highlights violence and has come to consider sex not central – enough so that it once again can function as a subtext, after a period of saturation and too much attention.

This return to subtextual meaning for sex operating in some contemporary films does not point to the same answers found in *Cabaret* and *The Night Porter*, but rather requires an awareness of the current appeal of the Daddy image which rests not on an unresolved Oedipal desire, but on a Daddy that never ex-isted in the first place. Between attacks on the morality of welfare mothers, and the Promise Keepers, a subgroup of the Men's Movement bent on reclaiming the image of the American Father by taking the independent American Mother down a few notches, Daddy is omnipresent in current conservative political rhetoric, whether at the root of the problem (the ultimate molester), or the an-swer. If this study of the Sexy Nazi is any indication, the study of desire and sex-uality in film therefore needs to take stock of the complex history of which it is a part in order to properly assess new psycho-sexual meanings as they emerge.

---

of criminals called "The Insiders," who are set against the rebelling gang of reformed crim-inals organized into a defensive, paternalistic community called "The Outsiders."

46 Created by Marc Greenberg, the program also included "a visit to the Los Angeles County men's central jail, a session with a federal judge, a discussion with college students from the American Jewish Committee's Hands Across the Campus, a tour of the Simon Wiesenthal Center's Museum of Tolerance and a meeting with the Rev. Cecil Murray of the First AME Church." (Allen: "Young, White and Surrounded," p. 84).

Bodies, Souls and Modern Warfare

Wolfgang U. Eckart
Universität Heidelberg

Aesculap in the Trenches:
Aspects of German Medicine in the First World War

Abstract: In many ways, World War I was a traumatic event for the participating soldiers as well as for civilian populations. The enthusiasm for the war, shared by doctors and nurses, soon turned into a permanent horror. The positional warfare took a heavy toll. In the trenches soldiers had to endure physical and mental agony mangling their bodies and torturing their souls. Common martial metaphors of Social Darwinism aestheticized the war in biological terms and were soon revealed as absurdities. Many front-line soldiers developed neuroses. Doctors tried to fight them in theory and practice by more or less violent methods. German psychiatrists were fascinated by the phenomenon of war neurasthenia. Other branches of medicine, in particular heart surgery, reaped the harvest of war's violence. This paper attempts to trace the relation between war, violence and medicine.

World War I has often been described as traumatic for German society, not only for those participating, but also for the generations to follow. The violating energy of this war has been openly discussed. It is surprising to note, however, that one group of war participants who dealt professionally with injuries, that is medical doctors, has so far attracted only scarce attention. It is the more surprising as the medical profession was one of the large and closed groups of academics among the participants of the war. They were also pillars of war propaganda producing war metaphors and ideologies. They restored the forces' *Kriegsverwendungsfähigkeit* (fitness to fight), and strongly believed in its scientific yield.

During the years of 1914 to 1918 a total of 8986 doctors were mobilized for military service in Germany, 1724 of whom died of injuries or diseases in the war. Moreover, many doctors worked as privates in the hospitals of the hinterland. In the beginning, 46 female doctors were among those serving in hospitals. They were being removed from military service, however, as early as 1915 by the medical board of the Ministry of War as unwanted persons. No previous war had involved such a large number of doctors. And no previous war had rendered them necessary to such an extent as the appalling figures prove: In 1918, 10 million out of 71 million soldiers mobilized worldwide had been killed, 1.8 million of them German. Twenty million had been injured, 4.24 million of them German.[1]

I. The medical profession and war propaganda

Like no other war before or after, the war of 1914 to 1918 can be characterized as a "war of cultures" right from the start, a battle of scholars and the intelligentsia. Leading figures of the sciences in Germany willingly accepted their spiritual mobilization at an early stage. When confronted with the war they were eager to demonstrate unity and patriotism and sign proclamations. Important members of German medical science joined the campaign. Among those who signed the *Erklärung deutscher Universitätslehrer* (Proclamation of German university teachers) of 7 September 1914[2] were Paul Ehrlich, the Nobel prize winner Emil von Behring, Vincenz Czerny, Wilhelm Erb, and Max Fürbringer (all three from the University of Heidelberg) and August Bier, Hermann Oppenheim, and Wilhelm Alexander Freund, members of Berlin University. The proclamation explained why British academic rewards should be rejected. Despite its "close blood ties with Germany," Great Britain had incited, it was argued, other countries against "us" for many years and finally declared war. Another, similar proclamation *An die Kulturwelt* (To the Civilized World), published on 4 October 1914,[3] was also signed by leading figures of German medicine, among them von Behring and Ehrlich, Albert Neisser (Breslau), Albert Plehn, Max Rubner, Wilhelm von Waldeyer, and August von Wassermann, the latter four from Berlin. Defying all evidence this appeal rejected the claim "that Germany was to blame for this war, ... that it had boldly violated Belgian neutrality," and even "that it affected the life and property of one single Belgian citizen." The medical profession was united in denying that Imperial German "troops had brutally caused havoc in Loewen" or that Germany had "disregarded international law." According to this thesis, the fight against German militarism was a fight against German culture.

Thanks to Ms. Ilse C. Wagner for the kind help with the translation.

1   Figures taken from *Sanitätsbericht über das Deutsche Heer* vol. 1.

2   Jeschal: *Politik und Wissenschaft deutscher Ärzte im Ersten Weltkrieg*, pp. 27–28.

3   Ibid., pp. 24–5; vom Brocke: "'Wissenschaft und Militarismus' – Der Aufruf der 93 'An die Kulturwelt!' und der Zusammenbruch der internationalen Gelehrtenrepublik im Ersten Weltkrieg," p. 718.

They were determined to fight "as a nation of culture to which the legacy of Goethe, Beethoven or Kant" would be "as important as home or country."

As could be expected, the doctors' enthusiasm for the war was reflected especially by the medical press. Readers of the *Deutsche Medizinische Wochenschrift* were pounded by its editor's propaganda that the war was fair and necessary. In his articles, Julius Schwalbe[4] defamed the enemies as mean creatures, especially England, the "perfidious albion." On 10 November 1914, Dr. Max Nassauer, a doctor from Munich, published a poem in the *Münchener Medizinische Wochenschrift* that very journal conveying his hate for England:

Im Nebel nur wagt es Engeland

Sie sagen es an der Wasserkant':
 'Im Nebel nur wagt es Engeland!
Peitscht aber der Sturm das tosende Meer,
Hoiho, dann kommt der Deutsche daher!

Wenn stinkender Nebel niederflennt,
Dann ist es Englands Element!
Es streckt die schleimigen Fühler aus
Und schleicht heran um Hof und Haus.

Doch wenn der Sturm die Nebel zerreisst,
Und sie in tausend Fetzen zerschmeisst,
Zieht Deutschland seine Flagge hoch
Und stürzt sich ins englische Nebelloch!

Die deutsche Kraft, der deutsche Zorn
Nimmt den Polypen sich aufs Korn
Und braust einher im ehrlichen Sturm,
Zerschmetternd den erbärmlichen Wurm.[5]

---

4 Deutsche Medizinische Wochenschrift 40 (1914), pp. 1623, 1662–1663. Eckart: "Julius Schwalbe."

5 Nassauer: "Im Nebel nur wagt es Engeland." *Münchener Medizinische Wochenschrift* 61 (1914), p. 2231: "They say it on the German coast: / Only in fog England is brave. / But if storm lashes the raging sea, / hoiho, then it's good for Germany. // When stinking fog is blubbering down, / then England is in her element. / She stretches out her slimy tentacles, / sneaking around house and court. // But when storm is rending fog, / smashing it to a thousand pieces, / then Germany's flag is hoisted up. / She plunges into such a hole of the fog. // German power and German fury / aiming at the polyp, / roaring along in an honest storm, / smashing this mean worm."

On both sides of the lines volunteers played an important role. Due to the al-
truistic devotion of German Red Cross nurses near and behind the lines hundreds of thousands of lives were saved. Following the patriotic tradition of the
Red Cross women's associations, these middle class women were not driven by
pure charity. Apart from motivations such as duty and humanist convictions,
they also showed open signs of patriotism. Emotionalized pictures and texts
in standardized war diaries, handed out to the Red Cross nurses along with
their equipment, were typical for the second part of the war. For these women
war was a *Heilige Zeit*. In 1917, the Red Cross nurses of the *Badischer Frauenver-
ein* were presented with a poem of the war poet Paul Enderlich. It was supposed to strengthen their courage and to stress the "holy purpose" of the war.

Heilige Zeit

Dämpfe Dein Lachen, allzu hell und froh!
Denke: ein Deutscher fällt jetzt irgendwo.
Ein glühendes junges Leben ward starr und kalt
Fern in Polens Sumpfe, im Argonner-Wald.

Irgend-, irgendwo in dieser Stunde
Blutet auf fremdem Boden die deutsche Wunde,
Deutsche Worte lallt ein zuckender Mund,
Deutsches Blut sickert in fremden Grund.

Unter des Meeres übersprühendem Schaum,
Oben in der Wolken durchstürmtem Raum,
Im Schatten der Palmen – allüberall
Blutet ein Deutscher jetzt auf dem Erdenball.

Du, dem sein Sterben Deutschtum und Leben gewann,
Kraft und Freiheit und Stärke, denke daran!
Dämpfe das Lachen! Senke die Stirn Du
Vor des Bruders Sterben und Grabesruh!

Heilig jede Stunde voll Wunden und Leid
Heilige Wunde in dieser Zeit:
Der dort in der Fremde zu früh verblich
Denke daran – er starb für Dich, für Dich.[6]

---

6   Albrecht: Aus meinem "Kriegs-Tagebuch": *Badischer mobiler Lazarett-Trupp*, pp. 37–8: "Sub-
    due your laughter, all too clear and merry. / Remember: A German is killed, now, some-
    where. / A glowing life turns cold and stiff / far in Polish swamps, in the forest of the Ar-
    gonnes. // Somewhere now, / a German wound is bleeding on foreign ground. / German
    words stammered by convulsive lips, / German blood oozing away on foreign soil. // May
    it be beneath the foaming sea, / or in cloudy skies, / in palm trees' shadows, all over the

II. Technology on the Battlefield

In contrast to earlier wars modern science and technology were systematically instrumentalized during World War I. The battlefield was turned into a perfect system to kill. Three examples may illustrate this thesis: the strategic use of machine guns, the precise directing of artillery fire by aerial reconnaissance and the various types of poison gas in the chemical warfare.

The new way of killing by poison gas in particular was one of the most appalling inventions of this war, its effects lasting until today. During the attack on the Belgian town of Ypres on 22 April 1915 Germans troops used poison gas for the first time. Within the years to follow all sides competed in chemical warfare,[7] first by gassing and, since 1916, by lobbing gas shells. In 1917, Germany lost its leading position which, until then, it had occupied due to the strength of its chemical industry. Nerve gases of different strengths, *Weisskreuz* and, above all, *Grünkreuz*, affecting the eyes and the nose, as well as phosgene, affecting the lungs, and the pesticide chlorpicrine or gases irritating the skin such as Lost, Yperit, and Mustard Gas (*Gelbkreuz*) soon became common. Severe irritations and even irreversible blindness occurred. The shocking pictures were similar on both sides of the front. Lines of gassed soldiers, eyes red and bulging, walked slowly, each soldier resting one hand on the shoulder in front of him became common sights. They were weak and exhausted, with pale greenish skin, blindfolded, their heads bent in pain and despair. This brutal warfare was rarely criticized by doctors. What was considered a real problem, however, was the separation of "malingering" soldiers from the group of truly blinded soldiers. In the third volume of *Ärztliche Erfahrungen im Weltkriege 1914/18*, published in 1921, this problem was illustrated by Oskar Minkowski, a professor of internal medicine and consulting internist of the IX. army.

> Die überwiegende Mehrzahl der den Verbandsplätzen und Krankensammelstellen zuströmenden 'Gaskranken' bildeten glücklicherweise […] leichte Fälle. Sie waren oft nur schwer von den 'Mitläufern' zu unterscheiden, die nur befürchteten, giftiges Gas eingeatmet zu haben, oder nur die Gelegenheit benutzen wollten, um das Schlachtfeld zu verlassen.[8]

---

globe / a German is bleeding now. // Thou, gaining life and Germaneness by death, / strength, liberty, and power, remember! / Subdue thy laughter, lower thy brow / before your brother's death. // Sacred every hour full of wounds and sorrow, / sacred wound in this time. / He, who died on foreign ground too early: / remember he died for you, for you."

7 For the Britsh situation see Richter: *Chemical Soldiers*.

8 Oskar Minkowski: "Die Erkrankungen durch Einwirkung giftiger Gase." Schjerning, ed.: *Handbuch der Ärztlichen Erfahrungen im Weltkriege 1914/1918* vol. 3, pp. 340–83, p. 350: "For-

For the medical profession this war became a laboratory and field for medical experimentations. Soon after the beginning of the war, some renowned doctors realized the opportunity to obtain results from a huge life experiment, in particular in the field of hygiene and bacteriology, an experience that was impossible to make during scientifically "meager" peace times. Thus, Karl Mense, doctor of hygiene and tropical medicine, expressed his enthusiasm in the *Archiv für Schiffs- und Tropenhygiene* in January 1915:

> Vor unseren Augen aber spielt sich der größte Versuch [...] ab, den die Einbildungskraft ersinnen kann. Menschen der verschiedensten Zonen werden gegeneinandergeführt und leben und ringen unter den ungünstigsten hygienischen Verhältnissen. Die Völker des Erdballs stellen dadurch ein so riesiges epidemiologisches Experiment auf, wie es die Seuchenforschung nie erträumen konnte. Aber erst wenn die Friedensglocken läuten, winkt der Lohn aller Mühen und Kämpfe – hoffentlich auch der Wissenschaft.[9]

Mense was not the only one who considered the war the "great master" for medicine. In fact, results could soon be obtained, in particular in the field of vaccination prophylactics of infectious diseases. Protective vaccination dramatically reduced the number of tetanus. Systematic vaccination during the first months of the war – following the results gained during the Colonial Wars in Africa – considerably reduced the number of typhoid infections. The causes for the development of typhus became known and the disease, common at the Eastern front, was contained through delousing. As a result of campaigns to chemically eradicate lice in the *Entlausungskammer* – also a collective male experience of this war –, the notion of "parasite" began to spread and was interpreted in anthropological terms.

---

tunately, the clear majority of gas-poisoned soldiers pouring to the dressing stations and sickbays had only minor injuries. Often enough it was quite difficult to distinguish them from the so-called 'followers' who only thought to have inhaled poisoned gas or from those who just took the chance to sidle off the battle-field."

9   Karl Mense: "Zum neuen Jahre." *Archiv für Schiffs und Tropen-Hygiene* 19 (1915), p. 1: "Surgeries and offices are empty. In the field and on board, right behind the lines and back home, each doctor - even the one who does not practice any more, but who is peacefully doing research - is now fervently trying to heal the wounds of the war. The creative pen is laid down, papers remain unfinished, as the scholar, too, participates in the actions of his people which completely fill our hearts: Primum vincere deinde philosophari! Directly in front of us, an experiment, so extensive that it could hardly derive from imagination, is taking place. People from the most different regions are brought together in order to live and fight under the most unfavourable hygienic conditions. The people of the globe are taking part in an epidemiological experiment so huge, scientists would have never been dreaming of. It will not happen before peace will be restored, however, that all our fights and efforts will be rewarded - hopefully this will apply for science, too."

By and large, German hygienists and bacteriologists were quite successful in fighting the classical epidemics. A battle they could not win, however, was that of the so-called *Spanische Grippe* (Spanish influenza)[10] in the summer of 1918. Millions were struck down by the largest pandemic of this century and the medical profession was helpless. From mid 1917 until July 1918, 708 306 soldiers were infected in Germany. The German ambulance report of 1934 stated only 999 lethal cases, a figure definitely much too low. Onboard the American ships on their way to Europe the pandemic was raging wildly, causing the death of 30,000 American soldiers. Until December 1918, the estimated number of infections went up to about 20 million. Faced with the influenza, doctors and nurses had little help to offer. At the end of the war, the "war laboratory" failed.

III. Experimental heart surgery

The war was looked upon as an excellent opportunity to do field studies by hygienists and bacteriologists. This attitude was also common among army surgeons, particularly in oral and heart surgery. For the latter, war was of prime importance. As a result of an unimaginable number of casualties this subdiscipline of surgery was born during the war. War offered innumerable opportunities for experiments. Among the physicians who seized the opportunity to help, even in desperate situations, thereby contributing to create a new discipline was Ludwig Rehn (1849–1930). Before 1914, Rehn was a professor of surgery at Frankfurt University and director of a municipal clinic. In 1896 he had been the first to successfully perform a heart operation. During the war he was a consulting surgeon of an army in the West. In 1922 he published his experiences.[11]

> In dem ungeheuren Kriege war, wie nie zuvor, die Gelegenheit, Herzverletzungen zu behandeln, zu operieren und zu obduzieren. Gewiß kam ein großer, sicher der weit größte Teil nicht in die Hand des Arztes, oder er kam in dessen Hand, ohne daß Hilfe möglich war. […] Indessen hatten die Friedenserfolge doch zuwege gebracht, daß sich Interne, pathologische Anatomen wie Chirurgen in gleicher Weise

---

10 Friedrich Münter: "Influenza." Schjerning, ed.: *Handbuch der Ärztlichen Erfahrungen im Weltkriege 1914/1918* vol. 3, pp. 322–34.

11 Ludwig Rehn: "Die Kriegsverletzungen des Herzens und des Herzbeutels." Schjerning, ed.: *Handbuch der Ärztlichen Erfahrungen im Weltkriege 1914/1918* vol. 1, pp. 799–816.

für die Herzverletzungen interessierten. Dadurch ist unser Wissen und Können außerordentlich gefördert worden. Es ist nicht nur die Vielseitigkeit der Verwundung des Herzens, die unser Erstaunen erregt, sondern immer wieder die erstaunliche Tatsache, was ein menschliches Herz verträgt.[12]

Ich erinnere nur noch einmal an die verschiedenartigen Steckschüsse, die Herzbeutel und Herz betreffen. Welche Toleranz besitzt das Herz in Bezug auf diese Verletzungen![13]

It is questionable whether the ordinary soldier in the trenches on the Western front shared the surgeon's practical and scientific enthusiasm. Soldiers experienced a helpless fear of being struck by sudden death, hit by those 'little things' which sometimes penetrated hearts. In his autobiographical war novel *Die Pflasterkästen — Ein Feldsanitätsroman* (1929) Alexander Moritz Frey (1881–1957) describes such a situation. In 1918, on the Western front, a tiny splinter, kills a young stretcher-bearer.

Und als sollte […] demonstriert werden, durch welche Kleingkeiten man um die Ecke gebracht werden kann […], bekommt eines Morgens der jüngere der beiden Kanzlisten ein Splitterchen in Linsengröße ab. […] Wo fehlt's ihm denn, ist er getroffen, wo ist er getroffen? Er blutet nicht, die Uniform ist heil – soweit eine deutsche Uniform 1918 heil genannt werden kann. Unbegreiflich, aber deutlich sichtbar, verfällt er in wenigen Sekunden. Hier ist ganz eindeutig zu sehen, wie der Tod das Leben erobert, Schritt um Schritt und Griff um Griff, mit sicherer Faust. […] Jener ist weiß, wird grau, dann gelb. Sein Mund schnappt einmal, zweimal kräftig – und ebensooft um eine Kraftstufe schwächer. Die Lippen werden farblos – unterm nächsten Zugriff schimmern sie blau. Er hat die Augen geschlossen – daß sie nun halb aufgehen, ist kein Erwachen, kein Zurückkehren, es ist das Erschlaffen der Lider, die auf Halbmast gehen und keinen Blick mehr enthüllen, nur das Gebrochene ehemaliger Blicke. […] Stabsarzt Fünfer faßt nur noch an einem Körper umher, der schon kalt wird. […] "Da ist offenbar etwas ganz Kleines mitten ins Herz gedrungen," formuliert Fünfer seine Diagnose ungewollt und ungewöhnlich albern.[14]

---

12   Ibid., p. 799: "As never before, this enormous war offered numerous chances to give medical attention to heart injuries, to perform operations or autopsies on the heart. Surely, we can be certain that, in this war, most injuries of the heart have never been inspected by a doctor. And most of those cases inspected were hopeless. However, pre-war success had led to a large interest in heart injuries among internists, pathologists, and surgeons. As a consequence, knowledge as well as our practical experience have grown enormously. Not only the variety of possible heart injuries but in so many cases the endurance of this very organ is just amazing."

13   Ibid., p. 815: "I just remind you again of the variety of retained missiles. How tolerant is the heart in regard to these injuries!"

14   Frey: *Die Pflasterkästen: Ein Feldsanitätsroman*, pp. 201–02: "As if to demonstrate what minor events can make a person kick the bucket, one morning the younger one of the two clerks

IV. Martial Metaphors

Some doctors compared World War I to well-known patho-physiological phenomena. By implication their attempt to 'explain' the war, however, aestheticized it in biological terms. A pathologist from Freiburg, Ludwig Aschoff, compared the fight of the nations to the "fight" of blood cells, referring in particular to leukocytes:

> Diese Zellen entstammen im wesentlichen den altbekannten Depots der Blutbildungsstätten, unter denen beim erwachsenen Menschen die verschiedenen Knochen mit ihrem Knochenmark als Hauptgarnisonsstädte in Betracht kommen. Wie leicht und schnell diese Mobilmachung der Leukocytentruppen vor sich geht, kann man am besten daraus ersehen, daß schon eine leichte Reizung des großen Telegraphensystems der Eingeweide [...] genügt, um sofort Truppen vom Knochenmark in die Blutwege übertreten zu lassen.[15]

Martial metaphors and images of fighting became popular in medical language. Large groups of the medical profession adopted the doctrine of Social Darwinism, transferring biological terminology from Charles Darwin's theory of evolution to the realm of social and political discourse.

---

is hit by a tiny fragment as big as a lentil. He was listening to the grenade going off in the garden, obviously near the wall, for we can hear wood creak and stones burst – and then noisy boots hurrying down the steps to the cellar. They carry and drag him along because he cannot walk any more. What's wrong with him? Has he been hit? Where has he been hit? He is not bleeding, his uniform is still decent as far as a German uniform can be called decent in 1918. Unbelievable, but clearly visible he collapses within seconds. Here you can clearly see death conquering life, step by step, grip by grip, with an iron fist. He is white, he turns to grey and then yellow. He vehemently gasps for breath once, twice, and then twice again, but weaker. The colour vanishes from his lips, they are turning blue. He keeps his eyes shut. They are now half open, but that does not mean he is awake, nor coming back. It simply means that his eyelids go limp, that they are at half-mast and do not unveil a glance, merely a mirror of former glances. Captain Fünfer of the medical corps touches a body that is turning cold. 'Obviously, something really small penetrated his heart', Fünfer's diagnosis was expressed in a silly way, which was not intended, however."

15 Aschoff: *Krankheit und Krieg: Eine akademische Rede*, p. 15; Schmiedebach: "Sozialdarwinismus, Bio logismus, Pazifismus – Ärztestimmen zum Ersten Weltkrieg," p. 104: "These cells essentially originate in the well-known deposits of sanguification, the different bones including the marrow being the major garrison towns in adults. How easily and how quickly these leukocytes can be mobilized can be concluded from the time it takes to rush legions from the marrow into the veins as soon as the large telegraph system of the entails is stimulated."

V. Social Darwinism and War

An application of ideas of Social Darwinism to positional warfare with its high casualty rate, wiping out the 'strongest' in the first lines while protecting the 'weak' and 'unfit' behind the front, was largely accepted by the medical profession regardless of individual doctors' personal attitude towards the war. However, conclusions and expectations resulting from this view differed a great deal. Max von Gruber, Bavarian hygienist (1853–1927), pan-German and radical Anglophobe, romantic and idealist mystic of German culture (*Deutschtum*), particularly feared for the life of those "healthy, strong, bold, active, dutiful, willing to sacrifice, born to be leaders and fighters."[16] Yet, he was basically optimistic about the possibility to fill this gap by "extensive reproduction" of the healthy survivors after the end of the war. Georg Friedrich Nicolai (1874–1964), physiologist and pacifist from Berlin did not share such fantasies. His ideas were determined by the Social Darwinist warning of "counterselective" mechanisms and "degeneration of the population" by demographic, that is biological, effects of the war. In his *Biologie des Kriegs* he states in 1919:

> Der Krieg schützt die Blinden, die Taubstummen, die Idioten, die Buckligen, die Skrofulösen, die Blödsinnigen, die Impotenten, die Paralytiker, die Epileptiker, die Zwerge, die Mißgeburten. All dieser Rückstand und Abhub der menschlichen Rasse kann ruhig sein, denn gegen ihn pfeifen keine Kugeln. [...] Der Krieg bildet also für sie geradezu eine Lebensversicherung, denn diese körperliche und geistige *Krüppelgarde*, die sich im freien Konkurrenzkampf des Friedens gegen ihre tüchtigen Mitbewerber kaum behaupten könnte, bekommt nun die fettesten Stellen und wird hoch bezahlt.[17]

Akin to the pacifist Nicolai, the leading neurologist and war psychiatrist Max Nonne (1861–1959) characterized the negative selection of the war in his pessimistic retrospective of 1922. According to Nonne, it is a "shame" that the war, by protecting the "inferior," selected successfully exactly contrary to Darwin's principles.

---

16 Ibid., p. 101; Eucken and Gruber: *Ethische und hygienische Aufgaben der Gegenwart*, pp. 27–8.

17 Schott: *Die Chronik der Medizin*, p. 385: "The war protects those blind, deaf, or hunchbacked, the idiots and lunatics, the ones tuberculous, impotent, or paralytic, the epileptics, the dwarfs, those deformed. All those retarded, the whole scum of the human race, they can be at peace, as no bullets threaten them. For them, the war is a mere life insurance, for this troop of physical and mental cripples, which can rarely compete with their competent fellowmen when applying for a job during peace times, without free competition they now get the best jobs and are very well paid."

Die besten werden geopfert, die körperlich und geistig Minderwertigen, Nutzlo-
sen und Schädlinge werden sorgfältig konserviert, anstatt daß bei dieser günstigen
Gelegenheit eine gründliche Katharsis stattgefunden hätte, die zudem durch den
Glorienschein des Heldentodes die an der Volkskraft zehrenden Parasiten verklärt
hätte.[18]

VI. Unveiling the Malingerers and Breaking Their Will

Soldiers were often unable to cope with technological warfare which produced an apocalyptic inferno of permanent shelling, dazzling lightning and
thunder, piercing sounds of exploding shells, perfidious twittering, humming
and whistling of projectiles and ricochets, shouts and groaning of the wounded and the sight of disfigured bodies during the "Stahlgewitter" in Flanders
and the Argonne.[19] Many soldiers suffered nervous breakdowns, began trembling, cramped, threw up, wetted themselves, fell silent, shut themselves off
the outside world or reacted to the conditions in other deviant ways. The psychiatrist J. Raecke remembered in 1919:

> So schor sich ein Soldat ein Kreuz ins Haupthaar, um angeblich gegen Flieger-
> bomben gesichert zu sein [...]. Ein anderer brachte bei der Aufnahme einen
> Frosch an der Leine mit und sagte, das sei ein Bär. Einige tranken Tinte und er-
> klärten dieselbe für guten Wein.[20]

'War neuroses' and 'shell shock' dominated German psychiatry during the
years of war.[21] War psychiatrists, however, remained wary of becoming their
patients' allies. They preferred to unveil "malingerers" and "moral weak-
lings." By unmasking opponents of the war and breaking their patients' un-
willingness to continue to fight, the doctors complied with the political objec-

---

18 Max Nonne: "Therapeutische Erfahrungen an den Kriegsneurosen in den Jahren 1914 bis
    1918." *Handbuch der ärztlichen Erfahrungen im Weltkriege 1914/1918* vol. 4, pp. 102–21, p. 112:
    "The best ones will be sacrificed, the physically and mentally inferior, the useless and the
    pests are carefully being conserved. Instead, a thorough catharsis should have been staged
    at that opportunity, additionally glorifying those who died on the battlefield, otherwise
    minimizing a nation's energy."
19 Jünger: *In Stahlgewittern.* 33. Aufl. (1992).
20 Raecke: "Über Aggravation und Simulation gei stiger Störung," p. 588: "In order to protect
    himself from the bomb raids, he cut a cross into his hair. Another one came with a frog on
    a leash pretending it to be a bear. Some were drinking ink pretending it to be wine." – Ried-
    esser and Verderber: *Aufrüstung der Seelen – Militärpsychiatrie und Militärpsychologie in Deutsch-
    land und Amerika.*
21 Fischer-Homberger: *Die traumatische Neurose,* pp. 136–70.

tives of the period. These objectives were as perverse as their methods of application: surprise attacks by electric shocks, painful electric sine currents often to be endured for hours – the so-called "Kaufmann-Kur" –, the coercion to swallow one's vomit, X-rays in darkrooms, solitary confinement for weeks, provoking the mortal agony of suffocation by inserting a laryngo bougie, mock operations under etherization which created the terror of execution.[22] Patients who had undergone such medical treatment ended up as broken characters and were sometimes sent back directly to the front. Many patients did not survive. After treatment by war psychiatrists only few patients were "kriegsverwendbar" (fit for the war). At best, they could be used in ordnance factories.

VII. Herzklopfer

A subgroup of the so-called *Kriegsneurotiker* was formed by the *Herzneurotiker*, heart neurotics. The war, in a figurative sense, had penetrated the soldiers' chests injuring their hearts. In his war novel "Aufbruch der Nationen" (1929) Franz Schauwecker (born in 1890) describes such a heart-rending situation. Although the experience of a bursting grenade was a common one, Schauwecker chooses an expressionist language to paint a dazzling picture of the explosion and its psychophysical effects on soldiers in the trenches. Thus, Schauwecker's autobiographical fragment converts into the brutal aesthetics of war. In a forward trench at the Eastern front Albrecht, a former student, experiences for the first time the death of a comrade.

> Ein Klumpen von Glut und Druck zerbarst schmetternd. Brocken spritzen weg. Dampf wirbelte kochend, und ein blendender Strahl von Hitze fuhr in den Graben. Schnurgrade über Albrechts Kopf weg stand ein hundertfacher Pfiff aus glühenden Ventilen, ein sausendes Gewirr von Motoren. Er begriff nichts. Er war eiskalt mit Würgen und Schlucken. Sein Herz loderte blutig in der vertrockneten Kehle. Jemand krächzte und schlug um sich. Jemand lag auf der Erde, an die Grabenwand geschleudert, ein schreiender Haufen, blödsinnig verdreht. Totenstille. Nur die Stimme schrie. Albrecht erhob sich taumelnd. Was war das? Da standen Herse, Merker, Wermig über den Haufen gebeugt, der jetzt mit einem Male nur ächzte, ganz tief aus der Brust heraus mit einem Brodeln in der Luftröhre. Brenn trat vorsichtig hinzu. Albrecht folgte ihm fassungslos. Was war das? Er starrte bebend durch das Gedränge hindurch, das durch rasch hinzukommende Soldaten

---

22 Riedesser and Verderber: *Aufrüstung der Seelen – Militärpsychiatrie und Militärpsychologie in Deutschland und Amerika*, pp. 11–20.

anwuchs. Da lag Helm auf der Erde. Er lag da wachsgelb, mit halbgeschlossenen Augen, halb auf der Seite und stöhnte leise, ein röchelndes Knurren von Krampf und Schmerz. Mit einem Male war er weggewischt aus der Reihe der andern. Im Graben entstand Bewegung. "Sanitäter!" rief eine Stimme. Ein Sanitätsunteroffizier erschien und kniete sachlich bei dem Verwundeten. "Bauchschuß von der Seite," sagte er. "Und'n Schulterschuß hat er auch noch. Da sitzt auch noch was am Bein. Den müssen wir in den Unterstand haben. Hier ist nichts zu wollen." Eine Bahre aus Weidengeflecht kam. Holm, der nur ein Gewimmer von sich gab, wurde vorsichtig hinaufgehoben. Er hielt die Augen geschlossen und die Hand an die rechte Seite gepreßt. Er hatte mit alldem hier nichts mehr zu tun. Man trug ihn fort.[23]

Soldiers traumatized by such shocking events and suffering from 'shell shock' were of special interest to war-psychiatrists. Soldiers whose reaction to the trauma was more of a physical nature as in cases of *Herzneurose* fell into the hands of internists. Among the latter we find August Hoffmann (1862–1929), Brigadier General of the Medical Corps during the war and in the twenties professor for internal diseases and director of a university hospital in Düsseldorf. Immediately after the war, Hoffmann wrote a detailed article on "Funktionelle and nervöse Herzkrankheiten" which was published in 1921 in the *Handbuch der ärztlichen Erfahrungen im Weltkriege 1914/1918*. On the origins of *Herzneurose* he offered his own ideas.

---

23 Schauwecker: *Aufbruch der Nation*, p. 59: "A lump of heat and pressure exploded with a bang. Scraps splashed. Boiling steam was swirling and a dazzling beam of heat spurted into the trench. Directly above Albrecht's head red-hot valves were whistling a hundredfold, a tangle of buzzing motors. He did not understand anything. He was freezing cold, he had to swallow hard. His heart was blee ding, and he was choked with fear. Somebody was screaming while lashing out. Somebody was lying on the ground, flung towards the side of the trench, a screaming lump, twisted unnaturally. Deathly silence. Merely the voice gave a yell. Albrecht stood up staggering. What was that? He saw Herse, Merker, and Wermig bent over this lump, which suddenly started to groan deep down from his chest with a seeting in his gullet. Brenn went near him cautiously. Albrecht followed him in complete bewilderment. What was that? Trembling he peered through the crowd which was enlarged by soldiers quickly arriving. It was Helm lying on the ground. He was lying on his side, his face was yellow, like wax, his eyelids half shut, cramps and pain made him groan, a death rattle. All of a sudden he was torn away from the others. There was motion all over the trench. 'Orderly!' a voice called. A medic appeared and knelt down beside the wounded. 'He was shot in the stomach from the side', he said. 'And he's got a shot in the shoulder as well. The leg is hurt, too. We have to bring him to the dugout. There is nothing to be done for him any more.' A wicker stretcher was brought. Helm was carefully bedded on it. He was merely whimpering now, his eyes were shut, his hand pressed on the right side. He had nothing to do with all that any more. He was carried off."

Mancher konstitutionell Schwächliche, der bei ruhiger Friedenstätigkeit vielleicht niemals etwas von seinem Herzen gespürt hätte, erkrankte unter den physischen und psychischen Einwirkungen des Kriegsdienstes, da er diesen von vornherein nicht gewachsen war. [...] Dazu kam die psychische Infektion, die nervös Erkrankte auf Disponierte ausübten, so daß sich von wenigen Neurotikern ganze Epidemien an geeigneten Stellen ausbreiten konnten.[24]

Hoffmann maintained that an earlier sense of duty and desire to defend the country was later replaced with selfish feelings. Moreover, the "negative effects" of poor nutrition and abuse of alcohol and nicotine (Genußgifte) had led to circulatory disturbances on a large scale as well as to a certain refractoriness towards medical treatment ("refraktäres Verhalten gegenüber ärztlichen Einwirkungen"). He also attributed adversary effects to false diagnoses. Soldiers, he argued, had been led to believe to be suffering from heart disease: "*Herzfehler, Herzerweiterung*, diese Worte fielen allzu oft und hafteten sich in dem Bewußtsein der Kranken fest, die darin die willkommene Bestätigung ihrer eigenen Ansicht, wirklich herzkrank zu sein, fanden und nicht wieder von diesem Glauben abzubringen waren."[25] Nevertheless, Hoffmann also was convinced that the experience of war in the trenches could lead to heart diseases "auf psychisch nervösem Wege." Physicians observed neurasthenic soldiers, in particular under shell-fire, and recorded quickened pulses and many extrasystols. In analogy to the shell-shocked soldiers who were discriminated against by being labeled *Kriegszitterer* all patients on the killing fields of the Western front who reacted to heavy shell-fire with quickened pulses were called *Herzklopfer*. According to Hoffmann, theirs was an understandable reaction of the body and not only characteristic of war conditions. In his opinion, similar phenomena could be observed in times of peace, for instance during sporting events.

Es ist eine, auch in Friedenszeiten bekannte Erfahrung, daß mangelnder Schlaf und übermäßige, namentlich mit seelischen Erregungen verbundene, körperliche

---

24 August Hoffmann: "Funktionelle und nervöse Herzkrankheiten." Schjerning, ed.: *Handbuch der ärztlichen Erfahrungen im Weltkriege 1914/1918* vol. 3, pp. 470–505: "Many a weakly disposed soldier fell ill under the physical and emotional stress of war service, which he was not able to cope with. Probably none of them would have even perceived his heart in quiet times of peace. Besides, there was a kind of mental infection of those disposed caused by soldiers who had already fallen sick with nervousness. At crucial points, a few neurotics only could really be starting off a mental epidemic."

25 Ibid., p. 477: "*Cardiac defect, dilatation of the heart*, too often could these words be heard. They stuck to the minds of the sick firmly who were truly convinced to suffer from heart disease. It was impossible to get them off this delusion."

Anstrengung, wie sie besonders beim Sport vorkommt, Störungen des Kreislaufs auslösen können. Auch hier sieht man Tachykardien, verbunden mit allgemeinen nervösen Störungen, auftreten. Es ist aber bei körperlichen Anstrengungen der Kriegsteilnehmer zu berücksichtigen, daß sie unter Umständen geleistet werden, bei denen das psychische Moment eine große Rolle spielt. Die stete Lebensgefahr, die Spannung aller geistigen und körperlichen Kräfte, die Ungewißheit des Ausganges und des Erfolges, all dies Psychische wirkt hier mit den körperlichen Anstrengungen zusammen ein. Beim Sport ist es ja ebenso.[26]

Sorrow for the beloved at home and homesickness should not be neglected either and Hoffmann was aware that many a heart was burdened or even broken by these emotions. But not only common emotional factors had to be taken into consideration. The war-internist also blamed the individual psycho-physical constitution and pre-war experiences for certain reactions to conditions at the front. While cautioning that oversimplifying schemes should be avoided, he observed:

> Ich habe hünenhafte Recken gesehen, die mit ihrem Herzen nervös zusammenbrachen, und zarte, schlanke Gestalten, die trotz großer aufregender Ereignisse und körperlichen Strapazen keine Symptome von Kreislaufstörungen zeigten. Sehr wichtig war dabei der bisherige Beruf. Kopfarbeiter und Leichtarbeiter erkrankten besonders häufig mit nervösen Kreislaufsymptomen.[27]

Hoffmann explained the fact that farmers were overrepresented among the *Herzneurotiker* by referring to the special character of this profession which, he said, is particularly peaceful

> und dessen Ausüber gegenüber den ins furchtbarste gesteigerten Wirkungen der technischen modernen Kampfmittel vielleicht leichter psychisch versagen. Die Schwerarbeiter, die das geringste Kontingent stellten, sind einerseits durch die ständige Muskelübung gegen Anstrengungen und Strapazen unempfindlicher, an-

---

26 Ibid., p. 485: "Lack of sleep, excessive phy sical stress accompanied by emotional strain, as in sporting competitions for instance, frequently cause circulatory disturbances. Even in times of peace this is a well-known experience. In these cases we find a high frequency of the heartbeat often combined with nervous disturbances. In wartime it has to be considered that extreme physical exertion is always accompanied with emotional stress. Permanent danger to life, strain of all mental and physical forces, uncertainty of ending and success, all these mental factors co-operate with physical exertion. In sporting competition it's just alike."

27 Ibid., p. 487: "I saw herculean built warriors with nervous breakdowns of their heart as well as sensitive and slim figures who although being under extreme psycho-physical stress do not show any sign of a circulatory disturbances. The pre-war profession played a dominant role in whether somebody had nervous circulatory disturbances, in particular men with braines or those doing light work were easily affected."

dererseits auch gegenüber den maschinellen Kampfmitteln weniger psychisch empfänglich.[28]

Therapies for neurosis of the heart and circulatory disorders were not very specific. Hoffmann was convinced that a lot, if not everything, depended on the physician's strong personality. Especially his suggestive power to fight against the soldier's auto-suggestion to be suffering from heart disease seemed to be of great importance to him. He added, however:

> Mit brüskem Vorgehen ist da nichts zu erreichen, es müssen eben hier andere Wege eingeschlagen werden, die in einer zielbewußten Persuasion, die durch entsprechende Allgemeinbehandlung unterstützt wird, bestehen. [...] Massage, passive Bewegung, Widerstandsgymnastik, [...] Gehübungen, Spazierengehen, später Bewegungsspiele und schließlich Exerzieren nach Kommando und Turnen nach Kommando brachten den besten Erfolg.[29]

VIII. "Iron Will" – Treatments of War Victims

With its new killing techniques, the effects of this first modern war were like Pandora opening her box on the battlefields of Europe. After the end of the war, many scars remained: topographic-ecological ones on the churned up landscapes of the Vosges, the Argonne, at the Somme and in Flanders, with trees destroyed, fields soaked with human blood and hundreds of thousands of hungry rats feeding on dead bodies; social and physical scars in the burnt down villages and broken rural communities, blown up by grenades; tormented bodies and souls of survivors with bitter wounds and bitter feelings.[30]

In the wake of the war the most striking aspect of the scene was the legion of the blind, amputees, deranged and disfigured men. This picture emerged as early as months after the outbreak of the war. In early 1915, prior to the huge battles of material in the west, the number of mutilated soldiers, according to estimations by Konrad Biesalski, a doctor of orthopedics, amounted to

---

28 Ibid., pp. 493–94: "which is a rather peaceful one. The farmer's nervous system probably breaks down more easily when he is faced with these most terrible effects of this war's modern technical weapons. The industrial heavy worker, hardened to exertion and drudgery by daily muscle training is less sensitive to mechanical weapons."

29 Ibid., pp. 496–97: "In these cases nothing can be achieved by harsh methods. Just the opposite has to be applied: Best results are produced by determined persuasion accompanied and supported by massage, passive movement of the limbs, gymnastics, walking exercises, outdoor games and finally drill and physical exercise on command."

30 Whalen: *Bitter Wounds: German Victims of the Great War, 1914–1939.*

30,000. Reactions back home were as different as the physical distortions themselves. There was a boom in the design and production of orthopedic prosthetics (among them the so-called "Sauerbrucharm") and of plastic surgery. There was the half-hearted attempt to secure the *Kriegskrüppel* (disabled war veterans) and their families financially, and there was the attempt to remove disfigured and ugly bodies from the peaceful street scenes of the cities as well as from the minds, the *Entkrüppelung*. An "iron will" was supposed to make those shattered by war, "die Kriegszermalmten" deal with their impairments and finally overcome them. Firm belief in medical and technical progress was believed to modify the souls of the victims as well as public opinion. An "iron will" was supposed to humanize the war by looking at it from afar. Every possible way to play down the war victims' problems was pursued, especially by the print media, that published photographs of disabled sportsmen, farmers reaping the corn or engineers with artificial arms producing precision tools.

The Weimar Republic tried to rapidly reintegrate the war victims into the working world by means of pensions at or below subsistence level, the brutal demand to increase efficiency, warnings not to pamper the war victims, appealing even to the wives of victims, the hysterical searching for fraudulent pension claims (*Rentenbetrügerei*), an insinuated crime that poisoned social-political discourse. The objective was to "disperse them among the working population as if nothing had happened."[31] In the end all attempts failed. What remained was a legion of men destroyed and unable to support themselves. They fell through the holes of a social net too thin and too small for them and their families. A situation that should have been avoided: injustice and dissatisfaction prepared a fertile soil for violence and political agitators who would lead to a new disaster.

---

31   Ulrich: "'… als wenn nichts geschehen wäre': Anmerkungen zur Behandlung der Kriegsopfer während des Ersten Weltkriegs." Hirschfeld and Krumeich: *Keiner fühlt sich hier mehr als Mensch …: Erlebnis und Wirkung des Ersten Weltkriegs*, pp. 115–29, p. 118.

LISABETH DURING
University of New South Wales, Sydney

The Failure of Love:
A Lesser Theory of the Great War

Abstract: In this paper I want to point out some reasons why war, in particular the war of 1914–1918, gets in the way of love, whether that be the transports of sexual bliss or the pleasures of private conversation. For various reasons my discussion is limited to heterosexual love. This was the love requiring intimate understanding between the two sexes, the love that flourishes when the sexes are recognised in their differences. *It* suffered the most by competition with this war which, as Freud remarked soon after it was over, developed libidinal structures all of its own. In an essay on group psychology Freud gives us some hints why this might be the case: Two people, coming together for the purpose of sexual satisfaction, in so far as they seek for solitude, are making a demonstration against the herd instinct, the group feeling.[1]

I.

I began this paper thinking about a history already much contested, the history of the fractured relations between literary modernism and the 'sexual question': the problem as it stood, by August 1914, between men and women.[2] Modernism covers a multitude of sins: the ones I am interested in have more to do with love than with language. I was intrigued by the moral uncertainties

---

1 Freud: "Group psychology and the analysis of the ego." *Civilization, Society and Religion,* p. 174.
2 The problem does not just affect modernism as a literary movement, of course. For the connections between pictorial modernism, war, sexual difference, and crises in the bedroom see Lisa Tickner's recent article "Men's Work? Masculinity and Modernism," p. 3: "The battle of the sexes (for pro- and anti-feminists, especially men) and the exploration of a modern self-determined identity (particularly by women) is *the* modern subject matter even where talk of speed, electricity, cars, planes, and war dominates the manifest content of the work."

of the pre-war and war period rather than the similar confusions in politics and the arts. Yet I doubt very much that these can be kept apart. Hence my reading of certain key moments in the war experience is a symptomatic reading. It pursues a pathology of love.

Psychologically speaking, love between the sexes disturbs the peace. Of those Europeans whose reflections on the Great War have still to be entirely assimilated by our culture, there were few who brooded about the meaning of war in the psyche to such effect as Freud. Two years after the Armistice, Freud published a description of the desire for death which is still astonishing. Its fascination, which I would like to exploit in this paper, is far in excess of its explanatory power.

In a pessimistic trilogy, *Civilisation and its Discontents, Beyond the Pleasure Principle*, and *Thoughts for the Time on War and Death*, Freud refuses an equation between war and the instincts of aggression. That equation had been a staple of the literature on war, at least since Homer. Yet many people have noticed something contradictory in two of the most basic human drives. With all our power we will to survive. Love fastens itself on children, on lovers, because it believes it sees in them an image of our future, our survival. Nothing else holds such a lure for our emotions. Yet the drive to go all the way to destruction, the belligerent streak in all human communities, appears equally primordial. To sing, as the classical poets did, of love and war, is not just to cover all the topics that could possibly attract an audience: it is also to announce a paradox. There is nothing unusual about seeing that. But when Freud looked at the ruins of the human and cultural landscape in 1918 he saw something much stranger.

War, Freud argues, does not express the masculine unconscious brutally unfettered.[3] Its intoxication, so euphoric in those first August days of war-

---

3 Here he sees something quite different from Elias Canetti in his brilliant book from another era: *Crowds and Power* (1960). There are "war crowds" and "packs" of women as well as men, who play an important part in the success of war-expeditions. But more important than the opposing "crowds" (Massen) of "us" and "our enemies," or men and women, are the antagonistic "masses" of living and dead: the fight between the living and the dead will always end with the victory of the dead: "for they are so many." "The living are always on the retreat. Nothing is ever really over." The activity of this "double crowd" is seen most clearly in war, says Canetti: "The aim is to transform a dangerous crowd of live adversaries into *a heap of dead* (my emphasis: Canetti elaborates this image: the relevant mounds could be hands, heads, sometimes penises) ... Death, which in truth threatens every man all the time, must have been proclaimed as a collective sentence before people will oppose it actively. There are, as it were, *declared times of death*, times when it turns on a definite arbitrarily selected group as a whole. It is "death to the French" or "death to the English." The enthusiasm with which men accept such declarations has its root in the individual's cowardice be-

fever, merely appears to be a regressive dream come true, a "discharge of tensions that had built up for years … which the outbreak of war had wiped away," as Magnus Hirschfield put it at the time.[4] Apocalyptic orgies failed to materialise: the hope that this modern, technological war meant a second coming of lost ancestral virility was fantasy, a seductive fantasy fed by nationalistic longings and fears of modernity. The spirit of war, Freud reflects with gloom, is the spirit of death. It has more to do with indifference than with excitement. For its aim is not the increase of tensions but their extinction. But what of the rhetoric of war, its drama, the stage it sets up for a sublime confrontation of fragile man and unrelenting force? No such Wagnerianisms for Freud. The 'purposes' of war do not belong to transcendence, he argues, but to a mundane economy, an economy which aims to control excess, expel surplus, lead the organic back to the 'nether world' of inorganic being. As Hegel understood, the warrior is willing to die in the service of his own sovereignty, but in fact he is all the while the servant of an industry indifferent to him and his desires. Heroism, sacrifice, the trials of human endurance, are the means by which war works its insidious ends; they are not its meaning. The shell-shock victims, whom Freud and other war-time psychologists identified as the first admissible male hysterics, revealed in their nightmares an unexpected signifying process: the effects of modern war, unlike the idealized wars of the past, tend towards paralysis, stillness, suffocation.[5] These men, not cowards,

---

fore death; no one likes facing it alone. The worst that can happen to men in war is to perish together; and this spares them death as individuals, which is what they most fear. Canetti: *Crowds and Power*, p. 74–84.

4   Cited in Leed: *No Man's Land: Combat and Identity in World War I*, p. 40. Leed looks at many similar statements, from the period and later (Stefan Zweig: "this surplus of force, a tragic consequence of the internal dynamism that had accumulated in those forty years of peace and now sought violent release." (p. 52, written in 1941), and equivalent analyses from our own contemporaries, e. g., Arno Mayer: "Both war and revolution release tensions that accumulate in modernizing societies," or Roger Caillois, who likens modern war to premodern festivals, similar in being outbreaks of collective energy that take place outside the normal social hierarchies and codes, liberating fraternal sentiments and libido alike. Leed's accounts stress the fluid, exciting, transitional character of the first days of the war; life, and love, seemed released like a stream of fire, will was "mobilised," collective life suddenly seemed urgent and all-welcoming; the immediacy of this nationalist passion wiped away the stresses and boredoms, the divisions and frustrations, of modern, overly rationalised life. The world was at once simplified and made insistent.

5   Showalter: *The Female Malady: Women, Madness and the English Culture, 1830–1980*, pp. 171–172. See also Rivers: *Instinct and the Unconscious*, Eissler: *Freud as an Expert Witness*, Ferenczi, Abraham, Simmel, and Jones: *Psychoanalysis and the War Neurosis* and Barker's novelisation of the intriguing therapeutic relationship between Rivers and Siegfried Sassoon in her *Regeneration*.

had enlisted expecting action and direction, passion and intensity, to suffuse their lives; what they found was the opposite. Virility, the excess of the creative force, may be necessary to the rhetoric of war, but the reality of war, in particular modernist war, is different; its logic is entropic, its economy nihilistic. So much energy devoted to so self-canceling an end. It's a puzzle. Perhaps its secret lies in the unconscious, that most reactionary of directors, always winding its way back to the past, in increasing circles of repetition:

> It would be in contradiction to the conservative nature of the drives if the goal of life were a state of things which had never yet been attained. On the contrary, it must be an *old* state of things, an initial state from which the living reality has at one time or another departed and to which it is striving to return by the circuitous paths along which its development leads.[6]

Why do men insist on their own destruction, wondered Freud? Because they are afraid of the new and the different. They are afraid of the ambivalence which is life itself and which, in particular, is desire.

The story Freud devises to explain the inexplicable tells of a primordial battle between eros and death, love and apathy. Yet the combatants are hard to keep apart: where, one wonders, will the aggressive instinct finally end up? When civilisations are on the ascent, Eros enlists on the side of survival; the interests of the race – that is, its reproductive imperative – coincides with the organism's need to expend (discharge). But in the stages of decline, the violent urges turn inward, like a disappointed love returning to the comforts of the narcissistic. When the complex structures of the secondary processes break down, and the delicate economy of pleasure and pain is no longer sufficient to reassure the psyche, then the species tries to head downward on the evolutionary chain. This can only be so because the drives, which Freud wants us to see as atavistic survivals of a more primitive organisation of the passions, secretly aim to restore an "earlier state of things." Never far advanced, despite all the interruptions of civilisation, from the inanimate substratum which gave them birth, the drives incline towards the "inertia inherent in organic life." They flee from the disturbances of new stimuli; they withdraw their energies into acts of repetition, osmosis. When Eros is in the ascendant it is reinforced by the aggressive drives. Drawn towards difference, the erotic energy here craves higher thresholds of excitation, in order that the release be all the more rewarding. But when Eros loses faith then its innate violence finds itself denied external expression. Swerving towards death, by "circui-

---

6   Freud: "Beyond the Pleasure Principle," Part V, in *The Pelican Freud Library*, vol. 11: "On Metapsychology," pp. 310–11.

tous paths," the system avoids novelty, resists interruption. The organism sinks to a lower state of quiescence, immobility, duplication. And this, Freud now fears, may be its true purpose: all that we have recognised and admired as productivity, thought, love, the serious games of humankind, can only be seen as "ever more complicated *detours*" before the organism is allowed to "reach its aim of death."[7]

In this paper I want to extend some of Freud's dark meditations about sex and death, narcissism and war. But I want to add to them my own preoccupation with sexual difference, with the way it structures the cultural and spiritual experience of war. Feminine difference, a difference in perception, in desire, even in the very workings of the mind itself, is something with which Freud was notoriously uncomfortable. Yet without the Freudian story and its categories, it is almost impossible to picture the peculiar involvement of sexuality and mass conflict, an involvement which, as Freud suspects, might have been fatal to civilisation. What Freud's story about the death instinct says is that human life contradicts itself. Drawn by an allure that is 'ancient,' long-gone, the species betrays its own instinctual will to self-preservation. Human desire, said Hegel (with a host of others), breaks out of the realm of the animal because it wants more than gratification: it wants acknowledgment, reciprocity, a frame of words in which to be recognised and preserved. Even more, it wants to be wanted. Becoming social, as it must to satisfy *this* want, nature's itch finds that its life is prolonged, its dominion extended. Harnessed to the future of the larger human organism, desire begins to look like the fundamental force of social production. And, after the internal struggle with religion is won, concludes Hegel, it is the State itself which is the biggest beneficiary of desire's industry; while Freud may repeat the received wisdom that the civilised community depends on the renunciation of instinct, he knows quite well that the modern social apparatus flourishes to the degree that it enlists, solicits, and repays desire.

Compared to this felicitous yoking of desire, the state, and violence, (for which the modern state claims monopoly),[8] there is something deeply anarchic in the human psyche. Not entirely the plaything of Eros (or life), the psyche is capable of contemplating the absence of desire. Never mind the threat to social productivity, to the very future of the organism, there are some things which are more seductive than survival itself. Ancient and opaque, on the far side of desire lies the promise of peace, repetition, conservation. The

---

7   Ibid.
8   Weber: *Economy and Society* vol. 1, p. 56.

dream of the death drive is a world without the differences of the sexes, a world which can neither reproduce itself nor summon the energies for its own conflicts. It is the psychic landscape of the infantile, but it is also the image (in some utopias) of a space at the far end of the struggle for human evolution.

This is the world of the neuter, the world where difference of every sort, logical as well as ontological, recedes, because what is there to be different from? With a certain amount of fear and skepticism Freud describes the appeal of the inorganic, that last desire that lies beyond the pleasure principle and is unspeakable, unrepresentable. The realm of the death drive is truly a liminal world, a Nirvana, Freud calls it, a twilight of life where all shapes are blurred, where there is no self or nothing but an anonymous self. Christian asceticism conjures this state in the words of St Paul: there will be no beast or human, no male or female, no danger of frightful hybrid forms, monstrous conjunctions and foreign copulations, because there will be no difference at all to threaten the endless narcissism of the same.

Compared to this, love between the sexes is disruptive. Eros, especially heterosexual eros, is on Freud's account a threat to the death-drive. For Eros lures us into a world of complexity, ambivalence, otherness. It demands that we awaken from our narcissism, our self-containment, our preference not to will or to desire at all. Modern war is in this respect different from ancient war. Foreign to the modern experience of combat is the heroic model of violence, for which love or abduction of women could be an exciting cause, a motive for aggression. The mass neurosis that was the Great War revealed to Freud the temporary victory of the death drive over life. But the turn against desire could only have taken place, he reasoned, if the world blocked out its profound and disquieting knowledge: that one is not alone in the world, that there are two sexes. The first wound in the history of human unhappiness is the discovery of the split between the sexes. Jacques Lacan, who returned this discovery to the center of psychoanalytic theory, used it to make lack the origin of desire. For Lacan, only partly in jest, there is in the Real "no sexual relation."[9] In the Great War this was not a joke.

What happened to the erotic in the Great War? Well, we learned a lot about all the substitutes for the mutual egoism of the heterosexual couple. An entire erotics of the mass, the group, the horde, grew up as if overnight. In a paper of 1920, Freud writes that love between the sexes is incompatible with the war machine. In war, the energies of the erotic and the ego are channeled

---

[9]   Lacan: *Freminine Sexuality*, p. 138.

here, at least initially, into the libidinal structures and ties of the military collective:

> In the great artificial groups, the Church and the army, there is no room for woman as a sexual object. The love relation between men and women remain outside these organisations. There is scarcely any sense in asking whether the libido which keeps groups together is of a homosexual or of a heterosexual nature, for it is not differentiated according to the sexes, and particularly shows a complete disregard for the aims of the genital organization of the libido.[10]

II.

Despite the disquieting insistence on the sexual, Freud's reflections in the 1920s moved within conventional channels. They repeated maxims which were rapidly becoming familiar: that war is a monosexual culture, that the war machinery was incompatible with the sublimation of heterosexual attraction on which culture depends, that the war was an experience which was powerful just to the degree it fed upon sublimated homo-erotic bonds and identifications. Yet Freud, against his better judgment, was also saying something different, not at all conventional. What he had to say would prove distasteful to the militarist and the pacifist alike; it would probably pose just as many problems to that feminist ideology for which it was important that masculinity and war be thought in tandem. For war is not virility under fire; it is not the love between men so long denied that its only image of satisfaction is violent and transgressive. While it has its own relation to the erotic, there is nothing in war that can be clearly assigned to either gender. The sexuality of war is enigmatic. That is its seductive charm.

It has become popular in recent debates over sexuality, identity and definition, to speak in terms of a 'category crisis.' In my reading of Freud, the category crisis which is coterminous with Modernism begins on the battlefield, where the European psyche, late in its career, began to doubt that there was anything fundamental and absolute about the binaries of its culture. To ex-

---

10 Freud: *Civilisation, Society and Religion*, p. 175. Freud also writes here that "there are abundant indications that being in love (*Verliebtheit*) only made its appearance late on in the sexual relations between men and women; so that the opposition between sexual love and group ties is also a late development." Love is, frankly, exceptional, not to say weird: Freud likens it to hypnosis under a lesser state of inhibition. It is a delicate balance between the expression of drives and their restriction, so strenuous in its achievement that, he adds, "it is a condition in which there is only room for the ego and the object." (p. 177).

press that doubt too explicitly might make life unlivable. But there was an option. In the shadowy regions where death and life seemed less distinct, where the soldier's "courtships," as Wilfred Owen wrote, solicited the ghosts of friend and foe, the 'natural' connection (and contrast) between man and woman fails finally to make sense.[11] Freud saw this: The attraction of war borrows from the attraction of the death drive, because both effectively deny sexual difference. In 1914 war was welcomed as a fantasmatic resolution of conflicts between men and women which were fast become unbearable.[12] Yet it was not just for males in mass, men in extremis, that the fact of sexual difference was disturbing. Culture in its most idealised forms had also tried to avert its eyes from the awkward duality of the race.

Even the emotion which most drags men away from barbarism, the sentimental or affectionate love for women, which Freud suspects may be the only card in civilisation's hand, could be seen as aspiring to a state where sexual difference would be minimised. In the idealised language of love, the lover would be a friend, the 'other self' which had been lost from eternity; two bodies, with their awkward discrepancies and asymmetries, would be one. An entire philosophy of eros depends on just this fiction, that true union transcends the differences of the body. This dream of a perfect understanding between lovers, where mutual loyalty, sympathy, dependence, makes the gender differences irrelevant, posed a problem for the politics of feminism. For it was a dream which early feminists convinced themselves they had to contest, even at the cost of renouncing the pleasures of love and the very real comforts of marriage. For the reformers of the fin de siècle and the pre-war period, there was no way a compromise could be accepted, not that easily. Indeed if sentimental bonding, approved by nature, can turn a blind eye to the asymmetry between the sexes, then the weapons of feminism are undone. But the anxieties provoked by early feminist agitation tell us something else. The ideal of harmony was a shallow one. Sexual difference uncovers the lie of a homogenous, ordered world, which belongs to the unspoken politics of patri-

---

11 Wilfred Owen: "Strange Meeting" (1918) – *The Poems*, pp. 125–6.
12 This point, essential to my argument, is also made strongly, and with a wealth of illustration, by Sandra M. Gilbert and Susan Gubar in their *Sexchanges*, vol. 2 of *No Man's Land: The Place of the Woman Writer in the Twentieth Century*. Paul Fussell (*The Great War and Modern Memory*) has been even more psychologically illuminating about the way the war destroyed the language, as well as the social reality, through which masculinity had been experienced, but he is less eager to interpret this as pertaining to the relations between the sexes. On the psychological forces alive in the immediate pre-war period, Leed: *No Man's Land: Combat and Identity in World War I*, is perhaps the most persuasive.

archy. And public displays of feminist discontent betrayed precisely this emptiness at the heart of middle class society ... It is now hard to imagine the shock caused by the spectacle of female armies charging into spaces marked out as single-sex, aloof, 'business-like.'

Indeed among the disorienting experiences of modernity the new visibility of women as a sex stood out as one of the hardest to assimilate. No ready cultural means existed to shape and recuperate that threat. (For it was not demonisable as was the threat of working-class revolt, which could always been portrayed as an anarchic contagion introduced by foreign agents, subversive enemies of the social order. The protest of wives, mothers, sisters, and daughters, presented a different level of criticism entirely.) Faced with this intimate and intractable intruder, bourgeois masculinity realised there was only one defense: deny the issue entirely. The first defense against erosion of the sexual order by feminism had been mounted by an intensified insistence on the 'natural' polarity and separateness of the sexes. And *fin de siècle* culture brooded deeply, irresolutely, on this strange mystery of sexual doubleness. But now, in the first decades of the 20th century, it looked as if the assertion of difference had backfired.

Women, reminded that they were women and not men, now reasonably wonde red why everything in the society had been tailored for only half of its members. In the pre-war suffrage movement, the political menace of sexual difference, represented by an unrepentant feminist movement, brought things to a head. And men reacted with a a conscious and unconscious display of indignation that has retrospectively been dignified with the name 'masculinity crisis.' Modernists in the avant garde capitals of Europe rose to the occasion. Here was a genuine worry, to take their mind off the bourgeoisie for a change: For how long could the destructive energies which are the mark of the 'real' modernist hope to thrive, once feminine qualities were allowed to take over even the least sought-after sectors of cultural space? Without the sexes in their place, things fall apart; the center will not hold. In *Le Figaro* of February 20, 1909, the Italian Futurist Marinetti declaimed on behalf of virile values: "We want to glorify war – the only cleansing act of the world – militarism, patriotism, the destructive act of the anarchists, beautiful ideas which kill, and contempt of women. We want to destroy museums, libraries, to combat moralism, feminism and all such opportunistic and utilitarian acts of cowardice."[13]

But Fascist spleen and posturing was a symptom of this anxiety around gender, not a victory over it; the aesthetics of the phallic modernist were so

13   Marinetti: *Selected Writings*, pp. 39–44.

far unable to imagine a satisfying alternate model of masculine identity, one that would withstand the erosion of will which, for Marinetti, love for women must represent. The counterpart to an aesthetic of power without reciprocity, vigour without sexuality, was the desexualised sentimental love which, as we saw, was one way of weakening the argument of the feminists, by simply denying that conflict between the sexes was necessary. Another option, closer in spirit to the Fascist, was to escape into onanism or a homoerotic metaphysics. None of these, of course, managed to resolve the crisis of masculinity. But in a few short years the outbreak of war, which at least in the beginning was hailed as the lost national identity of the masculine sex, made these problems irrelevant. Here at last was a space sacred to the "No Woman," as Freud noted when discussing the psychology of the 'artificial hordes' like the church and the army: if these collectivities lack any clear differentiation according to the recognisable systems of gender or desire, what they manage above all to 'lack' is the pressure, the presence of 'difference.'[14]

Not simply in the monastic or hierarchical structure of the 'group' but in its code of loyalty, its discourse of solidarity, 'bloodbrotherhood' and its simple wiping out of the fraught differential of sex, war was a refuge: A refuge from love, at least from heterosexual love, with its uncertainties, its pain, its confusing physicality and equally humiliating failure. When the generation of August 1914 glowed with exquisite anticipation of martyrdom, they saw themselves like Rupert Brooke's swimmers in his terrifying poem *Peace* (1914):

> Now, God be thanked Who has matched us with His hour,
> And caught our youth, and wakened us from sleeping,
> With hand made sure, clear eye, and sharpened power,
> To turn, as swimmers into cleanness leaping,
> Glad from a world grown old and cold and weary,
> Leave the sick hearts that honour could not move,
> And half-men, and their dirty songs and dreary,
> And all the little emptiness of love![15]

For it was no secret that the imagery of war depicted a place which, if it was wholly elsewhere, removed from any social reality one knew, was also gender-free. Likened to water, to fire, to a "powerful current of the national tide," elemental and unstoppable, erect and proud, wave-like and surging, war's gendered metaphors managed to cancel themselves out. When the young men who enlisted on August the 3rd saw the adventure they were embarking on as

---

14 Cf. above, Note 10.
15 Brooke: *Complete Poems*, p. 146.

a rite of purification, they believed that for them the sordid reality of an old world would be swept off and, like the clean machines of the future, the body would be once again intact, untouched by any secret places and internal sensations. They dreamt of a body that would be pure exteriority, armour without insides, a fantasy worthy of a Wilhelm Reich or an Ernst Jünger. They dreamt of a world without the taint of sexuality, and more particularly, without the contamination of the feminine. And they got their wish. But the repression – or avoidance, disavowal of that disturbing truth – exacted its price.

In fact the sinister revelation of the body, which made sex less than ideal and a woman 'something other' than a mate, did not disappear. Abject physicality returned, but this time not as the mingled limbs of sex and its secretions. Strung from the wires of No Man's Land, disaggregated bodies forced themselves onto the senses, dismembered not in passion but in decay. In the decades before 1914 European civilisation feared its own unmanning: there was too much peace, too much bourgeois complacency and comfort. If neurosis was a threat, surely it was from not having enough to do, from being offered nothing but an education that stultified and punished the spirit of experimentation. Advanced young women like Freud's patients Bertha Pappenheim and Ida Bauer, like Vera Brittain and her friends and Henry James' Olive Chancellor, became, in the jargon of the day, 'morbid' because of the lack of outlet for their wits and energies. But alarm bells did not at first go off, for this was no more than the usual fate of femininity. What was newly worrying in the pre-war period was the prospect of it happening to men: denied challenge, crushed out of a place in the open by the sheer weight of the old and the over – swelling population, a young masculine generation was in danger of becoming 'feminised,' impotent, decadent. To this problem war seemed an ideal solution. Who realised that the wounded and shell shock victims who crept home from the front would have reproduced precisely the conditions of feminine hysteria, futility and resentment, which they went to war to escape?

The culture that denied the co-presence of male and female reproduced them in its image world, in its unconscious. It was equally intolerable that there be no sexual difference, and that there be two sexes. When Freud, in the heady years of the *fin de siècle* and the pre-war, listened to his hysterical patients, the message he heard was this: I can't tell if I'm a man or a woman. The anxiety over sexual identity plagued the neurotics, for whom it was an indication of social unhappiness, a sign that one could not play one's part. And the anxiety over sexual identity plagued the feminists, the New Women, the sexual reformers, for whom it was a sign of political injustice, oppressive social arrangements, bad hygiene, and inept education. And it plagued the prophets of cultural despair, like Spengler and Weiniger, for whom it represented nothing less than the *degeneration* of the race, the final, syphilitic crisis of world civilisation. War, whatever else it might bring, would clarify this situation. Or would it?

III.

My reading of love, modernity and war challenges a rival sexual theory of the body and mind of the war generation. That other sexual theory of the war is Klaus Theweleit's now notorious inquiry into the masculine imaginary of fascism.[16] In Theweleit's thesis, the fascist mind had an opponent bent on its annihilation, and femininity was its secret name. Racism, which acquired a more and more menacing aspect in the history of National Socialism, borrowed its significance from this more totalising aversion, says Theweleit. For the fascist, all the clear and upright structures of identity and pride – culture, the nation, the Volk, the army – are helpless in the face of an insidious, formless mass. As that mass spreads, it brings dissolution and a painful decomposition of everything pure, defined, everything whole and clean and unified. In Theweleit's account, that abjected mass bears a gendered sign. The horrors it represents, whether the revolutionary mob *or* the shameless whores who prey on the 'clean' bodies of young men *or* the degenerate diseases seen as lurking in either, are interchangeable. And, for the Fascist imaginary, they are also interchangeable with their counterpart, the feminised man, the Jew.[17]

---

16 Klaus Theweleit: *Male Fantasies*.

17 Did Freud anticipate the conflations in the fascist imaginary? Sander Gilman has argued for the understanding of the unconscious links between "the stereotypical representations of race and those of gender in Freud's work and times." In these times, Gilman shows, "the relationship between the stereotype of the Jew and that of the woman (as parallel categories to the Christian and the male) became a central element in the structuring of Jewish identity. Neither image reflected an unmediated conceptual category. Each was constructed to present a means of influencing aspects of a world thought to be out of control." But how far was Freud complicit in these identifications? With Nietzsche and Otto Weininger he saw parallels between the "deviant" state of femininity – subjected because of their oppression and exclusion from culture to a higher degree of neurotic symptoms and defenses: they are "secretive," "insincere'; their desires are "obscure" – and the marginal state of the Jew. Gilman: *Freud, Race and Gender*, pp. 7; 37. Gilman suggests that Freud's assumption of the "persona of male scientist" was his defense against the feminisation of his race, as the scientist stood for the idealised construction of the masculine in the late nineteenth century. If not for this fragile identification, what could protect the male Jew from "turning into a woman," that is to say, into a "truncated man," a man with less of a penis, which is how, Gilman reminds us, the nineteenth century saw the circumcised Jew, and Freud, we know all too well, saw woman. "The 'Jew' is the male hidden within the body of the female for Freud. In Freud's discussion of the nature of the female body, the distinction between male

Theweleit's diagnosis is compelling. But from my reading of comparable experiences, especially those using the language of Modernism, gender functions in a different way. There are other names for alterity than Woman, other ways of signifying the critical erosion of masculine definition. I agree that the reality which the war generation found difficult to accept was a reality marked deeply by sexual difference, with all the ambiguity that presented. But I find Theweleit's continuation of sex mythology by other means avoids the opportunity for critique which he could have seized. I find myself asking the same question of him as of other anxious modernists: Ezra Pound, D. H. Lawrence, Wyndham Lewis.[18] Why is the unman read as woman? why are we

---

Aryan and male Jew is repressed, to be inscribed on the body of the woman." (Ibid., p. 40) Freud's most Oedipal disciple, Jung, was to make even greater mileage out of the prevalent association of "feminisation" and the Jew: if Jews are a "third sex," as the apostate Weininger certainly believed, then should we be taking our sexual problems to this new class of "Jewish doctors'? If modern culture is finding it harder and harder to tell the difference between masculine and feminine, it may be that the "Judification" of that culture has been to blame. The path between psychoanalytic "homologies" and fascist "facts" (a path Theweleit illustrates so vividly) starts looking very short indeed. – In a move that Freud would understand, the fascist imagination converts the death drive, as Julia Kristeva says, to a "terrified loathing of the mother's body," using this to conceal the counterpart Freud believed its double: "eroticised aggression against the father." Kristeva repeats the cultural truth: there is a "universal partnership between death and the penis-lacking feminine." Kristeva: *Black Sun: Depression and Melancholia*. And it is this interchangeability which the (male) neurotic reenacts in his guilt and his aggression.

18 Feminist analysis of the phallic anxieties of Modernist artists is now advancing into its second generation, yet the material itself has not lost its capacity to astonish. Sandra Gilbert and Susan Gubar's "Preface" to their major study *No Man's Land: The Place of the Woman Writer in the Twentieth Century*, vol. 2, gives a classic precis: "'Make it new,' Ezra Pound famously exhorted his contemporaries as he struggled to fashion a modernist aesthetic for a modern world. The statement would appear to be gender-free, but elsewhere the 'Sage Homme' who acted as midwife to *The Waste Land* (as opposed, presumably, to a 'sage femme,' whose intervention in the pregnancy would have the opposite effect, LD) strikingly sexualised his definitions of what was new and who could make it. Explaining in his translator's preface to Remy de Gourmont's *Natural Philosophy of Love* (1931) that 'the brain itself [is] only a sort of great clot of genital fluid.' Pound went on to conceptualize originality as 'the phallus or spermatozoid charging, head-on, the female chaos,' adding in a confessional aside, 'Even oneself has felt it, driving any new idea into the great passive vulva of London.'" (p. xi) Carolyn Baurke uses the same Poundian remark in her subtle discussion of American modernism and gender. Pound, she conjectures, was himself in these early days of the post-war unsure about the co-extension of poet and virile intellect: "Already at a disadvantage as a 'colonial,' an exile, and a man of letters, Pound's sense of himself as a member of the more powerful sex was further challenged be the apparent threat posed by the suffragists' political and literary agitation. Like the aggressive dress and behavior that he adopted in these years, his recourse to theories about the passive nature of the female may

asked to imagine that a body or culture without the marks and supports of masculine identity is therefore feminine? Why does the loss of sexual difference and sexual certainty, for a man, mean feminisation? Surely the sexual identity of an undifferentiated way of being is neuter, if it is anything at all. On what grounds can we fit femininity into the picture of the fascist and modernist nightmare: the decomposition which every civilised social individual learns to fear, where the organising structure departs, leaving nothing but soulless and base matter? Only, I would argue, if we continue to identify the masculine with the phallic and the feminine with the negative. Only if we have failed to notice the role of the neuter.[19]

Theweleit asks: What is a man without a phallus? And he notes the answer given by the masculine unconscious: a female. But the man without a phallus is merely un-sexed, neutralised, lacking, beyond sex or something else yet undefined. The temptation Theweleit has failed to resist is the one his psychoanalytic insights do so much to expose, and that is the belief that the undoing of man produces a man-of-lack, a man without qualities or structure, a man whom all men, especially all fascist men, fear as the feminine within. It should be clear by now that femininity, as practice and as identity, is something more

---

have functioned to shore up some of his uncertainties about his place in the world." Baurke: "Getting Spliced: Modernism and Sexual Difference," pp. 104–5. If genius is generative, hence penetrative, perhaps it can be saved from its old, suspicious links with a notion of the imagination as fluid, "plastic," receptive. Perhaps creativity is more like the chisel speaking to the stone – hard, uncompromising, unflinching – than like the mother cajoling shape out of a wet, needy mass. But if modernist language receives its characteristic temper in being brought to this masculine pitch, what are we to make of those female modernists whose language, just as spare and uncompromising, nonetheless uses feminine or non-heterosexual images for the forms they are inventing in? Burke's analysis suggests a way past the old sexual dichotomies: not simply by theoretical and deconstructive sleights of hand, but by returning to the "decentered, anti-hierarchical modes of writing" of the famous and not so famous women modernists.

19 Roland Barthes' thoughts on the "neuter" and his allusion to a traditional fourfold classification of the sexes, via reference to the phallus, must be remembered here, and I return to the "neuter" at the end of the paper: Briefly, as Barthes dissects the sexed positions in the text, there is one which is a mixture of "having the phallus" and "being the phallus", e. g., that exists in the interval between women and men, but that position is not neuter rather androgynous. Only the eunuch (here, Balzac's Zambinella), who neither is not has the phallus, is properly neuter. But, Barthes, argues, this classification should strike us as inadequate; defined by their relation to castration, the otherwise biologically sexed characters in Balzac's tale exhibit a wide range of sexual possibilities, and identifications across the differences of the body. Even the fact of castration doesn't fully define and delimit, for the castrato singer moves between active and passive, castrating and castrated. Barthes: *S/Z*, p. 43.

than the negation of masculinity. Perhaps it still needs to be said: it is time that the male and female sex stopped being each other's repressed selves, that femininity in particular not be dreamt of as the guilty conscience of masculine identity.

I want to end with some assertions and an anecdote. Men thought they went to war to escape feminisation. In reality they went to war to find a neutral space: not just a no woman's land, but a world innocent of the split into gender. If the death-drive tells us anything about the emotional dynamic of this war, then it tells us of a desire to transcend desire. This is in turn related to the cultural longing for innocence, and for a 'new creation' untainted by the past, hypocrisy, corruption. Innocence here would represent a state prior to any division between the active and the passive, a division whose very appearance signals the arrival of ambivalence. Such innocence had been the subject of religious idealisation even before Christians like Augustine worried about the flesh and depravity. Once the possibility of seduction has announced itself, there is no decisive way to turn against seduction it. (One must act as if knowledge was foreclosed.) Purity, in a world that knows the inevitability of moral imperfection, can not be achieved by judicious self-control. To demand it is to demand something beyond the world.

Thus the culture that could not give up a certain image of purity turned against the realities, and asymmetries, of gender. Psychoanalytically speaking, the discovery of bodily difference quickly becomes a source of mental anxiety, whose most notorious form is the castration complex. This association of gender difference with failure and flaw can be extended yet further. One canonical text (the Bible) connects the first fall from innocence to a later loss, the dissemination of human tongues. But Aristophanes' famous myth of the original hermaphrodites leads us to recognise a more general category: the human dislike of difference. What else, the myth implies, but the promise of a temporary relief from division, could give the act of love its allure?

If in some sense, the division of the sexes was the originary form of violence, and still, for the castration theory at any rate, represents a continual reminder of danger, it could be that one violence demands to be purged in another. War, terror, torture, and death are not simply at odds with the reproductive imperative; they are genuinely its rivals for attentions we must call sexual but which choose their ends outside the heterosexual couple. Masculine hardness and purity are the conscious forms of the soldier's desire – a purity that can only, as Theweleit's evidence proves, be marred by the proximity of women. On this account the soldier's desire is like the Christian desire of the eunuch. And as the war dragged on in the unconscious of the combatants, the soldier's desire turned in exhaustion to an asexuality easier to achieve. Death is the ethereal bridge, and purity the bleached bones which mingle finally with nothing but the earth itself. Freud's image of a regression to the immortal protozoa goes deeper than this ancient ascetic suspicion of the female sex and of the race's complicity in the rites of intercourse. Freud admits something (a point?) which Georges Bataille, seeking an experience that will shatter the bounds of the self, welcomes almost ecstatically: in the sexual act we die to our difference. It is the purity of death which defeats sexual anxiety (and in a way, consummates the ecstatic's desire), because it satisfies our narcissism: there is no other to oppose or attract us.

Did love die in the war? It depends on the love. For the sufferer from war neurosis – guilty because he has survived, guilty because his conscious mind cannot live with the erasures his memory requires – there seemed still one way out from the confusion of sex. The Utopian fantasy of a love beyond sexual polarity revived with the end of the war in Modernist writing. As a figure for the emotions it has much to recommend it. Fatigue speaks in favour of it as does the desire to regress in the face of an impossible and contradictory experience. One war neurotic, Christopher Tietjens, the damaged 'good soldier' of Ford Madox Ford's war trilogy, saw the tragedy of the sexes clearly. Like many young men of his generation, Richard Aldington and his anti-hero, George Winterbourne, do the same, Christopher went to war to get away from the mess of his emotional relationships, for, as Aldington remarks, "the amount of irreparable harm which can be done by a really good man is astounding." George Winterbourne, the subject of Aldington's *Death of a Hero*[20] stands up in the last battle of the Somme, on the morning of the 4th November, to stop a machine-gun bullet; nothing could be worse than the prospect of returning to the nightmare of his wife Elizabeth and his mistress Fanny, both New Women and sexual predators. And towards the end of the war Christopher Tietjens is visited in France by a general from the staff, who is, as it happens, his godfather. Christopher's love life is a public disaster. The general is going to send Christopher up the line "so that the morals of the troops in his command may not be contaminated by the contemplation of Christopher's marital infelicities." At this Christopher briefly contemplates suicide. But, he says,

> Suicide is no remedy for a twisted situation of a psychological kind. It is for bankruptcy. Or for military disaster. For the man of action, not the thinker. Creditor's meetings wipe the one out. Military operations sweep on. But my problem will remain the same whether I'm here or not. For it's insoluble. It's the whole problem of the relations of the sexes.[21]

---

20   Aldington: *Death of a Hero*, p. 4.
21   Ford Madox Ford: *Parade's End*, p. 491.

And yet, if he could only escape from the torturous involvement with his viciously unfaithful wife, there was always the promise of love: Like the exemplary English Protestant he is, Christopher's idea of love is Miltonian: it is conversation. Sex is only a sublimated form of the desire for talk:

> That was what a young women was for. You seduced a young woman in order to be able to finish your talks with her. You could not do that without living with her. You could not live with her without seducing her; but that was the by-product ... You have to wait together – for a week, for a year, for a lifetime, before the final intimate conversation may be attained ... and exhausted (Ford's ellipses). That in effect was love.[22]

The fantasy of a child-like world, love in a cottage with a virginal, slim and athletic suffragette, for Christopher's beloved is an intellectual of 'exact mind' and pure body, expresses a powerful longing of this epoch for a relationship not polarised into male and female species. The avant-garde fashion for brother-sister couples, most brilliantly represented by Musil's lovers Agathe and Ulrich, is another instance. It seems to me that these desires call out for explanation: they tell us of the poverty and confusion of the discourse of gender we are saddled with.

And feminists of our generation have been taking up this challenge, noting dryly that the discontents of this gender discourse have, since the Great War and its identity crisis, finally been noticed as damaging to men as well as to women. There is a certain irony in the fact that the dramatic entry of womens' voices and presences into the public sphere produced a desire to see the difference between the sexes disappear, as if by magic. Luce Irigaray and other feminists of difference note that the ideology of sexual difference was precious to European culture, just until the moment when women began to claim a stake in it. Without an ethics that brings justice to relations between the sexes, such feminists complain, there will be nothing we can know as love. Yet the desire for a better conception of social and symbolic arrangements which would allow decent relations between the two sexes is also, I believe, detectable in the Modernist longing for a brother-sister love without conflict, and in Christopher's dream of the erotic life of conversation. And it is expressed openly in Virginia Woolf's utopian vision of androgynous harmony. She writes in *A Room of One's Own*:

> Perhaps to think, as I had been thinking these two days, of one sex as different from the other is an effort. It interferes with the unity of the mind ... For certainly when I saw the couple get into the taxi-cab the mind felt as if, after being divided, it had come together again in a natural fusion. The obvious reason would be

---

22   Ibid., p. 629.

that it is natural for the sexes to co-operate. One has a profound, if irrational, in-stinct in favour of the theory that the union of man and woman makes for the greatest satisfaction, the most complete happiness. But the sight of the two people getting into the taxi and the satisfaction it gave me made me also ask whether the-re are two sexes in the mind corresponding to the two sexes in the body, and whether they also require to be united in order to get complete satisfaction and happiness.[23]

Woolf's vision of love, and Christopher's, and Ulrich's, remind us of what is missing. Yet none is really what we need. Instead of androgyny or asexuality, it is the space between the sexes, the no man's land, which needs to be re-claimed so it can be thought about, and talked about, in a different way. Luce Irigaray writes in a paper called "Love of Self": "It takes two to love. To know how to separate and how to come back together. Each to go, both he and she, in quest of self, faithful to the quest, so that they may greet one another, co-me close, make merry, or seal a covenant."[24] To create a space where the wo-men's voice can be heard, a space for the emergence of that female imagina-tion which has so far never existed, I believe we need something like Irigaray's ethics of sexual difference, where the first step, as she admits, is to reconsti-tute the ground of the neuter.[25] What is required, at the very least, is a differ-ent notion of bodily place: no longer a metaphor of "matter and form," but one that includes container, boundary, interval, opening, hence we are to think, between bodies and sexes, of a bridge, a "two-way journey" that did not destroy the "place" of each: "the habitat in which each wed without ceas-ing [...] to infinity," something that can happen only if the split between mas-culine and feminine "(in the division of both work and nature) were brid-ged."[26]

But where is the neuter? We have been saying this for a long time now: in fact there has been no neuter.[27] The meanings which our culture presents as neutral, unmarked by difference, are coded implicitly as masculine, assuming the absence of an 'other' sex. And correlative to this deceptive neutrality is the practice by which one sex provides the metaphorical resources for every-

---

23 Virginia Woolf: *A Room of One's Own / Three Guineas*, p. 127.
24 Irigaray: "Love of Self." Irigaray: *Ethics of sexual difference*, p. 71.
25 Irigaray: "Irigaray's ethics of sexual difference." Ibid., p. 133–150, for a vision of the age where there could be an ethic of the couple, which would require a "bridge," even a bridge which is negative space, a "crossing through the neuter." (p. 147).
26 Ibid., p. 37.
27 I believe this point is made also by Jacques Derrida in conversation with a group of Wom-ens Studies students and scholars. See Derrida "Women in the Beehive," in *Men in Feminism*.

thing the dominant sex needs to deny. (Or, counter-culturally, to reclaim, as when writers on the order of Derrida speak in the name of a "hymenisation" of philosophy, turning to positive account – as virtue for philosophy – the feminine and hysteric refusal to accept a world of "clean and proper" separation.[28]) What can a positive representation or discourse of femininity look like when the terms of the feminine have already been co-opted to explain the exhaustion of virility, the annihilation of the masculine? It is time to say that masculinity is simply a certain way of being marked by sex, and femininity is the same. Hence the opposite, the antithetical term to masculinity is not femininity, but neutrality, the non-sexed. Men and women, argues Irigaray, have no hope of ever engaging in an intimate and free conversation as long as the place of the woman is occupied by a metaphor of the "not," by a crowded and contradictory image-bank. Only if we recognise a common space between us, for which we independently share the responsibility, and for which we must now begin to develop new symbols, will there be any beginning of love on an equal footing, love that lives up to the 'exact' and precise speech which Christopher Tietjens lost twice: in war and in sex.

---

28 "Language, as a separation from a presumed state of nature," as "introduction of an articulated network of differences," involves, Kristeva says, a "logical operation of separation" which is the "common destiny of the two sexes, men and women. That certain biofamilial conditions and relationships cause women (and notably hysterics) to deny this separation and the language which ensues from it, whereas men (notably obsessionals) magnify both and terrified, attempt to master them – this is what Freud's discovery has to tell us on this issue." Julia Kristeva: "Women's Time."

CRYSTAL MAZUR OCKENFUSS
University of Virginia

Benn's Body:
Masculine Aesthetics and Reproduction in Gottfried Benn's Essays

Abstract: This paper seeks to excavate the theory of corporeal aesthetics implicit in several of Gottfried Benn's essays. Although I claim that Benn designs a version of the "fascist" body, his conception does not coincide with the one described in Hitler's *Mein Kampf.* Whereas Hitler locates the perfection of a race in its superior physis, Benn shifts the focus to the intellect. Evolution enhanced by scientific breeding provides no promise of constant progress. Instead, Benn envisions an expansion of the brain (and hence the skull) which ultimately leads to the extinction of the human species. For Benn, the final goal is to progress into regression, to over-breed to the point where the ultimate, ultra-specialized genius peaks and returns to the primitive. – The second part of the paper examines the consequence of Benn's interpretation of evolution. Since the hyperdeveloped genial skull will eliminate the possibility of successful vaginal birth, reproduction must be relocated. In the figure of Pallas, Benn finds an emblem of an alternate femininity, one which is not predicated by pregnancy. The conditions of her birth allow Pallas to remove the locus of generativity from its biological seat within the female and place it squarely within the artificial, cultural domain of the male, where it must be maintained by force. By designating the male as the site of reproduction, Pallas implicitly sanctions homosexuality. The homoerotic body is the body of construct, as art.

I. Introduction: "Don't shoot 'till you see the white of their eyes …!"

In the 1920s, August Sander photographed Germans. Although Gottfried Benn was not among his subjects, he would have fit in well. In the portrait shot by Franz Pfemfert in 1927, Benn stares out over his right shoulder.[1] I'm

---

1   See Walter Lenning: *Gottfried Benn*, p. 7.

sure it is his right shoulder because photography reverses the image and his gaze is opposite and away from my right. His eyes are light (I can see their whites!), but his hair appears dark and is receding. The suit is three-piece, gut-*bürgerlich*. He wears a wrist watch. Under his arm, he seems to have tucked a pair of gloves, whose round, compressed openings give the appearance of the looped handle of a riding crop. His arms are crossed, but one slender hand is visible. There is a cleft in his chin.

This essay is not about Benn's body, but about Benn's corpus. I describe Benn only because this particular photo embodies many of the characteristics of the body as Benn wrote it. It is a historical body. Benn was, whether he liked it or not, an artist in the age of mechanical reproducibility. His image, from birth to death, is recorded on film, where we can see it progress from that of a slim-hipped, pensive youth gazing over the moor (1910) to that of an aging man, rather heavy in the jowls, writing in a Churchillian pose, complete with cigar (1956). The passage of time is etched in the flesh. Lenning prints nineteen photos of Benn. In the vast majority of them, including the 1927 shot, Benn's gaze refuses to engage. It is always directed elsewhere; even when he looks straight ahead, his eyes seem to graze the top of the viewer's head. He aims beyond us. This disengaged pose is typical of the Bennean body – it seeks to resolve the particular into the bigger picture, be it form or *Urschleim*. It seems fitting that Benn's chin is cleft, for the body he writes is often divided into a series of dichotomies – mind/body, male/female, discipline/breeding. Benn's body is not, in and of itself, the "blueblonde" German body as Hitler conceived it. Benn no more sought to create his own body to Hitler's specifications than he did he did the body of his work. The body Benn bred is not the Nazi body, but it does look to the right.

II. The Blue-Blond-Brown Body

> "[…] with a Meinkampf look"
> Silvia Plath: *Daddy*

It is unlikely that Benn actually wore a Nazi uniform during his stint as an army physician. It doesn't really matter if he did or not. What is fascist in Benn's corpus goes much deeper than the skin. It goes back to the genes. In the introduction, I stressed that, although the Bennean body looks to the right, it does not (as Benn himself does not) have, in the words of Silvia Plath, "a Meinkampf look." In a certain sense, it is entirely correct to argue that Benn was not a Nazi. Judging from his 1933 publications, he seems to have been fairly convinced that he was, despite the fact that the party never quite chose to acknowledge him. If one is eager to "redeem" Benn, one can capitalize on this opportune discrepancy, and absolve him in the name of that ancient Aurelian principle that to truly know the good is to do the good and all evil is simply a case of ignorance. Squeezing Benn back into grace through a loophole, however, only strips him of one hindersome, incriminating mask – it does nothing to change the body of evidence against him. Even if Benn was not a "real" Nazi in that he misunderstood the nature and/or aims of the movement (see "Doppelleben," for instance), there were elements in it which corresponded, in principle, with some themes central to Benn's own work, even that prior to 1933. Hence, to term Benn "fascist," at least within the framework of this essay, is to call attention to his preoccupation with control of the body through both selective breeding and discipline.[2] It is in his treatment of these topics, however, that Benn separates himself from the banal "Blut und Boden" physical aesthetics.

We have become so used to the image of Nietzsche's "blonde Bestie" that we rarely feel the need to read Hitler's own thoughts on the subject.[3] Although it is often Nietzsche alone who is incorrectly cited as the source of Hitler's ideas on the superiority of a purebred Aryan race, it is more likely that the notion of actually breeding for such a population stems from Lanz von Liebenfels, a late 19th century religious dissident who foresaw the founding of a "Neutemplerordens."[4] This "new order" would be composed of "blondblaue Männer, die sich zur Reinzucht verpflichten, d. h. nur blaublonde Frauen heiraten würden, damit blondblaue Kinder zur Welt kämen."[5] According to Johannes Hampel, Hitler told Hermann Rauschning of his plan to form a scientifically-bred "Führerorden, d. h. die Auslese der besten Deutschen"

---

2   This interest was by no means limited to the National Socialist Movement. For an intelligent examination of other European intellectuals who attempted to figure a new aesthetic ideal within a broadly fascist context in a fashion similar to Benn's, see Alice Yaeger Kaplan: *Reproductions of Banality*, esp. pp. 10–11.

3   Although I use Hitler as a "spokesman" for eugenics, it is important to point out that the idea of genetic manipulation in a negative form (sterilization) or a positive one (selective breeding) was well-established and very popular prior to the advent of National Socialism in Germany. For a comprehensive discussion of the complex history and development of eugenics in an international context, see Weingart, Kroll and Bayertz: *Rasse, Blut und Gene*.

4   For the history of such experiments in Nordic breeding, see ibid., esp. pp. 34, 195.

5   Hampel, "Hitlers *Mein Kampf*: Die Weltanschauung der Nationalsozialisten," p. 104: "[…] blondblue men, who pledge themselves to pure breeding, i. e. who would marry only blue-blond women, so that blondblue children would be born […]." Why all the men are "blondblue," the women "blueblond," remains unclear. If these adjectives are truly gender-specific, then all the children, characterized as "blondblue", must be male – a technicality strangely in line with Benn's own musing on reproduction!

outside of the party.[6] This group would then eventually provide the ruling class for the burgeoning thousand-year Reich.

Hitler did not view this "scientific" selective breeding as in any way artificial, but rather as an extension of nature's will:

> The result of all racial crossing is therefore in brief always the following:
> (a) Lowering of the level of the higher race;
> (b) Physical and intellectual regression and hence the beginning of a slowly but surely progressing sickness.
> To bring about such a development is, then, nothing else but to sin against the will of the eternal creator. And as sin this act is rewarded. When man attempts to rebel against the iron logic of Nature, he comes into struggle with principles to which he himself owes his existence as a man. And this attack must lead to his own doom. Here, of course, we encounter the objection of the modern pacifist, as truly Jewish in its effrontery as it is stupid! "Man's rôle is to overcome nature."[7]

Hitler expects to achieve progress through calculated evolution. This improvement must be first located in the physical body: "[...] the folkish state must not adjust its entire educational work primarily to the inoculation of more knowledge, but to the breeding of absolutely healthy bodies. The training of mental abilities is only secondary."[8] Ultimately, the blue-blonde-brown body would realize the "Greek ideal of beauty," "the wonderful combination of the most magnificent physical beauty with brilliant mind and noblest soul."[9]

Dr. Benn, too, is willing to play Dr. Frankenstein and design "der deutsche Mensch."[10] The scenario in his theoretical laboratory looks quite different, however. From the onset, Benn (perhaps unwittingly) aligns himself with the Jewish-pacifist tradition[11] by acknowledging the unnaturalness of the custom pedigree:

---

6   Ibid., p. 104: "'Führer' order, i. e. a selection of the best Germans."

7   Hitler: *Mein Kampf*, pp. 86–87.

8   Ibid., p. 108.

9   Ibid.

10   Gottfried Benn: "Der deutsche Mensch." *Gesammelte Werke*, vol. 3: *Essays und Reden*, pp. 245–52. It is not surprising that Benn, a dermatologist by trade and a specialist in venereal disease, should express an interest in the eugenics discussion. The battle against the spread of sexually-transmitted diseases often played a role in these debates. See Weingart, Kroll and Bayertz: *Rasse*, pp. 280–83.

11   As Weingart, Kroll and Bayertz point out, Benn also participates in an established German literary tradition in which the Naturalists represent the critical, and the Decadents the enthusiastic pole. See ibid. pp. 2–63.

Dies muß man von vornherein beachten: Züchtung an sich gibt es nicht, die Degenerationsformen, wie das Aussterben der Arten, stammen ja auch aus der Natur, Züchtung ist gegen die Natur, ist Überlisten der Natur, ist Prägung, politische Entschließung, Weltanschauung, Werterklärung, Willensakt.[12]

The breeding principle, for Benn, must be relegated to the realm of the unnatural precisely because he does not accept the Darwinian law of "survival of the fittest": "Die Darwinische Theorie vom Kampf ums Dasein und vom Überleben des Stärksten und biologisch Tüchtigsten war ein Anthropomorphismus und genügt methodisch in gar keiner Weise zur Erklärung des psychologischen, paläontologischen und fossilen Materials."[13] In his essay, "Geist und Seele künftiger Geschlechter," while seemingly in accord with the necessity of breeding for the body, Benn questions whether any real progress can be made at the grass-roots level of the gene.

Zunächst muß man sich klarmachen, daß man ja keineswegs beliebig, visonär oder träumerisch in einem unbestimmbaren und unbestimmten deutschen Raum züchten kann und daß aus solchen Träumen durch irgendwelche eugenische Maßnahmen ein Zug heller nordischer Leiber hervortreten könnte [...].[14]

Even if it were possible, the blue-blond-brown body is not necessarily the ultimate realization of human potential – "Ist der gesunde Körper an sich eine Garantie für vollendete Menschheit? Genügt Gesundheit, um ein Volk zu universalgeschichtlicher Größe zu führen?"[15] In an almost tongue-in-cheek fashion, Benn cites the "Fußballsieger" as an oft-mentioned example of the combination of brawn and brains; an illustration which, for the discriminating reader, performs unsatisfactorily as the fulfillment of the "Greek ideal." True to the classic "mind vs. body" problematic, Benn is unwilling to con-

---

12 Benn: "Geist und Seele künftiger Geschlechter." *Gesammelte Werke*, vol. 3: *Essays und Reden,* pp. 253–59, here p. 253: "This must be understood from the outset: There is no such thing as breeding. Degenerate forms, such as the extinction of species, also occur in nature. Breeding is against nature; it is the out-witting of nature, is formative, political determination, world-view, a declaration of values, an act of will."

13 Benn: "Der Aufbau der Persönlichkeit," ibid., pp. 111–24, here p. 121: "The Darwinian theory of the struggle for existence and the survival of the strongest and biologically fittest is an anthropomorphism; it in no way suffices as an explanation of the psychological, paleontological and fossil material."

14 Benn: "Geist und Seele künftiger Geschlechter," ibid. p. 256: "Firstly, one must come to the realization that one cannot just arbitrarily, visionarily or fancifully breed in an unspecifiable and unspecified German space, and that such dreams could, by way of some sort of eugenic means, bring about the trait of fair Nordic bodies [...]."

15 Ibid., p. 258: "Is the healthy body a guarantee for consummate humanity? Is health enough to lead a people to universal historical greatness?"

ceive of the possibility of an acceptable balance between these two elements. He is trapped within an eternal either/or: "das biologische Natürliche und Gesunde oder die hohe Züchtung des Geistes?"[16] For Benn, the answer is clear:

> So viel wird man allerdings wohl vermuten können, daß es Rasse ohne Geist nicht gibt. Daß also Rasse züchten auch immer heißt: Geist züchten. Nur der Geist – Geist als Entscheidungsfähigkeit, Maßsinn, Urteilshärte, Prüfungsschärfe – bildet das Körperliche eines Volkes oder eines Einzelnen dahinaus, daß man von Rasse und Züchtung sprechen kann.[17]

Hitler states in *Mein Kampf*, "A decayed body is not made the least bit more aesthetic by a brilliant mind, indeed the highest intellectual training could not be justified if its bearers were at the same time physically degenerate and crippled, weak-willed, wavering and cowardly individuals."[18] Whereas for Hitler, a sound body is the prime qualification for greatness, for Benn, the reverse is true. Throughout his theoretical writings on genius and race, Benn demonstrates that the result of inbreeding is *bionegativ*, an anti-Darwinian development of potential to its ultimate climax and subsequent destruction. The Protestant minister population provides a suitable, closed "Erbmasse" (gene pool) with which to illustrate his point; in "Der deutsche Mensch," Benn states that 50 % of all German genius claims parentage from within this group.[19] However, in "Das Genieproblem," he adds that the appearance of genius signals the beginning of the "Entartung" (degeneration) of that particular family.[20] This "Entartung" takes the form of a "*körperliche Minusvariante*" (physical deficit) and a psychological or physical inability to reproduce naturally.[21] Benn proceeds to list a variety of ailments peculiarly common to geniuses: madness, suicidal tendencies, paralysis, alcoholism, drug addiction, homosexuality, as well as certain cosmetic defects.[22] Furthermore, the biolog-

---

16 Ibid.: "the biologically natural and fit, or the noble breeding of the spirit?"
17 Ibid.: "So much can be safely assumed: That there can be no spirit without race. That to breed for race always means: breeding spirit. But the spirit – spirit as decisiveness, as discretion, as critical judgment and acute analysis – trains the body of a people or an individual to the point where one can speak of race and breeding."
18 Hitler: *Mein Kampf*, p. 108.
19 Benn: "Der deutsche Mensch. Erbmasse und Führertum." *Gesammelte Werke*, vol. 3: *Essays und Reden*, pp. 245–252, here p. 246.
20 Benn: "Das Genieproblem," ibid., pp. 131–43, here p. 134. According to Weingart, Kroll and Bayertz, the question of degeneration is the primary preoccupation of psychopathological circles of the late 19th century. See, for instance: *Rasse*, pp. 48–49.
21 Benn: "Das Genieproblem." *Gesammelte Werke*, vol. 3: *Essays und Reden*, p. 135.
22 Very similar to those listed by Weingart, Kroll and Bayertz: *Rasse*, p. 49.

ical co-requisite of extreme intelligence, namely an exceptionally large head, could prove fatal, either to the mother (whose pelvis could be shattered during the birth) or the child (who could be trapped in the birth canal): "Diese Entwicklung ist so handgreiflich, daß die Rassenforscher schon davon sprechen, die kontinuierliche Schädelvergrößerung infolge Überspezialisierung des Großhirns könne als Geburtshindernis flagrant werden und das Weiterbestehen der Rasse gefährden."[23] If Darwin is correct, then breeding for increased intelligence, with its requisite larger skulls and brains, ultimately does not increase the species' potential for success, but rather causes it to advance towards extinction.[24] When Benn chooses this path for the white race, he is actually encouraging its glorious self-destruction: "Die weiße Rasse, das ist Deutschland, Jugend, vergiß es nie, ihre letzte Züchtung, ihr letzter Glanz bist du."[25]

For Benn, the final goal is to progress into regression, to overbreed to that point where the ultimate, ultra-specialized genius peaks and returns to the primitive:

> Eine militante Transzendenz, ein Richtertum aus hohen wehrenden Gesetzen, Züchtung von Rausch und Opfer für das Sein verwandelungsloser Tiefe, Härte aus tragischem Gefühl, Form aus Schatten! Züchtung gegen seinzerstörendes Gesicht: Vergehen der Welten, Musik, der Nornenzug: dies ganze verschloßen, nordisch, darüber Schwerter. Noch einmal die weiße Rasse, ihr tiefster Traum: Entformung und Gestalt, noch einmal im Norden: der Sieg des Griechen. Dann Asien, der neue Dschingis-Khan. Das ist die Perspective.[26]

---

23 Benn: "Der Aufbau der Persönlichkeit." *Gesammelte Werke*, vol. 3: *Essays und Reden,* p. 117: "This development is so striking that racial scientists are already considering the possibility that the continual expansion of the skull caused by the over-specialization of the cerebrum could become a conspicuous impediment to the birth process and thus endanger the survival of the race."

24 This fear plays into another one quite prevalent in the early 20th century revolving around the apparent low birthrate in intellectual circles. See, for instance, Weingart, Kroll and Bayertz: *Rasse*, p. 52.

25 Benn: "Lebensweg eines Intellektualisten." *Gesammelte Werke* vol. 2: *Prosa und Autobiographie*, pp. 305–479, here p. 341: "The white race, that is Germany, Youth, never forget, her last breed, her last splendor, that is you."

26 Benn: "Züchtung I." *Gesammelte Werke*, vol. 3: *Essays und Reden*, pp. 237–42, here p. 242: "A militant transcendence, a court of noble, safeguarding laws, breeding of intoxication and sacrifice for the being of unchanging depth, hardness made of tragic sentiment, form made of shadow! Breeding against its destructive face: passing of the worlds, music, the Norne's train: all this occult, Nordic, over it swords. One last time the white race, its deepest dream: unforming and shape, one last time in the North - the triumph of the Greeks. Then Asia, the new Ghenghis Khan. That is the perspective."

The "Entformung" (unforming) Benn refers to is no figurative trope, a return to Greece or Ghengis Khan in spirit, but rather a literal ontogenetic denaturation. In the essay "Der Aufbau der Persönlichkeit," the human genotype, the sum of all expressed and unexpressed genetic material, is presented geologically.[27] Layers of new traits (genes) cover, but do not destroy, older, more primitive ones. By breeding towards genius, a condition whose degenerative side-effects reduce the ability of younger genes to override their ancestors, Benn hopes to regain access to these deeper, aboriginal layers of the genetic strata. What attracts Benn to this genetically primal state is the apparent ability of primitive man to "think" with his body.

> Die Soziologen entdeckten beim Studium der primitiven Völker ganz andere geistigen Organisationen als hirnlich ableitbare, nämlich eine allgemein biologische Bewußtseinsgliederung mit dazugehörigen fremdartigen Körpergefühlen, einer an einer anderen Wirklichkeit gebildeten Erfahrung, einer Besitzergreifung der Welt mittels mystischen Partizipation, die auch zu einer Art Weltbild geführt hatte auf Grund einer universellen körperlichen Basis für die Erlebbarkeit des Seins.[28]

By relocating perception from the brain to the body proper, Benn radically designated the body as the locus of history, which is, physically inscribed in the flesh.

III. Zucht und Züchtigung: The Breeding and the Disciplined Body

> "Every woman adores a Fascist,
> the boot in the face, the brute
> Brute heart of a brute like you"
> Silvia Plath, *Daddy*

What sort of body is this, that will bear the deep brand of history? Biology offers Benn two options – the male or the female. Both sexes figure in his plan for the physical transcription of history, but in fundamentally different ways. Benn often writes of *Zucht*, but infrequently directly refers to its etymological cousin, *Züchtigung*, even though his work is full of images of corporal chastisement. It is through these twin means that Benn brings the body to articulate

---

27 Benn: "Der Aufbau der Persönlichkeit," ibid., p. 111, 118.
28 Ibid., p. 113: "During their research amongst primitive peoples, sociologists discovered an intellectual organization completely different from one reducible to the brain, namely a general biological arrangement of consciousness – complete with unfamiliar physical sensations, a sense of experience patterned on a different reality, and a comprehension of the world by means of mystic participation – that lead to a world-view founded upon a universal physical basis for the experience of being."

itself. Women reproduce the past continually. Men, however, lacking the capacity for birth, must literally be remodeled into appropriate vehicles for history, culture and art through violent means. Maybe those weren't gloves Benn was carrying after all, but indeed a fine, thin crop whose inflicted welts we read.

Since Benn's interest in *"Zucht"* is essentially a negative one, it is not surprising that he greatly devalues the maternal function. I earlier cited a excerpt in which Benn claims that a classical Darwinian evolution would produce skulls too large to be born comfortably. Such a development has several drastic implications. If the mother is to survive, the child must allow its skull to be crushed by the mother's pelvis, which would eventually lead to the extinction of the species. However, if the child is successfully born, the mother's pelvis is shattered – a situation which also precludes further reproduction. It is quite possible that the mother would not survive such an ordeal at all, in which case all women operating "as women" are doomed, leaving a world full of men and women acting as (pseudo-)men. The price of existence is, then, the sacrifice of femininity, insofar as this implies motherhood. Within the framework of fascism this is, of course, the only acceptable role for women, hence Benn's dilemma must always end in death.

The unrevenged death of the mother is what characterizes the "Oresteische Epoche" in which modern man finds himself.[29] Whereas the Nazis' wish to return to the "totale Schwangerschaft" ("total pregnancy") model of womanhood, Benn sees in Pallas the appropriate expression of modern feminine potential.[30] He recognizes the futility of an attempted return to earth-mother sensibilities, suggesting "daß es einen Naturzustand für uns überhaupt nicht mehr gibt."[31] Pallas represents the female after the triumph of culture (art, artifice, history) over nature.

Pallas, "never impregnated, narrow, childless goddess," creates, but she does not reproduce.[32] She herself was not conceived through the generative powers of sex and born of woman, but rather sprang from Zeus' head fully-formed, much like an idea. In many versions of the myth, Zeus is obliged to have another man, Haephaestus, cleave his skull with an ax so that she might emerge, clad in armor. From the moment of her birth, Pallas is a product of male violence – violence which, in her case, usurps the power and place of the mother. This is her birthright and she is committed to its defense, hence her

---

29   Benn: "Pallas," ibid., pp. 379–85, here p. 382.
30   Benn: "Zum Thema Geschichte," ibid., pp. 353–67, here p. 355.
31   Ibid., p. 383: "that a 'state of nature' no longer exists for us."
32   Ibid., p. 379.

protection of Orestes: "Pallas schützt Müttermörder!"[33] Her defense of ma-
tricide leads to the "deposition of woman as the primal and supreme gender"
and ushers in "Fluchzeit," cursed time.[34] She removes the locus of generativity from its traditional, biological seat within the female and places it squarely
within the artificial, cultural domain of the male, where it must be maintained
by force.[35] In Benn's words, patriarchy is a "unnatural poetic idea" and "the
indecent and violent spirit."[36]

By relocating the site of generativity from the female to the male, Pallas
destroys the primeval unity of community. "The religio-social miracle of the
beehive" becomes impossible.[37] Pallas is no longer the queen bee who produces intoxicating, nourishing honey and who fills mazes of catacombs with
life, but rather the inventor of the flute. The flute is hollow, matterless. Pure,
delineated form, it is the P(h)allas.

> Pallas erfand die Flöte – Rohr und Wachs – , ein kleines Ding. Auch unser Gehirn
> findet sich vor einer Raumbegrenzung. Wir können nur wenig umfangreiche Teil-
> zentren bilden; horizontal und zeitlich lange Perspectiven zu entwickeln, ist uns
> nicht gegeben. Kleine Räume beschicken, meisseln auf der Handfläche – große,
> enge Zusammenfassungen, knappe Thesen –: alles Weitere liegt außerhalb der
> Epoche.[38]

The male is incapable of sustaining social unity and continuity. His sexuality
(and thought) are explosive and expulsive, the Dionysian relief of "phallic
congestion" as opposed to the female "Neunmonatszauber" ("nine-month-
magic"), receptive and gestating.[39] Male creativity involves the infliction of
form, as sex is the infliction of the delineated penis on the undifferentiated
female genitalia, the medusa's head Pallas carries on her shield: "Das Un-

---

33 Ibid.
34 Ibid.
35 For a reading of Marinetti's novel, *Marfaka*, that unearths a similar strategy, see Kaplan: *Re-
    productions of Banality*, p. 6: "Womanhood is foremost among the 'leftover' human qualities
    the futurism relegates to non-human objects in the course of its metallicization of man."
    (See also pp. 11, 81–85.).
36 Benn: "Pallas," ibid., p. 380.
37 Ibid.
38 Ibid., p. 382: "Pallas invented the flute – reed and wax –, a small thing. Our brain, too, finds
    itself faced with limited space. We can only construct a few comprehensive partial centers;
    it is not ours to develop horizontal, protracted perspective over time. Filling small spaces,
    chiseling upon a palm-sized span, narrow summaries, concise theses – everything else lies
    beyond the epoch."
39 Ibid.

förmliche, Ungebildete, Unbegrenzte vertilgt er dann, dazu die Titanen und Giganten, das Grenzlose."[40] While on the surface "Pallas" appears to be an apotheosis of the male, the essay's subtext actually seems to present masculinity as a desperate measure. "Pallas, die den Mann beschützt, die Klare, wo doch alles Urgrund, Urschoß, Urdunkel und Urmunkel bleiben sollte?"[41] By designating the male as the site of generation, Pallas implicitly sanctions homosexuality:

> Wenn er doch Stier geblieben wäre, Riechstoff, Pfau, Äffchen, josephischer Stall-wächter, aber er ward das transzendentale Männersubjekt, androkratischer Irr-denker, Tempelpäderast, widernatürlicher, sittenverderbt und die Ursache aller Verbrechen. Cherchez l'homme! Warum läßt die Gesellschaft ihn freigewähren? Im Brustkoller das kindlichste und gefährlichste Wesen, noch schnalzt und pfeift er, dreht sich als der balzende Hahn, gleich darauf ist er besinnungslos und mor-det.[42]

The shift to the homosexual mode seems to be intimately bound up with the advent of the modern plagues of nihilism, schizophrenia and "progressive Zerebralisation."[43] 'It is but one step from Pallas to schizophrenia' – homo-sexuality borders on schizophrenia because it represents a separation of man from the "natural" order of things and a failure to access the unity promised by the attempt to reestablish connection with a womb. By associating homo-sexuality with increasing intellectualization, it seems as if Benn means to im-ply that homosexuality is sexuality dictated not by the body but by the mind. The homosexual's pleasure is somehow located less in the congested phallus than in the expanding "*Hirnrinde*." Diotima no longer mirrors herself in the polished sphere of Socrates' bald head, but rather he sees himself inverted "on the negative of the skull's ceiling."[44] Homosexuality becomes the lust of

---

40 Ibid., p. 384: "The ill-formed, unconstructed, unbounded he then annihilates, along with the titans and giants, the unlimited." (Although I do not directly cite him, my interpretation of the "Pallas" essay owes a great deal to Klaus Theweleit's seminal study, *Männerphan-tasien*).

41 Ibid., p. 381: "Pallas, who protects men, the clear, where everything should have remained originary ground, originary womb, originary darkness and originary murmur?"

42 Ibid.: "If only he had remained a bull, scent, peacock, little ape, Joseph's stableboy, but he became this transcendental man-subject, androcratic phantast, temple pederast, perverse, depraved and source of all crime. Cherchez l'homme! Why does society let him run free? In his mating frenzy, the most childish and dangerous creature; he roars and warbles, turns like the courting rooster; immediately afterward he is senseless and murders."

43 Ibid.

44 Benn: "Der Aufbau der Persönlichkeit," ibid., p. 112.

the mind to forcibly create its own body through the body of gender-identical other.[45]

Discipline, then, becomes the key to the development of the homoerotic body. The body must be prevented from remaining natural, but rather must have form imposed on it. This form, however, may not take the shape of "form-fitting corsets, brassieres" such as the Cretan women wear, or the "fantastic headdresses" of the little princes of Knossos.[46] These are only superficial alterations of the body, where Benn seeks real changes which affect the inner physical history:[47]

> Die Dorer arbeiten am Stein, er bleibt unbemalt. Ihre Figurn sind nackt. Dorisch, das ist die Haut, aber die bewegte, die über Muskeln, männliches Fleisch, der Körper. Der Körper, gebräunt von der Sonne, dem Öl, dem Staub, der Striegel und den kalten Bädern, Luft gewöhnt, rief, schön getönt. Jeder Muskel, die Kniescheibe, die Gelenkansätze, das ganze kriegerisch, doch sehr erwählt.[48]

The Doric youth is conditioned by the state for "killing and subjecting," yet in order to conquer he must first submit.[49] During the course of his education, he is forced to abstain from women and food: "Die Knaben schlafen nackt auf dem Schilf, das sie sich ohne Messer aus dem Eurotas reißen müssen, essen wenig und schnell [...]."[50] It is the responsibility of the state to make his body cubical ("kubisch"), flat ("schafft ihn Fläche") and "kunstfähig."[51] To be

---

45   It is beyond the scope of this paper to locate Benn's theories on homosexuality within the framework of current queer studies. I would argue they are most akin to those represented by the work of Hocquenghem, Foucault and Bersani. While it is impossible to characterize the work of three such important and independent thinkers in a few words, several traits link their theories to Benn's: the central interest in power relationships, the focus on anal intercourse, and on the "non-redemptive," dangerous quality of sex.

46   Benn: "Dorische Welt." *Gesammelte Werke*, vol. 3: *Essays und Reden*, p. 283.

47   This prefigures Leo Bersani's claim in "Is the Rectum a Grave?" (p. 15) that gay sadomasochistic rites function "to multiply or redistribute its [the body's] loci of pleasure."

48   Benn: "Dorische Welt. Eine Untersuchung über die Beziehung von Kunst und Macht." *Gesammelte Werke*, vol. 3: *Essays und Reden*, p. 295: "The Dorians worked stone, it remains unpainted. Their figures are naked. Dorian, that is skin, but in movement, that over muscles, manly flesh, the body. The body, tanned by the sun, the oil, the dust, the strap and the cold baths, used to the air, ripe, beautifully toned. Every muscle, the kneecap, the origin of the joints, all of it martial, but very select."

49   Ibid., p. 294.

50   Ibid., p. 293: "The boys sleep naked upon rushes they must rip without a knife from the banks of the Eurotas, eat little and quickly [...]." This corresponds to Foucault's views on the relation between the body and power in his book *Discipline and Punish*, esp. p. 5.

51   Benn: "Dorische Welt." *Gesammelte Werke*, vol. 3: *Essays und Reden*, p. 305.

"kunstfähig" does not mean to be able to create art, but rather to be physically capable of *being* art.

Hitler wrote in *Mein Kampf*, "This, too, is in the interest of the nation: that the most beautiful bodies find one another, and so help to give the nation new beauty."[52] Within the paradigm of Benn's Doric World, this can only mean men will find their way to each other, since women are not disciplined into art. Sexuality between men, however, must be maintained through force: "Dorisch war auch der Knabenraub: der Ritter entführte den Knaben der Familie, widersetzt sie sich ihm, ist das Entehrung, und er rächt sich blutig. Für einen Knaben aber ist es eine Schande, keinen Liebhaber zu finden, daß heißt nicht zum Helden berufen zu sein."[53] Within one's own ranks, honor demands submission and the desire to be a slave for the beloved.[54] Just as the boy wills and accepts his kidnapping (rape?), the lover promises to let himself be punished in the youth's stead, should the boy commit some crime.[55] Benn was acutely aware that the success of the state was based on the profitable exploitation of slavery, yet he seems reluctant to directly acknowledge that the sublimity of homosexual eroticism relied as well on the delicate interplay of submission and dominance.[56]

This theme, however, is woven so deeply into the essay "Dorische Welt" that even Benn's style reflects it. His images seem to follow one upon the other with the rhythmicity of whip lashes: "Sie durften kein langes Haar tragen, hatten keine Namen, man durfte sie verschenken, verpfänden, verkaufen, züchtigen mit Stöcken, Riemen, Peitschen, Fußblöcken, Halskrallen, Brandmarkung."[57] Although the quality of Nazi literary criticism is generally unremarkable, the author of "Der Selbsterreger," an article about Benn pub-

---

52 Hitler: *Mein Kampf*, p. 12.

53 Benn: "Dorische Welt." *Gesammelte Werke*, vol. 3: *Essays und Reden,* p. 294: "The theft of boys was also Dorian: the knight stole the boy from his family. If they resist, it is dishonor, and revenges himself bloodily. For a boy, however, it is shameful not to find a lover, since that means he is not called to be a hero."

54 As Bersani puts it in "Rectum," p. 209: "[…] they must never cease to feel the appeal of being violated."

55 Benn: "Dorische Welt." *Gesammelte Werke*, vol. 3: *Essays und Reden,* p. 295.

56 For an extensive analysis of the threat homosexuality poses to a society organized around reproduction and the patriarchal family, see Guy Hocquenghem's *Homosexual Desire*, esp. pp. 24–25. In Hocquenghem's view, the anus, the preferred site of homosexual desire, is, unlike the public phallus, radically private. A fascist "community" in the manner proposed by Benn would then ultimately be impossible.

57 Benn: "Dorische Welt." *Gesammelte Werke*, vol. 3: *Essays und Reden,* p. 289: "They were not permitted to wear their hair long, had no name, one was allowed to give them away, pawn them, sell them, discipline them with switches, straps, whips, stocks, collars, branding."

lished in *Das Schwarze Korps* in 1936, may have pegged him correctly.[58] Benn's language in this passage, as well in the one quoted earlier describing muscles and kneecaps, has a deliberately onanistic feel to it. The text (re)produces the act it describes in/for the reader. Does it seek to make us linear, erect and then flat and ready for art?

IV. Conclusion

Benn's bodies. The photographic body – immobilized for a moment by the shutter's shot. The written body – branded, bound. The body I have sketched, a chalky outline marked where it fell. *Corpus delicti*. Benn was hardly the criminal mastermind. Perhaps the bumbling accomplice. Or maybe just the not-so-innocent bystander trapped at the "Tatort." One thing is clear – Benn was there. We can read his traces.

Fluchzeit. Fluchtzeit. Ende.

---

58 "Der Selbsterreger," *Benn – Wirkung wider Willen*, pp. 196–99.

Phillip D'Alton
University of Wollongong, Australia

Women in the Military and the Cult of Masculinity

Abstract: The issue of women in the military can be examined on three levels. Whether they should be in the military at all, whether they should be able to hold command positions, and thirdly, whether they should be allowed to have a combat role. Issues of gender are inextricably linked to questions of power and dominance. Challenging traditional military roles calls into question the cult of masculinity and threatens the military's use of the 'code of manliness' to extract positive performance. Whether there can be a successful resolution in terms of equality and opportunity, given the pressures of gender attitude and the need for control, is poblematical.

Femininity and violence have traditionally been viewed as polar opposites. The belief that nurturing and caring, despite both attitude change and legislation in the private and public spheres as a result of the women's movement, is still the dominant expectation so far as a role for women in the military is concerned. While women in the broader, non-military sphere are gradually being accepted into what have always been seen as traditionally male occupations, *real* change in the composition of armed forces around the world has been either extremely slow or non-existent.

Western images of war and destruction have always been focused on the male. The male warrior is the center of attention and the assumed characteristics of the soldier are an affirmation of traditional male roles. Nor has the women's movement targeted the military, preferring to focus on the civilian sphere and thus, by default, the stereotypes about both men and women in the military have remained unchallenged.

The possibility of changing how we view warfare and women's place in it is in essence in limbo and demonstrates the power of both accepted popular beliefs and the resistance to change present in the various military establishments. Furthermore, the end of the Cold War, although it has clearly done little to reduce the number of armed conflicts worldwide, is more likely to act as a break on further 'liberalization' of female military roles particularly in the west. Coupled to the increasing sophistication of military equipment, the end of the superpower confrontation has meant that the actual number of military personnel, though not military expenditure, is in decline and this also reduces pressure for reform. While the need for filling the tables of organization had created a reluctant acceptance of women within the military, in more or less non-combat roles, the 'new world order' of the post-Cold War has no such need.

Compared to the changes in all other spheres of social activity and actual alterations in the structure of the military, changing images of women and femininity have had very little effect on the military role for women. Violence is and remains the province of the male. A proposition that the perceived wide gulf between civilian and military spheres both affirms and highlights. Running through all discussions about military activity is a confusing thread of accepted and basically unexamined assumptions about the nature of military performance. In total these assumptions create an idealized soldier, which is taken to be the norm, and it is from this false base that discussion and analysis then proceeds.

Stouffer's (1948) monumental work on American soldiers in World War II, Marshall's series of books between 1946–1976, and more recent works such as Keegan (1975), Gabriel and Savage (1978) and Hackworth (1991), are in the minority when they portray soldiers as *real* individuals rather than as interchangeable parts in a green (or gray) machine. Although these researchers are part of a long tradition of critical analysis of combat performance, which includes such classic works as du Picq's 'Battle Studies' (1864), it is a perspective which is largely ignored in favor of the ideal.

Furthermore, it is an ideal which is predicated upon the assumption that *real men* are the only suitable material for real soldiers. A real man is easy to pick, the military even offers detailed descriptions.

> The long column on the hard road … canteens empty but the cussedness burning in men's eyes – a fight ahead perhaps – that only a man can face and come out with his manhood intact … the company of God's own fighting gentlemen about you, the cussedest, doggedest, toughest men you'll ever walk with … and in your heart your soul satisfaction, a knowledge that you are a man.[1]

Whether it is a Lieutenant Colonel writing for an organ of the American Army, a German officer who told 11–12 year old cadets that their great and glorious purpose in life was to learn to die,[2] or a field psychiatrist in a tent in

---

1 Bellah: "Oh, the Infantry … With the Dirt Behind Their Ears." *Infantry Journal*, US Army, 53 (November 1943, No. 5), p. 54.
2 Laffin: *Jackboot*, p. 27.

Normandy interviewing psychiatric casualties who continually reinforced the line that real men can take it,[3] the message is a constant: the warrior is a man. The reality of combat is a direct contradiction of this cult of masculinity. Placed in the most lethal environment on the planet and rapidly coming to understand how small is his own chance of remaining alive, the combat soldier survives as best he can. This does not mean that the average soldier is either a coward or a hero but rather that the *norm* is one in which few soldiers function effectively.

Marshall's study of 400 American infantry companies in World War II showed that only 15–25 % of combat soldiers fired their guns in action.[4] The Wehrmacht between June 1944 and April 1945 lost 1,650,000 soldiers as prisoners, an average of 9,000 per day,[5] while the 5 % of American fighter pilots who achieved 'ace' standard in World War II accounted for 85 % of all enemy aircraft destroyed in combat.[6] The reality of combat can become so unpleasant for the human beings involved in it, that they come to identify their own leaders as the real enemy. The United States military for example, admits to having had over five hundred officers killed by their own men during the course of the Vietnam War.[7]

The confusion created for any serious examination of military performance by the unquestioning acceptance of the 'ideal' soldier, is compounded when there is any attempt to discuss a role for women within the military establishment. Attitudes within the military and outside it about a military function for women, reflect the wider cultural beliefs concerning men and women generally. Despite the changes in both attitudes and practices over the last two to three decades, changes which have in large measure been a result of the women's movement, females are still in a position of culturally defined inferiority.

In Australia for example, although there are now more women than men in the work force,[8] the positions they hold and the income they receive reflect this bias. Women are over-represented at the lower levels of both private and public organizations and virtually absent from these same organizations' upper echelons.[9] Although there are more female voters then males, only 15% of

---

3   Wagner: "Psychiatric Activities during the Normandy Offensive," pp. 341–46.
4   Marshall: *Men Against Fire.*
5   Shulman: *Defeat in the West*, p. 306.
6   Stouffer et al.: *The American Soldier* vol. 2, p. 57.
7   Gabriel and Savage: *Crisis in Command.*
8   ABS. Labor Force Statistics, 1992, Canberra, Australian Government Publishing Service.
9   ABS. The Labor Force, Australia, 1990, Canberra, A. G. P. S. Between 3–5 % in positions of authority.

all state and federal politicians are women.[10] Furthermore, despite equal opportunity and affirmative action legislation at both state and federal levels, the
ratio of female to male earnings remained basically constant at 0.78 between
1976–86 and the latest figures for 1993 show that this ratio has remained unchanged.[11]

Any attempt to evaluate a role for women in the military thus runs foul of
stereotypes about the 'real' combat soldier, blended with taken-for-granted
attitudes about women in general. The image of the male as the fighter, hero
and patriot, is magnified by our socialized images of women. Men are given a
cutting edge within the military itself by the use of the manliness ethic as a
method of selection and social control. Armies have always used training
methods which both stress and magnify the influence of manliness. Adjustment to army life is presented as a necessary prerequisite in the gaining of
one's birthright of self respect. The 'managers' of soldiers in combat are then
able to use manliness as a stiffener of their subordinates resolve. Simultaneously, the individual's attitude to himself and others, springing partly from his
pre-army beliefs about the manly thing to do and strengthened by army practices, reinforces the military's directives.

Changing the perception of who is or is not suitable to be a soldier; and
thence changing the composition of the military, is therefore not only difficult because of entrenched attitudes but also because the cult of masculinity
as it is practiced within the armed forces is one of the military's most effective
control mechanisms for extracting performance in combat. Given that a low
level of army positive behavior is the norm, then questioning suitability to be
a soldier inevitably produces opposition.

This also means that culturally internalized practices skews any serious
discussion away from whether women are capable of performing effectively,
to a debate on whether women *should* be allowed in the military and in combat. The male stereotype is paralleled by a female one centered around caring,
sensitivity and the need to be protected, attributes which obviously make
'real' women unsuitable for the demands of the military. In fact, up until the
end of World War II, the possible employment of women in combat roles or
even in support positions was seen by most of the involved countries as a sacrifice of the standards of civilization.

The arguments for and against women in uniform therefore operate on
three distinct but interrelated levels which are concerned far more with atti-

---

10   ABS, Canberra. Commonwealth Government Directory, December 1990, Canberra.
11   ABS. Earnings and Hours of Employees, 1993, Canberra, A. G. P. S.

tudes to and images of gender roles rather than upon empirical or historical evidence. The broadest issue is whether females should be in the military at all. The second, whether they should be in positions of authority, and lastly, if women should participate in combat. It is both command and combat roles that call into question the exclusivity of the male hero and it is these levels which attract the most opposition. The acceptance of a manliness ethic is only marginally challenged by women in non-combat positions – after all its 'nice' to have a pretty face to brighten up the place, but usurpation of command and combat functions is a direct threat to its existence.

Although most western countries do have a fair number of female military personnel, historically they have been viewed as warm bodies to release men, the real soldiers, for other duties. The most extreme position in modern day western armies is that taken by the then West German government.

The creation of the new German Army (the Bundeswehr) in May 1956, produced heated debates in the German parliament, but total agreement that the military would be all male. A decision which was reinforced by article 12 (a) of the constitution, that women "may not under any circumstances render service involving the use of arms."[12] Although there is no such total prohibition in most armies, the absence of a barrier against actual entry says very little about the acceptance of women, nor about their possibilities of having a genuine career. In practice, restrictions concerning command and combat functions means that women can never be anything more than sub-professionals with circumscribed careers.[13]

The current position for females in European and American military services (and this includes Australia) is that they are *legally* prevented from undertaking combat roles. This means that sex discrimination is institutionalized by the process of law and that it would require legal action to alter the situation. The initial American opening of additional specialties for women in the late 1960's produced no real breakdown in the established pattern. The services themselves have not been active in initiating changes; in fact the opening of more specialties was a result of action from the military's civilian superiors, and their reluctance and foot dragging is mirrored by the attitude of the US Congress which before, during and since World War II has been the major source of resistance to changes in the existing legislation.

---

12 Tuten: *The Utilization of Women in Combat: The Germans: Past Practice, Perspective and Prospects*, p. 17.

13 The Australian Army received a report in 1978 from its own Regular Officers Development Committee concerning this legally created inequality but, like all such studies, it has been largely ignored. *Study Five: Women Officers and Specialized Corps*, Canberra. A.G. P.S.

During the 1990's there has been some nibbling at the edges of this prohibition; for example female pilots being allowed to train on jet fighters, but it is questionable whether substantive change can be produced by a process of accretion. The current explosion over homosexuals in the US military is a reflection of the same unquestioned assumptions about 'real' soldiers and fits very nicely into the masculine stereotypes.

Israel is often alluded to as an example of female combat role participation. In fact, although females took part in the war of independence, are trained as irregulars for the defense of kibbutz, and are drafted compulsorily for military service, they are excluded from the combat units of armor, artillery and infantry in the Israeli Defense Forces (IDF). The image of women warriors is a useful propaganda device, but women only play out supporting, male releasing roles. Furthermore, Israeli women are able to obtain exemptions from military service far more easily than men, and they do not remain in the reserve units for as long as their male counterparts. Given that a substantial proportion of the Jewish electorate is by no means liberal in their attitude towards 'military females,' it is hardly surprising that their roles are circumscribed. The editors of the "Israeli Defense Forces Spokesman" have attempted to clarify the position for the benefit of outsiders and have pointedly observed that "CHEN (the Hebrew acronym for the Women's Corps of the Israeli Defense Forces) means charm."[14]

The closest role to a combat on that women have performed is that of nursing. In the carrying out of their tasks they have proved that females can withstand the pressures engendered by combat situations, and that they are able to undergo physical hardships equal to those endured by combat soldiers. However, their success has done very little to change the images and attitudes towards female abilities to perform in combat roles. Kalisch, writing on female nurses in American wars, demonstrates that there is little connection between the actual performance of nurses and the popular images held about them. He suggests that the reasons for this are fourfold. Nursing is seen as a natural extension of maternal and domestic responsibilities and only requires: a delicacy of touch, devotion to duty, a sense of responsibility and the maternal instinct. Commenting on this image, Kalisch dryly remarks that it fails to "draw attention to the violent environment and danger surrounding the nurse as she applies her delicate touch to mutilated stumps and grossly infected tissue."[15]

---

14   Quoted in Adams: "Jane Crow in the Army. Obstacles to Sexual Integration," p. 53.
15   Kalish and Scobey: "Female Nurses in American Wars," p. 227.

Secondly, the vague but pervasive feeling that nurses are somehow different to other women, and that becoming a nurse means that the individual is desensitized to hardship and suffering and is less likely to experience the emotional weakness of 'normal' women. Thirdly, there has been a direct carry over of traditional doctor-nurse relationships which perpetuate the role of nurse subordination. And lastly, the leadership of the nursing corps has accepted their subordinate position and, in endorsing the status quo, has not been active in pushing for rights for women. The image of nursing is therefore an amalgam of traditional male attitudes concerning the role of women and, on the part of the nurses themselves, an acceptance of the role into which they have been cast.

Although many countries provide basic (i. e.: combat) training for newly inducted female personnel, while evaluation of their performance may be fair, denial mechanisms mean that this does not necessarily change the stereotype. The particular female individuals who succeed are seen as exceptional and therefore their performance is not viewed as representative of women as a whole. Because of stereotypical ideals, women are seen as more emotional, more afraid of pain and violence, less cold-blooded and more likely to crack under pressure. Where this has proved not to be the case, as for example with nurses, then somehow these individuals aren't 'real' women.

While legislative changes regarding combat roles for females are important, they have to be paired with a shift in attitudes and beliefs. Combat teams need mutual trust and acceptance if they are to function effectively and therefore: "perhaps the most serious problem for women in combat will thus in the end be less what they can do, and more what their fellow soldiers think they can do."[16] Given current socialization practices, females in military service, despite basic combat training, do not see themselves as ready for combat. In the French Army in 1982 for example, 56 % of female officers and NCOs were against combat roles for women.[17] While an Australian study in 1985 found that 53 % of female service personnel felt the same way.[18] However, the fact that over 40 % of the personnel in the two studies did think that there was a combat role for women and that in the Australian study 43 % of the *male* military personnel agreed, reflects a change in attitude which it is hard to imagine surfacing in the military of the nineteen fifties and sixties.

As well as a lack of career prospects and the internalized attitudes of the authorities and of both male and female personnel, there are four additional

16   Queter: *Women in the Armed Forces: The US Experience*, p. 24.
17   See Martin: "From Periphery to Center: Women in the French Military.
18   See D'Alton: "The Role of Women in the Australian Armed Forces."

issues involved with moving females from the periphery to the center of military activities. These revolve around: physical features relating to women; the social and biological dimensions of sex; the attitude of allies and enemies to women in the forces; and lastly the importance of the small group. The way that these issues have been handled, highlights the culturally defined *inferiority* of females.

Physically the average male is stronger than the average female and, despite the technologizing of warfare, there do remain jobs that call for sheer brute strength not simply dexterity. However, although there are a percentage of females who fulfill the necessary strength criteria, what seems to be happening is that objective measures are only the visible part of a hidden agenda, one which excludes all females from combat roles *because* they are female, not because they are individually unsuitable for the job. Moreover, the technology of military hardware design is predicated upon the assumption that it will be used by the average male. Changing this assumption would diminish the 'problem' of physical strength. After all, when this had to be done for factory work during World War II to cater to females it was done with the minimum of fuss.

Women do menstruate, have sexual feelings and can become pregnant, but the biological realities of the female body are less significant than the way these issues have been addressed. The fact that most women *can* get pregnant, for example, is not an adequate reason for excluding them from combat assignments. After all, all men can get the flu or venereal disease and this type of category exclusion is not applied to them. It is rather specious to argue, as do some opponents of combat roles for women, that because society would never allow pregnant women in combat, that women as a group should be excluded.

The concern over sexual arousal, sexual activity and moral danger serves to underline some of the problems created by the culturally defined *inferiority* of women. Sexual activity in mixed gender units is a certainty, but it is not the only type of relations possible. To portray females as a problem because of their sexuality is not only demeaning and one-dimensional, it also offers an interesting side light on the thinking of those who are only able to see females in this way. Sexual arousal and protecting women from killing situations where they may be sexually aroused follows on from the 'problem' of sexual activity and is to my mind a very peculiar argument. The proposition seems to be based on a moral fear notion; that in some way sexual morality will be compromised if females are able to participate. It is presumably all right for men to be sexually aroused by killing, since this will not compromise the society's sexual morality which is apparently the repository of women.

Moral danger also seems to be behind the argument that since women could be raped by the enemy if they were captured, then this risk shouldn't be taken. Setting aside the general issue that people get *killed* in combat, the certainty that some soldiers will be tortured and/or killed when they are captured, has never been an argument advanced for keeping males out of combat. Moral danger is another of the visible faces of the hidden agenda. The excessive concern with women's sexuality has to be seen as providing information about male beliefs and attitudes rather than as a genuine perception of females as individuals.

A related argument against the inclusion of women in combat units that is also based on stereotypical ideas about gender, is the attitude of one's allies and ones enemies. Unless one is perceived as effective then the military cannot function as a credible deterrent against aggression and, following from this, that 'we' will be seen as weak if there are females in one's own combat units. Furthermore, that the presence of women would enrage the enemy's masculinity and that they would refuse to surrender to mixed sex units and thus increase casualties. This objection is also an illustration of the acceptance of the ideal soldier as a *reality*. In practice the normal behavior of European soldiers, for example, is not to fight to the death but rather to surrender when their situation is hopeless. It is therefore very difficult to support the contention that this desire to stay alive is going to be negated by the presence of female soldiers on the other side; particularly when the nature of modern combat makes close physical contact with the enemy the exception and not the rule. Furthermore, the refusal of an enemy to surrender is hardly a reason for determining the composition of one's own combat units. The Japanese soldiers in World War II generally did seem to choose death rather than surrender, often committing suicide rather than give in, but the American and British forces did defeat them. Nor was there ever any suggestion that the Japanese should not be fought because casualties might be higher as a consequence.

The last issue is the importance of the small group. Supporters of the status quo acknowledge its significance and take the anthropological line that group commitment is based on male bonding and that women would have a devastating effect upon the levels of cohesion.[19] One way of expressing this is to claim that women would be a problem because men would risk their lives to look after them instead of doing their job. The 'looking after' syndrome is of a piece with the image of 'inferiority' of women. It also places the performance of soldiers in the world of the ideal, where everyone is supposedly motivated to perform positively at all times regardless of the risks. The real world of combat shrinks the dimensions of the soldier's concerns down to those

---

19   See Segal: *Women in Combat.*

around them as the most important individuals in their world, and it is on this personal level that the soldier responds, not to some abstraction like cause or country.[20] Group cohesion is vital but it stems from interaction in a high stress environment, not simply as a function of maleness.

In fact, the argument about the inclusion of women having a devastating effect upon the small group, sounds remarkably like the dire warnings accompanying the integration of blacks into combat roles in the United States military, a policy change that only happened after World War II. The same type of stereotypes were appealed to, the same 'truths' which labeled a group because of the color of their skin or, in the present case, the sex of the individuals involved. Blacks now serve in all the traditional combat roles, performing tasks which it was solemnly asserted up until forty years ago were totally beyond them. However, the possible impact of females on a combat unit's performance is important for another reason; not because group cohesiveness is a function of masculinity, but because the military utilizes the manliness ethic as a way of obtaining positive performance. Properly applied, it creates a social climate for combat where deviance from expected behavior reduces the individual's manliness in his own eyes and in the judgment of those around him.

If the objection to the presence of females in a combat unit is seen in this light, then it is not the male bonding of the group per se which is the issue, but rather the use of this manliness as a covert control mechanism that is felt to be at risk. Extracting positive performance from soldiers is something that armies have had a long time to develop and refine and, in a hypothetical integrated combat unit of the future, one could argue that a variation on this theme could be used to shame men who can't take it by pointing to females who can.

The distinction between the three levels of involvement, in uniform, in command and in combat, is a useful tool for examining the parameters of the topic but it is an academic distinction not a real one. Although there is a general acceptance in most western countries of a non-combatant role for women but little endorsement of command and combat functions, the nature of combat makes nonsense out of these carefully delineated activities.

Developments in technology during this century have expanded the battlefield to include the entire territory of one's enemies, while guerrilla warfare with its total lack of front lines has blurred the old distinction between

---

20   In a sample of 634 German POWs captured in September 1944, only 5 % were worried about anything other than personal or familial problems. Shils and Janowitz: "Cohesion and Disintegration in the Wehrmacht in World War II", pp. 280–315.

combat and support roles. In fact a more meaningful definition would be to speak of areas of greater or lesser danger and this includes *all* service personnel. The reality of combat has therefore short-circuited the intentions of legislation and the avowed positions of politicians and military leaders. Servicewomen in areas of greater or lesser danger is a reality and the fact that they are barred from membership in the traditional combat arms, means that the only genuine 'combat' restrictions upon them is that they are not allowed to strike back at the enemy, or to control and direct those who do.[21]

Optimistically, the changes that have happened in the civilian sphere will, although real gender equality remains illusory, flow over into the military. The problem with moving females from the periphery to the center is that there are deeply embedded structural inequalities in our societies and these will not be easily overcome. Changes in images and attitude are occurring, albeit slowly, and hopefully one of the consequences of this will be the treatment of women as individuals, not as interchangeable units in an inferior gender category. The blanket exclusion of personnel from specific roles in the armed forces *because* they are female is neither legal in terms of equal rights, nor desirable given the changing nature of gender relations.

Pessimistically, the structural inequalities may be too embedded to change. After all, the legal exclusion of women from combat and command roles has remained basically unchallenged. Consider the upheaval that would result from a decision to establish a legal barrier excluding females from the more senior positions in state and federal public services or from management positions in the private sector and this lack of protest becomes even more striking.[22]

With no 'person-power' pressure to expand the talks and positions available to women in the future, it is likely that the military will remain a male bastion of *real* men which perpetuate the cult of masculinity. The irony is that,

---

21 This lack of a meaningful definition of combat was pointed out in 1978 in Australia but, like the whole of this study, the findings have generally been pigeonholed. "In summary, failure to analyze the concept of combat as a prelude to establishing policy on the employment of servicewomen presents basic logical difficulties which [...] seriously jeopardize the remainder of the policy." Regular Officer Development Committee (not. 13) p. 14, Canberra, A. G. P. S.

22 As McHugh discovered when she was interviewing respondents for her book on Australian women and the Vietnam War, although approximately a thousand women were 'in country' in a variety of positions during the conflict, several of the males she interviewed did not believe that there had been *any* Australian women in Vietnam. McHugh: *Minefields and Miniskirts.*

given the on-going changes in the civilian sphere, it is probable that it will be an increasingly feminized executive arm of government which directs them.

Artistic and Literary Representations
of Modern Warfare

RICHARD CORK
London

"A Murderous Carnival":
German Artists in the First World War

Abstract: The traumatic effects of the First World War are powerfully conveyed in the work produced by leading German artists on active service. Otto Dix, having gone to war filled with martial enthusiasm, changed from belligerence to disillusion in the self-portraits he produced. George Grosz, after producing several images focused on death, suffered a nervous breakdown. So did Ernst Ludwig Kirchner, who defined the vulnerability of the soldiers with unnerving force in his paintings of the period. Max Beckmann also gave way to a breakdown, and summarized his despair in gruelling etchings of a hospital operation and corpses in a morgue. Franz Marc had a more complicated attitude to the war, and in some respects regarded it as a necessary event which would purge European society. But he conveyed the greedy violence of the battlefield in his wartime sketchbook, and was killed himself in 1916. His death was perhaps the greatest single loss sustained by German art during the conflict.

I.

Although plenty of artists in Germany greeted the Great War with martial enthusiasm, they soon became unable to ignore the distressing reality of death. Initially caught up in a general sense of intoxicating excitement, bolstered by patriotic sentiment and military propaganda, even the most belligerent of them began, after a while, to recoil from the unprecedented savagery of the struggle.

The full, battering force of twentieth-century weaponry was unleashed during the conflict's protracted course, and the result forced everyone involved to revise their preconceptions about the nature of modern warfare. Machine-age armaments produced in immense quantities by highly organized industrial nations were capable of annihilation on a hitherto inconceivable scale. The spiralling human cost rapidly came to seem out of all proportion to the infinitesimal military gains made on either side.

The obscenity of the war's wasted lives, eventually mounting to a tally of ten million dead, created a deep-seated sense of incredulity, anger and revulsion. Anyone with a potent imagination was bound to be affected, and the generation which found itself embroiled in the fighting happened to contain an unusually high number of outstanding young artists. None was more forceful than in Germany, where the outbreak of war coincided with an exceptional period of ferment and innovative vitality in painting, sculpture and graphic art. The proliferation of avant-garde movements in the pre-war years had testified to a quickening pace, with vociferous and often highly competitive groups committing themselves to the principle of extreme renewal. Although the energy with which they pursued their insurrectionary goals was bound to be partially swallowed up in active service, an impressive range of artists refused to let the war prevent them from working altogether.

Much of that headlong determination can be found, above all, in the youthful frankness with which Otto Dix revealed his own pugnacity in *Self-Portrait as a Soldier* (Fig. 1). Painted soon after he enlisted as an artilleryman in August 1914, and brushed in with a speed that implies how little time the war left for art, this bull-necked presence offers a brusque image of Dix as a prizefighter. He strains his shaven head forward like a man eager to be let loose on the enemy, and the scarlet coat swathing his shoulders intensifies the bloodthirstiness of his stance. The bone-structure in his brutish, almost Neanderthal features is heightened by a fire as fierce as in the foundry where Dix's father worked as a mould-maker. Even the surname inscribed so prominently on a white space beneath the painting's date has the aggression of graffiti scrawled on a street wall.

This is a portrait of a man hungry for conflict, his belligerence backed up by a firm Nietzschean belief in the rebirth which the destruction of decadence can foster. *Self-Portrait as a Soldier* has the same jutting obstinacy as Dix's earlier bust of Nietzsche, and even in old age he was prepared to admit the extent of his initial excitement in 1914. "The war was a horrible thing," he declared, "but there was something tremendous about it, too. I didn't want to miss it at any price. You have to have seen human beings in this unleashed state to know what human nature is." Later in the same interview, Dix explained that he volunteered for the artillery out of an urgent "need to experience all the depths of life for myself,"[1] and in *Self-Portrait as a Soldier* he looks tough enough to withstand all the most degrading experiences which the war might hurl at him.

---

1   Otto Dix, interview, December 1963, quoted by Schmidt: *Otto Dix im Selbstbildnis*, p. 237.

1. Otto Dix: *Self-Portrait as a Soldier*, 1914, Galerie der Stadt Stuttgart.

On the other side of the paper, however, he is already prepared to present a more cautious and ambivalent viewpoint. Instead of rushing like an enraged dog towards the fray, without any apparent means of protecting himself, the

2. Otto Dix: *Self-Portrait with Artillery Helmet*, 1914, Galerie der Stadt Stuttgart.

soldier depicted here scrutinizes the world from the shelter of an elaborate artillery helmet (Fig. 2). Its gleaming star emblazons the painting, and Dix specifies braid, epaulettes and buttons with respect for military trappings. But

Dix's mood now seems restrained. His narrowed eyes look defensive as they stare sideways, shielded by the helmet's peak. Rather than immersing himself in the war with unqualified zeal, like his *alter ego* on the reverse of the painting, he appears withdrawn. His tightly buttoned uniform has a constricting effect, preventing him from any rash commitment to an impulsive action he may later regret. As for the signature positioned above his helmet, it no longer possesses the bravado of the capital letters spelling his name on the other self-portrait. This time it hovers uncertainly in space, and Dix has allowed the pigment to dribble down the picture like a presentiment of wounds he might soon be obliged to suffer.

At this early stage in the conflict, Dix's Nietzschean convictions were more powerful than any doubts he may already have entertained. A painting carrying the stark title *War* shows how energetically he could summarize the inferno of a full artillery barrage. Furious red zig-zags issue from the mouth of the great gun, which bristles with cogs and other mechanisms. The splintering effect of the explosions that tear their jagged paths through the air owe a formal debt to the Futurists, whose work had impressed Dix at a pre-war exhibition in the Galerie Arnold, Dresden. His cannon, however, is far more violent than its serio-comic counterpart in Severini's *Cannon in Action*. The playfulness of the Italian's word-spattered painting contrasts utterly with the singleminded ferocity of Dix's vision in *War*. He only permits himself a single terse word, "Spandau," inscribed around the rim of the gun's mighty wheel. Moreover, Severini's artillerymen carry out their duties quite calmly – whereas Dix's soldiers are reduced to a cluster of blanched and scarlet masks, wide-eyed as they shelter from the maelstrom around them.

Dix had a firmer and more tenacious grasp of war's capacity for destruction than the Futurists. After he witnessed the battlefield at first hand, his attitude grew grimmer still. *Self-Portrait as Mars* looks, at first, like a relatively straightforward attempt to identify the artist with the god of war. The artillery helmet which had appeared so defensive in his earlier self-portrait now sprouts an antique crest, as if to confirm Dix's new mythological status; and he occupies a focal position in the midst of the chaos whirling around him. The star on his helmet has lifted itself from a quiescent position and become a dancing star, just as Nietzsche recommended in *Zarathustra*. Dix alone seems to retain his composure while everything else in this wild, murderous universe is torn apart. Below his clenched head a gaggle of other faces can be discerned, their eyes sightless and mouths gushing blood. Horses rear and twist, wide-eyed with terror at the danger threatening their flame-reflecting bodies. And just below the upper right corner of the painting, a collapsing building metamorphoses into a skull with white teeth horribly exposed.

But is Dix as immune from the havoc as he initially appeared? Despite his evident determination to ride the storm, in the Nietzschean belief that a purified world will emerge from the catharsis, his own future is by no means assured. For Dix's eyes have enlarged as much as the horses', and he is invaded at every turn by the conflict. The Futurist-inspired 'lines of force' that cause the buildings to totter behind him slice through his head as well, while wheels and faces like death-masks penetrate his uniform. The god of war is himself battered by the forces he has unleashed, and Dix must have been aware of the irony involved. He was certainly prepared to admit the self-destructive absurdity of his life in the army by the time he painted *Self-Portrait as Shooting Target*. Proud Mars has now deteriorated into a helpless dummy, stripped of his helmet and fit only for remaining rigid while enemy bullets seek him out. It is a nihilistic image, where despair is countered solely by an obstinate ability to mock the mortal danger he confronts.

If Dix was torn between seeing himself as aggressor and victim, Max Beckmann possessed a clearer idea of his role in the war. As his *Weeping Woman* indicated, he knew from an early stage how much human tragedy the conflict would cause. Unwilling to be responsible for any killing, Beckmann volunteered in autumn 1914 for the German army's medical corps. Soon he was despatched to the ambulance service on the Russian Front, and his earliest letters voice an enthralled admiration for the spectacle he is witnessing. Describing the "incredibly grand noise of battle out there," he reported excitedly in October that "it's like the gates of eternity bursting open when a great salvo like this sounds across the fields. Everything evokes space, distance, infinity. I wish I could paint that sound. Oh, this expanse and uncannily beautiful depth!"[2]

His rapturous response to the distant battle did not survive a closer confrontation with suffering. Like Nevinson, whose duties as an ambulance driver exposed him to the worst consequences of injury and death, Beckmann was forced to scrutinize the most pathetic victims of war. Among the first images he produced from his experience at the Front is *Fallen Soldiers*, which insists on presenting the conflict solely in terms of the men it mowed down. They were the people whose bodies Beckmann and his colleagues handled, and in *Carrying the Wounded* he centers on the abject dependence of the soldier cradled in the medical orderly's arms. The stunned and disabled man clings to his helper's neck, so that their heads almost touch. But there is no psychological contact between them. The orderly looks to his left, possibly seeking as-

---

2   Beckmann, letter of 11 October 1914, Beckmann: *Briefe im Kriege*, p. 15.

sistance in the task of bearing his ungainly load; and the soldier's eyes are cast downwards, in bitter contemplation of the childlike state he endures.

Beckmann's sympathy for the injured was intensified when his brother-in-law Martin Tube sustained a serious head-wound on the Eastern Front. He produced a compassionate lithograph of the bandaged young man, who had predicted the war six years before and agreed with Beckmann that "it really would not be so bad."[3] The chastened soldier in *Portrait of my Wounded Brother-in-law Martin Tube* had doubtless altered his views by the winter of 1914, and Beckmann followed suit. For Tube died soon after the portrait was executed, and the tragedy affected Beckmann's work very dramatically. Enraged by the loss of his friend, and by the mounting evidence of pain among patients in the base hospital, he drew a protesting image of a cripple with the savagely ironic title *Théâtre du Monde-Grand Spectacle de la Vie*. The nervous, scrawling style of the drawing reveals the extremity of Beckmann's feelings. Here, only four days before Christmas 1914, he finds no demonstration of Christ's love for the world in this abused figure. As if the appalling wound on his face and paralyzed legs were not enough, the man also has to endure mental torment. That much is clear from his dishevelled hair writhing above eyes which still relive the shock and terror of the battlefield. He has been reduced to the level of a traumatized animal, and Beckmann recognizes the analogy by drawing the patient's exposed feet like a pair of claws.

The horror intensified when, in February 1915, Beckmann was transferred to a field hospital at Courtray in Flanders. For a moment, he found himself tempted to use his art as a form of escapism when invited to paint a fresco on the wall of a large delousing bath. Beckmann's letters disclose that he originally planned to depict an oasis festooned with palm trees in an Oriental desert.[4] But he quickly realized that the reality of war claimed priority now, and instead of depicting "an Oriental bath" he decided to "paint what is around me."[5] The outcome of his efforts did not last long: it was painted in a temporary building. But his graphic work of 1915 is motivated by a consistent desire to deal with "what is around me," and he did not flinch from concentrating on the most harrowing scenes imaginable.

A few months before, on the Eastern Front, he had witnessed an operation at the base hospital. The surgeon and nurses attending to the body on the table are disturbed by the arrival, in the foreground, of an orderly bearing the

3   Beckmann: *Leben in Berlin: Tagebuch 1908/09*, p. 22.
4   Beckmann, letter of 27 March 1915, Beckmann: *Briefe im Kriege*, pp. 31–2.
5   Max Beckmann, letter of 30 March 1915, ibid., p. 34.

3. Max Beckmann: *The Morgue*, 1915, Museum of Modern Art, New York.

next patients on a stretcher: the harassed nurse in the center seems divided between the rival demands of the two patients. But at least there is a prospect of tending the wounded, and the medical staff reassuringly outnumber the soldiers in their care. When Beckmann returned to the subject in 1915, however, he studied the dead rather than the injured. *The Morgue* (Fig. 3) is dominated by three corpses, and no comforting nurses bustle through the room to offset the finality of their stillness. Although a blanket still swathes one of the bodies, the dead man no longer benefits from its warmth. Members of the medical team gather round the corpse on the right, but the stiffness of the limbs proves that *rigor mortis* has set in. The destination awaiting all three figures is outlined on the floor beyond, where a makeshift open coffin has already been filled. The dignity of funereal custom cannot be observed in this bleak chamber, for another coffin is pushed awkwardly away by the only man available to carry it off to the grave.

As well as studying the corpses in the field hospital at Courtray, Beckmann was probably influenced by a visit he made to the Brussels Musée des Beaux Arts in April 1915. For he told his wife that he had admired some "wonderful" paintings by Rogier van der Weyden, "whom I like best of all the Belgian primitives."[6] Matthias Eberle speculated that van der Weyden's *Lamentation of Christ* may have provided Beckmann with specific inspiration for the bodies in *The Morgue*.[7] But the difference between Christ and the rigid corpses on their hospital tables is as great as any similarities they may possess. The limp figure stretched across the surface of van der Weyden's picture is graceful in death, for all his etiolation and the gashes puncturing his skin. Moreover, he is clasped with tenderness by both the people who support him, and the sorrow he arouses in the viewer is ameliorated by the knowledge that resurrection will ensue. Beckmann's bodies enjoy no such hope. With feet grotesquely up-turned and flesh disfigured by calamitous wounds, they await burial without ceremony in a foreign land. Instead of relatives and disciples, they are attend-ed by officials anxious only to complete a disagreeable job. If the *Lamentation* was indeed in Beckmann's mind when he etched the two orderlies bending over the corpse on the right, he can only have intended a sardonic contrast with the impassioned gestures of Christ's supporters. For the body's band-aged head precludes any possibility of sympathetic contact between the dead man and his attendants. In their eyes, he is simply one more cadaver-requiring summary dispatch, and they peer at his figure with the workaday detachment of refuse collectors clearing away litter.

Beckmann's work was haunted for years to come by the memory of those corpses, culminating in the bandaged tormentor who squats on an operating table in the center of *The Night*. The artist's quarters were positioned directly above the morgue, and he imagined once that dead bodies had invaded his room during the night. Nor were the wounded bodies any less troubling. In the summer of 1915 he described how "night-watch" had obliged him to look after "two stomach wounds and a severe brain contusion with delirium. Wrestled all night with the unconscious man. The room dimly lit, by night-lights and sheet lightning, and reeking of decay."[8] The cumulative effect of these duties took their toll on his mind and constitution alike. He succumbed to a nihilistic despair, asking in one anguished letter: "What would we poor mortals do if we didn't continually equip ourselves with ideas about God and country, love and art, in an attempt to hide that sinister black hole. This end-less desolation in eternity. This loneliness."[9] Meeting Erich Heckel and Lud-wig Meidner in Flanders did little to assuage this sense of isolation. An etch-ing of *Two Officers of the Motor Corps* suggests how alienated Beckmann felt

---

6   Ibid., p.36.
7   Eberle: *World War I and the Weimar Artists*, p. 92.
8   Beckmann, letter of 8 June 1915, Beckmann: *Briefe im Kriege*, p. 69.
9   Beckmann, letter of 24 May 1915, ibid., p. 63.

from the men with whom he came into contact in the army. Nothing in those cold and sullen faces indicates that Beckmann found in military service a gratifying sense of comradeship.

His accelerating agony received its most violent expression in *The Grenade* (Fig. 4), a large etching which Beckmann worried at and transformed in a sequence of five states. From the outset the grenade itself whirls in the air like a portent of cosmic catastrophe, and might well have been intended as a manifestation of the "sinister black hole." But he anchored the image in his experience of gas attacks at Ypres as well, for the commotion revolves around the soldiers' frantic attempts to escape the poisonous vapours. Some of the figures, even in the early states of the print, are incapable of fleeing. They lie in the foreground, felled by injuries which have gashed a hole in one man's cheek and exposed his teeth. But other infantrymen raise their rifles in a futile bid to fend off the threat, and the space directly below the bursting grenade is alive with the frantic gesticulations of a Meidner-like man whose arms are flung outwards in an unconscious echo of the crucifixion.

Subsequent states of the plate bear the mark of additional dry-point work, resulting in a general darkening of the mood. The sky, previously in a state of turmoil with strange fragments of dazed faces suspended in space, now becomes overcast. The pointing soldier on the right turns into a near-silhouette, and the disparity in scale between him and the wounded figures nearby becomes still more disquieting. Agitation permeates the entire composition, reflecting not only the men's fear but Beckmann's own nervous condition as well. The disposition of forms may owe a debt to the falling bodies in Bernard van Orley's *Altarpiece of the Visions of Job*, which Beckmann probably saw on a visit to the Brussels museum. But the sense of vertiginous disorder in *The Grenade* is an authentic reflection of his gathering inner panic, and in the final state of the print he accentuates the soldiers' hysteria more than ever. The silhouetted figures on the right have been deleted, enabling the man with outflung arms to thrust a leg into the vacated space. His rushing, yelling form thereby plays a more important part in the image as a whole, giving it a greater degree of urgency. The grenade gains in prominence too, for Beckmann has by now sliced off the top of the design and minimized the sky's former turbulence. A large figure appears in the upper left area of the composition, turning away and trying to shield his eyes from the blinding effects of the gas. But there is no escaping its evil vapours, just as Beckmann knew that the "sinister black hole" could never be evaded in the end.

He was certainly unable to prevent himself from being overwhelmed by the destruction surrounding him. "I suffer with every shot and have the wildest visions," he wrote during his time in the trenches, before implying that

4. Max Beckmann: *The Grenade*, 1915, British Museum, London.

thoughts of art saved him from collapsing under the strain: "My plans for plates that I want to make swell like a victory in Galicia."[10] But during the summer of 1915 his health was finally undermined by a nervous and physical breakdown. Although Beckmann never referred to the collapse later, it was severe enough to persuade the army that he should be allowed to convalesce at Strasbourg. From there he moved to Frankfurt and tried to regain a semblance of his earlier strength. For the time being, however, his hopes of recovery proved elusive. "Every day is a battle for me," he confessed in September. "A battle with myself and with the bad dreams that buzz around my head like mosquitoes. Singing: We'll be back again, we'll be back again. Work always helps me to get over my various attacks of persecution mania."[11]

Here, at least, Beckmann was able to take up the brush and palette he had longed to use in Flanders. "If I only think of grey, green, and purple, or of black-yellow, sulfur yellow, and purple," he had written in June, "I am overcome by a voluptuous shiver. I wish the war were over and I could paint again."[12] In Frankfurt his wish was at last realized, and the recuperating artist presented himself as a medical orderly in a small yet candid self-portrait.[13] Depicted in the act of applying pigment to canvas, Beckmann turns away as if startled by an unwelcome thought. His eyes have the strained, staring quality of a man transfixed by some painful memory. The presence of the red cross on his collar is surely intended to signify that army experiences have not gone away. They plague his waking hours as much as his dreams, and Beckmann's downturned mouth conveys the defensive grimness of a man condemned to struggle with recurrent nightmares.

Heckel, who had got to know Beckmann in Flanders, also served as a Red Cross orderly. That he did not succumb to the kind of collapse Beckmann suffered may partly be due to the enlightened understanding of his unit commander, the art historian Walter Kaesbach, who allowed artists in his charge to have every alternate day free for their own work. He enabled Heckel to contact other artists in the unit, and would certainly have encouraged him to execute woodcuts based on his experience at the Front. Like Beckmann, Heckel turned for subject-matter to the injured people in his care. The com-

---

10   Ibid., p. 60.

11   Beckmann, letter of September 1915, quoted by von Wiese: *Max Beckmanns zeichnerisches Werk 1903-1925*, pp. 171–72, note 125.

12   Max Beckmann, letter of 8 June 1915, Beckmann: *Briefe im Kriege*, pp. 72–3.

13   Although the word 'Strassburg' is inscribed beneath the signature in this self-portrait, it was probably painted in Frankfurt.

manding woodcut of *Two Wounded Soldiers* (Fig. 5) does not disclose the gashed
flesh Beckmann defined in his excoriating etchings. But Heckel's compassion
is evident at once. Obliged to remain inactive, two men sit hunched and for-
lorn as they contemplate their disablement. The figure with his arm in a sling
looks particularly dejected, and neither soldier displays the swaggering insou-
ciance with which they had probably marched off to war only a few months
before. Heckel's absolute refusal, in 1914, to display any hope or confidence
in the future course of the war is uncompromising. The powerful woodcut
self-portrait he executed soon afterwards has a furrowed intensity worthy of
Van Gogh. Indeed, the index finger extended by the frowning artist seems to
be insisting that we follow his gaze, and study with him the victims of the battlefields.

The convictions which had led him to volunteer for medical duties inform
all his war images, and in 1915 a second woodcut of *Two Wounded Soldiers*
shows a deepening pessimism. This time the picture-surface is presided over
by a man with an extensively bandaged head. Heckel's roughly scored treatment of his face makes him appear emaciated and weary, gazing forwards
with a sense of resignation about his chances of recovery. But at least he is
not confined to a bed like the man behind him. Here Heckel's cutting knife
achieves a macabre quality, so that the blanket covering the patient appears to
contain an X-ray of the skeleton beneath. It recalls Wyndham Lewis's remark
that German Expressionist woodcuts, "disciplined, thick and brutal,"
achieved nothing less than a "surgery of the senses."[14] Indeed, this prostrate
man with his upturned feet exposed at the bottom of the bed is eerily reminiscent of the corpses laid out for the last time in Beckmann's *The Morgue*.

The painting Heckel executed on two strips of an army tent for Christmas
1915 was far more optimistic.[15] The minuscule boat in the lowest area of the
picture is threatened by dauntingly high waves, and to that extent Heckel
acknowledges the reality of danger in his canvas. But any sense of alarm is
outweighed by the figure who rises from the sea and gives the painting its
name. For the *Ostend Madonna* is a colossus, and she is presumably meant to
help the beleaguered boatmen find a safe passage between the rocks. The
haloes irradiating both her and the child Jesus prove that Heckel's religiosity
could hardly be expressed with greater devotion. The angels and flowers
festooning the picture's borders vie with each other in their determination to
laud the holy pair. Donald E. Gordon convincingly proposed that *Ostend Ma-*

14   Wyndham: "Note [on some German Woodcuts at the Twenty-One Gallery]." *Blast* No. 1,
        p. 136.
15   The *Ostend Madonna* was destroyed in the Second World War.

5. Erich Heckel: *Two Wounded Soldiers*, 1914, Brücke Museum, Berlin.

donna contains a self-conscious tribute to Philipp Otto Runge's *Morning¹⁶*, and the tent painting proves how ardently Heckel wanted to believe in the imminence of a peaceful dawn breaking over Europe with the new year. Judging by the response which greeted his *Madonna,* its sentiments were widely shared in the German army. "How glad I was to paint that for the soldiers," Heckel wrote at the time:

> It was fine to see how much respect and even love for artistic things there is in people, in spite of everything. Who would have thought that my style, which seemed so modern and incomprehensible to the critics and urban public, would now speak and appeal to the men to whom I have freely given it.¹⁷

All the same, the hope conveyed in his tent painting was confounded by events, and seems far less convincing now than the disillusioned work he went on to produce in the later stages of the war.

II.

In this respect, George Grosz's images of 1915 turned out to be informed by a greater accuracy about the true nature of the conflict. For Grosz viewed the onset of hostilities with misgivings from the start. "The outbreak of war made it clear to me that the masses marching wildly cheering through the streets were without a will under the influence of the press and military pomp," he remembered later. "The will of the statesmen and generals dominated them. I also sensed that will above my head, but I was not cheering because I saw the threat to the individual freedom in which I had lived hitherto."¹⁸ All these forebodings had been ferociously conveyed in *Pandemonium*, a hectic drawing executed soon after war was declared. Crazed by an aggressive fever, civilians are caught up in an orgy of greed, lust and random violence all over the city. At the top of the drawing, where the commotion is least frenzied, religious authority is snubbed as the church burns. Further down the sheet, disorder accelerates. A tram is smashed and its passengers slaughtered indiscriminately, while nearby a pedestrian is hanged on a lamp-post with a mocking paper crown on his head. Exultation of the most depraved kind breaks out below, where a bare-breasted whore brandishing a skull is carried triumphantly along

---

16   Gordon: *Expressionism: Art and Ideal*, pp. 108–10.
17   Erich Heckel to Gustav Schiefler, Christmas 1915, quoted by Dube: *Expressionists and Expressionism*, p. 101.
18   Grosz and Herzfelde: *Die Kunst ist in Gefahr*, p. 19.

the road. She exults in the mayhem around her, while bloated and deranged figures go on the rampage with guns, knives and pickaxes. It is a vision of hell even more vicious than the drawing of civil chaos made in the same hysterical summer by Meidner, whose work influenced Grosz considerably at this time.

The hatred of the world "in all its ugliness, sickness and lies"[19] gave way, during his short-lived military career, to a more somber vision. Realizing that he would soon be called up, Grosz volunteered in November 1914 for the Second Kaiser Franz Grenadier Guards Ist Company in Berlin. The images he made from his army experience lack the manic, overheated intensity of *Pandemonium*. Like Beckmann's *The Grenade*, Grosz's drawing of *The Shell* seizes on the moment when destruction erupts in the sky. But none of the figures affected by the blast in Grosz's picture shares the mobility of Beckmann's running soldier as he attempts to escape. Most of them are felled by the explosion, and the man who crawls across the foreground lacks the energy to make a quick retreat. He might well collapse and expire at any moment, to end up like the corpses whose contorted forms lie beside their abandoned weapons in *Shell Crater*. Grosz draws a parallel here between the soldier's twisted limbs and the convoluted branches of the bare trees above them. Stripped of leaves and yet still obstinately upright, they are the only survivors of a conflict which has left all its human participants strewn over the gouged terrain.

Grosz's drawings and lithographs of 1915 are obsessed by corpses. Where *Pandemonium* had continued his pre-war preoccupation with frenetic decadence in the city, *Battlefield with Dead Soldiers* surveys an entire silent panorama of mangled bodies. Grosz's thin, precise contours define the attitudes of the fallen with consummate economy. One figure on the right seems to have died while praying: his clasped hands still point towards heaven, even though his thrown-back head has the inertness of a doll whose neck is broken. Elsewhere, soldiers lie entangled in the barbed wire which proved such a lethal obstacle during infantry offensives. Grosz revealed in a letter that he was close enough to corpses trapped by the wire to smell their rotting flesh,[20] and *Battlefield with Dead Soldiers* fulfills Meidner's vision in his apocalyptic canvases three years before. The posts holding up the wire lead back in a straggling diagonal towards the horizon, where blackened trees are ranged beside ruined buildings consumed by fire. Thick smoke fills the sky to an asphyxiating extent – a metaphor, perhaps, of the nausea Grosz experienced as he grew more and more unnerved by the wholesale slaughter.

---

19   George Grosz to Otto Schmalhausen, 15 March 1917, quoted by Hess: *George Grosz*, p. 47.
20   George Grosz to Robert Bell, September 1915, quoted by Schneede: *George Grosz: His Life and Work*, p. 30.

Looking back on his period in the army, where he was moved to the First Reserve Battalion in January 1915, Grosz described how "the time I spent in the stranglehold of militarism was a period of constant resistance – and I know there was not one thing I did which did not utterly disgust me."[21] The knowledge that he was implicated in the killing, either directly or indirectly, gives his graphic work of 1915 a terrible sense of desolation. Stillness pervades his charcoal drawing *Landscape with Dead Bodies*, broken only by the birds hanging with predatory curiosity over the horse and soldiers stretched out on the white ground. Death is inescapable here, and the building nearest the corpses assumes the shape of a coffin. Whether Grosz realized it or not, he now saw extinction in everything. The trees punctuating the distant hill like crosses on Calvary are scorched beyond recall, while the large nearby warehouse seems little more than a battered façade hiding a burned-out void behind. On the rare occasions when Grosz did depict live soldiers, most notably in a spiky lithograph called *Captured*, the figures' movements seem furtive, almost apologetic. The pipe-smoking German walking behind the prisoners displays no trace of satisfaction, let alone triumph. He seems as weary as the men in his charge, and looks away from them towards the true focus of the picture: the corpse thrown back on a hillside. Beside the body wild flowers have sprung up, the only sign of nature's resilience in a landscape otherwise scarred by ruins leaning at precipitous angles on the hills beyond.

By May 1915 Grosz had become sufficiently ill to be discharged as unfit for military service, albeit with the prospect of a recall in the future. He later explained that a very serious sinus condition had developed on his way to the Front. The mental strain which took its most severe toll in 1917, when Grosz was called up again, might well have contributed to his earlier ailment. But the army considered that his conduct had been good, and he reserved his jubilation for a letter to his friend Robert Bell. While rejoicing in the knowledge that he had become "a civilian again," Grosz couched his emotion in irony. "If it were not a sin against the prevailing sacred custom in patriotic matters, I would allow myself a feeling of happiness," he wrote, before finally making the gleeful admission that, "in short, I am free, free from the Prussian military."[22]

Although he enjoyed an exceptionally productive period of work after settling into his Berlin Südende studio in July 1915, Grosz showed no sign in his

---

21 George Grosz to Robert Bell, probably May 1915, quoted by Hess: *George Grosz*, pp. 47–8.
22 George Grosz to Robert Bell, probably late 1915 or early 1916, quoted by Schneede: *George Grosz*, p.32.

6. George Grosz: *Aerial Attack*, 1914, Museum of Modern Art, New York.

art of euphoria or complacency. As a drawing called *Aerial Attack* (Fig. 6) discloses, he was unable to find in city life a feeling of security after the perils of active service. The explosion which had caused such devastation in his earlier drawing of *The Shell* reappears now in an urban context, and the result is still more terrifying. Bursting within a confined space, the bomb causes buildings to crack and totter. As for passers-by, the ravening lawlessness which Grosz had pilloried in *Pandemonium* has now been replaced by panic. While the figures nearest the blast are thrown upwards and backwards by its impact, the rest of the crowd scatter with terror distorting their features. The clarity Grosz deploys to expose the citizens' hysteria has a merciless edge, reflecting his scornful belief that "to be a German means invariably to be crude, stupid, ugly, fat and inflexible."[23] But the horror in *Aerial Attack* could only have been expressed by an artist who was himself living in dread. For Grosz continually feared the threat of recall, and he described how "the sword of Damocles hangs over my head. Heavens, when shall we be strong enough to resist?"[24]

23 George Grosz to Robert Bell, end of September 1915, quoted by Hess: *George Grosz*, p. 50.
24 George Grosz to Robert Bell, postmarked 28 June 1915, ibid., p. 51.

Grosz's answer, commencing in the latter months of 1915, was to involve himself with great bravery in the dangers of the anti-war movement. He distributed among his friends postcards published by *Die Aktion*, a courageous literary journal which took an almost isolated but sturdy stand against the continuation of hostilities. He also recorded[25] that *Die Aktion* had accepted several of his drawings and a poem, while conceding that the attempt to resist German militarism was still a long way from practical realization. He had to content himself with writing about "a dream of mine: revolts will happen and one day spineless international socialism may gain the strength for open rebellion, and then W. II and the Crown Prince will be no more. They still post the call-up papers on the hoarding. To the slaughterhouse!"[26] The only weapon Grosz possessed was his draughtsmanship, and during 1915 the self-taught artist honed it to a new sharpness. In *Stick It Out!* his handling of pen and ink takes on a raw, scratchy brutality it had never exhibited before. A familiar war slogan is here turned on its head and exposed as an empty cry. The rapacious, furtive and putrefying Berlin crowd is dominated by the specter of a hearse moving through the street, accompanied by a downcast line of top-hatted mourners.

Within a year or so, Grosz began to gain wide notoriety through the publication of such drawings in Wieland Herzfelde's radical new periodical *Die Neue Jugend*.[27] But in 1915 other, far less well-known German artists were also giving vent to their rage against war with remarkable authority and eloquence. In a sustained suite of ten lithographs entitled *Memento,* the Breslau-born artist Willy Jaeckel produced one of the earliest and most impressive of all the print sequences devoted to the conflict. Ten years before Otto Dix was finally ready to produce his great series *War,* Jaeckel wasted little time in showing his fellow artists how the struggle could be depicted with a passionate indignation reminiscent of Goya. Several of the prints in *Memento* pay homage to the Spanish master's *Disasters of War* cycle, and all of them share Goya's abhorrence of the slaughter. Their condemnatory stance earned official disapproval: the entire suite was banned immediately after it appeared in 1915.

The most Goyaesque of the prints are found at the beginning of the sequence, where Jaeckel's priorities are announced with uncompromising vigor. The very first print (Fig. 7), which isolates a man among a heap of executed

---

25   George Grosz to Robert Bell, end of September 1915, ibid., p. 50.

26   *Stick It Out!* appeared in *Die Neue Jugend* in July 1916.

27   *Rightly or Wrongly*, plate 2 in the *Disasters* sequence, is related to *The Third of May 1808,* but it depicts a fight rather than the execution of a helpless, unarmed man.

7. Willy Jaeckel: *Memento (I)*, 1914–15, Bröhan Museum, Berlin.

bodies, refers to *The Third of May 1808* rather than the *Disasters* series.[28] There is a similar emphasis on the plight of the white-shirted figure confronting his imminent death, and Jaeckel's decision to omit the firing squad does not lessen the horror of the man's predicament. Although a woman kneels in front of him pleading for her life, she already seems to belong to the corpses and does not detract from the drama of his stance. He is still agonizingly alive. The energy implicit in his bent, straining legs is a measure of his unwilling- ness to accept death's inevitability, and he stares out at his executioners with an expression of terror so extreme that it takes on an accusatory power.

Throughout *Memento,* in fact, Jaeckel denounces the atrocity of war with the fiery indignation which Goya manifests. Women as well as men are seen in all their martyred degradation. The second print in the sequence concentrates on the brutal assault of a woman by soldiers who grab her leg and arms under

---

28   See the catalogue of the exhibition *Schrecken und Hoffnung*, p. 150.

the cold, appraising eye of an officer. She resists far more vigorously than her counterpart in the thirteenth plate of the *Disasters* cycle, who pleads desperately with her assailants. But Jaeckel's debt to Goya is evident enough, and even extends to the round-arched setting where the assault takes place. Despite the strength of the woman's struggle, Jaeckel holds out no more hope for her survival than Goya. Her exposed right breast suggests that multiple rape is about to be committed, and its victim must subsequently meet a fate as abject as the death presented in *Memento*'s third print.

Here the image is dominated by the body of a woman who has been raped, killed and then dumped ignominiously over the side of a fallen chair. Her pushed-up dress, which testifies to the depravity of her murderers, does not disguise the victim's blanched, blood-smeared face. Nor does it prevent Jaeckel from depicting the plight of the baby lying beside her, abandoned by the soldiers after they butchered its mother. The child is, at least, alive. But in every other respect Jaeckel's scene remains as grim as Goya's *Ravages of War*, a celebrated print from the *Disasters* cycle which likewise focuses on battered women civilians and even includes a similar chair within the ruins. A decade later, *Ravages of War* would also inspire Dix to pay an overt tribute in one of his *War* series, where inverted bodies are strewn across the ruins of a bombed house in Tournai.

The rest of Jaeckel's suite deals mainly with the writhings of those who have not yet succumbed to death. Even within the charnel house of the fourth print, where some of the figures have already been slaughtered in the most horrible way, the butchery is still proceeding on top of the corpses. One wounded man cowers on the floor, protecting head with hands and gazing wildly around in search of his assailants. There remains, however, no sign that the carnage above him will abate. Its inevitability is relentless, and in the next three lithographs *Memento* reveals just how destructive the battlefield can be. Threatened by colossal eruptions nearby, the two soldiers dominating the foreground in the fifth print struggle to carry the weight of a slaughtered comrade. The next lithograph brings the explosion closer, and shows how it devastates the man standing near its annihilating impact. But hand-to-hand combat can still be just as ugly. In the seventh print Jaeckel settles on the moment when a bayonet thrust enters the target's body. It is administered with all the formidable strength at the disposal of the heavily built assailant, and the ambiguity of the dying man's upraised arms makes the image even more disturbing. Did he lift his hands as a gesture of surrender before the fatal penetration, or are they clawing the air as a result of the wound? Even though Jaeckel leaves the question open, he certainly does not discount the possibility that the victim was defenseless when the bayonet skewered his chest.

In *Memento*'s final prints, attention is concentrated each time on a single soldier meeting a tragic destiny. The eighth lithograph is dominated by a figure who bestrides the corpse-strewn ground, where arms are still rising in search of help. The protagonist may have survived so far, but he is in no condition to provide that support. His swaying legs seem on the point of buckling, and he stares up at the sky as if to ask God why humanity has been deprived of heavenly protection. In order to supply the most despairing answer imaginable, Jaeckel devotes the penultimate print to a study of a man trapped in a shell-crater. He places both elbows on the side and strives to heave himself out of the pit. But barbed wire ensnares his body like the coiled serpents in the *Laocoon*, preventing him from making the decisive move. The man's haunted eyes betray exhaustion, too, and along with it the tacit acknowledgement that he is on the verge of sinking back in the earth for the last time.

Memento ends as it began, with an accusing stare. Now, however, a woman's eyes look out from the field of war, and they are even more fierce and direct than their predecessors in the first print. They belong to the grieving wife of a dead man, who remains upright only because of her efforts to hold him there. Clutching his wrist with one hand and stroking his cheek with the other, she seems at first to be pretending that her husband is still alive. After a while, though, her true motive becomes clear. She props him up in order to remain close to him, and also to display the reality of his corpse in front of us. "Here," she could well be saying, "is the pitiful outcome of all the elevated yet empty rhetoric which drives men to fight one another."

Jaeckel's bull-terrier refusal to be deflected from the fundamental obscenity of war helps to ensure that *Memento* retains its angry force today. As well as suffering an official ban, it earned him severe censure from critics who claimed, from the safety of civilian life, that it had more to do with the artist's overheated imagination than the 'real events' of the conflict.[29] But Jaeckel, who served as a trench cartographer and later as an aerial photographer on the Eastern Front, had witnessed the tragedy for himself. It prompted him, in 1915, to produce another protesting lithograph called *Battlefield,* where a trapped horse and a cavalryman shot in the chest both raise their heads to scream a collective cry of anguish towards the sky. This image of human and animal helplessness is in marked contrast to the saber-waving jingoism of Max Liebermann's cavalryman shouting *Now We Will Thresh You!*, published in *Kriegszeit* during the initial surge of enthusiasm for the conflict.

---

29   See Carey and Griffiths: *The Print in Germany 1880–1933: The Age of Expressionism*, pp. 112–13.

The plight of women in war, which Jaeckel highlighted at several points in *Memento,* was not often attended to by male artists. But Christian Rohlfs placed it at the emotional center of his work when, around 1915, he decided to devote a large painting to the conflict. In his mid-sixties when the hostilities broke out, Rohlfs belonged to a generation of German artists who refrained, on the whole, from dealing with the war in their work. He had developed late in his career, after meeting Emil Nolde in 1905 and turning away from Impressionism towards a more innovative style which paralleled the Expressionism of *Die Brücke.* Working now with oil and tempera on canvas or paper, he evolved a loose and emotionally heightened style during the latter decades of his long life. Although violent subjects played little part in Rohlfs's pacific vision, he felt impelled to tackle the theme of *War* once the death-toll began to mount. Rather than dealing with the subject in a literal way, which took account of conditions at the Front, he took a more symbolic path. It was a sensible decision. Lacking any first-hand knowledge of modern military life, Rohlfs capitalized on his removal from the struggle by painting a summation of war's essential bestiality.

The lowering, full-lipped brute who emerges in earth colors from the deep purple shadows could belong to any age. He is the archetypal monster of aggression, lumbering towards the fray as his heavily muscled thigh crashes against a woman already trapped in his grasp. The club in his left hand confirms the primordial nature of this marauder, and Rohlfs's brusque handling of tempera and oil accentuates the roughness he seeks to condemn. *War* is a forthright indictment of the barbaric impulse, and it eventually proved too outspoken for the Germans who sought to rebuild their country's military supremacy during the post-war period. In 1937 the painting was confiscated as 'degenerate' by the Nazis, who excluded Rohlfs from the Prussian Academy of Arts at the same time. Their persecution hastened his death a year later.

Ernst Ludwig Kirchner, who also died in 1938 after an even more savage hounding by the Nazis, underwent perhaps the most traumatic and protracted suffering of any artist during the war. The fact that he volunteered for service as a driver in an artillery regiment, soon after hostilities broke out, should not be taken as a demonstration of Kirchner's enthusiasm. The field artillery, where he was transferred in the spring of 1915, turned out to be intensely unnerving. Even *In the Barracks Yard: Two Artillerymen Riding*, a relatively straightforward and buoyant lithograph, carries a disturbing undertow. Kirchner finds a violence in the animals' lunging movements which suggests that they, as much as the men who ride them, are agents of annihilation. He would have been mindful that horses have traditionally played an important part in images of the apocalyptic riders, and the ostensibly harmless exercise conducted in the barracks could easily metamorphose into a full-blown scene of devastation.

Kirchner was quick to recognize that soldiers, once they leave their official duties, are far more vulnerable than they would care to realize. A large lithograph of his friend Hugo Biallowons, probably produced during a short break from artillery training in Halle when the two men returned to Berlin for the night,[30] explores the weariness and despondency engendered by military existence. Before the war Biallowons had been an irrepressible companion, who was photographed naked in Kirchner's studio and appeared in many of his most uninhibited prints. Here, by contrast, the once-brazen exhibitionist seems subdued as he reclines in his uniform, sadly meditating on the difference between pre-war abandon and the constraints of a life spent preparing for a combat which would kill him the following year.

In his most ambitious painting of army life Kirchner went a great deal further, presenting the soldiers shorn of all the accouterments which define and dignify their roles as fighting men. He shows, in a canvas grand enough for a history picture of the most heroic kind, naked figures crammed together on a steeply inclined floor for a communal shower (Fig. 8). The room is almost as forbidding as the chamber where Beckmann drew the hospital morgue, and water spurts from the ceiling in short, stabbing shafts. Some of the men shy away from the shower's impact as if they were threatened by falling bayonets. Their yellow flesh looks jaundiced, and none of them possesses a physique sturdy enough to withstand prolonged exposure to the rigours of the Front. With considerable temerity, Kirchner paints the ordinary members of the Kaiser's invincible army as he thought they really were: undernourished, gawky and lacking any of the camaraderie which soldiers are supposed to enjoy. The brushstrokes slashing their attenuated bodies reinforce the sense of assault, and the figure on the left jerks his head backwards as he shields himself from the jets. Sprayed water here becomes a metaphor for the gunfire which will soon decimate so many of these wan young men. No amount of uniforms and weaponry can save them, and their pale, forced nakedness signifies an underlying inability to protect themselves from the savagery of modern warfare.

A year earlier Beckmann had explored a similar mood in a prophetic print called *Mustering*, where the new recruits shiver with embarrassment as they strip for inspection. One man covers his genitals and stares awkwardly away

---

30   Ernst Ludwig Kirchner to Hannes Meyer, 11 July 1923, quoted by Gordon: *Ernst Ludwig Kirchner*, p.101.

8. Ernst Ludwig Kirchner: *Artillerymen in the Shower*, 1915, Guggenheim Museum, New York.

from the officer surveying his body, while another volunteer looks risible as he reveals his overweight buttocks to the rest of the room. Beckmann already implies that 'soldiers' are, in the flesh, no less frail and uncertain than their civilian counterparts. He sees the volunteers divested of all illusions, as they confront the daunting reality of the system which now makes them feel so ashamed. But *Musterung* seems almost lighthearted in comparison with Kirchner's painting, where the men lose their identity altogether as they merge in an anonymous herd. The regimentation which dominates army life even extends to the shower-room, for their ablutions are scrutinized by an officer who retains cap, uniform and boots. His cool, undemonstrative formality makes the gesticulating nudity of the other men seem still more defenseless. Indeed, the sinister aspect of the scene is accentuated by the soldier crouching beside the boiler. As he shovels coal, his face takes on a demonic aspect in front of the consuming flames.

Kirchner was unable to withstand such an environment for long. In October 1915 he obtained sick leave because of a lung infection and general debility, but his self-portraits reveal that he was afflicted by a profound malaise of the spirit as well as the body. A terse drawing reflects this inner tension. The sallow artist stares at his reflection with utter fatigue, scarcely capable of raising his eyelids to perform the task. He looks drugged and demoralized, and his close-cropped hair bears witness to the military requirements which have brought him so low. The act of portraying himself was clearly important in the struggle to recover his sense of individuality after the deadening standardization he had experienced in the army. But the paradox is that the more he laboured at these portraits, the less able he became to claim that selfhood had been restored.

The Drinker, painted in his Berlin studio "while day and night the military trains screeched past my window,"[31] amounts to a confession of despair. The aerial vantage chosen for the portrait imparts a feeling of disorientation to the scene, tilting up the table-top to an alarming extent as Kirchner clutches its edge for support. His other hand extends towards us, as if beseeching our help. But since the artist's eyes have narrowed into slits by this time, the gesture appears rhetorical rather than hopeful. A strange lilac tinge is beginning to spread across his withdrawn face, doubtless precipitated by the content of the green goblet beside him. Its magnified dimensions reflect the importance which alcohol has assumed in Kirchner's dazed existence. Since the picture was initially entitled *The Absinthe Drinker*, it is reasonable to assume that he identified with the addicts depicted in late nineteenth-century French paintings like Degas's *"L'Absinthe."* Kirchner's bizarre decision to array himself in a brilliant striped scarf and pointed high-heeled shoes, possibly loaned from his dancer-mistress Erna Schilling, also indicates that he felt part of his masculinity had been impaired in the war.

The Drinker does not, however, convey the absolute horror and disgust which he injected into *Self-Portrait as a Soldier*. Now the mesmeric goblet has disappeared, and Kirchner asserts the prime importance of his art by framing himself between an unfinished canvas and a nude model waiting to pose in his studio. The scene should be set for creative resurgence, but the figure who occupies so much of the foreground does not resemble a newly invigorated

---

31 Ernst Ludwig Kirchner to Karl Ernst Osthaus, quoted by Wieland Schmied: "Points of Departure and Transformations in German Art, 1905–1985." *German Art in the Twentieth Century*, p.26.

painter. Obsessed by the trauma of his military experience, he is clothed in his old uniform. The numbers specified with unusual care on his red epaulets confirm that it does indeed belong to the 75th Artillery Regiment, and Kirchner even wears the cap with its target-like badge in the center. The deep blue of the uniform is the dominant colour in the painting. It suggests, ominously, that the depressed artist has donned his army regalia in a last-ditch attempt to restore morale.

If that was the motive, however, the venture has failed. Reverting to uniform does nothing to give Kirchner's parchment-dry skin an infusion of vigour. He looks more sickly than before, and his pupils are no longer visible in eyes now entirely filled with the same shade of military blue. Is Kirchner indicating that his memories of the war have scarred him so permanently that he cannot see anything except the color of his uniform? He clearly feels that the army has maimed him beyond reparation. Rather than trusting in his capacity to build a new life, he dwells on his former existence and protests against the damage it has inflicted. Kirchner raises his right arm as though to begin painting again, but all he manages to display is a greenish-yellow stump severed at the wrist. This macabre amputation fantasy serves as a brutal symbol of his impotence now that illness has brought his military service to an end. Unable either to paint or fight, he brandishes the raw and useless limb like an accusation. "I feel half dead with mental and physical torment," he confessed to his patron Karl Ernst Osthaus,[32] and in this picture the feeling of injustice festers as an exposed wound.

Apart from signifying his loss of creativity as an artist, the bloody stump also announces the more general nervous disorder of a man who would be plagued by breakdown and psychically related paralysis for the rest of the war. It could be argued, in fact, that Kirchner never fully recovered from his military ordeal. He became haunted by the suspicion that his central identity had been lost at the Front, and shared Grosz's perpetual fear of the effect that a recall to the army might have on his work. "New draft calls of the reserves stay close at my heels and who knows when they will stick me in again," he wrote in December 1915, "and then one can't work any more; one is more afraid of that than any prostitute."[33] Kirchner's growing awareness of sexual ambivalence brought him closer, in his own feverish mind, to the condition of the whores he had painted with such strident assurance in the pre-war period.

---

32   Ernst Ludwig Kirchner to Dr. Carl Hagemann, 3 December 1915, quoted by Gordon: *Kirchner*, p. 26.

33   Ernst Ludwig Kirchner to Gustav Schiefler, 27 July 1919, quoted ibid., p. 102.

He turned this faltering grasp of selfhood to brilliant account in a cycle of seven woodcuts for *The Amazing Story of Peter Schlemihl.* Written in 1813 by the Romantic author Adelbert von Chamisso, the story concerns a Faust-like man who, after selling his shadow, came into conflict with his soul and then struggled fruitlessly to regain the shadow he had lost. Kirchner realized that von Chamisso's archetypal *Doppelgänger* parable could directly reflect his suffering in the war. "The story of Schlemihl, stripped of all romantic trimming, is strictly speaking the life story of the victim of persecution complex," he explained later, "that is, of the human being who through some fortuitous circumstance becomes conscious with a shock of his infinitesimal insignificance."[34] Fired by this insight, Kirchner produced a *tour de force* of the woodcutter's art. The head dominating the title sheet has the same withdrawn appearance as the artist's own self-portraits, and he seems to be assailed by a jarring multiplicity of eyes. In the third sheet from the cycle, *Conflict,* a murderous mood is explored. The Schlemihl/Kirchner figure is juxtaposed with a naked woman who, clutching a wound with one hand, dangles the other in front of him. The scarlet blood staining her body and fingers is smeared across his lips, making him resemble a gruesomely painted whore. The feeling of persecution mania, powerfully dramatized in this woodcut, sums up Kirchner's siege mentality during the later months of 1915.

Paranoia turns to outright panic in *Schlemihl's Encounter with the Shadow,* where the colors flare into a vehemence reminiscent of Van Gogh's *The Painter on his Way to Work.* In his description of this incandescent image, Kirchner admitted that self-representation had become his main motive for tackling the scene:

> Schlemihl sits sadly in the fields when, suddenly, his shadow approaches across the sunlit land. He tries to place his feet in the footprints of the shadow, under the delusion that he can thereby become himself again. An analogue is the mental process of one discharged from the military.[35]

Kirchner's wild and flaring interpretation of Schlemihl's struggle offers an unsettling insight into the hysteria which threatened to overwhelm the artist in the aftermath of his military service.

Despite the outstanding quality of the Schlemihl cycle, Kirchner remained aware that it was a precarious achievement. He became obsessed by the prospect of failing powers, even after Nolde's friend Hans Fehr finally obtained his discharge from the army in December 1915. Three spells in a sanatorium at Königstein followed over the next seven months, but he could not oust the

---

34   Ernst Ludwig Kirchner to Gustav Schiefler, 28 March 1916, quoted ibid., p. 27.
35   Ernst Ludwig Kirchner, 1916, quoted by Dube: *Expressionists and Expressionism*, p. 101.

continual suspicion that a crisis – both personal and political – was about to destroy everything. "More oppressive than anything else," he wrote in 1916,

> is the strain of war and the prevailing shallowness. It is like a murderous carnival. One feels that a decision is in the air, and everything is topsy-turvy. One is so jaded and faltering, one hesitates to work, when all work is fruitless and the onslaught of mediocrity carries all before it. We ourselves are now like the tarts I'm painting. Done with, and on the next occasion heard of no more. In spite of everything I keep trying to get my thoughts in order and out of the muddle to paint a picture of the times, which is what I am here for.[36]

III.

The urge to continue working, even in the face of fierce fighting at the Front, remained strong in many German artists. Marc, whose initial enthusiasm for the war had prompted him to volunteer for the cavalry in September 1914, never stopped planning the images he hoped to paint on his return to active service. At first he saw the conflict as nothing less than a Nietzschean 'cleansing of Europe', but when his great friend August Macke was killed only a month later he wrote a tribute filled with sadness and indignation about the "accident of the individual death which, with every fatal bullet, inexorably determines and alters the destiny of a race."[37] At the same time he admitted to Kandinsky that the war had created a virulent new nationalism, threatening all the hopes about a spirit of 'Europeanism' entertained by the *Blaue Reiter* artists before the conflict began. By Christmas Marc had come to see that "the most important lesson and irony of the Great War is certainly this: that precisely the great triumph of our 'technical warfare' has forced us back into the most primitive age of the cavemen."[38]

During the course of 1915, when he carried out an extended and incisive series of drawings in his "Sketchbook from the Battlefield," Marc's view of the war continued to fluctuate. He found release in these thirty-six pencil studies, executed on small sheets of paper at spare moments between March and June. "They lighten my load and help me to relax," he revealed, describing how "I'm drawing from time to time fragments for paintings, ideas for bible illustrations which I'm keen to do again, small compositions and the

---

36 Franz Marc, quoted by Tim Cross in *The Fallen*, p. 3.
37 Franz Marc, December 1914, quoted by Jill Lloyd: *The Fallen*, p. 47.
38 Ibid., p. 51.

like."[39] The most biblical studies in the sketchbook are drawings like *Arsenal for a Creation*, where Marc obstinately continues to associate the accumulation of armaments with the idea of primal renewal. A horse's head and body can be discerned in the upper area of the composition, recalling his pre-war paintings of animals caught up in an apocalyptic storm. A related disturbance undulates through this drawing as well, but it lacks any sense of overwhelming devastation. Indeed, regeneration seems about to emerge from the maelstrom, and in 1915 Marc reiterated his hope that the conflict would turn out to be a boon. "For several years we have been saying that many things in art and life were rotten and done for," he wrote, "and we pointed to new and better possibilities. No one wanted to know. What we couldn't know was that the great war would come with such terrible swiftness, pushing words aside, sweeping away death and decay to give us the future today."[40] These sentiments help to explain the optimism of a sketchbook drawing called *The Peaceful Horse*, where the animal grazes quietly in a wood after cosmic strife has almost come to an end.

By no means all the 'battlefield' drawings explore such a beneficent mood. Some of the six deer who pause before a mountain pass in a graceful untitled study raise their slender necks cautiously, and sniff the air for danger. They are reminiscent of the central deer in *The Fate of the Animals*, Marc's pre-war masterpiece, and below the looming crescent moon signs of imminent disturbance are beginning to manifest themselves. On the following page the promised eruption arrives, breaking out in a cataclysm which tears through the entire drawing. The sun and other planetary forms are threatened with eclipse by this turmoil, which explodes with the force of the shell-bursts Marc must often have witnessed at the Front. Even here, though, the outcome may be far from disastrous. Without any consciousness of irony he called the drawing *Magical Moment*, in the stubborn conviction that a purged and healing regeneration would result from "the ancient rite of sacrificial blood." Marc was still sufficiently under the influence of Nietzsche to write a hundred aphorisms inspired by the example of Zarathustra's creator. He wanted to believe in a better future, and most of the 'battlefield' studies lack a fully tragic awareness.

Marc did, however, acknowledge the devouring and grotesque aspects of the war. In a drawing entitled *The Greedy Mouth* (Fig. 9), a predatory yet oddly impish creature gorges itself on an abundance of prey. But the image is am-

---

39   Franz Marc, 1915, quoted by Herbert: *German Expressionism*, p. 186.
40   Franz Marc, letter of 12 April 1955, quoted by Levine: *The Apocalyptic Vision: The Art of Franz Marc as German Expressionism*, p. 164.

9. Franz Marc: *The Greedy Mouth*, 1915, Staatliche Graphische Sammlung, Munich.

biguous: the shafts entering its mouth could just as easily be thrusting outwards, like diagonal tongues of fire issuing from a flame-thrower. Part gigantic insect and part diabolic instrument of war, the creature simultaneously de-
vours and belches with a gleeful zeal that precludes all consciousness of
responsibility for its actions. Around the period Marc drew this apparition, he
confessed in a letter that there was a time when "animals seemed more beautiful, more pure. But then I discovered in them too, so much that was ugly and
unfeeling [...] until now, suddenly I have become fully conscious of nature's
ugliness and impurity."[41]

Marc's naive faith in the emetic function of war was wavering again, and
the later drawings in the sketchbook show a darkening mood. One of the
most violent is given the bleak title *Conflict*, and defines a world wholly consumed by the clash of opposing forces. As well as looking back to the deluge
paintings of his old friend Kandinsky, the drawing displays an increased
awareness of the lancing, penetrating potential of the forces at work in this
tumultuous universe. Nothing now counters their engulfing power as they
travel towards the center, burst, and then roll back in order to prepare for a
fresh assault. There is no sign here of the renewal Marc had once envisaged.

---

41   Franz Marc, letter from the field, June 1915, quoted by Lloyd: *The Fallen*, p. 48.

The annihilation appears to be caught up in a repetitive cycle, and death rather than rebirth seems the outcome in one of the final 'battlefield' studies. An untitled drawing, it depicts a shattered world where everything droops in mournful attitudes of extinction. A few disconsolate birds can be glimpsed among the broken plants, but they are waiting for the end rather than embodying a more resilient alternative. It is an elegiac image, sadly prophetic of Marc's own fate only nine months later. In a moment of exhaustion he wrote from the Front, at the time when this drawing was executed, that "there is only one blessing & release: Death; the destruction of form in order to release the soul."[42]

Marc did not remain in this resigned and melancholy state for long. He was soon yearning for the opportunity to enjoy a sustained period of work, declaring impatiently that "it's clear to me that I'll only be able to work properly again when I get home to Ried, with all my materials, my wooden stick and above all heavenly peace and quiet."[43] But his ambition was never fulfilled, and as the year wore on he became strangely detached from the world of suffering and carnage. Even the loss of Macke, which had earlier forced him to reconsider his Nietzschean view of the war, receded with the passage of time and the ceaseless deaths among his fellow soldiers. More than a year after he first heard about the slaughter of Macke, Marc received a photograph of his friend cheerfully riding a donkey in Tunis. "Admittedly this posthumous reminder of his *joie de vivre* fills me with twice as much grief," he wrote,

> but his sad departure at the hand of a foe's bullet – one is almost tempted to say friend's – it was after all a French one – seems no more absurd than the death of Moillet's wife or some other "natural" accident. Even the war is natural; it isn't valid to say, like you always do, that the war is a totally unnatural phenomenon. The epidemic that it has perforce become is just as much a result of nature as the tsetsefly or the plague bacillus. *My attention has long since been deflected from the war.*[44]

Perhaps Marc was forced to cultivate detachment in order to survive the military ordeal. He did not, after all, succumb to illness or breakdown like other artists, and in February 1916 he sounded a remarkably buoyant note when telling his wife about a congenial duty he had been asked to carry out. "Dearest, had you seen me today, you would surely have had to despair of 'reality' or of my reason in no time," he wrote. "I was standing in a massive barn (charming atelier!) and painting nine of what Walterchen [Macke's young son] calls

---

42   Ibid., p. 51.
43   Ibid., p. 4.
44   Franz Marc to his wife, February 1916, ibid., pp. 5–6.

'Kandinskys' on military tarpaulins!" Like the team of French army camouflage painters who included Villon and Segonzac, Marc had been given a task
more suited to his abilities than fighting. "The business has a totally practical
purpose," his letter continued,

> to hide artillery emplacements from airborne spotters and photography by cover-
> ing them with tarpaulins painted in roughly pointillistic designs in the manner of
> bright natural camouflage. The distances which one has to reckon with are enor-
> mous – from an average height of 2,000 metres – your enemy aircraft never flies
> much lower than that [...] I am curious what effect the "Kandinskys" will have at
> 2,000 metres. The nine tarpaulins chart a development "from Manet to Kandins-
> ky!"[45]

If Marc had been allowed to continue with such welcome work for the rest of
the war, he might well have survived. But his duties in the cavalry ensured that
he was exposed to heavy bombardment only a month after describing his interlude as a camouflage painter. Full of optimism about the art he looked forward to making when the war was over – "I was *never precocious* & am sure that
I will achieve more lively things at 40 & 50 than I did at 20 & 30"[46] – Marc was
killed at Gussainville Castle, Verdun, on 4 March 1916. He had just celebrated
his thirty-sixth birthday, and written a letter to his mother explaining his attitude towards death and the work he still wanted to produce as a painter. "It
has never occurred to me to seek out danger and death as I had done so often
in earlier years," he wrote, remembering how

> at that time death avoided me, not I it; but that is long past. Today I would greet it
> very sadly and very bitterly, not out of fear and anxiety about it – nothing is more
> soothing than the prospect of the *stillness of death* – but because I have half-finished
> work to be done that, when completed, will convey the entirety of my feeling. The
> *whole purpose of my life* lies hidden in my unpainted pictures.[47]

The cutting-short of Marc's life only a fortnight after he wrote this letter was
cruel indeed, and his commanding officer subsequently gave an account of
the tragedy. "It was a radiant early-spring afternoon, as we got ourselves
ready," he wrote.

> At the foot of a hill Marc mounted his horse, a tall chestnut bay, and as long-legged
> as he himself. We rode together for some length along a path that the day before

---

45 Ibid., p. 50.
46 Franz Marc to his mother, 17 February 1916, Marc: *Briefe aus dem Felde*, pp. 133–34.
47 Hans Schilling in Lankheit: *Franz Marc im Urteil seiner Zeit*, pp. 171–72.

had been subject to some very severe fire, but on this day the fire was relatively light. In Braquis (20 kilometres east of Verdun) we separated. Marc was supposed to reconnoitre the woods for a path for a munitions convoy. Barely twenty minutes later his horse-attendant, H., returned, covered with blood and slightly wounded. His eyes filled with tears, he pointed toward the woods where, just a few minutes earlier, his superior had been struck by a grenade fragment and had died in his arms. Whether it was an unfortunate accident or whether it was the French [...] will forever remain a mystery. Franz Marc was dead![48]

The news profoundly affected his close friend Paul Klee, who had visited Marc's house at Ried on several occasions when the latter was on leave. Klee was critical of Marc's attitude towards the conflict, noting in his diary that "he should hate the war game more than he does or, better still, be totally indifferent to it."[49] But Klee liked the "Sketchbook from the Battlefield," declaring that Marc "should paint again, then his quiet smile, that is so much a part of him would appear, at once simple and simplifying."[50] Marc was never given the chance to resume his painting, and Klee expressed his sense of the loss to modern German art in a foreword to the catalogue of Marc's Memorial Exhibition. By an irony of fate, he was himself called up only seven days after his friend's death. Commencing a diary at the recruiting depot in Landshut, he revealed that "the name Marc frequently comes to my mind, and then I am moved, for I seem to see something collapsing."[51]

An increasing number of German artists shared this dizzying sensation. The disastrous emphasis on offensives had been maintained throughout 1915; and although the outcome was stagnation and entrenchment, the slaughter had reached murderous proportions. Images of graveyards became more and more common, in an attempt to convey the otherwise unimaginable extent of the killings. *Peace* is the title of Friedrich August von Kaulbach's etching, where a military cemetery marks the scene of a costly battle. To the extent that the soldiers buried beneath the rows of crookedly installed crosses have been 'laid to rest,' as the euphemistic phrase insists, peace of a kind has indeed been attained. But von Kaulbach knew, as well as anyone, that the deaths had achieved nothing. The soldier playing the pipe of peace on the most prominent crucifix is the very opposite of an idyllic, beneficent figure. His hands are skeletal as they dance along the instrument, and the helmet cannot

48   Paul Kree, diary, quoted by Herbert: *German Expressionism*, p. 187.
49   Ibid.
50   Paul Klee, diary 1916, quoted by Grohmann: *Paul Klee*, p. 58.
51   Ibid.

10. Ernst Barlach: *Mass Grave*, 1915, Ernst-Barlach-Haus, Hamburg.

disguise the fact that it encloses a skull. True peace seemed far more elusive at the end of 1915 than it had done a year before. Von Kaulbach's decision to portray death as the messenger of peace acknowledges the grim fact that the slaughter would continue indefinitely, like the lines of crosses extending in his print to the horizon and beyond.

All the same, *Peace* did not convey the full horror of the death-toll. It had now reached such intolerable proportions that soldiers' corpses had to be thrown, indiscriminately and without coffins, into hastily dug pits. Von Kaulbach's etching implies that each body was at least accorded the dignity of its own grave and marker. But Barlach recognized the utter wretchedness of war burial in a drawing called *Mass Grave* (Fig. 10). Only a year earlier he had envisioned the conflict as *The Holy War*, in which a cloaked figure with an awesome sword strides towards victory. Since then, Barlach's views had undergone drastic modification. News of the ceaseless massacring, coupled with his own call-up for war service in 1915, made him appreciate that the reality was totally removed from the exalted crusade he had once defined with such religious fervour. The firm ground over which his avenging agent had previously advanced was now strewn with the dying and dead. Rather than pursuing an unstoppable, all-conquering advance, progress had to be halted while vast, anonymous holes were dug in the earth. There the corpses were deposited, to share the ignominy of a collective burial. Barlach's line becomes brusque and cursory as he defines the grey, abandoned and often unidentifiable forms occupying the pit to the point of congestion. Although it should already have been filled in, the grave-digger is so exhausted that he is forced to abandon his shovel for a moment and sit on the ground. Bowed with fatigue, he acts as an unofficial mourner for all these unregarded bodies. Soon the hole will be covered over; but the diminutive figures in the distance, carrying yet another victim from the battlefield, prove that the demand for further makeshift graves shows no sign of abating.

ROBERT COHEN
New York University

Arnold Zweig's War Novellas of 1914
and Their Versions:
Literature, Modernity, and the Demands of the Day

Abstract: In the fall of 1914 Arnold Zweig, the future author of a monumental series of anti-war novels, wrote several novellas enthusiastically welcoming the outbreak of the war. Though early on Zweig had rejected the modern condition in all
its aspects, just before the beginning of the war there occurred a remarkable turnaround. Zweig's efforts to live as an assimilated German Jew and his desire to embrace German culture in its totality lead him to a complex embrace of modernity,
which specifically included modern war machinery. This paved the way for Zweig's
celebration of Germany's entry into the war. Though Zweig's perception of the
war changed soon thereafter, during the following decades he republished most of
his war novellas of 1914, often revising them until their original meaning was completely reversed. Yet, he was never able to create a definite version of these texts.

I.

More than thirty years after the fact, exiled in Palestine from fascist Germany,
Arnold Zweig (1887–1968) still recalled with shame the inflammatory novellas he had written in the weeks and months following August 1914 and in
which he had saluted the outbreak of the First World War. Published before
the end of 1914 under the title *The Beast*, they had long since become a thorn
("Stachel") in the side of their author,[1] by now a world-renowned writer of
half a dozen humanist and pacifist epic novels on World War I. In the years
following the war, Zweig publicly blamed himself for having been an "accomplice to the horror of the times" ("Mitschuldige[r] der Zeit und des Grau-

---

This essay was translated from the German by Daniel Slager.
1   Zweig: "Nachbericht." *Westlandsaga,* pp. 129–32, here p. 130.

ens"), and for having succumbed to Germany's wartime lies.[2] He had been on the wrong side, and his stupidity, in his own words, had been unsurpassable ("unüberbietbar").[3]

Arnold Zweig's critics have dealt harshly with his chauvinist attitudes at the beginning of the war. As a consequence, the novellas collected in *The Beast* are often summarily dismissed as having no literary value,[4] they are considered an embarrassment for their "barbarism" ("Barbarei"),[5] and their author is said to have transgressed "all boundaries of humaneness" ("die Grenzen jeglicher Humanität").[6] Strong words indeed, such as one hardly ever hears even in the context of Ernst Jünger's writings on war. Arnold Zweig agreed with the harsh judgment of his critics – and then again he did not. For over the course of a long life he republished most of these novellas, some of them up to four times. They reappeared not only in the Weimar Republic and during Zweig's exile years, but also in the German Democratic Republic where he resided from 1948 until his death.

It is of course not unusual for writers to document their beginnings, even if in the course of their lives, these beginnings have become foreign to them. It often serves as a sort of calling-to-account, both before oneself and before one's public, of one's origins and of the path one has since traveled. Yet, for today's readers Arnold Zweig's wartime novellas have lost all value as documents of Zweig's early positions: they unequivocally condemn the First World War, identify its causes and its instigators, strive for an understanding of foreign cultures and peoples, and generally convey the kind of humanist and socialist decency ("Gesittung")[7] characteristic of the later work of this writer. For Zweig, to an extent that is unique in prose-fiction (unlike in drama), revised and rewrote these texts until the revised versions stood in direct opposition to their originals. Over the years he had become increasingly outspoken in his condemnation of the First World War and those he held responsible for its outbreak, as well as in his socialist convictions. Still, his revisions were not always dictated by moral and ethical considerations. At times, Zweig's sense of what constituted good writing came into conflict with what he considered to be the demands of the day in the struggle against ethnic hatred, violence, and war. In addition, the repeated reshaping of these texts over several decades

---

2   Zweig: *Das ostjüdische Antlitz* [1920], p. 166.
3   Zweig: "Warum ich schwieg. Notwendige Antwort auf überflüssige Fragen," p. 5.
4   See Müller: *Der Krieg und die Schriftsteller*, p. 127.
5   Kaufmann: *Arnold Zweigs Weg zum Roman*, p. 37.
6   Sternburg: *Arnold Zweig*, p. 81.
7   On Zweig's concept of "Gesittung," see Bernhard: "Wider den Verfall der Gesittung."

played out against the backdrop of Zweig's early struggle for modernity. As a young aesthete in an aestheticist age Zweig had roundly rejected all manifestations of modernity, only to embrace it during the euphoric days of August 1914; a struggle which today still resonates with ambivalence.

II.

During his university years Zweig had been an enthusiastic student of such Nietzsche disciples as Husserl and Scheler.[8] Along with a philosophical preoccupation with anti-rational thought went a total rejection of the material foundations of modernity: industrialization and rationalization, and above all capitalism, socialism, and democracy. Zweig's antimodernist thinking found various expression; foremost is his vehement rejection of the Wilhelminian bourgeoisie, as the materialist class of entrepreneurs and industrialists who pushed Germany into the modern age, thereby destroying its great cultural traditions, if not its very soul. This thinking drives many early novellas such as "Cinema" (1911), "Subjection" ("Unterwerfung," 1912), or "Departure" ("Abreise," 1912).[9] In the novella "Quartet by Schoenberg" (1913), highly cultured Eli Saamen feels nothing but disdain for a bourgeois theater audience clearly not up to the great performance it is about to witness, and his mind withdraws to the top of a tower "umgeben von einer Atmosphäre reinen Wasserstoffs, atembar ihm allein"[10] – in other words, to an ivory tower.

Zweig's rejection of the bourgeoisie is closely linked to his rejection of capitalism. In a lengthy essay of 1913, "Democracy and the Soul of the Jew," Zweig denounces modern society for judging people by their material possessions and for reducing all human worth to material values, thereby deforming the very souls of its members. A major part of this polemic is aimed at Jews who, just like prejudiced gentiles, or so Zweig thought, held *wealthy* Jews to be representative of German Jewry as a whole.[11]

Zweig's objections to capitalism grew out of idealistic and generally regressive positions. He had no sympathy for socialism or for the struggle of the rapidly growing industrial proletariat.[12] A tone of disdain accompanies

---

8   See Zweig: "Bekehrung zum Frieden."
9   All three novellas in: Zweig: *Novellen*, vol. 1.
10   Zweig: "Quartettsatz von Schönberg." *Novellen* vol. 1, pp. 301–307, here p. 304: "surrounded by an atmosphere of pure hydrogen which he alone would be able to breathe."
11   See Zweig: "Die Demokratie und die Seele des Juden," pp. 216–219.
12   See ibid., p. 213.

any mention of workers; the word "Arbeiter" (worker) itself seems too vulgar for the nineteen year-old aesthete who is repulsed by the "dirty fist of the *ouvrier*" ("Schmutzfaust des *ouvriers*").[13] The socialist-democratic project is seen as a leveling of differences which had been willed by God.[14] Even more than at socialism Zweig's critique is directed at the form of government which he saw as the root cause of socialism and the general mediocrity of his time – democracy. Already in the early "Notes on the Family Klopfer" (1909), Peter Klopfer, a writer and in many ways a figure close to its author, expresses his opposition to socialism and democracy.[15] And in the already mentioned lengthy essay of 1913, Zweig issues a broad warning against the effects of democracy on the 'soul of the Jews.'

Anti-bourgeois, anti-capitalist, anti-socialist, and anti-democratic: the young author stands in every respect in direct opposition to his time, in direct opposition to modernity. This anti-modern stance has left numerous traces in his literary production from the pre-war years. In the novella "Benarône" from 1909, the insistence of a pompous school inspector on "modernity" in the curriculum leads to the students having to write an essay on the ridiculous topic of "Welchen Nutzen und welchen Schaden muss man dem Automobilismus für das moderne Leben zumessen?"[16] This triggers a string of events which lead to the confrontation of a small Bavarian town with modernity. Zweig's ironic portrayal of this clash includes a critique of the growing emphasis on chauvinist nationalism,[17] the ideological byproduct of growing international economic competition. The rejection of nationalism is thus entirely in accordance with Zweig's anti-modern attitude, which eludes easy classification as conservative or reactionary. Two years after "Benarône" Zweig wrote a satire on another emerging icon of modernity: on the cinema. In the novella "Cinema" of 1911 a simpleminded young man attends a movie theater for the first time. Even though the events on the screen are ridiculously artificial, they so overwhelm the young spectator that he decides to do away with himself, an attempt which fails in a ludicrous way.

Zweig's struggle with European modernity culminates in the novella "Quartet by Schoenberg." It is the story of Eli Saamen, a Russian Jew who in

---

13 Zweig: "Die Entwickelung [!] der modernen Lyrik." Wenzel, ed.: *Arnold Zweig 1887–1968*, p. 512 (emphasis added).

14 See Zweig: "Die Demokratie und die Seele des Juden," p. 213.

15 See Zweig: "Aufzeichnungen über eine Familie Klopfer." *Novellen* vol. 1, pp. 60–103, here p. 89.

16 Zweig: "Benarône." *Novellen* vol. 1, pp. 104–14, here p. 123: "What is the Usefulness or Harm of the Automobile for Modern Life?"

17 Ibid., p. 109.

his childhood escaped from the horrors of pogroms in his homeland to Western Europe and who has grown into a cultured and bookish intellectual. He now resolves to emigrate to Palestine, for he has grown weary of a Europe which to him seems variously a factory ("Maschinenhalle"), a department store ("Warenhaus"), a mental institution ("Irrensaal"), and a military hospital ("Lazarett").[18] In these images Zweig summarily denounces all those matrices of modernity which he had already rejected in earlier texts: technical modernization and the industrial proletariat – in the image of Europe as a factory; the capitalist economy – Europe as a department store; and the deforming effects of modernization on the minds of human beings – Europe as a mental institution. The reference, finally, to Europe as a 'military hospital' seems uncanny. Aside from the distant Balkan wars, Europe in 1913 was at peace. What use could it possibly have for military hospitals? The answer, of course, would come only a few months later.

With the story of Eli Saamen's emigration to Palestine, Zweig's rejection of European modernity reaches its apogee. But the novella also contains a dramatic turnaround. In what must be considered a key passage in Zweig's own struggle with modernity, Saamen is led to reconsider. Spending the last hours before the departure of his train at a concert in Leipzig, he finds himself listening to a quartet by the composer Arnold Schoenberg, of whom he has never heard. Saamen experiences an epiphany. The music of this towering representative of modernity produces in the young antimodernist an overpowering sense of the vitality of the whole continent ("das ganze Leben dieses Erdteils")[19] and of the modern world of capitalist production. Schoenberg's music conjures up images of industrial landscapes, steel bridges, trains, airplanes, and radio towers, of a metropolis with its hectic pace, its workers, scientists, doctors, and teachers, with its artists and philosophers, and its youth in search of new ways. Saamen has visions of a Faustian, industrious world, of the power and greatness that is Europe, in short, of European modernity. He resolves to emigrate for no more than one year; his last thought in the departing train is: "Oh, to return!" ("O Wiederkehr!").[20]

Eli Saamen's embrace of modernity reflects Zweig's rapidly evolving thinking. The imminent war produced in Zweig, as in countless other Germans, a state of euphoria. In a letter from August 1914 he celebrates in ecstatic words the greatness of the moment. The hitherto hated bourgeoisie is

---

18 Zweig: "Quartettsatz von Schönberg." *Novellen* vol. 1, p. 301.
19 Ibid., pp. 304, 307.
20 Ibid., p. 307.

singled out for praise, for it had, in the eyes of the enthusiastic writer, over night renounced its greedy materialism and now embodied the best qualities of the German people.[21] This validation of the very class which was the agent of modernization signals Zweig's readiness to embrace modernity itself. The deprecating image of Europe as a factory was about to be replaced by a glowing tribute to military technology. In the war novellas one can find characterizations such as "angreifende[n] Kraft tauchender deutscher Boote" ("attacking power of German diving ships"), "stillschwebende[n] Mine" ("silently floating mine"), "gradhinjagende[s] Torpedo" ("torpedo rushing straight on"), and "kleine[n] metallene[n] Maschinen" ("little metallic machines") flying through the air.[22] The strained poeticism of these phrases hints at the effort involved in this type of glorification.

But there was also a continuity in Zweig's embrace of the war. In his erstwhile opposition to modernity Arnold Zweig, born and raised in Prussia, had always perceived the military as a kind of alternative world. The main character of "Departure," the young writer who has lost any hope for the future, thinks of the "glücklichen Zeit, in der er wild und asketisch wie ein Soldat gelebt [hatte]."[23] In "Subjection," Hubert Schnabel, the young man rebelling against the commercial world of his father, dreams of becoming a naval officer. During a stay in Göttingen Schnabel rhapsodizes about how the greatness of Germany, once embodied by Goethe and other literary figures, had now found its fullest expression in the German army and navy.[24] An incomprehensible equation, in which the young Zweig appears to have misread the Enlightenment and the classical tradition as thoroughly as he misunderstood the reality of war.

Zweig made every effort to incorporate this impossible equation of Goethe and the imperial armed forces of 1914 into his war novellas. The war is depicted as an irrational, inexplicable, and metaphysical event of awesome dimensions, one which permits no questioning of its justification or morality and eludes analysis of its economic causes and the class interests it serves. This characterization of a misrepresentation of the reality of war is taken from an analysis of Ernst Jünger's war writings which are contrasted with the realism of Arnold Zweig's war novels of the late twenties and after.[25] But the

21   See Zweig: Letter to Helene Weyl – Wenzel, ed.: *Arnold Zweig 1887–1968,* pp. 61–63.

22   Zweig: "Blick auf Deutschland." *Die Bestie,* pp. 7–22, here p. 76.

23   Zweig: "Abreise." *Novellen* vol. 1, pp. 260–273, here p. 263: "happy times, in which he had lived wildly and ascetically like a soldier."

24   See Zweig: "Unterwerfung." *Novellen* vol. 1, pp. 251–259, here p. 255.

25   See Hüppauf: "Erziehung durch Krieg?", p. 58.

characterization of Jünger is perfectly appropriate for Zweig's own war novellas of 1914 and for Zweig's thinking up to his experiences on the battlefields of Verdun and on the eastern front.

Yet, in spite of his siding with the national spirit in welcoming the war, Zweig continued to reject chauvinism. This contradiction needs to be understood in the context of the themes of Judaism, anti-Semitism, and Zionism in Zweig's early work. Whenever he confronts these topics, Zweig's discomfort is apparent. In the novella "Benarône" the title character is a baptized Jew and thus neither a Jew nor a Christian. In the novella "The Flight of the van Spandows" ("Die Flucht der van Spandows," 1912/13), the Christian baptism of a Jewish family leads to misfortune. The depiction of Jews in these novellas almost always contains passages on anti-Semitism. Indeed, anti-Semitism, Pogroms and Zionism are the main themes of many of Zweig's early works. In order to credibly deal with these issues the young aesthete was forced to leave his ivory tower and face reality; specifically, the reality of Jewish existence in Wilhelminian Germany. This is what may have prevented him from an unrestrained embrace of patriotic chauvinism in the days and weeks following the outbreak of the war. In *The Beast*, this hint of caution, of holding back, can be gleaned not from any individual novella, but rather from their selection. For the collection of war novellas surprisingly includes two novellas with a Jewish theme, "Pogrom" ("Episode aus Zarenland"), and "The Crow" ("Die Krähe") both of which had already been published a year earlier. The euphoric letter of August 1914 hints at the reason for their inclusion in *The Beast*. The new spirit of the German bourgeoisie, Zweig wrote, had created a "Kulturgemeinschaft" (cultural communion) between Jewish and non-Jewish Germans. All prejudice toward Jews had miraculously disappeared.[26] The inclusion of the two 'Jewish' novellas in *The Beast* seems like a assertion of this perception – while maybe at the same time cautiously testing it.

In his later years in the GDR Zweig maintained that his long-lasting interest in Jewish issues had been a mere a detour on his path toward socialism.[27] In reality, the significant change in his thinking induced by the First World War was closely linked to this interest in Jewish issues. For beyond the experience of the horror and senselessness of the war accessible to every soldier on the battlefield, it was Zweig's experience as a *Jewish* soldier which led to the profound shift in his thinking. In October 1916, a census was taken of Jews in the German army, supposedly in order to prove that they were serving in appropriate numbers. A measure which reeked of anti-Semitism and which

---

26   Zweig: Letter to Helene Weyl – Wenzel, ed., *Arnold Zweig 1887–1968*, p. 61.
27   See Zweig: "Briefe an Hilscher," p. 35 (letter from June, 1959).

deeply offended Zweig and many other Jews. He wrote a bitter satire of this event, in which the corpses of Jewish soldiers killed in the war emerge from their graves and stand at attention for the census count.[28] Where not too long ago Zweig had celebrated the new-found unity of all German people, he now felt himself to be a foreigner without a state ("staatenlose[r] Ausländer"). All that remained two years after his embrace of Germany at war was a feeling of "unerhörte Trauer über Deutschlands Schande und unsere Qual" ("enormous grief for Germany's disgrace and our [the Jews'] pain").[29]

III.

In the war novellas from 1914 then, Arnold Zweig welcomes and celebrates the war. Remarkably enough, however, the most essential soldierly virtue, the capacity for reckless killing of human beings, is ascribed predominantly to the enemy, while every civil and humane attitude, the elimination of which is the goal of any boot camp, is attributed to the Germans. The tone of these works is often one of kitsch and sentimentality, which, as will be shown, can not completely mask a deeper commitment to humanity. Zweig eventually reissued all but one of the novellas originally published in *The Beast*. The following analysis will be limited to the fate of three of them.

The novella "The Receipt" ("Die Quittung") tells in a frivolously light tone of a Private named Kruppa, who volunteers for a life-threatening mission to bring ammunition to a unit in the front lines. Kruppa's major commands him jokingly to bring back a receipt from the trenches. The simpleminded Kruppa obeys this command, thereby risking his life; for this he receives military honors. – For the first republication of this story in 1926, its insupportably euphoric tone is tempered. The explosion of grenades is no longer "jauchzend" ("exultant"), but "tödlich" ("deadly"), the "Hurrah!" of attacking soldiers no longer sounds "brüllend" ("thunderous"), but "angstvoll" ("terrified"), and the cannons no longer merely bring "Vernichtung" ("devastation"), but in a more accusatory tone, "bleiernen Mord" ("leaden murder").[30] (It is no small irony that in these novellas Zweig attempts to render the reality of war before he ever experienced it. After his years as a soldier

---

28 See Zweig: "Judenzählung vor Verdun." Wenzel, ed., *Arnold Zweig 1887–1968,* pp. 555–57. See also Midgley: *Arnold Zweig,* pp. 8–9.

29 Zweig: Letter to Martin Buber of February 15 – Wenzel, ed.: *Arnold Zweig 1887–1968,* p. 74.

30 Zweig: "Die Quittung." *Gerufene Schatten,* pp. 52–90. An identical version appears in Zweig: *Knaben und Männer* pp. 318–23.

at Verdun and at the eastern front, in the several thousand pages of his war novels, Zweig included very few battle scenes.) The grotesque joke the major plays on his subordinate, however, was not criticized until 30 years later. For the publication of "The Receipt" in the socialist German state, the frivolous tone of Zweig's narrative was entirely eliminated, as was the syrupy-sentimental relationship between Kruppa and the major. These revisions still did not satisfy Zweig. He added a short passage at the beginning of the novella which informs readers that the following tale reveals the machinations by which Europe had been led into the First World War. There is also a new concluding paragraph. It suggests that Kruppa would later fall, like hundreds of thousands of others. From this tragedy, readers are told, they should derive an obligation to construct a more humane and worthy society.[31] – Thus the novella's original meaning was now reversed. Still, this was not to be its final form. In a fourth republication of "The Receipt," for the 1961 edition of Zweig's collected works, both the opening and the concluding paragraph were dropped. Undoubtedly, both passages were aesthetically as well as intellectually unsatisfying. But without them the novella in its last version remains ambivalent, if not objectionable. Zweig had apparently been unable to reconcile his convictions with his literary and aesthetic demands.

The novella "The Enemy" ("Der Feind") confirms least of all the view of Zweig's war novellas as having overstepped all "boundaries of humaneness." A young Silesian carpenter, Paul Paschke, drafted in the first days of the war, finds himself after a minor accident in a German military hospital where he is placed in a ward with wounded and dying Russian prisoners. This proximity to the enemy leads to a lengthy dream in which Paschke relives a school episode and which in turn conjures up other episodes from early childhood. He remembers the conflicting messages about the Christian values of fairness and tolerance he had received from the adults. This passage shows the earliest influence of Freud on Zweig. Freud was to become the thinker who most influenced Zweig; the particular modernity of Zweig's oeuvre stems in large part from his absorption of Freudian theories. Zweig eventually befriended Freud. Paschke comes to realize that his enemies are humans like himself. Back in the field, he leads a night patrol which ends up killing four Russians. Overcome by sympathy and pity for the single surviving Russian, Paschke wants to spare him. The Russian misunderstands Paschkes intentions and shoots him.

The insights Paschke has gained in the military hospital are summed up in the following words: "Wie der Körper in der Uniform, dann in Wollwäsche, endlich im Hemde steckt und dahinter erst die Haut beginnt, genau so lag ge-

---

31 Zweig: "Die Quittung." *Neue deutsche Literatur* 3:2 (1955): 76, 79.

wickelt in den Feind etwas anderes, ein Nicht-Feind, ein Kerl, Handwerker, Bauer oder Vagabund – ein Mann, ein Mensch …"[32] Nowhere in the thousands of pages of Zweig's half dozen pacifist war novels, has such an insight been formulated more convincingly or more simply. Although he at the time sided with them, Zweig was clearly not a reliable ally of the instigators of the war. – When "The Enemy" was republished in 1933, the year its author was forced into exile, it only needed to be revised in one area. In the original, Paschke's humanity is asserted to be a specifically German trait. Zweig corrected this aspect of his story without any recourse to explanatory passages: by turning the nameless Russian who shoots Paschke into a fully developed character. Schimon Frug is a Lithuanian Jew, a Yeshiva student and bookstore assistant, as well as a socialist and member of the Russian Jewish workers' organization ("Arbeiter-Bund").[33] He sees through the capitalist interests which drive the war. In spite of his vigorously emphasized bravery, he loathes the war, and even at the moment of extreme peril feels a sense of solidarity with his German enemies.

Zweig made one more significant change. In the original version, the historical context remains unspecified, making the story appear unfathomable. In the new version, the events take place at a clearly defined historical and strategic moment of the war.[34] Thus, they become part of a historical continuum and are subject to rational analysis and critique.

"The Enemy" was revised yet again for its publication in the GDR in 1952. Zweig created a different ending. Both Paschke and Schimon Frug survive the war. They exchange letters and eventually come to understand that they had been attracted to the war by a mistaken sense of duty ("irregeleiteter Pflichtbegriff")[35] which went against their own interests. This was obviously also meant to apply to the Paschkes and Frugs of the Second World War, which had occurred in the intervening years. In view of its didactic function in the post-war Germany of the fifties, this version of "The Enemy" has its obvious merits. But once again, the revision of the ethical core of one of these war novellas had made it too artlessly obvious.[36]

---

32 Zweig: "Der Feind." *Die Bestie*, pp. 37–55, here p. 45: "As the body is hidden in the layers of the uniform, then in the woolens, and finally in one's shirt, behind which is one's skin; in exactly this way – wrapped up in the enemy is something else: not an enemy, but a chap; whether a craftsman, farmer, or vagabond – a man, a human …"

33 On the Bund, see Weinstock: *Zionism: False Messiah*, pp. 32–35.

34 See Zweig: "Der Feind." *Spielzeug der Zeit*, pp. 155–81 on Schimon Frug pp. 179–80, on the historical context, p. 172.

35 Zweig: "Der Feind." *Der Elfenbeinfächer* vol. 1, pp. 125–142, here p. 142.

36 Whether the GDR versions of Zweig's novellas were in any way influenced by pressures

Zweig was apparently aware of this. For the 1961 edition of his collected works he attempted yet again to find a satisfying form for this text. Surprisingly, he went back neither to the earlier GDR version nor to the revision of 1933, but rather to the original story of 1914. The passages in the 1933 version about the socialist Yeshiva student Schimon Frug, so significant for an ethical repositioning of the story, are dropped. Dropped, too, is the didactic ending of the 1952 version. Only a minor detail remains from the first GDR version – the name of a Sergeant Fröschel, which had been Peschel in the earlier versions. This detail is significant for an appreciation of the evolution of Zweig as a writer and thinker, for it shows how deliberately he proceeded. He obviously never lost oversight in the confusion of versions. The ethically and morally convincing version of 1952, one can reasonably conclude, was consciously abandoned for one whose tendency remains questionable but which is of a higher literary quality.

IV.

As one after another the novellas of 1914 were republished in revised form, there still remained a thorn in Zweig's side: the novella "The Beast" ("Die Bestie"). It had provided the slim volume of 1914 with its overall title. This most gruesome of the war novellas takes place during the first few weeks of the war, when Germany invaded Belgium. It tells of a simple-minded and devious Belgian peasant, Labrousse, who slaughters three well-intentioned German soldiers like cattle and feeds their entrails to his pigs. The crime is discovered soon after and Labrousse is shot by a German unit. This story is particularly odious in view of the fact that Germany without any provocation had attacked Belgium, a small and neutral country, and that the imperial German army had committed war crimes of such proportions that it created an outcry in much of the world. German propaganda then created the myth of the 'Belgian atrocities' ("belgische Kriegsgreuel") in order to blame the victims and justify its own armies' behavior.[37] In his novella, Zweig had done the work of the German propaganda machine. Could this distorted and hateful story be saved? The question was of special interest to Zweig, and for good reason: "The Beast" is a masterpiece, it is one of German literature's classic

---

from the cultural bureaucracy remains to be determined. One should keep in mind, however, that Zweig was always willing to listen to arguments and that he was in general agreement with the policies of his chosen homeland.

37 See Kramer: "'Greueltaten': Zum Problem der deutschen Kriegsverbrechen."

novellas; a fact which had been lost on most of Zweig's critics, until Jost Hermand recently suggested that "The Beast" belongs in a league with the novellas of Heinrich von Kleist.[38]

Decades earlier, in 1937, Lion Feuchtwanger, the novelist, and a friend of Zweig, had been one of the first to publicly praise "The Beast" as masterful ("meisterlich").[39] Zweig explicitly referred to Feuchtwanger's praise when, in 1942, he finally got around to revising "The Beast." It was not until ten years later, however, that the new version appeared. It was now the centerpiece of a new and much longer novella entitled *Westlandsaga*. Upon receiving the manuscript in 1952, Feuchtwanger, who was living in exile in the United States, confirmed once again that the section of *Westlandsaga* which contains "The Beast" belonged among the strongest pages of German prose.[40]

The republication of "The Beast" as part of a larger work had necessitated a number of changes.[41] Most notably, the three German soldiers now kill each other, with the reason for this explosion of hatred going back to the common childhood of two of them. The commander of the German unit which happens upon the scene divines the truth but decides to have the Belgian peasant shot anyway in order to obfuscate an event which might dishonor the German army. – Zweig's revision of his most objectionable war novella appears successful; its main elements have generally been preserved without recourse to moralistic or didactic passages, and its misinformation and hatred have been replaced by a realistic depiction of the behavior of the German army in Belgium.[42] Thus, the thorn had finally been removed from Zweig's side. – One could leave it at that were it not for the confounding fact that not only Feuchtwanger, but Zweig himself continued to prefer "The Beast" in its original form.

In 1956 Zweig asked Feuchtwanger for advice on the forthcoming edition of his collected works in the GDR: should he include *Westlandsaga* or perhaps "The Beast" in its original form? In his response Feuchtwanger recommends that the original text be included, adding that the novella represented "that which Lessing called 'exemplary'."[43] Not once in the many references to the

---

38   See Hermand: *Arnold Zweig*, p. 27.

39   Feuchtwanger: "Arnold Zweig," p. 1413.

40   Letter of September 3, 1952 – Feuchtwanger/Zweig: *Briefwechsel 1933–1958* vol. 2, pp. 177–78.

41   On Zweig's revisions of "Die Bestie" for *Westlandsaga*, see Wenzel: "'Si vis pacem ...' und die Folgen."

42   See Kramer: "'Greueltaten': Zum Problem der deutschen Kriegsverbrechen."

43   Letter of September 18, 1956, see Feuchtwanger/Zweig: *Briefwechsel 1933–1958* vol. 2, pp. 333–39.

novella in his letters to Zweig did Feuchtwanger ever reflect on the content of "The Beast." – Feuchtwanger died in 1958. In 1961 Zweig's collected works were published in the GDR, including two volumes of novellas. They contained most of the revised war novellas, as well as *Westlandsaga*. The original version of "The Beast" had not been included.

The extent to which Zweig revised and rewrote his war novellas shows that he was little concerned with preserving unchanged earlier works which he considered lacking. But neither does the pattern of revisions suggest that the last published versions of these texts should be regarded as definitive. They do not represent an authentic or 'ideal' text toward which Zweig labored over decades. The succession of versions draws attention not so much to any ultimate position Zweig evolved to, but rather to this evolution itself. Set off by the young author's struggle with modernity, Zweig's evolution appears as a long, meandering process, wherein creative and artistic demands would at times come into an unresolvable conflict with the demands of the day.

Harro Müller
Columbia University

War and Novel:
Alfred Döblin's Wallenstein and November 1918

Abstract: The historical novels *Wallenstein* and *November 1918* are novels on civil wars. I discuss the presentation of war, its implications concerning the theory of history and its anthropological assumptions especially with regard to the *Wallenstein*-novel. Then I draw comparisons to *November 1918* and comment of writing possibilities within modern times.

I.

Without a doubt Alfred Döblin's work is counted among the modern classics – a fame which rests chiefly on his urban novel *Berlin Alexanderplatz*. However, Döblin was an extremely prolific writer and the author of, among other works, historical novels such as *Wallenstein* and *November 1918*. Both of these are war novels, novels of civil war. The first of them was written during the First World War, and the second completed in Döblin's American exile during the Second. I will first discuss the presentation of war in *Wallenstein* and, in particular, elucidate the work's implications for the theory of history.[1] This will comprise the major part of my article. Finally I will draw comparisons to *November 1918* in a shorter section.

II.

Döblin wrote in retrospect in a text from 1930 about the circumstances surrounding the writing of *Wallenstein*:

The essay was translated by Jarsen Powell.
1   Müller: *Geschichte zwischen Kairos und Katastrophe*, pp. 78–96.

'Wallenstein' schrieb ich im Weltkrieg, und zwar in den Jahren 1916 bis 1918. […] In der ersten Zeit war ich Arzt in einem Lazarett für Infektionskrankheiten in Lothringen […] Nachmittags und abends konnte ich schreiben […]. Mein Zimmer war im obersten Stock des Hauses: hier breitete ich wieder und wieder mein Manuskript aus, wenn ich hinaufging, und war ich fertig, schleppte ich es zur Sicherheit hinunter. Nun es schlugen gar viele Bomben in der Nachbarschaft ein, aber weder mir noch meinem Manuskript geschah was. […] Vielleicht ist etwas von der furchtbaren Luft, in der das Buch entstand, Krieg, Revolution, Krankheit und Tod in ihm.[2]

Beyond the historical concept of sympathetic reconstruction ("Einfühlung") and of bringing the past to life, Döblin notes that the experience of the present (war, revolution, sickness, death, bombing, contingency) were decisive in his attempt "[den Toten des 30-jährigen Krieges] die Münder zu öffnen, ihre vertrockneten Gebeine zu bewegen."[3] The theme of the extraordinarily complex novel is the victory of the Emperor Ferdinand over the Winter King (early in 1621), and its end is an occurrence invented by Döblin: the murder of the emperor two years after the violent death of Wallenstein in late summer of 1636. The novel begins immediately and its end is open. It does not begin with the assumed causes leading to the outbreak of the Thirty Years' War, but with the description of an excessive victory dinner where "warlords" eat and drink with vast and animal gusto. In this manner they show that it is always a great pleasure for them to devour and digest their prey. At the novel's end one finds not the Kingdom of God, – with which so many novels, according to Friedrich Schlegel, like to end, – but a look ahead to further war developments and further battles:

Unter die aufmarschierenden Heere der Kaiserlichen Sachsen Schweden Bayern gerieten von allen Seiten die losgelösten verzweifelten Volksteile. Viele gingen zu den Truppen über, von Lohn und Nahrung verlockt. Was ihnen störend in den Weg kam zerklatschten die Heere.

---

2 Mayer: *Alfred Döblins 'Wallenstein'*, p. 11: "I wrote *Wallenstein* during the World War, and especially in the years 1916 to 1918. […] At first I was a doctor in a hospital for infectious diseases in Lorraine […] In the afternoons and in the evenings I could write […]. My room was in the top floor of the house: here I continually spread out my manuscripts whenever I went upstairs, and once I was ready, I would bring it downstairs for safekeeping. Many bombs hit in the immediate neighborhood, but none hit either me or my manuscript. […] Perhaps something of the terrible atmosphere, in which the book was written – war, revolution, sickness and death – has left its traces in the work."

3 Döblin: "Der historische Roman und wir." *Schriften zur Ästhetik, Poetik und Literatur (Ausgewählte Werke in Einzelbänden)*, pp. 291–316, here p. 310: "to open the mouths" of the dead from the Thirty Years' War and to "make their dried-up bones move."

> Die Söldnermassen selbst brachen gegeneinander los, schlugen nieder, verfolg-
> ten sich, metzelten sich von neuem, Kaiserliche Schweden Sachsen Bayern. Im
> Westen hatten sich die Welschen gesammelt. Sie warteten in frischer Kraft auf ihr
> Signal, um sich hineinzuwerfen.[4]

Between the immediate beginning and the open end of the book, horrifying
events from the war are represented. There is no thoroughgoing chronology
in the novel, which is characterized rather by repetitions, parallelisms and
fragmentations. The heterogeneity of history in its temporal and spatial aspects is strongly accented. History occurs both continuously and discontinu-
ously, and this is matched by an abrupt, fissured narrative which juxtaposes
fragments and allows for no larger vantage point. The work privileges a cinematic style in which it runs right up to the figures, pans or zooms, abruptly
veers with its lens, and then gives a total picture or offers orgies of description. The figures appear, disappear, reappear or never reappear at all, according to a principle of epic apposition which simultaneously relativizes the plot
as a narrative model. The most weight is placed on the level of histoire, which
is nonetheless extremely internally segmented. The level of discourse is not
only often completely absent, but also represents the place where chronological order is negated as a means of generating meaning. The figures, both individual and collective, are mostly described from outside, and large areas of
the figures' subjectivity remain obscure and resist any form of search for
meaning. Out of the extraordinarily numerous dramatis personae of the novel
– there are more than 60 figures – a few are singled out for sharper outlining:
Wallenstein, Ferdinand, Maximilian of Bavaria, Gustav Adolphus of Sweden,
Tilly, the Danish King Christian, actors and instruments, actors and sufferers
in opaque, labyrinthine struggles. Despite the great gains of power which may
be obtained in war there is no guarantee of success, and almost all of the
figures fail and come to violent death. No one figure can master the labyrinth
of history, which cannot be reduced to any personal conception. The heterogeneity of goals is in force here, and history is not containable in concepts of
dialectical or non-dialectical progress, development or education. Nor is it the
place for larger constructions of human history or the history of the race of
man – conceptions which are in any case mostly secularized rewritings of sal-

---

4   Döblin: *Wallenstein (Ausgewählte Werke in Einzelbänden)*, pp. 738–39: "Among the arriving ar-
    mies of the emperor and of Saxony, Sweden and Bavaria, disparate and despairing parts of
    the populace got mixed in from all sides. Many of them joined the troops, seduced by pay
    and food. The armies destroyed whatever got into their way. The masses of hired troops
    themselves fought against each other, killed and attacked each other again and again, Impe-
    rial troops, Swedes, Saxons, Bavarians. The foreigners had assembled in the West. They
    waited in full strength for the signal to hurl themselves against the enemy."

vation history. The novel undoes history as a transcendental signified; it is set up in such a way that no concept of significance can offer a way out. In *Wallenstein* there is no center of force from which history may be produced – which is not even to speak of a center of meaning. Beyond historical and natural determinism there is admittedly much that is undefined, undefinable, contingent. Contingency refers to modality, but the opening of the space of the play of possibilities does not mean that the histories which are not realized are better than those which are:

> Wallenstein zeigte sein grausiges Gesicht: Ein einiges deutsches Reich, eine einige Knechtung. Söldner breitbeinig durch die Gassen, über die Märkte, Trommeln und Pauken hinterher. Die Sprache des neuen Herrschers Armut Entrechtung Versklavung. In Tierställe verwandelten sie das Heilige Reich.[5]

The complex historical unwinding of events is, paradoxically formulated, at once definite and indefinite; it cannot be contained in assumptions of causality: "Die Kausalisten sehen alles nachher, von hinten. Vorher aber war es unklar. Ihre Welt verläuft gar nicht programmatisch [...], sondern metagrammatisch."[6]

The metagrammatical conception of history corresponds, in Döblin, to a scientific assumption: "Die Unordnung ist [...] ein besseres Wissen als die Ordnung,"[7] – and it is also bound to a postulate on the anthropological level: "Im Organismus liegt zwar eine Harmonie, aber keine vollständige. Es ist eine disharmonisierende Unruhe im Organismus, die mit der Harmonie kämpft."[8] Thus *Wallenstein* is a farewell to all materialist or idealist conceptions of history and to all anthropological attempts at grounding. The novel is anti-historical, anti-humanist and post-idealist.

Wallenstein is the only novel of Döblin's which was not banned by the Nazis, and Döblin refused to republish the book after the Second World War. This novel, linguistically virtuosic and written according to an aesthetics of

---

5   Ibid., p. 391: "Wallenstein showed his gruesome face: a unitary German empire, a single form of subservience. Hired troops striding broadly through the streets, over the marketplaces, drums beating in their wake. The language of the new ruler: poverty dispossession enslavement. They converted the Holy Empire into a barn for animals."

6   Döblin: *Unser Dasein (Ausgewählte Werke in Einzelbänden)*, p. 84: "The partisans of causality see everything in hindsight, from later on. Earlier, however, everything was unclear. Their world unfolds not programmatically [...] but metagrammatically."

7   Döblin: *Die beiden Freundinnen und ihr Giftmord*, p. 94: "Disorder is [...] a better form of knowledge than order".

8   Döblin: *Das Ich über der Natur*, p. 99: "There is indeed a harmony in the organism, but not a complete one. There is a disharmonizing unquiet in the organism, which struggles with harmony."

terror, with its eruptions of eccentricity and blind impulse, contains many extremely shocking scenes which demonstrate the bestialization of man in war. The war as an exceptional case calls forth patterns of behavior which had been successfully kept latent during peacetime. Both on the collective as well as on the individual level there are extreme forms of sadism and masochism, there are disgusting rape scenes, and the mountains of corpses rise to the sky. Both the representatives of Protestantism and those of Catholicism prove to be the purest form of imperialists. Many parts may be read as a plea for aesthetic amoralism, for historical nihilism, for complete naturalization of history or for a mythology of history. This allegorical historical novel with its hyperbolic procedures and futuristically inspired dynamizations is in any case no mere playing with confusion of sense: Thus there are unmistakable references to religion as an ideological screen and for capitalism as an instrument of exploitation: state and social institutions are crucially interested in preserving and producing power.

The orgies of aggression, destruction and regressions which are presented in the book produce ambivalent effects but are not employed simply as stimulants; the book is no mere affirmation of violence – that is, the representation of violence, which strongly colors the natural, human and social realism, does not amount to an apology for violence. There are gestures of humane protest which are not cynically relativized.

Wallenstein and others are mythologically charged and thus dehistoricized: "der Friedländer ihm gegenüber, ein gelber Drache aus dem böhmischen blasenwerfenden Morast aufgestiegen, bis an die Hüften mit schwarzem Schlamm bedeckt, [...]."[9]

That which is precarious in this war novel seems to rest precisely in its mixture of mythic, historical, natural and rationally explicable elements in such a way that the respective boundaries of these domains become unstable. The reader is given no black, red or green thread of sense with which he could orient himself in the labyrinth of history. Thus Wallenstein is on the one hand a captain of industry who acts rationally, and a mortal man who is afflicted by disease, and on the other hand he is a mythic monstrosity who produced apocalyptic effects. Thus the moment of terror and the moment of death can happen at any instant:

Vom Alten Markt zogen ihm [Tilly] fünfhundert kaisertreue Bürger, die rote Feldbande schwingend, Weiber und Kinder in der Mitte, entgegen. Waren im Augen-

---

9 Döblin: *Wallenstein (Ausgewählte Werke in Einzelbänden)*, p. 243: "The Friedlander was facing him, a yellow dragon risen up from the bubbling swamps of Bohemia, coated with black slime to his hips [...]".

blick von Kroaten und Wallonen bäuchlings rücklings seitlings hingestreckt und zertreten.[10]

This lack of possibility of orientation is however tied closely to the meta-grammatical conception of history, which ultimately refers to the absence of transcendental signified, or any helmsman or helmswoman who could give any general sense of direction, in modernity. In the regulated-unregulated movements towards chaos of the Thirty Years' War the entire risk of modernity appears under exceptional conditions, – a risk even today hardly bearable.

As Bertolt Brecht said about his furious play *Baal*, so also Döblin could have said about *Wallenstein*: the play, the novel lacks wisdom.[11] In an "Epilogue" the German Jew Alfred Döblin, who had in the meantime become Catholic, expresses his opinion about his historical novel *Wallenstein*, this colossal painting for the short- sighted (as it was termed in a review).[12] In this Epilogue one may read the following:

> Ich fand offen und insgeheim Gefallen an den grandiosen Phänomenen. Den Menschen, sein Ich, sein Leiden sah ich wohl. Aber ich erbarmte mich seiner und meiner nicht. [...] Denn alle weltfrohe Umhüllung der historischen Vorgänge täuschte mich nicht über die Schwäche der Position, über die Unentschiedenheit, die Mutlosigkeit.[13]

The novel *Wallenstein* criticizes, with its tendencies to naturalization and mythification, all concepts of humanism, and even religious proposals of meaning – whether institutionally mediated or not – cannot help here and prove to be either ideological deception or a plea for complete nihilism: "Die Welt hat einen Hauch von Verwesung. Es ist ein zarter Geruch, der bei mancher Witterung stärker wird."[14] This could be shown in an analysis of the sermons which are built into the novel. However, Döblin does not depart

---

10   Ibid., p. 503: "Five hundred subjects loyal to the Emperor marched against him [Tilly] from the Old Marketplace, waving the red field banner, with women and children in the middle. They were in an instant crushed backwards sideways into the stream by Croats and Walloons."

11   Brecht: "Bei Durchsicht meiner ersten Stücke." *Werke* vol. 23: *Schriften 3*, pp. 239–45, here p. 242.

12   Scherpe: "Ein Kolossalgemälde für Kurzsichtige", pp. 226–41.

13   Döblin: "Epilog." *Autobiographische Schriften und letzte Aufzeichnungen (Ausgewählte Werke in Einzelbänden)*, pp. 439–51, here p. 443: "I took both open and secret pleasure in the grandiose phenomena. I saw clearly the individual man, his ego, his suffering. But I had no pity either for him or for me. [...] For all world-celebrating drapery of historical events did not deceive me regarding the weakness of the position, the indecisiveness, the lack of courage."

14   Döblin: *Wallenstein (Ausgewählte Werke in Einzelbänden)*, p. 314: "The world smells of corruption. It is a delicate scent which gets stronger in certain atmospheric conditions."

from that which I would like to call the anthropological discourse. There are
many dispositional possibilities in it. What is Döblin's fundamental assumption? Döblin sees a close connection between man's aggressive and unharmo-
nizable disposition and war. "Der Krieg ist so wenig wie der Friede ein Natur-
gesetz."[15] Human society is the result of a process of civilization which has no
foreseeable end and for which no telos may be found. The development of
humanity has until now consisted in the taming and suppressing of the "wil-
den, bestialischen Impuls" ("wild, bestial impulse"). This struggle is in fact
extremely difficult, since the "alte Trieb [...] schon im einzelnen Menschen,
nun gar in den Massen eine so ungeheure Gewalt hat."[16]

III.

If the point of departure is set in this way, it is hardly surprising that Döblin,
who in the course of his long literary life was faced with such painful historical events, should have searched for possibilities to approach the problem in
other aesthetic and cognitive fashion than the *Wallenstein* novel did. This can
be well shown in the case of another historical novel of Döblin's. It has the
title *November 1918* and was written in the period between 1937 and 1943 in
French and American exile. A few comparative comments on this 4-volume
novel which is more than 2000 pages long:

1. The novel, with its multiple polyperspectival narrative procedures, thematizes the failure of the German revolution with all its good intentions in
1918–9. It begins in the first volume, *Citizens and Soldiers*, at the same place
where Döblin had written his *Wallenstein* novel under the above-described
dangerous conditions, that is, Alsace, and there is, as in *Wallenstein*, reference
to contingency as a historico- theoretical figure. The revolution and the revolt
might well have taken a different course. It is interesting in any case that there
are now positive figures set up in the book: Wilson and Rosa Luxemburg.

2. As in *Wallenstein*, there is a vast narrative panorama spread out and numerous novelistic characters are involved. However, here much more emphasis is placed on chronological order and the Futuristic boldness and stylistic
extravagances are considerably muted. Döblin mixes pathetic and ironic, re-

---

15 Döblin: "Krieg und Frieden." *Schriften zur Politik und Gesellschaft (Ausgewählte Werke in Einzel-
    bänden)*, pp. 152–69, here p. 152: "War is as little a natural law as is peace."

16 Ibid., p. 394: "old drive [...] has already such a tremendous force in individual humans, and
    then even more in masses."

alistic and experimental narrative techniques, typifies and individualizes characters.[17]

3. This strong tendency to individualization now makes global metaphors attractive for the purpose of directing the development of individual narratives. Döblin had rigorously excluded this sort of procedure when he wrote *Wallenstein* as an avantgardist and literary rebel inspired by Futurism and oriented to antihistoricism. These metaphors are those of development and education. With regard to the chief characters Friedrich Becker and Rosa Luxemburg, the secondary literature has justifiably spoken of a religious novel of development in which the characters' inner life is illuminated in many ways.[18] In contradistinction to the *Wallenstein* novel the inner life of the characters plays a great role here.

4. The accentuation of individuality as an irreducible base unity of history and society which cannot be further transposed into a merely functional nexus is closely tied to the fact that Döblin broadly quotes elements from the traditional cultural inheritance in *November 1918*, unlike *Wallenstein*. Individuals are socialized in a dialogue with Antigone, or with the help of religious traditions from Tauler to Kierkegaard. Nonetheless they know: "Wenn die Not groß ist, helfen auch Klassiker nicht."[19]

5. If *Wallenstein* is an antihistorical and antihermeneutical novel, hermeneutics plays a significant role in *November 1918* as a theory and a praxis of individual appropriation of meaning. The failed and well-intentioned revolution of 1918/9 with its tragic, comic and ridiculous aspects belongs to the prehistory of German fascism. Thus Döblin works here with a historical model of events in which his original anthropological premise is retained.

6. Thus the fundamental meaning which is presented in *November 1918* is ethically and religiously motivated, stresses the individual conscience and encourages engagement for those who suffer, for victims.

All aestheticist positions are strictly rejected, in contradistinction to *Wallenstein*. There are in *November 1918* no passages which blend horror and fascination, terror and pleasure in refined manner.

7. If, in *Wallenstein*, war history is the history of terror with strongly marked cyclical moments, then in *November 1918* there are no more orgies of violence of titanic dimensions, although horror, fear, suffering and death are certainly not hushed up. Döblin is now of the opinion that history is ultimate-

---

17   Blume: *Die Lektüren des Alfred Döblins*, p. 27.
18   Kiesel: *Literarische Trauerarbeit*, pp. 18–27.
19   Döblin: *November 1918. Teil I: Bürger und Soldaten 1918 (Ausgewählte Werke in Einzelbänden)*, p. 24: "In times of great need even the classics cannot help."

ly conceivable according to a model of interactivity and that there are always possibilities of intervention which are not merely the play of cyclical repetition. His motto now is: "Mit Geschichte will man was," and the author must write for the partisanship of those who are active.[20]

8. If in *Wallenstein* the transcendental signified 'history' is contradicted, in *November 1918* it returns, since what Helmut Kiesel termed the recognition of the right to resistance or insurrection (mediated by Christianity), can only arise from this transcendental signified[21].

9. Thus *November 1918* is no resigned novel. Precisely in the face of the extraordinarily painful experiences which he had with German Fascism, Alfred Döblin took a position in a religious and humanistic discourse which reminds the individual that he has his life before him and must be answerable for it before a metaphysical instance.

10. This valorization of a humanistic and religious discourse with its appeal to the individual conscience explains then why, despite its cinematic style and its great variety of writing procedures, which range from the emphatic to the strongly ironic and satirical, the novel *November 1918* has been often negatively evaluated relative to the *Wallenstein* novel with its consistently deathly-serious and grotesque sections. In fact it may appear questionable whether a religious, humanist and ethical discourse as 'discourse of discourses' may be a helpful means of orientation in modernity, with its differentiation of particular and functionally nonequivalent partial systems, with its tendencies away from morality and its increase of risk. This option is however a serious possible response which deserves to be taken seriously as long as one adopts an anthropological discourse. Döblin at least spent his entire life working out his relation to his own personally chosen 'pessimistic' variant, which irritated and shocked him and constantly served as an impetus to his large poetic productions.

In "Der historische Roman und wir" (1936) Döblin wrote, that historical novels can make possible "komplexeres Sehen und Denken, ein tieferes Einfühlen, ein rascheres Kombinieren." He then adds: "Mit jedem gelungenen Werk ist wieder einmal die Erde größer geworden, unser Reichtum ist vermehrt, eine neue Kolumbusfahrt ist geglückt, ein neues Indien entdeckt."[22]

---

20 Döblin: "Der historische Roman und wir." *Schriften zur Ästhetik, Poetik und Literatur (Ausgewählte Werke in Einzelbänden)*, pp. 301–02: "One intends something with history".

21 Kiesel: *Literarische Trauerarbeit*, pp. 482–88.

22 Döblin: "Der historische Roman und wir." *Schriften zur Ästhetik, Poetik und Literatur (Ausgewählte Werke in Einzelbänden)*, pp. 308–309: "[…] a more complex form of seeing and thinking, a deeper penetration into the material and more rapid ways of combination." "With every achieved work the earth has again become larger, our wealth is increased, a new expedition of Columbus has succeeded and a new India has been discovered."

Both *Wallenstein* and *November 1918* are evidently successfully achieved works. There are however different forms of successful achievement. With this text I wanted to offer some indices of how one might relate to these forms.

Tim Mehigan
University of Melbourne

Violent Orders in Robert Musil's "Der Mann ohne Eigenschaften" and Thomas Bernhard's "Kalkwerk"

Abstract: Modernity and modernism are inseparable from *violence*. However much the events of the twentieth century support this view, little is known about why such a relationship exists and what implications it might give rise to. Robert Musil's *Der Mann ohne Eigenschaften* and Thomas Bernhard's *Kalkwerk* can provide instruction. Both texts undertake analyses of the social circumstances of their time, Musil in the early part of the modernist period, Bernhard in the later part. What they uncover are not so much the effects of violence as the violence of effects – the idea that violence can inhabit form as its very precondition. I propose to analyze the circumstances that lead to violent acts in both works and to investigate their origin in formal orders that have come to condition perception in the modern era.

I. The Beginnings of Subjectivity

The process of separating object from ego, Freud argues, is a primary task of the child's earliest development. Sensations are sorted through on the basis of the pleasure principle – those things responsible for pain and displeasure are consigned to an outside realm, things inducing pleasure become part of an inner realm; this simple mechanism sets up the initial basis on which the ego can be distinguished from the outside world, although experience will tutor the child that pleasure can issue from non-ego related objects, and equally, not all ego is pleasure.[1] To put it another way, the absence of internal points of reference means that the child's earliest acts of representation are in fact quite impersonal; the movement by which the outside of the self finds an inside, and the inside a center, occurs only with experience and the due passage of time. A contemporary of Robert Musil, the philosopher Bergson, confirms

---

1   Freud: *Das Unbehagen in der Kultur*, p. 67.

the point that it is only gradually that representation comes to "adopt our body as a center and become our representation."[2] It cannot be assumed, however, that this process occurs in all cases as a matter of course. The study of pathological states, for example, reveals those factors which complicate the process of establishing a distinction between the ego and the world. In extreme cases, aspects of the body and self – perceptions, thoughts, feelings – appear completely inseparable from elements external to the ego. As a consequence, the subject's sense of self is turned over to the flux and random disturbances of the exterior world while the boundaries that otherwise hive off the subject from external objects become unreliable, disrupted,[3] or, at worst, are lost altogether.

Musil's sex-killer, Moosbrugger, certainly fits this picture of pathological disturbance, as we are told: "Es wurde gegen seinen Willen in ihm gedacht. Er sagte, Gedanken würden ihm gemacht."[4] Thought for, not thinking, Moosbrugger exists in the novel as an image of complete alienation at the point where exteriority appears to reclaim the interior space of the ego while leaving few remnants of the subject visible. Moosbrugger's function in the novel seems to be to provide a counterweight to the project of the protagonist, Ulrich, the eponymous "Mann ohne Eigenschaften." The ideal to which this state, this absence of qualities, alludes must be understood as a contrasting attitude of radical openness to the world at the level of subjective reflection, where the enclosure of the ego by the world is met – and disabled – by a strategy of "Eigenschaftslosigkeit," or of the indeterminability of the subject. Here, following Bergson, indeterminability "gives the exact measure of the extent of [...] perception."[5] The issue of the disappearance of subjective spaces evident in the study of pathological states is then recast as a problem of perception rather than of the world. At stake is now the reinitiation of action from a heavily indeterminate subjective center. This is the problem named later in the novel by the so-called "other condition" ("der andere Zustand").

---

2 Bergson: *Matter and Memory*, p. 46.
3 Freud: *Das Unbehagen in der Kultur*, pp. 66–7.
4 Musil: *Der Mann ohne Eigenschaften*, p. 240: "Things thought themselves in him against his will. He said that thoughts made themselves inside him." Note that all translations into English are by the author.
5 Bergson: *Matter and Memory*, p. 41.

II. The Crisis of Subjectivity

"Die Sache hat uns in der Hand." Musil advances this diagnosis of the contemporary condition at the outset. At issue is a severe imbalance between object and ego-world that bears upon the strategies invoked by the subject in fashioning notions of self and ego boundaries:

> Die Sache hat uns in der Hand. Man fährt Tag und Nacht in ihr und tut auch noch alles andere drin; man rasiert sich, man ißt, man liebt, man liest Bücher, man übt seinen Beruf aus, als ob die vier Wände stillstünden, und das Unheimliche ist bloß, daß die vier Wände fahren, ohne daß man es merkt …[6]

A watershed in the history of the subject is thereby announced: significant voluntary movements are no longer registered in the subject, but in objects which move that subject. The subject, in turn, becomes more acted upon than actor, reducible in the extreme to a random surface across which the relentless passage of objects can be traced. This shift occurs historically and has the widest possible implications for the subject – it is not a formal change that can be altered or reversed by new categories of thinking manipulated by the subject. It is for this reason that *Der Mann ohne Eigenschaften* sets up its imaginative program historically, debates conceptions of history[7] and of genius[8] which may be excepted from it, and merges its utopian union of sibling lovers with the historical framework "Ins tausendjährige Reich" in the novel's final section. The conclusion drawn from this interest in history is that there can be no self-willed return to former times, and no recourse to the familiar and predictable that prevailed under imperial Austria, where the fully centered human subject was the sovereign author of all thinking and action.[9] More than incidental context or backdrop, the sense of history the novel evokes becomes central to its imaginative project. The crisis of subjectivity is named historically, although it is never dated in terms other than a chronological before and after under which a reversal is forestalled. Equally, historical markers become the logical outgrowth of crisis, as a remark from the unpublished notes of the author makes clear: "*Grundidee*: Krieg. Alle Linien münden in den Krieg."[10]

---

6   Musil: *Der Mann ohne Eigenschaften,* p. 32: "Things have taken hold of us. Day and night we travel in them and do all sorts of things besides: we shave, eat, love, read books, follow a profession – as if our four walls stood still, and the terrifying thing is merely that these four walls are moving without our knowledge."

7   Ibid., p. 361, p. 364.

8   Ibid., p. 45.

9   Ibid., p. 32.

10   Ibid., p. 1851: "Basic idea: war. All lines lead to war."

An atmosphere of crisis pervades the assessment of social relations in the novel, although almost none of the characters is aware of it. The fascination the case of Moosbrugger begins to exercise over people and institutions is but one of the reference points of crisis, even though the official social interest in the case has the plausible motivation of adjudicating diminished responsibility in criminal cases. For the most part, however, the atmosphere of crisis is subdued, and is usually expressed in the abstract pronouncements of the protagonist ("wir [haben] immer mehr Ordnungen und immer weniger Ordnung,"[11] "das einzige, was den Ideen einigermaßen Halt gibt, ist der Körper, zu dem sie gehören"[12]) and in the curiously uncommitted attitude he strikes towards his environment. Crisis is sustained nevertheless as a structural moment around which a central division in the novel falls, the polarization of social forces and the asocial forces which resist them.

Social forces are centripetal and chiefly gather around the characters Diotima, Arnheim, Sektionschef Tuzzi and the so-called "Parallelaktion." Musil wants to sketch the collapse of society onto itself, its steady implosion, which he sees as the culmination of a long process of degeneration absorbing every facet of public and social life: the proliferation of orders but an increasing lack of order, everywhere values but ever less value, Musil finds for this particular encroachment of outer upon inner, in which the ego comes to lose control over its own processes of self-constitution, the term "Seinesgleichen":

> Es sind die fertigen Einteilungen und Formen des Lebens, was sich dem Mißtrauen so spürbar macht, das Seinesgleichen, dieses von Geschlechtern schon Vorgebildete, die fertige Sprache nicht nur der Zunge, sondern auch der Empfindungen und Gefühle. [13]

The subject encounters a fully pre-fabricated world of sense and emotion. Accordingly, the activity of the subject is not to organize a brokerage of external objects and ego demands, but is absorbed instead without conflict into the circulation of ready-made responses and attributes. Participation is assumed. Nothing is figurative because all is literal (or pre-figured). There is no opposition between genuine and phony, proper and improper, actual and fake, because everything now exists without reference to an original it is pre-

---

11   Ibid., p. 379: "There are ever more orders and ever less order."
12   Ibid., p. 380: "The only thing that gives our ideas a center is the body to which they are attached."
13   Ibid., p. 129: "It is finished divisions and forms of life which give grounds for suspicion – these enactments, that which the species has pre-formed, the finished language not only of speech but also of sensation and feeling."

sumed to have copied or corrupted. In the language of recent critical thinking, this is Baudrillard's second order of simulacrum based on the commercial
law of value. It follows the decline of the so-called classical period, whose
dominant scheme was an interdiction attending the imitation of its posited
natural law of value (namely, counterfeit).[14] The prototype of second generation simulacra is the Prussian industrialist, Arnheim, who insinuates himself
into the "Parallelaktion" in its early stages and whose wealth, learning and
prestige soon begin to dominate it. Arnheim reproduces the commercial law
of value perfectly in his thinking and action. He is possessed of a "selbstge-
fällig ausgebreitetes Denken"[15] and a belief that wealth conveys not only dignity, but also moral worth, upon a person. He declares God to be "im tiefsten
unmodern,"[16] conceives history as the steady unraveling of a positive dynamic of change and claims that fears of the moment concerning the saturation of
culture with over-refined knowledge and sophistication will be robustly answered by one thing alone – "das Auftreten einer neuen Person."[17] Unlike Ulrich, his natural counterpart and enemy in the novel, Arnheim is all immediacy, standing for that seamless overlapping of "Geist" ("intellect") and "Tat"
("action") Musil felt would lead irresistibly to war. As Ulrich tells General
Stumm in another context: "Geist ist Ordnung, und wo gibt es mehr Ordnung als beim Militär?"[18]

These, then, are what I'm calling the social forces – forces that regulate
ever greater areas of physical life, even as they leave the soul unordered (the
circulation of commercial value leaves the soul largely unaddressed). The
movement of these forces draws the description "Seinesgleichen geschieht"
the title of the novel's second part, and what it describes is the re-enactment
of finished processes: what happens, as one critic tells us, are happenings,
"Geschehen an sich."[19] It is fitting, therefore, that most of the discussion in

---

14 Baudrillard: *Simulations*, p. 83.
15 Musil: *Der Mann ohne Eigenschaften*, p. 187: "an expansive and self-satisfied type of thinking."
16 Ibid., p. 197: "profoundly unmodern."
17 Ibid., p. 198: "the emergence of a new figure."
18 Ibid., p. 377: "Intellect is order and where is there more order than in the military?"
19 Rothe: " 'Seinesgleichen geschieht.' Musil und die moderne Erzähltradition." Dinklage, Albertsen and Corino, eds., *Robert Musil*, p. 133. According to Graf, "Seinesgleichen" must be
understood as an historical process of socialization by which external forms come to condition human actions and responses – Graf: *Erfahrungskonstruktion*, p.25. For Baumann
"Seinesgleichen" is a structure outside time, a scheme of "authorized relations" which insinuates itself into "histories" without ever becoming historical – Baumann: *Robert Musil*, p.
23. This moves it into the ambit of Foucault's operational conception of power, which I
have analyzed elsewhere – Mehigan: "Brecht and 'Gestus.' The Place of the Subject." *Faultline*, vol. 2, 1993, pp. 81–2. Accordingly, "Seinesgleichen" would be consonant with a strat-

this section should be about a "parallel action," a staged re-enactment, which, in its breadth and ambition is to be more impressive than its original!

III. Forms of Resistance

The asocial forces in the novel gather around the characters Ulrich, Moosbrugger, the Nietzsche devotee Clarisse and Ulrich's sister, Agathe. They are asocial because they resist society's spiraling tilt to the center by their own eccentric movements: in Clarisse's case, by living every idea as real; in Ulrich's case, by being deliberately non-committal, or, as he proclaims at one stage, by following a conscious strategy of "active passivism": "Das Warten eines Gefangenen auf die Gelegenheit des Ausbruchs."[20] Ulrich's radical passivism is worked out against a complex background of excessiveness in both the social forces he despises and in the asocial forces to which he is more sympathetic. Typically, he is resisted by both. Diotima, who rejects his non-commitment as naive, is drawn instead to Arnheim's dynamic, secure-in-the-world activism; Arnheim, whom Ulrich fascinates as much as frustrates, attempts to co-opt Ulrich to his firm when he can't subdue him by other means. It is Walter, Clarisse's husband and Ulrich's one-time close friend, who first labels Ulrich "ein Mann ohne Eigenschaften,"[21] but in a thoroughly negative sense. Clarisse, for her part, initially finds appeal in the description, but later she calls him "a big criminal."[22]

Ulrich lives against the tenor of his age. His conviction is that attributes are born without reference to the individuals who assume them and in whom responsibility for them might otherwise be invested. The result of this invasion of the person from without is the loss of that private realm of self in which ethical judgments about behavior can form. Morality and ethics are normalized with reference to the social whole but with complete indifference to the person; this social whole in turn draws its existence from processes of legitimation now radically dismembered from its smallest and most vital element, the human individual. It is for this reason that the rise of an exclusively physical "culture of the body" is registered with such alarm — in the empty inner spaces of self the highly trained body reacts to every stimulus automati-

---

egy flowing through disciplinary codes, institutions, apparatuses and notions of truth and engendering not reality, but "reality effects." Cf. Deleuze: *Foucault*, pp. 25–36.

20 Musil: *Der Mann ohne Eigenschaften*, p. 356: "The prisoner's waiting for the moment to break out."

21 Ibid., p. 64.

22 Ibid., p. 357.

cally, its owner is left with the disturbing feeling of watching on[23] – and for this reason that Ulrich is forced to cultivate a seemingly futile policy of resistance and negation in an attempt to defend a private region capable of generating duties which are binding on the self.

In working out this diagnosis of the age, Ulrich comes to fix attention upon Moosbrugger, a carpenter by trade who attains notoriety through a particularly savage murder of a prostitute. The case is closely followed for its sensational value in the press, just as the actual case on which it is based was widely reported in Musil's own day.[24] Moosbrugger, like the historical Florian Großrubatscher, is deranged rather than debased, a naive soul with "ein Wille zum Rechten"[25] who kills not with any conviction of his own but in the context of things beyond him. As Ulrich remarks to himself: "wenn die Menschheit als Ganzes träumen könnte, müßte Moosbrugger entstehn."[26] Moosbrugger appears as private subjective spaces seem to disappear. His interrogators fail to find a satisfactory motive for the murder, and there is no sign of remorse in Moosbrugger in the wake of his crime. When reminded by the prosecuting judge of his earlier references to hate and anger, Moosbrugger concedes he might have displayed such emotion, although he has no recollection of it. In truth, he is interesting as much for the attention Viennese society devotes to him as for the nature of his crime, and Ulrich feels this greater social interest repeated in himself.

IV. "Deterritorialization"

Moosbrugger is no latter day Woyzeck, as has been argued[27] – he is less driven than Woyzeck, although similarly ridiculed in his battle for self-respect. He is rather more a cousin of Büchner's other lost soul, Lenz, in his fits and starts,

---

23 Cf. ibid., p. 30: "Das körperliche Treiben komme ja wirklich schon in Mode, und im Grunde schließe es ein grauenvolles Gefühl ein, weil der Körper, wenn er ganz scharf trainiert sei, das Übergewicht habe und auf jeden Reiz ohne zu fragen, mit seinen automatisch eingeschliffenen Bewegungen so sicher antworte, daß dem Besitzer nur noch das unheimliche Gefühl des Nachsehens bleibt […]." "Physical exertion was becoming quite fashionable and in fact in a rather disturbing way because the body, when highly trained, took over and would react so surely to any stimulus with its automatically programmed movements that its owner was left with the worrying feeling of looking on […]."

24 Cf. Karl Corino: "Ein Mörder macht Literaturgeschichte. Florian Großrubatscher, ein Modell für Musils Moosbrugger." Strutz, ed., *Robert Musil*, pp. 130- 47.

25 Musil: *Der Mann ohne Eigenschaften*, p. 67.

26 Ibid., p. 76.

27 Howald: *Ästhetizismus und ästhetische Ideologiekritik*, p. 213.

flows and intensities, and sudden complete absences of emotion. Viewed in this light, Moosbrugger comes to resemble one of Deleuze-Guattari's nomadic schizos produced within capitalistic social conditions. According to Deleuze-Guattari, there is always some escape from the heavily restrictive pattern of material production and desire under capitalism.[28] When escape occurs, desire – that ceaseless productive energy driven on to make ever new connections and couplings – breaks free and is "deterritorialized."

Deleuze-Guattari identify two aspects to the notion of territory: firstly, a regulation of space in which the coexistence of different members of the same species is achieved by keeping them apart; secondly, a further ordering of this space which maximizes the numbers of different species within this space by specializing them.[29] These are the conditions that allow for the performance of work in modern capitalism. If territorialization is the determination of movement within a space, deterritorialization is the movement which starts within this space but moves beyond it. Under these circumstances a machine can be said to be released. A machine, in turn, is defined as "a set of cutting edges that insert themselves into the assemblage undergoing deterritorialization, and draw variations and mutations of it."[30] Space is therefore continually subject to a process of stratification as well as a type of anti-stratification – the movement which forever goes beyond it. This movement, particularly visible at its edges, actually defines the space by moving outside it.

Deterritorialization proceeds by the vehicle of desire.[31] Desire moves out of the psychic and spatial boundaries which subdue and direct it and begins to range free over undetermined territory, engaging and disconnecting with other objects in a random flow of libidinal but otherwise meaningless material energy. These flows are generated by the unconscious without reference to particular objects or any center in human subjectivity. They emerge within a social field and can be coded or "territorialized," but, strictly speaking, exist prior to signifying schemes and regulative social practices. The deterritorial-

---

28 The critique of capitalism is particularly evident in *Anti-Oedipus*, where the point is made: "[…] capitalism, throughout its process of production, produces an awesome schizophrenic accumulation of energy or charge, against which it brings all its vast powers of repression to bear, but which nonetheless continues to act as capitalism's limit." This leads to the assertion that "schizophrenia is desiring-production as the limit of social production" – Deleuze-Guattari: *Anti-Oedipus*, pp. 34–5.

29 Deleuze/Guattari: *A Thousand Plateaus*, p. 320.

30 Ibid., p. 333.

31 Cf. ibid., p. 399: "Assemblages are passional, they are compositions of desire. Desire has nothing to do with a natural or spontaneous determination; there is no desire but assembling, assembled, desire."

ized body becomes known as the "body without organs" – not an organless body, but a body without "organization" that escapes from regulated subjectivity into undetermined physical spaces.

It is precisely this nomadic movement that is described in the novel. Moosbrugger becomes disengaged from the social field when mass processes of work distribution fail to include him – he finds himself turned over to the street for weeks at a time and is pushed further to the margins by repeated abuse and lack of respect: "[...] ein unheimliches Gefühl ergriff ihn dann, so als wäre er nicht fest in seiner Haut."[32] By the evening of the murder the feeling of dislocation is complete – spatial boundaries dissolve, Moosbrugger is driven onto an open field at the edge of town to relieve his disorientation, only encountering the girl at a bridge on the sweep back into town. The girl is a disarticulated "partial object"[33] like himself – "ein stellenloses davongelaufenes Dienstmädchen, eine kleine Person, von der man nur zwei lockende Mausaugen unter dem Kopftuch sah."[34] Their encounter is fitful and protracted: she pursues him relentlessly through streets and a park, he quickens his step, fearing violence from her pimp who in fact never emerges from the shadows. Instead of giving in to her entreaties, he stabs at her to get free, "und stach so lange auf sie ein, bis er sie ganz von sich losgetrennt hatte."[35]

Ulrich achieves a stay of execution for Moosbrugger in order to effect a further assessment of his mental condition, but he resolves to do no more than this for him. His interest is almost completely exhausted by the time he reaches his own understanding of Moosbrugger as "ein entsprungenes Gleichnis der Ordnung,"[36] and it is clear that the entry of Agathe into the novel in the third part more or less marks the end of the Moosbrugger section, although it is equally clear that Moosbrugger was part of the slow collapse of events into war and was therefore still an element in Musil's notes and chapter sketches in the late 1930's.

Moosbrugger can be viewed as one of those dismembered bodies without organization Musil assessed as resulting from the broader division of labor.[37]

---

32 Musil: *Der Mann ohne Eigenschaften,* p. 71: "[...] a terrifying feeling then seized him as if he wasn't securely within his own skin."

33 This is a term used by Deleuze-Guattari: *Anti-Oedipus,* pp. 5–6.

34 Musil: *Der Mann ohne Eigenschaften,* p. 73: "an unemployed servant girl on the run, a small person of whom one saw nothing but two captivating eyes beneath a bonnet."

35 Ibid., p. 74: "and stabbed at her until he had completely freed himself of her."

36 Ibid., p. 653: "an escaped metaphor of order."

37 Musil reflects on the division of labor through his protagonist in the following terms (ibid., p. 359): "Ulrich in seiner Achtung vor Fachlichkeit und Spezialistentum, war im Grunde entschlossen, nichts gegen eine solche Trennung der Tätigkeiten einzuwenden. Aber er

Participation in labor generates regulative socialization, just as exclusion from labor leads to alienation. Alienation in turn becomes a line of escape disengaging the subject from regulated processes of ego restraint and sublimation by which the system perpetuates itself. The result is the release of flows in all directions and intensities – the productive energy of desire Deleuze-Guattari ask us to conceive of as a machine driven on to make random couplings and equally random disconnections. In this sense Moosbrugger is indeed an "escaped metaphor of order," a nomad rambling in free space, repeating itself in flows and intensities, the ultimate ordered body without organization.

V. Identity and the End of Character

To sum up so far: the passage of history transfers the construction of identity from subjective spaces to the objective world. Hitherto stable processes of self-constitution are dismantled over time or rendered superfluous. An immediate casualty is the conventional structure by which subjectivity finds its lines in opposition to the material world. As this structure of opposition collapses, there appears to be no impediment to material practices which increasingly gain that autonomy the subject surrenders. As Bergson puts it, consciousness begins to derive itself from the interplay of material elements while at the same time giving rise to the hope that matter might be able to engender intellectual facts of the highest order.[38] According to this version of consciousness, enlightenment about the world is thought to proceed in the first instance from the discrete movement of objects rather than the independent exertions of human perception. As interest shifts away from the activity of subjective perception, a crisis is called forth within that subject – the artificial distinction between subject and object is ended, the subject gets absorbed into the circulation of material objects such as money (from which the true mysteries about

---

gestattete sich immerhin noch selbst zu denken, obgleich er kein Berufsphilosoph war, und augenblicklich malte er sich aus, daß das auf den Weg zum Bienenstaat führen werde. Die Königin wird Eier legen, die Drohnen werden ein der Wollust und dem Geist gewidmetes Leben führen, und die Spezialisten werden arbeiten." "Ulrich, in his respect for the merits of expertise and specialization, had basically resolved not to object to such a division of activity. But he did still allow himself to think although he wasn't a professional philosopher and it was his present view that that would lead to an empire of ants. The queen would lay eggs, the drones would lead a life given over to lust and the intellect and the specialists would do all the work."

38 Bergson: *Matter and Memory*, p. 72.

the world are now thought to issue), and human endeavor finds itself directed towards larger-than-life enactments of the eclipse of the person, notably the "Parallelaktion," where the now incontestable pre-eminence of objective historical processes proceeds through celebration into ritual.

The triumph of materialism is curiously not at all a triumph of action over thought – the "Parallelaktion" doesn't amount to action at all, even though endless hours of drawing-room talk are given over to planning it. Far more telling is the promise to duplicate significant action and thus dispense with the frustratingly diversionary nature of the everyday responses of the individual. The ideal of significant action celebrated by the "Parallelaktion" is won at the expense of characteristic human responses, indeed of character as such. The human being must be dislodged from the everyday and brought to the point of relinquishing the banal once and for all, discarding all that is individual and idiosyncratic – everything that is tied to place, subject, character and time. Reality can thereby be transformed into the sum of significant events on the plane of the abstract, rather than a series of contingent relations on the practical level of the everyday.[39]

Moosbrugger presents an eruption of character just as the grandiloquent lines of the "Parallelaktion" are being cast. This explains the fascination he exerts over his contemporaries. Banality appears to suspend itself as a moment of significant action apparently issues forth from the everyday. For Ulrich, Moosbrugger is the inverse of his own strategy of characterlessness, if not its foil. Moosbrugger enacts action where Ulrich forestalls it through reflection. Moosbrugger enters the circulation of objects as object, Ulrich withdraws from objects in order to salvage the subject. Ulrich's insight is that objective practices have rendered the subject inactive as character. Instead the idiosyncratic, the particular, the individually authentic has been progressively dismantled by the very idea of character – the subject instead turns into the surface across which an endless proliferation of "characteristics" *increasingly dislodged from the person* can be traced.[40] As these characteristics – more accurately to be referred to henceforth as "qualities" – become attached to objects and multiply, the individual relinquishes its hold on character and gives up pri-

---

39 As an early comment in the book makes clear, the newspaper culture of the novel's present age is synonymous with the view that significant events no longer occur on the plane of reality, that is, where action is constrained by the everyday, but on the plane of the abstract – Musil: *Der Mann ohne Eigenschaften*, p. 69.

40 "[…] der unendliche Schnittpunkt der verschiedenen öffentlichen Ansprüche" – Musil: *Gesammelte Werke*, vol. 8., p. 1249. Also quoted in Willemsen: *Das Existenzrecht der Dichtung*, p. 164.

vate spaces to the objective practices of ordered systems and institutions. Issues like morality, once debated at the localized level of the individual, now pass into the care of practices beyond the subject.

"Partial objects" like Moosbrugger become the sole memorials to character, where character is defined as a property of the person. At the same time they accelerate the movement towards objective practices by revealing the excesses of character. For Ulrich they provide confirmation of the end of character and make urgent an alternative defensive strategy of the person. While the subject gains enlightenment from the example of escape commended by renegade character (the case of Moosbrugger), it finds no instruction in the abandonment of complex subjectivity at whose expense this escape has been secured. Accordingly, a strategy must be forged by which a new notion of the person is made compatible with the inviolability of the person grounded independently in a conception of self. Such a strategy must first resist the steady encroachment of objects and objective practices in order ultimately to disable them. This is the task assigned to perception which is taken up in the unfinished (and possibly unfinishable) final section of the novel. In the meantime, the subject retreats from action to an area of protective inscrutability within the self. This interim condition is constituted as a temporary abandonment of characteristics and a seeming cultivation of inaction. It is from here that the moment of escape into a new authenticity of the person is to be planned.

The issue in Musil's *Mann ohne Eigenschaften*, viewed from another angle, is representation. The representation of the subject is destabilized by the encroachment of objective practices at its very center. Representation is thereby removed to the peripheral region of the body's motor responses (which explains why Musil is so trenchantly critical of his age's "culture of the body") from where in extreme cases it is cajoled, exhorted or seduced into joining the circulation of finished forms in the material world. This is the process by which characteristics, once typical of subjectivity, are turned into qualities and appear to accrue the reality of material practices. This becomes the basis of their claim to special significance.

VI. *Kalkwerk*

Bernhard's *Kalkwerk* announces a similar penetration of subjective representation under equally urgent conditions:

> [...] dem Zuschauer biete sich eine gleichmäßig von Fortschritts- und also Maschinenwahnsinn durchzogene Atmosphäre an, in welcher er, gleich wo, ob auf

dem Land oder in der Stadt, immer dieselben Voraussetzungen vorfinde. Wir alle
machten in allem einen von ihm so genannten Gesellschaftsvermischungsprozeß
durch, an dessen Ende der qualifizierte Mensch als Unmensch und das heißt als
Maschine herauskomme.[41]

At issue is the transgression of the boundaries of the subject by proliferating
exterior forms. The result is not only a destabilization of the subject, but its
provision with a new, non-human, mechanical substitute center. Under the
conditions of modern culture, as with Musil, this process alters the nature of
subjective spaces since the enforced and duly achieved transformation of the
person is now marked by a special qualification – an indication of quality as
well as the modification of a previous form, and in any case a verifiable gain
in material practice: "der qualifizierte Mensch als Unmensch und das heißt als
Maschine."

In Bernhard's *Kalkwerk* the experimenter Konrad takes possession of a
disused limeworks in order to further his investigations into human hearing.
Apart from an old employee who is part of the contractual terms of the purchase, Konrad's sole companion is his once beautiful, long crippled wife
whose confinement to a wheelchair makes her an ideal, if reluctant, analytical
subject. Accordingly, she is tyrannized with endless hours of hearing exercises, book readings and one-sided literary exegeses, while Konrad awaits the
time when the painstaking accumulation of data can be concentrated into a
moment of perfect calculation and so made into action: the moment when
thoughts can be put on paper and the study, in its true sense, begun. That moment never arrives. What happens instead is something quite unplanned: the
murder of his wife, for which there can only be one suspect – Konrad himself. As Konrad's arrest is related at the very outset, the course of the story is
represented as a lengthy interrogation not just of a likely murderer (where the
ostensible issue is the search for a motive), but also of consciousness, from
which the precise circumstances of profound dislocation must be recon-
structed. Konrad thus becomes the object of a study he unwittingly passes on
to the reader – one, as he says himself, of interminably lost heads inhabiting
interminably lost bodies on interminably lost continents.[42]

---

41 Bernhard: *Das Kalkwerk*, p. 173: "[...] the spectator enters an atmosphere pervaded in equal
   measure by the madness of progress and of machines, in which – regardless of whether he
   is in the city or the country – he always encounters the same set of conditions. In all things
   we are forced to undergo a process of so-called social mixing and come out of it as human
   beings qualified in inhumanity which is to say as machines."

42 Ibid., p. 135.

VII. Nature and Consciousness

At the heart of the study is the question of the separateness or otherwise of nature:

> [...] er beschäftige sich zwar ununterbrochen mit der Natur und keine andere Beschäftigung fülle sein Gehirn aus, aber er sei und zwar aus diesem Grunde der ununterbrochenen Naturbeschäftigung, kein Naturfreund, ja ganz im Gegenteil [...][43]

In terms of the story, the retreat to the limeworks furnishes Konrad with optimal conditions for the study of hearing. On another level, it presents the conditions under which nature itself can be elicited – not just the external physical nature of one's surroundings, but the true inner nature of the human being. To this extent Konrad's renovation of the limeworks is entirely logical: the returning of the factory to its original state is an excavation of the consciousness which created it. The simplified architectural form will unearth not only a typology of original consciousness, but, according to Konrad, will also reveal consciousness as being entirely coextensive with reflection. Reflection in turn is nothing other than the pure calculation of the human being responsible for engendering life. These are the circumstances in which nature can be merged with purified original culture and the endemic perversion of form of subsequent ages cast off. This also delivers the rationale for the study of human hearing since the most rigorous analysis of the physical state of the human being is certain to elicit the very architecture of human thought. Every exercise, endlessly repeated, will restore those conceptual spaces by design which nature itself has left absent or taken away. The disability of mind of Konrad's wife is therefore the pure surface upon which reason through experiment can demonstrate its priority. And since absolute precision is the goal of the study, nothing less than a moment of perfect reflection can allow the study to achieve its final written form.

The experiments which Konrad undertakes aim to show that perception, under special conditions, can be widened to include the whole of nature. This in turn will adduce the proof that human consciousness informs all natural things, just as all nature is consciousness. This is the idealist conception of nature. It turns the human being – under ideal conditions – into the self-conscious architect of life in the same way that it puts an end to the haphazard and the circumstantial, which only serve to frustrate the advance of the real.

---

43 Ibid., p. 19: "[...] he was forever busy with nature and no other activity filled his head but it was precisely because he was so absorbed with nature that he was no friend of nature, in fact quite the opposite [...]."

Konrad's work thus becomes a search for that unrepeatable moment which will begin and end the study: when spontaneity and reflection coincide, when pure perception can express the reality of the subject, when nature no longer figures forth from nature, but from the human being.

This is why ever more disciplined refinement through mechanical repetition is thought to provide the special moment of insight. Konrad's hearing experiments are designed to instill through habit a kind of ultimate model memory. Rigorous habit, under the special circumstances Konrad provides for, will bring forth by a sort of quantum leap a moment of supreme significance which will transcend habit and experiment to become unrepeatable in practice. This moment will banish from the present the alienation from natural states occasioned by the subject's uncorrected movement away from nature. By such a strategy time will in the end be conquered, the past not only retrieved but also joined seamlessly to the present. Only at this moment – the recovery of perfection – will the present become truly habitable.

Under the terms of Konrad's study, experiment is accorded such seriousness that it soon takes over the place of even minor day-to-day utterances such as greetings. Single words are repeated ceaselessly alongside vowels, consonants and whole sentences, as we are told: "mit dem Wort *Rinnsal* experimentiere er an die zehn Jahre."

> Obwohl er die Studie fertig im Kopf habe, denke er, experimentiere er immer weiter, um die Studie, obwohl er sie fertig im Kopf habe, immer noch mehr zu komplettieren, zu vervollkommnen, abgesehen von der Tatsache, daß er die Studie in jedem Augenblick niederschreiben könnte, ohne Angst haben zu müssen, daß er sie nicht ganz und gar im Kopf habe, wenn er die Möglichkeit hätte, sie plötzlich niederzuschreiben.[44]

Instead of narrowing the gap between performance and reality so that language can function as a reflex of the world and its practices, experiment in fact moves the moment of perfection – that is, when perception and nature are made coexistent – further and further away. Repetition creates habitual motor responses of the body,[45] a sort of impersonal learned recollection, but

---

44 Ibid., p. 92: "He had been experimenting with the word *rivulet* for around ten years." "Although he has completed the study in his mind, he thinks, he wants to go on experimenting – although he has finished the study in his mind – in order to refine it ever more completely, to perfect it, regardless of the fact that he could write the study up at any moment without having the fear that he didn't have it entirely in his head if he in fact had the opportunity of suddenly writing it up."

45 Virilio has interpreted the attempt to move the soul from the head, where it has resided since antiquity, to the body's motor responses in the science of modern sport in terms of the optimal reduction of the time needed for reflection. The body thus appears to act inde-

it is unable to liberate that ineffable connection between the image of memory and the image of the real. As Bergson tells us, to act is to induce the memory of the past to shrink.[46] Experiment increasingly finds itself occupying the present and forestalling real action to prevent the past, to which the image of perfection may be joined, from disappearing altogether.

Bernhard leaves us in no doubt that pathological circumstances are being described. Konrad is allowed an insight, but it occurs on the eve of the murder and coincides with the first sign of his own hearing loss:

> [...] kurz vor dem Unglück [...] sei er sich der Tatsache bewußt, daß es überhaupt keinen idealen, geschweige denn idealsten Moment oder Augenblick, die Studie niederschreiben zu können, gebe, weil es niemals und in keiner Sache und in nichts den idealen, geschweige denn den idealsten Moment oder Augenblick oder Zeitpunkt geben könnte.[47]

The merest indication of infirmity in any matter, let alone a matter so intimately connected to the study such as hearing, removes the hope that the study can be completed. The endlessly postponed moment of writing is therefore exposed as the pretext not to write at all, as the evasion of action under the influence of a contemptible idea – not the search for the real but the fear of it. It is presumably for this reason that Konrad compensates for inactivity with a moment of pure action which both ends the study as well as the life of his wife. His is therefore a double culpability: he is culpable not only on account of murder, but also because of a murderous loyalty to an idea in whose name a tyranny upon others as well as upon self was executed. In fact murder becomes entirely consistent with idealism. The search for the ideal conjunction of perception and the reality of the object is, properly speaking, only achievable by a death: the death of the subject in whom all perception can be extinguished forever.

It is above all here that I see a connection between Bernhard's *Kalkwerk* and Musil's *Der Mann ohne Eigenschaften*. Both works take up the issue of encroachments upon subjectivity and the defensive strategies they engender. They investigate the pathology of form and of forms. Here the link with violence in the external world becomes instructive. Musil's protagonist resists subjectivity because he fears the descent into the circulation of finished forms that have co-

---

pendently of thought and with an erasure of the past which serves to remove any trace of the doubt which might complicate or even prevent action – Virilio: *Die Eroberung des Körpers*, p. 103.

46 Bergson: *Matter and Memory*, p. 106.

47 Bernhard: *Das Kalkwerk*, p. 210: "[...] shortly before the disaster [...] he became aware of the fact that there was no ideal – let alone the most ideal – moment to write up the study because in no thing or things could it be said that there was such an ideal, let alone the ideal moment or point in time or instance."

me to condition it. He follows a utopian vision of the person that aims to rein-
state the individual and forestall that violence of forms of which Moosbrugger
becomes a prototype. Accordingly, Moosbrugger shows up the fate of a fully
determined subjectivity that has become synonymous with alienation under
the conditions of modern capitalism. Bernhard constructs a similar pathology
of forms in *Kalkwerk*. Konrad's investigations into hearing presuppose not only the dominance of reflection over action, but its tyranny. It is a tyranny under
which perfection is not merely the precondition that makes action possible, it is
action's only condition. The ideal conjunction of reflection and action is then
exposed as a moment of pure violence. It is the ideal itself which ultimately reveals the despotism of order. As the moment that precipitates the murder is the
moment when Konrad identifies his own loss of hearing, we may assume that
violence – the impatience with life that will brook no physical weakness – is now
cyclical (Konrad will later be punished for his own infirmity). Under such conditions there is no difference between the order of subjectivity and the organization of the external world – they become perfectly and violently coextensive.

JUSTUS FETSCHER
Zentrum für Literaturforschung, Berlin

"Les peuples meurent, pour que Dieu vive": Gertrud Kolmar's Consecration of the Protagonists in the Drama of the French Revolution[1]

Abstract: This paper raises the question whether the German poet Gertrud Kolmar's (1894–1940) texts on the French Revolution can be read as representative of those central European Jews who, according to Zygmund Bauman, were the foremost indicators of modernity's tendency to produce ambivalence while simultaneously aiming to eliminate it. Kolmar drew on Rolland's drama *Danton* and the enthusiastic reception it received among pacifist Germans after World War I. Writing in 1933, she countered the Nazi rise to power with her idealized reincarnation of St. Just and Robespierre and her interpretation of the combination of striving for justice and sacrifice. In suffering defeat they rescue divine justice, a concept which justifies violence and death.

I. Modern Culture and Ambivalence

"'Tis in ourselves that we are thus or thus," Iago says to Roderigo (I,iii). What sounds like an iambic verse turns out to be the opening of a radical precept: "Our bodies are our gardens, to which our wills are gardeners; so that if we will plant nettles or sow lettuce, set hyssop or weed up thyme, supply it with one gender of herbs or distract it with many – either to have it sterile with idleness or manured with industry – why, the power and corrigible authority of this lies in our wills." For modern man all options are or seem to be open,

---

1 I would like to thank the following persons who helped me with hints, objections and encouragement to write this article: Barbara Breysach, Bernd Hüppauf, Wolfgang Klein, Katharina Ochse, Helmut Peitsch, Brian Poole, Diana Zimmermann (for drawing my attention to Rolland's *Théâtre de la Révolution*) and the staff of the Schiller Nationalmuseum/Deutsches Literaturarchiv (Marbach). I am indebted to Jean Pietrowicz for bringing my text in line with the correct usage of the English language.

be it diversity or contraction of his spirit, a leisure class or an active life as a merchant or soldier.

What modernity was going to encompass as an object of its self-making though was not primarily the individual but the whole body politic. Zygmunt Bauman defines modernity as "an age of artificial order and of grand societal designs, the era of planners, visionaries and – more generally – 'gardeners' who treat society as a virgin plot of land to be expertly designed."[2] Modernity opened up the possibility of the Holocaust inasmuch as this era is characterized by a utopian thrust to perfect society and by a new organizational technique of implementing what the state, armed with a bureaucratic working force, is aiming at. This process breaks down a whole into pieces of discrete problems calling for expert knowledge to solve them. By definition this process cannot stay idle nor cultivate weed. Its gardening does not respect the botany of the human species characterized by Theophrastus. It sets out to utilize its ground by appropriating most of the plants for functional purposes and rooting out those considered undesirable. The violence inflicted on its human objects is a product of *this civilizing* process. Bauman, following and at the same time challenging Norbert Elias, maintains that this process implies "the redeployment of violence, and the redistribution of access to violence."[3] Violence is centralized and reassembled in the "modern state with its monopoly of physical violence and coercion."[4]

Two years after his *Modernity and the Holocaust*, Bauman elaborated on his theses in *Modernity and Ambivalence* (1991). He gives an historically more precise dating of the inception of what he means by modernity. It began when the state's monopoly of violence was advocated in the *Leviathan*: "[W]e can agree," Bauman writes, "with Stephen L. Collins, who [...] took Hobbes' vision for the birthmark of the consciousness of order, that is – in our rendition – of modern consciousness, that is of modernity."[5]

The crucial test this modernity exposed its contemporaries to, Baumann argues, is Jewish assimilation. The most conspicuous paradigm of the project of modernity being the fate of Central European Jewry between the early nineteenth century and the Shoah. This history serves as Bauman's key example for modernity's incessant production of its own ambivalence. Assimila-

---

2   Bauman: *Modernity and the Holocaust*, p. 113.
3   Ibid., p. 97; cf. p. 107.
4   Ibid., p. 111.
5   Bauman: *Modernity and Ambivalence*, p. 5. Bauman might thereby react to some objections raised by Zipes: "The Holocaust, Modernity and Tough Jews," and especially Oxaal: "Sociology, History and the Holocaust."

tion, as he puts it, is typically modern in that "[i]t derives its character and significance [...] from the bid of the modern state to linguistic, cultural and ideological unification of the population." For only in modern times "[t]he *nationalization of the state* (or, rather, *etatization of the nation*) blended the issue of political loyalty and trustworthiness (seen as conditions for granting the citizenship rights) with that of cultural conformity."[6]

This points to Bauman's other revision of the theory of modernity. What he calls *gardening* was first conceived, in *Modernity and the Holocaust*, as tantamount to modern science (social science, social engineering) as well as to modern culture and art, modern aesthetics.[7] Obviously, Bauman's implicit definition of modern art as based on the equation of beauty and order does not apply to all major tendencies in Western arts since Romanticism. In his new book, Bauman distinguishes between modernity and modernism. The latter he conceives as a constant appeal against the fallacy and failure of modernity. And therefore in his view modern culture is "a 'project' of *postmodernity* in a prodromal stage"[8] upheld by the foremost artists and theorists of the twentieth century.

In line with a number of other historians Bauman identifies the Jews of Central Europe as the group whose artistic and intellectual manifestations first and most sharp-sightedly reveal the taboos and inconsistencies of modernity: "The assimilatory process, that trademark of modern politics, cast the Jews in social contexts from which contradictions of modernity were most poignantly experienced and hence easier to scan, to comprehend and to theorize. Jewish contributions to modern culture are better understood not as expressions of 'Jewish struggle with modernity', but as by-products of 'modernity's struggle with itself'."[9] In contradistinction to the aforesaid cultural conformity, the modern state claims that the works of Jewish writers like Freud, Simmel, Kafka and Derrida constitute "the seminal contribution to the obstreperous, critical and rebellious culture of modernity."[10]

---

6   Both quotes from Bauman: *Modernity and Ambivalence*, p. 141. Bauman's italics.
7   See Bauman: *Modernity and the Holocaust*, p. 92.
8   Bauman: *Modernity and Ambivalence*, p. 4, n. 1.
9   Ibid., p. 154; cf. p. 157 and chapter 5.
10   Ibid., p. 195.

II. The Sublime of War and Revolution in Kant

As the strengths as well as intricacies of Bauman's argument hinge, in my view, on the schematical picture he gives of the history of the last three centuries, one might question the neatness of his clear-cut line between cultural conformity required by the modern state and rebellious culture performed by the outsiders of that state-run society. Bauman's historical analyses mostly rely on second-hand sources. They tend to give a rather static and *ex eventu* reading of what might have happened.[11] One should not, however disparage (as post-garde movements doomed to failure) all attempts by Central European Jews to make theirs the universalist promises of the modern age. For them it was not the English Civil War but the French Revolution that, implementing the nationalization of the state or, rather, etatization of the nation, cleared the way for their forced entry into modernity. The thinker to spell out the consequences of this entry was hence not Hobbes but Kant.

Inasmuch as modern aesthetics when it came into contact with politics turned out to be an aesthetics of the sublime (rather than of the beautiful), Kant's *Kritik der Urteilskraft* (*Critique of Judgment*, 1790) might be perceived as its magna charta. Aesthetically, Kant contends, the warrior is superior to the statesman because the former is capable of proving "die Unbezwinglichkeit seines Gemüts durch Gefahr." Even war itself, he goes on, "wenn er mit Ordnung und Heiligachtung der bürgerlichen Rechte geführt wird, hat etwas Erhabenes an sich, und macht sogleich die Denkungsart des Volks, welches ihn auf diese Weise führt, nur desto erhabener, je mehreren Gefahren es ausgesetzt war."[12]

This blunt contention does not seem to be reconcilable with Kant's later plea *Zum ewigen Frieden* (*Towards Perpetual Peace*, 1795). It should, however, be noticed that Kant's aesthetic vindication of war is bound to two preconditions of how to wage it, preconditions that date from 1789: First, that civil rights should be respected, even hallowed, and second, that it ought to be the people (and not the head of state) who are waging this war as theirs. Given the political geography of 1790, it becomes clear that Kant is thinking of revolutionary France and that he is predetermining the conditions under which war can be justified.

---

11   I should add, though, that Bauman cautions his readers against such a perspective (ibid., p. 164).

12   Kant: *Kritik der Urteilskraft – Gesammelte Schriften* vol. 5, pp. 165–485, quote pp. 262–3 (§ 28). A Baumanian reading would perhaps stress the postulate of order to be upheld in battling, whereas I shall underscore the other part of Kant's conditional clause, viz. the consecration of civil rights.

Kant revises and reaffirms his stance toward the Revolution in his *Der Streit der Fakultäten* (*The Conflict of the Faculties*, 1798). He argues that none other than a republican constitution would lead to conditions that will principally rule out offensive warfare. Moreover, the Revolution even in its failure has testified to a moral disposition in mankind. Buttressed by the German tradition to moralize and politicize theater as a medium of compensation for historical powerlessness and inaction, Kant adapts for his use the well-known self-representation of the Revolutionists as *dramatis personae*, a metaphor that will nourish a whole strand of modern Revolution dramas, from Büchner via Schnitzler and Rolland to Genet and Peter Weiss, blurring the spheres of histrionic and historical power play. In Kant's view, not the (French) actors but the (German) spectators of the Revolutionary drama of 1789ff. have proven this by the very fact of their aloofness from it.[13]

This line of argument introduces more than just a defense of the German bystanders of the Revolution who followed the developments on the other side of the Rhine with the theoretical enthusiasm of staunch idealists barred from entering history. As Kant put it, their *"Teilnehmung* dem Wunsche nach" (participation by wish) compensated their own passivity; also the apparent failure of the Revolution which, by 1978, had been tinged with "Elend und Greueltaten" (misery and atrocities).

The literary case I am outlining here constitutes both an extension and an extreme hypostatization of this German tradition of telepathic identification with and sympathetic restaging of the French Revolution. Gertrud Kolmar, a German-Jewish poet (1894–1943), took up the rhetoric, iconography and philosophical program of the Revolution because she interpreted them as promises granted to herself as to everyone else. She believed in the lasting validity of this historical offer – even after its failure, or rather due to it. Robespierre, she argued, had "declared the Revolution permanent. In leaving it unaccomplished, he made it possible that it could be taken up and be continued at any time. And the 'abyss of the Revolution'? He threw himself into that abyss as a victim like Marcus Curtius, not to close it but to keep it open."[14]

---

13   This and the following quotes are taken from Immanuel Kant: *Der Streit der Fakultäten – Gesammelte Schriften* vol. 7, pp. 1–116, quotes p. 85 (italics there). On the theatrics of the revolution, see Butwin: "The French Revolution as Theatrum Mundi"; Grimm: "Über Spiel und Ernst in einigen Revolutionsdramen"; Leiteritz: *Revolution als Schauspiel*. Testifying to the renewed interest in this relation in the wake of the Russian Revolution, but without theoretical interest: Widmann: *Theater und Revolution*, pp. 145–7.

14   Kolmar: "Das Bildnis Robespierres. Mitgeteilt von Johanna Zeitler", p. 580: "Man warf ihm vor, daß er 'die Revolution nicht geschlossen' habe. Nein, er hat sie in Permanenz erklärt. Indem er sie unvollendet ließ, ermöglichte er, daß sie jederzeit wieder aufgenommen

This event should in the end secure Kolmar a place in the tradition of the idea of a chiliastically perfected world. In Auschwitz where she was murdered she definitely did not find this place. She refrained, though, from escaping the Shoah by staying in Nazi Germany and sticking to an idea of Divine Justice in history that could embrace her and the sacrifice of entire nations. Following the lead of her revolutionary heroes, she tried, literally, to make sense of her own victimization. Thus she was not revealing modernity's ambivalences by laying bare its weaknesses. Rather, she spelled out a paradox of modernity: adherence by sacrifice. While Kolmar was clinging to the ideals of the French Revolution, she surpassed what Kant had called an "uneigennützige Teilnehmung" in the Revolution, one that is linked with the "Gefahr, diese Parteilichkeit könne [...] sehr nachteilig werden" ("risk that this partiality could turn out to be very disadvantageous"). Poetically re-establishing the Revolution of 1789, if not of 1793/94, she both rescinded and restated the self-declared national revolution of 1933.

Between these dates, the works of the expressionist poet Georg Heym might serve as a staging post, although *ex negativo*. His is the best-known poetic depiction of the French Revolution in Wilhelmine Germany.[15] Sonnet-shaped portraits of the protagonists of the Parisian stage from 1789 to 1794 testify to the boredom and frustration he experienced. It made no difference to him whether he evoked the execution of the deposed French King or the dismantled Jacobin leader Robespierre. Writing under the impact of Georg Büchner's tragedy *Dantons Tod* (1837), Heym drew on the colorful theatrical signals these events had to offer – regardless of whatever historically feasible consequences they may have had.

The one French hero with whom he seemed to identify in a more than transitory and playful manner is not a victim but the self-declared heir of the Revolution. Heym's first Napoleon poem is dated 1904.[16] And another cycle of sonnets written in 1910, a few months before those dedicated to the Revolution, celebrates the victories and camaraderie of the Napoleonic army. By naming a troop unit the "Express train of Brussels" ("Der Brüssler Eilzug"), said to "rush through the evening and darkness" ("Durchrast den Abend und die Dunkelheit"), Heym associated the innovative quality of the French Revo-

---

    und fortgeführt werden konnte. Und der 'Abgrund der Revolution'? Er warf sich selbst als Opfer hinein wie Marcus Curtius, nicht, ihn zu schließen, sondern ihn offen zu halten."

15   See Heym: *Dichtungen und Schriften*, esp. vol. 1: *Lyrik*, pp. 86–90, 134, 165, 181, 188, 228; vol. 2: *Prosa und Dramen*, pp. 6–18, 733–7; vol. 3: *Tagebücher, Träume, Briefe*, pp. 164, 203.

16   On Heym's admiration for Napoleon see Seiler: *Die historischen Dichtungen Georg Heyms*, pp. 142–52, 279–82, 287–8.

lution with technological progress, and Napoleon's campaign with the swiftness of the modern war machinery.[17]

III. Kolmar's Robespierre (between Büchner and Benjamin)

Whereas Heym's poetry was seeking to outdo the banality of life of his own
time, the series of poems Kolmar wrote on the French Revolution is based on
her experiences as a reader of Heym, Büchner and Romain Rolland, as a
woman and as a Jew. Like Heym, Gertrud Kolmar wrote about Robespierre's
death. Yet, as she explained in a letter to Walter Benjamin written in 1934 –
the same year, it is to be assumed, she produced her whole *Robespierre* cycle –
"there is nothing more different than these two poems," Heym's and hers.[18]
In fact, some of her verses can be understood as replies to Heym's sonnets.
Where he, for instance, imagines Louis XVI plucking at his shawl on the day
of the *états généraux* (181), Kolmar deliberately deceives the readers' wish for
omina: "The ruler moves/ Unconsciously his right hand to his neck, senses –
// Nothing" (383–4).[19]

It might therefore seem that this poet aims at greater historical accuracy.
We know from her sister that Gertrud Kolmar's French was perfect. She
worked as an interpreter and spent some time in Paris. Her most enduring im-
pressions concerning the Revolution stem, however, from dramas. She knew
by heart scenes from Büchner's *Dantons Tod*. Considering that she visited Max
Reinhardt's Berlin theaters (597), it is likely that she watched his famous mise

---

17 Heym: *Dichtungen und Schriften* vol. 2, p. 42.

18 "[…] es gibt nichts Verschiedeneres als jene beiden Gedichte," quoted from Kolmar:
"Zwei Briefe an Walter Benjamin," p. 123. – On Kolmar see two recent documentations:
Woltmann, ed.: *Gertrud Kolmar 1894–1943*; Eichmann-Leutenegger: *Gertrud Kolmar. Leben
und Werk in Texten und Bildern*. As to her poems on the French Revolution, Robespierre and
Napoleon compare: Wiesinger: "Gertrud Kolmar. Rue Saint-Honoré;" Byland: *Zu den Gedichten Gertrud Kolmars*; Smith: "Gertrud Kolmar's Life and Works," pp. 7–8, 34–7; Döhl:
"Gertrud Kolmars 'Ludwig XVI., 1775'"; Mattenklott: "Gertrud Kolmar. Metaphorischer
Schattenriß," pp. 200–2; Schlenstedt: "Suche nach Halt in haltloser Lage. Die Kulturarbeit
deutscher Juden nach 1933 in Deutschland und die Dichterin Gertrud Kolmar," pp.
737–40; Brandt: *Widerspruch und Übereinstimmung in Gertrud Kolmars Gedichtszyklus "Das Wort
der Stummen,"* esp. vol. 1, pp. 102–28, 218–25 and annex, vol. 2, pp. 7–9 (I am referring to
this version and not to the book version: Brandt: *Schweigen ist der Ort der Antwort: Eine Analyse des Gedichtzyklus "Das Wort der Stummen" von Gertrud Kolmar*); Erdle: *Antlitz – Mord – Gesetz. Figuren des Anderen bei Gertrud Kolmar und Emmanuel Lévinas*, pp. 247–57; Woltmann: *Gertrud Kolmar – Leben und Werk*, pp. 67–72, 187–97.

19 All quotations from Kolmar poems are taken from Kolmar: *Das lyrische Werk*.

en scène of Büchner's drama. It was shown there starting in 1916, only six years after the expressionist theater director Leopold Jessner had staged a spectacular version of this tragedy.[20]

Kolmar's poems represent a restaging of Büchner's drama turning upside down what Heym had made of it. Her Danton is despised as a hedonist and exhibitionist, a man who takes twice of what he gives. Time and again he is characterized by that shameless nakedness he proposes in Büchner's drama as a fitting attitude of avowing human sexuality. Two Kolmar poems present a confrontation between him and Robespierre along the lines of Büchner's tragedy (391–2, 426–7). But this time it is Robespierre who is the hero. He is Kolmar's icon. In Büchner, he evokes himself as a "blood Messiah who sacrifices without being sacrificed."[21]

In Kolmar's lyrical biography as well as necrology of his character Robespierre turns a true saint, if not a new Christ. He shares this role with Saint-Just who is called "the chosen" (401) and even more so with Marat whose blood is said to "stream over France into the world."[22] Kolmar's poems

20   See Boeser and Vatková, ed.: *Max Reinhardt in Berlin*, pp. 338 and 341–2: a list of Reinhardt's work in Berlin specifying two *mises en scènes* of *Dantons Tod*, namely at the Deutsches Theater, premiered Dec. 15, 1916, and at the Großes Schauspielhaus, premiered Dec. 17, 1921. For photographs from the show see p. 76 and 88, compare descriptions of Reinhardt's *Dantons Tod* given in this book pp. 193–5, 234. The distribution of roles is given in Huesmann: *Welttheater Reinhardt. Bauten Spielstätten Inszenierungen*. No. 1172. Reviews of this *mise en scène* are assembled in Fetting, ed.: *Von der Freien Bühne zum politischen Theater*, vol. 1, pp. 553–69 (concerning Reinhardt's 1916 staging of *Dantons Tod*). Another contemporary description of this *Dantons Tod* has been published by Herald: "Dantons Tod," in Stern and Herald, eds.: *Reinhardt und seine Bühne. Bilder von der Arbeit des Deutschen Theaters*, pp. 86- 91. Herald stresses the choreography of the masses, the atmospheric and dramatic effect of the distribution of shadow and light and the simultaneous acting of scenes in the *mise en scène*. Indirectly he links the dynamics of history displayed in this drama to the experience of WW I: "so wirkt [...] St. Justs große Revolutionsrede [...] vom Weg der Geschichte, auf dem die zertretenen Millionen erbarmungslos liegen bleiben müssen [...] doppelt stark." (p. 91) Compare Widmann: *Theater und Revolution*, pp. 145–7; Jacobsohn: *Max Reinhardt*, pp. 131–6; Kindermann: *Theatergeschichte Europas* vol. 8: *Naturalismus und Impressionismus*. 1st Part: *Deutschland/Österreich/Schweiz*, pp. 521–30 (there were times when Kindermann would not have heralded Reinhardt's fame). For an interpretation by a more reliable theater historian see Styan: *Max Reinhardt*, pp. 46–50.

21   I:6: "Jawohl, Blutmessias, der opfert und nicht geopfert wird." Büchner: *Dantons Tod – Werke und Briefe*, p. 90. Earlier (I:2), it is a woman that hails Robespierre as "den Messias, der gesandt ist, zu wählen und zu richten [...]. Seine Augen sind die Augen der Wahl, seine Hände die Hände des Gerichts!" (p. 75) Gertrud Kolmar might have identified with the character of Robespierre; she adores the Revolutionary leader as a chosen one who does not himself choose, like Danton, his loves but rather selects those who are to be sentenced.

22   Kolmar: *Das lyrische Werk*, p. 410: "[...] sein Blut / Über Frankreich strömend in die Welt."

amount to an epitaph for Jacobin martyrs. But it is Robespierre who is placed on top of that epitaph. The very first of her poems addresses him asking "Is your Easter now?"[23] And so he is named the sacrificial lamb (453), shown when forgiving his enemy (414), prayed to as the judge of the world (431–2) and, once killed, scorned as "You son of God, you pride of a ruler,/ Now you are similar again to men."[24] What Büchner's Desmoulins, an ally of Danton's, said about him, "He was always ominous and lonely,"[25] is here regarded as a tragic and honest feature. His rank lies in that there is no one equaling him (434), so that when he dies his hands are "untouched and pale and slender."[26]

In this purity Kolmar brings together physical abstention with the innocence of a saint. This quality differs from Christ's *noli me tangere* in that Robespierre has not yet found glorification and sanctification in a holy text. Kolmar's poems attempt to fill this gap but they are much too modest to be blasphemous. The voice of these texts takes on and takes over the accusations and, moreover, the lamentations of those who are shown defending and mourning the assassinated Jacobins. Like Simone Évard, the widow of Marat or Éléonore Duplay, the elder daughter of Robespierre's landlord, Kolmar might have considered herself the only person to whisper for the dead Robespierre "a disparaged prayer" ("ein verrufenes Gebet") as a "poor old one,"[27] a woman comparable to his mother who was the fictional speaker of a Robespierre poem some pages before. According to the sources from which Kolmar is likely to have drawn, Walter Wiesinger has identified this woman as Catherine Théot, a sectarian whom Robespierre declined to condemn and who called herself the mother of God.[28]

So it turns out to be the female task to preserve the heritage of things past and men who have died. Kolmar's intellectual reason for revering them is evident. They are celebrated for having overcome their selfish desires, for having sacrificed their well-being on behalf of humanity. They stand against a

---

23 "Sind deine Ostern jetzt?" Ibid., p. 376. The poem "Bildnis Robespierres" written in autumn 1933 but not pertaining to this cycle calls Robespierre "chosen and derided already" ("Erwählt und schon verlacht") and portrays him as a new, less powerful and thus more lamentable Christ of the enlightened eighteenth century. Kolmar: *Frühe Gedichte (1917–22). Das Wort der Stummen (1933)*.

24 Kolmar: *Das lyrische Werk*, p. 427: "Du Gottessohn, du Herrscherstolz, / Nun bist du Menschen wieder gleich."

25 Büchner: *Dantons Tod – Werke und Briefe*, p. 97: "Es war immer finster und einsam" (II:3).

26 Kolmar: *Das lyrische Werk*, p. 427: "Sie waren unberührt und bleich und schmal."

27 Ibid., p. 452: "[…] ein verrufenes Gebet," "eine arme Alte."

28 See Wiesinger: "Gertrud Kolmar. Rue Saint-Honoré," p. 525.

crowd of pettifoggers and fools, soon renamed thieves and fools,[29] against a "Nude and glittering [...] Golden Youth."[30] For these heroes are *just* – not in a legal but in a theological, eschatological sense. Robespierre, above any other, is depicted by Kolmar as the icon of justice, holding and attentively watching the scales of its balance and threatening with its sword (376, 442 etc.). He is the allegory of a *fiat mundus* thereby providing a poem on him with the title ... *et pereat mundus* (431–2). His portrait emerges as that of a just punisher and avenger as he retaliates for the pain and oppression suffered for "more than a thousand years" (397).

Evidently this Robespierre incarnates an experience of injustice inherited through the generations. Assuming such a function, he is paralleled by Kolmar with Isaiah and the other prophets of the Thora. He has "the tongue of the prophet" (392). Like Marat he incorporates the passion of Christ crucified, the early Christians persecuted (393–4) *and* the Jews witnessing "Light [...] helplessly flickering on stifling stale Ghetto mists."[31] Having transgressed, like Marat has, "the reflection of the pyres,/ When Spaniards baptized withered Jews,"[32] Robespierre's prophet tongue cries out for what the Jews could not yet claim. In a programmatic poem "We Jews", the chorus that gives the text its title says: "If only I could raise my voice to be a blazing torch/ Amidst the darkened desert of the world, and thunder:/ Justice! Justice! Justice!"[33]

Consistent as this pattern of projections may seem, it remains problematic that Kolmar in her poems "glorifies even the grandeur of the perpetrators to whose victims she is going to belong." According to Hans Byland, this irony points to Kolmar's strangeness vis-à-vis history. Modernity was to her, as he puts it, outright anti-lyrical and inhuman.[34] Therefore she had to counter the political reality in which she lived by means of her poetic visions. The French

---

29   Kolmar: *Das Lyrische Werk*, p. 456: "Die Krämer [...] und die Narren," "Diebe [...] Narren."

30   Ibid., p. 451: "Nackt und glitzend ritt die Goldne Jugend."

31   Ibid., p. 399: "Licht [...], / Gegen stickig schale Ghettodünste / Hilflos flackernd."

32   Ibid., p. 400: "Widerglanz der Scheiterhaufen, / Wenn Spanier welke Juden taufen."

33   This translation is Smith's: "Gertrud Kolmar's Life and Works," p. 115. The German text reads: "O könnt ich wie lodernde Fackel in die finstere Wüste der Welt / Meine Stimme heben: Gerechtigkeit! Gerechtigkeit! Gerechtigkeit!" – Kolmar: *Das Lyrische Werk*, p. 102. On this poem, compare Zeitler in Kolmar: "Das Bildnis Robespierres. Mitgeteilt von Johanna Zeitler," pp. 556–7; Schlenstedt: "Suche nach Halt in haltloser Lage," pp. 738–9.

34   Byland: *Zu den Gedichten Gertrud Kolmars*, p. 118: "Sie verherrlicht auch die Grösse der Täter, zu deren Opfern sie gehören wird." And: "Die Moderne ist ihr das Antilyrische und Unmenschliche schlechthin."

Revolution that she depicts in order to rehabilitate its name in front of, and against, the "national revolution" of the Nazi party is not identical with the events of 1789. She creates her own revolution. Not things past but permanence. Not a date in history *per se* but one in salvation history.

One might ask whether this enmity toward history could have had something in common with the revolutionary messianism that Kolmar's cousin Walter Benjamin tried to establish as a philosophy of history. Benjamin would certainly not have agreed in consecrating the revolutionists. The theocratic end of history should not be evoked by contaminating in advance its immanent (worldly) precinct. But when Kolmar and Benjamin point to the moment of revolution, their metaphors resemble each other. They suggest the suspension of time whose continuity is brought to a standstill that violently changes the world. Kolmar's Robespierre "Grasped at the dial of the world's time,/ Grasped as with claws both hands' ends/ And full of pain and trembling halted them."[35] In the fifteenth of his theses *Über den Begriff der Geschichte*, Benjamin speculated about the revolution's power to suspend time.[36]

IV. Rolland's *Théâtre de la Révolution* in Germany

As to their dramatic sources, Kolmar's visions differed from Heym's in that she viewed the French Revolution not only in the light of Büchner's *Dantons Tod* but even more so in the light of Romain Rolland's *Danton* and, arguably, his earlier *Les loups*. At the turn of the century, the French author embarked on producing a dramatic "Iliade du peuple français": his *Théâtre de la Révolution*. Of the ten plays planned, the first four, published between 1898 and 1902, made no lasting impression on the French public. Only after the experiences of WW I and the Russian Revolution the dramas were revived and esteemed, this time on the other side of the Rhine. In Germany they became fashionable between 1920 and 1925. Less than four years after his mise en scène of *Dantons Tod*, Max Reinhardt staged the German première of *Danton* at the Großes Schauspielhaus Berlin on February 14, 1920.[37]

---

35 Kolmar: *Das lyrische Werk*, p. 425: "Griff in das Zifferblatt der Weltenzeit, / Griff wie mit Krallen beide Zeigerenden / Und hielt sie mühevoll und zitternd an."

36 Quoted from Benjamin: *Gesammelte Schriften*, vol. 1, 2, pp. 701–2. Cf. his *Theologisch-politisches Fragment*.

37 Reviews of this *mise en scène* are accessible in Rühle, ed.: *Theater für die Republik im Spiegel der Kritik* vol. 1, pp. 204–9. Boeser and Vatková provide photographs from the *Danton* performance (Boeser and Vatková, eds.: *Max Reinhardt in Berlin*, pp. 38, 76, 195, 233) and a sketch of Reinhardt's stage setting (p. 212). For the distribution of roles see Huesmann: *Welttheater*

The motives for Reinhardt's interest in Rolland's plays might be inferred from two other contemporary German-speaking Jewish intellectuals. Both Wilhelm Herzog and Stefan Zweig owed to Rolland their conversion from war-abiding to the humanist and pacifist positions they upheld by the end of 1914. Herzog, since 1915 the foremost interpreter of Rolland's thought vis-à-vis the German public, opened the first post-War issue of his periodical *Das Forum* with his translations of excerpts from *Les loups* and of the full text of *Danton*.[38] Later on Zweig praised in his *Romain Rolland. Der Mensch und das Werk* (1921) the dramatic and moral qualities of the project of the Revolution dramas. It seems that Zweig's deep-felt sympathies for them centered on his gratitude for *Les loups* (1898). Zweig suggested to his German readers that the defenders of Dreyfus must have seen in it a "dramatic symbolization" of their commitment to justice.[39]

But some of the Dreyfusards had failed to do so because they were, in 1898, disappointed by the play. In their view, it mirrored, Rolland's distanced position.[40] Rolland believed in an all-encompassing natural harmony. However, feelings of resentment and contempt vis-a-vis the Jewish society let to a deeply ambivalent attitude toward the Dreyfus affair. He occasionally acted as an anti-Semitic defender of the fatherland and the honor of its army. "On lit en eux," that is on the Jews, he wrote in late 1897, "'*Pereat! Pereat* l'armeé, la patrie, la république, pourvu que notre Dreyfus soit vengé!'"[41]

Reinhardt, No. 1172. On the overall vogue Rolland's Revolution dramas enjoyed in the Weimar Republic cf. Kempf: *Romain Rolland et l'Allemagne*, pp. 241–2; Nedeljkovic: *Romain Rolland et Stefan Zweig. Affinités et influences littéraires et spirituelles 1910-1942*, p. 295.

38   See Rolland: *Die Wölfe* (III, 1) and *Rolland: Danton* in: *Das Forum* (1918/1919). In his editorial, Herzog praised Rolland as the leader of a yet to be founded pacifist international league of intellectuals (pp. 6–9). – René Cheval calls Herzog the leading spokesman for Rolland in Germany in 1915 (Cheval: *Romain Rolland, l'Allemagne et la guerre*, p. 403; cf. p. 433 n. 2). Recent articles on the correspondence between Zweig and Rolland emphasize the latter's key role in turning Zweig's stance into a clearly universalistic one: Natter: "Quelle Europe: Stefan Zweig et Romain Rolland face à la montée du nationalisme"; and Vergne-Cain and Rudent: "Lettres dans la mêlée."

39   Zweig: *Romain Rolland. Der Mann und das Werk*, pp. 90–1. Now easily accessible, together with Zweig's further statements on Rolland, in Zweig: *Romain Rolland*, ed. by Knut Beck.

40   On the disappointment Rolland's play met with on both sides when premiered in 1898 see Robichez: *Le symbolisme au théâtre: Lugne-Poe et les débuts de l'Œuvre*, pp. 183–7, Rolland: *Mémoires*, pp. 290–5, and Rolland: *Choix de lettres à Malwida von Meysenbug*, pp. 228, 231–3.

41   Quoted from Blum: *Romain Rolland, "Les loups" et l'affaire Dreyfus*, p. 158. I am indebted to this study. In Blum's view, *Les loups* is basically Dreyfusard and has been received as such in spite of Rolland's unrelenting efforts to declare it an aesthetic statement that declines to take sides (see his then unpublished preface to *Les loups* in: Péguy and Rolland: *Une amitié française. Correspondance*, pp. 311–7) and to revise it in that sense. – In a similar vein, Rolland

Rolland sent another strong anti-Dreyfusard letter to the theatre director Lugné-Poe three months before the latter staged the premiere of Les *loups*. This correspondence reveals Rolland's uneasiness in simultaneously veiling and unveiling the applicability of his drama to the Dreyfus case.[42] The connection with this debate was evident though. The play shows a quarrel among officers of the French revolutionary army during its campaign in the French-occupied German Rhineland. By means of a forged letter, officer Verrat accuses his comrade d'Oyron of spying for the coalition forces and a story emerges which in many respects mirrors the Dreyfus affair.

German readings of Les *loups* seem to have been misled by the character of commander Verrat, whose name is the German word for treachery. They failed to notice that Rolland wanted to counter their hero Teulier not with the infamous Verrat but with the respectable Quesnel.[43]

Later on, Rolland maintained that his Revolution dramas celebrated "la Vie," his "idéal de la collectivité," this means the political life of the French people in 1789 and in the following years.[44] This vitalistic and fatalistic confession reminds one of the conclusion of Rolland's letter to Lugné-Poe: "il n'y a qu'une France au monde, et je préfère les êtres aux idées. J'aime la justice, mais j'aime mieux la vie. Que m'importe que la justice règne sur un monde d'-on toute vie qui m'est chère aura disparu."[45] Rolland nationalizes the notion of life, life meaning French life. Using a rhetoric similar to that of his (yet unwritten) character Saint-Just in Les *loups*, Rolland states the very opposite of his final contention in *Danton*: "Les Idées n'ont pas besoin des hommes. Les peuples meurent, pour que Dieu vive."[46] ("The Ideas don't need man. Nations die in order that God may live.")

---

distances himself in his *Memoires* from some Jewish Dreyfusards, i. e. from "les indignations vertueuses de ces 'honnêtes gens,' qui eussent mis le feu à la France pour sauver l'innocent Dreyfus condamne" (p. 286). – Rolland's ambivalent position toward the Dreyfus case is plain from his letters to Malwida v. Meysenbug (Rolland: *Choix de lettres à Malwida von Meysenbug*, pp. 188, 213–6). A more sympathetic view on Rolland's stance vis-à-vis the affair is given by Duchatelet: "L'écho de l'affaire Dreyfus dans l'œuvre romanesque de Romain Rolland."

42 Rolland and Lugné-Poe: *Correspondance 1894–1901*, pp. 71–5, 116, 125.

43 Rolland, on May 22, 1898, to Malwida von Meysenbug, Rolland: *Choix de lettres à Malwida von Meysenbug*, p. 228.

44 Rolland and Gillet: *Correspondance*, p. 193. The letter is dated May 2, 1902.

45 Rolland to Lugné-Poe: *Correspondance 1894–1901*, ed. Jacques Robichez, p. 74.

46 Rolland: *Danton*, in his *Théâtre de la Révolution. Le 14 juillet – Danton – Les loups*, p. 119 (each play is paged seperately). This harks back to Robespierre's "La France jeûne pour que ses soldats mangent" (p. 58). The materialism of war and the idealism of modern philosophy of history coincide in the practice of capitalization for what ought to come first: la France,

In 1900, Rolland expounded the idealist implications of this line in a letter to his German friend Malwida von Meysenbug: "J'ai voulu exprimer là l'idéalisme sanglant de la Révolution, l'indifférence aux hommes, et la foi profonde en l'existence des Idées, supérieures aux hommes, seules existantes." According to Rolland, these ideal *entes realissima* were represented by the Jacobin leaders of the Revolution.[47]

Ignoring these aspects of Rolland's thinking and even, as we shall see, turning them around, Zweig had been lobbying for Rolland's dramas since 1912. He masterminded the Austrian première of *Les loups* in 1916 in Vienna.[48] In his *Romain Rolland*, he presented his friend's drama *ex eventu*; that is from the viewpoint of an admirer of Rolland's pacifist position during WW I. This reading, which deprived the text of its ambivalences, prevailed in Germany.[49] It seems that it was this play that attracted Reinhardt to Rolland's cycle. *Les loups* was advertised at his *Deutsches Theater* first for March 15, 1914 and then for December 8, 1918, this second time arguably as a theatrical reply to the *Dolchstoßlegende* of post-war anti-Semitic propaganda. The drama was

---

les Idées, Dieu. The German translation has: "SAINT-JUST. Die Idee bedarf des Menschen nicht. Die Völker sterben, auf daß Gott lebe." (Rolland: *Danton,* translated by Lucy v. Jacobi and Wilhelm Herzog, p. 174) The (unpublished) Danton manuscript had: "St.-Just: La République n'a pas besoin des hommes. Mieux vait la mort d'un peuple qui la mort d'une idée." Quoted after Steck: *Romain Rollands Revolutionsdrama "Danton,"* p. 21.

47 Rolland to Malwida von Meysenbug in Rolland: *Choix de lettres à Malwida von Meysenbug,* pp. 277–8 (dated February 17, 1900). – The protagonists of Rolland's dramas are capable of representing the ideas of the Revolution because they are inspired by the historical "extraordinaire idéalité de ce mouvement" (Ibid., p. 243). This ideality fits into Rolland's view on histoly and on the options historical drama has (see Blum: *Romain Rolland, "Les loups" et l'affaire Dreyfus,* pp. 110–29). It is therefore basically an aesthetic concept.

48 See Nedeljkovic: *Romain Rolland et Stefan Zweig,* pp. 290–3; Dumont: *Stefan Zweig et la France,* pp. 140, 154. This is now plain from the German translation of their correspondence: Rolland and Zweig: *Briefwechsel 1910-1940* vol. 1, pp. 41, 209–12, 237–41. Zweig publicly announced this mise en scène as early as 1914, see Zweig: *Romain Rolland,* ed. by Knut Beck, p. 29 n.*. – The play had then already been successfully staged in Munich (at the Kammerspiele) in 1914 – see Gumppenberg: "Rollands 'Wölfe' / Münchner Theater;" Curtius: *Die literarischen Wegbereiter des neuen Frankreich,* p. 84; Gerber: *Rolland als Dramatiker,* pp. 106–07. I could not verify Antoinette Blum's indication: "Selon l'auteur, *Les Loups* sont joués au début de 1914 à Munich, à Berlin, à Mayence, à Francfort et à Hannovre. En 1920, ils apparaissent à nouveau à Francfort et au Altes Theater de Leipzig," Blum: *Romain Rolland: "Les loups" et l'affaire Dreyfus,* p. 332, cf. p. 336 n. 50.

49 Lerch even surpassed Zweig in stating that Rolland "zögerte nicht, für ihn [Dreyfus] einzutreten" ("did not hesitate to argue for him"): Lerch: *Romain Rolland und die Erneuerung der Gesinnung,* p. 106; and that the whole cycle of Revolution dramas "entstand aus der Stimmung der Dreyfus-Krise heraus" ("was produced out of the mood of the Dreyfus crisis"), p. 109.

eventually staged at the *Deutsches Theater* in 1922.[50] The German success of *Les loups* sparked a staging of this play at the Yiddish Art Theater in New York in 1924. Rather maliciously commenting on what he had heard of its director Maurice Schwartz, Rolland wrote in his *Journal intime*: "Il est remarquable que ce soient, une fois de plus, les Juifs qui aient su flairer l'effet scénique infaillible de mes *Loups*."[51] "Once again": this means, I guess, after Zweig and Reinhardt.

How, then, was the German public to understand the anti-Semitic attacks on Danton and the Dantonists in *Danton* (1900), the play directed by Reinhardt in 1920 and lauded the following year by Zweig as the breakthrough of Rolland's dramatic genius?[52] Here the revolutionists send their former comrades and newly declared enemies to the guillotine, accusing them to be "la juiverie, les banquiers autrichiens" or "juifs de naissance, originaires de Moravie."[53] The contempt Rolland eventually had for this attitude is spelled out in a commentary he added to a 1909-revision of the text, which he dedicated to its first publisher, the famous Dreyfusard Charles Péguy.[54] He considered the events shown in his *Danton* the turning point of the Revolution, "la crise décisive, où fléchit la raison des chefs de la Révolution, où leur foi commune est sacrifiée à leurs ressentiments."[55] Resentments legitimize and cause dissent among those that had originally embarked on implementing the rights of man and thus on creating a nation of equal citizens. Rolland's sentence is, in retrospect, marked by the experience of the Dreyfus case. And it is accurate in that it criticizes all leaders of the Revolution. For in his play Danton himself tries to fend off the charges of the Jacobin Revolutionary Court by vilifying Robespierre with quasi anti-Semitic stereotypes.[56]

Stephan Zweig sums up the moral of Rolland's tetralogy as emerging from a conflict between patriotism and justice, devotion to the efficiency of the revolutionary means and insistence on the principle of justice the Revolution

---

50   See Huesmann: *Welttheater Reinhardt*, Nos. 732, 1047 and 1303.
51   Quoted from Blum: *Romain Rolland: "Les loups" et l'affaire Dreyfus*, p. 334.
52   Zweig: *Romain Rolland*, ed. by Knut Beck, p. 86: "In dieser Tragödie ist Rolland ganz Dramatiker geworden."
53   Rolland: *Danton* – Rolland: *Théâtre de la Révolution*, pp. 72, 80.
54   On the history of this first edition of *Les loups* see Rolland et Péguy: *Une amitié française*, pp. 13–24.
55   Rolland: "Préface" to Rolland: *Théâtre de la Révolution*, pp. v-viii, quote pp. vi-vii.
56   *Danton* – ibid., p. 96: "DANTON. [...] Exempt du malheur d'être né d'une race privilégiée et abâtardie, j'ai conservé [...] toute ma vigeur native. [...] parce qu'un vieux renard a la queue coupée, faut-il que nous perdions la nôtre?"

undertook to put into practice. In *Danton* Robespierre persuades Saint-Just to overcome his scruples against eliminating the Dantonists regardless of the law. This attitude is countered by characters like Teulier in *Les loups*. He gloriously fights a fight in which – according to an idea dear to Zweig and, later on, to Kolmar – "the defeated always is the winner and the loner the stronger one."[57] The cause they defend, justice, might eventually be lost, but what matters is not to lose faith in it. So Teulier, speaking *"avec une violence concentrée,"* states: "Que la justice se fasse, et que le ciel croule!"[58] Zweig later interprets this statement as a translation of the Latin saying *Fiat justitia et pereat mundus.*[59]

V. Kolmar's *Das Bildnis Robespierres*

Kolmar's writings display an intense and inverting reception of Rolland's *Danton.*[60] She must have seen Reinhardt's staging of the play and she might have read Zweig's book. She systematically shifts the features given to Danton, Robespierre and Saint-Just by Rolland, Reinhardt and Zweig. For the victim she identifies with is not Danton but Robespierre. And so she does not take on positions upheld by Danton but again adopts principles she believes incarnated in Robespierre the "Incorruptible" and Saint-Just, the Holy or Saint Just. In her biographical essay *Das Bildnis Robespierres*, written about 1934 the Jacobin is stylized as a "great lonely one"[61] just as Kolmar, in her *Robespierre* poems, had inferred it from Büchner's drama. Furthermore, Robespierre represents in her view a man of "unyielding justice": Calling for a life of purity to be practiced by him and you all ("ihr"). Her Robespierre aggravated things (whereas Danton facilitated them) and, thus, he might have been "from the very beginning a defeated one."[62] He had an unpleasant face.

---

57   Zweig: *Romain Rolland*, ed. by Knut Beck, p. 88: "[…] jener Kampf, in dem der Besiegte immer der Sieger und der Einsame der Stärkste ist."

58   Rolland: *Les loups* – Rolland: *Théâtre de la Révolution*, p. 74.

59   See Zweig: *Romain Rolland*, ed. by Knut Beck, p. 90.

60   A summary of Kolmar's admiration for Rolland and its consequences for her literary view on the French Revolution is to be found in Eichmann-Leutenegger: *Gertrud Kolmar*, pp. 98–9. Cf. Brandt: *Widerspruch und Übereinstimmung in Gertrud Kolmars Gedichtzyklus "Das Wort der Stummen,"* pp. 109–10.

61   Kolmar: *Das Bildnis Robespierres*, p. 571: "[…] ein großer Einsamer."

62   Ibid., p. 576: "[…] eine unbeugsame Gerechtigkeit"; "der mit strengem, steinharten Antlitz verlangt, […] daß ihr ein reines Leben führt" (p. 572; compare with Rolland's – then yet unpublished – remark that Robespierre wanted to accomplish "les Idées de République puritaine"); "[v]ielleicht […] war Robespierre von Anfang an ein Besiegter." (p. 579) When Kolmar underscores Robespierre's training as a lawyer (see p. 562) she must have had in

Kolmar compares it with a portrait of Dreyfus. Both could have been condemned for looking repulsive.[63]

Thus it is Robespierre who stands for an idea of justice that is upheld by him, whatever the consequences, against the assaults of egoist hedonism or pragmatist patriotism. Turning Zweig's reading aside, Kolmar claims to recognize this Robespierre in Rolland's *Danton* where he almost comes to a par with the hero, sometimes, it seems, 'with a mixture of hypocrisy and sincerity', but anyhow: a character." More important is Kolmar's conclusion: "Two opposites in the most literal meaning of the word. On the one side Danton: *Right or wrong, my country*. On the other side Robespierre: *Fiat justitia et pereat mundus*."[64] As in the title of her *Robespierre* poem, this *"... et pereat mundus"* (431) implies the *fiat justitia* by representing it. This might be the personal hallmark of Robespierre's challenges, of his "inexorably rigorous reason" and "hard, almost bitter philanthropy."[65]

The peremptory wording for this rigor is given in the final line of *Danton*: "Les Idées n'ont pas besoin des hommes. Les peuples meurent, pour que Dieu vive." This conclusion was criticized by a theater critic reviewing Reinhardt's mise en scène.[66] But the Saint-Just who represents these principles

---

mind that her adored father, too, is one of Robespierre's social fellows ("Robespierres Standesgenossen"), p. 566.

63 See ibid., p. 569. Zeitler states that in Kolmar's essay "der Leidensweg Robespierres wird ein Gleichnis für die Leiden der Dichterin und für diejenigen ihres Volkes." (p. 557). Cf. Erdle: *Antlitz – Mord – Gesetz*, pp. 250–1.

64 "Der Robespierre in Georg Büchners Drama ist keine bluttriefende Greuelgestalt, aber ein unheimlich-unmenschlicher Schemen [...]. Hinwieder ist er bei Romain Rolland dem Helden nahezu ebenbürtig, gelegentlich wohl 'mit einer Mischung von Heuchelei und Aufrichtigkeit', immerhin: ein Charakter. Zwei Gegensätze im wörtlichsten Sinne des Wortes. Auf der einen Seite Danton: Right or wrong, my country. Auf der anderen Seite Robespierre: Fiat justitia et pereat mundus." (Kolmar: *Das Bildnis Robespierres*, p. 565). Cf. Kolmar's poem "Danton und Robespierre." *Das lyrische Werk*, pp. 391–2.

65 Kolmar: *Das Bildnis Robespierres*, p. 576: "Eine unerbittlich strenge Vernunft, eine harte, fast bittere Menschenliebe."

66 Reviewing Rolland's drama, Herbert Jhering expressed some reserve about the final *gnomon* of the drama: "'Die Völker sterben, auf daß Gott lebe.' Wie in diesem Drama das Milieu abfällt, damit der Mensch, und der Mensch abfällt, damit der Gedanke lebt, so wird das Thema: Republik und Revolution, sublimiert, bis es sich selbst verzehrt und einsam, kalt die Abstraktion, der Sinn, die Konsequenz zurückbleibt." ("As in this drama social condition is deserted in order that man may live, and man is deserted in order that thought may live, so the issue: republic and revolution is being sublimated to the point where it consumes itself and what is left is, lonely and cool, the abstraction, the meaning, the consequence.") Jhering: *Von Reinhardt zu Brecht. Vier Jahrzehnte Theater und Film* vol. 1: *1909–1923*, p. 148. A 1920 article on Büchner, Rolland and their Danton plays had ended with the comment, Saint Just's final line may constitute "das Wort [...], das als Fragezeichen über Drama

might be the mouthpiece of the author of the *Théâtre de la Révolution* whose *Les loups* was, in fact, published under the pseudonym "St. Just."[67] The publishing house selling the German translation quoted his final sentences as the drama's ultimate lesson: "Aber 'die Idee bedarf des Menschen nicht. Die Völker sterben, auf daß Gott lebe'."[68] And it is this sentence that Gertrud Kolmar will cite twice between 1934 and 1942 that deserves more detailed comment.

VI. The "Mortalism" of the Revolution

According to Rolland's own explanation, the characters of *Les loups* are allowed to live and kill as long as they live up to the purest ideals of the Revolution. "Mes monstres de la Révolution se battent pour un haut idéal. Il arrive parfois que ces ideals se heurtent et produisent des actions meurtrières. N'importe: si quelques hommes en souffrent, l'âme n'en souffre pas, et c'est là ce qui seul importe."[69]

Rolland's play celebrates death because death is given a new meaning by the Revolution. This holds true for death on the guillotine as well as for death on the battlefield. It was not simply a device to mislead the public that *Les loups* was renamed *Morituri* once rumor had it that Rolland was the author. Rolland aimed at reconciling a country divided by the Dreyfus affair by reaffirming in all of his compatriots their allegiance to the ideals of the French Revolution. Dreyfusards and anti-Dreyfusards should end their quarrel and bow before a metahistorical power.[70] Confronted with this (quasi-divine) in-

---

und Revolution schweben bleibt" ("the word that remains hovering, as a question mark, over drama and revolution"), Angel: "Drama und Revolution. Zur Soziologie der Dantondramen," pp. 25–7, quote p. 27.

67   Rolland contaminated this name with the notion of justice – just as Kolmar will do. Evidently he had a parallel in mind that made exchangeable the names of commander Teulier, St. Just and "St. Just" (i. e. Rolland). Commenting on *Les loups* he wrote: "Quant à Teulier, c'est un St. Just, tranchant et fanatique de justice." Rolland: *Choix de lettres à Malwida von Meysenbug*, p. 230.

68   Quoted from the advertisement for *Danton* at the end of: Rolland: *Die Wölfe*, p. 136. Rolland praised in a letter contemporary to *Les loups* "Les maximes lapidaires et profondes de St. Just" Rolland: *Choix de lettres à Malwida von Meysenbug*, p. 246; the letter is dated November 7, 1898. Diana Zimmermann has shown the function of the epigrammatic closing lines of *Les loups* and *Danton* (Zimmermann: *Romain Rolland: Le Théâtre du Peuple et le Théâtre de la Révolution*. Paper written for a seminar at Paris VIII/St. Denis, 1993/94).

69   Quoted from Blum: *Romain Rolland: "Les loups" et l'affaire Dreyfus*, p. 83: letter to Auguste Bréal, May 17, 1898.

70   Ibid., p. 378: Blum gives an extract of earlier versions of *Les loups*. In one of them Teulier asks: "Crois-tu qu'un juge là haut pèse nos actions *mortelles*?" (Italics mine).

stance they might become aware of human mortality uniting them. And death they had to conceive along the lines of commander Teulier's Revolutionary principles, as the pledge the warriors of Jacobine France gave to future generations, thus to Rolland's 1898 public: "La mort comme but et comme moyen, et non plus les froides parties d'échec, les jeux tranquilles, les belles capitulations. La mort au bout du duel qui s'est engagé entre nous et les envahisseurs sacrilèges de la patrie. La mort pour eux, ou pour nous, peut-être pour nous deux. Et quand nous ne serons plus, d'autres armées sortiront de nos os, pour mourir et pour tuer, jusqu'à la liberté ait broyé les tyrans."[71]

As the radical pacifist Rolland emerged during WW I, though, he discarded this idealism as a stance he had left behind whereas his nationals still clung to it: "Sie wissen," he wrote to Zweig in 1915, "welche Macht Ideen wie Gerechtigkeit, Freiheit usw. immer in Frankreich gehabt haben. Für sie hat Frankreich Kriege geführt, Revolutionen gemacht. Immer hat es bei uns eine Rasse von Menschen gegeben, die bereit waren, für diese Ideen alles zu opfern: das eigene Leben und das Leben anderer. Mehr als einmal haben mir meine Pariser Freunde – *meine ehemaligen, jetzt von mir getrennten Freunde* – mich an den Satz erinnert und ihn mir vorgehalten, mit dem eines meiner Revolutionsstücke schließt – den Ausspruch Saint-Justs am Schluß des 'Danton': 'Die Völker sterben, damit Gott lebe!' Zwanzig Jahre ist es her, daß ich das geschrieben habe. Seither habe ich meinen Weg fortgesetzt. Aber das Publikum ist eine träge Herde, die erst viel später nachkommt, um die Spur unserer Schritte abzugrasen, und an unseren toten Worten hängenbleibt."[72]

Almost twenty years later, Kolmar used Saint-Just's sentence as a motto for *Gott*, a poem belonging to her *Robespierre* cycle of 1934: "Die Völker sterben, auf daß Gott lebe./ Saint-Just, nach Romain Rolland."[73] This crucial text evokes a God whose justice is founded on his distance and even radical separation from mankind. Kolmar defines Him as an absolute being present where men reach their limits, fail and die, as a negative sublime force effective in nature: "And is yet rock not levered up by Titans,/ The tree an ax threatens in vain,/ The strongest sea, never containable,/ Is not just life. God is Death."[74]

---

71 Rolland: *Les loups. Théâtre de la Révolution*, pp. 21–22. One understands at this stage that Rolland's vitalism implies a certain 'mortalism.' "[…] je vois et je chante la Vie. La Vie et la Mort. La Force éternelle," he said on his Revolution dramas in 1910 (to Gillet in Roland and Gillet: *Choix de lettres*, p. 192).

72 Rolland-Zweig: *Briefwechsel 1910–1940* vol. 1, pp. 174–75. The German translation has: "Die Menschen sterben, […]," p. 174. So either it translated "Les peuples" with "Die Menschen" or Rolland has misquoted himself, replacing "Les peuples" with "Les hommes."

73 Kolmar: *Das lyrische Werk*, p. 404.

74 Ibid.: "Und ist doch Fels, den nicht Titanen stemmen, / Der Baum, dem Axt vergeblich

had to give his *Théâtre de la Révolution*. It seems as if Kolmar not only was ideally prepared to receive this book but rather that the drama itself was prepared by what Kolmar had said in 1933/34 about Rolland's *Danton* and the French Revolution. Moreover, with this last drama, written in the time of the *Front populaire*, a Jacobin tendency in Rolland's whole cycle resurfaced. This tendency was programmatically explained in Rolland's early letters[79] and detectable in *Danton* (1900) but scarcely upheld in any reading except in Kolmar's. Rolland's *Robespierre* thus invigorates again what she had made of his *Danton*.

Rolland's drama celebrates Robespierre as the highpriest and sublime suggestor of justice. He impresses this principle on the Parisian crowd by means of a rhetoric of simplicity that reduces its message to the pure mention of key notions: "ROBESPIERRE […] *donnant son plein d'éloquence, les deux bras tendus [...].* […] Justice! (*La foule répète*: Justice!) Liberté! (*La foule répète*: Liberté!)."[80] As ever, this imploring of justice even if it seems to succeed remains firmly linked to the *imago* of the suffering and eventually defeated just. Robespierre has given up his cause, before rhetorically defending and propagating it. He anticipates his defeat and changes it into the sign and precondition of his eventually triumphant justice: "Mais pour les justes, la mort ouvre les portes de l'immortalité."[81]

Inasmuch as Robespierre's "last will" speech to the Jacobins resembles Christ's Sermon on the Mount, it becomes manifest that this revolutionist is, in fact, a saint; his teaching a gospel; his power a divine way of uttering words. Identifying with his hero, Rolland did not only rehabilitate Robespierre's renown as a rhetorician but recast his character into an ideal author making history by using language. At the beginning of the play, he still has to learn from his admirer Simon that the power of the word is "De tous les pouvoirs […] le plus beau et le plus exaltant."[82] But the Robespierre who has spoken his will to the Jacobin club eventually agrees in resorting to the peaceful means of language as being the sole weapon he should continue to wield: "je ne veux d'autre arme que ma parole, et d'autre bouclier que la loi. Tu vois quel

---

79 On Robespierre he wrote to M. v. Meysenbug as early as 1898: "[…] c'était la tête la plus forte de la Révolution, la seule capable d'établir un ordre nouveau et d'avancer l'humanité de plus d'un siècle […]. Il n'a point fait la Terreur; il y a été contraint; il l'a subie, dirigée, et il est mort d'avoir voulu l'enrayer. […] Le 9 thermidor […] a été la ruine de la République." Rolland: *Choix de lettres*, p. 245, cf. p. 247.

80 Rolland: *Robbespierre*, p. 201.

81 Ibid., p. 198.

82 Ibid., p. 44. Since 1898 Rolland held Robespierre's rhetorical gift in high esteem (see Rolland: *Choix de lettres*, pp. 245, 249). Cf. his letter in Rolland: *Un beau visage*, pp. 257–8.

est son pouvoir sur les âmes."[83] Language (la parole) and justice (la loi) correlate with each other. In theological terms: Abiding by God's commands, the just assumes the suggestive faculty for prophesizing his own rescue after death.

There is no female role in such a revolutionary passion play apart from that of a helpless admirer. An old woman hearing Robespierre's sermon calls him, "ecstatically": "Jésus! Jésus!"[84] But the sole female character that links this drama to *Danton* is Éléonore Duplay, the daughter of Robespierre's landlord. Once more, she passively adores the revolutionist, so that *Danton's* scene 4, act II is now mirrored in the fifth scene of *Robespierre* – just as they seem mediated by the Éléonore Duplay poem in Kolmar's *Robespierre* cycle. In Rolland, she urges Saint-Just's Henriette not to dare to teach humanity to their beloved. For she knows them to be no simple humans but divine harbingers of a future humanity.[85] The moment Robespierre enters in order to take leave, she cannot but betray her speechless and powerless adoration for him whom she would want to stay: "*Éléonore [...] joint les mains, mais sans parler.*"[86]

This attitude, however, foreshadows the "exaltation halucinée"[87] about Robespierre and the coming fulfillment of his program with which Rolland ends his play. So even if these female characters are speechless, they are right. They assume and send forth the message that history is a process in which the just is sacrificed and the sacrificed is a just in order that justice is saved for the future.

This simple distribution of gender roles is to be paralleled and contrasted with Kolmar's yet unpublished Robespierre drama *Cécile Renault*, a text she produced after the *Robespierre* poems and the essay *Das Bildnis Robespierre* between November 1934 and March 1935. A few weeks before his downfall, Robespierre yields to the Committee of Security the right to judge a group of sectarians. Among them is Cécile Renault, who is charged with having tried to stab Robespierre. Yet she has but sought to kill herself. Robespierre knows this and is aware of his own imminent end. He refuses, though, to save her with his testimony because he rejects to be hailed as a martyr and saint after his death.

Utmost justice is thus converted into legitimizing a deadly sacrifice, the reprieved Cathérine Théot to the innocently convicted Cécile Renault. Once again, this Robespierre is, as in Büchner, a "Blutmessias, der opfert und nicht

---

83   Rolland: *Robespierre*, p. 203.
84   Ibid., p. 204.
85   See ibid., p. 76.
86   Ibid., p. 82.
87   Ibid., p. 310.

geopfert wird." But more so, he sacrifices in order that he eventually will be sacrificed as pure as he wanted to remain to his death. In the precarious dialectics of this dramatic action Kolmar's Robespierre achieves his sanctification by means of his refusal to impose it, ostentatiously, on those coming after him: "'Nun bin ich allein. Allein ... Nun habe ich alles zum Opfer gebracht: auch mein Andenken bei der Nachwelt.'"[88] By sacrificing not only his life but even his own renown in the eyes of posterity, Robespierre pays homage to the God of historical justice and, thereby, becomes part of His divine power. Again, the female voice is silenced, this time even silenced to death. She therewith, however, offers the opportunity for Robespierre to accomplish his project of living a pure life. A life that was not in vain as it was without vanity. Kolmar's drama seems to both exalt and condemn Robespierre for this reason. This paradox is strongly linked with her poetic alteration of the Jacobin leader: Sacrificing in order to be sacrificed defines, in Kolmar's mythology, the woman and the artist as well. The former is bent to devote and thus give herself (her independence, her body, her life) to the man, the latter abstains from life for the sake of the work to be achieved at life's cost.[89]

In November 1942, then, trying to cope with her father's deportation from Berlin to, as she might have guessed, a concentration camp, Kolmar sought relief and solace in quoting, most disconcertingly, once again the last sentence from Rolland's *Danton*: "'Die Völker sterben, auf das Gott lebe,' dies Wort von Saint-Just fiel mir ein."[90] It is a God that kills, and to whom life is sacrificed. One would be able to distinguish here Kolmar's deification of justice from her justification of God and his deeds. In upholding her own (Rolland-inspired) image of a God who demands sacrifices, Kolmar seems to assent to what Büchner's Danton had rebelled against as the presumably transcendent force of history: "Sind wir Kinder, die in den glühenden Molochsar-

---

88   Quoted after Woltmann, ed.: *Gertrud Kolmar 1894–1943*, p. 97. Cathérine Théot plays, in fact, an important role in the *Cécile Renault* drama, see Woltmann: *Gertrud Kolmar*, pp. 196–7.

89   Marion Brandt has charted this dimension of Kolmar's writing. Brandt: "'Opfre ich mich auf schäumender Altars Stufe': Über das Bild des Opfers im Werk von Gertrud Kolmar (1894–1943)." She drew on theories on the anthropological function of sacrifice expounded by Walter Burkert and René Girard. Briefly dealing with the Robespierre texts of 1933/34 (see pp. 175–6), she stressed that the Jacobin stands out as the sole male person to sacrifice himself in Kolmar. It seems to me that her poem "Das Opfer" (1937) might be read as circumscribing the myths of Iphigeneia and Jephta: Kolmar: *Das lyrische Werk*, pp. 582–84.

90   Kolmar: *Briefe an die Schwester Hilde*, p. 180 (letter no. 75, dated November 18, 1942).

men dieser Welt gebraten und mit Lichtstrahlen gekitzelt werden, damit sich die Götter über ihr Lachen freuen?"[91]

By 1933, this question must have struck a chord in Gertrud Kolmar. As a faithful daughter she put herself at risk when she stayed in Nazi Germany to take care of her aging father. As a mother *manquée* she had consented to the abortion of her illegitimate child in spite of her lifelong urgent longing for children. To sacrifice them to an heterogamous God is what the Molech of the Old Testament required. The people of Israel complied time and again. But this is always mentioned by Jehovah by way of a reprimand or condemnation (Leviticus 20, 1–5; 2 Kings 23, 11; Jeremiah 32, 35). Thus to let the children fall victim might have seemed to Kolmar as both a ritual command and forbiddance to her Jewish ancestors.

VII. Kolmar's *Napoleon und Marie*

In March 1925, when Rolland's *Théâtre de la Révolution* had become almost fashionable in Germany, Zweig urged his French friend to add to his *Danton* a drama on Robespierre: "Robespierre," he wrote in 1926, "fascine encore comme prédécesseur de Napoléon. [...] Il est nécessaire à votre Danton comme pendant: ce sont les deux cariatides qui portent le bâtiment. Après leur mort, il croûlait et devait être reconstruit par Napoléon."[92] Some nine years later Kolmar, too, parallels Robespierre with Napoleon, whom she calls the witness for the defense of the great Jacobin.[93]

Through the agency of the literary 'I' of her *Robespierre* poems, Kolmar hoped for a political power that would assume the role of a liberator of the Jews. Historically, although against the chronology of the texts, this projection of wishes on Robespierre is followed by an investiture of Napoleon as a ruler protecting the Jews. In *Napoleon and Marie* (c. 1912/1914–15)[94] Kolmar

---

91 Büchner: *Dantons Tod – Werke und Briefe*, p. 129 (IV:5). Cf. another version of this depiction of the Revolution as an act of sacrifice, taken from Greek mythology: "Das Volk ist ein Minotaurus, der wöchentlich seine Leichen haben muß" p. 80 (I:4). See also Büchner's letter to Wilhelmine Jaeglé, dating from March 7, 1834: ibid., p. 287. The mythical metaphor was taken up by Rolland in the 1924 preface to *Le jeu de l'amour et de la mort*: "Depuis, nos demi-dieux et nos minotaures ont eu, en Moscovie, des réincarnations plus saisissantes." (p. 23).

92 Quoted from Nedeljkovic: *Romain Rolland et Stefan Zweig*, p. 302. Cf. Rolland-Zweig: *Briefwechsel 1910-1942*, Vol. 2, p. 162.

93 Kolmar: *Das Bildnis Robespierres*, p. 563, cf. p. 567.

94 According to the differing dates given in Woltmann, ed.: *Gertrud Kolmar 1894–1943,* p. 30, viz. in Woltmann: *Gertrud Kolmar – Leben und Werk,* pp. 69, 278–9 n. 80, and in Eichmann-Leutenegger: *Gertrud Kolmar. Leben und Werk in Texten und Bildern,* p. 70, respectively. Her sis-

recapitulates the love between the emperor and the Polish Countess Marie Walewska from a woman's perspective . Marie Walewska is jubilant as she considers that he who has conquered the world is defeated by affection.[95] Sometimes, though, she looks into the future envisaging her rejection and her old age that she will spend remembering of the time when she had been "a little flute that sang for the emperor."[96] So she bows to a God who has not yet brought about justice and is to be adored in spite of people's destiny.[97]

Most telling is that Marie Walewska seems to hail the same ruler who Polish nationals consider the "heritor and comrade of the king's butchers,"[98] Napoleon, a true successor of Robespierres. In a poem she declares him "consecrated to be the Lord of the old earth."[99] In another one she parallels herself with the biblical Esther and Napoleon with Ahasverus[100] and gives thereby a private lyrical version of what the Jews stage and watch at Purim. The title reads *Geschichte* and it resumes an earlier lyrical reworking of the book of Esther.[101] *Geschichte* could refer to the story of Gertrud Kolmar's life as a writer as well as the Babylonian and the Polish stories and histories. For legend has it that Poles cited to Marie Walewska the example of Esther and Ahasverus in an attempt to make her yield to Napoleon's wooing. Polish patriots asked her: "Do you think, Madame, that Esther gave herself to Ahasverus out of love?"[102] Her catholic countrymen, however, understood this as a biblical parabel with a Christian reading, its "Jewish" text being baptized by a quotation from Cardinal Fénelon.[103] Kolmar, recreating a typological read-

---

ter Hilde Wenzel remembered that Gertrud Kolmar adored Napoleon. She got angry when her classmates teased her by saying that Robespierre and Napoleon had been criminals (quoted in Woltmann: *Gertrud Kolmar – Leben und Werk*, pp. 320, 322). Obviously the lonely, extraordinarily gifted school girl identified with these men.

95 See Kolmar: *Das lyrische Werk*, pp. 352–3, 362.

96 Ibid., p. 368: "[…] kleine Flöte, die dem Kaiser sang."

97 See Ibid., pp. 404–5.

98 Ibid., p. 345: "Erbe und Genoß der Königsschlächter."

99 Ibid., p. 347: "[…] zum Herrn der alten Erde […] [ge]weiht."

100 See Ibid., p. 354. Hilde Wenzel tells us that her sister was not content with her name Gertrud and would have preferred to be called Esther or Judith (quoted from Woltmann: *Gertrud Kolmar – Leben und Werk*, p. 316).

101 See Kolmar: *Das lyrische Werk,* pp. 73–4.

102 "Glauben Sie, Madame, daß Esther sich dem Ahasverus gab aus Liebe?" Quoted from Masson: *Napoleon I. und die Frauen,* p. 152. This text I consider to be Kolmar's source. Its first publication dates from 1894 (Masson: *Napoleon et les femmes,* Paris 1894) and the first print of Bieberstein's translation from the following year (Leipzig 1895). – Marie Walewska seems to stand for a 'slavonic' side of Napoleon with whom Eastern Jews could identify.

103 See Kolmar: *Das lyrische Werk,* p. 153.

ing of the parallel leaves out the episcopal authority and thus makes possible a "Judaization" of the Polish Countess with whom she, Kolmar, identifies.

In the end Georg Heym and Gertrud Kolmar seem to converge in their glorification of Napoleon. Yet, a strong difference remains. For whereas Heym celebrates Napoleon's way of waging war as a primer of the new age of technology, Kolmar reminds her readers that her revolutionary God demands sacrifices. He is "not ready to carry along with Him your carriage like steam power on the rails."[104] The tracks designed by the dialectics of enlightenment and set up by the French Revolution drifted apart. One led to modern emancipation, and another to modern anti-Semitism.

---

104   Ibid., p. 405: "O wundert euch nicht, wenn er / [...] / Nicht willig wie die Dampfkraft auf den Schienen / Auch euer Wäglein mit sich reißt."

Wolf Kittler
University of California, Santa Barbara

Laws of War and Revolution: Violence in Heiner Müller's Work

Abstract: Warfare, in the twentieth century, has become an industry. Thus, from a socialist perspective, violence and destruction has to be thought of as a form of productivity. The question then is: what distinguishes fascist blitzkrieg strategy from revolutionary energy? It is a question which – in Heiner Müller's work – has to be asked in terms of territory, law and language.

The peripeteia of Heiner Müller's first play comes at the very end: mason Balke, hero of the drama and "hero of work" ("Held der Arbeit") within the drama, asks fellow mason Karras to give him a helping hand while working in the heat of a burning kiln which has to be repaired quickly in order to fulfill the plan. In doing this the hero contradicts himself, for in the preceding scene his last words were: "Mit Karras kann ich nicht arbeiten,"[1] a statement which is quite understandable since Karras was among those who went so far in obstructing Balke's work as to beat him up. Karras and his kind commit sabotage, claiming that Balke's extra-work is aimed at lowering the wages for the piece work of all workers (hence the title of the play, *Der Lohndrücker*, the one who lowers the wages of his coworkers), whereas Balke for his part insists that the goal of socialist work is not payment but the surplus-value that is produced by all and for all according to the motto: Our life style will be as good as our standard of work.

Balke's change of heart is all the more astonishing as it is induced by another saboteur, the secretary of the communist party, Schorn, who replies to Balke's phrase, "Mit Karras kann ich nicht arbeiten," with a sharp retort: "Wer hat mich gefragt, ob ich mit dir arbeiten kann?"[2]

---

1   "I cannot work with Karras." Müller: "Der Lohndrücker." Müller: *Stücke*, pp. 5–33, here p. 32.
2   "I cannot work with Karras." Schorn: "Who asked me whether I can work with you?" Ibid.

Balke and Schorn have been working together long before the founding of
the GDR. They produced hand-grenades in and for the war-industry of Nazi-
Germany. In 1944 Schorn was arrested for sabotage. Balke who was employed as an inspector had been the informer. Now he argues that, having
been a suspect under special surveillance, he was forced to report the crime.
"Ich war auch dafür, daß man den Krieg abkürzt," he says, "aber mir hätten
sie den Kopf abgekürzt, wenns ohne mich herauskam."[3] Even after this justification Schorn remains Balke's adversary or rather enemy – to Balke's hopeful question: "Was gewesen ist, kannst du das begraben?" his short reply is:
"Nein!"[4]

Schorn's resentment is more than personal. It concerns the reliability of
Balke and his like within the new socialist republic. "Es hängt viel von ihm
ab," Schorn muses in a conversation with the director of the plant: "Zu viel.
Pause. Ich habe mit ihm in der Rüstung gearbeitet, Handgranaten. Seine
Handgranaten waren immer in Ordnung. Er war ein guter Arbeiter. Er hat die
Aufrüstung nicht sabotiert. Ich frage mich: Wird er den Aufbau sabotieren?"[5]

Thus, the result of the action is an alliance of three enemies: Schorn, the
saboteur of Hitler's war-industry talks his former denouncer Balke into forming a team with Karras, the former saboteur of Balke's extra-work. An alliance, not a "friendship,"[6] that is, the transition or rather: the leap, from an enmity founded in past histories to a solidarity to come. Old hostilities are
neither forgotten nor forgiven but overcome in the name of a common 'objective' objective, so to say, as opposed to 'subjective' goals and resentments.

It is a violent solution after all – violent in so far as the subjection of subjective feelings under objective necessities seems to be more self mutilative
than the torture of working in a red-hot kiln. For what is at stake here is not
just some kind of renouncement on the part of the subject, but the death of
subjectivity itself, namely the painful recognition that it is (despite its appearance of glorious autonomy) a mere effect of a general process called history
which (in this case) can and must be traced back to the rise of Nazi-Germany
preceding World War II, to the consequent splitting of the country along this

---

3 "I was for shortening the war, too, but they would have shortened me if they had found out
   that I was covering for sabotage." Ibid., p. 19.
4 Balke: "Can you bury the past? Schorn: No." Ibid.
5 "Much depends on him, too much. We were together in the war-industry, producing hand-
   grenades. His grenades were always perfect. He was a good worker. He did not sabotage
   Hitler's armament. And so I ask: Will he sabotage the construction of socialism." Ibid., p.
   26.
6 Müller: "Der Lohndrücker." Müller: *Stücke*, pp. 5–33, here p. 32.

war's final front-line, and to the creation of a socialist republic in East Germany. To face the future in the name of an objective goal is to position oneself within a history of shared violence and to envision the possibility that one's own past was neither self-chosen nor self-made, but violently imposed by an alienated will. It is to recognize at the bottom of dear and painful memories both one's own and other's wounds.

The drama *Der Lohndrücker* is an attempt to think the transition from fascist to socialist Germany in terms of both differences and similarities. This implies that team-work and team-productivity in the GDR cannot be conceived of without notions of enmity and violence, and it implies that the total mobilization of Nazi-Germany, including the efforts of the German Armed Forces during World War II, has to be understood as a special form of collective work according to Karl Korsch's diagnosis of "blitzkrieg strategy as concentrated leftist energy" ("Blitzkrieg als gebündelte linke Energie"[7]). Hence Müller's question can be formulated thus: What turns work into war, that is, destruction, the contrary of productivity? And inversely: How is it possible to turn warfare into – what Müller calls in the terminology of his country – "Aufbau,"[8] socialist construction? These are questions which clearly evoke Ernst Jünger's concept of the "Gestalt" of the worker within – what he calls – "total mobilization."

Der Lohndrücker describes the conversion of war-industry into collective and that is communist productivity as a solution which has no justification in the past nor in the present but only in the uncertain dream of a deferred and different future. The "inverse" of this is Müller's *Philoctetes*[9] – the drama of three commanders who, like Balke, Schorn and Karras, are trying to overcome personal hostilities in the name of a common cause.

In order to understand Müller's version of the play, I need to refer briefly to the tragedy by Sophocles:[10] Philoctetes gained Hercules' famous bow when he lit the pyre which ended the hero's unbearable suffering from the Nessus robe. Being among the first and most valiant Greek noblemen setting out for Troy, he is bitten by a snake while making an offering on the altar dedicated to the goddess of the island Chryse. Forced by the stench of Philoctetes' wound and the noise of his moaning, the Greek commanders – following Ulysses' advice – maroon him on the island of Lemnos. Ten years pass. Achilles, Aias and others are dead, Troy is still unconquered, but an oracle announces that

---

7   Quoted from Müller: *Jenseits der Nation*, p. 84.
8   Müller: "Der Lohndrücker." Müller: *Stücke*, pp. 5–33, here p. 26.
9   Müller: "Zu Philoktet." Müller: *Herzstück*, pp. 102–109, here p. 103.
10 Sophokles: *Tragödien und Fragmente*.

its walls shall fall to the joined forces of Achilles' son Neoptolemos and Hercules' bow.

The question is how will it ever be possible to win back Philoctetes' support. It is again Ulysses who promises to solve the problem. He takes Neoptolemos with him and sets out for Lemnos. There he divises the following stratagem: He will hide himself while his companion, using a white lie, talks Philoctetes into entering their ship. Neoptolemos shall pretend that he has broken his alliance with the Greeks and is sailing home from Troy because they robbed him of his legitimate legacy by giving Achilles' weapons to Ulysses. Philoctetes, hoping to have found the man who will free him from exile and at the same time seized by a fit of pain, puts his bow into the hands of Neoptolemos who then tells him the truth – namely that he is acting in obedience of the Greek commanders. Ulysses appears and attempts to abduct Philoctetes by force, Philoctetes threatens to commit suicide whereupon Ulysses and Neoptolemos leave the scene – the latter carrying Hercules' bow. But too noble to deceive, Neoptolemos goes back and returns the weapon to Philoctetes. The coward Ulysses is put to flight. Only after the intervention of the deified Hercules ex machina is Philoctetes ready to make common cause with his former enemies and join his new friend Neoptolemos for the defeat of Troy.

According to Müller's interpretation, the Sophoclean *Philoctetes* describes the historical transition from clan to statehood, whereas his own version of the tragedy is a "Roman Philoctetes,"[11] that is to say, a play which happens at a time when the institution of the state has reached the summit of its power. One little detail shows the difference. In Müller's text, the hostility between Ulysses and Neoptolemos is not a pretense, they are enemies. The former carries Achilles' weapons neither for glory nor merit nor deceit, but out of a simple calculation concerning the requirements of command and control. Since battles in the name of statehood are no longer fought by single heroes, but by armies, the command of such large numbers becomes a question of mass psychology. Thus, when Ulysses's troops suffered heavy casualties in the battle over Achilles' corpse, there was only one way to prevent the surviving soldiers from imminent defection, namely to set a token as a substitute for their wounds and their dead. This symbol was Achilles' weapons which were given to their leader.

---

11   "'Philoktet' ist eine Übersetzung des Sophokles ins Römische, eine staatlichere Version. Die Maschine schneidet tief ins Lebendige und hat auch die Toten noch im Griff." Müller: *Jenseits der Nation*, p. 321.

The episode is significant in two respects. First, it assimilates the constellation of Müller's *Philoctetes* exactly to that of his earlier play *Der Lohndrücker*: As Schorn and Karras are related to Balke as old and new enemies so are Philoctetes and Neoptolemos both adversaries of Ulysses. Second, it shows that the subject of Müller's drama are not heroes and their magic weapons, but masses and signals, that is C3 modern strategy: command, control, communication. Hence, what the Greek army needs is neither Philoctetes' physical strength nor the power of his bow. Rather, it is the commander symbolized by his weapon, that is, a token which – to use a recurrent trope of the play – is judged to be worth "one thousand spears."[12] Violence is performed not just by human bodies or by technical instruments, but by symbols and words.

The Sophoclean tragedy deals with fierce and defiant individuals whose forces cannot be joined without the will of the gods who are the spirit of the 'polis'. Müller's text deals with the possibility of fusing large multitudes into a single body of work, that is, into a collective acting as a machine. This makes all the difference. Sophocles does not so much show a battle between falsehood and truth, but the superiority of nobility over cowardice. The problem of Müller's figures is motivation or better: ideology. This is why the power of persuasion is so important in the modern version of the play. It turns the figure of Ulysses from a minor character into a main actor. It changes the figure of Neoptolemos from an inexperienced but incorruptible nobleman into an undecided and feeble follower, and it accounts for the unexpected solution of the drama, namely that, with the appropriate arguments, Philoctetes' and even Ulysses' corpse is worth a living warrior.

By the end it seems as if Ulysses, acting for the cause of the Greek nation, was the winner of the game. But this would fail to notice that Ulysses, as Müller remarks,[13] is the most tragic figure of the play. To begin with, Müller invokes the cryptic tradition according to which Ulysses tried to avoid the draft for the Trojan campaign by feigning mental illness. Now, after ten years of war, attempting to win back Philoctetes' support, he is not at all motivated by patriotism but by the desperate desire to end a murderous war. This accounts for the paradox of his position – risking the lives of possible allies in order to end the killing of hundreds. His tragedy can be formulated thus: involuntarily fighting for a common cause, which is not his, he realizes that in order to finish the war one has to shift the front-line which divides friend and foe to within the ranks of one's own comrades-in-arms. This is the theme which is already invoked by the Sophoclean Ulysses' retort to Neoptolemos' defiance:

---

12   Müller: "Philoktet." Müller: *Mauser*, pp. 7–42, here pp. 10, 16, 28, 32, 39.
13   Müller: "Zu Philoktet." Müller: *Herzstück*, pp. 102–109, here p. 103.

"Also mit dir, nicht mit Troja kämpfen wir."[14] Hence the first battle is also the last: the battle that will end the war, is the war between brothers, a civil war.

The consequence is that in Müller's play the fight between Ulysses and Philoctetes is fought with real swords,[15] an action which accounts for the first as well as for the second turning point of the drama: The duel between Ulysses and Philoctetes is both the reason why Neoptolemos gets hold of Hercules' bow and the reason why Neoptolemos feels compelled to kill Philoctetes from behind in order to save Ulysses' life.

The fight among brothers is a recurring motive in Heiner Müller's work. In the short text *The Horatius*, a man kills two: a Curiatius, enemy of the republic, and his own sister, the fiancée of his first victim. How will he be treated by the community of Rome –: as savior of his country or as fratricide? The answer is twofold: he is sentenced for his crime and praised for his victory, praise and sentence forming a clashing conjunction according to the rule:

> Ein Schwert kann zerbrochen werden und ein Mann
> Kann auch zerbrochen werden, aber die Worte
> Fallen in das Getriebe der Welt uneinholbar
> Kenntlich machend die Dinge oder unkenntlich.
> Tödlich dem Menschen ist das Unkenntliche.
> [...]
> So stellten sie auf, nicht fürchtend die unreine
> Wahrheit
> In Erwartung des Feinds ein vorläufiges Beispiel
> Reinlicher Scheidung, nicht verbergend den Rest
> Der nicht aufging im unaufhaltbaren Wandel.[16]

Justice, as it is performed here in a moment of warfare, sets a standard for situations to come. It accounts for the difference between two forms of violence: necessary violence in the name of a common cause, that is, violence in the form of war waged by the republic of Rome, and unnecessary violence which (although Horatius pretends to perform it in the name of Rome) is a mere manifestation of personal rage, hence violence as a crime. Instead of neglecting the one in the name of the other the people of Rome decide to face

---

14 "So we are fighting you, not Troy." Sophokles: *Tragödien und Fragmente,* p. 555.
15 Müller: "Philoktet." Müller: *Mauser,* pp. 7–42, here p. 35.
16 "A sword can be broken and a man/Can be broken, but words/Fall into the mechanism of the world irretrievably/Making things knowable or unknowable./The unknowable means death to man./[...] Thus not afraid of impure truth/In expectation of the enemy they gave a preliminary example/Of a clear difference not hiding the never fading/Remainder inherent in unstoppable change." Müller: "Der Horatier." Müller: *Mauser,* pp. 45–54, here p. 53.

both, which is to say that the judges have to violate their own desire for unity and noncontradiction. In order to account for the difference between one form of violence and the other one of the basic principles of logic, namely the principle of contradiction needs to be jettisoned. In the face of violence, the language of judgement itself has to be violently administered. And the very fact that, in order to ban violence one has to perpetuate it by keeping its memory alive, explains why this solution can be but preliminary. In registering the contradiction instead of erasing it, the possibility of another and perhaps less violent solution is maintained, a solution which in the presence of an imminent war against the Etruscean army cannot be spelled out.

The distinction between necessary and unnecessary violence recurs and is rethought in Müller's play *Mauser*[17] which takes place in a different historical setting, shifting the scene from the founding of Rome to the Russian Revolution. This is not a shift from a conflict between two antique communities to one among the many civil wars of modernity, but to civil war as such, a war which, rather than in the name of one country or faction, is waged in the name of the proletariat in as far as it represents humanity. This utmost generalization of a war's cause leads to a reevaluation of violence as both dangerous and beneficial at one and the same time. Violence is necessary to put an end to a history of violence, and it is never just directed against the other but always already autoreferential to the extent that the one who enacts it cannot separate himself from the enemy. The global perspective of the world revolution abolishes any spatial difference by which one could tell apart friend and foe. At the same time it abolishes the difference between a past and a present by reading the latter as the result of an objective process which, by encompassing every individual, leads in the final analysis to the end of subjectivity itself. The only remaining difference is the one between a moment of history in which violence is used only because it is inherited from history and one which necessitates a different violence in the name of things to come. Violence can be justified through this gap between a present loaded with the weight of history and a future that is still unknown.

The text stages a dialogue between an anonymous individual, A, and a chorus, acting as vox populi. A was employed as an executioner killing peasants who fought on the side of the Russian White Army against the Bolsheviki. He did not show a weakness until the day when, after having discovered that he was killing people just like himself, he developed doubts and feelings, a change of mind which turned revolutionary work into subjective rage: henceforth he was unable to continue to simply kill, but attempted to annihi-

---

17   Müller: "Mauser." Müller: *Mauser*, pp. 69.

late the memory of the executed by trampling on their corpses. Forgetting his task and acting according to his own reasoning, the executioner turns into an enemy of the revolution which makes him fall within the scope of his own law: "TOD DEN FEINDEN DER REVOLUTION."[18]

The phrase echoes the famous ending of Kleist's *Prince Friedrich of Homburg*: "In Staub mit allen Feinden Brandenburgs!"[19] which is in itself a reversal of the older phrase: "Long live the king!" A succession of war-cries and political slogans which – even if it is incomplete – is apt to emphasize the fundamental difference in the justification of political power which marks the leap from the mediaeval period to modernity: The series not only proceeds from the king's body over the national territory to an abstract ideal, but also from life to death. In this last respect the Roman Republic, the national states of the 19th century, and the world revolution have one thing in common: they define themselves by their enemies.

This, however, does not mean that in these different forms of government, war and power are identical. Horatius was a representative of his republic. He stands as an individual both for his own and for the common cause. Therefore, he kills two, one friend, one foe. In the national wars of the 19th and 20th centuries the individual is erased, friend and foe become multiplicities, but there is still a clear line drawn between the two of them. It is a spatial line: the border of a country's territory. In this sense the idea of the proletarian revolution is not that of a war any more: friend and foe are in principle one and the same, people like the executioner.

The problem is that, with the transition from the national territory to a universal idea, there is no longer an outside where to seek or project a foe. The enemy of the revolution is at the limit of both: nobody or everybody, including the revolutionary fighter himself. After the end of the spatial definition of political power, there is only one category left to introduce difference as such – time. Hence, the verdict of the executioner in Müller's *Mauser* is justified as follows: "Nicht Menschen zu töten ist dein Auftrag, sondern / Feinde. Nämlich der Mensch ist unbekannt."[20]

The distinction between the criminal and the patriotic deed developed in Müller's *The Horatius* is transposed onto another stage of history, namely the proletarian revolution, where it reappears as difference between subjective

---

18 "DEATH TO THE ENEMIES OF THE REVOLUTION." Ibid., pp. 60, 64, 69.
19 "To the dust with every enemy of Brandenburg!" Kleist: "Prinz Friedrich von Homburg." Kleist: *Sämtliche Werke und Briefe* vol. 2, pp. 555–644, here 644.
20 "Your task was not to kill men, but enemies./Namely man, is still unknown." Müller: "Mauser." Müller: *Mauser*, p. 63.

feelings and objective goals – the former being rooted in and oriented towards the past and the latter opening up to the future. Hence, subjective interpretation conceives history as the mere recurrence of the identical in which man is a given and will never change, whereas objective consciousness is based on the notion of history as work which means that violence and destruction – even in their utmost form as killing – are not a simple setback for human progress, but a transition to another stage, a notion which implies that man is not the material, but the final cause of history, not a given, but a project to be achieved, even at the price of a murderous and fratricidal war.

In the final analysis the tragedy takes place, to quote Müller's *Wolokolamsk Highway V*: "Im Augenblick der Wahrheit Wenn im Spiegel / Das Feindbild auftaucht."[21] It is the moment to ask the question of guerrilla warfare one more time, namely the question: Who is the enemy? a moment indicating the last stage of history prior to the realization of the communist statement that all men are brothers, including not only one's brothers-in-arms but also the men beyond the front-line, the "real enemy" ("der wirkliche Feind")[22] to quote the German General York von Wartenburg.

Guerrilla warfare is revolutionary warfare as such since by abolishing the difference between soldiers and civilians it generalizes the cause of war to its utmost limit, namely to the point where the fighter is in principle indistinguishable any more from his opponent. This is why the revolutionary act can no longer be conceived of and perceived as fulfillment of subjective, that is, unmediated desires. It is not a passion, but a form of work. For while unmediated access to the identity of friend and foe leads to hate, the climax of subjectivity, revolutionary action guarantees both: identity (in terms of a deterministic past) *and* difference (in terms of a utopian future). If the killing of one's enemies is understood as a revolutionary task, it fulfills exactly the same function as the "general strike," which, in Walter Benjamin's rigorous conception, is "apt to diminish outbreaks of violence proper in the course of revolutions."[23] The same activity, killing, has two completely different meanings depending on the consciousness of the perpetrator. It is either a crime, accompanied by personal rage, or a necessary task, understood as revolution-

---

21 "At the moment of truth when/the image of the enemy appears in the mirror." Müller: *Wolokolamsker Chaussee II–V.* Müller: *Shakespeare Factory* 2, pp. 231–259, here p. 257 and p. 259.

22 Yorks letter to King Friedrich Wilhelm III of Prussia quoted from Droysen: *Das Leben des Feldmarschalls Grafen York von Wartenburg.* Vol. 1, p. 504.

23 "Inwiefern übrigens eine so rigorose Konzeption des Generalstreiks als solche die Entfaltung eigentlicher Gewalt in den Revolutionen zu vermindern geeignet ist, hat Sorel mit geistvollen Gründen ausgeführt." Benjamin: "Zur Kritik der Gewalt." Benjamin: *Angelus Novus*, pp. 42–66, quote p. 58. The reference is to Sorel: *Réflexions sur la violence.*

ary work. Müller's remark that "communism individualizes" whereas "capital-ism makes uniform"[24] is to be understood within this context.

This opens up a radical alternative: On the one hand, there is a mirror that turns identity into radical difference, friend into foe, on the other hand, the black mirror leaves no difference at all. It is the alternative between guerrilla warfare and the atomic bomb, in Müller's mythology, the last stage of the struggle between revolution and counterrevolution which will end either in total destruction or with the liberation of mankind.

Returning one last time to the tragedy of *Philoctetes*, one should not forget that the oracle that makes Ulysses look for Philoctetes' support creates a con-junction in the sense of formal logic or a metonymy in the sense of rhetoric: Troy will not fall before a man, Achilles' son Neoptolemos, and an instru-ment, Hercules's bow, will be combined for the common cause of the kings of Greece. It seems as if Heiner Müller overstated the importance of one of the two terms of the conjunction, namely of the man over the weapon which seems reduced to a mere representational sign. But the contrary is true. For if Philoctetes's bow is indeed downgraded to a signifier for enhancing the mo-rale of the troops, this operation produces a dialectical effect: while the in-strument is dematerialized to the status of a message, the receivers of this message are instrumentalized in turn. The magic of Hercules' bow is no longer active because the difference between man and his instrument is abol-ished, not by the humanization of instruments to be sure, but by the intru-mentalization of humans, including that of the dead. It is the last stage of warfare before the reign of the battles of machinery in World War I and World War II, an implication made explicit by Müller's stage direction to illus-trate the last scene of the drama with pictures from military history "begin-ning with the Trojan and ending with the Japanese war."[25] This amounts to a history of modern imperialism leading from the fall of an eastern city to the first reversal, namely the first victory of an Asian country over an occidental power. The actors of these battles were human, but the dream of the magic weapon was always alive.

Hence, it is not surprising to see one of the most advanced products of 20th century war-industry pop up in the imagery of Müller's pseudo-archaic language. I quote one of Philoctetes' curses: "Könnt ich mich umbaun selber zum Geschoß / Das tötet, und Gefühl hat für sein Tun."[26]

---

24 Müller: *Jenseits der Nation*, p. 25.
25 Müller: "Philoktet." Müller: *Mauser*, pp. 7–42, here p. 42.
26 "If only I could convert myself into a missile/That kills, and has a feeling for its action."
    Ibid., p. 27.

This is plainly the exact definition of Hitler's so-called 'miracle weapon', the instrument that kills and has control over its actions by means of feedback. Thus, the consequent thinking of mass-psychology in modern statehood, industry and warfare veers in a sudden turn into its dialectic counterpart, cybernetics, just as the suicidal mission of the German Sixth Army in Stalingrad has its technological correlate in the bombing of Hiroshima and Nagasaki.

It is evident that the drama *Philoctetes* is more than a mere critique of Stalinism. It shows the historic turn when traditional warfare shifts to the tragedy of modern mass destruction which is based on total mobilization of men and machines and which abolishes the difference between soldier and civilian as well as the difference between hinterland and battleground. Modern war is nothing but an industry, a form of human productivity.

This leads to Müller's *Wolokolamsk Highway I-V*.[27] The first two variants of the text are situated at one of the turning points of World War II, namely the highway of Wolokolamsk, 100 km West of Moscow, where the Red Army finally stopped the advancing tanks of the German Armed Forces. Variants number III and V mirror this beginning: They deal with a return in a twofold sense, namely with Russian tanks advancing from the East in order to stop two revolts, the one which took place in East Berlin on June 17, 1953, and the other one in 1968 which was called the 'Prague Spring'.

Variant number IV, according to Müller's own dictum the satyricon within a series of tragedies, describes the tragedy as farce.[28] Its subject is the metamorphosis of a bureaucrat into a writing desk, a joke with the German "Amtsschimmel,"[29] a word whose literal translation would be bureaucratic mare and which means red tape. This is a hint indicating the main subject of the cycle which is the coupling of men and machine in the double sense of the term: signifying the result of marriage as well as a mechanical or electrical connection.

What the writing desk is in the satyricon, the tanks are in the tragedies. They are the apparatus which threatens to immobilize history halting its movement towards the creation of human autonomy. The situation in *Wolokolamsk Highway I* is similar to that in Müller's plays *Mauser* and *Philoctetes*. The

---

27 Müller: "Wolokolamsker Chaussee I." Müller: *Shakespeare Factory 1*, pp. 241–250; Müller: "Wolokolamsker Chaussee II-V." Müller: *Shakespeare Factory 2*, pp. 231–259. Unfortunately there is not enough space within the scope of this article to discuss the different literary sources of the five pieces which allude to texts by Alexander Bek: n. I and II, Anna Seghers: n. III, Franz Kafka: n. IV, and Heinrich von Kleist: n. V.

28 Müller: *Shakespeare Factory 2*, p. 259.

29 Müller: "Wolokolamsker Chaussee IV," ibid., p. 245.

commander of a Soviet company, confronted with the approaching German tanks, has to solve a case of self mutilation in his troop. Subjective feelings such as compassion and understanding for the culprit's fears clash with the objective necessity of setting an example which will have the effect of fusing the different members of the company into a single body of men, a collective. The text enacts the dream of a possible pardon as well as the reality of the execution. The stage of the play is the consciousness of the commander who identifies with both: the executioner and the executed. Hence, another case of fratricide in the name of an objective task, another case of violence that is painful, but necessary.

In *Wolokolamsk Highway II* a Soviet battalion has been decimated to the size of a company. Now it is caught in a pocket surrounded by German tanks. All communication with the Red Army is cut off. The commander discovers that the ambulance train is lost, having been forsaken by the medical officer. This functionary, an academic, is of a higher rank than the battalion commander. Hence the question: How can the disciplinary offense be sentenced and punished and by whom? Who is the true representative of the Soviet-order in a situation of total isolation? It is the question of guerrilla warfare in which – as Clausewitz said – a single soldier can sometimes "claim to act in the name of an army" ("den Namen einer Armee in Anspruch [...] nehmen").[30] If the commander assumes the superiority of judgment over the medical officer, how will he prevent his men from assuming the same prerogative according to the maxim: "Und jeder ist sein eigner Kommandeur."[31] In the end, the medical officer is degraded and discipline restored. The reasoning of the commander is the following:

> Das Batallion ist die Sowjetarmee
> Der Boden unter unsern Stiefeln heißt
> Sowjetunion und ich bin die Sowjetmacht.[32]

This is the classical situation of Carl Schmitt's *Theory of the Partisan*,[33] the moment when the motivation of the fighter comes down to basics, that is, the double rooting of guerrilla warfare in an ideological and a telluric cause, or put another way: an idea to fight *for*, namely the order of the Soviet Union,

---

30   Clausewitz: *Vom Kriege*, p. 501.

31   "And everybody is his own commander." Müller: "Wolokolamsker Chaussee II." Müller: *Shakespeare Factory 2*, p. 236.

32   "The Batallion is the Soviet Army/The ground under our boots is called/Soviet Union and I am the Soviet Power." Ibid., p. 238.

33   Schmitt: *Theorie des Partisanen*.

and a land to fight *on*, "the ground under our boots" – the territory which Müller does not hesitate to evoke by the untranslatable word "Heimat."[34]

In the first two pieces of *Wolokolamsk Highway*, the conflict ensues from the confrontation of a body of men with a highly industrialized enemy force. The same is true for the last two variants of the play. But the sides have changed: The tanks are Russian and the men who are confronted with them are Germans, East Germans, to be exact. The front, however, where the battle is fought, is still the line that separates East and West, socialism and capitalism or – in Müller's words – revolution and counterrevolution. Thus in the last two pieces of *Wolokolamsk Highway* an uncanny reversal is taking place: Those who once stood up as single men against German tanks, now return to Germany themselves armed with tanks. "Denn bei Stalingrad hat die Rote Armee die Strategie der deutschen Wehrmacht verinnerlicht."[35]

Is this to say that the return of the tanks from Russia is nothing but fascism reversed, to wit Stalinism? Is the Berlin Wall an attempt to wall in the capitalists,[36] as one of Müller's heroes remarks, or is it the relapse into static warfare of World War I, sort of an identification with the aggressor, capitalism, that is, in the final analysis, fascism? Are the politics of the communist East nothing but the introjection of the blitzkrieg strategy which was the German attempt at avoiding trench warfare by encircling the enemy with quickly moving motorized forces?

The common theme of the different pieces of Müller's *Wolokolamsk Highway* is a certain form of heroic stoicism which enables the protagonists to overcome their inhibition against hurting their own men in the name of socialism: The Russian commanders sentence and derank their comrades despite the fact that they are members of their party, and the East German functionaries respectively criticize and denounce their protégé and adoptive son. But this is where the similarities come to an end. For if in *Wolokolamsk Highway I* and *II* the line between friend and foe is clear, this cannot be said about the last two pieces of the cycle. The invasion of the Russian tanks confronts East Germans not just with an enemy, but with a necessary choice between friend and foe. It confronts those who side with the Soviet Union to the others who are dissidents. It is the critical moment when the "bureaucratic terror"[37] of the GDR reveals its ugly face. In other words, it becomes clear

---

34 Müller: "Wolokolamsker Chaussee II." Müller: *Shakespeare Factory 2*, p. 238.
35 "For the Red Army introjected the German Armed Forces' strategy in the battle of Stalingrad." Müller: *Zur Lage der Nation*, p. 45.
36 "[…] jetzt/hab ich die Kapitalisten eingemauert." Müller: *Germania Tod in Berlin*, p. 78.
37 "[…] der bürokratische Terror," Müller: *Deutschland ortlos*, p. 264.

that what officially was and had to be called "REAL EXISTIERENDE[R] SOZIALIS-
MUS"[38] was and had been nothing more than just another form of a "principle
experience," namely "statehood as violence," the only difference being that
this time it is not "fascist violence," but "communist" and that is "stalinist
counterviolence" of the state.[39] This is the reason why the figure of the
enemy has to reappear:

> Der Staat ist eine Mühle die muß mahlen
> Der Staat braucht Feinde wie die Mühle Korn braucht
> Der Staat der keine Feinde hat ist kein Staat mehr
> Ein Königreich für einen Staatsfeind.[40]

In *Wolokolamsk Highway V* a precarious and significant phrase marks the turn-
ing point of the text: "ich bin das Volk."[41] These words are not without prece-
dent in Müller's work. In his play *The Life of Gundling Frederic of Prussia Lessing
Sleep Dream Cry*, it is Frederic the Great himself who – in remembrance of
Louis XIV's famous statement: "L'état c'est moi," claims: "I am the people if
you know what I mean."[42] Another of Müller's heroes jokes: "Du kannst mich
DDR nennen."[43] And within the context of the five pieces of *Wolokolamsk
Highway*, the phrase echoes the commander of the Russian Batallion assuming
the martial law of his country by maintaining: "I am the Soviet Power."[44]

What complicates things in a play which addresses the issue of the Russian
tanks in Prague, reflected in discussions of an East German family in 1973, is
the fact that there is no way of backing the phrase, "I am the people," with
any myth or notion of territory whatsoever as long as there is not one but two
Germanies. Thus, the German word "Volk," to which both fascism and socialism laid claim, had lost its historical correlate, that is, the connection to the
soil, to "Heimat" which – in *Wolokolamsk Highway II* – even an officer of the

---

38 "SOCIALISM EXISTING IN REALITY," Müller: *Deutschland ortlos*, p. 264.

39 "Meine Grunderfahrung war: Staat als Gewalt. Auf der einen Seite die faschistische Ge-
    walt, auf der anderen die kommunistische – in Klammern: stalinistische – Gegengewalt."
    Müller: *Zehn Deutsche sind dümmer als fünf*, p. 275.

40 "The state is a mill that has to grind / The state needs enemies as the mill needs grain / The
    state which does not have an enemy any more is not a state / A kingdom for an enemy of
    the state," Müller: "Wolokolamsker Chaussee IV." Müller: *Shakespeare Factory 2*, p. 246.

41 "I am the people," Müller: "Wolokolamsker Chaussee V." Ibid.,, p. 257.

42 Müller: "The Life of Gundling Frederic of Prussia Lessing Sleep Dream Cry." Müller:
    Herzstück, p. 31.

43 "You can call me GDR."

44 See Note 20.

Red Army is given to evoke. And one should note in this context that the popular word for the GDR was "Zone," that is, the term which after the re-thinking of trench warfare in 1916 was used to denote the space between the front-lines: no-man's-land.

This may be the reason why the phrase which identifies an individual with a country or a cause when it appears for the last time, keeps the situation in ambiguous suspense: In *Wolokolamsk Highway V* it is not possible to tell who legitimately claims to be the people, the father or his son, the foundling. But in the end and maybe for the very last time a clear distinction is achieved: the father reaches for the phone and denounces the enemy of what he thinks is the people of the GDR. The Russian commander did not have this option. His communications were cut off. He had to act on his own – demonstrating thus what Müller means when he states that what rules communism is the in-dividual whereas capitalism is characterized by the collective. One could also say: Warfare with regular troops is the ultimate form of capitalism, and com-munism is born out of the spirit of guerrilla warfare. It is, in Müller's words: "Die Wiedergeburt des Revolutionärs aus dem Geist des Partisanen."[45]

The phone which is disconnected for a short moment during the revolt of June 17, 1953, (*Wolokolamsk Highway III*) and which is being restored in 1968 connecting the secretary of the party with the central office of the Stasi, changes everything. It fulfills exactly the same function as the ominous "mis-sile/That kills, and has a feeling for its action."[46] It is the coupling of man and machine gone awry, the use of sophisticated technology in the service of an archaic form of power, namely the state.

Thus, the heroic isolation of the Russian officer is replaced with the bu-reaucratic cowardice of a German functionary who is unable to act without the backing of the secret service. It is the ugly sight which has been revealed sufficiently since the revolt of those who – with a small, but significant change in the wording – seemed to quote and parody texts like Müller's *Wo-lokolamsk Highway V* by carrying placards with the slogan: "We are the Peo-ple." Did the originators of the slogan realize that the "ego is a collective,"[47] as Müller states, or were they just alluding to article 20, paragraph 2, of the Constitution for the Federal Republic of Germany? It states: "Alle Staatsge-walt geht vom Volke aus. Sie wird vom Volke in Wahlen und Abstimmungen

45 "The rebirth of the revolutionary from the spirit of the guerrilla fighter." Müller: *Jenseits der Nation*, p. 347.
46 See note 25.
47 "Ich ein Kollektiv," Müller: "Medeamaterial." Müller *Herzstück*, pp. 91–101, here p. 101.

und durch besondere Organe der Gesetzgebung, der vollziehenden Gewalt und der Rechtsprechung ausgeübt."[48]

For Müller the fact that his compatriots were "voting with their hands and feet against the truth"[49] was caused by images, namely by the self representation of Western capitalism on East German TV-screens. Once the (Berlin) wall had fallen, the confrontation with the realities behind these images created a shock which "produces these outbreaks of violence" that have shocked the world.[50]

Violence, which Müller's work attempts to think in relation to both history and the utopian future relapses into an archaic state. For if the revolution did not take place in the East because of Soviet occupation, then the softer but more effective stranglehold of market economy had exactly the same result. And if this failure of the revolution marks the preliminary end of class struggle, this is not the end of violence, but its return in one of its most extreme forms: "Die Quittung für den gebremsten Klassenkampf ist der Umschlag in den Atavismus der Rassenkämpfe, die uns noch lange beschäftigen werden."[51]

This is why – after the cold war's end which might be called the end of World War II[52] – the battle lines along which violence may erupt in the future have to be rethought in terms of East, that is, Europe, and West, that is, Asia, as well as in terms of North and South, that is, in terms of an "economically dominated holding loop" ("in einer neuen ökonomisch dominierten Warteschleife")[53] as opposed to the so-called Third World.

---

48   "All power (Gewalt= power and violence) of the state emanates from the people. It is executed by the people by means of voting and elections and by means of special organs of legislation, of the executive power and of the judicial power." Grundgesetz für die Bundesrepublik Deutschland, Artikel 20, 2.

49   Müller: "Selbstkritik." Müller: *Daily News*, n. 3, p. 103.

50   "Die DDR-Bevölkerung konnte in der Vergangenheit durch das Fernsehen ganz abstrakt alles über den Kapitalismus lernen. Aber sie glaubten es nicht. Denn es gibt Differenzen zwischen den Bildern und der Erfahrung. In diesen Zwischenraum fallen die Leute jetzt. Das ist ein Schock und sicher eine Lehre. Dieser Schock produziert jetzt auch diese Gewaltausbrüche." Müller: *Zehn Deutsche sind dümmer als fünf,* p. 77.

51   "The price of the slowing down of class struggle is the dialectical turn into the struggles of race which will be occupying us for a long time to come." Müller: *Deutschland ortlos,* p. 414.

52   In his earlier works Müller states quite clearly: "Der Krieg ist nicht zu Ende." ("The war [that is WWII] is not finished yet." Müller: "Germania Tod in Berlin." Müller: *Germania Tod in Berlin*, pp. 37–78, here p. 55.

53   Müller: "Deutschland ortlos." Müller: *Deutschland ortlos,* p. 413.

Bibliography

The bibliographhy contains the full data of all titles cited by the contributors, the footnotes give only short-titles[1]

1. Primary Sources (Literary, Historical, Philosophical)

Academy Entertainment: "Romper Stomper" (Press materials for U. S. release). Los Angeles, CA: Academy Entertainment, 1992.

Aldington, Richard: *Death of a Hero: A Novel*. London: Chatto & Windus, 1929.

Allen, Jennifer: "Young, White and Surrounded." *Rolling Stone*, June 30, 1994: 55–61, 84.

Anton, Reinhold: *Am Pranger: Der Lügenfeldzug unserer Feinde: Eine weitere Gegenüberstellung deutscher, englischer, französischer und russischer Nachrichten über den Weltkrieg 1914/1915*. Vol. 2. Leipzig: Zehrfeld, 1915.

Aschoff, Ludwig: *Krankheit und Krieg: Eine akademische Rede*. Freiburg, Leipzig: Hans Speyer, 1915.

Avenarius, Ferdinand: *Das Bild als Verleumder: Beispiele und Bemerkungen zur Technik der Völkerverhetzung*. München: Callwey, 1915 (Flugschrift des Dürerbundes. 151).

Barker, Pat: *Regeneration*. London: Penguin, 1991.

Battock, Geoffrey, ed.: *The New Art: A Critical Anthology*. New York: Dutton, 1966.

Bauer, Max: *Konnten wir den Krieg vermeiden, gewinnen, abbrechen?* Drei Fragen, beantwortet von Oberst Bauer. Berlin: Scherl, 1919 (Flugschriften des "Tag". 2).

Becker, Maire Luise: *Ein Beitrag zur Aufklärung der feindlichen Greuelberichte*. Berlin: 1915.

Beckmann, Max: *Briefe im Kriege*. Gesammelt von Minna Tube. München: Piper, 1955.

Beckmann, Max: *Leben in Berlin: Tagebuch 1908/09*. Hrsg. von Hans Kinkel. München: Piper, 1966 (Piper-Bücherei. 216).

Bellah, James Walter: "Oh, the Infantry … With the Dirt Behind Their Ears." *Infantry Journal*, US Army, 53 (November 1943, No. 5): 54.

Benda, Julien: *The Treason of the Intellectuals*. New York: Norton, 1928.

Benn, Gottfried: *Gesammelte Werke in der Fassung der Erstdrucke*. Textkritisch durchgesehen u. hrsg. von Bruno Hillebrand. [Vol. 1:] *Gedichte*. 1982. – [Vol. 2:] *Prosa und Autobiographie*. 1984. – [Vol. 3:] *Essays und Reden*. 1989. – [Vol. 4:] *Szenen und Schriften*. 1990. Frankfurt a. M.: Fischer Taschenbuch Verlag 1982–1990.

---

1 In checking and completing the data of the bibliography Martin Andree, Oliver Cech, Diana Kurth, and Marcel Offermann, all of Cologne, provided valuable assistance.

Bergson, Henri: *Matter and Memory*. Authorized translation by Nancy Margaret Paul and W. Scott Palmer. New York: Zone Books, 1991.

Bernhard, Thomas: *Kalkwerk*. Frankfurt a. M.: Suhrkamp, 1973.

Bernhardi, Friedrich von: *Vom Kriege der Zukunft*. Berlin: Mittler, 1920.

Best, Werner: "Der Krieg und das Recht." Ernst Jünger, ed.: *Krieg und Krieger*. Berlin: Junker & Dünnhaupt, 1930. 135–62.

Blau, Albrecht: *Geistige Kriegführung*. Potsdam: Voggenreiter, 1937.

Blau, Albrecht: *Propaganda als Waffe*. Berlin: Bernard und Graefe, 1935.

Braun, Oberstleutnant: "Der strategische Überfall." *Militär-Wochenblatt (Berlin)*. No. 18 (spring 1938): 1135.

Brecht, Bertolt, Heiner Müller: *Der Untergang des Egoisten John Fatzer*. Bühnenfassung von Heiner Müller. Frankfurt a. M.: Suhrkamp, 1994 (Edition Suhrkamp. 1830).

Brecht, Bertolt: *Werke*. Große kommentierte Berliner und Frankfurter Ausgabe. Hrsg. von Werner Hecht, Jan Knopf, Werner Mittenzwei, Klaus-Detlef Müller. Berlin und Weimar: Aufbau-Verl.; Frankfurt a. M.: Suhrkamp, 1988–1995. – Vol. 23: *Schriften 3*. Bearb. von Barbara Wallburg unter Mitarb. von Marianne Conrad, Sigmar Gerung, Werner Hecht und Benno Slupiniak †. 1993. – Vol. 24: *Schriften 4. Texte zu Stücken*. Bearb. von Peter Kraft unter Mitarb. von Marianne Conrad, Sigmar Gerund und Benno Slupianek. 1991. – Vol. 26: *Journale 1*. Bearb. von Marianne Conrad und Werner Hecht unter Mitarb. von Herta Ranthun †. 1994. – Vol. 27: *Journale 2*. Bearb. von Werner Hecht. 1995.

Brooke, Rupert: *The Complete Poems*. London: Sidgwick & Jackson, 1958.

Buchfink, Ernst: *Der Krieg von Gestern und Morgen*. Langensalza: Beyer, 1930 (Schriften zur politischen Bildung. 6).

Büchner, Georg: *Werke und Briefe*. Münchner Ausgabe. Hrsg. von Karl Pörnbacher, Gerhard Schaub, Hans-Joachim Simm und Edda Ziegler. München: Hanser, 1988.

Calverhall, Randolph D.: *Serpent's Walk*. Hillsboro, W. V.: National Vanguard Books, 1991.

Chamberlain, Houston Stewart: "Deutsche Weltanschauung." *Deutschlands Erneuerung* 1, No. 1 (April 1917): 6.

Clausewitz, Carl von: *On War*. Ed. and trans. by Michael Howard and Peter Paret. Princeton: Princeton University Press, 1976. First ed. Berlin, 1832.

Clausewitz, Carl von: *Vom Kriege*. Hinterlassenes Werk. Vollständige Ausgabe im Urtext. 3 Teile in einem Band. Mit erneut erweiterter historisch-kritischer Würdigung von Werner Hahlweg. 19. Aufl. Bonn: Dümmler, 1980.

Curtius, Ernst Robert: *Die literarischen Wegbereiter des neuen Frankreich*. 3. Aufl. Potsdam: Kiepenheuer, 1923.

D'Annunzio, Gabriele: *La penultima ventura*. Opere di Gabriele d'Annunzio. Vol. 43. Verona: Mondadori, 1932.

Daudet, Léon: *La guerre totale*. Paris: Nouvelle librairie nationale, 1918.

Delbrück, Clemens v.: *Die wirtschaftliche Mobilmachung in Deutschland 1914*. Aus dem Nachlaß hrsg., eingel. u. erg. von Joachim von Delbrück. München: Verl. für Kulturpolitik, 1924.

Delbrück, Hans: *Regierung und Volkswille: Eine akademische Vorlesung*. Berlin: Stilke, 1914.

Denkschrift des OKW v. 4. 4. 1938 "Kriegführung als Problem der Organisation" mit Anhang "Was ist der Krieg der Zukunft."

Deutelmoser, Erhard: "Die amtliche Einwirkung auf die deutsche Öffentlichkeit im Kriege." *Die deutsche Nation* 1:10 (1919): 18–22.

Di Mattia, Joseph: "No More Happy Endings." Interview with Beth B. *Montage*, August/September 1990: 8–10.

Dobie, Kathy: "Long Day's Journey into White." *The Village Voice*, April 28, 1992: 22-32.

Döblin, Alfred: *Ausgewählte Werke in Einzelbänden*. Begründet von Walter Muschg. In Verb. mit den Söhnen des Dichters hrsg. von Anthony W. Riley. Olten und Freiburg i. Br.: Walter. – *Autobiographische Schriften und letzte Aufzeichnungen*. Hrsg. von Edgar Pässler. 1977. – *November 1918: Eine deutsche Revolution*. Erzählwerk in drei Teilen. Hrsg. von Werner Stauffacher. Vol. 1–3 (in 4). 1991. – *Schriften zur Ästhetik, Poetik und Literatur*. Hrsg. von Erich Kleinschmidt. 1989. – *Schriften zur Politik und Gesellschaft*. 1972. – *Unser Dasein*. 1964. – *Wallenstein: Roman*. 1965.

Döblin, Alfred: *Das Ich über der Natur*. Berlin: Fischer, 1928.

Döblin, Alfred: *Die beiden Freundinnen und ihr Giftmord*. Frankfurt a. M.: Suhrkamp, 1971.

Droysen, Johann Gustav: *Das Leben des Feldmarschalls Grafen York von Wartenburg*. Vols. 1–2. Berlin: Veit, 1851–52.

Eggebrecht, Axel: "Gespräch mit Remarque." *Die Literarische Welt* 5:24 (June 14, 1929): 1–2.

Eimannsberger, Ludwig Ritter von: *Der Kampfwagenkrieg*. München: Lehmann, 1934.

Eliot, Thomas Stearns: *Selected Prose*. Ed. by Frank Kermode. New York: Harcourt Brace Jovanovich, 1975.

Eltzbacher, Paul: "Die politische Propaganda der Franzosen." *Norddeutsche Allgemeine Zeitung*, No. 109, 28 February 1914.

Emilie, Albrecht: *Aus meinem "Kriegs-Tagebuch": Badischer mobiler Lazarett-Trupp XIV. A.-K.* 2. Zug. Heidelberg: Alfred Wolff, 1917.

Enzensberger, Hans Magnus: *Civil Wars: From L. A. to Bosnia.* Transl. by Martin Chalmers and Pier Spence. London: Penguin, 1994.

Eucken, Rudolf, and Max von Gruber: *Ethische und hygienische Aufgaben der Gegenwart.* Berlin: Springer, 1916.

Ferguson, Adam: *An Essay on the History of Civil Society.* 1767. Ed., with an introduction by Ducan Forbes. Edinburgh: Edinburgh University Press, 1966.

Feuchtwanger, Lion, and Arnold Zweig: *Briefwechsel 1933–1958.* Vols. 1–2. Frankfurt a. M.: Fischer, 1986.

Feuchtwanger, Lion: "Arnold Zweig." *Die neue Weltbühne* 33:45 (1937): 1412–15.

Ford, Ford Madox: *Parade's End.* Harmondsworth: Penguin, 1982.

Forsthoff, Ernst: *Der totale Staat.* München: Beck, 1933.

Freud, Sigmund: *Abriß der Psychologie: Das Unbehagen in der Kultur.* Frankfurt a. M.: Fischer Taschenbuch, 1972.

Freud, Sigmund: *Civilization and its Discontents. (Das Unbehagen in der Kultur,* German*).* Newly trans. from the German and ed. by James Strachey. New York, London: Norton, 1961.

Freud, Sigmund: *The Standard Edition of the Complete Psychological Works.* Trans. from the German under the general editorship of James Strachey, in collaboration with Anna Freud, assisted by Alix Strachey an Alan Tyson. Vol. 1–24. London: The Hogarth Press and the Institute of Psycho-Analysis, 1953–1974.

Freud, Sigmund: *Civilization, Society and Religion: "Group Psychology," "Civilization and its Discontents" and other Writings.*Trans. from the German under the general editorship of James Strachey. Ed. by Albert Dickson. Reprinted. Harmondsworth, Middlesex: Penguin 1985 (The Pelican Freud Library. 12).

Freud, Sigmund: *On Metapsychology: The Theory of Psychoanalysis: "Beyond the Pleasure Principle," "The Ego and the Id," and other writings.* Trans. from the German under the general editorship of James Strachey. Compiled and ed. by Angela Richard. Harmondsworth, Middlesex: Penguin 1984 (The Pelican Freud Library. 11).

Frey, Alexander Moritz: *Die Pflasterkästen: Ein Feldsanitätsroman.* Leipzig, Weimar: Kiepenheuer, 1984. First ed.: Berlin: Kiepenheuer, 1929.

Freyer, Hans: *Revolution von Rechts.* Jena: Diederichs, 1931.

Fromm, Erich: *Escape from Freedom.* New York: Avon, 1941.

Frosch, Dr.: "Die Dämonen der Lüge." *Die Welt am Montag,* 26. April 1915, Beilage.

Gandenberger v. Moisy, Fritz: *Luftkrieg – Zukunftskrieg: Aufbau, Gliederung und Kampfformen von Luftstreitkräften.* Berlin: Zentralverlag, 1935.

Gibbon, Edward: *The History of the Decline and Fall of the Roman Empire.* Vol. 1–6. London: Strahan & Cadell, 1776–1788.

Goebbels, Joseph: *Goebbels-Reden.* Hrsg. von Helmut Heiber. Vol. 1–2. Düsseldorf: Droste, 1972.

Goebbels, Joseph: "Rede vor der Presse, 16.3.33." Goebbels: *Revolution der Deutschen. 14 Jahre Nationalsozialismus: Goebbelsreden mit einleitenden Zeitbildern.* Hrsg. von Hein Schlecht. Oldenburg i. O.: Stalling 1933.

Goebel, Otto: *Deutsche Rohstoffwirtschaft im Weltkrieg einschließlich des Hindenburgprogramms.* Stuttgart, Berlin: Deutsche Verlags-Anstalt, 1930.

Golder, Frank Alfred, ed.: *Documents of Russian History 1914–1917.* Trans. by Emanuel Aronsberg. New York, London: The Century, 1927 (The Century historical series).

Gothein, Georg: *Warum verloren wir den Krieg?* 2., völlig umgearb. und erw. Aufl. Stuttgart: Deutsche Verlags-Anstalt, 1920.

Grass, Günter: "The Business Blitzkrieg." *The Guardian,* 20–21 October 1990: 6.

Groos, Otto: *Seekriegslehren im Lichte des Weltkriegs: Ein Buch für den Seemann, Soldaten und Staatsmann.* Mit einem Geleitw. von Großadmiral v. Tirpitz. Berlin: Mittler, 1929.

Grosz, George, and Wieland Herzfelde: *Die Kunst ist in Gefahr.* Berlin: Malik, 1925.

Grosz, George: "[Stick It Out!]." *Neue Jugend* 1 (1916) No. 7 (July): 127.

Guderian, Heinz: *Achtung Panzer.* Berlin: Union Deutsche Verlagsgesellschaft, 1937.

Guderian, Heinz: *Panzer – Marsch!* Vol. 1–2. München: Schild, 1957.

Gumppenberg, Hans von: "Rollands 'Wölfe' / Münchner Theater." *Der Kunstwart und Kulturwart* 27:3 (April-August 1914): 52–3.

Hadamovsky, Eugen: *Blitzmarsch nach Warschau: Frontberichte eines politischen Soldaten.* München: F. Eher, 1940.

Hadamovsky, Eugen: *Propaganda und nationale Macht: Die Organisation der öffentlichen Meinung für die Politik.* Oldenburg: Stalling, 1933.

Harnack, Adolf von, Otto Hintze, Friedrich Meinecke, Max Sering, and Ernst Troeltsch: *Die Deutsche Freiheit: Fünf Vorträge.* Gotha: Perthes, 1917.

Hauptmann, Gerhart: "Dresden." *Sämtliche Werke. Nachgelassene Werke. Fragmente.* Vol. 11. Frankfurt a. M.: Propyläen, 1974. 1205–06.

Heidegger, Martin, and Elisabeth Blochmann: *Briefwechsel 1918–1969.* Hrsg. von Joachim W. Storck. 2. Aufl. Marbach a. N.: Deutsche Schillergesellschaft, 1990 (Marbacher Schriften. 33).

Heidegger, Martin: "The Question concerning Technology." Heidegger: *Basic Writings.* Ed. by David Farrell Krell. New York: Harper and Row, 1977. 283–317.

Heidegger, Martin: "Zur Seinsfrage. Über 'die Linie'." *Gesamtausgabe.* Vol. 9. Frankfurt a. M.: Klostermann, 1977. 385–426.

Heldmann, Karl: *Kriegserlebnissse eines deutschen Geschichtsprofessors in der Heimat.* Ludwigsburg: Friede durch Recht, 1922.

Hesse, Kurt: *Der Feldherr Psychologos: Ein Suchen nach dem Führer der deutschen Zukunft.* Berlin: Mittler, 1922.

Heym, Georg: *Dichtungen und Schriften: Gesamtausgabe.* Hrsg, von Karl Ludwig Schneider. Vol. 1–3. Hamburg: Ellermann, 1960–1964.

Hierl, Constantin: *Grundlagen einer deutschen Wehrpolitik.* München: Eher, 1929 (Nationalsozialistische Bibliothek. 12).

Hirschfeld, Gerhard, and Gerd Krumeich, eds.: *Keiner fühlt sich hier mehr als Mensch … : Erlebnis und Wirkung des Ersten Weltkriegs.* Essen: Klartext, 1993.

Hitler, Adolf: *Mein Kampf.* A translation by John Chamberlain et al. New York: Reynal and Hitchcock, 1939.

Hitler, Adolf: *Mein Kampf.* A translation by Ralph Mannheim. Boston: Houghton Mifflin Company, 1971.

Hobbes, Thomas: *Leviathan, or the Matter, Form, and Power of a Common-Wealth Ecclesiastical and Civil.* London: Printed for Andrew Crooke, 1651.

Hochhuth, Rolf: *Soldaten. Nekrolog auf Genf: Tragödie.* Reinbek: Rowohlt, 1967.

Hochhuth, Rolf: "Vom Soldaten zum Berufsverbrecher. Brief an den Bundespräsidenten und Schirmherrn des Deutschen Roten Kreuzes." Hochhuth: *Krieg und Klassenkrieg. Studien.* Reinbek: Rowohlt, 1971. 106–29.

Isherwood, Christopher. *Goodbye to Berlin.* New York: New Directions, 1954.

Jaspers, Karl: *Die Atombombe und die Zukunft des Menschen.* München: Piper, 1958.

Jones, Tamara: "Germany's Troubles." *The Los Angeles Times Magazine,* March 7, 1993: 14–20.

Jünger, Ernst: *Der Arbeiter: Herrschaft und Gestalt.* Hamburg: Hanseatische Verlagsanstalt, 1932.

Jünger, Ernst: *Die totale Mobilmachung.* 2. Aufl. Berlin: Junker & Dünnhaupt, 1934.

Jünger, Ernst: *In Stahlgewittern.* Stuttgart: Klett-Cotta, 1992.

Jünger, Ernst: "Kriegerische Mathematik." *Der Widerstand* 5 (1930): 267–73. Also under the title "Feuer und Bewegung."

Kant, Immanuel: *Gesammelte Schriften.* Hrsg. von der Königlich Preußischen Akademie der Wissenschaften. Vol. 1–9. Berlin: Reimer, 1913.

Kant, Immanuel: *Werke in sechs Bänden.* Hrsg. von Wilhelm Weischedel. 5., erneut überprüfter reprographischer Nachdruck. Darmstadt: Wissenschaftliche Buchgesellschaft, 1983.

Kästner, Erhart: *Das Zeltbuch von Tumilat.* Frankfurt a. M.: Suhrkamp, 1976.

Kästner, Erhart: *Ölberge, Weinberge: Ein Griechenlandbuch.* Wiesbaden: Insel, 1953.

Kleist, Heinrich von: *Sämtliche Werke und Briefe in vier Bänden.* Hrsg. von Ilse-Marie Barth, Klaus Müller-Salget, Stefan Ormanns und Hinrich C. Seeba. Vol. 1–3 [thus far]. Frankfurt a. M.: Deutscher Klassiker Verlag 1987–1991 (Bibliothek deutscher Klassiker. 71, 26, 51).

Knesebeck, Ludolf Gottschalk von dem: *Die Wahrheit über den Propagandafeldzug und Deutschlands Zusammenbruch: Der Kampf der Publizistik im Weltkriege.* Im Anhang: 20 unveröffentlichte Briefe Ludendorffs aus dem Weltkrieg und die wahrscheinliche Denkschrift Bethmanns zur Entlassung Falkenhayns. München: Selbstverlag, Auslieferung: Fortschrittliche Buchhandlung, 1927.

Koester, Adolf: *Fort mit der Dolchstosslegende! Warum wir 1918 nicht weiterkämpfen konnten.* Berlin: Verlag für Politik und Wirtschaft, 1922.

Kolmar, Gertrud: *Briefe an die Schwester Hilde (1938–1941).* Hrsg. von Johanna Zeitler. München: Kösel, 1970.

Kolmar, Gertrud: *Das lyrische Werk.* München: Kösel, 1960.

Kolmar, Gertrud: *Frühe Gedichte (1917–22). Das Wort der Stummen (1933).* Hrsg. von Johanna Woltmann-Zeitler. München: Kösel, 1980.

Kolmar, Gertrud: "Das Bildnis Robespierres. Mitgeteilt von Johanna Zeitler." *Jahrbuch der Deutschen Schillergesellschaft* 9 (1965): 553–80.

Kolmar, Gertrud: "Zwei Briefe an Walter Benjamin." *Sinn und Form* 43 (1991): 122–24.

Köppe, H.: "Schriften über den Kriegssozialismus." *Archiv für die Geschichte des Sozialismus und der Arbeiterbewegung* 8 (1919): 76–115.

Kranold, Hermann: *Sozialisierung: Warum, Was, Wie, Wann?* Sonderabdruck aus der *Chemnitzer Volksstimme* [1919].

Laffin, John: *Jackboot.* London: Cassell, 1976.

Lehmann-Russbüldt, Otto: *Warum erfolgte der Zusammenbruch an der Westfront?* Mit einer dem General Ludendorff einstmals übermittelten Denkschrift eines deutschen Landsturmmannes. 2., erw. Aufl. Berlin: Berger, 1919. (Flugschriften des Bundes neues Vaterland. 3).

Lewin, Kurt: "Kriegslandschaft." Zeitschrift für angewandte Psychologie 11 (1916): 440–47.

Liddell Hart, Basil: *Infanterie von morgen.* Deutsch von Artur Eberhardt. Potsdam: Voggenreiter, 1934.

Liddell Hart, Basil: *The British Way in Warfare.* London: Faber & Faber, 1932.

Liebig, Hans Freiherr von: *Die Politik von Bethmann-Hollwegs: Eine Studie.* München: Lehmann, 1915.

Ludendorff, Erich: *Der totale Krieg.* München: Ludendorff, 1935.

Ludendorff, Erich, ed.: *Urkunden der Obersten Heeresleitung über ihre Tätigkeit 1916–18.* 3., durchges. Aufl. Berlin: Mittler, 1922.

Ludendorff, Erich: *Kriegführung und Politik.* Berlin: Mittler, 1922.

Ludendorff, Erich: *Ludendorff's Own Story. August 1914–November 1918: The great war from the siege of Liege to the signing of the armistice as viewed from the Grand Headquarters of the German army.* Vol. 2. New York, London: Harpers & Brothers, 1919.

Macdonald, Andrew: *Hunter.* Hillsboro, W. V.: National Vanguard Books, 1989.

Mach, Ernst: *Die Analyse der Empfindungen und das Verhältnis des Physischen zum Psychischen.* 2. Aufl. Jena: Fischer, 1890. First ed. 1886 under the title *Beiträge zur Analyse der Empfindungen.*

Malaparte, Curzio: *Der Staatsstreich.* Übertragen von Renée Adloff. Leipzig, Wien: Tal, 1932.

Malaparte, Curzio: *Die Wolga entspringt in Europa.* Mit einem Vorwort von Heiner Müller. Köln: Kiepenheuer & Witsch, 1989.

Mann, Thomas: *Tagebücher 1944 – 1.4.1946.* Hrsg. von Inge Jens. Frankfurt a. M.: S. Fischer, 1986.

Marc, Franz: *Briefe aus dem Felde.* Berlin: Rauschenbusch, 1940.

Marinetti, Filippo Tammaso: *Selected Writings.* Ed. by R. W. Flint, trans. by R. W. Flint and Arthur Coppotello. New York: Farrar, Straus and Giroux, 1972.

Masson, Fréderic: *Napoleon I. und die Frauen.* Vom Französichen ins Deutsche übersetzt von Oskar Marschall von Bieberstein. Berlin: Brandus'sche Verlagsbuchhandlung, 1913. First ed.: Leipzig: Schmidt & Günther, 1895.

Masson, Fréderic: *Napoléon et les femmes.* Paris: Ollendorf, 1894.

McLuhan, Marshall: "Marshall McLuhan: A Candid Conversation with the High Priest of Popcult and Metaphysician of Media." *Playboy Magazine,* March 1969.

Mense, Carl: "Zum neuen Jahre." *Archiv für Schiffs- und Tropen-Hygiene* 19 (1915): 1.

Metzsch, Horst von: *Krieg als Saat.* Breslau: Hirt, 1934.

Metzsch, Horst von: *Zeitgemäße Gedanken um Clausewitz.* Berlin: Junker u. Dünnhaupt, 1937 (Schriften der deutschen Hochschule für Politik. 1)

Miksche, Ferdinand Otto: *Blitzkrieg.* With an introduction by Tom Wintringham. London: Faber and Faber, 1941.

Moellendorf, Wichard von, ed.: *Von Einst zu Einst: Der alte Fritz, J. G. Fichte, Freiherr vom Stein, Friedrich List, Fürst Bismarck, Paul Lagarde über Deutsche Gemeinwirtschaft.* Jena: Diederichs, 1917.

Moellendorff, Wichard von: *Konservativer Sozialismus*. Hrsg. und eingeleitet von Hermann Curth. Hamburg: Hanseatische Verlagsanstalt, 1932.

Mühsam, Kurt: *Wie wir belogen wurden: Die amtliche Irreführung des deutschen Volkes*. München: Langen, 1918.

Müller, Heiner: *Germania Tod in Berlin*. Heiner Müller: *Texte 5*. Berlin: Rotbuch Verlag, 1977.

Müller, Heiner: *Herzstück*. Korrigierte Erstauflage. Heiner Müller: *Texte 7*. Berlin: Rotbuch Verlag, 1983.

Müller, Heiner: *Jenseits der Nation: Heiner Müller im Interview mit Frank M. Raddatz*. Heiner Müller: *Texte 11*. Berlin: Rotbuch Verlag, 1991.

Müller, Heiner: *Material: Texte und Kommentare*. Leipzig: Reclam, 1990.

Müller, Heiner: *Mauser*. Heiner Müller: *Texte 6*. Berlin: Rotbuch Verlag, 1978.

Müller, Heiner: *Shakespeare Factory 1–2*. Heiner Müller: *Texte 8–9*. Berlin: Rotbuch Verlag, 1985–89.

Müller, Heiner: *Stücke*. Mit einem Nachwort von Rolf Rohmer. Berlin: Henschelverlag, 1975.

Müller, Heiner: *Zur Lage der Nation: Heiner Müller im Interview mit Frank M. Raddatz*. Heiner Müller: *Texte 10*. Berlin: Rotbuch Verlag, 1990.

Müller, Heiner: "Daily News. Drei Lektionen." *Die neue Rundschau* 2 (1990): 101–04.

Müller, Heiner: "Deutschland ortlos. Anmerkung zu Kleist. Rede anläßlich der Entgegen nahme des Kleist-Preises." *Sinn und Form*. 2 (1991): 413–15.

Müller, Heiner: "Zehn Deutsche sind dümmer als fünf: Gespräch mit dem Dramatiker Heiner Müller." *Die neue Rundschau*. 2 (1992): 66–78.

Musil, Robert: *Der Mann ohne Eigenschaften*. Hrsg. von Adolf Frisé. Vol. 1–2. Reinbek: Rowohlt, 1988.

Nassauer, Max: "Im Nebel nur wagt es Engeland." *Münchener Medizinische Wochenschrift* 61 (1914): 2231.

Ortner, Eugen: *Gott Stinnes: Ein Pamphlet gegen den vollkommenen Menschen*. Hannover, Leipzig: Stegemann, 1922.

Owen, Wilfred: *The Poems*. Ed. by Jon Stallworthy. London: Chatto and Windus, 1985.

Paul, Wolfgang: *Dresden 1953*. Esslingen: Bechtle, 1953.

Philipp, Albrecht, ed.: *Die Ursachen des deutschen Zusammenbruchs im Jahre 1918*. Unter Mitwirkung von Eugen Fischer und Walther Bloch im Auftrag des Vierten Untersuchungsausschusses. Vol. 1–12. Berlin: Deutsche Verl.-Ges. f. Politik u. Geschichte 1925–1929 (Das Werk des Untersuchungsausschusses der Verfassunggebenden Deutschen Nationalversammlung und des Deutschen Reichstages 1919–28. 4. Reihe).

Plath, Sylvia: "Daddy." Plath: *The Collected Poems*. Ed. by Ted Hughes. New York: Harper Perennial, 1992. 222–24.

Plenge, Johann: *Deutsche Propaganda: Die Lehre von der Propaganda als praktische Gesellschaftslehre*. Bremen: Angelsachsen-Verlag, 1922.

Possony, Stefan Th.: *L'economia della Guerra Totale*. Torino: Einaudi, 1939.

Pound, Ezra: *Selected Poems*. Ed. with an introduction by Thomas Stearns Eliot. London: Faber and Faber, 1928.

Preuß, Hugo: *Das deutsche Volk und der Weltkrieg*. Jena: Diederichs, 1915.

Preuß, Hugo: *Obrigkeitsstaat und großdeutscher Gedanke: Zwei Vorträge*. Jena: Diederichs, 1916.

Raecke, J.: "Über Aggravation und Simulation geistiger Störung." *Archiv für Psychiatrie und Nervenkrankheiten* 60 (1919): 521–603.

Rathenau, Walther: *Gesammelte Schriften*. Vol. 1–5. Berlin: S. Fischer, 1918.

Rathenau, Walther: *Hauptwerke und Gespräche*. Hrsg. von Ernst Schulin. München: Müller; Heidelberg: Lambert Schneider, 1977 (Walther Rathenau-Gesamtausgabe. 2).

Rathenau, Walther: *Nachgelassene Schriften*. Vol. 1–6. Berlin: S. Fischer, 1928.

Reich, Wilhelm: *The Mass Psychology of Fascism* (*Massenpsychologie des Faschismus*, Engl.). A translation by Theodore P. Wolfe. New York: Orgone Institute, 1946.

Rodenberger, Axel: *Der Tod von Dresden: Ein Bericht über das Sterben einer Stadt*. Frankfurt a. M.: Müller-Rodenberger, 1963.

Rolland, Romain: *Choix de lettres à Malwida von Meysenbug*. Par Romain Rolland. Établi par Marie Romain Rolland. Avant-Propos de Edouard Monod-Herzen. Paris: Michel, 1948 (Cahiers Romain Rolland. 1)

Rolland, Romain, and Aurélien Lugné-Poe: *Correspondence 1894–1901*. Ed. par Jaques Robichez. Paris: L'Arche, 1957.

Rolland, Romain, and Louis Gillet: *Correspondence entre Louis Gillet et Romain Rolland: Choix de lettres*. Ed. par Louis Gillet et Mme Romain Rolland. Paris: Albin Michel, 1949 (Cahiers Romain Rolland. 2).

Rolland, Romain, and Charles Péguy: *Une amitié française: Correspondence entre Charles Péguy et Romain Rolland*. Ed. par Alfred Saffrey. Paris: Albin Michel, 1955 (Cahiers Romain Rolland. 7).

Rolland, Romain, and Stefan Zweig: *Briefwechsel 1910–1940*. Hrsg. von Waltraud Schwartze. Vol. 1–2. Berlin: Rütten & Loening, 1987.

Rolland, Romain: *Danton*. Trans. from French into German by Lucy v. Jacobi and Wilhelm Herzog. München: Georg Müller, 1920. First ed. 1919.

Rolland, Romain: *Die Wölfe*. Übersetzt von Wilhelm Herzog. 2. Aufl. München: Georg Müller, 1920.

Rolland, Romain: *Le jeu de l'amour et de la mort.* 18th thousand. Paris: Albin Michel, 1925. First ed.: Paris: Éditions du Sablier, 1924.

Rolland, Romain: *Mémoires et fragments des journal.* Paris: Albin Michel, 1956.

Rolland, Romain: *Robespierre. Drame en trois actes et vingt-quatres tableaux.* 5th thousand. Paris: Albin Michel, 1939.

Rolland, Romain: *Théatre de la Révolution: Le 14 juillet – Danton – Les loups.* Paris: Albin Michel, 1926.

Rolland, Romain: *Un beau visage à tous sens: Choix de lettres de Romain Rolland.* Paris: Albin Michel, 1967 (Cahiers Romain Rolland. 17).

Rolland, Romain: "Danton." Trans. from French into German by Lucy v. Jacobi and Wilhelm Herzog. *Das Forum* 3:1 (1918/19): 370–402, 428–89.

Rolland, Romain: "Die Wölfe (III,1)." *Das Forum* 3:1 (1918/19): 201–23.

Roth, Joseph: "Die hundert Tage: Roman." Roth: *Werke.* Vol. 5. Hrsg. von Fritz Hackert. Köln: Kiepenheuer & Witsch, 1990. 677–848.

Rühle, Günther, ed.: *Theater für die Republik im Spiegel der Kritik.* Vol. 1–2. Berlin: Henschel, 1988.

Salomon, Ernst von: "Der verlorene Haufe." Ernst Jünger, ed.: *Krieg und Krieger.* Berlin: Junker & Dünnhaupt, 1930: 101–26.

Sanitätsbericht über das Deutsche Heer (Deutsches Feld- und Besatzungsheer) im Weltkriege 1914/1918 (Deutscher Kriegssanitätsbericht 1914/18). Bearbeitet in der Heeres- Sanitätsinspektion des Reichskriegsministeriums. Vol. 1. Berlin: Mittler, 1935.

Schauwecker, Franz: *Aufbruch der Nation.* Berlin: Freundsberg, 1929.

Scherke, Felix, and Ursula Vitzthum: *Bibliographie der geistigen Kriegführung.* Berlin: Bernard & Graefe, 1938.

Schmidt, E. E. Hermann: *Das politische Werbewesen in der Umsturzzeit.* Berlin: Berwig 1919.

Schmidt, E. E. Hermann: *Das politische Werbewesen im Kriege.* Berlin: Berwig, 1919.

Schmitt, Carl: *Der Nomos der Erde im Völkerrecht des Jus Publicum Europaeum.* Köln: Greven, 1950.

Schmitt, Carl: *Die Wendung zum diskriminierenden Kriegsbegriff (1938).* Vol. 1–2. Berlin: Duncker & Humblot, 1988.

Schmitt, Carl: *The Crisis of Parliamentary Democracy.* Trans. by Ellen Kennedy. Cambridge, Mass.: MIT Press, 1985.

Schmitt, Carl: *Theorie des Partisanen: Zwischenbemerkung zum Begriff des Politischen.* Berlin: Duncker & Humblot, 1963.

Schmitt, Carl: *Völkerrechtliche Großraumordnung mit Interventionsverbot für raumfremde Mächte (1941).* Berlin: Duncker & Humblot, 1991.

Schmitt, Carl: *Völkerrechtliche Großraumordnung mit Interventionsverbot für raumfremde Mächte: Ein Beitrag zum Reichsbegriff im Völkerrecht.* Berlin, Wien: Deutscher Rechtsverlag, 1939 (Schriften des Instituts für Politik und internationales Recht an der Universität Kiel. N. F. 7).

Schmitt, Carl: "Der neue Raumbegriff in der Völkerrechtswissenschaft." *Raumforschung und Raumordnung* 1 (1940): 440–42.

Schmitt, Carl: "Diktatur und Belagerungszustand: Eine staatsrechtliche Studie." *Zeitschrift für die gesamte Strafrechtswissenschaft* 38 (1916/17): 138–62.

Schmitt, Carl: "Raum und Großraum im Völkerrecht." *Zeitschrift für Völkerrecht* 24 (1940): 145–79.

Schultze-Pfaelzer, Gerhard. *Propaganda, Agitation, Reklame: Eine Theorie des gesamten Werbewesens.* Berlin: Stilke, 1923.

Schwalbe, Julius: "Kleine Mitteilungen." *Deutsche Medizinische Wochenschrift* 40 (1914): 1623, 1662–1663.

"Der Selbsterreger." (1936) Peter Uwe Hohendahl, ed.: *Benn – Wirkung wider Willen.* Frankfurt a. M.: Athenäum, 1971. 196–99.

Soldan, George: *Der Mensch und die Schlacht der Zukunft.* Oldenburg: Stalling, 1925.

Sophokles: *Tragödien und Fragmente.* Griechisch-deutsch. Herausgegeben und übersetzt von Wilhelm Willige. Überarbeitet von Karl Bayer. München: Heimaran, 1966 (Tusculum-Bücherei).

Sorel, Georges: *Reflections on Violence.* Trans. by T. E. Hulme (1915). New York: Peter Smith, 1941.

Sorel, Georges: *Réflexions sur la violence (1906).* Edition définitive suivie du Plaidoyer pour Lénine. Paris: Riviere, 1946.

Spaight, James Molony: *Air Power and War rights.* 2nd ed. London, New York: Longmans, Green, & Co., 1933.

Spann, Othmar: *Der Wahre Staat: Vorlesungen über Abbruch und Neubau der Gesellschaft gehalten im Sommersemester 1920 an der Universität Wien.* Leipzig: Quelle & Meyer, 1921.

Stehr, Hermann, Walther Rathenau: *Zwiesprache über den Zeiten: Geschichte einer Freundschaft in Briefen und Dokumenten.* Hrsg. von Ursula Merides-Stehr. Leipzig, München: List, 1946.

Steinmetz, Sebald Rudolf: *Soziologie des Krieges.* Leipzig: Barth, 1929.

Stephinger, Ludwig: *Grundsätze der Sozialisierung.* Tübingen: Mohr, 1919.

Stern, Ernst, and Heinz Herald, eds.: *Reinhardt und seine Bühne: Bilder von der Arbeit des Deutschen Theaters.* 2. Tausend. Berlin: Eysler, 1918.

Stern-Rubath, Edgar: *Die Propaganda als politisches Instrument.* Berlin: Trowitzsch, 1921.

Sternberg, Fritz: *Der Dichter und die Ratio: Erinnerungen an Bertolt Brecht.* Göttingen: Sachse und Pohl, 1963.

Sternberg, Fritz: *Die deutsche Kriegsstärke: Wie lange kann Hitler Krieg führen?* Paris: Editions Sebastian Brant, 1939. Engl. ed.: *Germany and a Lightening War.* London: Faber and Faber, 1939.

Stouffer, Samuel et al.: *The American Soldier.* Vol. 2. Princeton, N. J.: Princeton University Press, 1949.

Thimme, Hans: *Weltkrieg ohne Waffen: Die Propaganda der Westmächte gegen Deutschland, ihre Wirkung und ihre Abwehr.* Stuttgart, Berlin: Cotta, 1932.

Tönnies, Ferdinand: *Der englische Staat und der deutsche Staat.* Berlin: Curtius, 1917.

Tönnies, Ferdinand: *Fortschritt und soziale Entwicklung: Geschichtsphilosophische Ansichten.* Karlsruhe: Braun, 1926.

Tönnies, Ferdinand: *Warlike England as seen by Herself.* New York: Dillingham, 1915.

Tönnies, Ferdinand: *Zur Kritik der öffentlichen Meinung.* Berlin: Springer, 1922.

Tönnies, Ferdinand: "Gemeinschaft und Gesellschaft. Vorrede zu der Dritten Auflage." Tönnes: *Soziologische Studien und Kritiken.* Vol. 1. Jena: Fischer, 1925.

Troeltsch, Ernst: *Der Kulturkrieg. Rede am 1. Juli 1915.* Hrsg. von der Zentralstelle für Volkswohlfahrt und dem Verein für volkstümliche Kurse von Berliner Hochschullehrern. Berlin: Heymann, 1915.

Troeltsch, Ernst: "Das Wesen des Weltkrieges." Max Schwarte, ed.: *Der Weltkrieg in seiner Einwirkung auf das deutsche Volk.* Leipzig: Quelle & Meyer, 1918.

Vonnegut, Kurt: *Slaughterhouse Five or the Children's Crusade: A Duty-Dance with Death.* New York: Delacorte, 1971.

Walser, Martin: *Die Verteidigung der Kindheit.* Frankfurt a. M.: Suhrkamp, 1991.

Walser, Martin: "Über Deutschland reden: Ein Bericht." Walser: *Über Deutschland reden.* Frankfurt a. M.: Suhrkamp, 1989. 76–100.

Weber, Max: *Economy and Society.* Vol. 1. Ed. by Guenther Roth and Claus Wittich. Berkeley: University of California Press, 1978.

Werner, Bruno E.: *Die Galeere.* Frankfurt a. M.: Suhrkamp, 1949.

Wolff, Theodor: "[Untitled.]" *Berliner Tageblatt,* No. 534, 10. November 1918, (Morgen).

Woolf, Virginia: *A Room of One's Own / Three Guineas.* Oxford: Oxford University Press, 1992.

Wrisberg, Ernst von: *Der Weg zur Revolution 1914–1918.* Leipzig: Koehler, 1921.

Wyndham, Lewis: "Note [on some German Woodcuts at the Twenty-One Gallery]." *Blast.* No. 1, London 1914: 136.

Ziegler, Leopold: "Haß." *Die Schaubühne* 1 (1915): 5.

Zimmering, Max: *Im herben Morgenwind: Ausgewählte Gedichte aus 25 Jahren.* Berlin: Dietz, 1958.

Kolmar locates God in the last word of the no less famous Revolutionary slogan: *Liberté, égalité, fraternité, ou la mort.* This black deity triumphs as an absolute principle ignoring and devaluing individual suffering. In Kolmar's eyes, Saint-Just and Robespierre were priests if not saints of a God of Justice who affirms His rule by destroying men's projects and lives.

In the period between the publication of Saint Just's fatal phrase in German (1919/20) and its quotation by Kolmar (1934), Rolland had resumed his work on the cycle of Revolution dramas. His next contribution to his cycle, the drama *Le jeu de l'amour et de la mort*, appeared in 1924. It opened with a dedication whose German translation reads: "à Stephan Zweig/ Je dédie affectueusement ce drame qui lui doit d'être écrit."[75] In Germany, the play had an unprecedented success. In September 1925, it was, according to Zweig, performed by forty German theaters.[76] Rolland's *Robespierre* might be indebted to Zweig and the theater of the Weimar Republic,[77] but we do not even know whether Kolmar was able to avail herself of this book.

What is documented is that she did not stop reading on Robespierre up to 1941.[78] And we should assume that hardly any other text could have been as intriguing, affirmative and comforting for her at that time as Rolland's *Robespierre*. Here, Rolland finally embarks on rehabilitating this ill-reputed revolutionist. The play was destined to be the definitive reconception this dramatist

---

droht, / Der Meere stärkstes, niemals einzudämmen, / Ist nicht nur Leben. Gott ist Tod." On the metaphysically paradox disparity between man and nature in Kolmar see the brilliant study by Bayerdörfer: "Die Sinnlichkeit des Widerlichen. Zur Poetik der 'Tierträume' von Gertrud Kolmar."

75   Rolland: *Le jeu de l'amour et du hazard*, p. 7; cf. p. 18. The first edition appeared in Paris: Editions du Sablier, 1924. Nedeljkovic goes so far as to assume that Rolland would never have resumed the work on his *Théâtre de la Révolution* without Zweig's encouragement: Nedeljkovic: *Romain Rolland et Stefan Zweig*, pp. 287, 308.

76   Zweig to Rolland: *Briefwechsel 1910–1940* vol. 2, p. 122; cf. pp. 75–7, 79–80, 89. Kempf speaks of thirty German *mises en scènes* repertoired in August 1925: Kempf: *Romain Rolland et l'Allemagne*, p. 242.

77   Since 1924, Zweig time and again put pressure on Rolland to complete his *Robespierre* (Nedeljkovic: *Romain Rolland et Stefan Zweig*, pp. 297, 299, 302–3; Rolland-Zweig: *Briefwechsel 1910–1940*, e. g., vol. 2, pp. 20, 49–50, 162, 287). The drama, written in c. 1936–1938, seems to have adopted its typified juxtaposition of the "Incorruptible" with Joseph Fouché from the third chapter of Zweig's 1929 biography *Joseph Fouché* (cf. Dumont: *Stefan Zweig et la France*, pp. 231–2, 306; on Rolland's reading of *Joseph Fouché* and Zweig's reaction to the finished text of *Robespierre* see their *Briefwechsel 1910–1942*, vol. 2, pp. 688- 91, 698–703). In its scenographical means, Rolland might have borrowed from Max Reinhardt's 1920 *mise en scène* of *Danton* (the mass scenes) as well as from Erwin Piscator's spectacular blurring of theatrical and filmic shows (Robespierre's "visions" in scene 23).

78   Kolmar: *Briefe an die Schwester Hilde (1938–1941)*, p. 105 (letter no. 38, dated July 22, 1941).

Zimmering, Max: *Phosphor und Flieder: Vom Untergang und Wiederauferstehung der Stadt Dresden.* Berlin: Dietz, 1954.

Zweig, Arnold: *Das ostjüdische Antlitz [1920].* Wiesbaden: Fourier, 1988.

Zweig, Arnold: *Der Elfenbeinfächer: Ausgewählte Novellen.* Vol. 1. Berlin: Aufbau-Ver lag, 1952.

Zweig, Arnold: *Die Bestie: Erzählungen.* München: Albert Langen, 1914.

Zweig, Arnold: *Gerufene Schatten.* Leipzig: Reclam, 1926.

Zweig, Arnold: *Knaben und Männer.* Berlin: Kiepenheuer, 1931.

Zweig, Arnold: *Novellen.* Vol. 1–2. Frankfurt a. M.: Fischer, 1987.

Zweig, Arnold: *Spielzeug der Zeit: Erzählungen.* Amsterdam: Querido, 1933.

Zweig, Arnold: *Westlandsaga.* Frankfurt a. M.: Fischer Taschenbuch, 1985.

Zweig, Arnold: "Bekehrung zum Frieden." *Illustrierte Rundschau* (East Berlin) 5:20 (1950): 6.

Zweig, Arnold: "Briefe an Hilscher." *Neue deutsche Literatur* 15:11 (1967): 33–42.

Zweig, Arnold: "Die Demokratie und die Seele des Juden." Verein jüdischer Hochschüler "Bar Kochba" in Prag, ed.: *Vom Judentum.* Leipzig: Wolff, 1913. 210–35.

Zweig, Arnold: "Die Quittung." *Neue deutsche Literatur* 3.2 (1955): 76, 79.

Zweig, Arnold: "Warum ich schwieg: Notwendige Antwort auf überflüssige Fragen." *Die literarische Welt* No. 12/13, December 25, 1925: 5.

Zweig, Stefan: *Joseph Fouché: Bildnis eines politischen Menschen.* Leipzig: Insel, 1929.

Zweig, Stefan: *Romain Rolland: Der Mann und das Werk.* Frankfurt a. M.: Rütten & Loening, 1923.

Zweig, Stefan: *Romain Rolland.* Hrsg. von Knut Beck. Frankfurt a. M.: S. Fischer, 1987.

2. Secondary Sources

Adams, Veronica: "Jane Crow in the Army: Obstacles to Sexual Integration." *Psychology Today* 14:5 (1980): 53.

Adorno, Theodor W., Else Frenkel-Brunswik, Daniel J. Levinson, and R. Nevitt Sanford: *The Authoritarian Personality.* New York: Harper and Brothers, 1950.

Adorno, Theodor W.: *Aesthetic Theory.* A translation by C. Lenhardt. London: Routledge & Kegan Paul, 1984.

Adorno, Theodor W.: *Erziehung zur Mündigkeit: Vorträge und Gespräche mit Hellmut Becker. 1959–69.* Hrsg. von Gerd Kadelbach. Frankfurt a. M.: Suhrkamp, 1970.

Allen, Thomas B. and Norman Polmar: *Code-Name Downfall: The Secret Plan to Invade Japan – and why Truman Dropped the Bomb.* New York: Simon and Schuster, 1995.

Alperowitz, Gar et al.: *The Decision to use the Atomic Bomb and the Architecture of an American Myth.* New York: Alfred Knopf, 1995.

Amis, Martin: "Kurt Vonnegut: After the Slaughterhouse." Amis: *The Moronic Inferno and Other Visits to America.* London: Penguin, 1986. 132–37.

Anderson, Benedict: *Imagined Communities: Reflections on the origin and spread of nationalism.* London: Verso, 1983.

Angel, Ernst: "Drama und Revolution: Zur Soziologie der Dantondramen." *Das junge Deutschland* 3 (1920): 25–27.

Arato, Andrew, and Eike Gebhardt, eds.: *The Essential Frankfurt School Reader.* New York: Continuum, 1975.

Arazi, Doron: "Horchdienst und Blitzkrieg: die deutsche militärische Funkaufklärung im Unternehmen 'Barbarossa'." Bernd Wegner, ed.: *Zwei Wege nach Moskau: Vom Hitler-Stalin-Pakt bis zum 'Unternehmen Barbarossa'.* München, Zürich: Piper, 1991. 221–33.

Armstrong, Nancy, and Leonard Tennenhouse, ed.: *The Violence of Representation: Literature and the History of Violence.* London, New York: Routledge, 1994.

Baddock, Geoffrey: *Art and Culture.* London: Thames and Hudson, 1973.

Bahlke, Friedrich: "Unsere Lage. Carl Schmitt am Golf. In suo esse perseverare." *KultuR Revolution* 25 (1991): 21–27.

Balfour, Michael: *Propaganda in War, 1939–1945: Organisations, Policies and Publics in Britain and Germany.* London: Routledge & Kegan Paul, 1979.

Barclay, David E.: "A Prussian Socialism? Wichard von Moellendorff and the dilemmas of Economic Planning in Germany, 1918–1919." *Central European History* 11 (1978): 50–82.

Barkai, Avraham: *Das Wirtschaftssystem des Nationalsozialismus: Ideologie. Theorie. Politik 1933–45.* Erweiterte Neuausgabe. Frankfurt a. M.: Fischer Taschenbuch-Verlag, 1988 (Fischer-Taschenbuch. 4401).

Barthes, Roland: *S/Z.* Paris: Editions du Seuil, 1970.

Bartov, Omer: *The Eastern Front 1941–45: German Troops and the Barbarisation of Warfare.* Basingstoke, Hampshire: Macmillan, 1985.

Baudis, Dieter, and Helga Nussbaum: *Wirtschaft und Staat in Deutschland vom Ende des 19. Jahrhunderts bis 1918/19.* Vaduz: Topos, 1978 (Wirtschaft und Staat in Deutschland. 1).

Baudis, Dieter: "Vom 'Schweinemord zum Kohlrübenwinter.' Streiflichter zur Entwicklung der Lebensverhältnisse in Berlin im Ersten Weltkrieg (August 1914 bis Frühjahr 1917)." *Jahrbuch für Wirtschaftsgeschichte* 1986: 129–52.

Baudrillard, Jean: *Simulations*. Trans. by Paul Foss, Paul Patton and Philip Beitchmann. New York City: Semiotext(e), 1983.

Bauman, Zygmund: *Modernity and Ambivalence*. Cambridge: Polity Press, 1991.

Bauman, Zygmund: *Modernity and the Holocaust*. Ithaca, New York: Cornell University Press, 1989.

Baumann, Gerhart: *Robert Musil: Zur Erkenntnis der Dichtung*. Bern München: Francke, 1965.

Baurke, Carolyn: "Getting Spliced: Modernism and Sexual Difference." *American Quarterly* 39:1 (1987): 98–121.

Bayerdörfer, Hans-Peter: "Die Sinnlichkeit des Widerlichen. Zur Poetik der 'Tierträume' von Gertrud Kolmar." Hansgert Delbrück, ed.: *Sinnlichkeit in Bild und Klang: Festschrift für Paul Hoffmann zum 70. Geburtstag*. Stuttgart: Heinz, 1987. 449–63.

Becker, Jean-Jacques, Annette Becker, Stéphane Audoin-Ruzeau, Gerd Krumeich, and Jay M. Winter, eds.: *Guerres et cultures: Vers une histoire comparée de la grande guerre*. Paris: Armand Colin, 1994.

Bellebaum, Alfred: "Ferdinand Tönnies". Dirk Käsler, ed., *Klassiker des soziologischen Denkens*. Vol. 1. München: Beck, 1976. 232–66.

Bendixen, Peter: *Das Staatsdenken Walther Rathenaus*. Kiel, Phil. Diss. 1971.

Beniger, James R.: *The Control Revolution: Technological and Economic Origins of the Information Society*. Cambridge, Mass., London: Harvard University Press, 1986.

Benjamin, Walter: *Angelus Novus*. Ausgewählte Schriften 2. Frankfurt a. M.: Suhrkamp, 1966.

Benjamin, Walter: *Gesammelte Schriften*. Hrsg. von Rolf Tiedemann und Hermann Schweppenhäuser. Vol. 1–7 (in 14). Frankfurt a. M.: Suhrkamp, 1972–1989.

Benjamin, Walter: *Illuminations*. Ed. and with an introduction by Hannah Arendt; trans. by Harry Zohn. New York: Harcourt, Brace & World, 1968.

Bergander, Götz: *Dresden im Luftkrieg*. Köln, Wien: Böhlau, 1977.

Berking, Helmuth: *Masse und Geist: Studien zur Soziologie in der Weimarer Republik*. Berlin: Wissenschaftlicher Autoren-Verlag, 1984.

Bernhard, Hans-Joachim: "Wider den Verfall der Gesittung – zu einem zentralen Motiv im Werk Arnold Zweigs." Helmut Müssener, ed., *Anti-Kriegsliteratur zwischen den Kriegen (1919–1939) in Deutschland und Schweden*. Stockholm: Almqvist & Wiksell, 1987. 39–51.

Bernstein, Barton J.: "Understanding the Atomic Bomb and the Japanese Surrender: Missed Opportunities, Little-Known Near Disasters, and Modern Memory." *Diplomatic History* 19:2 (1995): 227–73.

Bersani, Leo: "Is the Rectum a Grave?" *October* 43 (1987): 197–222.

Bessel, Richard: "The Rise of the NSDAP and the Myth of Nazi Propaganda." *Wiener Library Bulletin* 33 (1980): 20–29.

Bickel, Cornelius: *Ferdinand Tönnies: Soziologie als skeptische Aufklärung zwischen Historismus und Rationalismus.* Opladen: Westdeutscher Verlag, 1991 (Studien zur Sozialwissenschaft. 82).

Biechele, Eckhard: *Der Kampf um die Gemeinwirtschaftskonzeption im Jahre 1919: Eine Studie zur Wirtschaftspolitik unter Reichswirtschaftsminister Wissell in der Frühphase der Weimarer Republik.* Berlin, Phil. Diss. 1972.

Bitzel, Uwe: *Die Konzeption des Blitzkrieges bei der deutschen Wehrmacht.* Frankfurt a. M., New York: Lang, 1991 (Europäische Hochschulschriften. Reihe III: Geschichte und ihre Hilfswissenschaften. 477).

Blackbourn, David: "The Politics of Demagogy." *Past and Present* 113 (November 1986): 152–184.

Blum, Antoinette: *Romain Rolland, "Les Loupes" et l'affaire Dreyfus.* Ph. D. Yale University 1977.

Blume, Jürgen: *Die Lektüre des Alfred Döblin: Zur Funktion des Zitats im Novemberroman.* Frankfurt a. M.: Lang, 1991.

Boeser, Knut, and Renata Votková, eds.: *Max Reinhardt in Berlin.* Berlin: Edition Hentrich, Frölich und Kaufmann, 1984.

Bogacz, Ted W.: "'A Tyranny of Words': Language, Poetry, and Antimodernism in England in the First World War." *Journal of Modern History* 58 (1986): 643–68.

Bogacz, Ted W.: "War Neurosis and Cultural Change in England, 1914–22: The Work of the War Office Committee of Enquiry into 'Shell-Shock.'" *Journal of Contemporary History* 24 (1989): 227–56.

Böhme, Helmut, and Fritz Kalkenberg, eds.: *Deutschland und der Erste Weltkrieg.* Ringvorlesung an der Technischen Hochschule Darmstadt im Wintersemester 1984/85 veranstaltet vom Institut für Geschichte. Eine Dokumentation. Darmstadt: Präsident, 1987 (THD-Schriftenreihe. Wiss. u. Technik. 37).

Böhmel, Bernd: "Das Geheimnis des Sieges. Duell mit Schlieffen." *Sinn und Form* 44 (1992): 434–58.

Bohrer, Karl-Heinz, ed.: *Mythos und Moderne: Begriff und Bild einer Rekonstruktion.* Frankfurt a. M.: Suhrkamp 1983 (Edition Suhrkamp. 1144).

Boldt, Hans: *Rechtsstaat und Ausnahmezustand: Eine Studie über den Belagerungszustand als Ausnahmezustand des bürgerlichen Rechtsstaates im 19. Jahrhundert.* Berlin: Duncker & Humblot, 1967.

Bolz, Norbert: *Auszug aus der entzauberten Welt: Philosophischer Extremismus zwischen den Weltkriegen.* München: Fink, 1989.

Bolz, Norbert: "Peri Trans Beyond." Friedrich A. Kittler, Georg Christoph Tholen, eds.: *Arsenale der Seele: Literatur und Medienanalyse seit 1870.* München: Fink, 1989. 171- 85.

Bork, Siegfried: *Mißbrauch der Sprache: Tendenzen nationalsozialistischer Sprachregelung.* Bern: Francke, 1970.

Bowen, Ralph H.: *German Theories of the Corporate State: With Special Reference to the Period 1870–1890.* New York: Russell & Russell, 1971.

Bracco, Rosa: *Merchants of Hope: Middlebrow Writers of the First World War.* Oxford: Berg, 1993.

Bradbury, Malcolm, and James McFarlane, eds.: *Modernism 1890–1930.* Harmondsworth: Penguin, 1976 (Pelican Guides to European Literature).

Brandt, Marion: *Schweigen ist der Ort der Antwort: Eine Analyse des Gedichtzyklus "Das Wort der Stummen" von Gertrud Kolmar.* Berlin: C. Hoffmann, 1993.

Brandt, Marion: *Widerspruch und Übereinstimmung in Gertrud Kolmars Gedichtszyklus "Das Wort der Stummen."* Vol. 1–2. Ph. D., Berlin (Humboldt University) 1990.

Brandt, Marion: "'Opfre ich mich auf schäumender Altars Stufe': Über das Bild des Opfers im Werk von Gertrud Komar (1894–1943)." Inge Stephan et al., eds.: *Jüdische Kultur und Weiblichkeit in der Moderne.* Köln, Weimar, Wien: Böhlau, 1994. 173–85.

Braun, Klaus: *Konservatismus und Gemeinwirtschaft: Eine Studie über Wichard von Moellendorff.* Duisburg: Braun, 1978 (Duisburger Hochschulbeiträge. 11).

Brocke, Bernhard vom: "'Wissenschaft und Militarismus' – Der Aufruf der 93 'An die Kulturwelt!' und der Zusammenbruch der internationalen Gelehrtenrepublik im Ersten Weltkrieg." William M. Calder III, Hellmut Flashar, and Theodor Lindken, eds.: *Wilamowitz nach 50 Jahren.* Darmstadt: Wissenschaftliche Buchgesellschaft, 1985. 649- 719.

Bruch, Rüdiger vom: *Weltpolitik als Kulturmission: Auswärtige Kulturpolitik und Bildungsbürgertum in Deutschland am Vorabend des Ersten Weltkrieges.* Paderborn: Schoeningh, 1982 (Quellen und Forschungen aus dem Gebiet der Geschichte. 1).

Bruch, Rüdiger vom: *Wissenschaft, Politik und öffentliche Meinung: Gelehrtenpolitik im Wilhelminischen Deutschland (1890–1914).* Husum: Matthiesen, 1980 (Historische Studien. 435).

Brunner, Otto, Werner Conze, Reinhart Koselleck, eds.: *Geschichtliche Grundbegriffe: Historisches Lexikon zur politisch-sozialen Sprache in Deutschland.* Vol. 1–7. Stuttgart: Klett-Cotta, 1972–92.

Buck-Morss, Susan: *The Dialectics of Seeing: Walter Benjamin and the Arcades Project.* Cambridge, Mass.: MIT Press, 1991.

Burchardt, Lothar: *Friedenswirtschaft und Kriegsvorsorge: Deutschlands wirtschaftliche Rüstungsbestrebungen vor 1914.* Boppard a. Rh.: Boldt, 1968 (Wehrwissenschaftliche Forschungen. Abt. Militärgeschichtliche Studien. 6).

Burchardt, Lothar: "Die Auswirkungen der Kriegswirtschaft auf die Zivilibevölkerung im Ersten und Zweiten Weltkrieg." *Militärgeschichtliche Mitteilungen* 15 (1974): 65–97.

Burchardt, Lothar: "Walther Rathenau und die Anfänge der deutschen Rohstoffbewirtschaftung im Ersten Weltkrieg." *Tradition: Zeitschrift für Firmengeschichte und Unternehmerbiographie* 15:4 (1970): 169–96.

Burchardt, Lothar: "Zwischen Kriegsgewinnen und Kriegskosten: Krupp im Ersten Weltkrieg." *Zeitschrift für Unternehmensgeschichte* 32 (1978): 71–123.

Buruma, Ian: "War over the Bomb." *The New York Review of Books*, 21 September 1995: 26–34.

Butwin, Joseph: "The French Revolution as Theatrum Mundi." *Research Studies* (Washington State University) 43 (1975): 141–52.

Byland, Hans: *Zu den Gedichten Gertrud Kolmars.* Zürich, Phil. Diss. 1971.

Califia, Pat: "Feminism and Sadomasochism." *Heresies* no 3, 1981: 32.

Calinescu, Matei: *Five Faces of Modernity: Modernism, Avant-garde, Decadence, Kitsch, Postmodernism.* 2nd enlarged edition of *Faces of Modernity.* Durham, N. C.: Duke University Press, 1987.

Canby, Vincent: "'Porter' is Romantic Pornography." *The New York Times*, October 14, 1974: 284.

Canetti, Elias: *Crowds and Power.* Trans. by Carol Stewart. Harmondsworth: Penguin, 1973.

Cannadine, David: "War and death, grief and mourning in modern Britain." Jo Whaley, ed.: *Mirrors of Mortality: Studies in the Social History of Death.* London: Europa Publications, 1981. 187–219.

Carey, Frances, and Anthony Griffiths: *The Print in Germany 1880–1933: The Age of Expressionism.* London: British Museum Publications, 1984.

Charmley, John: *Churchill: The End of Glory: A Political Biography.* London: Hodder & Stoughton, 1993.

Charnay, Jean-Paul: "Vitesse et stratégie." *La Vitesse (Exhibition catalogue).* Paris: Flammarion, 1992. 144–50.

Chefdor, Monique, Ricardo Quinones, and Albert Wachtel, eds.: *Modernism: Challenges and Perspectives.* Urbana: University of Illinois Press, 1986.

Cheval, René: *Romain Rolland, l'Allemagne et la guerre.* Paris: PUF, 1963.

Chickering, Roger: *We Men Who Feel Most German: A Cultural Study of the Pan-German League 1886–1914.* Boston: Allen & Unwin, 1984.

Clark, Suzanne: *Sentimental Modernism: Women writers and the revolution of the word.* Bloomington, Indiana: Indiana University Press, 1991.

Cobley, Evelyn: *Representing War: Form and Ideology in First World War Narratives.* Toronto: University of Toronto Press, 1993.

Cocks, Geoffrey: *Psychotherapy in the Third Reich: The Göring Institute.* New York and Oxford: Oxford University Press, 1985.

Coker, Christopher: *War and the Twentieth Century.* London: Brassey's, 1994.

Corino, Karl: "Ein Mörder macht Literaturgeschichte. Florian Großrubatscher, ein Modell für Musils Moosbrugger." Josef Strutz, ed., *Robert Musil und die kulturellen Tendenzen seiner Zeit.* München, Salzburg: Fink, 1983. 130–47.

Crew, David F: "'Wohlfahrtsbrot ist bitteres Brot.' The Elderly, the Disabled and the Local Welfare Authorities in the Weimar Republic 1924–1933." *Archiv für Sozialgeschichte* 30 (1990): 217–45.

D'Alton, Phillip: "The Role of Women in the Australian Armed Forces." Tom Jagtenberg and Phillip D'Alton, eds.: *Four Dimensional Social Space: Class, Gender, Ethnicity and Nature: A Reader in Australian Social Sciences.* Sydney: Harper & Row, 1989. 294–298.

Dahm, Georg: *Völkerrecht.* Vol. 1. Stuttgart: Kohlhammer, 1958.

De Lauretis, Teresa: "Cavani's *Night Porter.* A Woman's Film?" *Film Quarterly* 30:2 (1976/1977): 35–38.

Deighton, Len: *Blitzkrieg: From the Rise of Hitler to the Fall of Dunkirk.* With a foreword by W. K. Nehring. London: Cape, 1979.

Deist, Wilhelm, ed.: *Militär und Innenpolitik im Weltkrieg 1914–1918.* Vol. 2. Düsseldorf: Droste, 1970. (Quellen zur Geschichte des Parlamentarismus und der politischen Parteien. 2. Reihe: Militär und Politik. 1).

Deist, Wilhelm: "Der militärische Zusammenbruch des Kaiserreichs. Zur Realität der 'Dolchstoßlegende.'" Ursula Büttner, ed.: *Das Unrechtsregime: Internationale Forschung über den Nationalsozialismus. Band I. Ideologie – Herrschaftssystem – Wirkung in Europa.* Festschrift für Werner Jochmann zum 65. Geburtstag. Hamburg: Christians 1986. 101–29.

Deleuze, Gilles, and Félix Guattari: *Anti-Oedipus: Capitalism and Schizophrenia.* With a preface by Michel Foucault. Minneapolis: University of Minnesota Press, 1990.

Deleuze, Gilles, Felix Guattari: *Capitalisme et Schizophrenie.* Vol. 2: *Mille plateaux.* Paris: Editions de Minuit, 1980.

Deleuze, Gilles, Felix Guattari: *Capitalism and Schizophrenia.* Vol. 2: *A Thousand Plateaus.* Trans. by Brian Massumi. Minneapolis: University of Minnesota Press, 1987.

Deleuze, Gilles: *Foucault.* Minneapolis: University of Minnesota Press, 1988.

Derrida, Jacques: *Grammatologie.* (*De la grammatologie*, dt.) Übersetzt von Hans-Jörg Rheinberger und Hanns Zischler. Frankfurt a. M.: Suhrkamp 1983 (Suhrkamp Taschenbuch Wissenschaft. 417).

Derrida, Jacques: "Women in the Beehive." Alice Jardine and Paul Smith, eds: *Men in Feminism.* New York: Methuen, 1987. 189–203.

Dieckmann, Wilhelm: *Die Behördenorganisation in der deutschen Kriegswirtschaft 1914–1918.* Hamburg: Hanseatische Verlagsanstalt, 1937 (Schriften zur kriegswissenschaftlichen Forschung und Schulung).

Dilke, Oswald Ashton Wentworh: *The Roman Land Surveyors: An Introduction to the Agrimensores.* Newton Abbott: David and Charles, 1917.

Döhl, Reinhard: "Gertrud Kolmar Ludwig XVI., 1775." Walter Hinck, ed.: *Geschichte im Gedicht: Texte und Interpretationen. (Protestlied, Bänkelsang, Ballade, Chronik).* Frankfurt a. M.: Suhrkamp, 1979. 171–82.

Domansky, Elisabth: "Die gespaltene Erinnerung." Manuel Köppen, ed.: *Kunst und Literatur nach Auschwitz.* In Zusammenarbeit mit Gerhard Bauer und Rüdiger Steinlein. Berlin: Erich Schmidt, 1993. 178–96.

Döring, Herbert: *Der Weimarer Kreis: Studien zum politischen Bewußtsein verfassungstreuer Hochschullehrer in der Weimarer Republik.* Meisenheim: Hain, 1975 (Mannheimer sozialwiss. Studien. 10).

Drescher, Horst: "Der Alte Wilhelm Rudolph." *Sinn und Form* 33:5 (1981): 955–77.

Dube, Wolf-Dieter: *Expressionists and Expressionism.* Geneva: Skira, 1983.

Duchatelet, Bernard: "L'echo de l'affaire Dreyfus dans l'œuvre romanesque de Romain Rolland." Geraldi Leroy, ed.: *Les écrivains et l'affaire Dreyfus.* Orléans: Presse Universitaire, 1983. 287–94.

Dumont, Robert: *Stefan Zweig et la France.* Paris: Didier, 1967.

Eagleton, Terry: *The Ideology of the Aesthetic.* Cambridge, Mass.: Basil Blackwell, 1990.

Eberle, Matthias: *World War I and the Weimar Artists.* New Haven, London: Yale University Press, 1985.

Eckart, Wolfgang Uwe: "Julius Schwalbe." Wolfgang Uwe Eckart and Christoph Gradmann, eds.: *Ärztelexikon: Von der Antike bis zum 20. Jahrhundert.* München: Beck, 1995 (Beck'sche Reihe. 1095).

Eckert, Max: "Die Kartographie im Kriege." *Geographische Zeitschrift* 26 (1920): 273–86.

Ehlert, Hans Gotthard: *Die wirtschaftliche Zentralbehörde des Deutschen Reiches 1914 bis 1919: Das Problem der "Gemeinwirtschaft" in Krieg und Frieden.* Wiesbaden: Steiner, 1982 (Beiträge zur Wirtschafts- und Sozialgeschichte. 19).

Eichmann-Leutenegger, Beatrice: *Gertrud Kolmar: Leben und Werk in Texten und Bildern.* Frankfurt a. M.: Jüdischer Verlag, 1993.

Eissler, K. R.: *Freud as an Expert Witness: The Discussion of War Neurosis Between Freud and Wagner-Jauregg*. Trans. from the German by Christine Trollope. New York: International Universities Press, 1986.

Eksteins, Modris: *Rites of Spring: The Modern in Cultural History*. New York: Bantam Books, 1990.

Eley, Geoff: *Reshaping the German Right: Radical Nationalism and Political Change after Bismarck*. Second edition. Ann Arbor: Bowker, 1990.

Elias, Norbert: *Über den Prozeß der Zivilisation: Soziogenetische und psychogenetische Untersuchungen*. Vol.1–2. Frankfurt a. M.: Suhrkamp, 1976 (Suhrkamp Taschenbuch Wissenschaft. 158–59). First edition: Basel 1939.

Engelmann, Gerhard: *Die Internationale Weltkarte 1:1 Million: Ihre Anfänge aus deutschen Quellen 1891–1914*. Gotha: Perthes, 1980.

Epkenhans, Michael: *Die wilhelminische Flottenrüstung 1908–1914: Weltmachtstreben, industrieller Fortschritt, soziale Integration*. München: Oldenbourg, 1991 (Beiträge zur Militärgeschichte. 32).

Erdle, Birgit R.: *Antlitz – Mord – Gesetz: Figuren des Anderen bei Gertrud Kolmar und Emmanuel Lévinas*. Wien: Passagen, 1994.

Eysteinsson, Astradur: *The Concept of Modernism*. Ithaca, New York: Cornell University Press, 1990.

Farber, Stephen: "Cabaret May Shock Kansas … " *The New York Times*, February 20, 1972: Sec. II, 1.

Farias, Victor: *Heidegger und der Nationalsozialismus*. Frankfurt a. M.: Fischer, 1989.

Faulkner, Peter: *Modernism*. London: Methuen, 1977.

Faye, Jean Pierre: *Totalitäre Sprachen: Kritik der narrativen Vernunft. Kritik der narrativen Ökonomie*. Frankfurt a. M.: Ullstein, 1977.

Feingold, Henry L.: "How unique is the Holocaust?" Alex Grobman and Daniel Landes, eds.: *Genocide: Critical Issues of the Holocaust. A Companion to the film, Genocide*. Los Angeles: Simon Wiesenthal Center; Chappaqua, N. Y.: Rossel Books, 1983.

Feldman, Gerald D.: *Armee, Industrie und Arbeiterschaft in Deutschland 1914 bis 1918*. Aus dem Engl. übers. von Norma von Ragenfeld-Feldman. Berlin, Bonn: Dietz, 1985.

Feldman, Gerald D.: "Die Demobilmachung und die Sozialordnung der Zwischenkriegszeit in Europa." *Geschichte und Gesellschaft* 9 (1983): 156–77.

Feldman, Gerald D.: "War Economy and Controlled Economy: The Discrediting of 'Socialism' in Germany during the First World War." Hans-Jürgen Schröder, ed.: *Confrontation and Cooperation: Germany and the United States in the Era of World War 1, 1900–1924*. Providence, R. I, Oxford: Berg, 1993 (Germany and the United States of America. 2). 229–52.

Ferenczi, S., Karl Abraham, Ernst Simmel, and Ernest Jones: *Psychoanalysis and the War Neurosis*. London: International Psychoanalytical Press, 1921.

Fetting, Hugo, ed.: *Von der Freien Bühne zum politischen Theater: Drama und Theater im Spiegel der Kritik*. Vol. 1–2. Leipzig: Reclam, 1987.

Fiebig-von Haase, Ragnhild: "Die deutsch-amerikanischen Wirtschaftsbeziehungen, 1890- 1914, im Zeichen von Protektionismus und internationaler Integration." *Amerikastudien* 33:3 (1989): 329–57.

Fischer, Klaus: *Nazi Germany: A New History*. New York: Continuum, 1995.

Fischer-Homberger, Esther: *Die traumatische Neurose: Vom somatischen zum sozialen Leiden*. Bern, Stuttgart, Wien: Huber, 1975.

Fokkema, Douwe W.: *Literary History, Modernism and Postmodernism*. Amsterdam: Benjamins, 1984 (Utrecht publications in general and comperative literature. 19).

Fornari, Franco: *The Psychoanalysis of War*. Garden City, New York: Anchor, 1974.

Förster, Georg: *Totaler Krieg und Blitzkrieg: Die Theorie des totalen Krieges und des Blitzkrieges in der Militärdoktrin des faschistischen Deutschland am Vorabend des zweiten Weltkriegs*. Berlin: Deutscher Militärverlag, 1967 (Militärhistorische Studien. N. F. 10).

Foucault, Michel: *Discipline and Punish: The Birth of the Prison*. Trans. from the French by Alan Sheridan. New York: Vintage Books, 1979.

Foucault, Michel: *The History of Sexuality Volume I: An Introduction*. (*La Volenté de savoir*, Engl.). A translation by Robert Hurley. New York: Vintage Books, 1980.

Foucault, Michel: "'Film and Popular Memory': An interview conducted by the editors of *Cahiers du Cinema*, trans. by Martin Jordin." Sylvère Lotringer, ed.: *Foucault Live: Interviews, 1966–1984*. New York: Semiotext(e), 1989.

Foucault, Michel: "History of Systems of Thought." Foucault: *Language, Counter-Memory, Practice: Selected Essays and Interviews*. Ed. with an introduction by Donald F. Bouchard. Trans. from the French by Donald F. Bouchard and Sherry Simon. Ithaca, N. Y.: Cornell University Press, 1977. 199–204.

Fourquin, Guy: *Les soulèvements populaires au Moyen Age*. Paris: Presse Universitaire, 1972.

Frank, Manfred: *Der kommende Gott: Vorlesungen über die Neue Mythologie*. Frankfurt a. M.: Suhrkamp, 1982.

Frank, Manfred: *Gott im Exil: Vorlesungen über die Neue Mythologie*. Frankfurt a. M.: Suhrkamp, 1988.

Friedlander, Henry: *The Origins of Nazi Genocide: From Euthanasia to the Final Solution*. Durham: University of North Carolina Press, 1995.

Fries-Thiessenhusen, Karen: "Politische Kommentare deutscher Historiker 1918/19 zu Niederlage und Staatsumsturz." Eberhard Kolb, ed., *Vom Kaiserreich zur Weimarer Republik*. Köln: Kiepenheuer & Witsch, 1972. 349–68.

Fuller, J. F. C.: *Pegasus: Problems of Transportation*. London: Kegan Paul, Trench, Trübner; New York: Dutton, 1925.

Fuller, J. F. C.: *The Conduct of War, 1789–1961: A Study on the Impact of the French, Industrial, and Russian Revolutions on War and its Conduct*. London: Da Capo Press, 1962.

Fussell, Paul: *The Great War and Modern Memory*. London, Oxford, New York: Oxford University Press, 1975.

Fustel de Coulange, N. D.: *Histoire des Institutions Politiques de l'ancienne France*. Vol. 4: L' Alleu et le domaine rural pendant l'époque mérovingienne. Paris: Hachette, 1889.

Gabriel, Richard, and Paul Savage: *Crisis in Command*. New York: Hill and Young, 1978.

Galtung, Johan: *Strukturelle Gewalt*. Reinbek: Rowohlt, 1975.

Gärtringen, Friedrich Freiherr Hiller von: "'Dolchstoß'-Diskussion und 'Dolchstoßlegende' im Wandel von vier Jahrzehnten." Waldemar Besson and Friedrich Freiherr von Gärtringen, eds.: *Geschichte und Gegenwartsbewußtsein: Historische Betrachtungen. Festschrift für Hans Rothfels zum 70. Geburtstag*. Dargebracht von Kollegen, Freunden und Schülern. Göttingen: Vandenhoeck & Ruprecht, 1963: 122–60.

Gentile, Emilio: "Fascism as Political Religion." *Journal of Contemporary History* 25 (1990): 229–51.

Gerber, Richard: *Romain Rolland als Dramatiker*. Münster, Phil. Diss. 1933.

Geuter, Ulfried: *Die Professionalisierung der deutschen Psychologie im Nationalsozialismus*. Frankfurt a. M.: Suhrkamp, 1984.

Geyer, Michael; "Ein Vorbote des Wohlfahrtsstaates: Die Kriegsopferversorgung in Frankreich, Deutschland und Großbritannien nach dem Ersten Weltkrieg.'" *Geschichte und Gesellschaft* 9 (1983): 230–77.

Gilbert, Sandra M., and Susan Gubar: *No Man's Land: The Place of the Woman Writer in the Twentieth Century*. Vol. 2: *Sexchanges*. New Haven, London: Yale University Press, 1989.

Gilman, Sander: *Freud, Race and Gender*. Princeton: Princeton University Press, 1993.

Girard, René: *La Violence et Le Sacré*. Paris: Bernard Grasset, 1972.

Giroux, Henry: "The Challenge of Neo-fascist Culture." *Cineaste* 1:4 (1975): 31–2.

Glucksmann, André: *Le discours de la guerre*. Paris: Editions de L'Herne, 1974.

Glum, Friedrich: *Zwischen Wissenschaft, Wirtschaft und Politik: Erlebtes und Erdachtes in vier Reichen*. Bonn: Bouvier, 1964.

Gollin, Gillian Lindt, and Albert E. Gollin: "Toennies on Public Opinion." Werner J. Cahnman, ed., *Ferdinand Tönnies: A New Evaluation, Essays and Documents*. Leiden: Brill, 1973. 181–203.

Goodrich, Peter: "Eating Law: Commons, Common Land, Common Law." *The Journal of Legal History* 12 (1991): 246–67.

Gordon, Donald E.: *Ernst Ludwig Kirchner.* Cambridge, Mass.: Havard University Press, 1968.

Gordon, Donald E.: *Expressionism: Art and Idea.* New Haven, London: Yale University Press, 1987.

Graf, Werner: *Erfahrungskonstruktion: Robert Musils Roman "Der Mann ohne Eigenschaften."* Berlin: Volker Spieß, 1981.

Gray, Glen: *On Understanding Violence Philosophically.* New York: Harper and Row, 1970.

Greenberg, Clement: "Beginnings of Modernism." Monique Chefdor, Ricardo Quinones, and Albert Wachtel, eds.: *Modernism: Challenges and Perspectives.* Urbana, Chicago: University of Illinois Press, 1986. 17–24.

Greenberg, Clement: "Modernist painting." Geoffrey Battock, ed.: *The New Art: A Critical Anthology.* New York: Dutton, 1966. 100–10.

Greenspun, Roger: "Liza Minelli Stirs a Lively Cabaret." *The New York Times*, February 14, 1972: 22.

Grewe, Wilhelm: *Epochen der Völkerrechtsgeschichte.* Baden-Baden: Nomos, 1984.

Grimm, Reinhold: "Über Spiel und Ernst in einigen Revolutionsdramen." *Basis* 1 (1969): 49–93.

Grohmann, Will: *Paul Klee 1879–1940.* Trans. from the German by Frank Whitford. London: Tillotsons (Bolton), 1965.

Grohmann, Will: *Paul Klee: A Critical Examination of his Work.* London: Lund Humphries, 1954. New ed. 1965

Grossman, Dave: *On Killing: The Psychological Cost of Learning to Kill in War and Society.* Boston, New York etc.: Litle, Brown, 1995.

Grotjahn, Karl-Heinz, and Reinhard Oberschelp, eds.: *Stahl und Steckrüben: Beiträge und Quellen zur Geschichte Niedersachsens im Ersten Weltkrieg (1914–1918).* Vol. 1–2. Halle: Niemeyer, 1993.

Grundy, Kenneth W., and Michael A. Weinstein.: *The Ideologies of Violence.* Columbus, Ohio: Merrill, 1974.

Gumbrecht, Hans Ulrich: *I Redentori della Vittoria: Über Fiumes Ort in der Genealogie des Faschismus.* Typescript, 1993.

Gurr, Ted Flobert, ed.: *Handbook of Political Conflict: Theory and Research.* New York: Free Press. 1980.

Gutsche, Willibald, Fritz Klein, and Joachim Petzold: *Der Erste Weltkrieg: Ursachen und Verlauf. Herrschende Politik und Antikriegsbewegung in Deutschland.* Köln: Pahl-Rugen-stein, 1983.

Gutsche, Willibald: "Die Entstehung des Kriegsausschusses der deutschen Industrie und seine Rolle zu Beginn des Ersten Weltkriegs." *Zeitschrift für Geschichtswissenschaft* 18 (1970): 877–98.

Habermas, Jürgen: "Vom öffentlichen Gebrauch der Historie: Das offizielle Selbstver-
ständnis der Bundesrepublik bricht auf." *Historikerstreit: Die Dokumentation der Kontroverse um die Einzigartigkeit der nationalsozialistischen Judenvernichtung.* München:
Piper, 1987. 243–55.

Hachamovitch, Yifat: "The Ideal Object of Transmission: An essay on faith which
attaches to instruments (de fide instrumentorum)." *Law and Critique* 2 (1991):
85–101.

Halberstam, Joshua: "From Kant to Auschwitz." *Social Theory and Practice* 14:1 (Spring
1988): 41–54.

Hampel, Johannes: "Hitlers *Mein Kampf:* Die Weltanschauung der Nationalsozialisten."
Der Nationalsozialismus. Hrsg. von Johannes Hampel. Vol 1: *Machtergreifung und
Machtsicherung 1933–35.* München: Bayerische Landeszentrale für politische Bil-
dungsarbeit, 1985 (Arbeitsheft. Bayerische Landeszentrale für politische Bildungs-
arbeit. 72): 89–115.

Handwörterbuch zur deutschen Rechtsgeschichte. Hrsg. von Adalbert Erler und Ekkehard
Kaufmann. Mitbegründet von Wolfgang Stammler. Vol. 1. Berlin: Erich Schmidt,
1971.

Hardach, Gerd: *Der Erste Weltkrieg 1914–1918.* München: Deutscher Taschenbuch
Verlag, 1973 (Geschichte der Weltwirtschaft im 20. Jahrhundert. 2).

Harrison, Tom: *Living through the Blitz.* London: Collins, 1976. Reprint: New York:
Schocken Books, 1989.

Hartrecht, Stephen: "The Ideologies and Semiotics of Fascism: Analyzing Pound's
Cantos." *Boundary* 2 (1993): 65–93.

Hartung, Günther: "Walter Benjamins Anti-Kriegsschriften." *Weimarer Beiträge* 3
(1986): 404–19.

Haug, Wolfgang Fritz: *Der hilflose Antifaschismus: Zur Kritik der Vorlesungsreihen über Wissenschaft und NS an deutschen Universitäten.* Frankfurt a. M.: Suhrkamp, 1967 (Edition
Suhrkamp. 236).

Haupts, Leo: *Deutsche Friedenspolitik 1918–1919: Eine Alternative zur Machtpolitik im Ersten Weltkrieg?* Düsseldorf: Droste, 1976.

Hecker, Gerhard: *Walther Rathenau und sein Verhältnis zu Militär und Krieg.* Boppard a.
Rhein: Boldt, 1983 (Wehrwissenschaftliche Forschungen: Abt. militärgeschichtliche Studien. 30).

Heider, Paul: "Der totale Krieg – seine Vorbereitung durch Reichswehr und Wehrmacht." Ludwig Nestler, ed.: *Der Weg deutscher Eliten in den Zweiten Weltkrieg: Nach-
trag zu einer verhinderten deutsch-deutschen Publikation.* Berlin: Akademie-Verlag, 1990:
35–80.

Heinemann, Ulrich: *Die verdrängte Niederlage: Politische Öffentlichkeit und Kriegsschuldfrage in der Weimarer Republik.* Göttingen: Vandenhoeck & Ruprecht, 1983 (Kritische Studien zur Geschichtswissenschaft).

Helms, Hans G.: "Adler-Orden aus der Hand des Führers: Wie Helfershelfer aus Übersee den Nationalsozialismus stützten." *Vorwärts* No. 51/52 (21 December 1978): 26–27.

Herbert, Barry: *German Expressionism: "Die Brücke" and "Der blaue Reiter."* London: Jupiter Books, 1983.

Hermand, Jost: *Arnold Zweig: Mit Selbstzeugnissen und Bilddokumenten.* Reinbek: Rowohlt, 1990 (Rowohlts Monographien. 381).

Hess, Hans: *Georg Grosz.* New Haven, London: Studio Vista, 1974.

Heydte, F. A. Freiherr von der: "Discovery and symbolic Annexation and virtual Effectiveness." *American Journal of International Law* 29 (1935): 448–71.

Hilberg, Raul: *The Destruction of the European Jews.* Rev. and definitive ed. Vol. 1–3. New York: Holmes & Meier, 1983.

Hirschfeld, Magnus, et al.: *The Sexual History of the World War* (*Sittengeschichte des Weltkrieges*, Engl.). New York: Falstaff Press, 1937.

Hocquenghem, Guy: *Homosexual Desire.* A translation by Daniella Dangoor, with an introduction by Jeffrey Weeks. London: Allison and Busby, 1978.

Hoffer, Eric: *The True Believer: Thoughts on the Nature of Mass Movements.* New York: Harper and Row, 1966 (Perennial Library. 71).

Holden, Stephen: "Of Skinheads High on Hate and Violence." *The New York Times,* June 9, 1993: Section C, 17.

Holmes, Robert L.: *On War and Morality.* Princeton: Princeton University Press, 1989.

Holzapfel, Friedrich: *Politische Propaganda.* Münster, Jur. Diss., 1926.

Horak, Jan-Christopher: *Anti-Nazi-Filme der deutschsprachigen Emigration von Hollywood 1939–1945.* Münster: Maks Publikationen, 1985.

Horne, John, and Alan Kramer: "German 'Atrocities' und Franco-German Opinion, 1914: The Evidence of German Soldier's Diaries." *Journal of Modern History* 66:1 (1994): 1–33.

Houston, Beverle and Marsha Kinder: "The Night Porter as Daydream." *Literature and Film Quarterly* 3:4 (1975): 363–70.

Howald, Stefan: *Ästhetizismus und ästhetische Ideologiekritik: Untersuchungen zum Romanwerk Robert Musils.* München: Fink, 1984. (Musil-Studien. 9).

Howard, Michael: *War in European History.* London, Oxford, New York: Oxford University Press, 1976.

Howlett, Jana, and Rod Mengham, eds.: *The Violent Muse: Violence and the Artistic Imagination in Europe, 1910–1939.* Manchester: Manchester University Press, 1994.

Huber, Georg: *Die französische Propaganda im Weltkrieg gegen Deutschland 1914 bis 1918.* München: Pfeiffer, 1928 (Zeitung und Leben. 1).

Hubert, Ulrich: *Best: Biographische Studien über Radikalismus, Weltanschauung und Vernunft, 1903–1989.* Bonn: Dietz, 1996.

Huesmann, Heinrich: *Welttheater Reinhardt: Bauten Spielstätten Inszenierungen.* München: Prestl, 1983.

Hunt, Lynn: *Politics, Culture, and Class in the French Revolution.* Berkeley: University of California Press, 1984 (Studies in the history of society and culture. 1).

Hüppauf, Bernd: *Ansichten vom Krieg: Vergleichende Studien zum Ersten Weltkrieg in Literatur und Gesellschaft.* Königstein: Anton Hain, 1984.

Hüppauf, Bernd: "Die Stadt als imaginierter Kriegsschauplatz." *Zeitschrift für Germanistik* N.F 2 (1995): 317–35.

Hüppauf, Bernd: "Erziehung durch Krieg? Arnold Zweigs Frage nach einer moralischen Begründung des modernen Kriegs." David Midgley, Hans-Harald Müller, and Geoffrey Davis, eds.: *Arnold Zweig – Poetik, Judentum und Politik.* Bern: Lang, 1989. 54–77.

Hüppauf, Bernd: "Mythisches Denken und Krisen der deutschen Literatur und Gesellschaft." Karl-Heinz Bohrer, ed.: *Mythos und Moderne: Begriff und Bild einer Rekonstruktion.* Frankfurt a. M.: Suhrkamp 1983 (Edition Suhrkamp. 1144). 508–27.

Hüppauf, Bernd: "Räume der Destruktion und Konstruktion von Raum: Landschaft, Sehen, Raum und der Erste Weltkrieg/Space of Destruction and Construction of Space. Landscape, seeing, space and the First World War." *Krieg und Literatur/War and Literature* 3 (1991): 105–23.

Hüppauf, Bernd: "Walter Benjamin's Imaginary Landscape." Gerhard Fischer, ed.: *"With the sharpened Axe of Reason": Approaches to Walter Benjamin.* Oxford, Washington: Berg, 1996. 33–54.

Huyssen, Andreas: *After the Great Divide: Modernism, Mass Culture, Postmodernism.* Bloomington, Indiana: Indiana University Press, 1986.

Hynes, Samuel: *A War Imagined: The Great War and English Culture.* London: Bodley Head, 1991.

Irigaray, Luce: *An Ethics of Sexual Difference.* Trans. by Carolyn Burke and Gillian C. Gill. Ithaca, NY: Cornell UP, 1993.

Irving, David: *Die Tragödie der deutschen Luftwaffe.* Aus den Akten und Erinnerungen von Feldmarschall Milch. Aus dem Englischen von Erwin Duncker. Frankfurt a. M., Berlin: Ullstein, 1970.

Irving, David: *The Destruction of Dresden.* New York: Holt, Rinehart & Winston, 1964.

Jacobsohn, Siegfried: *Max Reinhardt.* 4. und 5. Aufl. Berlin: Reiss, 1921.

Jay, Martin: *Force Fields: Between intellectual history and cultural critique.* London: Routledge, 1993.

Jeschal, Godwin: *Politik und Wissenschaft deutscher Ärzte im Ersten Weltkrieg: Eine Untersuchung anhand der Fach- und Standespresse und der Protokolle des Reichstags.* Pattensen, Hannover: Wellm, 1977.

Jhering, Herbert: *Von Reinhardt zu Brecht: Vier Jahrzehnte Theater und Film.* Vol. 1: *1909–1923.* Berlin: Aufbau-Verlag, 1958.

Justrow, Karl: *Der technische Krieg im Spiegelbild der Kriegserfahrungen und der Weltpresse.* Berlin: Claassen, 1938.

Kaehler, Siegfried: "Neuere Geschichtslegenden und ihre Widerlegung." Kaehler: *Studien zur deutschen Geschichte des 19. und 20. Jahrhunderts: Aufsätze und Voträge.* Hrsg. u. mit einem Nachwort versehen von Walter Bussmann. Göttingen: Vandenhoeck & Ruprecht, 1961. 306–35.

Kael, Pauline: "Stuck in the Fun." *The New Yorker* 50:7 (1974): 151–52.

Kalish, Patricia, and Marilyn Scobey: "Female Nurses in American Wars." *Armed Forces and Society* 9:2 (1983): 215–44.

Kaplan, Alice Yaeger: *Reproductions of Banality: Fascism, Literature and French Intellectual Life.* With a foreword by Russell Berman. Minneapolis: University of Minnesota, 1986. (Theory and History of Literature. 36).

Kaplan, Robert D.: "The Coming Anarchy." *Atlantic Monthly* 273 (1994): 44–76.

Karl, Frederick: *Modern and Modernism: The Sovereignty of the Artist, 1885–1925.* New York: Atheneum, 1985.

Kaufmann, Eva: *Arnold Zweigs Weg zum Roman.* Berlin: Rütten und Loening, 1967.

Kempf, Marcelle: *Romain Rolland et l'Allemagne.* Paris: Nouvelles Editions Debresse, 1962.

Keyser, Lester J.: "Three Faces of Evil: Fascism in Recent Movies." *Journal of Popular Film* 4:1 (1975): 21–31.

Kiefer, Klaus H.: "Erster Weltkrieg und Avantgarde – Ein Projekt." *Krieg und Literatur / War and Literature* 3:5/6 (1991): 140–56.

Kiesel, Helmuth: *Literarische Trauerarbeit: Das Exil- und Spätwerk Alfred Döblins.* Tübingen: Niemeyer, 1986 (Studien zur deutschen Literatur. 89).

Kindermann, Heinz: *Theatergeschichte Europas.* Vol. 8: *Naturalismus und Impressionismus.* 1. Teil: *Deutschland/Österreich/Schweiz.* Salzburg: Otto Müller, 1968.

Kirkpatrick, Clifford: *Nazi Germany: Its Women and Family Life.* Indianapolis: The Babbs- Merrill Company, 1938.

Kitchen, Martin: *The Silent Dictatorship: The Politics of the German High Command under Hindenburg and Ludendorff 1916–1918.* London: Croom Helm, 1976.

Kittler, Friedrich: "Media Wars: Trenches, Lightening, Stars." *1800* (Amherst), No.1 (Fall 1989): 3–9.

Klemperer, Klemens von: *Germany's New Conservatism: Its History and Dilemma in the Twentieth century.* Princeton: Princeton University Press, 1957.

Knorenschild, Wilhelm: *Die Geschichtlichen Grundlagen der Revolutionsdramen Romain Rollands.* Münster, Phil. Diss. 1934.

Kocka, Jürgen: "Kriegssozialismus? Unternehmer und Staat 1914–1918." *Berlin und seine Wirtschaft: Ein Weg aus der Geschichte in die Zukunft – Lehren und Erkenntnisse.* Ed. by the Industrie- und Handelskammer zu Berlin. Berlin, New York: de Gruyter, 1987. 155–76.

Kocka, Jürgen: "Organisierter Kapitalismus im Kaiserreich." *Historische Zeitschrift* 230 (1980): 613–63.

Koeth, Joseph: "Rohstoffbewirtschaftung." Gerhard Anschütz et al., eds: *Handbuch der Politik.* Vol. 2: *Der Weltkrieg.* Berlin, Leipzig: Rothschild, 1920. 224–35.

Kolakowski, Leszek: *The Presence of Myth.* Trans. by Adam Czerniawski. Chicago: University of Chicago Press, 1989.

Könke, Günter: *Organisierter Kapitalismus, Sozialdemokratie und Staat: Eine Studie zur Ideologie der sozialdemokratischen Arbeiterbewegung in der Weimarer Republik (1924–1932).* Stuttgart: Steiner, 1987 (Studien zur modernen Geschichte. 37).

Koselleck, Reinhart: "Bilderverbot: Welches Totengedenken?" *Frankfurter Allgemeine Zeitung,* 8. April 1993.

Koselleck, Reinhart: "Der Einfluss der beiden Weltkriege auf das soziale Bewußtsein." Wolfram Wette, ed.: *Der Krieg des kleinen Mannes: Eine Militärgeschichte von unten.* München: Piper, 1992. 324–43.

Koselleck, Reinhart: "Kriegerdenkmale als Identitätsstiftungen der Überlebenden." Odo Marquard and Karlheinz Stierle, eds.: *Identität.* München: Fink, 1979 (Poetik und Hermeneutik. 8). 237–76.

Kramer, Alan: "'Greueltaten': Zum Problem der deutschen Kriegsverbrechen in Belgien und Frankreich 1914." Gerhard Hirschfeld and Gerd Krumreich, eds.: *Keiner fühlt sich hier mehr als Mensch … Erlebnis und Wirkung des Ersten Weltkriegs.* Essen: Klartext, 1993. 85–114.

Kristeva, Julia: *Black Sun: Depression and Melancholy.* A translation by Leon S. Roudiez. New York: Columbia University Press, 1989.

Kristeva, Julia: "Women's Time." [Trans. by Alice Jardine and Harry Blake] Nannerl O. Keohane, Michelle Z. Rosaldo, and Barbara C. Gelpi, eds: *Feminist Theory: A Critique of Ideology.* Brighton, Sussex: Harvester Press, 1982. 31–53.

Kroener, Bernhard R.: "Der 'erfrorene Blitzkrieg': Strategische Planungen der deutschen Führung gegen die Sowjetunion und die Ursachen ihres Scheiterns." Bernd Wegner, ed.: *Zwei Wege nach Moskau.* München, Zürich: Piper, 1991 (Serie Piper. 1346). 133–48.

Krüger, Dieter : *Nationalökonomen im wilhelminischen Deutschland.* Göttingen: Vandenhoeck & Ruprecht, 1983 (Kritische Studien zur Geschichtswissenschaft. 58).

Kruse, Wolfgang: *Krieg und nationale Integration: Eine Neuinterpretation des sozialdemokratischen Burgfriedensschlusses 1914/15.* Essen: Klartext, 1993.

Kruse, Wolfgang: "Kriegswirtschaft und Gesellschaftsvision. Walther Rathenau und die Organisierung des Kapitalismus, in: Walther Rathenau 1867–1922." Hans Wilderotter, ed.: *Die Extreme berühren sich: Eine Ausstellung des deutschen historischen Museums in Zusammenarbeit mit dem Leo Baeck Institute New York.* Berlin: Argon, 1993. 151–68.

Kügelgen, Werner von: *Kriegswirtschaft und Sozialismus: Die sozialistische Ordnung der deutschen Volkswirtschaft im Weltkrieg, dargestellt unter besonderer Berücksichtigung der Kriegsrohstoffbewirtschaftung.* Heidelberg, Staats- u. wirtschaftswiss. Diss. 1935.

Kuhn, Annette: *Cinema, Censorship and Sexuality, 1909–1925.* London: Routledge, 1988.

L., E.: "Ruinenromantik. Ruinendämonie." *Bildende Kunst* 2:7 (1948): 16–18.

Lacan, Jacques: *Feminine Sexuality: Jacques Lacan and the École Freudienne.* Ed. by Juliet Mitchell and Jacqueline Rose, trans. by Jacqueline Rose. London: Macmillan, 1982.

Lankheit, Klaus: *Franz Marc im Urteil seiner Zeit.* Köln: DuMont, 1960.

Lasswell, Harold Dwight, Ralph D. Casey, and Bruce Lannes Smith: *Propaganda and Promotional Activities: An Annotated Bibliography.* Minneapolis, Minn.: University of Minnesota Press, 1935.

Lederer, Emil: *Deutschlands Wiederaufbau und weltwirtschaftliche Neueingliederung durch Sozialisierung.* Tübingen: Mohr, 1920.

Leed, Eric J.: *No Man 's Land: Combat and Identity in World War I.* Cambridge, London, New York: Cambridge University Press, 1979.

Leiteritz, Christiane: *Revolution als Schauspiel: Beiträge zur Geschichte einer Metapher innerhalb der europäisch-amerikanischen Literatur des 19. und 20. Jahrhunderts.* Berlin, New York: de Gruyter, 1993 (Komparatistische Studien. 18).

Lembcke, Oliver: "Die Auseinandersetzung Tönnies' mit Grelling und Kautsky." Lars Clausen and Carsten Schlüter, eds.: *Hundert Jahre "Gemeinschaft und Gesellschaft": Ferdinand Tönnies in der internationalen Diskussion.* Opladen: Leske und Budrich, 1991. 495–504.

Lenning, Walter: *Gottfried Benn in Selbstzeugnissen und Bilddokumenten.* Reinbek: Rowohlt Taschenbuch Verlag, 1966 (Rowohlts Monographien. 71).

Lerch, Eugen: *Romain Rolland und die Erneuerung der Gesinnung.* München: Max Hueber, 1926.

Leser, Paul: *Entstehung und Verbreitung des Pfluges.* Münster: Aschendorff, 1931.

Levenson, Michael H.: *A Geneology of Modernism: A Study of English Literary Doctrine, 1908–1922.* Cambridge: Cambridge University Press, 1984.

Levin, Harry: "What Was Modernism?" *Massachusetts Review (August 1960)*. Reprinted in Levin: *Refractions: Essays in Comparative Literature*. London: Oxford University Press, 1966. 271–95.

Levine, Frederick S.: *The Apocalyptic Vision: The Art of Franz Marc as German Expressionism*. New York, San Francisco, London: Harper & Row, 1979.

Lifton, Robert Jay and Greg Mitchell, *Hiroshima and America: Fifty Years of Denial*. New York: Putnam's Sons, 1995.

Lifton, Robert Jay and Eric Markusen: *The Genocidal Mentality*. New York: Basic Books, 1990.

Limbaugh, Rush: *The Way Things Ought to Be*. New York: Pocket Star Books, 1992.

Link, Jürgen: "Über die strategische Funktion normalistischer Medien im exterministischen Krieg." *KulturRRevolution 25* (1991): 28–31.

Lorenz, Konrad: *Das sogenannte Böse: Zur Naturgeschichte der Aggression*. Wien: Borotha-Scheler, 1963.

Lotringer, Sylvère: *Overexposed: Treating Sexual Perversion in America*. New York: Pantheon Books, 1988.

Mai, Gunther: *Das Ende des Kaiserreichs: Politik und Kriegführung im Ersten Weltkrieg*. München: Deutscher Taschenbuch Verlag, 1987.

Mai, Gunther: "'Aufklärung der Bevölkerung' und 'vaterländischer Unterricht' in Württemberg 1914–1918. Struktur, Durchführung und Inhalte der deutschen Inlandspropaganda im Ersten Weltkrieg." *Zeitschrift für württembergische Landesgeschichte* 36 (1977/79): 199–235.

Maier, Charles: "Zwischen Taylorismus und Technokratie. Gesellschaftspolitik im Zeichen industrieller Rationalität in den zwanziger Jahren in Europa." Michael Stürmer, ed.: *Die Weimarer Republik: Belagerte Civitas*. Königstein/Ts.: Athenäum., 1980 (Neue Wissenschaftliche Bibliothek. 112: Geschichte). 188–213.

Man, Paul de: *Blindness and Insight: Essays in the Rhetoric of Contemporary Criticism*. Minneapolis: University of Minnesota Press, 1983.

Marshall, 'Slam': *Men Against Fire*. New York: The Infantry Journal and William Morrow and Co., 1948.

Martin, Margaret: "From Periphery to Centre: Women in the French Military." *Armed Forces and Society* 8:2 (1983): 302–33.

Mason, Timothy W.: "Die Bändigung der Arbeiterklasse im nationalsozialistischen Deutschland." Carola Sachse, Tilla Siegel, Hasso Spode, Wolfgang Spohn, eds.: *Angst, Belohnung, Zucht und Ordnung: Herrschaftsmechanismen im Nationalsozialismus*. Opladen: Westdeutscher Verlag, 1982. 11–53.

Masson, Philippe: *Une guerre totale 1939–1945: Stratégies – moyens – controverses*. Paris: Tallandier, 1990.

Mattenklott, Gert, and Mattenklott, Gundel: "Gertrud Kolmar. Metaphorischer Schatten riß." Gert and Gundel Mattenklott: *Berlin Transit: Die Stadt als Station*. Reinbek: Rowohlt, 1987. 189–206.

Mayer, Dieter: *Alfred Döblins "Wallenstein": Zur Geschichtsauffassung und zur Struktur.* München: Fink, 1972.

Mayer, Dieter: *Linksbürgerliches Denken: Untersuchungen zur Kunsttheorie, Gesellschaftsauffassung und Kulturpolitik in der Weimarer Republik (1919–1924).* München: Fink, 1981 (Literaturgeschichte und Literaturkritik. 2).

McClelland, J. S: *The Crowd and the Mob: from Plato to Canetti.* London: Unwin Hyman, 1989.

McHugh, Siobhan: *Minefields and Miniskirts.* Sydney: Doubleday, 1989.

Mehigan, Tim: "Brecht and 'Gestus': The Place of the Subject." *Faultline* 2 (1993): 73–94.

Melzer, Yehuda: *Concepts of Just War.* Leyden: Sijthoff, 1975.

Messenger, Charles: *The Art of Blitzkrieg.* London: Allen, 1976.

Meynen, Emil: *International Bibliography of the "Carte Internationale du monde au millionième."* Bad Godesberg: Bundesanstalt für Landeskunde und Raumforschung, 1962 (Bibliotheca Cartographica. Sonderheft 1).

Michalka, Wolfgang, ed.: *Der Erste Weltkrieg: Wirkung, Wahrnehmung, Analyse.* München: Piper, 1994 (Serie Piper. 1927).

Michels, Helmut: *Ideologie und Propaganda: Die Rolle von Joseph Goebbels in der Nationalsozialistischen Außenpolitik bis 1939.* Frankfurt a. M.: Lang, 1992 (Europäische Hochschulschriften. Reihe III. 527).

Midgley, David R.: *Arnold Zweig: Eine Einführung in Leben und Werk.* Frankfurt a. M.: Athenäum, 1987.

Millet, Kate: *Sexual Politics.* New York: Avon, 1969.

Milward, Alan S.: *The Economic Effects of the Two World Wars on Britain.* London: Basinstoke, 1984.

Mitzman, Arthur: *Sociology and Estrangement: Three Sociologists of Imperial Germany.* New York: Knopf, 1973.

Mizejewski, Linda: *Divine Decadence: Fascism, Female Spectacle, and the Makings of Sally Bowles.* Princeton, N. J.: Princeton University Press, 1992.

Möding, Nori: "Die domestizierte Masse: Gedanken zu den Affinitäten von 'Massen'- und 'Volks'-Begriff." Urs Jaeggi, et al., eds.: *Geist und Katastrophe: Studien zur Soziologie im Nationalsozialismus.* Berlin: Wisenschaftlicher Autorenverlag, 1983. 136–73.

Mommsen, Theodor: "Zum römischen Bodenrecht." *Hermes. Zeitschrift für classische Philologie* 27 (1892): 79–112.

Mommsen, Wolfgang J., ed.: *Die Organisierung des Friedens: Demobilmachung 1918–1920* Göttingen: Vandenhoeck & Ruprecht, 1983 (Geschichte und Gesellschaft. IX, 2).

Moraw, Peter: *Von offener Verfassung zu gestalteter Verdichtung: Das Reich im späten Mittelalter 1250–1490.* Frankfurt a. M., Berlin: Propyläen, 1989 (Propyläen-Geschichte Deutschlands. 3).

Mosès, Stéphane: *L'ange de l'histoire: Rosenzweig, Benjamin, Scholem.* Paris: Editions du Seuil, 1992.

Mosse, George L.: *Fallen Soldiers: Reshaping the Memory of the World Wars.* New York, Oxford: Oxford University Press, 1990.

Mosse, George L.: "National Cemeteries and National Revival: The Cult of the Fallen Soldiers in Germany." *Journal of Contemporary History* 14 (1979): 1–20.

Müller, Alfred: *Die Kriegsrohstoffbewirtschaftung 1914–1918 im Dienste des deutschen Monopolkapitals.* Berlin: Akademie-Verlag, 1955.

Müller, Hans-Harald: *Der Krieg und die Schriftsteller: Der Kriegsroman der Weimarer Republik.* Stuttgart: Metzler, 1986.

Müller, Harro: *Geschichte zwischen Kairos und Katastrophe: Historische Romane im 20. Jahrhundert.* Frankfurt a. M.: Athenäum, 1988.

Müller, Ingo: *Furchtbare Juristen: Die unbewältigte Vergangenheit unserer Justiz.* Vollständige Taschenbuchausg. München: Droemer Knaur, 1989 (Knaur. 3960).

Mulvey, Laura: "Visual Pleasure and the Narrative Cinema." *Screen* no 16, 1975: 6–18.

Natter, Monika: "Quelle Europe: Stefan Zweig et Romain Rolland face à la montée du nationalisme." *Europe*, 73, no. 794–795 (Juin-Juillet 1995): 104–11.

Nedeljkovic, Dragoljub-Dragan: *Romain Rolland et Stefan Zweig: Affinités et influences littéraires et spirituelles 1910–1942.* Paris: Éditions Klincksieck, 1970.

Negt, Oskar, and Alexander Kluge: "Einige 'Beobachtungen zum Entstehungsprozeß' des Blitzkriegs." Kluge und Negt: *Geschichte und Eigensinn.* Vol. 1–3. Vol. 3: *Gewalt des Zusammenhangs.* Frankfurt am Main: Suhrkamp, 1993. 1187–97.

Nobile, Philip, ed.: *Judgment at the Smithsonian's 50th Anniversary Exhibit of the Enola Gay.* New York: Marlowe, 1995.

Nolte, Ernst: "Vergangenheit, die nicht vergehen will. Eine Rede, die geschrieben, aber nicht gehalten werden konnte." *Historikerstreit: Die Dokumentation der Kontroverse um die Einzigartigkeit der nationalsozialistischen Judenvernichtung.* München: Piper, 1987. 39–47.

Ott, Hugo: *Martin Heidegger.* Frankfurt a. M.: Campus, 1988.

Owen, David: *Balkan Odyssey.* New York: Harcourt Brace, 1996.

Oxaal, Ivar: "Sociology, History and the Holocaust." [Rev. of: Zygmunt Bauman: *Modernity and the Holocaust.* 1989]. *Theory, Culture and Society* 8:1 (1991): 153–66.

Paret, Peter, ed.: *Makers of Modern Strategy: From Machiavelli to the Nuclear Age.* With the collaboration of Gordon A. Craig and Felix Gilbert. Princeton, N. J.: Princeton University Press, 1990.

Paul, Gerhard: *Aufstand der Bilder: Die NS-Propaganda vor 1933.* Bonn: Dietz, 1990.

Penck, Albert: "Die Weltkarte 1:1.000.000." *Jahrbuch der Kartographie*, Leipzig 1941: 81–82.

Peterson, Jens: "Mussolini: Wirklichkeit und Mythos eines Diktators." Karl-Heinz Bohrer, ed.: *Mythos und Moderne: Begriff und Bild einer Rekonstruktion.* Frankfurt a. M.: Suhrkamp 1983 (Edition Suhrkamp. 1144). 242–60.

Petzold, Joachim: *Die Dolchstoßlegende: Eine Geschichtsfälschung im Dienst des deutschen Imperialismus und Militarismus*. Berlin: Akademie-Verlag, 1963 (Schriften des Instituts für Geschichte. I, 18).

Pottage, Allain: "The Measurement of Land." *Modern Law Review* 57 (1994): 361–84.

Prescott, John R.: *Boundaries and Frontiers*. London: Croom Helm, 1978.

Prosch, Wilhelm: *Die Propaganda: Ihre Anwendung in der Politik und ihre Bedeutung für Deutschlands Wiederaufstieg*. Hamburg, Phil. Diss., 1924.

Prost, Antoine: "Les représentations de la guerre dans la culture française de l'entre deux guerres." *Vingtième siècle* 41 (1994): 23–31.

Puhle, Hans-Jürgen: "Historische Konzepte des Industriekapitalismus: 'Organisierter Kapitalismus' und 'Korporativismus'." *Geschichte und Gesellschaft* 10 (1984): 165–84.

Queter, Geoffrey Harold: *Women in the Armed Forces: The US Experience*. Chicago, Inter-University Seminar, Armed Forces and Society, October 23–25 1980: 24.

Raulff, Ulrich: *Ein Historiker im 20. Jahrhundert: Marc Bloch*. Frankfurt a. M.: S. Fischer, 1995.

Read, James M.: *Atrocity Propaganda, 1914–1919*. New York: Arno Press, 1941.

Readings, Bill: "Sublime Politics: The End of the Party Line." *Modern Language Quarterly* 53 (1992): 409–25.

Rhodes, James M.: *The Hitler Movement: A Modern Millenarian Revolution*. Stanford: Hoover Institution Press, 1980 (Hoover Institution Publication. 213).

Richter, Donald: *Chemical Soldiers: British Gas Warfare in World War I*. Lawrence, Kansas: University Press of Kansas, 1992.

Riedesser, Peter, and Axel Verderber: *Aufrüstung der Seelen: Militärpsychiatrie und Militärpsychologie in Deutschland und Amerika*. Freiburg: Dreisam, 1985.

Ringer, Fritz: *The Decline of the German Mandarins: The German Academic Community, 1890–1933*. Cambridge, Mass.: Harvard University Press, 1969.

Ritter, Gerhard: *The Sword and the Sceptre: The Problem of Militarism in Germany*. Trans. by Heinz Norden. Vol. 1–4. Coral Gables, Florida: University of Miami Press, 1969–1973.

Rivers, W[illiam] H[alse]: *Instinct and the Unconscious: A Contribution to a Biological Theory of Psycho-neuroses*. Cambridge: Cambridge University Press, 1992 (The Cambridge medical series).

Robert, Jean-Louis, and Jay M. Winter: *Paris, London, Berlin: Capital cities at war 1914–1919*. Cambridge: Cambridge University Press, 1995.

Robichez, Jaques: *Le symbolisme au théâtre: Lugné-Poe et les débuts de l'Œuvre*. Paris: Perrin, 1957.

Roerkohl, Anne: *Hungerblockade und Heimatfront: Die kommunale Lebensmittelversorgung in Westfalen während des Ersten Weltkreiges*. Stuttgart: Steiner, 1991 (Studien zur Geschichte des Alltags. 10).

Rose, Ramona M.: *The Position and Treatment of Women in Nazi Germany: As viewed from the perspective of the English Language press 1933–1945*. London: Tantalus Research Limited, 1984.

Rosenberg, Hans: "The Pseudo-Democratisation of the Junker Class." Georg Iggers, ed.: *The Social History of Politics: Critical Perspective in West German Historical Writing since 1945*. Dover, N. H.: Berg, 1985. 81–112.

Rothe, Wolfgang: "'Seinesgleichen geschieht': Musil und die moderne Erzähltradition." Karl Dinklage, Elisabeth Albertsen, and Karl Corino, eds.: *Robert Musil: Studien zu seinem Werk*. Reinbek bei Hamburg: Rowohlt Verlag 1970. 131–69.

Rowley, Brian A.: "Anticipations of Modernism in the Age of Romanticism." Janet Garton, ed.: *Facets of European Modernism: Essays in Honour of James McFarland Presented to him on his 65th Birthday, 12 December 1985*. Norwich: University of East Anglia, 1985. 1–22.

Ruddy, F. S.: "Res nullius and Occupation in Roman and International Law." *University of Missouri at Kansas City* 2 (1967/68): 274–87.

Sarris, Andrew: "The Nasty Nazis: History or Mythology." *The Village Voice*, October 17, 1974: 77–78.

Scherpe, Klaus R.: "'Ein Kolossalgemälde für Kurzsichtige'. Das Andere der Geschichte in Alfred Döblins *Wallenstein*". Hartmut Eggert et al., ed.: *Geschichte als Literatur*. Stuttgart: Metzler, 1990. 226–41.

Schieck, Hans: *Der Kampf um die deutsche Wirtschaftspolitik nach dem Novemberumsturz 1918*. Heidelberg, Phil. Diss. 1958.

Schieder, Theodor: "Rathenau und die Probleme der deutschen Außenpolitik." Marc Sieber, ed.: *Discordia Concors: Festgabe für Edgar Bonjour zu seinem 70. Geburtstag am 21. August 1968*. Vol. 1–2. Basel, Stuttgart: Helbing & Lichtenhahn, 1968. 239–68.

Schjerning, Otto von, ed.,: *Handbuch der ärztlichen Erfahrung im Weltkriege 1914/1918*. Vol. 1–9. Leipzig: Barth 1921–22. Vol. 1–2: *Chirurgie*. Hrsg. von Erwin Prayr und Carl Franz. 1922. Vol. 3: *Innere Medizin*. Hrsg. von Ludolf von Krehl. 1921. Vol. 4: *Geistes- und Nervenkrankheiten*. Hrsg. Karl Bonhoeffer. 1922. Vol. 5: *Augenheilkunde*. Hrsg. von Theodor Axenfeld. 1922. Vol 6: *Gehörorgan, obere Luft- und Speisewege*. Hrsg. von Otto Voss und Gustav Killian. 1921. Vol. 7: *Hygiene*. Hrsg. von Wilhelm Hoffmann. 1922. Vol. 8: *Pathologische Anatomie*. Hrsg. von Ludwig Aschoff. Vol. 9: *Röntgenologie*. Hrsg. von Rudolf Grashey. 1922.

Schlenstedt, Silvia: "Suche nach Halt in haltloser Lage: Die Kulturarbeit deutscher Juden nach 1933 in Deutschland und die Dichterin Gertrud Kolmar." *Sinn und Form* 41 (1989): 727–42.

Schmid, Dieter: *Wichard von Moellendorff: Ein Beitrag zur wirtschaftlichen Selbstverwaltung.* Berlin, Diss. 1970.

Schmidt, Dieter: *Otto Dix im Selbstbildnis.* Berlin (East): Henschel, 1978.

Schmidt, Gustav: *Deutscher Historismus und der Übergang zur parlamentarischen Demokratie: Untersuchungen zu den politischen Gedanken von Meinecke, Troeltsch, Max Weber.* Lübeck and Hamburg: Matthiesen, 1964 (Historische Studien. 389).

Schmied, Wieland: "Points of Departure and Transformations in German Art, 1905–1985." Christos M. Joachimides, ed.: *German Art in the Twentieth Century: Painting and Sculpture 1905–1985.* Exhibition catalogue, Royal Academy of Art, London, 11 October – 22 December 1985. London: Weidenfels and Nicolson, 1985.

Schmiedebach, Heinz-Peter: "Sozialdarwinismus, Biologismus, Pazifismus: Ärztestimmen zum Ersten Weltkrieg." Johanna Bleker and Heinz-Peter Schmiedebach, eds.: *Medizin und Krieg: Vom Dilemma der Heilberufe 1865 bis 1985.* Frankfurt a. M.: Fischer Taschenbuch Verlag, 1987: 93–121.

Schneede, Uwe M.: *George Grosz: His Life and Work.* London: Fraser, 1979.

Schneidau, Herbert N.: *Waking Giants: The Presence of the Past in Modernism.* Oxford: Oxford University Press, 1991.

Schott, Heinz: *Die Chronik der Medizin.* Dortmund: Chronik Verlag, Harenberg, 1993.

Schrecken und Hoffnung: Künstler sehen Frieden und Krieg. Gemeinsame Ausstellung der Deutschen Bank und des Ministeriums für Kultur der UdSSR, Moskau. Hamburger Kunsthalle, 1. Oktober – 15. November 1987 [also in Munich, Moscow, Leningrad]. Hrsg. von Werner Hofmann. Hamburg: Hamburger Kunsthalle, 1987.

Schulin, Ernst: "Krieg und Modernisierung. Rathenau als philosophierender Industrieorganisator im Ersten Weltkrieg." Thomas Hughes, ed: *Ein Mann vieler Eigenschaften: Walther Rathenau und die Kultur der Moderne.* Berlin: Wagenbach, 1990 (Kleine kulturwissenschaftliche Bibliothek. 21). 55–69.

Schürgers, Norbert J.: *Politische Philosophie in der Weimarer Republik: Staatsverständnis zwischen Führerdemokratie und bürokratischem Sozialismus.* Stuttgart: Metzler, 1989.

Schwichtenberg, Cathy, ed.: *The Madonna Connection: Representational Politics, Subcultural Identities, and Cultural Theory.* Boulder: Westview Press, 1992.

Segal, Martin: *Women in Combat.* Chicago inter-University Seminar, Armed Forces and Society, October, 3–25 1980.

Seiler, Bernd W.: *Die historischen Dichtungen Georg Heyms: Analyse und Kommentar.* München: Fink, 1972.

Seydewitz, Max: *Zerstörung und Wiederaufbau von Dresden.* Berlin: Kongress, 1955.

Shils, Edward: *Tradition.* Chicago: University of Chicago Press, 1981.

Shils, Evelyn, and Morris Janowitz: "Cohesion and Disintegration in the Wehrmacht in World War II." *Public Opinion Quarterly* 12 (Summer, 1948). 280–315.

Showalter, Elaine: *The Female Malady: Women, Madness and the English Culture, 1830–1980.* London: Virago, 1987.

Shulman, Milton: *Defeat in the West.* London: Mercury Books, 1980.

Siegert, Bernhard: "Luftwaffe Fotographie: Luftkrieg als Bildverarbeitungssystem 1911- 1921." *Fotogeschichte: Beiträge zur Geschichte und Ästhetik der Fotografie* 12 (1992): 41–54.

Silver, Ken: *Esprit de Corps: The Parisian Avant-garde in the Period of the Great War.* London: Thames & Hudson, 1988.

Simoneit, Max: *Wehrpsychologie: Ein Abriß ihrer Probleme und praktischen Folgerungen.* Berlin: Bernard & Graefe, 1933.

Skelton, R. A.: "The military surveyor's contribution to British cartography in the 16th century." *Imago Mundi* 24 (1970): 77–83.

Slane, Andrea: *The Erotics of Violence: Sexy Nazis and the Transformation of Psycho-Sexual Explanation and Political Rhetoric in Film, Video and Fiction, 1930–1994.* Ph. D., University of California, San Diego, 1995.

Smith, Henry A.: "Gertrud Kolmar's Life and Works." Gertrud Kolmar: *The Selected Poems.* Ed. and trans. by Henry A. Smith. New York: Seabury Press, 1975. 1–52.

Sodhi, Kripal Singh: "Zur Problematik der Massenpsychologie." *Kölner Zeitschrift für Soziologie* 10 (1958): 209–21.

Sonnenberg, Stephen M., Arthur S. Blank, and John A. Talbott, eds.: *The Trauma of War: Stress and Recovery in Viet Nam Veterans.* Washington: American Psychiatric Press, 1985.

Sontag, Susan: "Fascinating Fascism." *The Susan Sontag Reader.* New York: Farrar, Strauss, and Giroux, 1982. 305–25.

Sontag, Susan: "Waiting for something that does not arrive." *The Guardian Weekly* 149/6, August 8, 1993: 24.

Sontheimer, Kurt: *Antidemokratisches Denken in der Weimarer Republik: Die politischen Ideen des deutschen Nationalismus zwischen 1918 und 1933.* München: Nymphenburger Verlagshandlung, 1968.

Star, Susan Leigh: "Swastikas: The Street and the University." Robin Ruth Linden, Darlene R. Pagano, Diana E. H. Russell, and Susan Leigh Star, eds., *Against Sadomasochism: A Radical Feminist Analysis.* E. Palo Alto: Frog in the Well, 1982. 131-36.

Stark, Michael: "'The Murder of Modernism': Some Observations on Research into Expressionism and the Post-Modernism Debate." Richard Sheppard, ed.: *Expressionism in Focus.* Blairgowrie, Scotland: Lochee Publications Ltd, 1987. 27–46.

Starr, William Thomas: *Romain Rolland: One against All.* Den Haag, Paris: Mouton, 1971.

Steck, Rainald: *Romain Rollands Revolutionsdrama "Danton"*. Witterschlick bei Bonn: Richard Schwarzbold, 1973. Tübingen, Phil. Diss. 1972.

Stern, Joseph P.: *Hitler: The Führer and the People*. Berkeley: University of California Press, 1975.

Sternburg, Wilhelm von: *Arnold Zweig*. Frankfurt a. M.: Hain, 1990.

Sterritt, David: "Romper Stomper." *Christian Science Monitor*, June 11, 1993: 12.

Stolper, Gustav: *Deutsche Wirtschaft seit 1870*. Tübingen: Mohr, 1964.

Strandmann, Harmut Pogge von: *Walther Rathenau: Industrialist, Banker, Intellectual, Politician. Notes and Diaries 1907–1922*. Oxford: Clarendon Press, 1985.

Strandmann, Hartmut Pogge von: *Unternehmenspolitik und Unternehmungsführung: Der Dialog zwischen Aufsichtsrat und Vorstand bei Mannesmann 1900 bis 1919*. Düsseldorf, Wien: Econ, 1978.

Strandmann, Hartmut Pogge von: "Rathenau zwischen Politik und Wirtschaft." Franz Otmar, ed.: *Am Wendepunkt der europäischen Geschichte*. Göttingen, Zürich: Muster-Schmidt, 1981. 88–106.

Struve, Walter: *Elites Against Democracy: Leadership Ideals in Bourgeois Political Thought in Germany 1890–1933*. Princeton, N. J.: Princeton University Press, 1973.

Styan, J. L.: *Max Reinhardt*. Cambridge: Cambridge University Press, 1982.

Tatar, Maria: *Lustmord: Sexual Murder in Weimar Germany*. Princeton, N. J.: Princeton University Press, 1995.

The Fallen. Exhibition catalogue, Museum of Modern Art, Oxford, 5 November 1988 – 15 January 1989. Oxford: Museum of Modern Art, 1988.

Theweleit, Klaus: *Männerphantasien*. Vol. 1–2. Reinbek: Rowohlt, 1980.

Theweleit, Klaus: *Male Fantasies*. Trans. by Stephen Conway, Erica Carter and Chris Turner. Vol. 1: *Women, Floods, Bodies, History*. Minneapolis: University of Minnesota Press, 1987; vol. 2: *Male Bodies: Psychoanalyzing the White Terror*. Oxford: Polity Press, 1989.

Thimme, Annelise: *Flucht in den Mythos: Die Deutschkonservative Volkspartei und die Niederlage von 1918*. Göttingen: Vandenhoeck & Ruprecht, 1969.

Tickner, Lisa: "Men's Work? Masculinity and Modernism." *differences: a journal of feminist cultural studies* 4:5 (1992): 1–37.

Toch, Josef: *Vergesellschaftung in Österreich*. Wien: Verlag des Österreichischen Gewerkschaftsbundes, 1963.

Tönnies, Ferdinand: *Community and Society. (Gemeinschaft und Gesellschaft*, Engl.). New Brunswick: Transaction Books, 1988.

Trepp, Gian: *Bankgeschäfte mit dem Feind: Von Hitlers Europabank zum Instrument des Marshallplans. Die Bank für internationalen Zahlungsausgleich im Zweiten Weltkrieg*. Zürich: Rotpunkt, 1993.

Tuten, Jean: *The Utilization of Women in Combat: The Germans*: Past Practice, Perspective and Prospects. Chicago, Inter-University Seminar, Armed Forces and Society. 23–25 October 1980. 17.

Ullmann, Hans-Peter: *Interessenverbände in Deutschland*. Frankfurt a. M.: Suhrkamp, 1988.

Ulrich, Bernd: "Nerven und Krieg: Skizzierung einer Beziehung." Bedrich Loewen-stein, ed.: *Geschichte und Psychologie: Annäherungsversuche*. Pfaffenweiler: Centaurus, 1992 (Geschichte und Psychologie. 4). 163–92.

Vergne-Cain, Brigitte, and Gérard Rudent: "Lettres dans la mêlée." *Europe*, 73, no 794-795 (Juin-Juillet 1995): 112–21.

Verhey, Jeffrey: "Ferdinand Tönnies Kritik der 'öffentlichen Meinung': das Demokra-tieverständnis eines Vernunftrepublikaners." Wolfgang Bialas and Georg Iggers, eds.: *Intellektuelle in der Weimarer Republik*. Frankfurt a. M.: Lang, 1996 (Schriften-reihe zur politischen Kultur der Weimarer Republik. 1). 159-176

Verkamp, Bernard J.: *The Moral Treatment of Returning Soldiers in Early Medieval and Modern Times*. Scranton: University of Scranton Press, 1993.

Villinger, Ingeborg, ed.: *Verortung des Politischen: Carl Schmitt in Plettenberg, Beiträge zur Plettenberger Stadtgeschichte* Vol. 2. Hagen: Stadt Plettenberg, 1987.

Virilio, Paul: *Der reine Krieg*. (*Pure Ware*, dt.) Berlin: Merve, 1984.

Virilio, Paul: *Die Eroberung des Körpers: Vom Übermenschen zum überreizten Menschen*. Mün-chen Wien: Hanser, 1994.

Virilio, Paul: *War and Cinema: The Logistics of Perception*. London: Verso, 1989.

Visconti-Prasca, Sebastiano: *Der Entscheidungskrieg*. Oldenburg-Berlin: Stalling, 1935.

Vondung, Klaus: "Propaganda oder Sinndeutung?" Klaus Vondung, ed.: *Kriegserlebnis: Der Erste Weltkrieg in der literarischen Gestaltung und symbolischen Deutung der Nationen*. Göttingen: Vandenhoeck & Ruprecht, 1980. 11–37.

Wagner, Philip: "Psychiatric Activities during the Normandy Offensive." *Psychiatry* 9:4 (1946): 341–46.

Wallach, Jehuda L.: *Das Dogma der Vernichtungsschlacht: Die Lehren von Clausewitz und Schlieffen und ihre Wirkungen in zwei Weltkriegen*. Frankfurt a. M.: Bernard & Graefe, 1967.

Walzer, Michael: *Just and Unjust Wars: A Moral Argument with historical Illustrations*. New York: Basic Books, 1977.

Weidauer, Walter: *Inferno Dresden*. Berlin: Dietz, 1987.

Weingart, Peter, Jürgen Kroll, and Kurt Bayertz: *Rasse, Blut und Gene: Geschichte der Eugenik und Rassenhygiene in Deutschland*. Frankfurt a. M.: Suhrkamp, 1992.

Weinstock, Nathan: *Zionism: False Messiah* (*Sionisme contre Israël: Genèse d'Israël, 1882–1948*, Engl.). A translation by Alan Adler, with an introductory interview by Mosche Machover. London: Pluto Press, 1989.

Weisstein, Naomi: "'Kinder, Küche, Kirche' as Scientific Law: Psychology Constructs the Female." Robin Morgan, ed.: *Sisterhood is Powerful: An Anthology of Writings from the Women's Liberation Movement*. New York: Random House, 1970. 228-45.

Welch, David: *The Third Reich: Politics and Propaganda*. New York: Routledge, 1993.

Wellek, René: "The Term and Concept of Symbolism in Literary History." Wellek: *Discriminations: Further Concepts of Criticism*. New Haven, Connecticut: Yale University Press, 1970. 90–121.

Wendt, Bernd-Jürgen: "Vom Interventionsstaat zum Industrieparlament: Ordnungspolitische Vorstellungen in England nach dem Ersten Weltkrieg." *Geschichte und Gesellschaft* 12 (1986), Sonderbd.: Richard H. Tilly, ed.: *Nachkriegsprobleme 1918–1924 im Vergleich*. 5–33.

Wenzel, Georg, ed.: *Arnold Zweig 1887–1968*. Berlin, Weimar: Aufbau-Verlag, 1978.

Wenzel, Georg: "'Si vis pacem … ' und die Folgen. Die Verantwortung des Schriftstellers Arnold Zweig für den Frieden im Spiegel der Erzählungen 'Die Bestie' (1914) und 'Westlandsaga' (1952)." *Wissenschaftliche Beiträge der Ernst-Moritz-Arndt-Universität Greifswald*. 1985 (Greifswalder Germanistische Forschungen 6): 80–86.

Werckmeister, Otto K.: *The Making of Paul Klee's Career, 1914–1920*. Chicago: University of Chicago Press, 1989.

Wette, Wolfram, ed.: *Der Krieg des kleinen Mannes: Eine Militärgeschichte von unten*. München: Piper, 1992.

Wette, Wolfram: "Reichstag und 'Kriegsgewinnerei' (1916–1918). Die Anfänge parlamentarischer Rüstungskontrolle in Deutschland." *Militärgeschichtliche Mitteilungen* 36 (1984): 31–56.

Whalen, Robert Weldon: *Bitter Wounds: German Victims of the Great War, 1914–1939*. Ithaca and London: Cornell University Press, 1984.

Whaley, Joachim, ed.: *Mirrors of Mortality: Studies in the Social History of Death*. London: Europa Publications, 1981.

Widmann, Wilhelm: *Theater und Revolution: Ihre gegenseitigen Beziehungen und Wirkungen im achtzehnten, neunzehnten und zwanzigsten Jahrhundert*. Berlin: Oesterheld, 1920.

Wiedenfeld, Kurt: *Die Organisation der Kriegsrohstoff-Bewirtschaftung im Weltkrieg*. Hamburg: Hanseatische Verlagsanstalt, 1936.

Wieland, Lothar: *Belgien 1914: Die Frage des belgischen "Franktireurkrieges" und die deutsche öffentliche Meinung von 1914 bis 1936*. Frankfurt a. M.: Lang, 1984 (Studien zum Kontinuitätsproblem der deutschen Geschichte. 2).

Wiese, Stephan von: *Max Beckmanns zeichnerisches Werk 1903–1925*. Düsseldorf: Droste, 1978.

Wiesinger, Walter: "Gertrud Kolmar. Rue Saint-Honoré." Rupert Hirschenauer and Albrecht Weber, ed.: *Wege zum Gedicht II: Interpretationen von Balladen*. München, Zürich: Schnell & Steiner, 1963. 517–26.

Wilenski, Reginald Howard: *The Modern Movement in Art*. New York: Stokes, 1927.

Willemsen, Roger: *Das Existenzrecht der Dichtung: Zur Rekonstruktion einer systematischen Literaturtheorie im Werk Robert Musils*. München: Fink, 1984.

Williams, Raymond: "When Was Modernism?" Williams: *The Politics of Modernism: Against the New Conformists*. Edited and Introduced by Tony Pinkney. London, New York: Verso, 1989. 55–69.

Williamson, David Graham: "Walther Rathenau and the KRA: August 1914 – March 1915." *Zeitschrift für Unternehmensgeschichte*, 23 (1978): 118–36.

Winkler, Heinrich August, ed.: *Organisierter Kapitalismus: Voraussetzungen und Anfänge*. Göttingen: Vandenhoeck & Ruprecht, 1974.

Winter, Jay M.: *The Experience of World War I*. London: Macmillan, 1988.

Winter, Jay M.: *The Great War and the British People*. London: Macmillan, 1985.

Wohl, Robert: "The Generation of 1914 and Modernism." Monique Chefdor, Ricardo Quinones, and Albert Wachtel, eds.: *Modernism: Challenges and Perspectives*. Urbana: University of Illinois Press, 1986. 66–78.

Wolff, Robert Paul: "On Violence." *Journal of Philosophy* 66 (1969): 601–16.

Woltmann, Johanna, ed.: *Gertrud Kolmar 1894–1943*. 2. Aufl. Marbach a. Neckar: Deutsche Schiller-Gesellschaft 1993 (Marbacher Magazin. 63).

Woltmann, Johanna: *Gertrud Kolmar – Leben und Werk*. Göttingen: Wallstein, 1995.

Young, James E.: *The Texture of memory: Holocaust Memorials and Meaning*. New Haven, Conn.: Yale University Press, 1993.

Zeman, Z. A.B., ed: *Germany and the Revolution in Russia, 1915–1918: Documents from the Archives of the German Foreign Ministry*. London, New York: Oxford University Press, 1958.

Zimmerman, Paul D.: "Trampling on Rampling." *Newsweek* 84, Oct 7, 1974: 95.

Zimmermann, Diana: *Romain Rolland: Le Théâtre du Peuple et le Théâtre de la Révolution*. Paper written for a seminar at Paris VIII/St. Denis, 1993/94.

Zipes, Jack: "The Holocaust, Modernity and Tough Jews." *Telos* 86 (Winter 1990–91): 170–83.

Zolling, Peter: *Zwischen Integration und Segregation: Sozialpolitik im 'Dritten Reich' am Beispiel der 'Nationalsozialistischen Volkswohlfahrt' (NSV) in Hamburg.* Frankfurt a. M.: Lang, 1986.

Zunkel, Friedrich: *Industrie und Staatssozialismus: Der Kampf um die Wirtschaftsordnung in Deutschland* 1914–1918. Düsseldorf: Droste, 1974 (Tübinger Schriften zur Sozial- und Zeitgeschichte. 3).

List of Illustrations

1. Otto Dix: *Self-Portrait as a Soldier*, 1914, Galerie der Stadt Stuttgart.
2. Otto Dix: *Self-Portrait with Artillery Helmet*, 1914, Galerie der Stadt Stuttgart.
3. Max Beckmann: *The Morgue*, 1915, Museum of Modern Art, New York.
4. Max Beckmann: *The Grenade*, 1915, British Museum, London.
5. Erich Heckel: *Two Wounded Soldiers*, 1914, Brücke Museum, Berlin.
6. George Grosz: *Aerial Attack*, 1914, Museum of Modern Art, New York.
7. Willy Jaeckel: *Memento (I)*, 1914–15, Bröhan Museum, Berlin.
8. Ernst Ludwig Kirchner: *Artillerymen in the Shower*, 1915, Guggenheim Museum, New York.
9. Franz Marc: *The Greedy Mouth*, 1915, Staatliche Graphische Sammlung, Munich.
10. Ernst Barlach: *Mass Grave*, 1915, Ernst-Barlach-Haus, Hamburg.

Notes on Contributors

KARLHEINZ BARCK
specializes in Romance Philology and Comparative Literature. Publications on Spanish, (Góngora, Ortega y Gasset, generación del 27) and French (Baudelaire, surrealism) literature. Area of current research: theory and history of aesthetics. Co-editor of the work in progress: *Historical Dictionary of Aesthetic Concepts*. Recent publication: "Poésie und Imagination. Studien zu ihrer Reflexionsgeschichte zwischen Aufklärung und Moderne".

ROBERT COHEN
is adjunct Associate Professor of German, New York University. His major areas of research are the literature of the Weimar period, the Exile, and anti fascist literature, as well as the work of Peter Weiss. His books include *Versuche über Weiss 'Ästhetik des Widerstands'* and *Understanding Peter Weiss* (1993). He has published articles on Anna Seghers, Ernst Ottwalt, Karl Kraus, Arnold Zweig, and Peter Weiss.

RICHARD CORK
is an art historian, exhibition curator, and chief art critic of *The Times* in London. His books include the standard work on Vorticism and, most recently, *A Bitter Truth: Avant-Garde Art and the Great War* (1994). He has organized major exhibitions in Berlin, Milan, Paris and London. In 1989–90 he was Slade Professor of Fine Art at Cambridge University, and he is now Henry Moore Fellow at the Courtauld Institute of Art, London. He has recently been appointed Chairman of the Visual Arts Panel at the Arts Council of England.

PHILIP D'ALTON
teaches sociology at the University of Wollongong (Australia). Among his areas of specialization is the sociology of the military with particular emphasis on issues of gender and equality.

LISABETH DURING
teaches Philosophy and Gender studies at the University of New South Wales in Sydney, Australia. She has previously taught at Macquarie University and

Melbourne University. A visiting scholar at Columbia University in 1995, she is writing a book called *Virtue and the Way of the Worked: Chastity, Marriage, and Femininity*. Recent publications include 'The Muse Abused,' in *Creative Agonistics* (1995) and 'Clues and Intimations: Foucault, Freud, Holmes,' in *Cultural Critique* (1996).

WOLFGANG U. ECKART
is Professor of the History of Medicine at Heidelberg University, Germany. Born in 1952 in Schwelm, he studied medicine and history at the University of Münster. His Ph. D. thesis was on Daniel Sennert (1572–1636): *Grundlagen des medizinisch wissenchaftlichen Erkennens bei Daniel Sennert* (1978). His research and teaching activities include the history of science in early modern Europe; medical iconography of the 17th century; the history of medical ethics and medicine in German colonial imperialism.

JUSTUS FETSCHER
(born 1961) studied German Literature, Drama and History at Berlin´s *Freie Universität*. Ph. D. on Heinrich von Kleist´s *Amphitryon* (1990). Visiting Fellow at Cornell University (Western Societies Program) Ithaca/NY (1990). 1990–1995 Assistant (wissenschaftlicher Mitarbeiter) at the Institute for General and Comparative Literature at the FU. Co-edited (with Eberhard Lämmert and Jürgen Schutte) *Die Gruppe 47 in der Geschichte der Bundesrepublik* (1991). Articles on Kleist, theater history and post-War German literature.

BERND HÜPPAUF
Professor of German and chair of Department, New York University. He has previously taught at the universities of Tübingen, Regensburg, Berlin, and UNSW (Sydney, Australia). His areas of specialization include the Weimar Republic, literature and other discourses, representations of violence. Publications include essays on literature of the First World War, Photography, Skepticism, Musil, Döblin, Roth, Kunert.

WOLF KITTLER
Professor and Chair of Germanic, Slavic and Semitic Studies at the University of California, Santa Barbara. Ph. D. 1979, Erlangen-Nürnberg; Habilitation 1986, University of Freiburg; teaching experience at the Universities of Erlangen/Nürnberg, Freiburg, Munich, Konstanz. – Publications: *Der Turmbau zu*

Babel und das Schweigen der Sirenen: Über das Reden, das Schweigen, die Stimme und die Schrift in vier Texten von Franz Kafka (1985); *Die Geburt des Partisanen aus dem Geist der Poesie: Heinrich von Kleist und die Strategie der Befreiungskriege* (1987); essays on Hölderlin, Goethe, Kleist, Beckett, Borges, on literary theory, mediatechnology and warfare.

TIM MEHIGAN
is a Professor of German language and literature at the University of Melbourne (Australia). He has published on Kleist, Eichendorff, Brecht and Musil as well as in the area of foreign language pedagogy. He regularly directs theater productions.

WOLFGANG MICHALKA
specializes in modern military history and is the editor-in-chief of the „Militärgeschichtliches Forschungsamt" in Potsdam. He is also an adjunct professor (Lehrbeauftragter) at the University of Freiburg. He has published extensively on twentieth century German political history and is co-editor of Walther Rathenau's complete works.

HARRO MÜLLER
is Professor of German at the Department of Germanic Languages at Columbia University. Selected book publications: *Geschichte zwischen Kairos und Katastrophe: Historische Romane im 20. Jahrhundert* (1988); *Giftpfeile. Zu Theorie und Literatur der Moderne* (1994); *Diskurstheorien und Literaturwissenschaft* (ed. together with Jürgen Fohrmann, 1988), *Literaturwissenschaft/Systemtheorie* (1996).

CRYSTAL MAZUR OCKENFUSS
born 1967 in Buffalo, NY, received her BA in German and Cultural Anthropology from SUNY Buffalo in 1989, currently a President's Fellow and Ph. D. candidate at the University of Virginia. – Publications on Elfriede Jelinek, Kafka, Clemens Brentano.

ANDREA SLANE
is a media artist and Assistant Professor of Film Studies in the English Department of Old Dominion University. She received her Ph. D. from the University of California, San Diego, in 1995, with a dissertation entitled *Family Values and Nazi Perversion: Anti-Fascist Rhetoric on Sexuality in American Theory, Film and Commentary (1930–1995)*. Her film/video works include *The Alleged* (1992) and *Irresistible Impulse* (1994).

ANDY SPENCER

Ph. D. from Ohio State University, 1992: *Of Literature and Legend: German Writers and the Bombing of Dresden.* Forthcoming: "Die Zerstörung Dresdens: Symbol und Ereignis in Publizistik und Historiographie" in *Die Zerstörung Dresdens am 13./14. Februar 1945. Antworten der Künste.*

FRANK TROMMLER

is Professor of German and Comparative Literature at the University of Pennsylvania. Publications in the fields of modern German literary and cultural history, on theater, technology, and German-American cultural relations. Among his works are *Die Kultur der Weimarer Republik* (1978, repr. 1996), *America and the Germans* (coed. 1985).

JEFFREY VERHEY

studied history at UC Berkeley, Ph. D. thesis on *The Myth of the "Spirit of 1914" in Germany, 1914–1945.* He is presently a member of the "Graduiertenkolleg" at the University of Siegen. He has taught at UC Berkeley, UC Davis, and the Free University in Berlin, and has been a fellow at the Center for European Studies, Harvard University. He has published articles including, most recently, "Die Moralische Perspektive: Die Produktion von Selbst- und Feindbildern in Großbritannien in der ersten Hälfte des 20. Jahrhunderts," in Lutz Ebering, ed.: *Kommunikationsraum Europa* (1995).

CORNELIA VISMANN

studied law and philosophy; lawyer in Berlin and assistant at the Department of Cultural Studies, Europa Universität Viadrina, Frankfurt (Oder), is completing a doctoral thesis on *Files and Filing-Systems as Media for in Law.* Publications: „St. Benedict, Inc.: Zur Rechtsförmigkeit von Gemeinschaft," in Günter Frankenberg, ed.: *Auf der Suche nach der gerechten Gesellschaft* (1994), and "Terra Nullius: Zur Unterscheidung von Freund und Feind," in Armin Adam, Martin Stingelin, eds.: *Übertragung und Gesetz: Gründungsmythen, Kriegstheater und Unterwerfungsstrategien von Institutionen* (1995).

JAY M. WINTER

is University Lecturer in History and Fellow of Pembroke College, Cambridge. A specialist on the history of the First World War, he is a director of the research center of the Historial de la grande guerre, at Péronne, Somme,

France. Among his books are *Socialism and the challenge of war* (1974); *The upheaval of war: family, work and welfare in Europe 1914–1918* (1978); *The Experience of World War I* (1988); *Guerres et cultures: 1914–1918, La très grande guerre* (1994); *Sites of Memory, Sites of Mourning* (ed., 1995) and *Paris, London, Berlin: Capital Cities at War* (1996).

Index

European Cultures
Studies in Literature and the Arts

The Turn of the Century / Le tournant du siècle
Modernism and Modernity in Literature and the Arts
Le modernisme et la modernité dans la littérature et les arts

Edited by / Edité par Christian Berg, Frank Durieux, Geert Lernout

1995. x, 660 pages. Bound. ISBN 3-11-014018-7 (Volume 3)

Hanna Leitgeb
Der ausgezeichnete Autor
Städtische Literaturpreise und Kulturpolitik in Deutschland 1926–1971

1994. viii, 428 pages. Bound. ISBN 3-11-014402-6 (Volume 4)

Robert S. Leventhal
The Disciplines of Interpretation
Lessing, Herder, Schlegel and Hermeneutics in Germany 1750–1800

1994. xi, 351 pages. Bound. ISBN 3-11-014424-7 (Volume 5)

Icons — Texts — Iconotexts
Essays on Ekphrasis and Intermediality

Edited by Peter Wagner

1996. viii, 406 pages. With 63 illustrations and 8 tables. Bound. ISBN 3-11-014291-0 (Volume 6)

Daniel Fulda
Wissenschaft aus Kunst
Die Entstehung der modernen deutschen Geschichtsschreibung 1760–1860

1996. x, 547 pages. Bound. ISBN 3-11-015014-X (Volume 7)

Walter de Gruyter  Berlin · New York